John Wilkes Booth:
Day by Day

John Wilkes Booth: Day by Day

ARTHUR F. LOUX

McFarland & Company, Inc., Publishers

Jefferson, North Carolina

Publisher's note: Arthur F. Loux died on December 29, 2013,
after completing the writing of this book.
Special thanks are given to Jennifer R. Loux,
who subsequently prepared the manuscript for publication.

Library of Congress Cataloguing-in-Publication Data

Loux, Arthur F.
John Wilkes Booth: day by day / Arthur F. Loux.
p.   cm.
Includes bibliographical references and index.

ISBN 978-0-7864-9527-6 (softcover : acid free paper) ∞
ISBN 978-1-4766-1709-1 (ebook)

1. Booth, John Wilkes, 1838–1865.   2. Assassins—
United States—Biography.   3. Lincoln, Abraham,
1809–1865—Assassination.   I. Title.
E457.5.L78 2014   973.7092—dc23   [B]   2014017300

British Library cataloguing data are available

On the cover: John Wilkes Booth, 1865, Alexander Gardner,
photographer to the Army of the Potomac, Washington, D.C.:
Philp & Solomons (Library of Congress); *background*: John
Wilkes Booth diary page (Library of Congress)

Printed in the United States of America

*McFarland & Company, Inc., Publishers
Box 611, Jefferson, North Carolina 28640
www.mcfarlandpub.com*

To
the memory of
John C. Brennan

Acknowledgments

The late John C. Brennan of Laurel, Maryland, provided his wide knowledge of the Lincoln assassination as well as an incredible number of copies of articles, books, and manuscripts. John also introduced me in 1991 to the eventual publisher of this book, McFarland.

The late James O. Hall, unequaled in graciousness and knowledge of the Lincoln assassination, generously provided the benefit of his research, encouragement, and advice.

Lincoln assassination and John Wilkes Booth scholar nonpareil Michael W. Kauffman provided much of his wide-ranging research.

Erik Jendresen contacted me when he was writing the screenplay for the National Geographic film *Killing Lincoln*. Soon I was happily supplying source documents for various events to satisfy Erik's dedication to historical accuracy. That effort re-generated my enthusiasm for completing this book.

I am most grateful to Jennifer R. Loux, a historian by profession, who brought her considerable editing talents, organizational skills, and eagle eye to bear on my manuscript, which was started about the same time as she was born. While I take full responsibility for this work, it is much improved by her efforts.

The knowledge and assistance of many "Booth buffs" and Lincoln assassination experts contributed to this book. Among them are: Bob Allen, Terry Alford, the late Louise Mudd Arehart, Randal Berry, Joan Chaconas, Jeannine Clarke Dodels, the late Dinah Faber, Joseph George, Jr., Nancy Griffith, Richard and Kellie Gutman, William Hanchett, the late Constance Head, Frank Hebblethwaite, the late Rev. Alfred Isacsson, the late Rev. Robert Keesler, Arthur Kincaid, Deirdre Kincaid, the late Dr. John K. Lattimer, the late Ernest Miller, Steven G. Miller, Roger Norton, Betty Ownsbey, the late Bert Sheldon, Richard E. Sloan, Angela Smythe, John Stanton, Louise Taper, Dave Taylor, Laurie Verge, and Sandra Walia.

Others who provided assistance are: Herb Adams, Steve Archer, the late Jack Brown, Tim Daniels, the late Donald Dow, the late Howard and Dorothy Fox (proprietors of Tudor Hall), Randall Haines, Roger Hunt, Dale Jirik, George Kackley, the late Franklyn Lenthall, E.A. "Bud" Livingston, Vicki Lockhart, Robert C. Marcotte, Mrs. Jean Struthers Newell, Judy and William Newell, and Gerald Trueson.

My wife, Kathleen, planned research trips, assisted in library research, and performed many services which propelled the completion of this book. Thanks also are due our children, Jennifer and Lauren, who spent parts of many spring and summer vacations touring Booth sites, cemeteries, and libraries.

—A.F.L.

Contents

Preface

On a memorable day in 1977, I was among a busload of people on the first Surratt Society Booth Escape Route tour. James O. Hall, a mellifluous-voiced, white-haired man who immediately commanded respect, guided the tour. I met John C. Brennan, an energetic force of nature, and Mike Kauffman, a young man who seemed to be as knowledgeable about the people and events surrounding the assassination as Mr. Hall. I met Richard Sloan, Laurie Verge, Joan Chaconas, Nancy Griffith, Betty Ownsbey, and Louise Arehart (a granddaughter of Dr. Samuel A. Mudd). At Port Royal, Virginia, the group visited Maude Motley, who described how she had obtained the piece of John Wilkes Booth's crutch she cradled in her hands. For a historian, days don't get much better than that.

Several days after the tour I found my mailbox jammed with letters from John Brennan. I was hooked. My mailbox remained full for many years with correspondence from Brennan and others who were researching every possible aspect of the Lincoln assassination. I began to record information about Booth in a day-by-day format by typewriter and on the computers of the day. I scoured libraries and museums. I visited the cities where Booth performed and the region where he prospected for oil. In 1990 I self-published twelve copies of *John Wilkes Booth: Day by Day*. I considered this to be a preliminary version that would be useful to my fellow researchers while I completed a more thorough rendition.

In the years after the initial publication, *John Wilkes Booth: Day by Day* has been cited in virtually all serious books and dissertations about Booth and the Lincoln assassination. With varying degrees of frequency, an email or phone call would bring a request for a copy of the book. A number of great friendships developed from these contacts.

Each page of the first edition of *Day by Day* was in the format of a weekly calendar from Sunday to Saturday. When I could identify an activity or event in the life of John Wilkes Booth, I made an entry in the appropriate date. Days and even weeks were blank when no information was available. On the other hand, there was such a wealth of information for some days that important material had to be severely abbreviated or left out because of limited space. Another deficiency of the format was difficulty in presenting certain findings that could not be assigned a specific date. In this new edition, the one-week-per-page format has been abandoned, allowing as many entries per day as necessary. Each entry notes the city in which Booth ended the day (when known), followed by his activities on that date. Information not specifically about Booth but which is considered pertinent closes the entry. A narrative, necessary to tie together and make sense of what was happening, begins each chapter.

Sparse information survives about John Wilkes Booth's youth. I have included notices of his father's theatrical appearances in his home city of Baltimore to indicate the frequency of his being home, where his presence influenced his son's development. I have traced Booth's acting career through newspapers, advertisements, reviews, and personal accounts of observers. I have included many reviews verbatim to allow the reader to form an opinion of Booth as an actor. In the day-by-day entries, reviews appear on the date of the performance rather than on the date they were published.

In examining the sources, those closest to the event receive the most credence. Sources far removed—for example, recollections in a newspaper article fifty years later—are given little or no credit, unless they are corroborated. In several instances, rather than ignore what I judge to be prejudiced or inaccurate accounts, I include them with commentary so as to allow the reader to form an independent opinion.

This book focuses on the life and actions of John Wilkes Booth. It is not intended to address all the mysteries of the Lincoln assassination. Priority is given to events in which Booth was directly involved. By consolidating Booth's actions and the sources here in one place, I hope to give the reader a new perspective from which to comprehend the complexities of the conspiracy against Lincoln. The dramatic story of the plot to kidnap President Lincoln, the assassination itself, and Booth's twelve-day escape has been told many times. My aim is to tell the story concisely with the emphasis on Booth's actions.

John Wilkes Booth was loved by his family and had hosts of friends. He was a successful actor and managed his career in a business-like manner. He had achieved a measure of fame, with a promise of more, and was accumulating a fortune. He had the mental capacity to interpret and memorize numerous plays and to perform five or six of them in the course of a week. Yet he gave up his career, his family, his friends, and his life for his misguided principles. John Wilkes Booth's life had the dimensions of a novel encompassing major historical events, with elements of sex, violence, and tragedy. Born to a prominent acting family, he rose nearly to the top of his profession in only four years. Toward the end of his brief life, he suddenly left his acting career to speculate in Pennsylvania oil exploration. He abandoned this endeavor after a short time to lead a nine-months-long conspiracy to abduct President Lincoln, take him south, and barter him for Confederate soldiers held captive by the Union. When the Civil War was over and Booth's cause was lost, he brutally assassinated the president, believing the Union commander-in-chief to be a tyrant responsible for the devastation wrought upon the South. Booth undertook this senseless act in full recognition that it would probably cost him his life.

1

Youth: 1838–1857

Junius Brutus Booth, the father of John Wilkes Booth, was one of the foremost actors in the United States during the first half of the nineteenth century. He was born in London in 1796, the son of Richard Booth, an attorney.[1] Junius, despite the objections of his father, became an actor and soon attracted a large and enthusiastic following. In 1815 Junius married Adelaide Delannoy, whom he had met in Brussels. Their son, Richard, was born in 1819. Two years later, Junius met and fell in love with Mary Ann Holmes, the daughter of a London nurseryman. The young actor resolved the difficult situation by making provisions for the support of his wife and child and then emigrating to the United States with his new love.[2]

Junius's fame on the stage had preceded him to America. He easily established himself as a "star," a performer who traveled from city to city appearing in lead roles supported by the local stock company. Junius demonstrated eccentricities which frequent and copious alcohol consumption magnified. He took to the rafters of a theatre during one performance and crowed like a rooster. He rode a horse through one town mounted backwards. He held a funeral service for dead pigeons. Only a week before the birth of John Wilkes Booth, a Baltimore newspaper referred to the elder Booth as "the mad tragedian." Despite, or perhaps because of, these eccentricities, his audiences were usually large, as was his share of the proceeds.

Junius was a loving and attentive father to his ten children born in America. The letters he wrote to Mary Ann while he was on the road convey a deep affection and solicitude for his family. During the acting season, ranging from late August through early June, he often performed at theatres in Baltimore, where he and his family resided. During the summer months he was at home on his farm near Bel Air, twenty miles from Baltimore. He required his family to follow his vegetarian diet and did not allow the slaughter of animals on the farm.[3]

Junius's son John Wilkes Booth was born on May 10, 1838, at the farm. The baby's great-grandmother, Elizabeth Wilkes, was related to the English republican politician John Wilkes, a fervent supporter of the American colonies in the eighteenth century.[4] Perhaps the middle name was chosen to honor the famous relative. Perhaps it was used for reasons of family tradition.

Four of John Wilkes Booth's nine siblings died in childhood. John's eldest brother, Junius Brutus Booth, Jr., sixteen years older than John, embarked on an acting career when John was an infant. Junius Jr., called June by his family, became a respected, if not first-rank, actor and theatre manager.

John's older sister Rosalie Booth never married. She was introverted and became more so with age. Family letters occasionally refer to her as an invalid. She lived with her mother until Mary Ann's death; then she lived with her brother Joseph until she died in 1889.[5]

3

Edwin Thomas Booth, born in 1833, became even more prominent on the American stage in the second half of the nineteenth century than his father had been in the first half. As a youth, Edwin organized amateur theatricals in which friends and his brother John took part. Fourteen-year-old Edwin began to accompany his father on his travels to keep the elder Booth from drinking and to care for him in times of mental confusion. Edwin was at home often during the theatrical season and for extended periods during the summer months. John must have admired and envied Edwin's glamorous life of travel.

Edwin first appeared on the professional stage in 1849. In 1852 he and his father traveled to California, where they acted under the management of Junius Jr. Edwin stayed in California after his father departed and continued his theatrical career there until 1854, when he left San Francisco and toured Australia. On his return to America he toured the eastern states as a star for several years. In the 1860s he traveled less frequently and concentrated his performances in New York and Boston. During the Civil War he was at the top rank of his profession.

John Wilkes Booth had a close relationship with his sister Asia, who was three years his senior. They practiced Shakespearean plays and elocution to while away the long, hot days on the farm. Asia and John planned to write a biography of their father, a task Asia completed when she published *Booth Memorials: Passages, Incidents and Anecdotes in the Life of Junius Brutus Booth* in 1866. She also wrote a memoir of her brother John titled *The Unlocked Book*. Asia married actor-comedian John Sleeper Clarke in 1859.[6] Their marriage suffered many strains.

Joseph Adrian Booth, two years younger than John, was his closest sibling in age. The two brothers attended various schools together. Joseph was a medical student in Charleston, South Carolina, in 1861 when hostilities broke out at Fort Sumter. Joe abandoned his studies and did little of conse-

quence during the Civil War. After the war he became the treasurer of a theatre Edwin opened in New York. At the age of forty-nine Joseph completed his medical education and became a successful doctor.[7]

By 1840 the Booth family resided in Baltimore on the east side of High Street, just north of Gay Street. A few years later they lived at 72 Front Street. In 1845 Junius bought a home at 62 North Exeter Street. He acquired property from neighbors to expand the size of his rear lot. Soon Junius began to make changes to the lot for the enjoyment of his children. An observer reported that

> a circle of trees [was] planted in the yard by the tragedian.... On the outer edge of this circle was a pathway on which the boys of the neighborhood would ride on a horse. It was discerned by them a veritable racetrack. On a summer evening Mr. Booth would place several of these youngsters on the back of the fiery steed and start the equine on a canter around the circle. He apparently enjoyed the spectacle immensely.... He would take them to a small shop on Exeter Street near Necessity Alley and treat them to ice cream.... A peculiarity of his was to call at the house of an opposite resident of the street and request the matron of the premises to favor him in sending her sons to his residence with instructions to arouse John Wilkes and Joe from their early morning slumber.[8]

An arbor in the rear yard served as a stage background for amateur plays mounted by Edwin Booth, John Sleeper Clarke, and several others. They performed classic works, both romantic and dramatic, as well as minstrel shows for the neighborhood youth, including John Wilkes Booth and the boys who lived across the street, Michael and William O'Laughlen.[9] A few years later John put on plays in the back yard, in a stable, and in a hotel cellar with his friends Sam Chester and Stuart Robson. Edwin and John Sleeper Clarke joined in at times. One of the shows had a run of several weeks.[10]

John Wilkes Booth's first school, according to the journalist David Rankin Barbee, "was a select school for boys, kept by an old classical scholar named Smith. To this school [Booth] was sent while yet in breeches, and here he was given the rudiments of an education."[11] Asia described her brother's approach to learning:

> John Wilkes was not quick at acquiring knowledge, he had to plod, progress slowly step by step, but that which he once attained he never lost.... He had great power of concentration, and he never let go a subject once broached until he had mastered it or proved its barrenness. From early boyhood he was argumentative and fervid in debate.[12]

Edwin, John Wilkes, Joseph Booth, and their friend John Sleeper Clarke subsequently attended a school taught by Susan Hyde. They then moved to a school in a one-story brick building on Exeter Street, between Baltimore and Fayette Streets, where the head of instruction was Martin J. Kerney, a graduate of Mount St. Mary's College in Emmittsburg, Maryland.[13] In 1846 Booth began three years of study at the Bel Air Academy, located in Bel Air at the corner of Main Street and the Bel Air Turnpike.[14] The schoolmaster described John as very handsome "in face and figure although slightly bowlegged."[15]

In the fall of 1849 Booth began studies at the Milton Boarding School in Cockeysville, Maryland. John E. and Eli M. Lamb had founded the institution, also known as Lamb's School, in 1847. A three-story stone building contained classrooms and a dining hall on the first floor and a dormitory on the top floor.[16] One year when the Milton Boarding School broke up for the summer, John performed Shylock in a scene from *The Merchant of Venice* at ceremonies attended by his mother and sister Asia.[17]

In 1852 John and his brother Joseph began studies at St. Timothy's Hall, a military academy, in Catonsville, Maryland.[18] According to the school handbook:

> The object of those who have the charge of St. Timothy's Hall, is to make it an institution of strict discipline, of good morals, and,

by the grace of God, a religious home for the young. [St. Timothy's is] a literary institution, for the education of young gentlemen whose appreciation of knowledge, and love of order, have made them diligent and patient of restraint.[19]

The Rev. Libertus Van Bokkelen, an Episcopal clergyman,[20] and Professor Henry Onderdonk[21] ran the school. Van Bokkelen was an abolitionist, a rarity in Maryland outside Quaker circles. He had run night and Sunday schools in New York for blacks. Because the students at St. Timothy's Hall were largely from slave-holding families, it is likely that Van Bokkelen held his social views in check.[22]

In 1853 a "rebellion" occurred at St. Timothy's. When several boys killed some of his chickens, Van Bokkelen punished the entire student body. The freshman and sophomore classes, including the Booth brothers, protested by camping in nearby woods. The scholars refused to be dislodged for three days, after which hunger, one would expect, compelled them to emerge from the woods.[23] Perhaps as a result of this incident, Van Bokkelen reduced the size of the school by more than a hundred pupils for the term beginning in the fall of 1853. No students above age fifteen were to be admitted.[24] John Wilkes Booth did not return for the fall term.

One of Booth's fellow students and close friends was Samuel Arnold, the son of a Baltimore baker.[25] Years later Booth would renew the acquaintance, to Arnold's everlasting regret.

Booth may have attended Charles Henry Bland's boarding school in York, Pennsylvania, for about three weeks in 1853.[26] John's formal education ended when he reached the age of sixteen. In January 1854 he considered learning a trade, but he soon abandoned that goal and attempted farming. Sometime in the autumn of 1854 Asia wrote to a friend: "John is trying to farm."[27]

Junius Brutus Booth had begun the construction of a new country home on his farm in Bel Air in 1851. He died in 1852 before work on the mansion was completed. By the middle of 1853 Mary Ann Booth rented out the Baltimore house and moved to the still-unfinished home, called Tudor Hall. The building was soon completed and made habitable for year-round use.[28]

John had a particular love of horses. Asia described her brother's affection for his colt:

> Wilkes had a beautiful black colt without a white hair or spot.... He had an *Ivanhoe* forehead, on which was imprinted many a loving kiss by his master, who had broken him in himself and named him Cola di Rienzi. Wilkes taught me to ride, with and without a saddle, to go through all the graceful maneuvers of a wild and daring horsewoman, and as he was a fearless rider, I kept by his side through many dangerous and isolated miles of country.... We took early morning rides before sun-up when the dew lay like rain on the grass.[29]

At harvest time it was customary for the hired help to take the midday meal with the family of the house. Booth, however, refused to allow his mother or sisters to join the laborers, showing, as his sister described it, his "first evidence of an undemocratic feeling."[30]

In 1854 Booth attended meetings of the American (or Know Nothing) Party, which emerged as a national organization that year. The party had its origins in secretive societies that had supported many successful candidates for local and statewide offices in 1852. Adherents favored limiting immigration, primarily of the Irish, and thus reducing the competition presented to domestic labor by immigrants. They also wished to curtail the influence of Catholics, arguing that loyalty to the pope was incompatible with republican government. Maryland, where Know Nothingism was especially popular, was the only state in which the party's candidate for president was victorious in 1856. Booth served as a steward at an American Party rally addressed by congressional candidate Henry Winter Davis.[31]

In the summer of 1854, John had an al-tercation with G.B. Hagan, who was farming the Booth fields on shares. Hagan was very ambitious and worked the Booth horses and hired men to exhaustion. He bought large quantities of guano fertilizer at Mary Ann Booth's expense. When she objected, Hagan became insolent and called her vile names. John, upon learning of the incident, cut a stout stick, sought out the farmer, and beat him. He wrote to his friend William O'Laughlen: "We had a client on the place whom we could not agree with. we had several sprees with him in one he called my sister a Liar. I knocked him down, which made him bleed like a butc[he]r we got the Sherrf to put him off the place. he then Warrented me. and in a coupple of weeks. I have to stand trial. For assault. and battery, as you call it."[32]

The farmer's complaint resulted in the following warrant:

> State vs. John Booth
> Copies J.L. Dallam Shff.
> John Booth & Mary A Booth each & severally Recognized for the sum of fifty Dollars
> To J.L. Dallam sheriff of Harf Co., State of Maryland, Harford Co. to wit,
>
> Whereas complaint hath been made before me the subscriber one of the justices of the peace in & for said state and county upon the information & oath of G.B. Hagan who charges John Booth with assaulting him by striking him with a club on the evening of the 30th Day of July 1854, you are therefore hereby commanded immediately to apprehend the said John Booth and bring him before me the subscriber or some other justice of the peace of the said state & county to be dealt with according to laws. hereof fail not, & have you there this warrant.
>
> Given under my hand & seal this 31st Day of July 1854.
> Jas. A. Fulton (seal)[33]

John Wilkes Booth had appeared in many amateur theatricals. Now he began to think seriously about performing on the professional stage. His friend John Sleeper Clarke invited him to appear in his benefit performance at the Charles Street Theatre in

Baltimore on August 14, 1855, as Richmond in the battle scene of *Richard III*. A Mr. Ellis played the part of Richard III, and John's friend John Albaugh played a supporting role. Upon his return to Tudor Hall, Booth told Asia, "Guess what I've done! I've made my first appearance on any stage, for this night only, and in big capitals." She recorded that his "face shone with enthusiasm, and by the exultant tone of his voice it was plain that he had passed the test night. He had made his venture in life, and would soon follow on the road he had broken."[34]

John had supported his mother and sisters by running the farm for four years after the death of his father. Edwin's return to the East Coast as a financially successful actor allowed John to start his own career. In July 1857 John advertised the sale of two horses and offered Tudor Hall for rent.[35] He had obtained a job in the stock company of the Arch Street Theatre in Philadelphia.

1838 *from April 6*

April 6, Saturday
The *Baltimore Sun* reported: "Mr. [Junius Brutus] Booth, the mad tragedian, has arrived in our city."[36]

April 30, Monday
Junius Brutus Booth failed to appear at the Holliday Street Theatre in Baltimore for a scheduled performance.[37]

May 1, Tuesday
Junius Brutus Booth celebrated his forty-second birthday. He appeared at the Holliday Street Theatre as Pescara in *The Apostate*.[38]

May 3, Thursday
The *Baltimore Sun* reported:
BOOTH AGAIN. Is this man a maniac?.... On Monday, he was announced to appear at the Holliday Street [Theatre] as Pescara; but when the hour of performance arrived the little eccentric was returned *non est*. "Booth is a genius" is the cry; and he has heard it reiterated so often that he imagines his vagaries will be overlooked.... This affectation of madness ... is disgusting.[39]

May 10, Thursday Bel Air[40]
John Wilkes Booth was born at his family's log cabin home in Harford County, Maryland, near Bel Air. Wilkes was a family name; the baby's great-grandfather had married Elizabeth Wilkes in 1747.[41]

May 15, Tuesday
Junius Brutus Booth appeared at the Holliday Street Theatre on this and several succeeding nights. The *Sun* commented: "Having recovered from his late indisposition, and being anxious to regain the good opinion of the Baltimore audience, there will, we are assured, be no disappointment this time."[42]

June 12, Tuesday
Junius Brutus Booth appeared as Pescara in *The Apostate* in a benefit performance at the Holliday Street Theatre.[43]

1839

July 15, Monday
Junius Brutus Booth began a week-long engagement at the Holliday Street Theatre.[44]

October 22, Tuesday
Junius Brutus Booth opened an engagement at the Front Street Theatre in Baltimore.[45]

October 26, Saturday
Junius Brutus Booth appeared in a benefit performance for his son Junius at the Front Street Theatre.[46]

December 28, Saturday
Junius Brutus Booth's father, Richard Booth, died in Baltimore at the age of seventy-six.[47]

December 29, Sunday
The body of Richard Booth was placed in a vault at the Christ Church burying ground in Baltimore.[48]

1840

January 24, Friday
Junius Brutus Booth began an engagement at the Front Street Theatre, a short walk from his home on High Street.[49]

February 8, Saturday

Mary Ann Booth gave birth to her last child, Joseph Adrian Booth, at the Booth home in Baltimore.[50]

March 2, Monday

Junius Brutus Booth began a short engagement at the Baltimore Museum.[51]

June 11, Thursday

Junius Brutus Booth had the body of his father removed from the Christ Church vault in Baltimore for burial. The undertaker wrote:

Contrary to my advice he [Junius] had the coffin opened; I drew off with the men, but from where we stood I was able to see that he bent down and kissed the face of the dead.... I saw him cut off a lock of hair from the dead.[52]

June 23, Tuesday

Junius Brutus Booth, in Philadelphia, wrote to Mary Ann at their home in Baltimore:

I took a slight cold which has rendered me rather hoarse but am nearly recovered from it. I hope the children are quite well. Kiss them for me, and give my love to each and all from Rosalie down to Joey. The time seems long while away from you and them; and I almost regret having made so protracted an engagement.[53]

July 9, Thursday

Junius Brutus Booth, in New York, wrote to Mary Ann:

Your counsel and advice have been and always are of the utmost benefit to me—my love for you is still undiminished—to avoid drinking I wake every effort—accept my blessing and give it to our dear children with kisses for all of them. I hope their colds have left them and that they are perfectly recovered ere this.[54]

September 21, Monday

Junius Brutus Booth began an engagement at the Front Street Theatre.[55]

1841

March 8, Monday

Junius Brutus Booth began an engagement at the Front Street Theatre.[56]

April 1, Thursday

Junius Brutus Booth began a two-day engagement at the Front Street Theatre.[57]

July 26, Monday

Junius Brutus Booth began an engagement at the National Theatre.[58]

October 9, Saturday

Junius Brutus Booth began a two-week engagement at the Front Street Theatre.[59]

1842

April 12, Tuesday

Junius Brutus Booth appeared at the Front Street Theatre.[60]

June 13, Monday

Junius Brutus Booth began an engagement at the Front Street Theatre.[61]

September 5, Monday

Junius Brutus Booth began an engagement at the Front Street Theatre.[62]

1843

March 16, Thursday

Junius Brutus Booth began an engagement at the Holliday Street Theatre.[63]

September 29, Friday

Junius Brutus Booth opened an engagement at the Front Street Theatre.[64]

November 9, Thursday

Junius Brutus Booth appeared at the Holliday Street Theatre.[65]

1844

April 2, Tuesday

A daughter, Blanche, was born to John Wilkes Booth's brother, Junius Brutus Booth, Jr., and his wife, Clementine DeBar. In later years Blanche used her mother's surname and went by Blanche Booth DeBar.[66]

April 29, Monday

Junius Brutus Booth opened an engagement at the Holliday Street Theatre.[67]

May 1, Wednesday

The Whig National Convention, meeting in Baltimore, nominated Henry Clay for president.

1845

March 27, Thursday

Junius Brutus Booth began a short engagement at the Egyptian Saloon in Baltimore.[68]

July 1, Tuesday

Junius Brutus Booth began an engagement at the Front Street Theatre.[69]

September 26, Friday

Junius Brutus Booth bought a house at 62 North Exeter Street in Baltimore.[70]

> The Booth residence is so placed that there is a pleasant atmosphere in the sidewalk in front of the house generally. This in conjunction with a deep gutter way which collected water from a neighboring pump made the spot the favorite resort of boys who delighted in sailing boats.[70]

1846

December 17, Thursday

Junius Brutus Booth's abandoned wife, Adelaide, who had recently arrived in the United States, wrote to her sister in England that her lawyer would "fall on [Booth's] back like a bomb" with a divorce suit. She would delay the proceedings until Booth had made as much money as possible on his winter tour.[71]

1847

January 21, Thursday

In a diary entry headed "Mississippi River, January 21, 1847" Junius Brutus Booth wrote:

> As I was dressing ... heard a report of pistols, and shortly after, Mr. Durivage came to say a man was shot dead in the bar-room adjoining the theatre. His skull was also broken by a cudgel, by two men. This injured our receipts materially but we played to about 57 dollars.[72]

March 8, Monday

Junius Brutus Booth began an engagement at the Baltimore Museum.[73]

April 5, Monday

Junius Brutus Booth opened an engagement at the Baltimore Museum.[74]

May 1, Saturday

Junius Brutus Booth agreed to pay his estranged wife, Adelaide, $1,000 as a ten-year advance on her annual separate maintenance payments, which had been arranged in 1826. To secure these funds he relied on an inheritance from his grandmother, which consisted of rents on lands in London "devised to and held by John Wilkes Booth [a cousin] of that city in trust."[75]

May 17, Monday

Junius Brutus Booth began a short engagement at the Holliday Street Theatre.[76]

May 20, Thursday

Junius Brutus Booth bought several adjoining lots to expand his back yard in Baltimore.[77]

June 30, Wednesday

Junius Brutus Booth began an engagement at the Baltimore Museum.[78]

July 2, Friday

Junius Brutus Booth played *Richard III* at the Baltimore Museum.[79]

October 20, Wednesday

Junius Brutus Booth began an engagement at the Front Street Theatre.[80]

November 5, Friday

Junius Brutus Booth, Sr. appeared with his daughter-in-law, Mrs. Junius Brutus Booth, Jr., at the Front Street Theatre.[81]

November 10, Wednesday

Junius Brutus Booth began a short engagement at the Holliday Street Theatre.[82]

1848

May 29, Monday

Junius Brutus Booth played the title role in *Hamlet* at the Front Street Theatre.[83]

July 10, Monday

Junius Brutus Booth appeared as Sir Giles Overreach in *A New Way to Pay Old Debts* at the Howard Athenaeum in Baltimore. His engagement lasted four days.[84]

July 13, Thursday

Junius Brutus Booth closed his engagement at the Howard Athenaeum with *Richard III*.[85]

August 14, Monday

Junius Brutus Booth opened an engagement in Albany, New York. Fourteen-year-old Edwin accompanied his father on this tour.[86]

November 25, Saturday

Junius Brutus Booth opened an engagement at the Baltimore Museum with *Richard III.*[87]

1849

June 18, Monday

Junius Brutus Booth appeared as Cassius in *Julius Caesar* at the Front Street Theatre.[88]

September 10, Monday

Edwin Booth made his debut as Tressel supporting his father in *Richard III* at the Boston Museum in Massachusetts.[89]

September 14, Friday Cockeysville

The fall term at the Milton Boarding School began on or about this date.[90] John Wilkes Booth began his first year of study there.

December 31, Monday

Richard Booth, Junius's son by his first wife, married Sarah Ware.[91]

1850

February 10, Sunday Cockeysville

The fall term at the Milton Boarding School ended on or about this date.[92]

April 1, Monday

Junius Brutus Booth was scheduled to perform *Richard III* at the Marshall Theatre in Richmond, Virginia, but he was drunk and did not appear.[93]

April 2, Tuesday

The Marshall Theatre playbill carried the message: "The management respectfully inform the public of Richmond they cannot allow Mr. Booth to appear again this season, after the disappointment he caused last evening to a brilliant audience."[94]

April 3, Wednesday

Edwin Booth went to Richmond to find his father. With the help of theatre manager John Sefton, he found him at a friend's plantation. Junius Brutus Booth borrowed $50 from Sefton for passage home and repaid the loan within two weeks.[95]

May 27, Monday

Junius Brutus Booth began a week-long engagement at the Holliday Street Theatre with a performance of *Richard III.*[96]

June 24, Monday Cockeysville

The census taken on this date lists John Booth, age twelve, as a student in the home of John E. Lamb, teacher.

July 6, Saturday Cockeysville

The academic year at Milton Boarding School ended on or about this date.[97]

August 2, Friday Bel Air

Edwin Booth and John Sleeper Clarke gave a reading at the court house in Bel Air. Among those in the audience was Junius Brutus Booth and, most likely, the entire Booth family. Edwin had been accompanying his father on his professional travels to care for him in his distracted periods and to keep him from drinking.[98]

September 14, Saturday Cockeysville

The fall term of the Milton Boarding School began on or about this date.[99] John Wilkes Booth may have begun a second year of study at the school.

October 31, Thursday

Junius Brutus Booth performed *Richard III* at the Holliday Street Theatre.[100]

November 1, Friday

Junius Brutus Booth appeared in the title role of *Hamlet* at the Holliday Street Theatre.[101]

November 2, Saturday

Edwin Booth and his father, Junius, appeared at the Holliday Street Theatre. This was the first advertised appearance in Baltimore of Edwin Booth. Edwin played Titus, and Junius played Brutus.[102]

1851

February 10, Monday Cockeysville

The fall term of the Milton Boarding School ended.[103]

February 27, Thursday

Junius Brutus Booth's legal wife, Adelaide Booth, filed a divorce bill in Baltimore stating that her husband had abandoned her in January 1821, that he had lived in the United States with a woman in an adulterous relationship, and that he had a large family by his mistress.[104]

March 11, Tuesday

The body of Richard Booth was removed from Christ Church burying ground, which was being abandoned, and was re-interred in Baltimore Cemetery.[105]

March 26, Wednesday

Junius Brutus Booth answered the charges of Adelaide Booth by admitting the facts stated in her bill of February 27. He agreed to a decree of divorce.[106]

April 18, Friday

Judge John C. Legrand granted a divorce to Junius Brutus Booth and Adelaide Booth. Junius was assessed the costs of the proceedings.[107]

April 21, Monday

Junius Brutus Booth, accompanied by Edwin, began a two-week engagement at the Marshall Theatre in Richmond.[108] Asia later wrote: "My father usually traveled from his farm to Philadelphia or to Richmond in his carryall, with two horses, 'Captain,' a very large animal, and the favorite but diminutive 'Peacock,' driven in tandem."[109]

April 25, Friday

Edwin Booth appeared at the Marshall Theatre in Richmond with his father in *The Iron Chest*.[110]

April 29, Tuesday

Junius Brutus Booth continued his engagement at the Marshall Theatre in Richmond, appearing with Edwin in *King Lear*.[111]

May 10, Saturday

Junius Brutus Booth married Mary Ann Holmes on the thirteenth birthday of their son, John Wilkes Booth.

July 6, Sunday   Cockeysville

The academic year of the Milton Boarding School ended about this date.[112]

July 20, Sunday

Junius Jr. arrived in San Francisco, California.[113]

September 14, Sunday   Cockeysville

The fall term of the Milton Boarding School began on this date.[114] John Wilkes Booth probably began a third year of study at the school.

October 3, Friday

Junius Brutus Booth appeared in *Othello* at the Holliday Street Theatre.[115]

October 4, Saturday

Junius Brutus Booth played *Richard III* at the Holliday Street Theatre.[116]

October 21, Tuesday

Junius Brutus Booth, in Philadelphia, wrote to his neighbor John Rogers and asked him to supervise several details in the construction of a new Booth house, known as Tudor Hall, on the farm in Harford County.[117] James Gifford, a theatre architect, designed and built the structure.[118]

1852

January 1, Thursday

Junius Brutus Booth began an engagement at the Holliday Street Theatre with *Richard III*.[119]

January 2, Friday

Junius Brutus Booth appeared at the Holliday Street Theatre.[120]

January 3, Saturday

Junius Brutus Booth appeared as Cassius in *Julius Caesar* at the Holliday Street Theatre.[121]

January 10, Saturday

Junius Brutus Booth appeared in *The Stranger* with Julia Dean at the Holliday Street Theatre.[122]

February 12, Thursday

Junius Brutus Booth played the title role in *Brutus*, with Edwin Booth as Titus, at the Holliday Street Theatre.[123]

February 24, Tuesday

Junius Brutus Booth played Pescara in *The Apostate* at the Holliday Street Theatre.[124]

March 16, Tuesday

Junius Brutus Booth appeared in *Venice Preserved* at the Holliday Street Theatre.[125]

March 17, Wednesday

Junius Brutus Booth played Cassius in *Julius Caesar* at the Holliday Street Theatre.[126]

May 4, Tuesday

Jane Booth Mitchell, Junius Brutus Booth's sister, died in Baltimore.[127]

May 31, Monday

Junius Brutus Booth began a six-day engagement at the Holliday Street Theatre in the role of *Richard III*. This would be his last engagement in Baltimore.[128]

June 1, Tuesday

Junius Brutus Booth played *Brutus*.[129]

June 2, Wednesday

Junius Brutus Booth played *Hamlet*.[130]

June 3, Thursday

Junius Brutus Booth played *King Lear*, supported by Edwin.[131]

June 4, Friday

Junius Brutus Booth played Sir Giles Overreach in *A New Way to Pay Old Debts* and Jerry Sneak in *The Mayor of Garratt*.[132]

June 5, Saturday

Junius Brutus Booth closed his engagement at the Holliday Street Theatre with a performance of *Richard III*.[133]

June 21, Monday

Junius Brutus Booth and his sons Edwin and Junius Jr. left on the steamer *Illinois* for San Francisco.

July 28, Wednesday

Junius Brutus Booth and his party arrived in San Francisco.[134]

September Catonsville

[Date approximate] John Wilkes Booth and his brother Joseph began studies at St. Timothy's Hall.[135]

October 1, Friday

Junius Brutus Booth left San Francisco for home.[136]

November 14, Sunday

Junius Brutus Booth began an engagement at the St. Charles Theatre in New Orleans, Louisiana.

November 19, Friday

Asia celebrated her seventeenth birthday. Junius Brutus Booth closed his engagement in New Orleans.[137] He had earned $1,084 for six nights.[138]

November 25, Thursday

On or about this day, Junius Brutus Booth left New Orleans on the steamer *J.S. Chenoweth*.

November 26, Friday

A fellow traveler on the steamer later wrote: We had been one day out from New Orleans, when I noticed a man walking back and forth in the saloon, with his hands behind him, his head bowed in deep thought. I sat observing him closely, trying to recollect when and where I had

seen him. A gentleman came up to me and remarked "That is the tragedian Booth."[139]

November 27, Saturday

Junius Brutus Booth's condition became of concern.
The second day out he [Booth] was absent from the saloon, and on inquiry I found that he was confined to his stateroom, very sick of a diarrhea.... I at once visited him, apologizing for my intrusion, and offered my services to him in any manner that might be useful. After scanning me with a look of penetration and surprise that I can never forget, he accepted the offer.... He wasted away very fast.[140]

November 28, Sunday

Junius Brutus Booth's health continued its rapid decline.
The third day after he [Booth] was taken sick, he could not turn over without help. I saw that he was getting in a hopeless condition, and thinking to stimulate his energies, gave him some brandy and water, having to saturate a rag and place it between his teeth, his jaws having become rigid; but on tasting it, he made an effort to remove it from his lips, and spoke with difficulty: "No more in this world."[141]

November 29, Monday

Junius Brutus Booth was near death.
On the fourth day after he [Booth] was taken, I asked him if I should read to him from my Testament. He seemed anxious that I should, when I selected an encouraging chapter and read, while he gave the deepest attention. I then asked him if I might pray for him. His eyes became dim with moisture, and he signified his consent, when I knelt by his bunk....[142]

November 30, Tuesday

Junius Brutus Booth died on the river boat as it approached Louisville, Kentucky. His last words were "Pray, Pray, Pray." A metallic coffin was procured in Louisville.[143] The body was taken to Cincinnati, Ohio. The Masons of Cincinnati took up a collection to help Mary Ann with expenses.

December 9, Thursday Baltimore

The body of Junius Brutus Booth arrived in Baltimore.[144]

December 11, Saturday Baltimore

Friends and theatrical acquaintances of the late actor gathered at the Irving House on Gay Street and went in a group to the funeral at the Booth home on North Exeter Street. Bands led the procession and played a solemn dirge as the remains were deposited in a vault at the Baltimore Cemetery.[145]

December 13, Monday Catonsville

John Wilkes Booth and his brother Joseph had returned to school.[146]

1853

January 11, Tuesday

The body of Junius Brutus Booth was interred in Lot 241 in Baltimore Cemetery.[147]

January 23, Sunday Catonsville

John Wilkes Booth and his brother Joseph were baptized at St. Timothy's Church. The Reverend John Stephenson and Henry Onderdonk sponsored the baptisms.[148]

July 28, Thursday Catonsville

The school term at St. Timothy's Hall ended on this date.[149] John Wilkes Booth had completed his formal education. His primary occupation during the next three years was farming.

October 10, Monday Bel Air

Asia and John rode about eighteen miles.[150]

December 20, Tuesday Bel Air

Asia wrote to Jean Anderson:
I believe William O'Laughlin [O'Laughlen] wants to visit us in Christmas week. John and I anticipate a fine ride to the rocks of Deer Creek tomorrow afternoon. Rose brought him home a new saddle. I ride to Bel Air very often to the Post Office and Store.[151]

1854

January 4, Wednesday Bel Air

In a letter to her friend Jean Anderson later in the week, Asia reported that "June [Junius Jr.] is here with his wife and baby. On Tuesday Mother and June went to town and returned the following afternoon. John and I rode horseback to Bel Air to meet them."[152]

January 25, Wednesday Bel Air

Booth wrote to his friend William O'Laughlen: "I may—perhaps—come to town to learn a trade in the summer but I am going to school in Bel Air to morrow if nothing happens."[153]

February 1, Wednesday Bel Air

Booth doodled in his arithmetic book: "John W. Booth Bel Air Harford Co. Md. Feb. 1st 1854."[154]

April 28, Friday

Booth had been invited to a ball in Bel Air, but a storm prevented him from attending.[155]

April 30, Sunday Bel Air

Booth wrote to William O'Laughlen:
The country is beautiful now, evry thing is in blossom. and in about three weeks time Squirls will be fit for shooting. I should like you to come up then and give them a round.... I have got my eye on three girls out here. I hope I'll get enough.... J.W.B. alias. Billy. Bow. Legs. J.W.B.[156]

Asia later wrote: "There was a celebrated Indian Chief named Billy Bowlegs, and Wilkes went by this name among his companions at Catonsville."[157]

June 13, Tuesday Bel Air

Samuel H. Patterson, husband of one of John Wilkes Booth's cousins, died at the Booth home in Bel Air.[158]

June 22, Thursday Baltimore

Presumably John Wilkes Booth and his family attended the burial service of Samuel H. Patterson at Baltimore Cemetery.[159]

July 30, Sunday

When John Wilkes Booth learned that G.B. Hagan, who was farming the Tudor Hall lands on shares, had been insolent with his mother and sister, he sought out the farmer and beat him with a stick.[160]

A troupe of actors led by Edwin Booth and Laura Keene, a popular actress and theatre manager, sailed from San Francisco for Australia.[161]

August 8, Tuesday Bel Air

John Wilkes Booth, at Tudor Hall, writing to William O'Laughlen, described his difficulty getting home after drinking quantities of champagne. He also recounted how he had thrashed farmer Hagan. The sheriff warranted Booth to stand trial for assault and battery. Finally, Booth related that he had recently made a "visit to the Rocks of Deer Creek."[162]

October 23, Monday

Edwin Booth and Laura Keene opened an engagement in Sydney, Australia.[163]

November 8, Wednesday Bel Air

John Wilkes Booth wrote to his friend William O'Laughlen:

My Dear Friend, Indeed you must excuse me for not writting to you sooner, also for not calling on you when I was in the City. when next I see you I will give you my reasons for not calling on you.... It is very cold up here now, there was ice an inch thick the other day ... if nothing happens I expect to be in Baltimore in a few weeks.[164]

1855

January 25, Thursday Churchville

John Wilkes Booth wrote to William O'Laughlen:

I am at present seated in a very snug bar room by a comfortable log fire.... You said in your last letter that on Christmas day Bac[c]hus took the lead. Why my dear fellow, he always reigns in church ville either he or some other spirrit maker I don't know which. Bac[c]hus I believe was the god of whine but it seems that here Old Rye is the generel cry.... John W. Booth[165]

March 30, Friday

[Date approximate] Edwin Booth and his party sailed from the Sandwich Islands [Hawaii] for San Francisco.[166]

May 22, Tuesday Bel Air

Asia wrote to Jean Anderson: "If ever there was perfect love, it was between my father and mother.... They [neighbors] had only one ball this winter. John and I were there; it was rather a dull affair."[167]

June 18, Monday Bel Air

John Wilkes Booth wrote to William O'Laughlen:

The first week in June I was taken up by a Fair...I spent more time than money on it ... for I was there night and day and you must not think I was blowing when I say I cut quite a dash. I saw pretty girls home from the Fair at ten o'clock at night, some at the distance of four or five miles....[168]

June 29, Friday Bel Air

John Wilkes Booth attended a picnic at the Deer Creek rocks.[169]

August 1, Wednesday

Asia wrote to Jean Anderson: "My dear brother Ned [Edwin] made a fortune [in Australia] but expects to lose it before returning to the States."[170]

August 14, Tuesday Baltimore

John Wilkes Booth made his professional debut at the Charles Street Theatre in Baltimore as Henry, Earl of Richmond, in *Richard III*. The performance was a benefit for John Sleeper Clarke. Another young actor in the cast, John Albaugh, would later perform with Booth in many cities throughout the country.[171]

September 14, Friday Bel Air

John Wilkes Booth wrote to William O'Laughlen. After casually mentioning his acting debut, he noted that he was bored and that, with the Crimean War in progress, "I am thinking of moveing to Sebasterpol [Sevastopol] you know there is some excitement there. and yet the country has been very lively lately and next week are two pick nicks...."[172]

September 25, Tuesday Bel Air

John Wilkes Booth attended a large ball in Bel Air.[173]

October 1, Monday Baltimore

John Wilkes Booth's letter to William O'Laughlen of September 14 stated that he would be in Baltimore in October.[174]

November 12, Monday Bel Air

In a letter to William O'Laughlen, John Wilkes Booth apologized for missing him at the fountain in Baltimore. Commenting on the political situation in Harford County, he then wrote: "Things are going on fine in the Country. but I am getting tired—the excitement is all over. American ticket was elected by 1749 Majority in this County. Three Cheers for Amerrica."[175]

1856

September 5, Friday

Edwin Booth left San Francisco for the East Coast.[176]

September 10, Wednesday Bel Air

Asia wrote to Jean Anderson:

Twice I was at a Camp Meeting some ten miles from here, I believe. Mother and I drove down one afternoon, or rather John took us....The men are all gone deranged over their politics. We have two small flags crossed over the door, Know Nothingism, of course.[177]

October 15, Wednesday Baltimore?

Edwin Booth opened an engagement at the Front Street Theatre with *Hamlet*.[178]

October 25, Saturday Baltimore?

Edwin Booth closed his engagement at the Front Street Theatre.[179]

November 12, Wednesday Baltimore?

John Wilkes Booth's friend, Samuel Knapp Chester, made his debut in a supporting role at the Baltimore Museum.[180] He had appeared with John Wilkes Booth and others in amateur theatricals.

November 19, Wednesday

Asia celebrated her twenty-first birthday.

1857 *through July 18*

July 18, Saturday Baltimore

Two advertisements under the name of "John Booth, Baltimore" appeared in the *Bel Air Southern Aegis*. The first offered two horses for sale. The second read:

> FOR RENT—The splendid and well-known residence of the late J. B. Booth, in Harford County, about three miles from Bel Air on the road leading to Churchville. This place will be rented to a good tenant if immediate application be made. There is 180 acres of land, 80 of which is arable. John Booth, Baltimore, Md.[181]

2

Philadelphia: 1857–1858

Junius Brutus Booth encouraged his sons to avoid the stage, yet he did not object when Junius Jr. and Edwin entered the profession. John Wilkes Booth, despite his lamented father's desire for him to become a farmer, decided to become an actor in the summer of 1857. He accepted, for eight dollars a week, the position of Third Walking Gentleman in the stock company of the Arch Street Theatre in Philadelphia, which was under the management of veteran actor William Wheatley.[1] As Third Walking Gentleman, Booth was assigned small, supporting roles, some with speaking parts and some without.

Wheatley had known Junius Brutus Booth, as had all the prominent actors of the era. The circumstances of the younger Booth's hiring are unknown. Perhaps Wheatley felt an obligation to his deceased friend. Perhaps young Booth showed talent. Wheatley's friend John Sleeper Clarke was courting Asia Booth and may have put in a good word for his future brother-in-law. John Wilkes Booth had himself billed under the name of John Wilkes. He wanted recognition on his own merit, and perhaps he wished to develop his skills before he used the family name.

Edward Loomis Davenport played most of the lead roles at the Arch Street Theatre. John Sleeper Clarke appeared in comedic parts. The season opened on August 15 with a performance of *The Belle's Stratagem*, in which John Wilkes Booth played Second Mask.[2] By November 10 the theatre was on the brink of closing. The *Philadelphia Press* reported:

> We perceive with surprise, and we may add, with regret, that the present is announced as the last week of the season at the Arch Street Theatre. This certainly cannot be caused by want of success, for Mr. Wheatley has been able to fill his house every evening. The prices to all parts of the house (except boxes and orchestra seats) are reduced to 25 cents.[3]

Somehow Wheatley kept the theatre open. By January 4 matters had improved. The *Philadelphia Press* noted that "[t]he hard times, which have sensibly affected public amusements in this city, appear to have subsided of late."[4]

On December 14 Elizabeth Crocker Bowers (known as Mrs. D. P. Bowers) left Wheatley's employ to lease the rival Walnut Street Theatre, which she opened on the following Saturday night.[5] February brought the withdrawal of E. L. Davenport and his wife, Fanny Vining Gill Davenport, from the Arch Street Theatre. "Without doubt," the *Philadelphia Press* remarked, the Davenports "occupy the foremost place, not only here, but in England in the theatrical world."[6]

Young Booth formed a lasting friendship with fellow stock company actor John McCullough, an Irishman who was also learning the profession.[7] Their colleague Walter Benn related that Booth was often late for rehearsals. One day Booth excused his tardy arrival by explaining that John Sleeper Clarke's horse had escaped, and that he had jumped out of bed to capture it. Booth, according to Benn, was staying with Clarke and Clarke's mother in West Philadelphia. Benn and Booth courted two sisters who lived near the theatre.[8]

As a minor actor in the stock company, Booth usually had few lines to speak and few real chances to act. In many plays he had no speaking part but appeared in crowd scenes. Sometimes his roles were prominent enough that he was listed on the playbill. During the season his acting skills improved as he learned by observing the excellent actors in the stock company as well as the visiting stars.

On February 19, 1858, Booth had the chance to take on a larger role than was usual for him; John Sleeper Clarke had asked him to perform on Clarke's benefit night. When an actor had a benefit, he chose the play, selected the actors who would support him, and received the receipts of the evening after expenses. Clarke played scenes from *Richard III*, with Booth portraying Richmond.[9] The *Philadelphia Evening Bulletin* noted that "Clarke is the greatest favorite ever upon the Arch Street boards, and as he plays three parts on the occasion of his benefit, we can promise fun enough."[10]

Several days later, according to newspaperman George Alfred Townsend, Booth flubbed his lines on consecutive nights, and the audience hissed him. Townsend's account, written in the heat of the passion that followed the Lincoln assassination, does not seem entirely reliable. In the midst of the play *Lucretia Borgia*, Booth reportedly fluffed his line, "Madame, I am Petruchio Pandolfo," saying instead, "Madame, I am Pondolfio Pet—Pedolfio Pat—Pantuchio Ped—; Dammit! What am I?" The audience, the cast, and Booth himself howled with laughter.[11] Booth seems to have handled the incident with grace and humor, which escaped Townsend's notice. Despite Townsend's recollection, Booth was actually playing the part of Ascanio Petrucci that night; Townsend seems to have forgotten the name of the character, as did

Booth. The *Philadelphia Evening Bulletin* did not mention the incident, reporting only that the performance was so well received that the theater repeated it two nights later.[12] On the next evening, according to Townsend, Booth invited a lady friend to witness his portrayal of Dawson in *The Gamester*. When Booth appeared, "[t]he audience, remembering the Petruchio Pandolfo incident of the previous night, burst into laughter, hisses, and mock applause, so that he was struck dumb, and stood rigid, with nothing whatever to say."[13]

Little additional information about Booth during his career at the Arch Street Theatre survives. Townsend provided some interesting observations:

> I saw John Wilkes Booth during the whole period of his connection with the Arch Street Theatre.... He had a handsome face, with rich contrasts in it, and a good voice, and was much affected by the careless class of women who are always looking out for acquaintance with actors.[14]

Townsend also reported that Booth "was compelled to pay a considerable sum of money to settle a romantic affair at his boarding house."[15] The truth of the report is dubious because Booth, according to another source, was not living at a boarding house but at the home of John Sleeper Clarke.

Townsend recalled Booth's physical appearance in detail:

> None of the printed pictures that I have seen do justice to Booth. Some of the *cartes de visite* get him very nearly. He had one of the finest vital heads I have ever seen. In fact, he was one of the best exponents of vital beauty I have ever met. By this I refer to physical beauty in the Medician sense—health, shapeliness, power in beautiful poise, and seemingly more powerful in repose than in energy. His hands and feet were sizable, not small, and his legs were stout and muscular, but inclined to bow like his father's. From the waist up he was a perfect man; his chest being full and broad, his shoulders gently sloping, and his arms as white as alabaster, but hard as

marble. Over these, upon a neck which was its proper column, rose the cornice of a fine Doric face, spare at the jaws and not anywhere over-ripe, but seamed with a nose of Roman model, the only relic of his half–Jewish parentage, which gave decision to the thoughtfully stern sweep of two direct, dark eyes, meaning to woman snare, and to man a search warrant, while the lofty square forehead and square brows were crowned with a weight of curling jetty hair, like a rich Corinthian capital. His profile was eagleish, and afar his countenance was haughty. He seemed throat full of introspections, ambitious self-examinings, eye-strides into the future, as if it withheld him something to which he had a right. I have since wondered whether this moody demeanor did not come of a guilty spirit, but all the Booths look so.[16]

Mary Ann Booth, in a letter to Junius Jr., related that John Sleeper Clarke thought John would become "a very good actor." Wheatley and Clarke planned a joint management at the Arch Street Theatre for the next season. When Clarke asked John to continue in the stock company, he declined.[17] Booth may have left the employ of the Arch to avoid Clarke; in later years a strong mutual dislike developed between them.

Shortly after the theatre closed for the season, John Wilkes Booth traveled to New York and registered at the St. Nicholas Hotel on Broadway. Edwin Booth had checked in several hours earlier.[18] Actor Charles Pope wrote of first meeting John Wilkes Booth at this time:

> It was in a billiard room next to Grace Church [in New York], managed by Michael Phelan, the champion of the cue. We played several games; he was an expert. Indeed, he excelled in all athletic sports. Like his brother "June" [Junius Jr.], he was a master of fence.... I was struck with his easy movements of alluring, springy grace. The classic Booth head sat above broad shoulders and deep chest. Taller than any of the other Booths, his frame was compactly knit and instilled with virile life in every fibre.[19]

On August 27 Edwin Booth had a benefit at Baltimore's Holliday Street Theatre in the title role of *Richard III*, with John taking the part of Richmond.[20] A fellow actor described the performances: "Both ... were superb. I shall never forget the fight between Richard and Richmond ... an encounter which was terrible in its savage realism."[21]

1857 *from August 11*

August 11, Tuesday Philadelphia

An Arch Street Theatre advertisement noted: "Mr. J. B. Wilks [*sic*]—from the N. York Theatres, his 1st appearance in Phila."[22]

August 12, Wednesday Philadelphia

The *Philadelphia Public Ledger & Daily Transcript* of August 11 had announced: WHEATLEY'S ARCH ST. THEATRE, PHILADELPHIA. NOTICE—The ladies and Gentlemen engaged at this establishment are requested to meet in the GREEN ROOM, on WEDNESDAY next, August 12, 1857, preparatory to opening, on Saturday, August 15.[23]

August 13, Thursday Philadelphia

August 14, Friday Philadelphia

Arch Street Theatre manager William Wheatley held a pre-theatrical season banquet on the stage of the theatre. Members of the press attended.[24]

August 15, Saturday Philadelphia

The Arch Street Theatre opened its season to a full house.[25] Booth played Second Mask in *The Belle's Stratagem*.[26]

Advertisements for the sale of horses and the rental of Tudor Hall had appeared each Saturday in the *Bel Air Southern Aegis*. The horses must have been sold, for on this date the advertisement for Tudor Hall appeared alone.[27]

August 16, Sunday Philadelphia

August 17, Monday Philadelphia

Booth played a courier in *The Wife*.

August 18, Tuesday Philadelphia

The Arch Street Theatre presented *Charity's Love*.[28]

August 19, Wednesday Philadelphia

The Arch Street Theatre presented *Charity's Love*.

August 20, Thursday Philadelphia

The Arch Street Theatre presented *Charity's Love*.

August 21, Friday Philadelphia

The Arch Street Theatre presented *Charity's Love*.

August 22, Saturday Philadelphia

The Arch Street Theatre presented *Richard III* with E. L. Davenport and *The Toodles* with John Sleeper Clarke.

August 23, Sunday Philadelphia

August 24, Monday Philadelphia

The Arch Street Theatre presented *The Lady of Lyons; or, Love and Pride* with E. L. Davenport as Claude Melnotte.[29]

August 25, Tuesday Philadelphia

The Arch Street Theatre presented *Love's Sacrifice*.

August 26, Wednesday Philadelphia

The *Philadelphia Press* announced: "The very great success of *Richard III*, on Saturday evening, fully warrants its repetition this evening. *The Toodles*, in which Mr. J. S. Clarke leads, will be the afterpiece."[30]

August 27, Thursday Philadelphia

The Arch Street company played *St. Marc; or, A Husband's Sacrifice*. Booth probably played the part of Stefano Lodari. The *Philadelphia Press* reported: "We can say, from a twenty minutes' presence in the house, that there was a very large audience, and that (as far as we saw and heard) the play went off admirably."[31]

August 28, Friday Philadelphia

Booth played Stefano Lodari in *St. Marc*.

August 29, Saturday Philadelphia

Booth played Stefano Lodari in *St. Marc*.

August 30, Sunday Philadelphia

August 31, Monday Philadelphia

The Arch Street Theatre presented *The Stranger* with Mrs. D. P. Bowers, who had not appeared at the theatre for several months. The *Philadelphia Press* noted that "the house was filled to excess before the curtain was up, and much disappointment was manifested among those turned from the house." E. L. Davenport, cast for *The Stranger*, was taken ill, and his place was filled by William Wheatley, "who is always

'up' when any of the stars of his company are down."[32]

September 1, Tuesday Philadelphia

Booth played Simpson in *The Hunchback*.

September 2, Wednesday Philadelphia

Booth played Antonio in *Fazio; or, The Italian Wife's Revenge*.

September 3, Thursday Philadelphia

Booth played Simpson in *The Hunchback*.

September 4, Friday Philadelphia

The Arch Street Theatre presented *Jane Shore*, followed by *The Toodles*.

September 5, Saturday Philadelphia

William Wheatley and Fanny Davenport played *Romeo and Juliet*. In the afterpiece Booth played First Officer in *The Golden Farmer*.

September 6, Sunday Philadelphia

September 7, Monday Philadelphia

Booth played Conrade in *Much Ado About Nothing*.

September 8, Tuesday Philadelphia

The Arch Street Theatre presented *The Merchant of Venice* with E. L. Davenport as Shylock, followed by *The Toodles*.

September 9, Wednesday Philadelphia

The Arch Street Theatre presented *Charity's Love*.

September 10, Thursday Philadelphia

The Arch Street Theatre presented *The Serious Family*.

September 11, Friday Philadelphia

The Arch Street Theatre presented *The Merchant of Venice*.

September 12, Saturday Philadelphia

Booth played First Spaniard in *The Apostate* and Nabhem in *Cape May*.

September 13, Sunday Philadelphia

September 14, Monday Philadelphia

Booth played Watchall in *A New Way to Pay Old Debts* and Nabhem in *Cape May*.

September 15, Tuesday Philadelphia

Booth played Stefano in *St. Marc* and Nabhem in *Cape May*.

September 16, Wednesday Philadelphia

Booth played Guildenstern in *Hamlet* and Nabhem in *Cape May*.

September 17, Thursday Philadelphia
Booth played the Earl of Oxford in *Richard III* and Nabhem in *Cape May*.

September 18, Friday Philadelphia
Booth played Guildenstern in *Hamlet*.

September 19, Saturday Philadelphia
Booth played Watchall in *A New Way to Pay Old Debts*.

September 20, Sunday Philadelphia

September 21, Monday Philadelphia
Booth played Guildenstern in *Hamlet*. E. L. Davenport played Hamlet, while Clarke played First Gravedigger.[33] The *Philadelphia Press* commented:

> At the Arch Street Theatre, this evening, *Hamlet* will be repeated. The characters are judiciously cast. Mr. Wheatley, as Laertes, has a part which exactly suits him.... His fencing scene with Mr. Davenport, in the last act, is one of the most beautiful trials of skill imaginable. Both these gentlemen are first class swordsmen.... It is a treat to see them fence.[34]

September 22, Tuesday Philadelphia
Booth played a servant in *Camille; or, The Fate of a Coquette*.

September 23, Wednesday Philadelphia
Booth played a brigand in *The Brigand* and appeared as Bubblemere in *The Willow Copse*.

September 24, Thursday Philadelphia
Booth played Second Mask in *The Belle's Stratagem* and appeared as a brigand in *The Brigand*.

September 25, Friday Philadelphia
Booth played a servant in *Camille* and appeared as a brigand in *The Brigand*.

September 26, Saturday Philadelphia
Booth played Guildenstern in *Hamlet*.

September 27, Sunday Philadelphia

September 28, Monday Philadelphia
Booth played Antonio in *Othello*.

September 29, Tuesday Philadelphia
Booth appeared as a brigand in *The Brigand*. Mrs. D. P. Bowers played the lead role.

September 30, Wednesday Philadelphia
The Arch Street Theatre presented *Victims*.

October 1, Thursday Philadelphia
The Arch Street Theatre presented *Victims*.

October 2, Friday Philadelphia
Booth appeared as a brigand in *The Brigand*.

October 3, Saturday Philadelphia
Booth played First Robber in *The Robbers*.

October 4, Sunday Philadelphia

October 5, Monday Philadelphia
Booth played a brigand in *The Brigand*.

October 6, Tuesday Philadelphia
Booth played Antonio in *Othello*.

October 7, Wednesday Philadelphia
Booth played First Robber in *The Robbers*.

October 8, Thursday Philadelphia
Booth played a servant in *Camille* and appeared as a brigand in *The Brigand*.

October 9, Friday Philadelphia
Booth appeared as First Robber in *The Robbers*.

October 10, Saturday Philadelphia
The Arch Street Theatre presented *Jack Cade*.

October 11, Sunday Philadelphia

October 12, Monday Philadelphia
Booth played a brigand in *The Brigand*.

October 13, Tuesday Philadelphia
Booth played Conrade in *Much Ado About Nothing*.

October 14, Wednesday Philadelphia
The Arch Street Theatre presented *Jack Cade*.

October 15, Thursday Philadelphia
The Arch Street Theatre presented *Jack Cade*.

October 16, Friday Philadelphia
The Arch Street Theatre presented *Jack Cade*.

October 17, Saturday Philadelphia
The Arch Street Theatre presented *Jack Cade*.

October 18, Sunday Philadelphia

October 19, Monday Philadelphia
The Arch Street Theatre presented *Jack Cade*. The *Philadelphia Press* reported that "*Jack Cade* has drawn the most crowded houses of the present season."[35]

October 20, Tuesday Philadelphia

The Arch Street Theatre presented *Jack Cade*.

October 21, Wednesday Philadelphia

The Arch Street Theatre presented *Jack Cade*.

October 22, Thursday Philadelphia

The Arch Street Theatre presented *Jack Cade*.[36]

October 23, Friday Philadelphia

Booth played Hortensio in *Katharine and Petruchio*.

October 24, Saturday Philadelphia

Booth played the Marquis de Villarceaux in *Civilization*.

October 25, Sunday Philadelphia

October 26, Monday Philadelphia

Booth played Second Officer in *Macbeth*.

October 27, Tuesday Philadelphia

Booth played the Marquis de Villarceaux in *Civilization*.

October 28, Wednesday Philadelphia

E. L. Davenport and company appeared in *Julius Caesar*.[37] Booth may have played the part of Metellus Cimber.[38]

October 29, Thursday Philadelphia

Booth played the Marquis de Villarceaux in *Civilization* and the sergeant in *Guy Mannering; or, The Gipsey's Prophecy*.

October 30, Friday Philadelphia

Booth played John in *The Jealous Wife* and the sergeant in *Guy Mannering*.[39]

October 31, Saturday Philadelphia

Booth played Metellus Cimber in *Julius Caesar* and Hortensio in *Katharine and Petruchio*.

November 1, Sunday Philadelphia

November 2, Monday Philadelphia

Booth played First Lord in *Queen of Spades* and Lieutenant Pike in *Black-Eyed Susan; or, All in the Downs*. The *Philadelphia Press* noted that the Arch Street Theatre was the "best-paying" theatre in the city during increasingly bad economic times.[40]

November 3, Tuesday Philadelphia

Booth appeared as First Lord in *Queen of Spades* and Lieutenant Pike in *Black-Eyed Susan*.

November 4, Wednesday Philadelphia

Booth appeared as First Lord in *Queen of Spades* and Lieutenant Pike in *Black-Eyed Susan*.

November 5, Thursday Philadelphia

Booth appeared as First Lord in *Queen of Spades* and Lieutenant Pike in *Black-Eyed Susan*.

November 6, Friday Philadelphia

Booth appeared as First Lord in *Queen of Spades* and Lieutenant Pike in *Black-Eyed Susan*.

November 7, Saturday Philadelphia

Booth played Elphinor in *Ingomar, the Barbarian* and Lieutenant Pike in *Black-Eyed Susan*.

November 8, Sunday Philadelphia

November 9, Monday Philadelphia

Booth played John in *The Jealous Wife* and Lieutenant Pike in *Black-Eyed Susan*.

November 10, Tuesday Philadelphia

The Arch Street Theatre presented *The King's Rival; or, The Court and the Stage*.

The *Philadelphia Press* announced that this would be the last week of the season at the Arch Street Theatre.[41]

November 11, Wednesday Philadelphia

The Arch Street Theatre presented *Jack Cade*.[42]

November 12, Thursday Philadelphia

Booth played a servant in *Camille* and Mouser in *The Robber's Wife*.

November 13, Friday Philadelphia

Booth played First Officer in *The Golden Farmer*.

November 14, Saturday Philadelphia

Booth played the Earl of Oxford in *Richard III*.

November 15, Sunday Philadelphia

November 16, Monday Philadelphia

Booth played Guildenstern in *Hamlet*. The *Philadelphia Press* noted that "[a]t the Arch Street Theatre, (which did not close, as threatened, on Saturday), pretty fair business has been done during the week, and we suspect that this would improve if Mr. Wheatley were himself to appear more frequently.[43]

November 17, Tuesday Philadelphia

Booth played Andrew Fairservice in *Rob Roy MacGregor; or, Auld Lang Syne* and a waiter in *Laugh When You Can*.

November 18, Wednesday Philadelphia
Booth played the sergeant in *Guy Mannering*.

November 19, Thursday Philadelphia
Booth played Andrew Fairservice in *Rob Roy MacGregor*.

November 20, Friday Philadelphia
Booth played First Courtier in *Richelieu; or, The Conspiracy*.

November 21, Saturday Philadelphia
Booth played Jano, a sailor, in *The Sea of Ice*.[44]

November 22, Sunday Philadelphia

November 23, Monday Philadelphia
Booth played First Courtier in *Richelieu*.

November 24, Tuesday Philadelphia
Booth played Jano in *The Sea of Ice*.[45]

November 25, Wednesday Philadelphia
Booth played Antonio in *Fazio*.

November 26, Thursday Philadelphia
Booth played a waiter in *Out for Thanksgiving* and Jano in *The Sea of Ice*.

November 27, Friday Philadelphia
Booth played Garnier in *Retribution; or, The Doom of the Libertine*.

November 28, Saturday Philadelphia
Booth played Garnier in *Retribution*.

November 29, Sunday Philadelphia

November 30, Monday Philadelphia
Booth played a waiter in *A Day Well Spent*.

December 1, Tuesday Philadelphia
Booth played Grosmere in *Madelaine; or, The Foundling of Paris*.

December 2, Wednesday Philadelphia
Booth played Grosmere in *Madelaine*.

December 3, Thursday Philadelphia
The Arch Street Theatre presented *London Assurance*.

December 4, Friday Philadelphia
The Arch Street Theatre presented *Still Waters Run Deep*.

December 5, Saturday Philadelphia
Booth played Antonio in *Othello*.

December 6, Sunday Philadelphia

December 7, Monday Philadelphia
The Arch Street Theatre presented *London Assurance*.

December 8, Tuesday Philadelphia
Booth played Frederick Morden in the afterpiece *Annette: The Forsaken*.

December 9, Wednesday Philadelphia
Booth played a waiter in *Laugh When You Can*.

December 10, Thursday Philadelphia
Booth played John in *The Jealous Wife*.

December 11, Friday Philadelphia
Booth played Major Desmoulins in *The Lady of Lyons*.

December 12, Saturday Philadelphia
E. L. Davenport appeared in *Richard III*.[46] It is likely that Booth played the Earl of Oxford.

December 13, Sunday Philadelphia

December 14, Monday Philadelphia
Booth played Frederick Morden in *Annette: The Forsaken*. The *Philadelphia Press* reported:
The theatrical event of the week in our fair city is the retirement of Mr. E. A. Marshall from the Walnut Street Theatre, and the announcement by Mrs. D. P. Bowers that she has entered into the lesseeship, and will open it next Saturday evening.... The public are tired with seeing the same old faces, season after season....[47]

December 15, Tuesday Philadelphia
Booth played Second Officer in *The Carpenter of Rouen; or, The Secret Order of the Confrerie*.

December 16, Wednesday Philadelphia
The Arch Street Theatre presented *Beatrice; or, The False and the True*, starring E. L. Davenport.[48]

December 17, Thursday Philadelphia
The Arch Street Theatre presented *Beatrice*.

December 18, Friday Philadelphia
The Arch Street Theatre presented *Beatrice*.

December 19, Saturday Philadelphia
Booth played Second Officer in *The Carpenter of Rouen*.
Mrs. D. P. Bowers opened the Walnut Street Theatre under her own management.[49]

December 20, Sunday Philadelphia

December 21, Monday Philadelphia
The Arch Street Theatre presented *Beatrice*.

December 22, Tuesday Philadelphia
The Arch Street Theatre presented *Beatrice*.[50]

December 23, Wednesday Philadelphia
The Arch Street Theatre presented *Beatrice*.

December 24, Thursday Philadelphia
The Arch Street Theatre presented *Beatrice*, followed by *Adventures of a Christmas Eve*.

December 25, Friday Philadelphia
Booth played Lieutenant Pike in *Black-Eyed Susan* at a two o'clock matinee. The evening performance included *The Last Days of Pompeii* and *Sarah's Young Man*.

December 26, Saturday Philadelphia
The Arch Street Theatre presented *The Last Days of Pompeii*, starring E. L. Davenport.[51]

December 27, Sunday Philadelphia

December 28, Monday Philadelphia
Booth played a sentinel in *The Rival Pages*.

December 29, Tuesday Philadelphia
Booth appeared as a sentinel in *The Rival Pages*.

December 30, Wednesday Philadelphia
The Arch Street Theatre presented *The Last Days of Pompeii* and *Still Waters Run Deep* with E. L. Davenport and William Wheatley.[52]

December 31, Thursday Philadelphia
The Arch Street Theatre presented *The Last Days of Pompeii*.

1858 *through August 27*

January 1, Friday Philadelphia
The Arch Street Theatre presented *The Last Days of Pompeii*.

January 2, Saturday Philadelphia
Booth played St. Vrain in *The Scalp Hunters*.

January 3, Sunday Philadelphia

January 4, Monday Philadelphia
Booth appeared as St. Vrain in *The Scalp Hunters*. "The hard times, which have sensibly affected public amusements in this city, appear to have subsided of late," noted the *Philadelphia Press*, which continued:

> At the Arch Street Theatre, which Mr. Wheatley, by good management and liberal expenditure has elevated to one of the most respectable establishments in this country, the company is very effective. Mr. Wheatley himself is entitled to draw anywhere as a Star. He acts well, and dresses well. Mr. Davenport is one of the best actors we have, with a very wide range of character.[53]

January 5, Tuesday Philadelphia
Booth appeared as St. Vrain in *The Scalp Hunters*.

January 6, Wednesday Philadelphia
The run of *The Scalp Hunters* continued with Booth as St. Vrain.

January 7, Thursday Philadelphia
The run of *The Scalp Hunters* continued with Booth as St. Vrain.

January 8, Friday Philadelphia
The run of *The Scalp Hunters* continued with Booth as St. Vrain.

January 9, Saturday Philadelphia
The run of *The Scalp Hunters* closed with Booth as St. Vrain.

January 10, Sunday Philadelphia

January 11, Monday Philadelphia
Booth played Pacolo in *Don Caesar de Bazan*.

January 12, Tuesday Philadelphia
The Arch Street Theatre presented *The Last Days of Pompeii*.

January 13, Wednesday Philadelphia
Booth played Salanio in *The Merchant of Venice*.

January 14, Thursday Philadelphia
Booth played St. Vrain in *The Scalp Hunters*.

January 15, Friday Philadelphia
Booth played Major Desmoulins in *The Lady of Lyons*.

January 16, Saturday Philadelphia
Booth played Clarence Lindon in *Fraud and Its Victims; or, The Poor of Philadelphia*.

January 17, Sunday Philadelphia

January 18, Monday Philadelphia
Booth played Clarence Lindon in *Fraud and Its Victims* and the sentinel in *The Rival Pages*.

January 19, Tuesday Philadelphia
Booth played Clarence Lindon in *Fraud and Its Victims.*

January 20, Wednesday Philadelphia
Booth played Clarence Lindon in *Fraud and Its Victims* and also played John in *The Married Bachelor; or, Master and Man.*

January 21, Thursday Philadelphia
Booth played Clarence Lindon in *Fraud and Its Victims.*

January 22, Friday Philadelphia
Booth appeared as Clarence Lindon in *Fraud and Its Victims* and also played a sentinel in *The Rival Pages.*

January 23, Saturday Philadelphia
The run of *Fraud and Its Victims* continued with Booth as Clarence Lindon.

January 24, Sunday Philadelphia

January 25, Monday Philadelphia
Booth played Clarence Lindon in *Fraud and Its Victims.*

January 26, Tuesday Philadelphia
Booth played Clarence Lindon in *Fraud and Its Victims.*

January 27, Wednesday Philadelphia
Booth played Clarence Lindon in *Fraud and Its Victims.*

January 28, Thursday Philadelphia
Booth played Clarence Lindon in *Fraud and Its Victims.*

January 29, Friday Philadelphia
The run of *Fraud and Its Victims* closed with Booth as Clarence Lindon. Booth appeared as a waiter in *Laugh When You Can.*

January 30, Saturday Philadelphia
Booth may have played the role of James in *A Cure for the Heartache.*[54] He also may have appeared as the Earl of Fife in *Wallace, The Hero of Scotland.*[55] Playbills indicate he played those roles in later performances.

January 31, Sunday Philadelphia

February 1, Monday Philadelphia
Booth played Second Senator in *Damon and Pythias.*

February 2, Tuesday Philadelphia
Booth played the Earl of Fife in *Wallace, The Hero of Scotland.*

February 3, Wednesday Philadelphia
Booth played the Earl of Fife in *Wallace, The Hero of Scotland.*

February 4, Thursday Philadelphia
The Arch Street Theatre presented *Brian Boroihme; or, The Maid of Erin.*
Booth wrote "John W. Booth, Feb. 4th, Arch St." in a copy of Shakespeare's *Julius Caesar.*[56]

February 5, Friday Philadelphia
The Arch Street Theatre repeated *Brian Boroihme.*

February 6, Saturday Philadelphia
The Arch Street Theatre presented *Speed the Plough.*

February 7, Sunday Philadelphia

February 8, Monday Philadelphia
Booth played a soldier in *Virginius* with E. L. Davenport.

February 9, Tuesday Philadelphia
Booth played Second Officer in *The Carpenter of Rouen.*

February 10, Wednesday Philadelphia
Booth played Sir Thomas Nalvern in *Ambition; or, The Tomb, the Throne, and the Scaffold.*

February 11, Thursday Philadelphia
Booth appeared as Sir Thomas Nalvern in *Ambition.*

February 12, Friday Philadelphia
Booth appeared as Sir Thomas Nalvern in *Ambition.*

February 13, Saturday Philadelphia
Booth appeared as Sir Thomas Nalvern in *Ambition.*

February 14, Sunday Philadelphia

February 15, Monday Philadelphia
Booth appeared as Sir Thomas Nalvern in *Ambition.*

February 16, Tuesday Philadelphia
Booth appeared as Sir Thomas Nalvern in *Ambition.*

February 17, Wednesday Philadelphia
Booth appeared as Sir Thomas Nalvern in *Ambition.*

February 18, Thursday Philadelphia
The run of *Ambition* ended with Booth as Sir Thomas Nalvern.

February 19, Friday Philadelphia

John Sleeper Clarke played scenes from *Richard III*. Booth, listed on the playbill under his own name, "Mr. Wilks [*sic*] Booth," played Richmond. Clarke performed a comic version of Richard, while Booth played "straight." The *Philadelphia Evening Bulletin* advertised the event:

Mr. J. S. Clarke will take a benefit, when he will present a very attractive bill. Tragedy, comedy and serio-comic tragedy. Clarke is the greatest favorite ever upon the Arch Street boards, and as he plays three parts on the occasion of his benefit, we can promise fun enough.[57]

February 20, Saturday Philadelphia

The Arch Street Theatre presented *The Stranger* with Mary Ann Russell Farren,[58] who in later years toured as a star with John Wilkes Booth.

The *Philadelphia Press* critic noted:

With extreme regret, we notice the withdrawal of Mr. and Mrs. E. L. Davenport from the Arch Street Theatre. Thereby, Mr. Wheatley loses two of the best cards in his hand. It is said that they are engaged for Boston. Without doubt, they occupy the foremost place, not only here, but in England in the theatrical world.[59]

February 21, Sunday Philadelphia

February 22, Monday Philadelphia

Mary Ann Farren played the lead role in *Bertram* at the Arch Street Theatre.

The *Philadelphia Press* noted:

It will be extremely difficult to fill the void in the Arch street company made by the secession of Mr. and Mrs. Davenport. We perceive that Mrs. Farren and Mr. Vezin are engaged. We do not think them at all equal to the two admirable performers ... whom they succeed.[60]

February 23, Tuesday Philadelphia

In the midst of the play *Lucretia Borgia*, Booth, portraying Ascanio Petrucci, reportedly fluffed his line, "Madame, I am Petruchio Pandolfo," saying instead, "Madame, I am Pondolfio Pet—Pedolfio Pat—Pantuchio Ped—;Dammit! What am I?" The audience, the cast, and Booth himself howled with laughter.[61]

February 24, Wednesday Philadelphia

Booth appeared as Dawson in *The Gamester*.

E. L. Davenport had left the Arch Street company. He appeared this night in a benefit performance at Mrs. D. P. Bowers's Walnut Street Theatre.[62]

February 25, Thursday Philadelphia

Booth played Elphinor in *Ingomar, the Barbarian* and Ascanio Petrucci in *Lucretia Borgia*.

The Tuesday performance of *Lucretia Borgia* received a favorable review in the *Philadelphia Evening Bulletin*.

February 26, Friday Philadelphia

Booth portrayed Lord Gardiner in *Mary Tudor*.

February 27, Saturday Philadelphia

The Arch Street Theatre presented *Romeo and Juliet* with Susan Denin[63] as Juliet and Mme. Ponisi[64] as Romeo. The afterpiece was *The Toodles*.

February 28, Sunday Philadelphia

March 1, Monday Philadelphia

Booth played a servant in *Jane Shore*. Susan Denin had the lead role.[65]

Mary Ann Farren's acting has "not been improved in the South and West, where she has long been a favorite," opined the *Philadelphia Press*.[66]

March 2, Tuesday Philadelphia

The Arch Street Theatre presented *Money*.

March 3, Wednesday Philadelphia

Booth played Antonio in *Fazio*.[67]

March 4, Thursday Philadelphia

The Arch Street Theatre presented *Romeo and Juliet*.

March 5, Friday Philadelphia

Booth played Vasio in *Rule a Wife and Have a Wife* and a gamekeeper in *A Roland for an Oliver*.

March 6, Saturday Philadelphia

The Arch Street Theatre presented *Douglas; or, The Noble Shepherd*, in which Booth may have played Second Officer, and *The Willow Copse*, in which he may have played Bubblemere.[68]

March 7, Sunday Philadelphia

March 8, Monday Philadelphia

Booth appeared as Captain Danforth in *The Declaration of Independence; or, Philadelphia in the Olden Time*.

Adelaide Delannoy Booth died in Baltimore. She had married Junius Brutus Booth in 1815, had been abandoned by him in 1821, and was granted a divorce in Baltimore on April 18, 1851. She followed him to America in 1846.[69]

March 9, Tuesday Philadelphia
Booth appeared as Captain Danforth in *Declaration of Independence*.

March 10, Wednesday Philadelphia
Booth appeared as Captain Danforth in *Declaration of Independence*.

March 11, Thursday Philadelphia
Booth appeared as Captain Danforth in *Declaration of Independence*.

March 12, Friday Philadelphia
Booth appeared as Captain Danforth in *Declaration of Independence*.

March 13, Saturday Philadelphia
Booth appeared as Captain Danforth in *Declaration of Independence*.

March 14, Sunday Philadelphia

March 15, Monday Philadelphia
Booth appeared as Captain Danforth in *Declaration of Independence*.

March 16, Tuesday Philadelphia
Booth appeared as Captain Danforth in *Declaration of Independence*.

March 17, Wednesday Philadelphia
Booth appeared as Captain Danforth in *Declaration of Independence* and as First Officer in *The Golden Farmer*.

March 18, Thursday Philadelphia
Booth appeared as Captain Danforth in *Declaration of Independence*.

March 19, Friday Philadelphia
Booth appeared as Captain Danforth in *Declaration of Independence*.

March 20, Saturday Philadelphia
Booth played Second Officer in *Douglas* and Bubblemere in *The Willow Copse*.

March 21, Sunday Philadelphia

March 22, Monday Philadelphia
The Arch Street Theatre presented *Asmodeus*.

March 23, Tuesday Philadelphia
Booth played Duc de Rohan in *The Husband of an Hour*. John Sleeper Clarke played Jacques Strop in *Robert Macaire*.

March 24, Wednesday Philadelphia
The Arch Street Theatre presented *Speed the Plough*.

March 25, Thursday Philadelphia
The Arch Street Theatre presented *The Rivals*.

March 26, Friday Philadelphia
Booth played Duc de Rohan in *The Husband of an Hour*.

March 27, Saturday Philadelphia
Booth played Elliot in *Venice Preserved*.

March 28, Sunday Philadelphia

March 29, Monday Philadelphia
The *Philadelphia Evening Bulletin* noted: This evening, the tragedy of *Ugolino*, written by the tragedian [Junius Brutus] Booth, is to be presented with a superior cast, including all the augmented star company. It has been a long time since this piece was played, and its revival will undoubtedly attract.[70]

Susan Denin played the part of Angelica in the performance of *Ugolino*.

March 30, Tuesday Philadelphia
The Arch Street Theatre presented *The Heir at Law*.

The *Philadelphia Press* reported: *Ugolino*, by the celebrated Junius Brutus Booth, was revived at the Arch Street Theatre last night. The play is attractive, as written by such a man as Booth, and as a comparative novelty here. But it is not a first-class piece, by any means. The house was crowded.[71]

March 31, Wednesday Philadelphia
Booth played Careless in *The School for Scandal*.

April 1, Thursday Philadelphia
Booth played Duc de Rohan in *The Husband of an Hour*, followed by *Ugolino*.

April 2, Friday Philadelphia
Booth played Captain D'Esterre in *The Gambler's Fate* and also appeared as James in *A Cure for the Heartache*.

April 3, Saturday Philadelphia
Booth played Careless in *The School for Scandal* and Captain D'Esterre in *The Gambler's Fate*.

April 4, Sunday Philadelphia

April 5, Monday Philadelphia
Booth played a messenger in *Brutus; or, The Fall of Tarquin*.

April 6, Tuesday Philadelphia

The Arch Street Theatre presented *Richard III*. E. L. Davenport played Richard, William Wheatley played Richmond, and Susan Denin played Lady Anne.[72]

April 7, Wednesday Philadelphia

Booth played Augustus Fogg in *Fashion* and also appeared as Rodolph in *William Tell*.[73]

April 8, Thursday Philadelphia

Booth played Augustus Fogg in *Fashion* and Almagro in *Pizarro; or, The Conquest of Peru*.

April 9, Friday Philadelphia

Booth played Tenellus in *The Egyptian* and Lieutenant Pike in *Black-Eyed Susan*.

April 10, Saturday Philadelphia

Booth played Second Senator in *Damon and Pythias* and Second Officer in *The Carpenter of Rouen*.

April 11, Sunday Philadelphia

April 12, Monday Philadelphia

Booth played Frank Linwood in *Paul Pry in America* and Sergeant Sam in *Jonathan Bradford; or, The Murder at the Road-Side Inn*.

April 13, Tuesday Philadelphia

Booth played Lamp in *Wild Oats*.

The monument for the Booth cemetery plot arrived in Baltimore.

A MONUMENT, to be erected to the memory of Junius Brutus Booth, was brought to Baltimore on April 13th, from Boston by the steamboat *William Jenkins*. It was an obelisk of marble resting on a granite base four and one half feet in height, by five feet square, tapering to a top of three and a half feet square. The work was executed by Joseph Carew of Boston.[74]

April 14, Wednesday Philadelphia

Booth played Sergeant Sam in *Jonathan Bradford* and Frank Linwood in *Paul Pry in America*.

April 15, Thursday Philadelphia

About this date Booth signed a card: "J. W. Booth, Arch St. Theatre, Philad. April 1858."[75]

Booth played an undertaker in *The Way to Get Married*.

April 16, Friday Philadelphia

Booth played Robin in *Town and Country*.

April 17, Saturday Philadelphia

Booth appeared as an undertaker in *The Way to Get Married* and as Sergeant Sam in *Jonathan Bradford*.

April 18, Sunday Philadelphia

April 19, Monday Philadelphia

Booth played Sergeant Sam in *Jonathan Bradford*.

April 20, Tuesday Philadelphia

Booth played John, Prince of Lancaster, in *King Henry IV* with James Hackett as Falstaff.

April 21, Wednesday Philadelphia

The Arch Street Theatre presented *The Merry Wives of Windsor*.

April 22, Thursday Philadelphia

Booth played John in *King Henry IV*.

April 23, Friday Philadelphia

Booth played John in *King Henry IV* and Hortensio in *Katharine and Petruchio*.

April 24, Saturday Philadelphia

The Arch Street Theatre presented *The Dramatist*.

April 25, Sunday Philadelphia

April 26, Monday Philadelphia

The Arch Street Theatre presented *Jessie Brown; or, The Relief of Lucknow*. Dion Boucicault, the play's author, played the part of Nena Sahib, the villain.[76]

April 27, Tuesday Philadelphia

The Arch Street Theatre presented *Jessie Brown*.

April 28, Wednesday Philadelphia

The Arch Street Theatre presented *Jessie Brown*.

April 29, Thursday Philadelphia

The Arch Street Theatre presented *Jessie Brown*.

April 30, Friday Philadelphia

The Arch Street Theatre presented *Jessie Brown*.

May 1, Saturday Philadelphia

Asia Booth Clarke later wrote:

On Edwin's arrival from California, he erected a monument over his father's grave. The sculpture was executed in Boston and completed in the spring of 1858 and the monument was placed over the tomb on the first of May, his father's birthday.[77]

The Arch Street Theatre presented *Jessie Brown*.

May 2, Sunday Philadelphia

May 3, Monday Philadelphia
The Arch Street Theatre presented *Jessie Brown.*

May 4, Tuesday Philadelphia
Booth played Squire Robert in *The Irish Broom-maker; or, A Cure for Dumbness.*

May 5, Wednesday Philadelphia
Booth played Squire Robert in *The Irish Broom-maker.*

May 6, Thursday Philadelphia
The Arch Street Theatre presented *Jessie Brown.*

May 7, Friday Philadelphia
The Arch Street Theatre presented *Jessie Brown.*

May 8, Saturday Philadelphia
Booth played Squire Robert in *The Irish Broom-maker.*

May 9, Sunday Philadelphia

May 10, Monday Philadelphia
Booth, on his twentieth birthday, played Squire Robert in *The Irish Broom-maker.*

May 11, Tuesday Philadelphia
The Arch Street Theatre presented *Jessie Brown.*

May 12, Wednesday Philadelphia
Booth played Henry Dunderford in *Teddy the Tiler.*

May 13, Thursday Philadelphia
Booth played Henry Dunderford in *Teddy the Tiler.*

May 14, Friday Philadelphia
The Arch Street Theatre presented *Jessie Brown.*

May 15, Saturday Philadelphia
The Arch Street Theatre presented *Jessie Brown.*

May 16, Sunday Philadelphia

May 17, Monday Philadelphia
The Arch Street Theatre presented *Jessie Brown.*

May 18, Tuesday Philadelphia
The Arch Street Theatre presented *Jessie Brown.*

May 19, Wednesday Philadelphia
The Arch Street Theatre presented *Jessie Brown.*

May 20, Thursday Philadelphia
The Arch Street Theatre presented *Jessie Brown.*

May 21, Friday Philadelphia
The Arch Street Theatre presented *Jessie Brown.*

May 22, Saturday Philadelphia
The Arch Street Theatre presented *Jessie Brown.*

May 23, Sunday Philadelphia

May 24, Monday Philadelphia
Charlotte Cushman[78] opened her engagement at the Arch Street Theatre in *The Stranger.*[79] The *Philadelphia Press* critic commented in the next day's newspaper: "Each effective scene was greeted with prolonged and cordial applause— an evidence at least of the great popularity of this lady."[80]

May 25, Tuesday Philadelphia
Booth played First Apparition in *Macbeth.*
Laura Keene and Charles Wheatleigh were appearing at the Walnut Street Theatre in Philadelphia.[81]

May 26, Wednesday Philadelphia
The Arch Street Theatre playbill lists Booth as Capucius in *Henry VIII*, but his name is crossed out and replaced by "Hess."[82]

May 27, Thursday Philadelphia
The Arch Street Theatre presented *Guy Mannering.*

May 28, Friday Philadelphia
Charlotte Cushman appeared in *As You Like It* for her benefit. She was supported by a luminous cast that included William Wheatley, John Sleeper Clarke, and John McCullough, with Booth as Silvius.[83]

May 29, Saturday Philadelphia
Booth played Garnier in *Retribution* and Rodolph in *William Tell.*

May 30, Sunday Philadelphia

May 31, Monday Philadelphia
Booth played Bubblemere in *The Willow Copse.* C. W. Couldock played the lead role.[84] The *Philadelphia Press* critic commented: "We

never have had to record a duller theatrical week than that which has just closed."[85]

June 1, Tuesday Philadelphia

The Arch Street Theatre presented *The School of Reform*.

June 2, Wednesday Philadelphia

The Arch Street Theatre presented *Louis IX*.

June 3, Thursday Philadelphia

The Arch Street Theatre presented *Louis IX*.

June 4, Friday Philadelphia

The Arch Street Theatre presented *Louis IX*.

June 5, Saturday Philadelphia

Booth played the Duke of Burgundy in *King Lear*.

June 6, Sunday Philadelphia

June 7, Monday Philadelphia

Booth played Captain Tancred in *Sketches in India*. Laura Keene closed her engagement at the Walnut Street Theatre.[86]

June 8, Tuesday Philadelphia

The Arch Street Theatre presented *David Copperfield*.

June 9, Wednesday Philadelphia

Booth played Lord Lounge in *The Nervous Man* and William Jones in *Po-ca-hon-tas; or, The Gentle Savage*.

June 10, Thursday Philadelphia

Booth appeared as William Jones in *Po-ca-hon-tas*.

June 11, Friday Philadelphia

Booth appeared as William Jones in *Po-ca-hon-tas*.

June 12, Saturday Philadelphia

Booth appeared as William Jones in *Po-ca-hon-tas*.

June 13, Sunday Philadelphia

[Date approximate] Booth's mother wrote to her son Junius Jr.: "Now Edwin writes to me every week unless he is sick—& John also he never misses a Sunday." She related that John Sleeper Clarke had told her John would be "a very good actor, nothing great." John had refused Clarke's offer to continue at the Arch Street Theatre.[87]

June 14, Monday Philadelphia

John Brougham starred in *Columbus El Filibustero!!* According to the *Philadelphia Press*:

The public amusements of the past week have been of small account, indeed. At the Walnut Street Theatre, ere half the week was through, Miss Laura Keene's management, suddenly, but not unexpectedly, collapsed.[88]

June 15, Tuesday Philadelphia

The Arch Street Theatre presented *Columbus El Filibustero!!*

June 16, Wednesday Philadelphia

Booth played Captain Spruce in *Lend Me Five Shillings*.

June 17, Thursday Philadelphia

The Arch Street Theatre presented *Columbus El Filibustero!!*

June 18, Friday Philadelphia

The Arch Street Theatre presented *Po-ca-hon-tas*, with Booth as William Jones.

June 19, Saturday Philadelphia

The season at the Arch Street Theatre was brought to a close with performances of *The Happy Man*, *Columbus El Filibustero!!*, and *Brian O'Lynn*.

July 13, Tuesday New York

Edwin Booth registered at the St. Nicholas Hotel on Broadway, followed several hours later by his brother John Wilkes Booth.[89]

July 14, Wednesday New York

July 15, Thursday New York

July 16, Friday New York

Booth checked out of the St. Nicholas Hotel by this date.[90]

August 7, Saturday

An article in the *New York Times* by Edwin Booth's friend Adam Badeau discussed a recent visit by the two to Tudor Hall in Bel Air. Badeau described the six-year-old house and noted that the Booths "now prefer a town residence...."[91]

August 18, Wednesday

John Sleeper Clarke joined William Wheatley as co-manager of the Arch Street Theatre in Philadelphia.[92]

August 27, Friday Baltimore

Edwin Booth appeared at the Holliday Street Theatre in a benefit as *Richard III*. John played the part of Richmond.[93] A fellow actor related that "[b]oth performances were superb. I shall never forget the fight between Richard and Richmond, in the last act, an encounter which was terrible in its savage realism."[94] John and Edwin's mother attended the performance and observed that John "is more like Edwin than anybody else."[95]

John's brother Joseph had a job at Baltimore's Holliday Street Theatre box office and earned $4 a week.[96]

3

Richmond: 1858–1860

On August 27, 1858, Edwin Booth played a benefit performance of *Richard III* in Baltimore. John Wilkes Booth, billed under his own name, appeared as Richmond. A week later John was in Richmond, Virginia, for the opening of the Marshall Theatre (also known as the Richmond Theatre), where he had been engaged as a member of manager George Kunkel's stock company at a salary of $11 per week.[1] Still not confident enough to use his family name on a regular basis, he used the name "John Wilkes."

Booth enjoyed the acquaintance of his fellow stock company actors. Samuel Knapp Chester, a boyhood friend, was in the company. Booth roomed with veteran actor Harry Langdon at the Powhatan Hotel at Eleventh and Broad Streets.[2] Noted actress Anna Cora Mowatt, wife of William F. Ritchie, editor of the *Richmond Enquirer*, took a special interest in the stock company, frequently entertaining the actors in her home. She occasionally directed performances at the theatre.[3]

Building on his experience in Philadelphia, Booth continued to learn the trade and prepared to become a star. The *Richmond Daily Dispatch* critic aptly wrote of the role of the stock company:

A stock company has many disadvantages in playing to a star of the profession. He has his round of characters which he has studied and played over again and again—they [members of the company] must learn each day, their parts, to appear in each piece, in rapid succes-

sion. It is impossible that they can be perfect ... and therefore the critic should always be liberal and forbearing....[4]

Stars appeared at the Marshall Theatre for two-week engagements. Star benefits were performed on Friday nights, the star receiving proceeds above house expenses. While in Richmond, Booth learned at close hand from the nation's leading actors, including his former employer William Wheatley, Maggie Mitchell, J. W. Wallack, Julia Hayne (formerly known as Miss Julia Dean), A. J. Neafie, and James E. Murdock. Booth's sister Asia wrote that Murdock was Booth's "ideal of grace and perfect elocution."[5] Murdock, an actor since 1829, had operated a school of elocution for eleven years. Murdock was an original, not imitating Junius Brutus Booth or Edwin Forrest, the theatrical giants of his day.[6]

Irish actor Barry Sullivan, who had been in America for only a few months, played an engagement at the Marshall Theatre in April 1859. During a stint in Baltimore he had made a pilgrimage to Bel Air to roam the woods where his idol, Junius Brutus Booth, had lived.[7] A review of Sullivan's acting in Washington, D.C., revealed his merits as a performer, which John Wilkes Booth tried to emulate: "The appearance of an actor who does not rant, who does not swagger, who does not snuff the air with his nose, but contents himself with taking nature by the hand, and going cheek by jowl with her, and her alone, should be hailed as little less than a blessing...."[8] Sullivan's rendition of *Richard III* strongly influenced Booth's portrayal of the character. As Sullivan's biographer notes:

Sullivan threw an amount of energy and realism into his action that almost bewildered the actors with fright.... He set aside most of the old traditions of the stage, ignored the methods of other players ... [t]he concluding scene of the tragedy was invariably the most brilliant.[9]

A resident of Richmond described John Wilkes Booth at this time:

He was a man of high character & sociable disposition, & liked by every one with whom he associated. Was considered very handsome having coal black hair & eyes, & frequently wore, when on the streets, a fur trimmed over-coat.... His intimate associates often joked him about his bow-legs.[10]

Fellow actor John Barron provided interesting insights into Booth's personality:

He, like his brothers, was as generous as the balmy air on a glorious summer eve. Modest as a maiden, gentle, kind and considerate. While he was not much as a conversationalist, he was exceedingly companionable. As to determination, he was the incarnation of all that the term implies, but so cool, so calm, that no man would dream of that "I will" as so predominant an element in the quiet, unruffled youth.... John was quick in action and had eyes that were piercing and most expressive, with a perfect physical beauty and stately bearing.[11]

Edward M. Alfriend, a friend of Booth, commented:

When John Wilkes Booth was in the Richmond Stock Company, he was very young. In his early twenties he weighed about 175 pounds, was a little taller than his brother Edwin, possessed his marvelously intellectual and beautiful eyes, with great symmetry of features, an especially fine forehead, and curly, black hair.... He was a great social favorite, knowing all the best men and many of the finest women. With men John Wilkes was most dignified in demeanor, bearing himself with insouciant care and grace, and was a brilliant talker. With women he was a man of

irresistible fascination by reason of his superbly handsome face, conversational brilliancy ... and a peculiar halo of romance.... His ability was unquestionable and his future assured.... His social success was hereditary, having been possessed by his father and also by his brother, Edwin.[12]

Another acquaintance observed:

I remember encountering in one of my afternoon walks uptown a handsome young gentleman, who was dressed a la mode, and carried himself like a Virginia gentleman to the manner born. I had seen him on the boards of the Marshall Theater in a subordinate role, and recognized by face and figure the notorious J. Wilkes Booth. It is said commonly, that one may know an actor off stage by the formal strut, the affected manner he uses on it. If so, Mr. Booth was an exception to the rule.[13]

John wrote to Edwin shortly after arriving in Richmond: "I called on Dr. Beeal [Beale].... He and his Lady seem a very nice couple. I like them very much."[14] Dr. James Beale, a leading Richmond physician, lived in a home several blocks from the theatre. Edwin Booth had formed a friendship with Beale on previous visits to Richmond. Beale, who seemed to know everybody, was an admirer of drama, literature, music, and the arts in general. His elegantly furnished house was always open to friends.[15] One guest recalled:

I never saw more lavish hospitality or greater profusion of the good things to eat and drink. About ten sat down to supper. The earth, the air, and the water had been called on to furnish the repast; and each guest was forced to try as much as his powers would permit. The writer, and I daresay some others, paid the penalty the next day of a headache, never to be forgotten....[16]

Dr. Beale often used his box at the theatre. He would frequently have actors come home with him for a late supper. Booth would wake Beale's four- or five-year-old daughter, Mary; on one occasion, he took her downstairs and sat her on the table, an action which upset Mary's nanny. One morning

Mary awoke and found a ring on her finger, placed there in the night by Booth. Mary's mother took the ring for safe-keeping.[17]

Mrs. Beale was no less a friend and mentor to young Booth than her husband. Booth sought her counsel when a stage-struck girl from a good Richmond family began to pay him unsolicited and ardent attention. She repeatedly sent him letters and, desperate after receiving no reply, wrote asking him to meet her in Capitol Square near the statue of Washington. Booth wanted to treat the girl chivalrously; if he did not, he knew the resulting scandal would ruin him in Richmond. Following advice from Mrs. Beale, he met the girl and gently let her down.[18]

Booth encountered the cream of Richmond society at the Beale home.[19] John Barron "remember[ed] with gratitude the Ritchies, Caskeys, Frys, Courtneys, Mountcastles, and many other old and prominent families for the cordiality with which they received and respected us."[20] The Ritchies published the *Richmond Enquirer*. John Caskie was a leading attorney. The Frys owned several stores. The Courtney family owned a hosiery and fancy goods store. William Mountcastle was a tin and sheet iron manufacturer. All lived within blocks of the theatre and Booth's hotel.[21]

A month into his first season at the Marshall, Booth attracted attention from the critic of the *Richmond Examiner*, who wrote that "[t]here is a young gentleman named Wilkes a good deal like Edwin Booth in face and person. He is a man of promise, and might, with the approbation of the audience, be cast for a higher position than he usually occupies."[22]

Booth's mother wrote to her son Junius to let him know that "John is doing well at Richmond. He is very anxious to get on faster. When he has a run of bad parts he writes home in despair."[23] John wrote to his mother every Sunday.[24] Edwin appeared at the Marshall late in September and on two occasions asked John to play Richmond to his *Richard*

III. In a letter to Junius, Edwin remarked: "I don't think he [John] will startle the world ... but he is improving fast, and looks beautiful on the platform."[25]

The *Dispatch* critic described the opening performance of Edwin's engagement in Richmond:

> The applause was hearty and long continued—not that kind of furious greeting kept up by a few admirers and friendly claquers to sustain the wavering reputation of mediocre talent—but that earnest and cordial expression of appreciation of true genius, which bursts spontaneous from a whole audience.[26]

A week later, the critic continued to be appreciative, asserting that Edwin's "career is steadily ascending. No actor of his age in our day, has taken so high a stand."[27] The *Dispatch* further noted:

> He [Edwin] has personated the highest role of characters in the range of the Drama, and we are earnest and confident in saying that, in some of them, he played scenes in a manner not equaled by any actor we ever saw. We are clearly of the opinion that all-in-all, he is superior to any man of his day on the stage.[28]

Three months after Edwin's engagement in Richmond, John Wilkes Booth won acclaim when, upon noticing that the dress of a juvenile actress had been ignited by the footlights, he quickly extinguished the fire and saved the girl from severe injury.[29]

Booth became familiar with the play *Our American Cousin* in February 1859, when William Wheatley and John Sleeper Clarke performed it on nine consecutive nights at the Marshall. Laura Keene, a popular actress and theatre manager, had introduced the play at her theatre in New York the previous October and continued to perform the hit for six months. In May the Marshall Theatre stock company played an afterpiece titled *Our Eastern Shore Cousin in Richmond*, a variant of the immensely popular *Our American Cousin*.[30]

Edwin Booth returned to Richmond for another engagement in mid–April 1859. The newspapers do not note whether John Wilkes Booth played Richmond to Edwin's *Richard III*, which the Marshall presented on April 22. On May 2 Edwin performed in a benefit to reward John for his supporting roles. John played Othello with Edwin as Iago.

Asia Booth married John Sleeper Clarke in Baltimore on April 28, 1859. John Wilkes Booth traveled all day to get to Baltimore for the wedding. Asia recalled that John "was not pleased at my marriage, and the strange words he whispered to me were, 'Always bear in mind that you are a professional stepping-stone. Our father's name is a power—theatrical—in the land. It is dower enough for any struggling actor.'"[31]

Booth began his second season in Richmond in September 1859, now boarding at Ford's Hotel.[32] His friend Sam Chester likewise returned as a member of Kunkel's stock company. Among the new members was Clementine DeBar, who had been married to, and divorced from, Junius Brutus Booth, Jr. Edwin Adams also joined the company. Booth and Adams immediately developed a lasting rivalry.[33] Once again Booth observed and learned from star actors such as Maggie Mitchell, Barry Sullivan, James E. Murdock, Helen and Lucille Western, and Frank Chanfrau.

On October 16 John Brown and a band of abolitionists attempted to seize the United States Arsenal at Harpers Ferry with the objective of using captured weapons to arm a slave revolt. Two days later, Marines led by Colonel Robert E. Lee captured Brown and his men. Following a swift trial before a Virginia judge and jury, Brown was sentenced to death only sixteen days after he had launched the invasion.

On November 19 the commander of the troops guarding John Brown in Charlestown, Virginia (now Charles Town, West Virginia), sent a telegram to Virginia Governor Henry A. Wise asking for reinforcements to forestall an anticipated attack to free Brown. Wise received the telegram at 6 p.m., and soon the Capitol Square bell tower signaled the city's volunteer militia companies to convene. Uniformed soldiers as well as curious citizens quickly gathered in the square. When Governor Wise announced the call for troops, excitement gripped his audience. A special train was to leave from the Broad Street depot at nine o'clock that night. A crowd of as many as 10,000 people wildly cheered the various military companies as they formed and boarded the train.[34]

Captain Wyatt M. Elliott of the Richmond Grays was in temporary command, under Governor Wise, of the First Virginia Regiment, which consisted of the Grays, the Richmond Light Infantry Blues, the Virginia Riflemen, the Howitzer Company, the Young Guard, Company F, and the Montgomery Guard. The seventy-six men of the Grays, under the temporary command of Lieutenant Louis J. Bossieux, marched through the large crowd to the depot at Eighth and Broad and boarded the train. An observer saw John Wilkes Booth, accompanied by his friend Edward M. Alfriend, emerge from the Marshall Theatre and board the coach occupied by the Grays.[35] Booth was not a member of the Grays, but he knew many of the members, including Alfriend, and he attended their social functions.[36] Grays Captain Elliott gave Booth his approval to board.

George W. Libby, one of the Grays, wrote:

> Booth appeared at the door of the car and asked if he could go with us to Harpers Ferry. We informed him no one was allowed on the train but men in uniform. He expressed a desire to buy a uniform, since he was very anxious to go. So, after some consultation with him, [Louis F.] Bossieux [son of Lieutenant Bossieux] and I each gave him a portion of our uniforms....[37]

The train, averaging about twelve miles an hour, carried Governor Wise and his 400 men to Aquia Creek, arriving at four o'clock in the morning. The regiment boarded a steamer and arrived in Washington, D.C., three hours later. Wearing a tall beaver hat, Wise led the troops from the Sixth Street Wharf to the White House, where the flamboyant governor expected to be greeted by President Buchanan. No such greeting was forthcoming, so the regiment marched down Pennsylvania Avenue to the Baltimore and Ohio Railroad depot. One report has Booth, his overcoat slung over his arm, marching behind Wise.[38] It seems likely that Booth, rather than occupying a conspicuous position near the governor, marched with the Grays behind their color bearer and company flag, which bore the Virginia state motto, "Sic Semper Tyrannis." The troops boarded the train and departed at 10:30 that morning. Several companies went on to Harpers Ferry, while the Grays and three other companies proceeded to Charlestown, arriving at 6 p.m.[39]

Booth and Louis F. Bossieux were appointed quartermaster sergeants under regimental quartermaster Robert A. Caskie, their duty being to issue rations.[40] The Black Horse Troop, commanded by Turner Ashby, was quartered close to the Grays. Ashby's supply wagon was liberally stocked with liquor, which flowed freely.[41]

Richmond Gray Edward M. Alfriend wrote:

> While at Charlestown the Richmond Grays occupied as their quarters an old tin factory, and here John Wilkes Booth slept every night when he was not doing duty as a sentinel, with Wirt Harrison, on a straw pallet, which was laid next to my own.... Nearly every night before taps he would entertain us with dramatic recitations from different plays. He was very fond of reciting, which he did in such a fiery, intense, vigorous, brilliant way as to forecast that great genius he subsequently showed on the stage.[42]

The wife of the rector of the Zion Episcopal Church in Charlestown recorded in her diary that "John Wilkes Boothe [sic], who is here as one of the guards of the John Brown Jail, has been giving Shakespearean readings each evening in the Episcopal Meeting House, to quell the population."[43] George Libby, who

had helped provide Booth with a uniform, recalled that the actor "was a remarkably handsome man, with a winning personality and would regale us around the camp fire with recitations from Shakespeare."[44] Booth also gave readings in the front parlor of resident Arthur "Sunshine" Hawks.[45]

The *Dispatch* reported news of the Richmond boys:

> THE RICHMOND GRAYS—In the extensive correspondence from Charlestown we see in our exchanges, a great many of the letters have highly complimentary notices of the Richmond Grays. Their splendid drilling and their behavior off duty, elicit much praise. Their name is used in other cities to urge effective military organizations.[46]

Booth was in a group of about twelve Grays who guarded the jail in which John Brown was imprisoned. All of these men had the opportunity to shake hands with the prisoner. One night Booth volunteered to investigate suspicious lights that were visible in the distance. He reported that the lights were merely sparks from a cabin's chimney.[47]

Booth and his fellow jail guards engaged local photographer Lewis Dinkle to take their pictures. The men gathered on George Street opposite the jail yard, perhaps in the front yard of the house in which they were then billeted. In the resulting series of three ambrotypes, the jail yard wall is visible in the background as the men strike different poses. One of the pictures, obviously staged, shows Edward M. Alfriend restraining Booth, with dagger in hand, from attacking another man. Another of the images shows Booth restraining Alfriend.[48]

On December 1 the *Richmond Dispatch* humorously noted:

> General Content. Old [John] Brown says he is ready to die; the abolitionists say they want a martyr; the Conservatives think he ought to be hung, and the Virginians will swing him off with great gratification. We never heard of a public execution which promised so much satisfaction to everybody concerned.[49]

At eleven o'clock on the day of the hanging, the Richmond Grays stood guard as John Brown exited the jail and mounted a waiting wagon. Six companies of infantry, including the Grays and Booth, marched with the wagon about a half mile to the site of the hanging. The military units formed a "v," with the gallows at the open end. The Grays were on the left arm about twenty yards from the gallows; the company on their right extended to the point of the "v."[50] Philip Whitlock, a member of the Grays, observed:

> ...our company was present as a Body Guard, being about 30 feet from the gallows. John Wilkes Booth, being about the same height as I, was right next to me in rank. When the drop fell, I noticed that he got very pale, and I called his attention to it. He said that he felt very faint and that he would give anything for a good drink of whiskey.[51]

On December 3 the Richmond Grays departed for Washington and stayed overnight at the National Hotel before returning to Richmond.[52] Theatre manager Kunkel had discharged Booth for leaving the stock company without notice. The Grays, upon learning of Booth's plight, marched to the theatre and demanded his reinstatement, which was granted.[53]

John's military adventure worried his family. Mary Devlin,[54] a young actress who had previously been a member of the Marshall Theatre stock company, wrote to her fiancé, Edwin Booth:

> Your news regarding the mad step, John has taken—I confess did not surprise me—if you remember, I told you I thought he would seize the opportunity. 'Tis a great pity he has not more sense—but time will teach him—although I fear the discipline is hardly severe enough to sicken him immediately with a soldier's life.[55]

Booth's attention soon returned to acting. On February 29, 1860, he played the role of Romeo Jaffier Jenkins in the afterpiece, *Too Much for Good Nature*. Booth continued to play this role even after he became a star.

On May 29, at the final play of the regular season, the Marshall Theatre gave away a painting of Edwin Booth as an inducement to attend. John Wilkes Booth and fellow actor James W. Collier[56] had a benefit two nights later. The *Daily Richmond Enquirer* advertised the performance and advised Booth:

> Have a little more confidence—and to Collier, take care how you fall into certain mannerisms at variance with good taste. We would yet maintain that they are good actors, and good fellows too. Indeed, our stock company has not been appreciated, even by manager Kunkel himself, as they ought to have been.[57]

At the benefit, Booth appeared as Victim in *Son of Malta*, as Sayers in *My Fellow Clerk*, and as "The Crook'd Back Tyrant ... Richard" for the "first time" in the fifth act of *Richard III*.[58] The *Enquirer* commented:

> Booth has proved, as we always thought he one day would, that he inherits no small share of his father's genius, but he has never had sufficient confidence in himself to show it. On Thursday night, however, he got over *that* to a considerable extent, and his success was proportionate, as was manifested by the hearty and sincere applause bestowed on him. But Booth is young in years, and as he grows older he will gather more pluck, and pluck more laurels. Collier, too, was much applauded. Why has not a full night been given to each of these actors?[59]

At the close of the season, Booth thought he had learned enough in his apprenticeship to become a star. In March 1860, Mary Devlin informed Edwin that Joseph Jefferson, a prominent actor and Booth family friend, had promised to write to John and help him obtain an engagement.[60]

1858 *from August 30*

August 30, Monday Richmond
August 31, Tuesday Richmond

September 1, Wednesday Richmond

September 2, Thursday Richmond

September 3, Friday Richmond

September 4, Saturday Richmond

The season at the Marshall Theatre, also known as the Richmond Theatre, opened with a performance of *Town and Country*, followed by *Wanted, 1000 Spirited Young Milliners for the Gold Diggings*. The theatre was uncomfortably crowded. Although ten of the actors were mentioned in a review, Booth did not attract sufficient attention to be included.[61]

September 5, Sunday Richmond

September 6, Monday Richmond

The Marshall Theatre presented *The School for Scandal*.

September 7, Tuesday Richmond

The Marshall Theatre presented *Extremes* and *Jenny Lind; or, The Swedish Nightingale*.[62] Booth played Herr Scheroot in later presentations of *Jenny Lind*.

September 8, Wednesday Richmond

The Marshall Theatre presented *The Wife* and *The Swiss Swains*.

September 9, Thursday Richmond

Booth played Cool in *London Assurance*.[63] The *Daily Richmond Enquirer* critic praised the acting of stock company actors Sam Chester and Julia Irving.

September 10, Friday Richmond

The Marshall Theatre presented *Old Heads and Young Hearts*.

In a letter to Edwin, John Wilkes Booth related that the climate in Richmond did not agree with him; he was taking medicine that made him "languid and stupid." He mentioned that audiences had called for him by his real name on one or two occasions. He was preparing parts for Maggie Mitchell's upcoming engagement in Richmond.[64]

September 11, Saturday Richmond

The Marshall Theatre presented *La Tour de Nesle; or, The Chamber of Death, The Lottery Ticket*, and *The Lawyer's Clerk*.

September 12, Sunday Richmond

September 13, Monday Richmond

The *Enquirer* noted the opening of actress Maggie Mitchell's engagement at the Marshall Theatre:

> This favorite of the young gentlemen, the popular and much lauded little Maggie Mitchell, makes her appearance this evening at the Richmond Theatre. She takes the part of Prince Frederic in the comic drama of *The Young Prince*.[65]

The afterpiece was *The Four Sisters*.

September 14, Tuesday Richmond

The Marshall Theatre presented Maggie Mitchell in *Margot, The Poultry Dealer*, followed by *The Young Prince; or, The Privileges of a King's Son*.

September 15, Wednesday Richmond

The Marshall Theatre presented *Milly, the Maid with the Milking Pail, Katy O'Shiel*, and *The Lottery Ticket*.

September 16, Thursday Richmond

The Marshall Theatre presented Maggie Mitchell in *The Wept of Wish-Ton-Wish* and *Margot, The Poultry Dealer*.

September 17, Friday Richmond

The Marshall Theatre presented *The Pet of the Petticoats, Katy O'Shiel*, and *The Lady of the Lions*.

September 18, Saturday Richmond

The Marshall Theatre presented *The French Spy* and *La Tour de Nesle*. The management extended Maggie Mitchell's engagement for another week.

September 19, Sunday Richmond

September 20, Monday Richmond

The Marshall Theatre presented Maggie Mitchell in *The Wild Irish Girl* and *Milly, the Maid with the Milking Pail*.

September 21, Tuesday Richmond

The Marshall Theatre presented *The Wept of Wish-Ton-Wish* and *The Wild Irish Girl*.

September 22, Wednesday Richmond

The Marshall Theatre presented *The French Spy* and *A Husband at Sight*. The *Enquirer* critic suggested:

> ... in order to elevate the tone of dramatic performances to what they were of yore, when our classic critics filled the seats of the Richmond Theatre, a considerable reform in acting and wording must take place. As matters are [at the theatre], ardent boys and verdant men help to make matters disagreeable by whooping, whistling and applauding at the *wrong* time, and

exhibit much want of taste as well as good sense in their notions of wit or talent.[66]

September 23, Thursday Richmond

Maggie Mitchell played *Satan in Paris* and *The Wandering Boys*.

September 24, Friday Richmond

Maggie Mitchell appeared in *Jessie Brown; or, The Relief of Lucknow* and *Captain Charlotte*.

September 25, Saturday Richmond

Maggie Mitchell closed her engagement at the Marshall Theatre with *The Green Bushes; or, A Hundred Years Ago* and *Jessie Brown*.

September 26, Sunday Richmond

September 27, Monday Richmond

Edwin Booth began an engagement at the Marshall Theatre with *The Apostate*, which was followed by *Family Jars*. The *Richmond Daily Dispatch* critic wrote:

> This young actor was received ... by a large audience, and was warmly cheered upon his appearance upon the stage. The applause was hearty and long continued.... His performance of *Pescara* was most excellent, and the audience were enraptured with his representation, expressing their approbation in the most emphatic manner.[67]

September 28, Tuesday Richmond

Edwin Booth appeared in *Richelieu; or, The Conspiracy*, which was followed by *Nature and Philosophy*.

September 29, Wednesday Richmond

Edwin Booth played Sir Giles Overreach in *A New Way to Pay Old Debts*, which was followed by *Family Jars*.

September 30, Thursday Richmond

Edwin Booth appeared in *The Iron Chest* and *Katharine and Petruchio*. The *Enquirer* remarked:

> Good Dramatic talent at any time will receive encouragement in Richmond, as may be seen by the crowded houses which have nightly, during this week, greeted the excellent young tragedian, Booth, at our Theatre. He, as when formerly here, has created an excellent impression upon all Theatre-goers, by his classic and natural acting....[68]

October 1, Friday Richmond

Edwin Booth played the title role in his benefit performance of *Richard III*.

The *Enquirer* announced that "Junius Brutus Wilkes Booth" (meaning John Wilkes Booth)

would appear as the Earl of Richmond. Richmond sculptor Edward V. Valentine recorded in his diary that he met Edwin Booth.[69]

October 2, Saturday Richmond

Edwin Booth played *Macbeth*. The afterpiece was *Nature and Philosophy*. The *Dispatch* commented that "Saturday night wound up one of the most brilliant periods at the Theatre for a long time. The audiences throughout the week were large."[70]

Describing Edwin, the *Dispatch* remarked that "Mr. Booth's playing commands the highest mark of admiration, silence. His exhibition of that passion, Remorse—so difficult to counterfeit—produced almost breathless silence: a silence which was not broken at the close of the scenes."[71]

October 3, Sunday Richmond

In a letter to her son Junius, Mary Ann wrote: "Edwin is playing now in Richmond.... John is in Richmond too & Edwin thinks he will get along first rate—he plays some very good parts ... his Voice is so like Edwin's you could scarcely tell them apart."[72]

October 4, Monday Richmond

Edwin Booth appeared in *Romeo and Juliet*, followed by *All the World's a Stage*.

October 5, Tuesday Richmond

John Wilkes Booth played Horatio to Edwin's *Hamlet*. At the conclusion of the performance, Edwin brought John forward and asked the audience, "I think he has done well. Don't you?"[73] The *Enquirer* critic mentioned several supporting actors but ignored John Wilkes Booth.

October 6, Wednesday Richmond

Edwin Booth appeared in *Macbeth*. The afterpiece was *The Secret; or, A Hole in the Wall*.

October 7, Thursday Richmond

Edwin Booth played Iago in *Othello*, followed by *All the World's a Stage*. The *Dispatch* noted:

> Edwin Booth continues to command the warm praise of the critics and the playgoers.... In the fiercer tragedies, exhibiting very much of physical action, he occasionally relapses into a style we may say is a little too didactic. This remark is applicable to both *Richard* and *Macbeth*; in both of which, however, there were scenes in which his performance could not be excelled.[74]

October 8, Friday Richmond

Edwin Booth starred in *The Merchant of Venice* and *Katharine and Petruchio*.

October 9, Saturday Richmond

Edwin and John Wilkes appeared together again in *Richard III* as Richard and Richmond, respectively.[75] The afterpiece was *Poor Pillicoddy*.

October 10, Sunday Richmond

October 11, Monday Richmond

Edwin Booth played *King Henry V*. The afterpiece was *Poor Pillicoddy*.

October 12, Tuesday Richmond

Edwin Booth played *King Henry V*. The afterpiece was *The Lottery Ticket*.

October 13, Wednesday Richmond

Edwin Booth performed *King Lear*. The *Richmond Whig* critic wrote:

...the performance was one of the most impressive we have ever seen upon the stage. The scenes in which Lear has his interviews with Edgar and the eyeless Gloster, were exquisitely rendered.... Mr. Booth presented the character, throughout, in a manner which could hardly admit of improvement.[76]

October 14, Thursday Richmond

Edwin Booth appeared in *Brutus; or, The Fall of Tarquin,* which was followed by *All the World's a Stage*.

October 15, Friday Richmond

Edwin Booth closed his engagement at the Marshall Theatre with *Much Ado About Nothing*. The afterpiece was *In and Out of Place*. The *Dispatch* noted:

Mr. [Edwin] Booth has the keen, critical sense to perceive the brilliant points of Shakespeare's plays, and the genius to bring them out in the happiest and most impressive manner.... Mr. Booth has played one of the most successful engagements that was ever made at our theatre.[77]

October 16, Saturday Richmond

The Marshall Theatre presented *The Factory Girl; or, All That Glitters Is Not Gold,* followed by *La Tour de Nesle*.

The *Enquirer* noted: "EDWIN BOOTH— This excellent actor has received more honor in Richmond nightly since his advent to our boards, than at any time previously.... For this evening he is advertised to appear in Baltimore as *Richard III*."[78]

October 17, Sunday Richmond

October 18, Monday Richmond

The Marshall Theatre presented *The Sea of Ice*, followed by *The Alpine Maid*.

In New York, Laura Keene starred in the premier of Tom Taylor's new play, *Our American Cousin*.[79]

October 19, Tuesday Richmond

The Marshall Theatre presented *The Sea of Ice* and *Jenny Lind*. It is probable that Booth appeared as Herr Scheroot in the latter play.

October 20, Wednesday Richmond

The Marshall Theatre presented *The Sea of Ice* and *The Factory Girl*.

October 21, Thursday Richmond

The Marshall Theatre presented *The Shoemaker of Toulouse* and *Family Jars*.

October 22, Friday Richmond

The Marshall Theatre presented *The Shoemaker of Toulouse* and *Nature and Philosophy*.

October 23, Saturday Richmond

The Marshall Theatre presented *The People's Lawyer* and *Jessie Brown*.

October 24, Sunday Richmond

October 25, Monday Richmond

The Marshall Theatre presented *David Copperfield*, in which Booth played the part of Traddles, and *Family Jars*.[80]

October 26, Tuesday Richmond

The Marshall Theatre presented *Jessie Brown*, followed by *The Factory Girl; or, All That Glitters Is Not Gold*.

October 27, Wednesday Richmond

The Marshall Theatre presented *The Dutch Governor*, *Poor Pillicoddy*, and *In and Out of Place*.

October 28, Thursday Richmond

The Marshall Theatre presented *The Sea of Ice* and *The Lottery Ticket*.

October 29, Friday Richmond

The Marshall Theatre presented *Triple Murder; or, The Chamber of Death* and *The Yankee Teamster*.

October 30, Saturday Richmond

On his evening walk, Richmond sculptor Edward Valentine ran into Booth. Later that night he attended the theatre and saw *La Tour De Nesle* and *Dombey and Son*.[81]

November 1, Monday Lynchburg

Seventeen members of George Kunkel's Marshall Theatre stock company, including John Wilkes Booth, opened an engagement at Dudley Hall in Lynchburg, Virginia. Among the cast were Sam Chester and Julia Irving. Harry Langdon appeared in *The Wife*, with Booth taking the part of Count Florio. The afterpiece was *Poor Pillicoddy*.[82]

The New Orleans English Opera Troupe was engaged for a week at the Marshall Theatre.

November 2, Tuesday Lynchburg

Harry Langdon and Mrs. I. B. Phillips played *Romeo and Juliet*, which was followed by *The Lottery Ticket*. The *Lynchburg Daily Virginian* remarked: "Mr. Langdon, who comes strongly recommended from our neighboring cities of Baltimore and Richmond, will sustain the character of Romeo."[83] The weather reduced the size of the audience.

November 3, Wednesday Lynchburg

Kunkel's company presented *David Copperfield*, followed by *Family Jars*. The *Virginian* noted that the performance of *Copperfield* "was the greatest success yet achieved by the Company. Uriah Heep was personated by Mr. Johnston, with unwonted power and effect." [84]

Booth played Traddles in later presentations of *David Copperfield* and likely assumed the role in this one as well.

November 4, Thursday Lynchburg

Kunkel's company performed *Othello* before a large audience. The *Virginian* noted that "Mr. Langdon, as *Othello*, executed his part to the entire satisfaction of all present. His voice was clear and distinct, and his manner earnest and true to nature."[85]

The afterpiece was *The Swiss Swains*.

November 5, Friday Lynchburg

Kunkel's company presented *Romeo and Juliet*. The *Virginian* reported that the performance "was a perfect triumph, with one exception.... [T]he weather ... necessarily precluded a large attendance of ladies."[86] The afterpiece was *The Lottery Ticket*.

November 6, Saturday Lynchburg

Kunkel's company presented *The Factory Girl*, followed by *La Tour De Nesle*.

November 7, Sunday Lynchburg

November 8, Monday Lynchburg

Kunkel's company presented *School for Scandal*, which the *Virginian* regarded as "one of the best comedies extant."[87]

Booth may have played the part of Sir Benjamin Backbite. The afterpiece was *In and Out of Place*.

November 9, Tuesday Lynchburg

Kunkel's company presented *Macbeth*, followed by *The Secret*.

November 10, Wednesday Lynchburg

The *Virginian* remarked: "On this evening *The Sea of Ice*, so justly celebrated wherever it is performed, will be produced in a style of unsurpassed splendor with a strong cast of characters, and with the same beautiful and costly scenery with which it met such unbounded success in ... Richmond."[88]

November 11, Thursday Lynchburg

Kunkel's company performed *The Sea of Ice*. According to the *Virginian*, "[t]he house was filled with the beauty and fashion of our city."[89]

November 12, Friday Lynchburg

Kunkel's company performed *The Sea of Ice*.

November 13, Saturday Lynchburg

The *Virginian* noted: "*Sea of Ice*—This splendid production will be produced this afternoon, commencing at precisely 3 o'clock, for the express accommodation of ladies and children who are unable to attend at night."[90] Kunkel's company concluded its engagement in Lynchburg with evening performances of *Richard III* and the second act of *The Sea of Ice*.

November 14, Sunday Richmond

November 15, Monday Richmond

The Marshall Theatre presented Richmond native Avonia Jones in *Evadne; or, The Statue*, which was followed by *Poor Pillicoddy*.[91]

November 16, Tuesday Richmond

The Marshall Theatre presented *Ingomar, the Barbarian* and *The Lottery Ticket*.

November 17, Wednesday Richmond

The Marshall Theatre presented *The Bride of Lammermoor* and *Sudden Thoughts*.

November 18, Thursday Richmond

Avonia Jones appeared in *Armand*, which was followed by *The Swiss Swains*.

November 19, Friday Richmond

Avonia Jones starred in *Adrienne, The Actress* with Booth playing Poisson. Booth also played Herr Scheroot in the farce *Jenny Lind*.[92]

November 20, Saturday Richmond

The Marshall Theatre presented a "Grand Saturday night gala" of *Lucretia Borgia* and *Paul Pry*.

November 21, Sunday Richmond

November 22, Monday Richmond

Avonia Jones appeared in *Sybil*. The afterpiece was *Sudden Thoughts*.

November 23, Tuesday Richmond

Avonia Jones appeared in *Sybil*, followed by *Our Gal*.

November 24, Wednesday Richmond

Avonia Jones appeared in *La Tisbe; or, The Spy of St. Marc* and *Boots at the Swan*.

November 25, Thursday Richmond

Booth played the part of Poisson in *Adrienne, The Actress*, which was followed by *Our Gal*.

November 26, Friday Richmond

Avonia Jones played *Sybil*, which was followed by *Katharine and Petruchio*.

November 27, Saturday Richmond

Avonia Jones appeared in the last three acts of *Sybil*, followed by the second and third acts of *Lucretia Borgia* and *The False Heir*.

November 28, Sunday Richmond

November 29, Monday Richmond

The Marshall Theatre presented J. W. Wallack in *The Iron Mask*.[93]

November 30, Tuesday Richmond

The Marshall Theatre presented *The Iron Mask*.

December 1, Wednesday Richmond

The Marshall Theatre presented *The King of the Commons* and *Boots at the Swan*.

December 2, Thursday Richmond

The Marshall Theatre presented *Virginius* and *Dead Shot*.

December 3, Friday Richmond

The Marshall Theatre presented J. W. Wallack in *Werner*, followed by *My Aunt*.

December 4, Saturday Richmond

The *Dispatch* advertised J. W. Wallack's *Richard III* as "Cibber's adaptation of *Life and Death of Richard III*, with further restorations from the text of Shakespeare."[94] The afterpiece was *Our Gal*.

December 5, Sunday Richmond

December 6, Monday Richmond

The Marshall Theatre presented J. W. Wallack in *Civilization*, followed by *Boots at the Swan*.

December 7, Tuesday Richmond

J. W. Wallack appeared at the Marshall Theatre in *The Iron Mask*.

December 8, Wednesday Richmond

The Marshall Theatre presented *Civilization* and *Dead Shot*.

December 9, Thursday Richmond

The Marshall Theatre presented *The King of the Commons* and *Sudden Thoughts*.

December 10, Friday Richmond

J. W. Wallack appeared as *Macbeth*, followed by *A Day in Paris*.

December 11, Saturday Richmond

The Marshall Theatre presented *William Tell, Black-Eyed Susan; or, All in the Downs*, and *The Robbers of the Heath*.

December 12, Sunday Richmond

December 13, Monday Richmond

Julia Dean Hayne[95] opened an engagement at the Marshall Theatre with *The Hunchback*, followed by *The Lottery Ticket*.

December 14, Tuesday Richmond

Julia Hayne appeared in *Evadne*, which was followed by *Love in All Corners*.

December 15, Wednesday Richmond

The Marshall Theatre presented Julia Hayne in *Love in all Corners*, followed by *Dead Shot*.

December 16, Thursday Richmond

The Marshall Theatre presented *Old Heads and Young Hearts*, followed by *Our Gal*.

December 17, Friday Richmond

Julia Hayne appeared in *The Italian Wife*, which was followed by *The Love Chase*.

December 18, Saturday Richmond

Julia Hayne appeared as Madelaine in *The Orphan of Paris*, which was followed by *The Warlock of the Glen*.

December 19, Sunday Richmond

December 20, Monday Richmond

 The *Enquirer* advertised the first night of Mademoiselle Louise Wells and her Equestrian Troupe in *Buck Bison; or, Baby Blanche, the Child of the Prairie.*[96] The afterpiece was *Family Jars.*

December 21, Tuesday Richmond

 Louise Wells repeated *Buck Bison*, followed by *A Day in Paris.*

December 22, Wednesday Richmond

 The Marshall Theater company performed the farce of *Our Gal* prior to the appearance of Louise Wells's trained horses. During the play, actress Kate Fisher's merino dress took fire from the footlights. The *Whig* reported: "The ignition being observed by some of the audience, several voices made known the actress' peril to Mr. Wilkes Booth who promptly extinguished the fire...."[97]

December 23, Thursday Richmond

 The Marshall Theatre presented *Putnam, the Iron Son of '76* and *Boots at the Swan.*

December 24, Friday Richmond

 The Marshall Theatre presented *Buck Bison.*

December 25, Saturday Richmond

 The Marshall Theatre presented a matinee performance of *Monster of St. Michael; or, Harlequin and the Golden Sprite of the Sulphur Mines.* In the evening Louise Wells appeared in *The Swamp Fox.*

December 26, Sunday Richmond

December 27, Monday Richmond

 Louise Wells's Equestrian Troupe played *Kit Carson* and *The Swamp Fox.*

December 28, Tuesday Richmond

 Louise Wells's Equestrian Troupe played *Kit Carson* and *El Hyder.*

December 29, Wednesday Richmond

 The Marshall Theatre presented *A Day in Paris* and *Rookwood.*

December 30, Thursday Richmond

 The Marshall Theatre presented *Poor Pillicoddy* and *Rookwood.*

December 31, Friday Richmond

 The Marshall Theatre presented *Wizard Steed* and *The Secret.*

1859

January 1, Saturday Richmond

 Louise Wells closed her engagement with *Wizard Steed*, followed by *Kit Carson.*

January 2, Sunday Richmond

January 3, Monday Richmond

 The Marshall Theatre featured Signor Felix Carlo, acrobat, gymnast, and clown, and "His Wonderful Sons and Baby Clown" through January 15. The plays in the evening were *Belle of the Faubourg* and *The Married Rake.*

January 4, Tuesday Richmond

 The Marshall Theatre presented *Sweethearts and Wives; or, Before and After Marriage* and *In and Out of Place.*

January 5, Wednesday Richmond

 The Marshall Theatre presented *Theresa's Vow; or, The Oak of Croissey* and *A Day After the Wedding.*

January 6, Thursday Richmond

 The Marshall Theatre presented *Don Caesar de Bazan*, with Harry Langdon in the lead role, and *Nick of the Woods; or, the Jibbenainosay; a Tale of Kentucky.*

January 7, Friday Richmond

 The Marshall Theatre presented *David Copperfield.* Felix Carlo followed.

January 8, Saturday Richmond

 The Marshall Theatre presented *The Rake's Progress* in a benefit for W. H. Bailey, who played the part of Snump. *Naval Engagements* followed.

January 9, Sunday Richmond

January 10, Monday Richmond

 The Marshall Theatre presented *Ernest Maltravers; or, A Father's Curse* and *Faint Heart Never Won Fair Lady.* Felix Carlo continued his engagement.

January 11, Tuesday Richmond

 The Marshall Theatre presented *Dame Trot.*

January 12, Wednesday Richmond

 The Marshall Theatre presented *The Marble Heart; or, The Sculptor's Dream.*

January 13, Thursday Richmond

 The Marshall Theatre presented *Don Caesar de Bazan* in a benefit for "the baby clown," a member of Felix Carlo's troupe.

January 14, Friday Richmond

The stock company of the Marshall Theatre played *Victims*.

January 15, Saturday Richmond

The Marshall Theatre presented "a grand Saturday night carnival" performance of *Rather Excited*. Felix Carlo closed his engagement.

January 16, Sunday Richmond

January 17, Monday Richmond

Touring star A. J. Neafie[98] began an engagement at the Marshall Theatre with a performance of *The Corsican Brothers*.

January 18, Tuesday Richmond

A. J. Neafie played *Hamlet*.

January 19, Wednesday Richmond

A. J. Neafie played *Richelieu*.

January 20, Thursday Richmond

A. J. Neafie appeared in *Pizarro; or, The Conquest of Peru*.

January 21, Friday Richmond

A. J. Neafie appeared in *Harrolde; or, The Merchant of Calais*, which was followed by *Faint Heart Never Won Fair Lady*.

January 22, Saturday Richmond

The Marshall Theatre presented *The Corsican Brothers* and *Black-Eyed Susan* in A. J. Neafie's closing performance.

January 23, Sunday Richmond

January 24, Monday Richmond

An advertisement in the *Dispatch* noted: "First night of the magnificent, spectacular dramatized from Alexander Dumas' great work of fiction, entitled *Monte Cristo*." "J. B. Wilkes" played Danglars.[99]

January 25, Tuesday Richmond

January 26, Wednesday Richmond

The Marshall Theatre presented *Monte Cristo*.

January 27, Thursday Richmond

The Marshall Theatre presented *Monte Cristo*.

January 28, Friday Richmond

The Marshall Theatre presented *Monte Cristo*.

The *Whig* reported:

Everyone is going to see *Monte Cristo*.... We are sure that juveniles will be greatly diverted by the carnival, and the trained animals, the giants, and the troop of cavalry. As a burlesque upon the "grand entrees" of a circus, it is richly successful.... The principal characters are cleverly sustained by Mesdames Phillips and Proctor and Messrs. Langdon, Harkins, Bailey and Booth.[100]

January 29, Saturday Richmond

The Marshall Theatre presented *Monte Cristo* as a matinee and repeated it in the evening.

January 30, Sunday Richmond

January 31, Monday Richmond

Monte Cristo continued its run at the Marshall Theatre.

February 1, Tuesday Richmond

The Marshall Theatre presented *Monte Cristo*. The *Whig* noted that "[i]n addition to the grand spectacle a great band of Ethiopian minstrels will nightly appear in a variety of the most popular songs, duets, etc."[101]

February 2, Wednesday Richmond

The Marshall Theatre presented *The Cricket on the Hearth*, *The Printer's Apprentice*, and a scene from *Monte Cristo* in a benefit for Kate Fisher.

February 3, Thursday Richmond

The Marshall Theatre presented *Theresa's Vow; or, The Oak of Croissey*, *The Printer's Apprentice*, *Monster of St. Michael*, and *Addledeboudle*.

February 4, Friday Richmond

The Sergeant's Wedding and *The Spirit of Seventy-Six* were advertised as a benefit for Pat Redford.[102]

February 5, Saturday Richmond

The Marshall Theatre presented *The Spirit of Seventy-Six* and *The Chamber of Death*.

February 6, Sunday Richmond

February 7, Monday Richmond

Maggie Mitchell opened an engagement at the Marshall Theatre in *Margot, The Poultry Dealer*, followed by *Katy O'Shiel*.

February 8, Tuesday Richmond

The Marshall Theatre presented *The French Spy* and *Milly, the Maid with the Milking Pail* with Maggie Mitchell.

February 9, Wednesday Richmond

Maggie Mitchell appeared in *The Wept of*

Wish-Ton-Wish with Booth playing the part of Uncas, an Indian.

February 10, Thursday Richmond
The Marshall Theatre presented *The Young Prince* and *Olympia, Queen of the Abruzzi.*

February 11, Friday Richmond
Maggie Mitchell played Miami in *The Green Bushes* and five characters in *A Lady's Stratagem.*

February 12, Saturday Richmond
The Marshall Theatre presented *The French Spy* and *Katy O'Shiel.*

February 13, Sunday Richmond

February 14, Monday Petersburg
Kunkel's Marshall Theatre stock company, along with Maggie Mitchell, opened at Phoenix Hall in Petersburg with *Margot, The Poultry Dealer* and *Katy O'Shiel.*[103]

February 15, Tuesday Petersburg
Kunkel's company presented *The Young Prince* and *A Lady's Stratagem.* The *Petersburg Daily Express* noted:

The petite and pretty MAGGIE MITCHELL ... again attracted a fine audience.... The company is a decided improvement upon the old stock of a year since. Mrs. Proctor, Mrs. Reid and Mrs. Taylecke are deemed excellent "leading characters." Mr. J. B. Wilkes possesses fine histrionic talent, conducting himself invariably in a manner which seems to say, "Excelsior!"[104]

February 16, Wednesday Petersburg
Maggie Mitchell starred in *The Pet of the Petticoats* and *The Four Sisters.* The *Express* reported: "The weather prevented the attendance of a very large number of ladies, yet the 'fair' were well represented."[105]

February 17, Thursday Petersburg
Maggie Mitchell performed *Satan in Paris* and *Milly, the Maid with the Milking Pail.*[106]

February 18, Friday Petersburg
Kunkel's company played *The French Spy* and *Katy O'Shiel.* The *Express* noted that "[t]he skies frowned savagely ... and occasionally leaked, greatly against the will and wishes of some thousand or two of pretty Maggie Mitchell's enthusiastic friends. Nevertheless, her benefit was a success."[107]

February 19, Saturday Petersburg
Maggie Mitchell starred in *The Wept of*

Wish-Ton-Wish in which Booth played Uncas. The afterpiece was *The Wandering Boys.*

February 20, Sunday Petersburg

February 21, Monday Petersburg
Maggie Mitchell appeared in *The Green Bushes* and *Nature and Philosophy.*[108]

February 22, Tuesday Petersburg
Maggie Mitchell appeared in *The French Spy* and *A Husband at Sight.*

February 23, Wednesday Petersburg
Maggie Mitchell appeared in *Olympia, Queen of the Abruzzi* and *The Pet of the Petticoats.*

February 24, Thursday Petersburg
Maggie Mitchell appeared in *Romeo and Juliet* with Booth as Paris. The afterpiece was *The Four Sisters.*

February 25, Friday Richmond
Kunkel's Marshall Theatre company returned to Richmond. The Theatre presented *Romeo and Juliet* and *The Widow's Victim.* Maggie Mitchell portrayed Romeo, and Mrs. I. B. Phillips played Juliet. Booth played Paris, while Sam Chester played Tybalt.

The actors of Kunkel's company published a letter in the *Dispatch* offering their services in a benefit for theatre manager Thomas L. Moxley. Booth signed as "J. W. Booth."[109]

February 26, Saturday Richmond
Maggie Mitchell appeared in *The French Spy* and *Katy O'Shiel.*

February 27, Sunday Richmond

February 28, Monday Richmond
William Wheatley and John Sleeper Clarke began an engagement at the Marshall Theatre with *Our American Cousin,* followed by *The Widow's Victim.*

March 1, Tuesday Richmond
John Sleeper Clarke performed *Our American Cousin,* which was followed by *Rather Excited.* The part Booth played, if any, is not listed in the bill. William Wheatley portrayed Lord Dundreary.[110]

The front page of the *Dispatch* carried an article (borrowed from the *Petersburg Daily Express*) about Junius Brutus Booth's first appearance in the United States, which had taken place in Richmond.[111]

March 2, Wednesday Richmond

John Sleeper Clarke performed *Our American Cousin*. The afterpiece was *The Quiet Family*.

March 3, Thursday Richmond

The Marshall Theatre presented *Our American Cousin* and *The Sergeant's Wedding*.

March 4, Friday Richmond

The Marshall Theatre presented *Our American Cousin*, *The Toodles*, and *Hypocrite*.

March 5, Saturday Richmond

The Marshall Theatre presented *Our American Cousin* as well as *P.P.; or, The Man and the Tiger* and *The Spectre Bridegroom*. The *Dispatch* commented:

> This laughable comedy has crowded the theatre for five nights this week. The extremely comic situations in the piece and the acting of "Our Cousin" and Lord Dundreary make it the most popular play ever put on our stage.[112]

March 6, Sunday Richmond

March 7, Monday Richmond

John Sleeper Clarke appeared in *Our American Cousin*, which was followed by *The Dramatist*.

March 8, Tuesday Richmond

The Marshall Theatre presented *Our American Cousin* and *The Willow Copse*.

March 9, Wednesday Richmond

The run of *Our American Cousin* concluded. The afterpiece was *Laugh When You Can*.

March 10, Thursday Richmond

The Marshall Theatre presented *Wild Oats* and *Turning the Tables*.

March 11, Friday Richmond

William Wheatley appeared in *Inconstant*, while John Sleeper Clarke appeared in *The Midnight Watch* and *Summer Thoughts*. The *Whig* noted:

> Mr. Wheatley has been educated in the old school of actors.... He has at times a declamatory manner which in tragedy is unpleasant, but only enables him to utter with sparkling gaiety the brief sententious dialogues of comedy.... He is a fine elocutionist....[113]

March 12, Saturday Richmond

The Marshall Theatre presented William Wheatley as *William Tell*, followed by *Our American Cousin* and the second act of *The Toodles*. The engagement of William Wheatley and John Sleeper Clarke concluded.

March 13, Sunday Richmond

March 14, Monday Richmond

Touring star James E. Murdock began an engagement at the Marshall Theatre, appearing in *Wine Works Wonders*.

March 15, Tuesday Richmond

James E. Murdock appeared as *Hamlet*, which was followed by *The Married Rake*.

March 16, Wednesday Richmond

The Marshall Theatre presented *The Gamester* and *The Swiss Swains*.

March 17, Thursday Richmond

The Marshall Theatre presented James E. Murdock in *Macbeth*, which was followed by *The Married Rake*.

March 18, Friday Richmond

James E. Murdock played *The Stranger*, which was followed by *My Aunt*.

March 19, Saturday Richmond

The Marshall Theatre presented *The Robbers* and *Our Gal*.

March 20, Sunday Richmond

March 21, Monday Richmond

James E. Murdock starred in *De Soto*. The supporting cast included Sam Chester as Anasco and Booth as Gallegos.

March 22, Tuesday Richmond

James E. Murdock played *De Soto*.

March 23, Wednesday Richmond

The Marshall Theatre presented *De Soto*.

March 24, Thursday Richmond

The Marshall Theatre presented *Victims* and *The Old Guard*.

March 25, Friday Richmond

The Marshall Theatre presented *The Marble Heart*. James E. Murdock's engagement ended.

March 26, Saturday Richmond

Mr. and Mrs. W. J. Florence began an engagement at the Marshall Theatre with *The Irish Immigrant*, followed by *Mischievous Annie*.[114]

March 27, Sunday Richmond

March 28, Monday Richmond

The Marshall Theatre presented *Paudeen*

O'Rafferty, Guilty or Not Guilty; or, A Lesson for Husbands, and The Happy Man.

March 29, Tuesday Richmond

W. J. Florence appeared in *The Knights of Arva*, which was followed by *The Young Actress* and *Paddy Miles' Boy*.

March 30, Wednesday Richmond

The Marshall Theatre presented *Irish Assurance* and *Mischievous Annie*.

March 31, Thursday Richmond

The Marshall Theatre presented *Irish Assurance*, *Yankee Modesty*, and *Working the Oracle*.

April 1, Friday Richmond

W. J. Florence played Tim Moore in *The Irish Lion*. The Marshall Theatre also presented *How to Get Out of It* and *Yankee Housekeeper*.

April 2, Saturday Richmond

The Marshall Theatre presented *Ireland as It Is*, *The Young Actress*, and *Florence Worried by Johnston*.

April 3, Sunday Richmond

April 4, Monday Richmond

The Marshall Theatre presented *White Horse of the Peppers*, *Lola Montez*, and *The Good For Nothing*.

April 5, Tuesday Richmond

W. J. Florence appeared in the Marshall Theatre's productions of *The Irish Mormon*, *Thrice Married*, and *Lord Flanagan*.

April 6, Wednesday Richmond

The Marshall Theatre presented *Iron Hand* and *The Sergeant's Wedding*.

April 7, Thursday Richmond

The Marshall Theatre presented *The Naiad Queen; or, The Nymphs of the Rhine*. Booth probably played the role of Amphibio.

April 8, Friday Richmond

The Marshall Theatre presented *The Naiad Queen*.

April 9, Saturday Richmond

The Marshall Theatre presented *The Naiad Queen* and *Love in Seventy-Six*.

April 10, Sunday Richmond

April 11, Monday Richmond

Barry Sullivan began his star engagement

at the Marshall Theatre in *Richelieu*, followed by *An Organic Affection*.

April 12, Tuesday Richmond

Barry Sullivan played *Richelieu*, with Booth as Baradas. The afterpiece was *An Organic Affection*.

April 13, Wednesday Richmond

Barry Sullivan played *The Gamester*, which was followed by *The Sergeant's Wedding*.

April 14, Thursday Richmond

Barry Sullivan played *Hamlet*.

April 15, Friday Richmond

Barry Sullivan appeared in *The Merchant of Venice*, which was followed by *Katharine and Petruchio*.

April 16, Saturday Richmond

The Marshall Theatre presented a matinee performance of *The Naiad Queen*. In the evening Barry Sullivan played *Richard III*, which was followed by *Matrimonial Squabbles*.

April 17, Sunday Richmond

April 18, Monday Richmond

Edwin Booth, having returned to Richmond, began an engagement at the Marshall Theatre with *The Apostate*, followed by *The Phenomenon*. The *Enquirer* noted: "This highly gifted young tragedian [Edwin] has just returned from a most favorable tour through the South, in which he has received the highest encomiums of the press."[115]

April 19, Tuesday Richmond

Edwin Booth appeared in *The Iron Chest*, which was followed by *A Day in Paris*.

April 20, Wednesday Richmond

Edwin Booth played *King Lear*.

April 21, Thursday Richmond

Edwin Booth played *Macbeth*.

April 22, Friday Richmond

Edwin Booth appeared as *Richard III*, which was followed by *The Phenomenon*.

April 23, Saturday Richmond

Edwin Booth played *Brutus*, which was followed by the farce *P.P.*

April 24, Sunday Richmond

April 25, Monday Richmond

Edwin Booth played *King Lear*.

April 26, Tuesday Richmond

Edwin Booth performed *A New Way to Pay Old Debts*. The afterpiece was *The Phenomenon*.

The *Enquirer* critic wrote:

In the dramatic line we notice the re-engagement for this week of "Richmond's favorite," Edwin Booth. During this period we may expect some fine acting, with an occasional touch in the tone of G sharp minor, in music, when, "His lips do move with inward mutterings, And his fix'd eye is riveted fearfully, on something that no other sight can see."[116]

April 27, Wednesday Richmond

Edwin Booth played *Hamlet*. The *Dispatch* announced that Edwin Booth would play in Petersburg on Thursday and Friday.[117]

April 28, Thursday Baltimore

Asia Booth married John Sleeper Clarke in Baltimore.[118] John Wilkes Booth traveled all day to get to Baltimore for the wedding.[119]

April 29, Friday Baltimore?

Edwin Booth performed in Petersburg.[120]

April 30, Saturday

Edwin Booth played *Richard III* in Petersburg.

May 1, Sunday Richmond?

May 2, Monday Richmond

The *Whig* advertised: "Benefit of J. Wilkes Booth who will for the first time sustain the arduous character of *Othello* and his brother Edwin Booth, who will remain this night only, will appear in his great character Iago."[121]

May 3, Tuesday Richmond

Mrs. W. C. Gladstane opened her engagement at the Marshall Theatre in *Lucretia Borgia*. *Sudden Thoughts* followed.

May 4, Wednesday Richmond

The Marshall Theatre presented *London Assurance* and *Irishman's Shanty*. Booth usually played the part of Cool in the former play.

May 5, Thursday Richmond

The Marshall Theatre presented *Louise de Lignerolles*.

May 6, Friday Richmond

Mrs. W. C. Gladstane appeared in *The Hunchback*. Booth played Lord Tinsel. *Rough Diamond* followed.

May 7, Saturday Richmond

The Marshall Theatre presented Mrs. W. C. Gladstane in *The Robber's Wife* and *Our Eastern Shore Cousin in Richmond*, a variant of the immensely popular *Our American Cousin*.

May 8, Sunday Richmond

May 9, Monday Richmond

The Marshall Theatre presented Mrs. W. C. Gladstane in *Peg Woffington*.

May 10, Tuesday Richmond

Booth celebrated his twenty-first birthday. Mrs. W. C. Gladstane played *Louise de Lignerolles*. The afterpiece was *Our Eastern Shore Cousin in Richmond*.[122]

May 11, Wednesday Richmond

The Marshall Theatre presented *Agnes de Vere; or, The Wife's Revenge* followed by *Our Eastern Shore Cousin in Richmond*.

May 12, Thursday Richmond

The Marshall Theatre presented *The Serious Family*, followed by *Our Eastern Shore Cousin in Richmond*.

May 13, Friday Richmond

Mrs. W. C. Gladstane appeared in *The Ladies' Battle* and *Masks and Faces; or, Before and Behind the Curtain*.

May 14, Saturday Richmond

The Marshall Theatre presented *The Female Gambler* with Mrs. W. C. Gladstane. *The Lottery Ticket* followed.

May 15, Sunday Richmond

May 16, Monday Richmond

The Marshall Theatre presented Tom Taylor's comedy, *Masks and Faces*, for the grand climax of the 1858–1859 season in Richmond.

May 17, Tuesday Lynchburg

George Kunkel's theatrical company traveled to Lynchburg and played *The Lady of Lyons; or, Love and Pride* to an audience reduced in numbers because of inclement weather.[123] Booth played the part of Gaspar.

May 18, Wednesday Lynchburg

Kunkel's company performed *Old Heads and Young Hearts*. The farce *The Lottery Ticket* followed.[124]

May 19, Thursday Lynchburg

The *Virginian* noted:

On this evening we have a bill of unusual merit, comprising *The Stranger* and *Taming a Shrew*. The *Stranger* was performed last season with decided success, and, in connection with the Shakespearean comedy (performed for the first time in our city) of *Taming a Shrew*, we have an evening's entertainment which no lover of the drama should miss.[125]

May 20, Friday Lynchburg

The *Virginian* stated: "The bill for this evening is a glorious one, which will scarcely fail to draw a crowded house. The beautiful comedy of *The Love Chase* has proved a favorite wherever performed.... We predict a full house of ladies, *weather* or no *weather*." *Honeymoon* followed.[126]

May 21, Saturday Lynchburg

Kunkel's company performed *Love in Seventy-Six*, *The Married Rake*, and *The Quiet Family*.

May 22, Sunday Lynchburg

May 23, Monday Lynchburg

The *Virginian* noted:

Messrs. Kunkel & Co. have engaged the services, for a few nights only, of the celebrated Druid Ox-Horn Players, being imitators of the ancient Druids, whose groves have often resounded with the music of their horns. This is a novel and attractive feature, and, in conjunction with the Dramatic Company [performing *Day After the Wedding*], will form a lucky card.[127]

May 24, Tuesday Lynchburg

May 25, Wednesday Lynchburg

Kunkel's company performed *Naval Engagements* and *P.P.*, and the Druid Ox-Horn Players finished their brief engagement in Lynchburg.[128]

May 26, Thursday Lynchburg

Kunkel's company performed *David Copperfield*. Booth had previously played the part of Traddles and probably reprised the role here. The *Virginian* remarked:

To the enterprising managers of our Theatre, Messrs. Kunkel & Moxley, we are indebted for an advance sight of the gorgeous scenery to be used in the representation of *The Naiad Queen*, shortly to be exhibited in our city. To say that it is beautiful does but poorly convey our idea of the grand and gorgeous in scenery.[129]

May 27, Friday Lynchburg

Kunkel's company performed *The Naiad Queen*, with Booth probably playing the part of Amphibio. The *Virginian* noted that the company, "with indomitable energy to leave nothing undone to contribute to the amusement of our citizens, have determined to produce, in the best style, the popular and moral spectacular drama of the *Naiad Queen*, with all its original scenery, effects, dramatic situations, &c."[130]

May 28, Saturday Lynchburg

Kunkel's company played *The Naiad Queen*. According to the *Virginian*, "Mr. Wilkes accredited himself handsomely in the part of Amphibio, in which part he excels. He is a promising young actor."[131]

May 29, Sunday Lynchburg

May 30, Monday Lynchburg

Kunkel's company played *The Naiad Queen*.

May 31, Tuesday Lynchburg

Kunkel's company played *The Naiad Queen*. The *Virginian* noted that the production "is nightly drawing full and fashionable audiences. As it must shortly be removed, to give way for other attractions, all who have not witnessed this grand spectacle should take early opportunity for so doing."[132]

June 1, Wednesday Lynchburg

Kunkel's company presented "a grand performance of the *Naiad Queen* on Wednesday afternoon, for the special accommodation of ladies and children," according to the *Virginian*.[133] The play was repeated in the evening.

June 2, Thursday Lynchburg

Kunkel's company played *The Naiad Queen*.

June 3, Friday Lynchburg

Kunkel's company played *The Naiad Queen*. *Rough Diamond* followed.

June 4, Saturday Lynchburg

Kunkel's company played *The Naiad Queen* at the matinee and again in the evening along with *Our Cousin at Richmond*.[134]

June 5, Sunday Lynchburg

June 6, Monday Lynchburg

Maggie Mitchell opened her engagement with Kunkel's company in Lynchburg.

June 7, Tuesday Lynchburg

Maggie Mitchell appeared in *Margot, The Poultry Dealer* and *A Lady's Stratagem*.

June 8, Wednesday Lynchburg

Maggie Mitchell's engagement continued.

June 9, Thursday Lynchburg

Maggie Mitchell appeared in *The Pet of the Petticoats* and *A Husband at Sight*.

June 10, Friday Lynchburg

In her benefit performance, Maggie Mitchell appeared in *Satan in Paris* and *Nature and Philosophy*.

June 11, Saturday Lynchburg

Maggie Mitchell appeared in *The Brigand Queen* and *Katy O'Shiel*.

June 12, Sunday Lynchburg

June 13, Monday Lynchburg

Maggie Mitchell appeared in *The French Spy* and *The Young Scamp*.

June 14, Tuesday Lynchburg

Maggie Mitchell appeared in *Miami; or, The Wild Huntress of the Mississippi* and *The Four Sisters*.

June 15, Wednesday Lynchburg

Maggie Mitchell's engagement in Lynchburg closed with *The Young Prince* and *Margot, The Poultry Dealer*.

June 16, Thursday Petersburg

June 17, Friday Petersburg

Maggie Mitchell, with Kunkel and company, opened at Phoenix Hall in Petersburg with *Katy O'Shiel* and *The Four Sisters*.

June 18, Saturday Petersburg

Maggie Mitchell appeared in *The French Spy* and *Milly, the Maid with the Milking Pail*.

June 19, Sunday Petersburg

June 20, Monday Petersburg

Maggie Mitchell appeared in *The Green Bushes* and *Nature and Philosophy*.

June 21, Tuesday Petersburg

Maggie Mitchell appeared in *The Young Prince* and *Margot, The Poultry Dealer*.

June 22, Wednesday Petersburg

Maggie Mitchell appeared in *The Wept of Wish-Ton-Wish*. Booth probably played the part of Uncas.

June 23, Thursday Petersburg

Maggie Mitchell appeared in *The Brigand Queen* and *The Pet of the Petticoats*.

June 24, Friday Petersburg

Maggie Mitchell appeared in *Satan in Paris* and *The Young Scamp*.

June 25, Saturday Petersburg

Kunkel's company closed its engagement in Petersburg with *The Wandering Boys* and *Katy O'Shiel*.

June 26, Sunday Richmond

June 27, Monday Richmond

Maggie Mitchell and the company presented *The Wept of Wish-Ton-Wish*, *A Day After the Wedding*, and *The Young Scamp* in a benefit for Kunkel, the last performance of the season.

August 27, Saturday

Colonel Edwin L. Drake struck oil near Titusville, Pennsylvania. In 1864 John Wilkes Booth entered the oil business.

August 29, Monday Richmond

John Wilkes Booth was probably in Richmond for rehearsals at least a week before the opening of the theatrical season. The trip from Washington to Richmond required seven hours. A steamer carried the passengers from Washington to Aquia Creek on the Potomac River. From there it was seventy-five miles to Richmond by rail.

August 30, Tuesday Richmond

August 31, Wednesday Richmond

September 1, Thursday Richmond

September 2, Friday Richmond

September 3, Saturday Richmond

The season opened at the Marshall Theatre with *The Heir at Law* and *Out to Nurse*. "J. B. Wilkes" appeared as Henry Moreland (in *The Heir at Law*), and Sam Chester portrayed Steadfast. According to the *Richmond Daily Dispatch*:

> The opening ... was successful beyond all hopes of those friends of the drama who were anxious to see the season open "brilliantly." The house was densely crowded and many, unable to get even comfortable standing room, left the building.[135]

September 4, Sunday Richmond

September 5, Monday Richmond

The Marshall Theatre presented *The Marble Heart* and *A Kiss in the Dark*.

September 6, Tuesday Richmond

Booth played the part of Icebrook in *Everybody's Friend*, which was followed by *Your Life's in Danger*.

September 7, Wednesday Richmond

The Marshall Theatre presented *The Rivals* and *Paddy Miles' Boy*.

September 8, Thursday Richmond
The Marshall Theatre presented *Everybody's Friend*, followed by *Our Country Cousin*, an adaptation of the New York hit play *Our American Cousin*.

September 9, Friday Richmond
The Marshall Theatre presented *Nine Points of Law*, *The Stage Struck Barber*, and *American Farmers*.

September 10, Saturday Richmond
Edwin Adams played the lead role in *Richard III*, while John Wilkes Booth had the supporting role of Buckingham. The review in the *Richmond Daily Whig* did not mention Booth.[136] The afterpiece was *Your Life's in Danger*.

September 11, Sunday Richmond

September 12, Monday Richmond
Touring stars D. W. and Emma Waller appeared in *The Duchess of Malfi*, which was followed by *A Kiss in the Dark*.

September 13, Tuesday Richmond
D. W. and Emma Waller appeared in *The Duchess of Malfi*, which was followed by *Why Don't She Marry*.

September 14, Wednesday Richmond
The Marshall Theatre presented *Macbeth*.

September 15, Thursday Richmond
The Marshall Theatre presented *Othello*.

September 16, Friday Richmond
D. W. Waller starred in *Guy Mannering; or, The Gipsey's Prophecy*, which was followed by *Therese; or, The Orphan of Geneva*.

September 17, Saturday Richmond
D. W. and Emma Waller appeared in *Bertram*, which was followed by *Horse-shoe Robinson; or, The Battle of King's Mountain*.

September 18, Sunday Richmond

September 19, Monday Richmond
The Marshall Theatre presented *Pauline; or, The Assassins of the Chateau* and *Buried Alive*.

September 20, Tuesday Richmond
The Wallers played the last three acts of *The Stranger* and *The Lady of Lyons*.

September 21, Wednesday Richmond
The Marshall Theatre presented *Pauline* and *A Deed of Dreadful Note*.

September 22, Thursday Richmond
The Marshall Theatre presented *Therese* and *Midas*.

September 23, Friday Richmond
The Wallers appeared in *The Hunchback*. Booth played Lord Tinsel. The evening closed with the last three acts of *Guy Mannering*.

September 24, Saturday Richmond
The Wallers closed their engagement with *Eleanor; or, The Masked Riders* and *Midas*.

September 25, Sunday Richmond

September 26, Monday Richmond
Jane Coombs opened her engagement with the play *Love's Sacrifice*, which was followed by *A Deed of Dreadful Note*.

September 27, Tuesday Richmond
Jane Coombs appeared in *The School for Scandal*. Booth probably played Sir Benjamin Backbite.

September 28, Wednesday Richmond
Jane Coombs appeared in *Romeo and Juliet*, with Edwin Adams as Romeo. Booth played Paris. *A Kiss in the Dark* followed.

September 29, Thursday Richmond
The Marshall Theatre presented *Ingomar, the Barbarian*. Booth played Alastor. *Ireland As It Is* followed.

September 30, Friday Richmond
Jane Coombs appeared in *The Lady of Lyons* with Booth playing Glavis. Booth played the romantic lead Trueworth opposite Miss Coombs in the afterpiece, *The Love Chase*.

October 1, Saturday Richmond
Booth probably played Alastor in *Ingomar, the Barbarian*, which was followed by *Tom and Jerry; or, Life in London*.

October 2, Sunday Richmond

October 3, Monday Richmond
Booth had a minor role in *Fazio; or, The Italian Wife's Revenge*. *His Last Legs* followed.

October 4, Tuesday Richmond
Jane Coombs starred in *London Assurance*, with Booth sustaining the role of Cool.

October 5, Wednesday Richmond
The Marshall Theatre presented *Actress of Padua* and *My Friend in the Straps*.

October 6, Thursday Richmond

The Marshall Theatre presented *The Stranger* and *Ireland As It Is*.

October 7, Friday Richmond

Jane Coombs appeared in the "screen scene" from *The School for Scandal*, the fourth act of *The Hunchback*, and the balcony scene from *Romeo and Juliet*.

October 8, Saturday Richmond

The Marshall Theatre presented *Black Rangers; or, The Battle of Germantown* and *Tom and Jerry*.

October 9, Sunday Richmond

October 10, Monday Richmond

Maggie Mitchell opened her engagement with *The Young Prince*, *Katy O'Shiel*, and *Black Rangers*.

October 11, Tuesday Richmond

Maggie Mitchell played *Margot, The Poultry Dealer* and *The Pet of the Petticoats*.

October 12, Wednesday Richmond

The Marshall Theatre presented *The Wept of Wish-Ton-Wish*, *The Little Savage*, and *My Friend in the Straps*.

October 13, Thursday Richmond

The Marshall Theatre presented *The French Spy* and *The Four Sisters*.

October 14, Friday Richmond

Maggie Mitchell played *The Green Bushes* and *A Lady's Stratagem*.

October 15, Saturday Richmond

The Marshall Theatre presented *Beauty and the Beast* and *Asmodeus*.

October 16, Sunday Richmond

At about 11 p.m. John Brown and a band of abolitionists crossed the Potomac River from Maryland to Harpers Ferry, Virginia, to begin their raid.

October 17, Monday Lynchburg

A contingent of George Kunkel's Marshall Theatre company, including Booth, opened at Dudley Hall in Lynchburg in *The Lady of Lyons*, with Edwin Adams as Claude Melnotte and Booth as Glavis. The play was followed by the farce *Our Country Cousin*.[137] Maggie Mitchell continued her engagement in Richmond.

October 18, Tuesday Lynchburg

The *Lynchburg Daily Virginian* advertised "Comedy Night" at the theatre, consisting of three farces: *The Stage Struck Barber*, *The Loan of a Lover*, and *The Wandering Minstrel*.

Shortly after dawn, Marines commanded by Colonel Robert E. Lee attacked the engine house in Harpers Ferry, which John Brown and his followers were defending. Brown was captured alive.

October 19, Wednesday Lynchburg

At Dudley Hall, Edwin Adams had the lead role in *College Boy*, G. W. Wren performed comic songs, W. Johnson played Jumbo in *Jumbo Jum; or, The Honest Shoe Black*, and Edwin Adams closed the evening in *The Farmer's Story*.

October 20, Thursday Lynchburg

Kunkel's company played *My Aunt, Rough Diamond*, and *Paddy Miles' Boy*. The *Virginian* critic wished to draw the "particular attention of the thousands now in our city, to the elegant entertainments provided by the enterprising managers of this popular resort [Dudley Hall], for their amusement."[138]

October 21, Friday Lynchburg

The *Virginian* carried the Dudley Hall advertisement for *The Stranger* and *The Loan of a Lover* above a notice titled "NEGROES AND OTHER PROPERTY FOR SALE." Maggie Mitchell closed her engagement in Richmond.

October 22, Saturday Lynchburg

Kunkel's company closed its week of performances in Lynchburg with a benefit for Mrs. I. B. Phillips and Edwin Adams. *Dumb Belle* and *Richard III* were followed by *A Kiss in the Dark*.

October 23, Sunday Richmond

October 24, Monday Richmond

The Marshall Theatre presented *Everybody's Friend*. Booth probably played Icebrook. The afterpiece was *Horse-shoe Robinson*.

October 25, Tuesday Richmond

The Marshall Theatre presented *The Heir at Law* with Booth as Henry Moreland. *The Illustrious Stranger; or, Married and Buried* followed.

October 26, Wednesday Richmond

The Marshall Theatre presented *Black-Eyed Susan*, *Going to the Cattle Show*, and *Beauty and the Beast*.

October 27, Thursday Richmond

The Marshall Theatre presented *Ireland as It Is*, *College Boy*, and *Going to the Cattle Show*.

October 28, Friday Richmond

The Marshall Theatre presented *Eustache*, *The Condemned*, and *The Farmer's Story*.

October 29, Saturday Richmond

The Marshall Theatre presented *The Maniac Lover*, *Irish Assurance*, and *Turning the Tables*.

October 30, Sunday Richmond

October 31, Monday Richmond

Barry Sullivan opened an engagement with *Hamlet*, in which Booth played Horatio. *Family Jars* followed.

In Charlestown, Virginia (later Charles Town, West Virginia), John Brown was found guilty of treason and sentenced to hang.

November 1, Tuesday Richmond

Barry Sullivan played *Richelieu*, which was followed by *Family Jars*.

November 2, Wednesday Richmond

Booth played Dawson in *The Gamester*, with Barry Sullivan as Beverley. *The Good for Nothing* followed.

November 3, Thursday Richmond

The Marshall Theatre presented Barry Sullivan as Alfred Evelyn in *Money*. *Paddy Miles' Boy* followed.

November 4, Friday Richmond

Barry Sullivan appeared in *The Merchant of Venice* and *Taming a Shrew*.

November 5, Saturday Richmond

The Marshall Theatre presented *Richard III*. Booth probably played the role of the Duke of Buckingham. *Your Life's in Danger* followed.

November 6, Sunday Richmond

November 7, Monday Richmond

The *Enquirer* noted that Booth was one of those "who have come up generally well in their parts."[139] The Marshall Theatre presented *A New Way to Pay Old Debts* and *More Blunders Than One*.

November 8, Tuesday Richmond

Sullivan played *King Lear* supported by Booth as Edmund.

November 9, Wednesday Richmond

The Marshall Theatre presented *King Henry IV* with Barry Sullivan as Falstaff.

November 10, Thursday Petersburg

Booth's fellow actor John Barron claimed that Booth had rehearsed the part of Don Pedro in *Much Ado About Nothing* but had, at the last moment, skipped the show and gone to Petersburg without explanation. His sudden absence marred the performance.[140] The afterpiece was *The Loan of a Lover*.

November 11, Friday Petersburg

Barry Sullivan played *The Iron Chest* at the Marshall Theatre in Richmond. According to the account of John Barron, Booth was in Petersburg.[141]

November 12, Saturday Petersburg

November 13, Sunday Richmond

Booth returned from Petersburg on or about this date.[142]

November 14, Monday Richmond

Comedian William E. Burton[143] opened an engagement with *A Breach of Promise* and *The Toodles*.

November 15, Tuesday Richmond

W. E. Burton appeared in *The Serious Family* at the Marshall Theatre.

November 16, Wednesday Richmond

The Marshall Theatre presented *The Loan of a Lover*, *Wanted, One Thousand Spirited Young Milliners for the Gold Diggings*, and *The Mummy*.

November 17, Thursday Richmond

The Marshall Theatre presented W. E. Burton in his popular *Dombey and Son*, followed by *The Wandering Minstrel*.

November 18, Friday Richmond

W. E. Burton played *Paul Pry* and *The Blue Devils*.

November 19, Saturday En route to Washington

Governor Henry Wise of Virginia ordered several military units composing the First Virginia Regiment to Charlestown to defend against any attempt to rescue John Brown. Booth borrowed a uniform from friends in the Richmond Grays and boarded the train with the unit. The train departed Richmond at 9:30 p.m. bound for Aquia Creek on the Potomac.[144]

November 20, Sunday Charlestown

The train bearing the regiment arrived at Aquia Creek at 4 a.m. The troops boarded a steamer and landed at Washington at 7 a.m. Governor Wise marched the men to the White House and then down Pennsylvania Avenue to the train depot. The men traveled by rail to Relay, Maryland, and on to Harpers Ferry. A few companies stayed in Harpers Ferry, while the Grays and several other companies continued to Charlestown, arriving at 6 p.m.[145]

November 21, Monday Charlestown

A crowd gathered at the courthouse square at 9 a.m. to witness a parade and review the regiment. When the parade and review were postponed, the Grays filled in with drills "which could hardly be excelled."[146]

The Grays wore new "blanket over-coats" supplied by Smith's clothing store in Richmond.[147]

Booth served as a quartermaster sergeant under regimental quartermaster Robert A. Caskie.[148]

November 22, Tuesday Charlestown

The Grays were stationed in Charlestown.

November 23, Wednesday Charlestown

Most evenings Booth performed Shakespearean recitations at the Episcopal Meeting House.[149]

November 24, Thursday Charlestown

November 25, Friday Charlestown

November 26, Saturday Charlestown

November 27, Sunday Charlestown

November 28, Monday Charlestown

Mary Devlin wrote to Edwin Booth saying that John had taken a "mad step."[150]

A correspondent of the *Daily Richmond Enquirer* described the Richmond contingent in Charlestown:

The Richmond Grays and Company F, which seem to vie with each other in the handsome appearance they present, remind one of uncaged birds, so wild and gleesome they appear.... Amongst them I notice Mr. J. Wilkes Booth, a son of Junius Brutus Booth, who, though not a member, as soon as he heard the tap of the drum, threw down the sock and buskin, and shouldered his musket with the Grays to the scene of deadly conflict.[151]

November 29, Tuesday Charlestown

November 30, Wednesday Charlestown

On or about this date Asia Booth Clarke wrote to her friend Jean Anderson: "John is crazy or enthusiastic about going for a soldier."[152]

December 1, Thursday Charlestown

Booth asked Charlestown's sheriff, James Campbell, for permission to visit John Brown and his fellow prisoners in their cells.[153] Booth and others spent the night in the court room across Washington Street from the jail.[154]

December 2, Friday Charlestown

John Brown was hanged at 11 a.m. The Richmond Grays, with John Wilkes Booth present, stood close to the gallows. Booth appeared to be shaken after the drop fell and desired a drink of whiskey.[155]

December 3, Saturday Washington

The Richmond Grays traveled to Washington and stayed at the National Hotel.[156]

December 4, Sunday Richmond

December 5, Monday Richmond

According to the *Richmond Daily Dispatch*, the "Richmond Grays and Company F returned from Charleston [*sic*] ... and speak in the highest terms of the kindness of the people among whom they have been sojourning and performing duty."[157]

The *Dispatch* also noted:

Not only the city, but the State owes the volunteers a debt of gratitude for the promptness with which they shouldered their muskets and left their homes to defend from invasion the soil of Virginia, and we can see no other way by which they can so easily partially repay it, as by giving those that have arrived, and those that are to come, a public reception at the cars.[158]

The Marshall Theatre performed *The Hidden Hand*.

December 6, Tuesday Richmond

The Marshall Theatre presented *The Hidden Hand* with Mrs. Charles Howard.

December 7, Wednesday Richmond

The Marshall Theatre presented *The Hidden Hand*.

December 8, Thursday Richmond

The Marshall Theatre presented *Smiles and Tears* and *Your Life's in Danger*.

December 9, Friday Richmond

Mrs. Charles Howard appeared in *Fortunes of War* at the Marshall Theatre.

December 10, Saturday Richmond

Mrs. Charles Howard appeared in *The Pioneer Patriot; or, The Maid of the Warpath* and *It Takes Two to Quarrel* at the Marshall Theatre.

December 11, Sunday Petersburg

December 12, Monday Petersburg

Kunkel's Marshall Theatre stock company opened an engagement in Petersburg with *The Hidden Hand*. The Marsh Juvenile Troupe of comedians opened a two-week engagement at the Marshall Theatre.[159]

December 13, Tuesday Petersburg

Kunkel's company performed *The Hidden Hand*.

December 14, Wednesday Petersburg

Kunkel's company performed *The Bride of an Evening; or, The Gipsy's Prophecy* and *Forty Winks*.

December 15, Thursday Petersburg

Kunkel's company performed *Smiles and Tears* and *A Kiss in the Dark*.

December 16, Friday Petersburg

Kunkel's company performed *The Pioneer Patriot* and *Jenny Lind*.

December 17, Saturday Petersburg

Kunkel's company played *The Pioneer Patriot* and *It Takes Two to Quarrel*.

December 18, Sunday Petersburg

December 19, Monday Petersburg

Kunkel's company performed *The Hunchback* and *Crimson Crimes*.

December 20, Tuesday Petersburg

Kunkel's company presented *Time Tries All* and *The Love Chase*.

December 21, Wednesday Petersburg

Kunkel's company performed *London Assurance*. Booth usually played the part of Cool.

December 22, Thursday Petersburg

The Petersburg engagement closed with *Fortunes of War*, *Who's Who*, and *Rough Diamond*.

December 23, Friday Richmond

The Marshall Theatre presented *Simon Seigal; or, The Miser and the Three Thieves*.

December 24, Saturday Richmond

The Marsh Juvenile Troupe ended its engagement at the Marshall Theatre with *Cinderilla* [sic]; *or, The Glass Slipper*.

December 25, Sunday Richmond

December 26, Monday Richmond

The Marshall Theatre presented *Poor Smike* and *A Christmas Pantomime* in the matinee. In

the evening Mrs. Charles Howard appeared in *The Hidden Hand*.

The militia company Virginia Rifles held its annual ball at the Hall of the Mechanics' Institute in Richmond; Booth's recent service in the Grays may have induced him to drop by.[160]

December 27, Tuesday Richmond

Booth played Lord Arthur Brandon in *Dreams of Delusion* and Lamp in the afterpiece, *Wild Oats*.

December 28, Wednesday Richmond

Mary Devlin wrote to Edwin Booth, who was performing in Montgomery, Alabama: "I grieve for John's trouble—foolish boy, what can he be thinking of—talk to him Edwin seriously, ere he destroys his youth."[161] The "trouble" was, most likely, a reference to John Wilkes Booth's escapade with the Richmond Grays.

December 29, Thursday Richmond

The Marshall Theatre presented *A Sheep in Wolf's Clothing*.

December 30, Friday Richmond

Mrs. I. B. Phillips played the lead in *A Sheep in Wolf's Clothing*. *Everybody's Friend* and *Siamese Twins* followed.

December 31, Saturday Richmond

The Marshall Theatre presented *The Pioneer Patriot*.

1860 *through June 4*

January 1, Sunday Richmond

January 2, Monday Richmond

Caroline Richings and her father, Peter Richings, opened an engagement at the Marshall Theatre with *The Daughter of the Regiment*.[162]

January 3, Tuesday Richmond

Caroline Richings appeared in *Louise Muller* and *The Bonnie Irish Wife*.

January 4, Wednesday Richmond

The Marshall Theatre presented *Chaplain of the Regiment* and *The Little Savage*.

January 5, Thursday Richmond

The Marshall Theatre presented *Immortal Washington*, *The Spirit of the Rhine*, and *Chaplain of the Regiment*.

January 6, Friday Richmond
The Marshall Theatre presented *Fashion* and *Immortal Washington*.

January 7, Saturday Richmond
The Marshall Theatre presented *Napoleon's Old Guard, The Spirit of the Rhine*, and *Immortal Washington*.

January 8, Sunday Richmond

January 9, Monday Richmond
The Marshall Theatre presented *Fashion* and *Immortal Washington*. The Richings continued their engagement.

January 10, Tuesday Richmond
The Marshall Theatre presented *The Blind Man's Daughter, Chaplain of the Regiment*, and *The Spirit of the Rhine*.

January 11, Wednesday Richmond
The Marshall Theatre presented *The Enchantress*, starring Caroline Richings.

January 12, Thursday Richmond
The Marshall Theatre presented *The Enchantress*.

January 13, Friday Richmond
The Marshall Theatre presented *The Enchantress*.

January 14, Saturday Richmond
The Marshall Theatre presented *The Enchantress*.

January 15, Sunday Richmond

January 16, Monday Richmond
The Marshall Theatre presented *The Enchantress*.

January 17, Tuesday Richmond
The Marshall Theatre presented *The Enchantress*.

January 18, Wednesday Richmond
The Marshall Theatre presented *The Enchantress*.

January 19, Thursday Richmond
The Marshall Theatre presented *The Enchantress*.

January 20, Friday Richmond
The Marshall Theatre presented *Prima Donna* and *Immortal Washington*.

January 21, Saturday Richmond
The Marshall Theatre presented *The Enchantress*.

January 22, Sunday Richmond

January 23, Monday Richmond
The Richings continued the long run of *The Enchantress* at the Marshall Theatre.

January 24, Tuesday Richmond
The Marshall Theatre presented *The Enchantress*.

January 25, Wednesday Richmond
The Marshall Theatre presented *The Blind Man's Daughter, The Bonnie Fish Wife*, and *The Spirit of the Rhine*.

January 26, Thursday Richmond
The Marshall Theatre presented *The Daughter of the Regiment* and *The Little Savage*.

January 27, Friday Richmond
The Marshall Theatre presented *Extremes* and *Immortal Washington*.

January 28, Saturday Richmond
The Richings' engagement at the Marshall Theatre closed with *Clari; or, The Maid of Milan, Private and Confidential*, and a program of songs.

January 29, Sunday Richmond

January 30, Monday Richmond
James E. Murdock opened an engagement at the Marshall Theatre as Rover in *Wild Oats*, which was followed by *Your Life's in Danger*.

January 31, Tuesday Richmond
James E. Murdock appeared as Alfred Evelyn in *Money*, which was followed by *A Kiss in the Dark*.

February 1, Wednesday Richmond
James E. Murdock appeared in *Hamlet*. Booth usually played the part of Horatio.

February 2, Thursday Richmond
Booth played Dawson in *The Gamester* with James E. Murdock as Beverley. In the afterpiece, *Buzzards*, Booth played Mr. Glimmer.

February 3, Friday Richmond
James E. Murdock appeared in *Inconstant*, which was followed by *My Aunt*.

February 4, Saturday Richmond
James E. Murdock appeared as Charles de Moor in *The Robbers*, which was followed by *The Buzzards*.

February 5, Sunday Richmond

February 6, Monday Richmond

The Marshall Theatre presented *Doom of Deville* and *Dreams of Delusion*.

February 7, Tuesday Richmond

The Marshall Theatre presented *The Marble Heart* and *Crimson Crimes*.

February 8, Wednesday Richmond

The Marshall Theatre presented *Grandfather Whitehead*, *A Sheep in Wolf's Clothing*, and *Glance at New York*.

February 9, Thursday Richmond

The Marshall Theatre presented *Horse-Shoe Robinson* and *A Glance at New York*.

February 10, Friday Richmond

The Marshall Theatre presented *A Sheep in Wolf's Clothing*, *Ireland As It Is*, and *Buzzards*.

February 11, Saturday Richmond

The Marshall Theatre presented *A Husband to Order* and *Bacon's Rebellion*.

February 12, Sunday Richmond

February 13, Monday Richmond

The Marshall Theatre presented *A Husband to Order* and *The Drunkard*.

February 14, Tuesday Richmond

The Marshall Theatre presented *A Husband to Order* and *Bacon's Rebellion*.

February 15, Wednesday Richmond

The Marshall Theatre presented *Don Caesar de Bazan* and *A Husband to Order*.

February 16, Thursday Richmond

The Marshall Theatre presented *Idiot Witness* and *The Doom of Deville*.

February 17, Friday Richmond

W. T. Johnson starred in *Broken Sword*. Booth played Claudio. *Village Lawyer* and *Jumbo Jum* followed.

February 18, Saturday Richmond

The Marshall Theatre presented *Wrecker's Beacon* and *Broken Sword*. Booth wrote an acrostic in the autograph album of Mary C. White, an actress in the stock company.[163]

February 19, Sunday Richmond

February 20, Monday Richmond

J. B. Roberts began an engagement with *Richard III*, in which Booth usually played Buckingham. *Omnibus* followed.

February 21, Tuesday Richmond

J. B. Roberts starred in *A New Way to Pay Old Debts*. *Village Lawyer* followed.

February 22, Wednesday Richmond

The Marshall Theatre presented *Louis Eleventh* and *Omnibus*.

February 23, Thursday Richmond

The Marshall Theatre presented *Louis Eleventh*.

February 24, Friday Richmond

J. B. Roberts played *Louis Eleventh*. *Faint Heart Never Won Fair Lady* followed.

February 25, Saturday Richmond

The Marshall Theatre presented *The Moors in Spain* and *Too Much for Good Nature*. Booth played the part of Romeo Jaffier Jenkins in the latter play.

February 26, Sunday Richmond

February 27, Monday Richmond

Julia Hayne began an engagement at the Marshall Theatre with *The Lady of Lyons*, which was followed by Booth as Romeo Jaffier Jenkins in *Too Much for Good Nature*.

Abraham Lincoln spoke at Cooper Union in New York City.

February 28, Tuesday Richmond

Julia Hayne played *Ingomar, the Barbarian*, which was followed by *Too Much for Good Nature*.

February 29, Wednesday Richmond

Booth played Lord Tinsel in *The Hunchback* and took the role of Romeo Jaffier Jenkins in the afterpiece, *Too Much for Good Nature*.

March 1, Thursday Richmond

Julia Hayne appeared in *London Assurance* with Booth as Cool, which was followed by *The Rifle, and How to Use It*.

Mary Devlin wrote to Edwin Booth: "Mr. [Joseph] Jefferson, promises to write to John—for though he may not be in management himself he can always procure him an engagement."[164]

March 2, Friday Richmond

Julia Hayne played *Evadne* in her benefit performance. Booth played Ludovico and was the only actor called before the audience for applause.[165] The afterpiece was *Rough Diamond*.

March 3, Saturday Richmond

Julia Hayne played *Lucretia Borgia*, which was followed by *Aunt Charlotte's Maid*.

March 4, Sunday Richmond

March 5, Monday Richmond

Louise Wells and her Equestrian Troupe returned to the Marshall Theatre and opened with *Buck Bison* and *Americans Abroad*.

March 6, Tuesday Richmond

Louise Wells and her Equestrian Troupe performed *Vesuvius*.

March 7, Wednesday Richmond

Louise Wells appeared in *Eagle's Eye*, which was followed by *Paddy Miles' Boy*.

Asia Booth Clarke wrote to her friend Jean Anderson: "John Booth desired that his love might be sent to Janey [Jean]."[166]

March 8, Thursday Richmond

The Marshall Theatre presented *The Female Horse Thief* and *Break of Day Boys*.

March 9, Friday Richmond

The Marshall Theatre presented *Rookwood*.

March 10, Saturday Richmond

The Marshall Theatre presented *Jack Sheppard on Horseback*. Booth appeared as Romeo Jaffier Jenkins in *Too Much for Good Nature*.

March 11, Sunday Richmond

March 12, Monday Richmond

Louise Wells continued at the Marshall Theatre in *Mazeppa* and *Aunt Charlotte's Maid*.

Booth's sister Rosalie wrote to Edwin: In regard to Wilkes' fight at Richmond it was with a man named Pat Redford or Redman in the box office who had insulted him.... He played *Ludovico* the other night for Julia Hayne's benefit and was the only one called before the curtain and had a six minute call. He seems very much pleased at it.[167]

March 13, Tuesday Richmond

The Marshall Theatre presented *Mazeppa*, followed by *Too Much for Good Nature*.

March 14, Wednesday Richmond

The Marshall Theatre presented *Rookwood* and *Crimson Crimes*.

March 15, Thursday Richmond

The Marshall Theatre presented *Putnam*, *Irish Assurance*, and *Yankee Modesty*.

March 16, Friday Richmond

The Wells Equestrian Troupe closed its engagement with *The Wept of Wish-Ton-Wish* and *Jack Sheppard on Horseback*.

March 17, Saturday Richmond

The Marshall Theatre presented *The French Spy*, the fifth act of *Richard III on Horseback*, and *Paddy the Piper*.

March 18, Sunday Richmond

March 19, Monday Richmond

John Sleeper Clarke opened a one-week engagement at the Marshall Theatre with *Leap Year*.

Part of Kunkel's company was in Petersburg from March 19 through March 24.[168]

March 20, Tuesday Richmond

John Sleeper Clarke played *Jonathan Bradford*, which was followed by *Leap Year* and *Aunt Charlotte's Maid*.

March 21, Wednesday Richmond

The Marshall Theatre presented *School of Reform* and *The Spectre Bridegroom*.

March 22, Thursday Richmond

John Sleeper Clarke appeared in *Paul Pry*, *The Toodles*, and *The Hypocrite*.

March 23, Friday Richmond

John Sleeper Clarke appeared in *Our American Cousin*. The afterpieces were *Old Times in Virginia* and *Jack the Exciseman*.

March 24, Saturday Richmond

John Sleeper Clarke and Booth again appeared in *Our American Cousin*, which was followed by *Old Times in Virginia* and *Jack the Exciseman*.

March 25, Sunday Richmond

March 26, Monday Richmond

The Marshall Theatre presented *A Sheep in Wolf's Clothing*, *Everybody's Friend*, and *Aunt Charlotte's Maid*. Part of Kunkel's company appeared in Petersburg with the Wells Equestrian Troupe this week.

March 27, Tuesday Richmond

The Marshall Theatre presented *Dreams of Delusion* and *Don Caesar de Bazan*.

March 28, Wednesday Richmond

The Marshall Theatre presented *All That Glitters Is Not Gold* and *Black-Eyed Susan*.

March 29, Thursday Richmond

The Marshall Theatre presented *The Stranger* and *Whitebait at Greenwich*, with Booth as Mr. Glimmer.

March 30, Friday Richmond

The Marshall Theatre presented *The Willow Copse* and *Aunt Charlotte's Maid*.

March 31, Saturday Richmond

The Marshall Theatre presented *The Rake's Progress* and *Solitary of the Heath*. Booth played the parts of Fred Florid and Sieur Arnaud, respectively.

April 1, Sunday Richmond

April 2, Monday Richmond

Helen and Lucille Western appeared in *The Flowers of the Forest* and *The Swedish Nightingale*. The Marshall Theatre's advertisement in the *Dispatch* read:

> First night of the beautiful and accomplished young American Star sisters, the Misses Lucille and Helen Western! The management, always anxious to meet the wishes of their patrons, and eager to secure the best talent which the country affords, has the pleasure to announce the engagement of the above Talented Young Artistes.[169]

April 3, Tuesday Richmond

Helen and Lucille Western starred in *A Lady's Stratagem*, *The French Spy*, and *The Wandering Boys*, with Booth as Count de Courcy.

April 4, Wednesday Richmond

The Marshall Theatre presented *Belle of Ireland*, *Our Female American Cousin*, and *Young Student*.

April 5, Thursday Richmond

The Marshall Theatre presented *The Wept of Wish-Ton-Wish*, followed by *Jack Sheppard*.

April 6, Friday Richmond

The Western sisters appeared in *Satan in Paris* and *Our Female American Cousin*.

April 7, Saturday Richmond

The Marshall Theatre presented *Hot Corn Girl* with Booth as Eugene Sedley, followed by *The French Spy*.

April 8, Sunday Richmond

April 9, Monday Richmond

The Marshall Theatre presented *The Three Fast Men*.

April 10, Tuesday Richmond

The Marshall Theatre presented *Our Fe-*

male American Cousin and *Nature and Philosophy*.

April 11, Wednesday Richmond

The Marshall Theatre presented *The Flowers of the Forest* and *The Loan of a Lover*.

April 12, Thursday Richmond

The Marshall Theatre presented *Green Bushes* and *A Lady's Stratagem*.

April 13, Friday Richmond

The Western sisters played *The Hidden Hand* and *Love's Disguises*.

April 14, Saturday Richmond

Booth submitted a claim for payment for his service with the Richmond Grays: "I claim as Quartermaster Sergeant of 1 Reg. V. Vol. for nineteen days service from 19 Nov. to Dec.—[signed] John Booth." He received a payment of $64.58.[170]

The Marshall Theatre presented *Hot Corn Girl* and *The French Spy*.

April 15, Sunday Richmond

April 16, Monday Richmond

The Marshall Theatre presented *The Three Fast Men; or, The Female Robinson Crusoes* with Booth as George Middleton. The Western sisters' engagement continued.

April 17, Tuesday Richmond

Helen and Louise Western appeared in *The Three Fast Men*.

April 18, Wednesday Richmond

The Marshall Theatre presented *The Three Fast Men*.

April 19, Thursday Richmond

The Marshall Theatre presented *The Three Fast Men*.

April 20, Friday Richmond

The Marshall Theatre presented *The Three Fast Men*.

April 21, Saturday Richmond

The Marshall Theatre presented *The Three Fast Men*.

April 22, Sunday Petersburg

April 23, Monday Petersburg

A contingent of Kunkel's Marshall Theatre stock company, including John Wilkes Booth, appeared in Petersburg this week.

April 24, Tuesday Petersburg

April 25, Wednesday Petersburg

Kunkel's company played *Hot Corn Girl* with Booth in the role of Eugene Sedley and *The Wandering Boys of Switzerland* with Booth as Count de Courcy.

April 26, Thursday Petersburg

April 27, Friday Petersburg

Kunkel's company played *The Three Fast Men* with Booth as George Middleton.

April 28, Saturday Petersburg

Kunkel's company closed its engagement in Petersburg with *The Three Fast Men.*

April 29, Sunday Norfolk?

Asia Booth Clarke wrote to her friend Jean Anderson: "John Booth has an eye on you—so I understand."[171]

April 30, Monday Norfolk

The traveling contingent of Kunkel's Marshall Theatre stock company opened an engagement in Norfolk.[172] In Richmond, comedian Frank Chanfrau[173] opened an engagement with *The Toodles, The Widow's Victim,* and *Swiss Cottage.* He performed "his wonderful imitations of the celebrated actors widely known—Booth, Forrest, Kean, Burton, Rice, Barney Williams."[174]

May 1, Tuesday Norfolk

May 2, Wednesday Norfolk

May 3, Thursday Norfolk

May 4, Friday Norfolk

May 5, Saturday Norfolk

May 6, Sunday Norfolk

May 7, Monday Norfolk

The Marshall Theatre was closed this week, perhaps because of stiff competition from a circus then playing in Richmond.[175]

May 8, Tuesday Norfolk

Booth wrote a letter to Robert Whittle, a clerk in the Richmond Manufacturing Company.[176]

May 9, Wednesday Norfolk

May 10, Thursday Norfolk

May 11, Friday Norfolk

May 12, Saturday Norfolk

May 13, Sunday Richmond

May 14, Monday Richmond

The Marshall Theatre presented *The Three Guardsmen* with John Wilkes Booth as Aramis, Sam Chester as Porthos, and James W. Collier as Athos. Edwin Adams played D'Artagnan.

May 15, Tuesday Richmond

The Marshall Theatre presented *The Three Guardsmen.*

May 16, Wednesday Richmond

The Marshall Theatre presented *The Flying Dutchman; or, The Phantom Ship.*

May 17, Thursday Richmond

The Marshall Theatre presented *The Flying Dutchman.*

May 18, Friday Richmond

Mrs. I. B. Phillips appeared in *The Romance of a Poor Young Man.* Booth played M. de Bevannes, a man of the world. *The Queen's Own* followed.

The convention of the Republican Party in Chicago nominated Abraham Lincoln for the presidency.

May 19, Saturday Richmond

The Marshall Theatre presented *The Flying Dutchman* and *Horse-shoe Robinson.*

May 20, Sunday Richmond

May 21, Monday Richmond

The Marshall Theatre presented *The Wood Demon.*

May 22, Tuesday Richmond

The Marshall Theatre presented *The Wood Demon.*

May 23, Wednesday Richmond

The Marshall Theatre presented *The Wood Demon.*

May 24, Thursday Richmond

The Marshall Theatre presented *The Wood Demon.*

May 25, Friday Richmond

Mrs. Edwin Adams appeared in *The Romance of a Poor Young Man.* Booth played M. de Bevannes. This was a farewell benefit for Mr. and Mrs. Edwin Adams "prior to their departure from Richmond."[177]

May 26, Saturday Richmond

The Marshall Theatre presented *Poor Smike* and *The Lost Ship; or, The Man of War's Man and the Privateer.*

May 27, Sunday Richmond

May 28, Monday Richmond

The Marshall Theatre presented *Poor Smike*, followed by *The Lost Ship*.

May 29, Tuesday Richmond

A Husband to Order was the play of the evening. The theatre gave away paintings, including one of Edwin Booth, as an inducement to attend the final play of the season.

May 30, Wednesday Richmond

May 31, Thursday Richmond

In a joint benefit for J. W. Collier and John Wilkes Booth, Booth appeared as Victim in *Son of Malta*, as Sayers in *My Fellow Clerk*, and as Richard in the fifth act of *Richard III*. This performance closed the season.[178]

The *Enquirer* advertised the benefit and advised Booth to have more confidence.[179]

June 1, Friday Richmond

June 4, Monday

The *Enquirer* critic wrote that Booth had demonstrated improved confidence in his Thursday night performance.[180]

4

Novice: 1860–1861

With three years of experience as a stock actor behind him, John Wilkes Booth decided to tour as a star. New York, the nation's center of theatrical activity, was the best place to arrange engagements for the upcoming season. Theatre manager Matthew W. Canning, who had leased a new theatre in Montgomery, Alabama, came to New York early in July 1860 to recruit both a stock company and stars. Booth had met Canning in Philadelphia when he was in the Arch Street Theatre company; Canning, trained as an attorney, was then the treasurer of a rival theatre. Booth's friends Samuel Knapp Chester and John Albaugh joined Canning's new stock company for the 1860–1861 season, and Canning hired Booth for a five-week period. While Booth was to be a member of the company, he would be performing starring roles. He would be paid as a stock player and would not receive a portion of the profits, as would a star.[1]

By late in September Canning's troupe arrived in Columbus, Georgia, where it would perform a three-week engagement at Temperance Hall before settling into the theatre in Montgomery. An advertisement in the *Columbus Daily Times* proclaimed: "Mr. John Wilkes has been engaged for a limited number of nights and will be supported by an excellent Stock Company."[2] In his first ten performances, Booth starred in *Romeo and Juliet, The Stranger, Evadne; or, The Statue, The Wife, Richard III, The Apostate, The Marble Heart, The Lady of Lyons,* and *Everybody's Friend.* This formidable feat must have re-

quired extensive preparation. Newspaper reviews were favorable. "The Columbus papers continue to speak in the most glowing terms of the theatrical performances of Mr. Canning's popular company in that city," noted the *Montgomery [Alabama] Daily Mail.* "Mr. Wilkes and Miss [Mary] Mitchell are highly complimented."[3]

Misfortune struck Booth near the end of the second week of his first starring engagement. On Friday, October 12, an hour before he was to play *Hamlet,* he was accidentally shot in the thigh. There are several contradictory accounts of the incident. One holds that Booth and John Albaugh were practicing their lines in Booth's room when Canning came in and playfully threatened to shoot them; the pistol accidentally went off. Another report indicates that the incident occurred at a shooting gallery.[4] The most reliable account, perhaps, has Booth and Canning cleaning a pistol when it unexpectedly discharged.[5]

The *Columbus Daily Sun* reported: "It is with a feeling of sincere regret that we announce that Mr. J. W. Booth, the young and talented Tragedian ... was seriously wounded ... by the accidental discharge of a pistol." The ball had entered Booth's thigh, taking a downward course. A severe wound resulted, but no major blood vessels were ruptured.[6]

Booth spent much of the next week convalescing in his room at Cook's Hotel attended by a Dr. Stanford.[7] Canning's company resumed performances; lead roles went to Mary Mitchell and John Albaugh, who had taken Booth's place in *Hamlet* the night of the accident and had done well.[8] A reviewer in the *Columbus Daily Times* reported that patronage at Temperance Hall had decreased since Booth had been disabled. He continued: "Mr. Wilkes, we are happy to announce, is doing quite as well as could be expected, and may possibly play by the close of the week."[9] Bad luck continued when inclement weather forced the cancellation of a benefit for Booth scheduled for the evening of October 19, a week after the shooting.[10]

The next day, the *Columbus Daily Sun* reported that Booth, while still feeble, would that night recite Marc Antony's address over the dead Caesar. A large audience saw Booth's return to the stage. "Curiosity to see the rising young Tragedian, and sympathy for his late misfortune, drew more to the theatre than the bill for the evening," the *Sun* remarked. The newspaper further commented that Booth performed his recitation "in a manner entirely above criticism, notwithstanding his suffering."[11]

Canning and his company left Columbus for Montgomery on October 21. Booth's injury prevented his departure until the morning of Tuesday, October 23.[12] The *Sun* reported: "With extreme caution he may reach that city without harm to his wound, but for some time he will be unable to fulfill his engagement upon the boards." Although the Monday issue of the *Montgomery Daily Mail* had indicated that "Mr. John Wilkes" would appear on stage the next day, the Tuesday issue advertised John Albaugh in *Poor Gentleman*, with no mention of Booth.

A reporter for the *Montgomery Daily Mail* interviewed Booth during the week:

> We had the pleasure of an introduction to this young tragedian ... at the theatre. He is rapidly recovering from his unfortunate accident in Columbus, some time since, and informed us that he would make his first appearance on our boards Monday night [October 29].[13]

Booth resumed regular performances seventeen days after the shooting and was greeted by a fair audience. The next night's production was also a success, drawing the largest crowd of the season. The *Daily Mail*'s review praised Booth, Mary Mitchell, John Albaugh, and Sam Chester.[14] Canning had engaged Booth to appear in Columbus and Montgomery for a total of five weeks. During that period Booth lost two weeks of performances and income because of his injury.

Booth stayed in Montgomery for four weeks after his engagement ended. On November 16 he appeared in *Romeo and Juliet* with Kate Bateman,[15] who then was starring with Canning's company. The joint appearance was so successful that Booth and Bateman discussed touring England together.[16] In his "Grand complimentary benefit" on December 1, Booth appeared in a two-act drama titled *Rafaelle the Reprobate*. He concluded the evening with the fifth act of *Richard III*.[17] On this night and ever after he was billed as John Wilkes Booth.

Booth's sojourn in Montgomery coincided with the fractious presidential election of 1860. Inflammatory editorials appeared in the *Montgomery Daily Mail*:

> If the South could be stupid enough to submit to such an administration as Lincoln's, for one moment, it ought to be plundered and mulattoized, both—made no better than the North! But the white people of the South are very different from those of Massachusetts, and we think they will resist free Negro rule at all hazards.[18]

On the evening of October 25, U.S. Senator Robert Toombs of Georgia, a secessionist and later a candidate for the presidency of the Confederate States, spoke from the balcony of his hotel room to a throng gathered in the street. He assured his audience that "the freemen of this great cotton State see and appreciate the issues and dangers of this contest and are prepared, like freemen, to meet them."[19] The next night Toombs addressed a crowd of 2,000 at the Montgomery Theatre.

An editorial in the *Daily Mail* commented on Toombs's message: "It was a speech to Southern people for Southern Union. It taught us to resist Lincoln at all hazards. And the people received it with shouts of applause such as have seldom been heard here."[20]

On November 1 Stephen A. Douglas, U.S. Senator from Illinois and a presidential candidate, arrived in Montgomery; he spoke the next day at the state capitol. On November 5 former Alabama Congressman William L. Yancey, an outspoken, single-minded defender of Southern rights, spoke at the theatre. The *Daily Mail* captured the tone of the event: "Never before, in the history of Montgomery, was such a welcome tendered to any man, as greeted our great townsman, Hon. Wm. L. Yancey, last night, on the occasion of his return from a political missionary tour among the Black Republican heathen of the North."[21] The next day Abraham Lincoln was elected President of the United States.

Booth reportedly expressed Union sentiments while in Montgomery. John Ellsler, a theatre manager and later a business partner of Booth, wrote:

> Wilkes was leading man in the stock company at Montgomery and his sympathy for, and utterances on behalf of the Union were so unguarded in their expression that his life was in jeopardy, and it became necessary for the manager of the theatre to resort to strategy and spirit Wilkes Booth out of the city to save his life. This I had from the lips of the manager [Matthew Canning] himself.[22]

In an unconfirmed and unreliable account, Louise C. Wooster, a young woman who later operated a brothel in Birmingham, claimed she had a relationship with Booth during his stay in Montgomery. She wrote:

> I was madly in love with J. Wilkes Booth. My love for him seemed to be reciprocated. He was my idol.... He had advised me to adopt the stage as a profession, to enter upon a theatrical career. Then we would always be together.... He [Booth] came in hurriedly one evening and said: "I must go home tonight or I can not get away at all. I will let you hear from me soon, and you shall come to me. This thing [the sectional crisis] can not last longer than a few weeks or a few months at the longest. Such a glorious country as ours can not be broken up by a few fanatics."[23]

Early in December Booth left Montgomery for Philadelphia. The most straightforward itinerary required a 400-mile train trip to Savannah, Georgia.[24] In Savannah he boarded the steamship *Huntsville*, which arrived in New York on December 9.[25]

By December 16 Booth was in Philadelphia staying with his mother and sister.[26] The nation's political crisis continued to evolve and deteriorate. In South Carolina, a state convention voted to secede from the Union on December 20. Citizens in many cities across the North and the South held public meetings. Ten thousand people attended a Grand Union meeting in Philadelphia on December 13. It is possible that Booth heard the speeches or read them in the local newspapers. Either way, he was inspired to write his own speech sometime between December 22 and 27. The text is heavily influenced by Marc Antony's oration over the dead body of Caesar, which Booth had delivered in Columbus only two months before.

Booth's speech voiced his dread for the future of the Union he claimed to love. He demanded equal rights and justice for the South on the issue of slavery. He thought slavery was a blessing rather than a sin and insisted that abolitionists be prosecuted as traitors to the Constitution. Booth predicted that if the Union applied force against South Carolina, the other Southern states would come to her aid:

> I am no alarmest. But I am surprised to see men look on with so much indifference at a sinking count[r]y Meny laugh at the cecession of South Carolina thinking that she will come back or that we will force her back or that if she stays out, we will never miss her.... The first attempt at force will be the cue for every Southern State to aid her.

He considered slavery a benign institution:

> What has been the cause of all this why nothing but the constant agitation of the slavery question.... And instead of looking upon slavery as a sin (mearly because I have none) I hold it to be a happiness for themselves and a social & political blessing for us.... I have been through the whole South and have marked the happiness of master & of man. Take every individual and you will find the happiness greater there than here. True, I have seen the Black man w[h]ip[p]ed but only when he deserved much more than he received. And had an abolitionist used the lash, he would have got double.

He continued to espouse the Union sentiments he had expressed in Montgomery:

> Now, I believe in *country* right or wrong, but gentlemen the whole union is our country and no particular state. We should love the whole union and not only the state in which we were born. We are all one people, and should have but one wish one object, one heart.

He added dramatic froth:

> Weep fellow countrymen, for the brightest half of our stars upon the nations banner have grown dim. Once quite out my friends, all will be dark and dreary, where once reigned such dazzling & celestial light to strike with awe the enthroned Monarchs of the universal world. I tell you sirs it is now the time to act, not to think.[27]

Booth never finished writing the speech.

At the end of December Booth was "sick" of starring and traveling. He told Edwin he was determined to join a stock company.[28] Nevertheless, he continued starring. His next acting engagement began on January 21, 1861, in Rochester, New York. The long hiatus between Booth's engagements is unexplained; he may have needed time to recuperate from his wound, or he may have had trouble finding work. Sisters Henrietta and Maria Irving shared billing with Booth during the engagement.

During a performance of *Richard III* in Rochester, Booth's sword struck the actor playing Richmond above the eye. The *New York Clipper*, a newspaper that reported sporting and theatrical news, described the accident: "During the combat between Richard and Richmond [Mr. Miles], the latter was severely injured by the breaking of Richard's sword, the point of which struck Mr. Miles just above the eye, inflicting quite a wound."[29]

Booth subsequently traveled to Albany, where he opened an engagement at the Gayety Theatre on February 11, and, according to the *Albany Evening Journal*, made an "immense hit." The misfortunes of this season continued on the next night, however, when Booth inflicted a slight cut with his rapier on the head of a fellow actor, J. H. Leonard, during a performance of *The Apostate*. Then, the *Clipper* reported, Booth "met with a mishap himself, by falling on his dagger, which entered his side, and glancing from the ribs, cut away the muscles for some three inches."[30] The stage of the theatre was tiny, only seven by nine feet, leaving little room for error.[31] The *Albany Atlas and Argus* reported that Booth's "acting was so fearfully real in some of the scenes as to cause a thrilling sensation to pervade the audience, and when at the conclusion of the play, in answer to the repeated calls, it was announced that he had seriously wounded himself, it seemed as though the climax of the Tragedy had indeed been reached."[32] A Dr. Crounse, who happened to be in the audience, was called and dressed the wound.[33] Booth could not perform for the remainder of the week.

On February 18 the *Atlas and Argus* reported Booth "quite recovered," adding:

> The Tragedian's many friends and admirers will be glad to learn that he is able once more to appear before them. The Tragedy of *The Apostate* has been selected at the repeated request of numerous patrons of the Gayety, and all who are fortunate enough to secure seats for its representation, will obtain a rare dramatic treat.[34]

Booth fenced his way through *The Apostate* using his left hand, since his right arm was bandaged and tied to his side.[35] The *Albany Evening Journal* reviewer commented:

Although Mr. B. is deprived of the use of his right hand and arm, he made a tremendous hit.... Mr. Booth has great power, not the power of turbulence, which breaks forth in bombast, but genuine force of feeling. He feels a passion naturally, and portrays vividly that which he feels. He never resorts to grimace, or by distorting his features, seeks to counterfeit a feeling which the most untutored audience can perceive is only skin deep. Mr. Booth makes an impression on you by the mere force of intellect.... In the fourth act, he uttered the word "Damnation" with such a gust of genuine passion that the audience were quite carried "off their feet."[36]

Leonard may have been more severely injured than Booth; he did not return to the stage until February 22, when he bravely played Richmond to Booth's Richard III. The house was full and applauded Booth enthusiastically.[37] The performance brought forth encomiums from the *Atlas and Argus* critic:

The sensation created by this extraordinary representation will long live in the memory of all who had the good fortune to witness Booth's impersonation.... Our oldest habitues of the Theatre, who were present, unite in the opinion that the Gloster ... has never been equaled in this city since the elder Booth played [here]....[38]

Booth returned to form quickly. Albany resident Henry Pitt Phelps observed Booth on the stage and wrote:

Booth, at this time, was ... as handsome a man as ever graced the stage.... The fame of his dead father, prepared the way for his reception, and the good reports of his brother Edwin, raised anticipation in relation to this younger aspirant, who was said to be equally, if not still more highly gifted.[39]

The *Atlas and Argus* was also complimentary:

The young gentleman [Booth] has succeeded admirably in gaining many warm admirers in this city, all of whom he never fails to delight with his masterly impressions. Mr. Booth is

full of genius, and this with his fine face and figure, and his artistic conceptions of the characters he performs, will always render him a favorite.[40]

On February 18, the day Booth returned to the stage, President-elect Lincoln, traveling to Washington, D.C., for his inauguration, arrived in Albany. Booth, who was staying at Stanwix Hall, reportedly expressed secessionist opinions quite openly at the hotel. Jacob C. Cuyler, treasurer of the Gayety Theatre, cautioned the new star against further comment on the subject. Booth asked, "Is this not a democratic city?" and received the reply, "Democratic? yes; but disunion, no!"[41] Only two months previously Booth had been an adamant proponent of proslavery Unionism. If the incident with Cuyler was reported accurately, Booth had become a secessionist.

Booth opened in Portland, Maine, on March 18. His one-week engagement was extended by a week. The *Portland Daily Advertiser* mistook John Wilkes for Edwin when it reported that "Mr. Edwin Booth a son of the great Junius Brutus Booth, and who is highly spoken of as a Tragedian by the press, is engaged by Mr. English, and will appear on Monday evening as *Richard III.* We bespeak for Mr. Booth a warm reception."[42]

Nathan Gould, a Portland resident, recalled:

Booth remained in the city for a time after his engagement. I saw him on the street, and remember his appearance. He was a young man who would be called handsome; had black curly hair, black eyes, a pale complexion, a moustache and was of good height and of good figure. He wore a black suit, a Prince Albert coat and a soft black hat.[43]

Booth stayed on in Portland, apparently not having secured an engagement elsewhere. The next star to appear was Mary Ann Farren, who had become acquainted with Booth when she performed in Philadelphia.[44] She asked Booth to appear in her benefit on the first Friday of her engagement. The combination must have been successful, for the following week the two stars appeared together every night. Several years earlier, the *Philadelphia Press* had noted the financial success of Farren's engagement in that city, but concluded that her style was "not adapted to these latitudes" and had "not been improved in the South and West, where she has long been a favorite. We last saw her at the Bowery Theatre, in New York, and, even there, her acting was exaggerated."[45]

When Booth left Portland, he failed to pay an advertising bill to the *Advertiser*:

> Our experience with him shows that he lacks the requisites of a gentleman.... He was extremely liberal in his offers, and not sparing of promises. Just before his departure, we called on him for the amount of his indebtedness, but were referred to his agent.... To cut the story short, we have not seen the color of the gentleman's money.[46]

On April 22 Booth opened an engagement in Albany, where, after performing for several days, he was stabbed by an actress with whom he had worked in Rochester. The *New York Clipper* reported:

> Miss Henrietta Irving, actress of Buffalo, considering herself a victim of unrequited affection, in a frenzied state of mind, entered Mr. Wilkes Booth's room at Stanwix Hall, Albany, armed with a dirk knife and stabbed him in the face. She then retired to her own apartment and stabbed herself but not fatally. Mr. Booth, it is said, trifled with her affections, which caused the knife work.[47]

What actually happened, according to Matthew Canning, was that Irving, in a jealous rage, stabbed Booth when she observed him coming out of her sister Maria's room.[48]

The stabbing was Booth's final injury of this disastrous season. During his six engagements, he had been shot by Canning in Columbus, had stabbed Miles in Rochester and Leonard in Albany, and had fallen on his dagger and been stabbed by Henrietta Irving in Albany. He played only eighteen of his scheduled thirty-six nights in Columbus and Mont-

gomery, lost four nights of his first Albany engagement, and played only five nights of his second Albany engagement before the Irving incident ended his season.

William A. Howell shared a room with Booth on High Street when Booth returned to Baltimore late in April. Howell, an actor, stated that Booth, while recovering from the wound inflicted by Irving, was planning to raise troops for the Confederate cause and march them to Richmond.[49] Booth was prone to exaggeration and "talking big." No corroborating evidence of Booth trying to raise troops has been found. Howell wrote:

> Before Wilkes Booth and myself could perfect our arrangement and organize our company and while we were waiting for instructions from Richmond, the Federal troops took possession of Baltimore and cut off all communication with the South, as well as knocked on the head our project about raising a company.[50]

Federal troops occupied Baltimore on May 13.[51]

Booth may have performed at the Holliday Street Theatre one night that spring. On May 16 the theatre's advertisement in the *Baltimore Sun* announced three pieces, *William Tell*, *The Dutchman's Ghost*, and *Gudgeons at the Relay House*. William Tell was played by Harry Langdon, Booth's Richmond roommate, Furst by William A. Howell, Booth's Baltimore roommate, and Aaron by an otherwise unidentified "Booth."[52]

Booth and his brother-in-law, John Sleeper Clarke, had a mutual antipathy. Actor Charles Wyndham[53] recalled:

> Soon after the war began, Booth and his brother-in-law John Sleeper Clarke were traveling on a train when Clarke made a disparaging remark about Jefferson Davis. As the words were uttered, Booth sprang up and hurled himself upon Clarke in a wild tempest of fury, catching him by the throat.... His face was drawn and twisted with rage.[54]

By June 27 Booth was "pursuing his [theatrical] studies" at Tudor Hall.[55] Adam Badeau, Edwin Booth's friend, later wrote:

There are stories in the [Booth] family of his [John Wilkes's] strange behavior at various times; of his talking and muttering to himself; of his living at the solitary farm near Baltimore with no one but one old servant, whom he frightened with his ravings, his brandishing of theatrical swords....[56]

Booth was rehearsing. One of his goals, it may be assumed, was prevention of injury to himself and to others on the stage.

While at Tudor Hall, Booth may have been involved with the Harford Riflemen, a local militia. In the early morning hours of July 14, several hundred Union soldiers of the 12th Pennsylvania Volunteers marched into Bel Air. The unit detained several militia leaders and issued orders for the arrest of Herman Stump, Jr., commander of the Harford Riflemen. Stump could not be found, and the troops soon left town.[57] On the night of the invasion, Stump had escorted a lady home after a dance and had not returned to Bel Air. The next morning, Booth stole through the picket lines and warned Stump that the soldiers were searching for him.[58]

1860 *from June 30*

June 30, Saturday New York?
The *New York Clipper* reported:
Mr. M.W. Canning has leased the theatre, now in course of completion in Montgomery, Ala. Its estimated cost will be $45,000, and altogether, it is a very handsome building; its decorations being in progress of manufacture in New York, where Mr. Canning expects to be about the 30th inst., in relation to the opening of his theatre.[59]

July 7, Saturday New York
Mary Devlin and Edwin Booth were married in the home of the Rev. Samuel Osgood, at 118 W. Eleventh Street.[60] Edwin's friend Adam Badeau was present, as was John Wilkes Booth.[61]

July 9, Monday New York?
The *New York Clipper* noted that Matthew Canning, manager of the theatre in Montgomery, Alabama, was in New York to recruit a stock company for the coming season. He stayed at the

Brandreth House at the corner of Broadway and Canal Street.[62]

John Wilkes Booth met Canning about this time and agreed to play in Columbus, Georgia, and in Montgomery.

September 12, Wednesday
The *Montgomery Advertiser* announced the list of members of Matthew Canning's company, headed by "Mr. John Wilkes, brother of Edwin Booth, the eminent young tragedian."[63]

September 25, Tuesday Columbus
Canning's company probably arrived in Columbus to rehearse before the engagement began.

September 26, Wednesday Columbus

September 27, Thursday Columbus

September 28, Friday Columbus

September 29, Saturday Columbus

September 30, Sunday Columbus
Booth received top billing in newspaper advertisements the day before Canning's company opened at Temperance Hall. The *Columbus Daily Times* noted:
Mr. John Wilkes has been engaged for a limited number of nights and will be supported by an excellent Stock Company. The piece selected for the opening will be Shakespeare's Romantic Tragedy, entitled, *Romeo and Juliet*, Mr. John Wilkes as Romeo, Miss Mary Mitchell as Juliet.[64]

October 1, Monday Columbus
Booth played Romeo for the first time in his career.

The *New York Clipper* followed events in Columbus:
Mr. Canning's company in Columbus opened on the 1st inst. in *Romeo and Juliet* with Mr. John Wilkes Booth (brother of Ned) as Romeo, and Miss Mary Mitchell as Juliet. The company embraces the following ladies and gentlemen: Manager, Mr. M. W. Canning; Acting Manager, C. H. Morton, Stage Manager, J. W. Albaugh.... J. W. Booth plays six weeks, to be followed by Miss Maggie Mitchell, [and] Miss Bateman....[65]

October 2, Tuesday Columbus
Booth played the title role in *The Stranger* for the first time in his career. The *Columbus Daily Sun* critic opined that Booth was more suited to this role than to that of Romeo.[66]

A large crowd had attended the opening, but weather limited the audience on Tuesday.

October 3, Wednesday Columbus

Booth played Ludovico in Richard Lalor Sheil's *Evadne; or, The Statue*, supported by Mary Mitchell. Booth's father had introduced the play in the United States at the Bowery Theatre in New York in 1847. Booth appeared in the role only rarely, probably because the lead part was intended to be shared with a leading lady, and a "star" usually did not share the lead.[67]

The *Sun* found Booth "not so much experienced as Edwin, but bids fair soon to equal him. He has all the promise, and in personal appearance is handsome and prepossessing."[68]

October 4, Thursday Columbus

Heavy rain limited the size of the audience for the performance of *The Wife*. Booth portrayed Julian St. Pierre, while Mary Mitchell played Marianna.

October 5, Friday Columbus

On his benefit night, Booth played the title role in a full production of *Richard III* for the first time in his career. The *Columbus Daily Times* urged readers to attend:

[Booth] has other claims upon the support of a Southern Community ... which we think should be ... acknowledged by a community somewhat noted for its intense Southern feeling. When John Brown made his raid ... he did faithful service until peace and quiet were restored.[69]

October 6, Saturday Columbus

Booth played Pescara in *The Apostate*.

October 7, Sunday Columbus

October 8, Monday Columbus

Booth appeared in the dual role of Phidias and Raphael in *The Marble Heart; or, The Sculptor's Dream*. The *Sun* remarked that he "acted the despairing sculptor perfectly."[70]

October 9, Tuesday Columbus

Booth played Claude Melnotte and Mary Mitchell represented Pauline in *The Lady of Lyons; or, Love and Pride*. The afterpiece was *The Loan of a Lover*.

October 10, Wednesday Columbus

Canning repeated *The Wife*, in which Booth portrayed Julian St. Pierre, in order to give the company an opportunity to perfect the new drama *Everybody's Friend*. *The Swiss Swains* was the afterpiece.[71]

October 11, Thursday Columbus

Booth starred as Icebrook and Mary Mitchell as Mrs. Featherly in Sterling Coyne's three-act comedy *Everybody's Friend*. The *Sun* voiced its approval: "*EVERYBODY'S FRIEND* has been performed but few times in this country, and it reflects credit upon Mr. Canning and his troupe that they give us something beside the old and hackneyed pieces that have been so often played here."[72]

October 12, Friday Columbus

Booth was to play *Hamlet* in his own benefit, but an hour before the performance he:

...was hurt though not seriously ... by an accidental discharge of a pistol in the hand of Mr. Canning while practicing at a shooting gallery....The ball pierced the fleshy part of Mr. Booth's leg. He was prevented from performing that night.[73]

Another report placed the shooting in Booth's room.

October 13, Saturday Columbus

John Albaugh took Booth's place in *Hamlet* and performed well.[74] The *Sun* commented: "It is with a feeling of sincere regret that we announce that Mr. J. W. Booth, the young and talented Tragedian ... was seriously wounded ... by the accidental discharge of a pistol...."[75]

October 14, Sunday Columbus

October 15, Monday Columbus

Booth spent much of the next week convalescing in his room at Cook's Hotel under the care of a Dr. Stanford.[76]

Canning's company resumed performances with Mary Mitchell and John Albaugh in *Six Degrees of Crime*.

October 16, Tuesday Columbus

The *Montgomery Daily Mail* reported:
The Columbus papers continue to speak in the most glowing terms of the theatrical performances of Mr. Canning's popular company in that city. Mr. Wilkes and Miss Mitchell are highly complimented. Our city will be favored with the appearance of this splendid corps of performers in a few days.[77]

October 17, Wednesday Columbus

A reviewer in the *Daily Times* reported that the patronage at Temperance Hall had decreased during Booth's forced absence. He continued: "Mr. Wilkes, we are happy to announce, is doing quite as well as could be expected, and may possibly play by the close of the week." Canning presented a triple bill of *The Gunmaker of Moscow*, *Eaton Boy*, and *Poor Pillicoddy*.[78]

October 18, Thursday Columbus

John Albaugh and Mary Mitchell had the lead roles in *The School for Scandal*.

The *Montgomery Daily Mail* noted that Canning would open the Montgomery Theatre on Monday, October 22.[79]

October 19, Friday Columbus

A benefit for Booth was canceled on account of inclement weather. It was rescheduled for the following night.[80]

October 20, Saturday Columbus

The *Sun* reported:

It is with pleasure we announce that Mr. J. Wilkes Booth is so far recovered from his accident, that he will be able to appear upon the stage this evening, although he is still far too feeble to take an active part in the performance. At the earnest solicitation of numerous friends, he will attend the play and recite Antony's address over the dead body of Caesar.[81]

The *Sun* reviewed the performance two days later:

The announcement that J. Wilkes Booth would appear at the theatre Saturday night drew a large crowd.... Curiosity to see the rising young Tragedian, and sympathy for his late misfortune, drew more to the theatre than the bill for the evening.... Between the plays Mr. Booth recited Mark Antony's address ... in a manner entirely above criticism, notwithstanding his suffering."[82]

October 21, Sunday Columbus

Canning and his company left Columbus for Montgomery. Booth's wound prevented his departure.[83]

October 22, Monday Columbus

The *New York Clipper* noted that the "new Theatre at Montgomery, Alabama opened on the 22nd ult. Manager Canning presented a short address to the audience. This week Mr. J. Wilkes Booth who is fast recovering from his late accident will appear."[84]

October 23, Tuesday Montgomery

Booth started for Montgomery in the morning. The *Sun* noted: "With extreme caution he may reach that city without harm to his wound, but for some time he will be unable to fulfill his engagement upon the boards." Although the Monday issue of the *Montgomery Daily Mail* had advertised that "Mr. John Wilkes" would appear the next day, the Tuesday issue advertised Albaugh in *The Poor Gentleman*, with no mention of Booth.[85]

October 24, Wednesday Montgomery

Canning's company presented *Ingomar, The Barbarian*. The *Daily Mail* noted that the audience was not large and added:

The *Ingomar* of Mr. Albaugh was faultlessly portrayed—life-like and natural. The performance brought general satisfaction, and at the close of the play Miss Mitchell and Mr. Albaugh were called before the curtain amidst loud cheering....[86]

October 25, Thursday Montgomery

Georgia Senator Robert Toombs, in Montgomery to give a speech the following night, addressed a crowd from his hotel room balcony.[87]

Inflammatory items appeared in the *Daily Mail*:

If the South could be stupid enough to submit to such an administration as Lincoln's, for one moment, it ought to be plundered and mulattoized, both—made no better than the North! But the white people of the South are very different from those of Massachusetts, and ... will resist free Negro rule....[88]

October 26, Friday Montgomery

A reporter for the *Montgomery Daily Mail* wrote of Booth:

We had the pleasure of an introduction to this young tragedian ... at the theatre. He is rapidly recovering from his unfortunate accident in Columbus, some time since, and informed us that he would make his first appearance on our boards Monday night.[89]

Senator Robert Toombs spoke to a crowd of 2,000 at the Montgomery Theatre. Passions were high before the November election. An editorial in the *Daily Mail* noted that "[i]t was a speech to Southern people.... It taught us to resist Lincoln at all hazards."[90]

October 27, Saturday Montgomery

The theatre advertisement in the *Daily Mail* called attention to "Mr. John Wilkes," who would appear Monday. The *Daily Mail* critic noted that John Albaugh and Samuel Knapp Chester supported Mary Mitchell "very creditably" in *Eustache*, her closing performance.[91]

October 28, Sunday Montgomery

October 29, Monday Montgomery

Booth made his debut at the Montgomery Theatre in *The Apostate*. According to the *Daily Mail*:

A very fair audience greeted Mr. John Wilkes in his first appearance in the character of Pescara in *The Apostate*. While we do not think this character a good one to show to great advantage Mr. Wilkes' talents, and considering his late accident from which he was not entirely recovered, still the performance ... stamps him as a chip off the old block which was received by the large audience with outbursts of applause."[92]

October 30, Tuesday Montgomery

Booth played Julian St. Pierre in *The Wife*. The *Daily Mail* reported:

There was a rousing crowd at the theatre, decidedly the largest of the season. This great play of *The Wife* ... was thoroughly presented and rendered quite effectively, to the entire satisfaction of all, judging from the demonstrations of approval which they received. Mr. John Wilkes, Miss Mitchell, Mr. Albaugh and Mr. Chester won new laurels in the fine rendition of their respective parts.[93]

October 31, Wednesday Montgomery

Booth played the title role in *Hamlet*. The *Daily Mail* reported that the performance was "a refresher to Manager Canning's pockets, for his large theatre was full from pit to dome. [The play] seemed to give pretty general satisfaction."[94]

An item in the *Daily Mail* noted that there had been four crowds in the city on Wednesday night: one at the theatre, one at a performance at Congress Hall, and two at political rallies on the street. The theatre had the largest crowd.[95]

November 1, Thursday Montgomery

Booth played *Richard III*. The *Daily Mail* reviewer reported "another jam at the theater...."[96]

Illinois Senator Stephen A. Douglas arrived in Montgomery in the evening. The *Daily Mail* referred to him as "the Squatter candidate for the Presidency."[97]

November 2, Friday Montgomery

Booth and Mary Mitchell played *Romeo and Juliet*. The *Daily Mail* commented: "Mr. John Wilkes as Romeo, was all that could be desired, and his rendition was received with applause and approbation by the large number present. The same may be said of the beautiful Miss Mary Mitchell."[98]

A large crowd heard Senator Douglas's speech at the state capitol. Booth was probably in the audience.

November 3, Saturday Montgomery

Booth closed his engagement with a portrayal of Charles de Moor in *The Robbers*. The *Montgomery Post* opined: "As the leader of the robber band he embodied the character in the most perfect and complete manner imaginable."[99]

November 4, Sunday Montgomery

November 5, Monday Montgomery

Former Alabama Congressman William L. Yancey, a Montgomery resident, was led by a crowd of 300 people from his home to the theatre "on the occasion of his return from a political missionary tour among the Black Republican heathen of the North."[100] Several crowds, unable to fit inside the theatre, were addressed by speakers in the streets who exhorted Southern secession in response to the impending election of Lincoln.

November 6, Tuesday Montgomery

Actress Kate Bateman began a two-week engagement at the Montgomery Theatre.[101]

Abraham Lincoln was elected President of the United States.

November 7, Wednesday Montgomery

November 8, Thursday Montgomery

November 9, Friday Montgomery

November 10, Saturday Montgomery

The legislature of South Carolina voted for a convention to consider secession.[102]

November 11, Sunday Montgomery

November 12, Monday Montgomery

November 13, Tuesday Montgomery

November 14, Wednesday Montgomery

November 15, Thursday Montgomery

The *Daily Mail* reported:

Mr. Wilkes has in the kindest manner volunteered his valuable services, and will appear as Romeo, Friday evening.... We apprehend, that the fashionable night of the season will prove to be tomorrow at the complimentary benefit tendered to Miss Bateman by a large number of our families and leading young men. On that occasion, as full dress as possible will be desirable on the part of the audience....[103]

November 16, Friday Montgomery

Booth played Romeo in Kate Bateman's benefit performance of *Romeo and Juliet*. The *Daily Mail* thought the performance "was given smoothly and effectively.... Mr. Wilkes showed that he can learn to play Romeo with great power, though as yet his conception is crude."[104]

Booth was billed as "John Wilkes" in the theatre's advertisement.

November 17, Saturday Montgomery

The *New York Clipper* noted: "At the Montgomery (Ala.) Theatre, Mr. John Wilkes has been playing an engagement—appearing principally in Shakespearean tragedies, in connection with Mary Mitchell."[105]

November 18, Sunday Montgomery

November 19, Monday Montgomery

A long review in the *Daily Mail* extolled the virtues of Kate Bateman's Friday night performance.

November 20, Tuesday Montgomery

November 21, Wednesday Montgomery

November 22, Thursday Montgomery

November 23, Friday Montgomery

November 24, Saturday Montgomery

The *New York Clipper* noted:

Mr. Booth's engagement [at Montgomery] was very successful, and his friends predict for him a brilliant future. Nature has done much for him, and if a close application to study (for he works hard) be rewarded, he will soon be on the uppermost round of the ladder. Miss Kate Bateman commenced on Tuesday evening, 6th inst.... Owing to the election, and the excitement attending it, Miss B.'s engagement has not been very profitable.[106]

November 25, Sunday Montgomery

November 26, Monday Montgomery

November 27, Tuesday Montgomery

November 28, Wednesday Montgomery

November 29, Thursday Montgomery

Maggie Mitchell opened an engagement at the Montgomery Theatre.[107]

November 30, Friday Montgomery

The Montgomery Theatre newspaper advertisement, listing M. W. Canning as Lessee and Manager and J. W. Albaugh as Stage Manager, announced a Saturday appearance by Maggie Mitchell. A "Grand Complimentary Benefit BY THE CITIZENS OF MONTGOMERY, TO MR. J. WILKES BOOTH" was to be a part of the same bill.[108] Before the play, at 5 p.m., Booth attended the anniversary dinner of the St. Andrews Society, a charitable organization of Scotsmen and their descendants.[109]

December 1, Saturday Montgomery

In his "Grand complimentary benefit," Booth appeared in a two-act drama titled *Rafaelle, the Reprobate*, followed by Maggie Mitchell in *Katy O'Shiel*. Booth concluded the evening with the fifth act of *Richard III*.[110] For this performance and ever after he was billed as John Wilkes Booth.

The review of the performance in the *Daily Mail* stated:

A fine audience attended the complimentary benefit of Mr. J. Wilkes Booth.... *Rafaelle* was well personated by Mr. Booth, and was well received by the audience, and at the close of the first piece, he was called before the curtain amidst loud cheering, then he returned his thanks in a very neat but short speech....[111]

December 2, Sunday Montgomery

December 3, Monday En route to Savannah

Booth left Montgomery for the North.[112]

The United States senators from South Carolina resigned.

December 4, Tuesday En route to Savannah

December 5, Wednesday En route to Savannah

December 6, Thursday Savannah and en route to New York

December 8, Saturday En route to New York

Secretary of the Treasury Howell Cobb of Georgia, believing that the election of Lincoln justified secession, resigned from President James Buchanan's cabinet.

December 9, Sunday New York

Booth arrived in New York on the steamship *Huntsville*.[113]

December 10, Monday New York

December 11, Tuesday New York

December 12, Wednesday New York

Secretary of State Lewis Cass of Michigan resigned because President Buchanan refused to reinforce the forts in Charleston Harbor.

December 13, Thursday New York

Ten thousand people attended a Grand Union meeting in Philadelphia. Booth possibly heard the speeches or read them in the local newspapers.

December 14, Friday New York

Wilkes' Spirit of the Times, a New York newspaper that covered sports, literature, and the theatre, reported that John Wilkes Booth was in New York this week.[114]

The Georgia legislature asked South Carolina, Alabama, Florida, and Mississippi for delegates to a convention to consider a Southern Confederacy.

December 16, Sunday Philadelphia

Asia Booth Clarke wrote to a friend: "John Booth is at home. He is looking well, but his wound is not entirely healed yet: he still carries the ball in him.... Mother & Rose are boarding in Marshall Street at a private house. John also."[115]

December 17, Monday Philadelphia

The South Carolina convention met in Columbia, South Carolina.

December 18, Tuesday Philadelphia

The South Carolina convention reconvened in Charleston.

December 19, Wednesday Philadelphia

At a benefit for Matthew Canning in Montgomery, John Albaugh presented the manager with a set of silverware.[116]

December 20, Thursday Philadelphia

The South Carolina convention voted to secede from the Union.

December 21, Friday Philadelphia

December 22, Saturday Philadelphia

Between this date and December 27, Booth, deeply affected by the secession crisis, wrote a speech expounding his views on the subject.[117]

December 23, Sunday Philadelphia

Edwin, in a letter to a friend, wrote that John was "sick" of his short tour as a star and was determined to join a stock company.[118]

December 24, Monday Philadelphia

December 25, Tuesday Philadelphia

December 26, Wednesday Philadelphia

December 27, Thursday Philadelphia

December 28, Friday Philadelphia?

There is no record of Booth having delivered his speech before any political meeting during this week of crisis. His speech was left unfinished.

December 31, Monday

Edwin Booth and Charlotte Cushman gave the first of ten performances at the Academy of Music in Philadelphia.[119]

1861 *through August 30*

January 9, Wednesday

Delegates in Mississippi voted to secede from the Union.

January 10, Thursday

Florida seceded from the Union.

January 11, Friday

Alabama became the fourth state to secede from the Union.

January 19, Saturday

Georgia voted to secede from the Union.

January 21, Monday Rochester

John Wilkes Booth and Henrietta Irving played *Romeo and Juliet* before a large audience at the Metropolitan Theatre, on South Saint Paul Street near Main. The *Rochester Union and Advertiser* critic wrote that Booth and Irving "won warm applause for the manner in which they acquitted themselves.... On the whole, the expectations of the playgoers in regard to these new candidates for favor at our Theatre were realized, we believe."[120]

January 22, Tuesday Rochester

Booth appeared in *The Lady of Lyons*. The *Union and Advertiser* noted:

> Tonight *The Lady of Lyons* will be played—Mr. Booth as Claude Melnotte, Miss Maria Irving as Pauline. Miss Henrietta Irving will take the part of *Sally Scraggs* in *Sketches in India*—a character in which she is reported to excel. The bill offered tonight is a good one, and will be especially pleasing to the ladies.[121]

January 23, Wednesday Rochester

Booth played *Othello* at the Metropolitan Theatre. He had been suffering from a severe cold for several nights.[122]

January 24, Thursday Rochester

Booth appeared as Julian St. Pierre in a rare performance of *The Wife*. The *Rochester Evening Express* declared Booth "the most talented young man upon the American stage."[123]

January 25, Friday Rochester

Booth played *Richard III* with Henrietta

Irving. The *Union and Advertiser* reported: "The distinguished actor, Mr. Booth, has been honored with good houses since he commenced his engagement and has won golden opinions...."[124]

January 26, Saturday Rochester

Booth played Rafaelle in *Rafaelle, the Reprobate*.

Wilkes' Spirit of the Times noted: "Theatricals are very dull throughout the entire South, and this city [New York] is thronged with members of the profession out of employment."[125]

Louisiana seceded from the Union.

January 27, Sunday Rochester

January 28, Monday Rochester

Booth appeared as Phidias and Raphael in *The Marble Heart*.

January 29, Tuesday Rochester

Booth appeared as Ludovico in *Evadne*.

January 30, Wednesday Rochester

Booth played the title role in *Don Caesar de Bazan* for the first time.

The *Union and Advertiser* critic wrote: [Booth] has played here for ten nights to full and crowded houses, at a time when theatricals were languishing.... This fact speaks more than anything else that can be said as a tribute to this genius. He has played a round of characters calculated to show the scope and versatility of his power. And all he has done well, making new friends and admirers in each new phase of character that he assumed. His *Othello*, *Richard* and *Romeo* were as faultless as the same characters in the hands of his illustrious sire at the same age, and there is no reason to doubt that he is destined to fill his place upon the stage, and add new luster to the name he bears.[126]

January 31, Thursday Rochester

Booth played *Richard III* with Maria Irving. The *New York Clipper* noted: "During the combat between Richard and Richmond [Mr. Miles], the latter was severely injured by the breaking of Richard's sword, the point of which struck Mr. Miles just above the eye, inflicting quite a wound."[127]

February 1, Friday Rochester

Booth played the double role of Fabien and Louis dei Franchi in *The Corsican Brothers*.

February 2, Saturday Rochester

On the last night of his engagement in Rochester, Booth played Fabien and Louis in *The Corsican Brothers*. He also appeared as Robert Shelley in *The Momentous Question*.

February 4, Monday

A convention of seceded states met in Montgomery, Alabama.

February 9, Saturday

The advertisement in the *Albany Atlas and Argus* for the Gayety Theatre, located on Green Street a few doors south of Beaver Street, noted that "Mr. Wilkes Booth will appear Monday."[128]

Jefferson Davis was elected provisional President of the Confederacy.

February 10, Sunday Albany

At his hotel in Albany, Stanwix Hall on Broadway, Booth expressed secessionist opinions. Jacob C. Cuyler, treasurer of the Gayety Theatre, cautioned the new star against further declarations. Booth asked, "Is this not a democratic city?" and received the reply, "Democratic? yes; but disunion, no!"[129]

February 11, Monday Albany

John Wilkes Booth and Annie Waite played *Romeo and Juliet* at the Gayety Theatre on the first night of Booth's engagement.

President-elect Abraham Lincoln left Springfield, Illinois, for Washington, D.C. Jefferson Davis left Mississippi for Montgomery.

February 12, Tuesday Albany

Booth fell on his dagger while playing Pescara in *The Apostate*. He seriously injured his right armpit and bled profusely.[130]

February 13, Wednesday Albany

The *Albany Evening Journal* reported that Booth had made an "immense hit" before his accident. The scheduled performance of *Othello* was canceled.[131]

February 14, Thursday Albany

The *Journal* reported that Booth was "quite comfortable."[132]

The advertisement for the Gayety Theatre in the *Atlas and Argus* noted Booth's "continued illness."[133]

February 15, Friday Albany

February 16, Saturday Albany

The theatre advertisement in the *Atlas and Argus* announced that Booth would appear on Monday.

February 17, Sunday Albany

February 18, Monday Albany

President-elect Lincoln arrived at Albany and stayed at the Delavan House.[134]

Booth resumed his engagement at the Gayety Theatre. He fenced his way through *The Apostate* using his left hand, since his bandaged right arm was tied to his side.[135]

Booth's friend, John Albaugh, witnessed the inauguration of Jefferson Davis as President of the Confederate States of America in Montgomery.

February 19, Tuesday Albany

The Gayety Theatre presented *The Wife* with Booth as Julian St. Pierre.

February 20, Wednesday Albany

Booth played the title role in *Othello*. A reviewer from the *Albany Times and Courier* commented:

The Othello of young Booth, last night, at the Gayety Theatre, was one of the most spirited pieces of acting that we have ever witnessed. He looks and acts the Moor admirably. He exhibits the workings of the green-eyed monster—jealous in a most terrible manner. In this part of the piece he is the exact counterfeit of his father. The scene where he doubts the honesty of Iago, and threatens to annihilate him unless he brings forth ocular proof, was most effectively and artistically executed. The last scene was also well acted, and elicited universal applause from the large and intelligent audience in attendance. Among the latter, were some old theatre-goers of our city, who highly appreciated the personation of Othello by young Booth, and gave vent to that appreciation by rapturous applause. His costumes throughout the piece were of the richest and most appropriate kind.[136]

February 21, Thursday Albany

Booth played *The Stranger*.

February 22, Friday Albany

Booth played *Richard III*. The *New York Clipper* noted:

Mr. Leonard, who was injured ... several days since at the Gayety in Albany, has recovered and appeared as Richmond [in *Richard III*] on the occasion of Mr. Wilkes Booth's benefit. The beneficiary was greeted with an overwhelming house. When the play reached its climax ... the most intense excitement prevailed.... As the curtain fell a tremendous call was given when Mr. Booth, much exhausted came before [the audience].[137]

February 23, Saturday Albany

Booth closed his engagement with a portrayal of Charles de Moor in *The Robbers*.

February 24, Sunday Albany

February 25, Monday Albany

Booth spent this week in Albany, still recovering from his wound.[138]

February 26, Tuesday Albany

February 27, Wednesday Albany

February 28, Thursday Albany

March 1, Friday Albany

March 2, Saturday Albany

The *Albany Atlas and Argus* noted:
The admirers of the legitimate drama will be pleased to learn that this talented and favorite actor [Booth] has been re-engaged by the management of the Gayety Theatre. Mr. Booth has been sojourning in Albany since last Saturday, having been released from other engagements elsewhere, that he might fully recover from his recent injuries.[139]

The provisional Confederate Congress voted to admit Texas.

March 3, Sunday Albany

March 4, Monday Albany

The Gayety Theatre presented Booth in *Richard III*. The *Albany Express* critic thought Booth played:

...with an ability which left us nothing to desire. His fifth act was a prodigious piece of acting, while the last scene of the fifth act was truly terrible. No such fighting has ever been seen in this city. In his battle scenes young Booth is far ahead of any actor we ever saw. He throws his whole soul into his sword, giving to the contest a degree of earnestness never approached, even by his father. At the end of the tragedy, three cheers were proposed.... They were given with a power that almost took the roof off.[140]

Abraham Lincoln was inaugurated President of the United States.

March 5, Tuesday Albany

Booth played *Richard III*.

March 6, Wednesday Albany

Booth played *Hamlet*. The *Express* noted of Booth:

This gentleman has rapidly risen in favor with the habitues of the Gayety, more from his chaste and powerful renditions of Shakespearean characters than from his personal qualities as a gentleman and scholar, which have made for him many friends; even amongst those who never visit our Theatre.[141]

March 7, Thursday Albany

Booth appeared as Claude Melnotte in *The Lady of Lyons*.[142]

March 8, Friday Albany

Booth played *Macbeth* for the first time as a star.[143]

March 9, Saturday Albany

Booth again played *Macbeth*. The *New York Clipper* reported that the theatrical season in Montgomery, Alabama, "has been good.... Miss Mary Mitchell, sister of Maggie and leading lady of the theatre, is represented as having become, a great favorite there, as also the juvenile man, Mr. J. W. Albaugh."[144]

March 10, Sunday Albany

March 11, Monday Albany

Booth appeared as Shylock in *The Merchant of Venice* in his benefit. The *Atlas and Argus* was "pleased to learn that this talented and favorite tragedian will remain at the Gayety Theatre a few nights longer. This will give our citizens an opportunity of witnessing him in characters in which he has not appeared at this Theatre."[145]

The *Albany Times and Courier* critic wrote: As Romeo, Claude Melnotte and Raphael, the cloak [rests] ... gracefully upon the young tragedian's shoulders. As the misanthropic, melancholy Stranger or Shylock, Mr. Booth identifies himself with either character in a forcible and artistic manner.[146]

March 12, Tuesday Albany

Booth performed the trial scene from *The Merchant of Venice*, Act 5 of *Richard III*, and Act 3 of *Hamlet*.

March 13, Wednesday Albany

Booth played Phidias and Raphael in *The Marble Heart*.

March 14, Thursday Albany

Booth played Fabien and Louis in *The Corsican Brothers*.

March 15, Friday Albany

Booth repeated *The Corsican Brothers*. The *Times and Courier* summarized Booth's engagement:

During his engagement in Albany, Mr. Booth has appeared in a round of characters that have plainly demonstrated his great histrionic power. His *Richard III*, *Macbeth* and *Apostate* have been impersonated in a manner such as a Booth only can delineate. The above characters require great tragic power. He possesses it.[147]

March 16, Saturday Albany

Closing his engagement in Albany, Booth appeared in some of his favorite roles: Fabien and Louis in *The Corsican Brothers* and Rafaelle in *Rafaelle, the Reprobate*.[148]

The *Atlas and Argus* announced that Miss Henrietta Irving would begin an engagement at the Gayety Theatre on Monday.

March 18, Monday Portland

Booth opened at the Portland Theatre, also known as Deering Hall, with *Richard III*. During this engagement he was supported by Helen and Lucille Western, daughters of the second wife of William B. English, the manager of the Portland Theatre.[149]

March 19, Tuesday Portland

Booth played the title role in *Othello* with Helen Western as Desdemona. According to the *Portland Eastern Argus*:

Mr. Booth is one of the brightest ornaments on the American stage. He is yet young in years, but possesses in a remarkable degree all the requisite qualities, which makes the finest actor. The character that he has chosen ... he is well adapted for, and one in which, it is said, he has few if any superiors.[150]

March 20, Wednesday Portland

Booth played *Hamlet*.[151]

March 21, Thursday Portland

Booth played *Richard III*.

March 22, Friday Portland

Booth played *Macbeth* with Lucille Western as Lady Macbeth. The *Portland Daily Advertiser* reported that Booth "will be sustained by the valuable aid of Mr. John McCullough, the favorite tragedian of the Howard Athenaeum, Boston. With such an array of talent, we have no doubt the theatre will be crowded."[152]

March 23, Saturday Portland

Booth appeared in a matinee. The *Eastern Argus* advertised:

THEATRE THIS AFTERNOON—An unusual bill of attraction is offered this afternoon, consisting of the new comic pantomime *Harlequin Jack the Giant Killer*, and the beautiful play of *The Lady of Lyons*, in which Mr. Booth, who has been especially engaged, appears as Claude Melnotte to the Pauline of the beautiful Helen [Western]. The price of admission [is] one cent for children and 15 for adults.[153]

March 24, Sunday Portland

March 25, Monday Portland

Booth appeared in *Romeo and Juliet*. The *Advertiser* noted:

The great desire that has been manifested to witness the performance of Mr. Booth has induced Mr. English to re-engage him for another week, and he appears this evening in Shakespeare's beautiful piece of *Romeo and Juliet*, the favorite Helen [Western] playing the gentle Juliet. The piece is otherwise finely cast, and will no doubt draw a full house.[154]

The *Baltimore Sun* stated: "J. Wilkes Booth, a brother of Edwin, is now playing in Albany, N.Y. [*sic*]. He is quite young, and will not venture to play in New York until confident of success."[155]

March 26, Tuesday Portland

Booth played Shylock in *The Merchant of Venice*, which was followed by *Our Female American Cousin*.

March 27, Wednesday Portland

Booth appeared as Pescara in *The Apostate*.

March 28, Thursday Portland

Booth played Phidias and Raphael in *The Marble Heart*.

March 29, Friday Portland

Booth appeared as Rafaelle in *Rafaelle, the Reprobate* and as Fabien and Louis in *The Corsican Brothers* in his benefit.

March 30, Saturday Portland

Booth appeared as Fabien and Louis in *The Corsican Brothers*. A patron recalled his performance:

He was dressed in a loose white shirt and had on black pants and was bareheaded. He stood with a rapier in his right hand raised up and his left arm, about the same position and was looking backward. He was to be slid across the stage under an illumination of red fire. I suppose he stood on a plank which had not been properly greased, for it would stop, then start, with a jerk so pronounced, that he or his shirt could not stand without a sympathetic movement each time, which destroyed the impressiveness of the scene.[156]

April 1, Monday Portland

Mary Ann Farren opened an engagement at the Portland Theatre in her famous role of *Lucretia Borgia*.

April 2, Tuesday Portland

Mary Ann Farren continued her engagement.

April 3, Wednesday Portland

Mary Ann Farren played *The Wrecker's Daughter*.

April 4, Thursday Portland

April 5, Friday Portland

The *Eastern Argus* carried this item: MRS. FARREN'S BENEFIT—A great combination is announced for the Benefit of Mrs. Farren this evening, on which occasion the talented tragedian, Mr. Booth, will appear in his world renowned character of *The Stranger*, Mrs. Farren as Mrs. Haller.[157]

The *Advertiser* reported that Booth would support Mary Ann Farren in two plays, *The Stranger* and *The Hunchback*.

April 6, Saturday Portland

Mary Ann Farren played *The Wrecker's Daughter*.

April 7, Sunday Portland

April 8, Monday Portland

Booth may have supported Mary Ann Farren in *Camille*. The *Advertiser* noted:

Mrs. Farren and Mr. Booth are to appear every night this week. These two eminent artists will afford each other support, and cannot fail to satisfy the patrons of drama. Tonight *Camille* with new scenery and dresses.[158]

April 9, Tuesday Portland

Booth and Mary Ann Farren appeared in *Evadne*. The *Advertiser* remarked: "We saw Mr. Booth in the part of Ludovico ... and thought it the best piece of real acting we have witnessed in this city."[159]

April 10, Wednesday Portland

Booth appeared in *The Wife* and in the fifth act of *Richard III*. The *Advertiser* noted:

BENEFIT OF MR. BOOTH—The farewell benefit performance of this talented young actor takes place this evening and a bill of great attraction is announced, consisting of Knowles' great play of *The Wife*, in which Mrs. Farren appears in her celebrated character of Marianna, and Mr. Booth as St. Pierre, followed by the 5th act of *Richard III*, with Mr. Booth as the crook backed tyrant.[160]

April 11, Thursday Portland

Maine's governor had proclaimed this a day of "Humiliation, public fasting and prayer" on account of the threat of war between the Confederacy and the Union.

The newspapers carried items announcing

"Fast Day" at the theatre. Booth played *William Tell* in the afternoon and *Macbeth* in the evening. The afterpiece in the evening was titled *Brothers and Sisters; or, The Soldiers of Fort Sumter*.

April 12, Friday Portland

Mary Ann Farren performed *Of Love* for her farewell benefit. The theatre advertisement noted that Booth would perform the third act of *Hamlet*.

The *New York Clipper* reported that the season of the Montgomery Theatre ended on this date.[161]

Confederate forces fired on the Federal garrison at Fort Sumter in Charleston, South Carolina.

April 13, Saturday Portland

Booth made his farewell appearance in Portland, performing as Fabien and Louis in *The Corsican Brothers* and as Rafaelle in *Rafaelle, the Reprobate*.[162]

Federal forces at Fort Sumter surrendered.

April 17, Wednesday

The convention authorized to determine Virginia's course in the sectional crisis passed an ordinance of secession, after having rejected such a measure on April 4.

April 19, Friday

President Lincoln proclaimed a blockade of the Confederate States from South Carolina to Texas.

The Sixth Massachusetts regiment reached Washington, D.C., after fighting a mob in Baltimore.

April 21, Sunday Albany

April 22, Monday Albany

Booth performed *Richard III* at the Gayety Theatre in Albany. The theatre advertisement in the *Albany Atlas and Argus* noted a "Double Attraction" consisting of "Mr. Wilkes Booth and Signor Canito, the man monkey." Booth's performance was followed by a farce titled *Jack Robinson and His Monkey*, featuring Canito.[163]

April 23, Tuesday Albany

Booth played Charles de Moor in *The Robbers*. Signor Canito performed in the afterpiece.

April 24, Wednesday Albany

Booth appeared as Ludovico in *Evadne*. Signor Canito performed in *Jocko, the Brazilian Ape*.

April 25, Thursday Albany

Booth played Ludovico in *Evadne*.

April 26, Friday Albany

Henrietta Irving attacked Booth with a knife. According to the *Madison [Indiana] Courier*:

> Miss Henrietta Irving, well known as an actress in Buffalo, entered the room of J. Wilkes Booth, at Stanwix Hall ... and attacked him with a dirk, cutting his face badly. She did not, however, succeed in inflicting a mortal wound. Failing in this, she retired to her own room and stabbed herself, not bad enough "to go dead."[164]

April 27, Saturday Albany

The *Atlas and Argus* advertised Booth as Ludovico in *Evadne*.

April 28, Sunday En route to Baltimore?

Booth probably left Albany for Baltimore. The Albany newspapers did not report the stabbing incident.

April 29, Monday Baltimore or Bel Air?

April 30, Tuesday Baltimore or Bel Air?

May 1, Wednesday Baltimore or Bel Air?

May 2, Thursday Baltimore or Bel Air?

May 3, Friday Baltimore or Bel Air?

President Lincoln issued a proclamation calling for three-year volunteers and increasing the size of the Army and Navy.

May 4, Saturday Baltimore or Bel Air?

The *New York Clipper* reported: "The Albany Theatre has closed for want of patronage, notwithstanding two stars were playing there, viz. J. Wilkes Booth and Signor Cairito [*sic*]."[165]

May 5, Sunday Baltimore or Bel Air?

May 6, Monday Baltimore or Bel Air?

Arkansas and Tennessee passed secession ordinances.

May 7, Tuesday Baltimore or Bel Air?

May 8, Wednesday Baltimore or Bel Air?

May 9, Thursday Baltimore or Bel Air?

May 10, Friday Baltimore or Bel Air?

Booth celebrated his twenty-third birthday.

May 11, Saturday Baltimore or Bel Air?

May 12, Sunday Baltimore or Bel Air?

May 13, Monday Baltimore or Bel Air?
Union troops occupied Baltimore.

May 14, Tuesday Baltimore or Bel Air?

May 15, Wednesday Baltimore or Bel Air?

May 16, Thursday Baltimore or Bel Air?
The Holliday Street Theatre advertised three pieces, *William Tell*, *The Dutchman's Ghost*, and *Gudgeons at the Relay House*. Harry Langdon played William Tell, W. A. Howell played Furst, and an unidentified "Booth" played Aaron.[166]

May 17, Friday Baltimore or Bel Air?

May 18, Saturday Bel Air
Booth began a ten-week stay, at $4 a week, at the Eagle Hotel in Bel Air. According to proprietor R. N. Hanna, Booth used the time to study and memorize plays.[167]

May 19, Sunday Bel Air

May 20, Monday Bel Air
A convention in North Carolina voted for secession.

May 21, Tuesday Bel Air

May 22, Wednesday Bel Air

May 23, Thursday Bel Air
The citizens of Virginia ratified the ordinance of secession in a statewide referendum.

May 24, Friday Bel Air

May 25, Saturday Bel Air

May 26, Sunday Bel Air

May 27, Monday Bel Air

May 28, Tuesday Bel Air

May 29, Wednesday Bel Air

May 30, Thursday Bel Air

May 31, Friday Bel Air

June 1, Saturday Bel Air

June 2, Sunday Bel Air

June 3, Monday Bel Air

June 4, Tuesday Bel Air

June 5, Wednesday Bel Air

June 6, Thursday Bel Air

June 7, Friday Bel Air

June 8, Saturday Bel Air

June 9, Sunday Bel Air

June 10, Monday Bel Air

June 11, Tuesday Bel Air

June 12, Wednesday Bel Air

June 13, Thursday Bel Air

June 14, Friday Bel Air

June 15, Saturday Bel Air

June 16, Sunday Bel Air

June 17, Monday Bel Air

June 18, Tuesday Bel Air

June 19, Wednesday Bel Air

June 20, Thursday Bel Air

June 21, Friday Bel Air

June 22, Saturday Bel Air

June 23, Sunday Bel Air

June 24, Monday Bel Air

June 25, Tuesday Bel Air

June 26, Wednesday Bel Air

June 27, Thursday Bel Air
Asia Booth Clarke wrote that "John is at the farm [Tudor Hall] pursuing his [theatrical] studies."[168]

June 28, Friday Bel Air

June 29, Saturday Bel Air

June 30, Sunday Bel Air

July 1, Monday Bel Air

July 2, Tuesday Bel Air

July 3, Wednesday Bel Air

July 4, Thursday Bel Air

July 5, Friday Bel Air

July 6, Saturday Bel Air

July 7, Sunday Bel Air

July 8, Monday Bel Air

July 9, Tuesday Bel Air

July 10, Wednesday Bel Air

July 11, Thursday Bel Air

July 12, Friday Bel Air

July 13, Saturday Bel Air

July 14, Sunday Bel Air

Several hundred men of the 12th Pennsylvania Volunteers marched into Bel Air at 4:30 a.m. and arrested local militia leaders.[169] John Wilkes Booth slipped through the lines and warned Herman Stump, Jr., commander of the Harford Riflemen, that Union troops were looking for him.[170]

July 15, Monday Bel Air

July 16, Tuesday Bel Air

July 17, Wednesday Bel Air

July 18, Thursday Bel Air

July 19, Friday Bel Air

July 20, Saturday Bel Air

July 21, Sunday Bel Air

The Confederate Army routed the Union Army at the First Battle of Bull Run (or Manassas).

July 27, Saturday

George B. McClellan assumed command of Union forces in Washington, D.C., and Virginia.

August 30, Friday

Union Major General John C. Frémont, without authorization, proclaimed martial law and announced the emancipation of slaves belonging to disloyal masters in Missouri.

5

Rising Star: 1861–1862

John Wilkes Booth was busy during the summer of 1861 setting up engagements for the coming season; as late as October 9, he was still writing to theatre managers for that purpose. He spent part of the summer in Boston, where he met Joseph H. Simonds, an officer at the Mechanics Bank. Simonds's father ran the bank, and his well-to-do family lived in the bank building. In time, Simonds would became Booth's confidant and business manager.[1]

Booth's acting season began on October 21 at the Pine Street Theatre (also known as the Providence Theatre) in Providence, Rhode Island. The five-night engagement was followed by a two-week appearance at the Metropolitan Theatre in Buffalo, New York. The *Buffalo Daily Courier* advised its readers to see John, a "worthy scion of the house of Booth," perform great Shakespearean roles.[2] The young tragedian, considering his experiences the previous season, must have been relieved to get through his first two engagements without injury to himself or others.

Sometime during the Buffalo engagement, according to an unverified account printed several years later in the *Chicago Tribune*, Booth broke a plate glass window in a store where war trophies were displayed. The paper reported that Booth "was arrested, paid the charge and a fine of fifty dollars, and the affair was kept out of the papers. He broke the window in his rage at seeing the exhibition of weapons taken from the rebels."[3]

Booth next appeared in Detroit, Michi-gan, at the 1,200-seat Metropolitan Theatre, where he was reunited with his friend John Albaugh, then a member of the theatre's stock company. Agnes Perry, wife of Harry A. Perry, manager of the theatre, later became the third wife of Junius Brutus Booth, Jr.[4] The terms of Booth's engagement gave him fifty percent of each night's proceeds after the first $60. Booth earned $116.92 for his seven performances, or $16.70 a performance. Maggie Mitchell, a more prominent star than Booth, had earned $22.67 a night at the same theatre two weeks earlier.[5]

Booth demonstrated his versatility as an actor by appearing on occasion as Romeo Jaffier Jenkins in the comic afterpiece *Too Much for Good Nature*. A fellow actor thought Booth was "exceedingly good in light and eccentric comedy," remembering that "Booth kept the audience in a roar of laughter all the time he was on stage."[6]

Kate Bateman, who had performed in Montgomery with Booth, was slated to begin an engagement in Detroit after Booth's ended, but she was unable to appear on her scheduled opening night. Booth substituted with *Richard III*.

Booth arrived in Cincinnati, Ohio, on November 23 and, while waiting for his room, penned a letter to Joe Simonds. He explained his reticence in writing letters:

I know you will forgive me, this long delay in answering your letters; if you knew me better you would not wonder at it, as I avail myself of any excuse to get rid of writing. No matter how I may long to hear from the person to whom I have to write, and I confess I should like to hear from you every day....[7]

Booth's engagement at Wood's Theatre, on the southeast corner of Sixth and Vine Streets, again followed an appearance by Maggie Mitchell. The *Cincinnati Daily Commercial* eagerly awaited his performances, noting that the "genuine furor he has everywhere excited, leads us to anticipate another theatrical triumph at Wood's."[8] Booth's engagement demonstrated his potential. The *Commercial* critic later recalled that Booth "left the impression that, though rather an unequal actor, as might be expected of one of his limited experience, he gave unmistakable evidence of genuine dramatic talent."[9]

In Kentucky, the *Louisville Daily Democrat* looked forward to Booth's December appearance at the Louisville Theatre, calling him "an Adonis in person," and complimenting "his genius."[10]

When Booth moved on late in December to Indianapolis, Indiana, the critics were no less enthusiastic than those in other cities. The *Indianapolis Daily Journal* remarked of Booth's performances at Metropolitan Hall that "his rendering of the text is always remarkably exact, and in good taste. We have heard no one who makes the sense of Shakespeare so clear, or delivers him with so evident a purpose to make the sense distinct and striking."[11] The *Indianapolis Daily Sentinel* told its readers that "[f]or some days past we have been bewildered, amazed, and delighted at the performances of Mr. J. Wilkes Booth."[12] At the end of Booth's engagement, the *Journal* noted:

Our Theater has been patronized during the week by the fashionable and elite of the city.... Mr. Booth is, beyond doubt, the most promising young actor of the day. His renditions of Richard, Hamlet, Othello, DeMoor, etc. would put to the blush many of the older actors....[13]

Albert G. Porter, a future governor of Indiana, observed Booth in Indianapolis:

He was of medium size, a well-formed, compactly built, agile young man, about 5 ft. 9, with a good healthy complexion, clear, ringing voice of good range (compass), & of rich and melodious tone, he was easy, graceful, vivacious, active, and singularly free from rant and staginess; cool and self-possessed; with black hair and eyes, and esteemed quite handsome.

During his Indianapolis engagement, he appeared in one of his best characters, in which occurs a touching and most affecting love scene, the other party (the heroine), to which was Marian Macarthy. Both played unexceptionally well. The writer with some friends occupied the second tier private box, and had a fair and close view of the facial features of hero and heroine in the affecting love scene referred to.

It was a part of the play that at a certain point the lady should simulate tears, but on this occasion (for some reason we could not then understand) poor Marian cried in sure enough earnest as though her heart would break, the tears poured down her cheeks in a flood, and the astonished star had his hands full to keep her from falling prostrate at his feet. A slight break in her lines (the words) was skilfully covered by Booth, and the play went on to its conclusion in a very satisfactory manner.

After the theatre closed for the evening, our party adjourned for refreshments to the "Exchange" now the Young Mens Ch. Assn. Buildg on N. Ills. St., where an elegant hot lunch was spread every night at about 11 o'clock. Mr. Booth soon came in and fell to with apparent good appetite, and we had a good opportunity to "sift him" in form and feature with our eyes, somewhat curious to inspect the personal appearance of one who was the immediate descendant of the illustrious Junius Brutus Booth. Dressed with modest but becoming taste in plain citizen's garb, and sitting directly opposite to us, apparently indifferent or at least careless of our scrutiny, he appeared to be a thoughtful, self-possessed gentleman.[14]

Booth opened in St. Louis, Missouri, on January 6, 1862. He lodged at the Planters' House, a large hotel occupying the block on Fourth Street between Chestnut and Pine Streets. Ben DeBar,[15] the proprietor of the St.

Louis Theatre, was family, in a way, to Booth. DeBar's sister, Clementine, had married Junius Brutus Booth, Jr., in 1844, and DeBar brought up their daughter, Blanche. The theatre, located on the north side of Pine Street between Third and Fourth Streets, had a capacity of 2,500. Eight saloons were provided for thirsty patrons.[16] Ben DeBar's pro–Southern feelings were well known. A local Southern-leaning newspaper, the *Missouri Republican*, often carried items favorable to DeBar and his theatre.[17] The provost marshal admonished DeBar several times for "pandering to rebel tastes on the stage."[18]

The *New York Clipper*'s St. Louis correspondent commented on the financial success of Booth's engagement. "Business at the St. Louis is very good and considering the times remarkably so," he noted.[19] Later the correspondent went on to say: "With cold near zero, our places of amusement are still doing a good business, and J. Wilkes Booth so far has played one of the best engagements of the season. He has reason to be satisfied with his first visit to St. Louis which we hope will be the precursor of many more."[20] The *St. Louis Missouri Democrat* added that "Mr. Booth is nightly attracting full and fashionable houses."[21]

During the St. Louis engagement a remarkable set of photographs was taken of Booth, two Union officers, and a civilian.[22] Booth stands alone in one picture. A seven-picture series depicts Booth standing between a seated Henry M. Day, Lieutenant Colonel of the 91st Illinois Infantry, and a civilian who bears a resemblance to Ben DeBar. The three men are shown conversing. Booth bends over and gestures in four of the pictures, and in one the men light cigars. Charles C. Campbell, a major in the 1st Illinois Light Artillery, joins the group in another photograph. Campbell stands in one of the pictures and is flanked by Booth and the civilian.[23] It is possible, of course, that one or more of the photographs is a composite.

Late in January Booth traveled to Chicago for an engagement at McVicker's Theatre. The *Chicago Tribune* predicted:

> That he [Booth] will receive a hearty welcome we cannot doubt, and should he possess the requisites to aspire to his father's mantle of greatness, Chicago will be quick to acknowledge it. For the short time he has been before the public he has received high praise, some critics even placing him in advance of his father as a tragedian.[24]

The *Chicago Evening Journal* critic, having watched Booth's opening performance in *Richard III*, observed:

> If originality is a virtue, Mr. Booth is virtuous to an intense degree. No actor ever displayed more independence of and less regard for the old beaten path than does he.... His bearing in the closing scene, on the battlefield, was that of an enraged tiger, goaded to madness. It was terrible; and those who had listlessly followed the interminable scene-shifting through long and dreary sets without deigning a token of applause, went wild over his furious combat with Richmond.[25]

After witnessing three performances, the critic from the *Journal* thought highly of the talents of the young actor:

> He established the fact that he was a reader of great merit, that his elocution was as near faultless as could be, that his form was slight, almost to delicacy, and suggestive of a wondering inquiry to those who saw his vigorous and terrific conflict with Richmond, on Monday night. His voice is light, but decidedly pleasant to the ear, and is attuned to the most delicate modulations.[26]

Three Chicago newspapers asked Booth to repeat a performance of *The Apostate*. One critic expressed surprise that Booth excelled in the reflective role of Hamlet. Jennie Hosmer, the leading lady of McVicker's stock company, thought John was a "greater actor" than Edwin, but believed that he did not have Edwin's "refinement, grace and crystal clearness of elocution."[27]

Booth was a decided success in his first engagement in Chicago. The *Journal* critic summarized:

Mr. Booth possesses all the virtues and none of the vices of the profession. Young, ambitious, resolute, and unswerving in honest integrity, we bespeak for him a future position in the history of the drama to which few may aspire, and but one or two in a generation attain.[28]

Booth next traveled to Baltimore, where the *Baltimore Sun* looked forward to the actor's first star engagement in his hometown:

Even in these days of sterner excitement, the popular pulse will beat more quickly at the apparition of a second son of the elder Booth on the boards of the old Holliday.... Apart from the classic traditions which surround his name, Mr. Booth brings to his task a person eminently suited to his high vocation; a face flashing with the light of genius; the eye and voice of his well-remembered father. We have never seen a set of features so admirably cast to reflect all the stormy changes of the tragic muse. While their rare beauty cannot fail to attract the sympathy of all, their intense earnest power will compel that critical approval which only surrenders to superior might. Mr. Booth possesses all the elements not only of success but of supremacy.[29]

Later in the week, the *Sun* continued:

Mid the galaxy of stars that have illuminated our theatrical firmament ... none have shown with greater brilliancy than our young artist; admiring audiences throughout the country, comprising the learned, the discriminating, and the ... people at large ... have conferred upon him their warmest admiration; and here in his native city, crowded audiences have nightly listened to his personations with ... riveted attention....[30]

After a week of performances, the *Sun* raved: "That this young tragedian is destined to achieve great distinction ... there can be no doubt. There is a freshness, energy, physical vigor, earnestness and dash in his personations...."[31]

Mary Ann Farren, Booth's one time co-star in Portland, had been hired to provide strong support for Booth during this engagement. Samuel Knapp Chester, Booth's old friend, was in the stock company. Farren went

on to New York with Booth in March. Actress Mary Provost[32] had chosen Booth as the first star to perform under her management at her theatre in that city. Booth played his signature role, *Richard III*, eleven times in three weeks, generating much attention from the critics. "We cannot name a better Richard," stated the *New York Times*.[33] *Wilkes' Spirit of the Times* added:

Young Booth makes Richard a stirring, active villain, busy with his grand ambition; soliloquizing, scheming, making love, dissembling.... With a firm step he hastens on from point to point, his eye constantly seeing in the near future the crown.... His soliloquies are full of restless gesture....[34]

Theatrical historian T. Allston Brown, writing years later, observed:

As *Richard III* Wilkes was different from all other tragedians. He imitated no one, but struck out into a path of his own, introducing points which older actors would not dare to attempt. In the last act he was truly original.... He would dart across the stage as if he "meant business."... His face covered with blood from his wounds ... he panted and fumed like a prize fighter.[35]

A critic who had seen Junius Brutus Booth in 1838 wrote that he was vividly reminded of the father by John Wilkes Booth: "He reads admirably and ... especially excels in the last act, which was a masterpiece of acting. He is perfectly self-possessed."[36] A year after this engagement, *Wilkes' Spirit of the Times* recalled that "John Wilkes Booth played ... his unrivaled Richard and several other notable characters with true Boothian vigor and talent."[37]

Rehearsing for *Richard III*, Booth casually walked through his lines and gave stage directions to the cast. Afterwards he spoke to each member of the cast, indicating that he would put more "fire" in the actual performance and offering occasional criticism.[38] One account of a performance during this engagement in New York relates that the actor Edward L. Tilton:

... was doing Richmond in the good old style to [Booth's] Gloster, and in the fencing scene the infuriated tyrant got so excited that he forced his opponent over the footlights into the musicians' inclosure. Although Tilton's shoulder was broken by the fall, he continued the part after being lifted to the stage, and fenced on with his left hand, amid the cheers of the spectators.[39]

Booth sought a fine line between infusing fire in the performance and avoiding injury. One source quotes Tilton claiming that Booth broke his arm with a sword blow; another, more tame, account has Tilton accidentally stepping off the stage and dislocating his shoulder.[40]

The critics made many flattering remarks about Booth's engagement in New York.

We think Mr. J.W. Booth has great natural gifts for the stage, and an amount of intellectual breadth in one so young that is most remarkable. Mr. Booth is a head and shoulders above those who ordinarily attempt Richard III.[41]

Care, study and experience will place him in the very first rank of his profession.[42]

In person he is very much like his brother Edwin, though considerably stouter.... He has a fine presence, but lacks in grace and dignity of carriage—a slight fault, a country habit.... His voice is so much like Edwin's that it is only in its greater power a casual hearer can detect the difference.[43]

Mr. Booth was admirable, and in the scenes with the father was great.... Booth's playing rose gradually in power and intensity to this grand point [the fourth act], where he wrought his audience to the wildest enthusiasm.[44]

His forte is in melodramatic rather than in quiet, classical, intellectual characters.[45]

Not everyone was impressed. Walt Whitman, having heard Booth's talents praised, attended a performance and thought the acting was as much like Booth's father as the "wax bust of Henry Clay" was to Clay himself.[46]

The *Herald* critic wrote:

[Booth] has had an opportunity of testing before a metropolitan audience the abilities that have won him such a reputation in the provinces. That he has passed through the ordeal with so fair a success is a proof that there is the stuff in him to make a first class tragedian, if he chooses to correct by study the extravagances that disfigure his impersonations....[47]

The critic from *Wilkes' Spirit of the Times* offered a long and thoughtful review of Booth's New York performances late in March. He found Booth's Hamlet not to his liking, but understood that others might well appreciate the interpretation. He thought Booth was "perfectly at home" in melodramatic efforts such as *The Apostate*. He found Booth's Richard "thrilling." He did not gush with enthusiasm, nor was he vitriolic in criticism. This serious and generally positive review is revealing of the merits of Booth as an actor.[48]

After his stay in New York, Booth took two weeks off before beginning his next engagement, in St. Louis. Stuart Robson, one of Booth's boyhood friends, was in the St. Louis stock company.[49] A journey from the east coast to St. Louis in those days was no small matter; travel by rail took over fifty hours. Booth returned to St. Louis for a good reason; he had been one of the biggest draws of the season in that city.[50]

Years later a military officer reported:

Both Ben DeBar [of the St. Louis Theatre] and Blanche Booth state that John Wilkes was exceedingly fond of money, that he was niggardly and avaricious and they never knew him to squander money in rioting or excesses of any kind, except possibly with women. They had noticed this as a marked trait in his character.[51]

At the time of the statement, DeBar may have thought that making negative comments regarding Booth would be in his best interest.

Booth moved on to Boston for a two-week engagement in May. Boston theatre-goers had idolized Junius Brutus Booth, Sr., and they adored Edwin. Comparisons of

John Wilkes Booth to these family members were inevitable. A Boston critic who had seen Booth perform *Richard III* in New York looked forward to his performances:

> We would by no means be considered as thinking that Wilkes Booth has yet attained the top of the ladder; but from witnessing this one performance, we are convinced that he has a sure footing in the position which he has so early reached, and that his ascent will be certain. Mr. Booth is yet very young, and time will undoubtedly do much toward ripening the powers which he now possesses. With him the present is full of merit, and the future big with promise....
>
> We never again expected to receive a new sensation at a representation of this hackneyed character [Richard III]. So many have we seen in the part, and so thoroughly has it been studied by all tragedians, that we had no hope of ever again being startled by a new "point"; but we were most agreeably surprised by Mr. Booth. He has in no way mistaken his vocation. The one performance of his that we have seen, satisfied us that he is by nature, as he is by education, an actor. His acting belongs to the very best school—that wherein a passion is expressed as the heart, wrought by tumult, itself directs; not that which teaches an actor, after stopping to select his position, to traverse the stage in short shuffling jumps, and throw himself through a series of horrible contortions. In fact, he seems perfectly natural, and *is* the character itself; so identified with the part, that, for the time, we forget Booth and think only of Richard.
>
> Mr. Booth is decidedly an original actor. There is no appearance of imitation in anything he does; although it is not unlikely this charge will be made against him, as there are naturally many points of similarity between him and the other members of his family. As Edwin is like and unlike his father, so is Wilkes like and unlike both. He has a voice very much like Edwin's—the same smooth, silvery tones, with no nasal twang, no mouthing of words; no disposition to rant, and yet, at times, electrifying the audience with powerful expressions of deep passion. His reading is beautiful in the extreme, and the hidden meanings of Shakespeare's lines are all unfolded by the power of genius and thorough study. That he has been a deep and earnest student, we well know, and it is evidenced by his performances; he has made critical analyses of all the characters he plays, which he carefully follows. With a handsome and prepossessing personal appearance, easy and graceful in his movements upon the stage, Mr. Booth pleases the eye as well as the ear, which goes far toward satisfying an audience.[52]

Booth received a warm welcome from the Boston critics and audiences at his opening. The *Boston Post* noted:

> His appearance was the signal for a stunning round of applause, which was continued for several minutes. In appearance, Mr. J. Wilkes Booth is taller than Edwin, but the first sight of him as Richard III makes one almost doubt his senses, so like are the twain. When he speaks, it is the same voice to a tone. It is soon discovered, however, that the younger brother has a handsomer countenance and a facial expression much more plastic than the other possesses. He is remarkably easy, nonchalant, and entirely devoted to the business before him, and in the various situations affords a study that all who see him delight to be absorbed in. We miss, however, the intensity and reflective nature of Edwin's method. It may be volatility or it may be genius that is shaping out some new development, which may supersede the stiff, rigid form that we have been accustomed to witness. Meantime we are prepared to say that he is an actor we shall delight to witness often; and the facts that he is peculiarly talented and that he is the son and brother of two of the most popular tragedians of their time, insure consideration from a Boston audience.[53]

After observing Booth in several performances, the critics further analyzed his style. The *Boston Post* offered:

> Edwin has more poetry, John Wilkes more passion; Edwin has more melody of movement and utterance, John Wilkes more energy and animation; Edwin is more correct, John Wilkes more spontaneous; Edwin is more Shakespearean, John Wilkes more melo-dramatic; and in a word, Edwin is a better *Hamlet*, John Wilkes a better *Richard III*.[54]

The *Boston Advertiser* critic thoughtfully wrote:

> With a view to observing if Mr. Wilkes Booth were winning for himself his father's triumphs, or if he were likely to do so, we have taken pains to see him in each of the characters which he assumed during the last week.... We have been greatly pleased and greatly disappointed. In what does he fail? Principally, in knowledge of himself—of his resources, how to husband and how to use them. He is, apparently, entirely ignorant of the main principles of elocution. We do not mean by this word merely enunciation, but the nature and proper treatment of the voice, as well. He ignores the fundamental principle of all vocal study and exercise—that the chest, and not the throat or mouth, should supply the sound necessary for singing or speaking.... When Mr. Booth wishes to be forcible or impressive, he produces a mongrel sound in the back of the mouth or top of the throat, which by itself would be unintelligible and without effect; by a proper use of his vocal organs he might draw from that fine trunk of his a resonant, deep tone whose mere sound in the ear of one who knew not the language should give a hint of the emotion to be thereby conveyed. In this connection we need simply say that his proclivity to a nasal quality is more apparent, and bodes great harm to his delivery if not checked at once.
>
> When he [Booth] moves, he does so with that aptness of motion, which forbids the observer to define it; he was there, he is here—he was seen to pass—but how he went, with what step upon the stage, or if borne through the air, can scarcely be told.... He has a physique, in short, which is equal to any demands which he need make upon it.[55]

After one of Booth's matinee performances, women gathered in a crowd at the stage door. They soon became unruly and tried to enter the door. Stage manager Edwin F. Keach came out and restored order.[56]

At the end of May Booth made another long trip to the Midwest, this time to Chicago for a return engagement. The *Chicago Evening Journal* commented:

> He has certainly improved since he was here, a few weeks ago, though we can scarcely con-

ceive how, inasmuch as his style is all his own, original, bold and masterly. It is no wonder that he took the Bostonians and Gothamites by storm, and certainly no actor of late years has received such encomiums from the press of the Atlantic cities as has J. Wilkes Booth.[57]

A week into the engagement, the *Journal* critic looked forward to a particular performance:

> While everyone is delighted with the delineation of the old characters by this excellent actor [Booth], there will be a curiosity to witness him in one that has hitherto not been deemed worthy the attention of our tragic hero. We allude to Raphael, The Sculptor in the play of *The Marble Heart*....[58]

The *Journal* critic was still enraptured with Booth's *Apostate*:

> Mr. Booth's greatest character is unquestionably that of *Pescara* in *The Apostate*. With him in this role we would rather witness *The Apostate* than any other tragedy extant. For grandeur of conception, terrible effect, startling incident, and beautiful stage effect, we know of no drama which surpasses it.[59]

At the beginning of Booth's third week in town, the *Chicago Tribune* noted:

> Mr. Booth's engagement thus far has been the success of the season, and we have no doubt his last week will be the most successful. In every character he has gained new admirers, while he may consider himself one of Chicago's greatest favorites. He should repeat *Raphael* in *The Marble Heart*. The large audience who witnessed it on Friday are loud in praise of its beauties.[60]

Booth drew large audiences during his three-week engagement—a worthy achievement considering the warm weather of June. According to the *Tribune*, "Mr. Booth's engagement has proved a complete triumph, of which he may well feel proud. It will be a hard task for any actor to supplant him with a Chicago audience."[61]

Booth, worn out by the labors of the long season, had a final engagement in Louisville late in June. The *Louisville Daily Journal* reported on June 23, the day of Booth's first scheduled performance, that "[a]n indisposition will prevent Mr. Wilkes Booth from appearing for a few nights."[62] He missed two performances, made five appearances, and then closed his acting season.

In the previous season (1860-1861), his first as a star, Booth had played a few engagements, mostly in small towns and cities. Injuries had reduced his performances and his income. When his second starring season closed in June 1862, he must have been proud of his accomplishments. He had performed fourteen engagements in eleven cities. He had given 162 performances, losing none through injury and only two to illness. His press reviews were positive, almost without exception. His audiences had crowded the theatres so much in Chicago, St. Louis, and Louisville that he was called back for return engagements. He had performed in the major theatrical cities of Baltimore, Philadelphia, New York, and Boston. He had succeeded in each of those cities, particularly in Boston. His earnings were good. He was young, and had much to learn, but he had shown signs of greatness.

1861 *from September 11*

September 11, Wednesday
President Lincoln revoked General Frémont's proclamation of August 30, which ordered the emancipation of slaves who belonged to Confederate-sympathizing masters in Missouri.

September 13, Friday Philadelphia?
Joseph Simonds, a cashier at the Mechanics Bank in Boston, wrote to Booth to keep him informed of the activities of mutual friends.[63]

September 30, Monday
Edwin Booth made his London debut at the Haymarket Theatre Royal.[64]

October 9, Wednesday Philadelphia
John Wilkes Booth, from 1004 Chestnut Street in Philadelphia, wrote to his friend Joe Si-

monds in Boston: "I know you will forgive me for not answering yours of Sept: 13th."[65] Booth related that he was negotiating an engagement with Edward Loomis Davenport, now manager of Boston's Howard Athenaeum.

October 19, Saturday
The *New York Clipper* reported that "Miss Helen [Kate] Bateman and J. Wilkes Booth will shortly appear at the Metropolitan, Buffalo."[66]

October 21, Monday Providence
Booth played Julian St. Pierre in *The Wife* at the Pine Street Theatre, also known as the Providence Theatre. The *Providence Daily Post* noted:

> The American stage still has a Booth. The reputation of his father, and of his brother, now in England, will, we predict, be equaled by his own. In word, look, gesture, tone, motion and position, the youngest Booth reminded us of the high-toned actors of days gone by. No vulgar rant, no mouthing, nothing artificial or unnatural, but all in keeping with the character assumed....[67]

The *Post* reported that Booth was "young, modest, and of prepossessing appearance, and in conversation evidences much cultivation, and also knowledge of his arduous profession."[68]

October 22, Tuesday Providence
Booth appeared as Pescara in *The Apostate*. The *Post* was enthusiastic:

> We were satisfied that the genius of Booth the senior has descended in no small measure to the son.... It was not Booth on the stage, but Pescara [in *The Apostate*] in Grenada. It did not seem like acting, but it was, for the time being, the reality. This, we are aware, is great praise of merit; but there was merit that deserves great praise.[69]

October 23, Wednesday Providence
Booth played *Macbeth*. At the same time as Booth's performance, Senator Charles Sumner of Massachusetts presented a lecture in Providence in which he argued that slavery was the sole cause of the war and that the destruction of slavery would lead to Confederate defeat.[70]

October 24, Thursday Providence
Booth played *Hamlet*. The *Providence Journal* commented on Booth's engagement:

> The eminent young American tragedian, Mr. J. Wilkes Booth, is playing a round of his celebrated characters this week at the Providence Theatre. It is seldom that we have an opportunity of witnessing so chaste and sterling an actor in our city.... Strongly resembling his gifted father in his

younger days he possesses talent and genius of a high order.[71]

October 25, Friday Providence

Booth closed his engagement with *Richard III*. The *Post* noted that Booth was a:

...young tragedian of very superior genius and of superlative artistic accomplishments.... [He gave] chaste, forcible and, in many respects, original personations of Macbeth and Hamlet.... We shall watch his career after he leaves our city with much interest, for we have written him down on our tablets as a name that will stand ... with the names of the first and best....[72]

October 28, Monday Buffalo

Booth, hampered by a severe cold, opened his engagement at the Metropolitan Theatre with a portrayal of Pescara in *The Apostate*. The critic from the *Buffalo Post* wrote:

J. Wilkes Booth was greeted by an appreciative audience.... The part of *Pescara* was given with a fire and vigor, that gave evidence of a strong natural talent and of future eminence in his profession. In person, Mr. Booth resembles his talented brother Edwin....[73]

October 29, Tuesday Buffalo

Booth played *Hamlet*. The *Buffalo Daily Courier* reviewed the performance, noting that the audience was:

... respectable as to size, but not so large as the merit of his acting should have brought together. He took to the character of the noble Dane as one to the manner born. Throughout the play ... the beauty of the impersonation came splendidly out.[74]

The *Buffalo Morning Express* remarked: That he shares with Edwin Booth the inherited genius which that youthful artist has so splendidly proven, is as certain as that he is stamped with the same familiar features. His powers are yet scarcely developed from their germ, and a patient task lies before him in their cultivation and training; but there is no mistaking the force that gives energy and inspiration to his acting.[75]

The *Courier* critic described Booth's style: [Booth has] the strange power and effect [of his father and brother] and ... the great ... feature, and gesture, the quiet intense by-play of eye and nerve, yet with more of grotesqueness of person and style than any of the family.... We do not flatter him when we say he has extraordinary physiognomical power, almost electric feeling and weird and startling elocutionary effects.[76]

October 30, Wednesday Buffalo

Booth played the title role in *Othello*. Years after this Buffalo engagement, an observer claimed that Booth had asked the stage

carpenter in Buffalo to construct a special set for the second act of *Othello*. A terrace and steps would allow Booth to make a grand entrance by running onto the terrace. Booth performed *Othello* only once in Buffalo.[77]

October 31, Thursday Buffalo

Booth appeared as Julian St. Pierre in *The Wife*.

November 1, Friday Buffalo

Booth played *Richard III*. The *Courier* remarked that "[t]he attendance at Mr. J. Wilkes Booth's benefit [*Richard III*] was but a fitting compliment to the genius and worthy [*sic*] of the actor." The critic favorably compared Booth's representation to that of Edwin Booth, which he believed was the standard for the part. He thought the combat scene was "especially great." [78]

The *Courier* observed:

[Booth's] engagement has fallen upon an unfortunate time, when war and politics so completely absorb the public attention, but we wish to have our readers realize, nevertheless, that they have now an opportunity not often, in our theatrical season, offered, for seeing great Shakespearean parts rendered by one who has the manner of the great actors, and who has shown himself a worthy scion of the house of Booth.[79]

November 2, Saturday Buffalo

Booth appeared in *The Robbers*. The *Courier* noted that "[Booth] has won the highest encomiums from our critics, and none more warm than awarded to his representation of Charles de Moor in Schiller's *Robbers*—a masterly performance full of new points and strangely fascinating."[80]

November 3, Sunday Buffalo

November 4, Monday Buffalo

Booth played Romeo in *Romeo and Juliet*. The *Express* reported:

A good audience occupied the benches ... to witness [Booth's] personation of the lover Romeo. It was an excellent bit of carefully studied acting, modeled upon the principles of good taste by a correct judgment. There are few actors who can appreciate the exquisite sentimentality of Shakespeare's *Romeo and Juliet*.[81]

November 5, Tuesday Buffalo

Booth played Claude Melnotte in *The Lady of Lyons; or, Love and Pride*.[82]

November 6, Wednesday Buffalo

Booth played *Macbeth*.[83]

November 7, Thursday Buffalo

Booth played *Richard III*. The *Express* noted:

Acceding to numerous requests, Mr. Booth will this evening repeat his great performance in the character of *Richard III*. This will afford a last opportunity for witnessing one of the finest pieces of acting that we have been allowed to enjoy in Buffalo for many a day.[84]

Booth wrote to Joe Simonds, "My second week in Buffalo was so, so."[85]

November 8, Friday Buffalo

Booth played Phidias and Raphael in *The Marble Heart; or, The Sculptor's Dream* in his farewell benefit. The *Courier* critic stated that Booth deserved a large crowd to honor the high quality of his acting.[86]

The U.S. Navy started an international incident when it seized James M. Mason and John Slidell, Confederate envoys to Great Britain and France.

November 9, Saturday Buffalo

Booth closed his engagement in Buffalo with a portrayal of Fabien and Louis in *The Corsican Brothers*. The *Express* reported:

We regret to see it announced that Miss Howard ... receives her farewell benefit [in *The Corsican Brothers*] this evening, prior to departing for California.... This evening is further specialized, theatrically, by its termination of the engagement of Mr. John Wilkes Booth, the young tragedian whose success in winning ... friendship and admiration ... has been only exceeded by that of his brother Edwin.[87]

November 11, Monday Detroit

Booth opened his engagement in Detroit by playing Julian St. Pierre in *The Wife* at Mrs. H. A. Perry's Metropolitan Theatre. Booth's friend John Albaugh was in the cast.[88]

November 12, Tuesday Detroit

Booth played *Macbeth*. The *Detroit Free Press* reported:

A large and highly appreciative audience was present ... to witness Mr. J. W. Booth's rendition of *Macbeth*, and we doubt whether an audience ever went away more thoroughly satisfied.... It [the play] has been *played*, it has been played *at*, and it has been murdered. The first is what may be said of Mr. Booth's representation.... The closing scene, the combat, was probably never excelled, if even equaled, in this city.[89]

November 13, Wednesday Detroit

Booth played the title role in *Othello*.

November 14, Thursday Detroit

Booth played the title role in *Othello*. The *Free Press* remarked:

Notwithstanding the unfavorable portent of the weather last evening, there was a goodly assemblage at the theatre to witness Mr. Booth's impersonation of *Othello*. The play was a most decided success. Mr. Booth fully sustained all that has previously been said of his superior qualities as an actor. Mr. Albaugh won new laurels by his masterly rendition of Iago, as also did Mrs. Perry in the character of Desdemona.[90]

November 15, Friday Detroit

Booth, in his benefit, played *Richard III* and appeared as Romeo Jaffier Jenkins in the afterpiece, *Too Much for Good Nature*. John Albaugh portrayed Richmond. The *Free Press* noted that *Richard III* "was admirably produced ... the sword combat in the last act between Richard and Richmond being decidedly the best and most thrilling scene that has ever been produced on the stage of the Metropolitan."[91]

November 16, Saturday Detroit

Booth played *Hamlet*. The *Free Press* anticipated the performance:

To-night Mr. Booth concludes a highly successful engagement.... The announcement that it is his last performance will be sufficient to pack the house. An admirable bill is presented in *Hamlet*.... Mr. Booth, during his short engagement has won a host of friends, who will heartily welcome him to the boards of the Metropolitan again.[92]

November 17, Sunday Detroit

November 18, Monday Detroit

Kate Bateman could not appear on the first night of her engagement, and Booth substituted with *Richard III*.

November 19, Tuesday Detroit

Booth's Russell House hotel bill listed charges of $1 for "Segars," $5.50 for "Bar," and $1 for "Washing." Room charges for nine and a quarter days totaled $14.58.[93]

November 20, Wednesday Detroit

Booth wrote an acrostic for a friend:
"To Fanny, In the following initials you will
F ind a soul made up of truth,
A nd yet in mortal form.
N ot clouded by the vanities of youth
N or shaded by pride's fitful storm
Y es, she's one to serve, as, *instar omnium*.

Yours with all respect. J. Wilkes Booth Detroit. Nov 20th/61"[94]

November 23, Saturday. Cincinnati

Booth wrote to Joe Simonds: "I played 7 nights in Detroit to a good Bus:[iness], Open here Monday night, 25th:, they count high on me but I am doubtful as to my success ... my dear Joe excuse this as I am standing in the Office with about a hundred people about me blowing at a fearful rate, I am not fixed yet, so I cannot go to my room."[95]

November 24, Sunday Cincinnati

November 25, Monday Cincinnati

Booth began his engagement at Wood's Theatre with *Richard III*. The *Cincinnati Daily Commercial* critic wrote:

The impression created ... by Mr. Booth's *Richard III*, was altogether favorable to that gentleman.... Mr. Booth is a rapid reader, full of fire, exhaustless in energy, and, though hurried on by the heat of his own emotions, never forgetful of the art, without which the actor fails of the highest realizations of his art. If lacking in anything, it is in physical force and vocal power. It is sometimes difficult, when his energies are wrought-up to their full tension, for the listener to catch his language, though the force of his acting never fails to clearly interpret his meaning. Altogether, he is an actor well worth seeing, whose genius is unmistakably apparent, and for whose future it is safe to anticipate a high professional renown.[96]

The *Cincinnati Daily Gazette* critic wrote: J. W. Booth is RICHARD—Notwithstanding the suicidal weather ... a very fair audience assembled at Wood's Theater to witness the young tragedian, J. W. Booth in the character of Richard III....

Those who have seen the elder Booth and Edwin both in the character of Richard have been forcibly struck with the close resemblance, in many respects, at least, of the impersonations, and the nearer Edwin's became a copy of the original the more he was applauded.

J. W. Booth resembles Edwin as nearly as Edwin did the old man. His portraiture of the "humpbacked tyrant," however, is not as finished a piece of acting as Edwin's, although one might readily imagine it was the latter who was "strutting his brief hour upon the stage." Their persons and voices are not unlike, and the "make-up," the same in all actors, makes them resemble each other still more closely. In J. W. we miss most the brilliant luster of Edwin's remarkable eyes, which, more than anything else, made him such a decided favorite with the fair sex.

The Richard ... impressed us very favorably, and was enough to stamp Mr. Booth as an actor of decided merit. Some of his readings are new, and we

think an improvement upon the usual method of delivery. We noted, especially, the line—Off with his head! So much for Buckingham. The rubbing of the hands and the darting forward toward the foot-lights added intensity to the satisfaction the announcement of Buckingham's death gave. Mr. Booth was not well-supported....[97]

November 26, Tuesday Cincinnati

Booth played *Othello*. The *Commercial* reviewer, Murat Halstead,[98] wrote:

Of Mr. Booth's *Othello* we have heard but one opinion, that, while an unequal performance as a whole, there were passages in which he attained the highest dramatic art, and gave the same evidence of uncommon genius that was apparent in his Richard. We were present only during the final act, in which he certainly displayed the terrible and convulsive passions of the scene. Nothing could have been finer, and no pathos more touching, than his remorse and the tone in which he exclaims, "O fool, fool, fool,"... His transitions from anguish to fiery indignation were absolutely electrifying.[99]

November 27, Wednesday Cincinnati

Booth appeared in *The Lady of Lyons*. The *Commercial* reported: "Mr. Booth's Claude Melnotte is conceded to have been the most even and successful of his renditions as yet, and confirmed the favorable opinions hitherto expressed."[100]

November 28, Thursday Cincinnati

A full house saw Booth play Charles de Moor in *The Robbers*. The *Commercial* remarked that Booth's "address to his band, and that scene altogether, was electrifying in character. It is plain that Mr. Booth has caught some of the fire that animated his great father."[101]

A. J. Neafie was appearing at Pike's Opera House in Cincinnati, also in Shakespearean characters. The *Commercial* critic suggested that theatregoers might find it interesting to compare Booth's portrayal of Othello to that of Neafie.[102]

November 29, Friday Cincinnati

Booth played *Macbeth*. The *Commercial* opined:

Mr. Booth is no common genius. He has the natural advantages of a good figure, a musically full and rich voice of rare compass and modulation, a face that talks.... His transitions are absolutely electrifying, and in this respect those who have seen the elder Booth observe a family resemblance. To these material aptitudes he adds a very clear perception of character, with the ability to assume it, to enter into and become part of it. He is evidently a close student, and not forgetful of those minor graces of art which complete and make perfect the interpretation of character. Like most young actors who wish to stamp with their own individuality the parts they assume, he varies frequently from the "old business" and gives them original interpretations, which while they may be characterized as experimental, may eventually meet with critical approval.[103]

November 30, Saturday Cincinnati

Booth played *Richard III*. An actor who played with Booth in Cincinnati later wrote:

In one scene he had a portion of his armor put on in the presence of the audience, and in that of the battle he had the stump of a tree set in the center of the stage as far back as possible. After parrying the first blow of Richmond he deliberately turned and ran up the stage, his foot tripped against the stump, and he fell headlong backward. Richmond ran up after him and as he fell aimed a blow at his head. This was immediately caught by Richard, who was on his feet in an instant raining blow after blow at his adversary and driving him down the stage to the footlights. This had an electrical effect upon the audience, especially as this stubborn fight was kept up for several minutes, Richard dying very hard indeed.[104]

The *Gazette* noted that heavy rains during the week had reduced audience size at the local theatres but that Wood's was least affected and "business has been good."[105]

December 1, Sunday Cincinnati

December 2, Monday Cincinnati

Booth played the dual role of Phidias and Raphael in *The Marble Heart*, about which the *Commercial* critic thought:

It is one of the best plays put upon the stage within the last ten years. A painful interest attaches to the young artist, whose infatuation has all the madness of love and a full share of its sufferings. It is a sharp, clear exposition of the struggle between ambition and love, duty and passion, and in ... perpetual strife....

Mr. Booth displays triumphantly his genius as an actor.... When it [the play] finds one who can interpret it thoroughly, whose art is so studied as to seem nature, who gives to that experience all the vividness of life, and invests himself so completely in it as to center in him all the interest and sympathy which we feel for the character, then the charm is complete and the fascination irresistible. Those who saw Mr. Booth ... will testify to his success in this particular, and acknowledge that they are rarely so spell-bound by the delineations of any actor.[106]

December 3, Tuesday Cincinnati

Booth again played Phidias and Raphael in *The Marble Heart*.

The *Cincinnati Daily Press* noted:

This classical production [*The Marble Heart*] is meeting with a decided success at our cosy dramatic temple. J. Wilkes Booth, as "Raphael Duchatlet," is winning the applause and good opinion of many, who look on with indifference at his "Othello," "Richard the Third," and other heavy characters. It's no fault of Booth, for he is a polished actor, and careful in his renditions.[107]

December 4, Wednesday Cincinnati

Booth appeared in *Hamlet*. The *Commercial* stated:

It was our misfortune, and we count it truly such, not to be present at the representation of *Hamlet* and cannot, therefore, speak pro or con of Mr. Booth's assumption of the part of the Prince.... It should be borne in mind that Mr. Booth's engagement is rapidly drawing to a close ... and those who wish to know something of one of the most promising actors of the day, should not fail in attending at Wood's.[108]

December 5, Thursday Cincinnati

Booth appeared as Julian St. Pierre in *The Wife*, and, by particular request, performed the last act of *Macbeth*. According to the *Commercial*:

During Mr. Booth's engagement the attendance at Wood's Theatre has constantly increased, as the reputation of the young actor extended. He has exerted himself to please, and has been in the main, fairly supported by the company.[109]

December 6, Friday Cincinnati

Booth played Shylock in *The Merchant of Venice* and Romeo Jaffier Jenkins in *Too Much for Good Nature*. The *Commercial* stated:

Mr. Booth, in the face of the prevailing taste for sensational drama, adheres to the legitimate, and is striving hard to revive an interest in it. His Shylock is a model piece of acting.... We have never seen it better rendered.... Mr. Booth's success, professionally, has been unquestioned.[110]

December 7, Saturday Cincinnati

Booth closed his engagement with *The Robbers*, in which he played Charles de Moor. The *Commercial* later offered this assessment:

In his transition from the quiet and reflective passages of a part to fierce and violent ... passion, his ... impetuous manner had in it something of that electric force and power which made the elder Booth so celebrated and called up afresh to the memory of men of the last generation the presence, voice and manner of his father.[111]

The *Gazette* critic wrote:

The engagement of Mr. Booth at Wood's will terminate to night. It has been moderately successful—more so, indeed, than we believed a fortnight of the legitimate could be made. Mr. Booth has in him the elements of a good tragedian, if he be not that already; but much of his acting is marred by poses, starts, gesticulations and readings peculiar to the "blood and thunder" school, which must be discarded ere he can hope to reach the pinnacle of histrionic fame. Moreover, he should let go the skirts of his father and Edwin, and strike out for himself. The efforts to imitate them, if directed in another channel, would make of him a much better actor.[112]

December 8, Sunday En route to Louisville

December 9, Monday Louisville

Booth opened his engagement, as usual, with *Richard III*. The *Louisville Daily Democrat* anticipated the performance:

Mr. J. Wilkes Booth, a scion of that noble race of actors whose fame belongs to the history of the last half century, makes his first bow before this audience. He appears in *Richard III*, a character in which his father never had an equal.... We recommend the young gentleman, who is said to be an Adonis in person, to the lovers of the drama here.[113]

After the production, the *Democrat* offered a review: "[Booth] has fire, energy, fine personal appearance, and good talent. Some eccentricities of style and some apparent imitations of other actors alone marred the beauty of his personation."[114]

December 10, Tuesday Louisville

Booth appeared as Claude Melnotte in *The Lady of Lyons*. The *Louisville Daily Journal* carried this item:

He reminds us more of his father than his brother Edwin does.... Mr. Wilkes Booth is a young man of extraordinary genius, and when his voice is matured by practice and he has succeeded in shaking off some mannerisms, he will become a great actor.... We have never seen the last act of *Richard III* played with more power, spirit and originality.[115]

December 11, Wednesday Louisville

Booth appeared in *Macbeth*. The *Democrat* commented:

Mr. Booth performed *Macbeth* ... to an excellent house, and in a style worthy of his growing reputation, showing conclusively that genius is sometimes hereditary.... His recitation of Macbeth, though somewhat unequal, was marked by great

beauties, original conception, and at times illuminated by those electric bursts characteristic of the elder Booth, which his admirers have never forgotten. In the fight between Macbeth and Macduff, there was a terrible intensity and appearance of reality that carried the audience by storm. In all our recollection of the stage we have never seen anything to surpass it....[116]

December 12, Thursday Louisville

Booth played *Richard III*. The *Democrat* reported:

A large and beautiful audience of ladies and gentlemen were attracted ... to witness Mr. Booth's personation of *Richard III*, and no audience ever left a theatre more entirely satisfied with the performances. The utmost quiet and order prevailed, and, in many passages, the breathless silence of the audience indicated the interest with which the performance was regarded.[117]

December 13, Friday Louisville

Booth appeared in *Hamlet*. According to the *Democrat*:

A very fashionable audience greeted Mr. Booth on the occasion of his benefit.... Mr. Booth's personation of *Hamlet* was a chaste and scholarly performance. A graceful and thoroughly appreciative idea of the character, beautiful elocution, and an elegant person, made Mr. B's performance one of unusual merit.[118]

December 14, Saturday Louisville

Booth appeared in *The Robbers*. The *Democrat* reported:

Mr. Booth played to another excellent house.... His rendering of Charles DeMoor in Schiller's play of *The Robbers* was marked by evidence of originality and boldness of conception characteristic of his *Richard III* and *Macbeth*. Mr. Booth is the most original actor we have seen in a great many years. In the strength of his genius he pursues his path to fame regardless of the means (not knowing them probably) which the great luminaries of the drama have used to seize and hold the plaudits of the world. The hackneyed term, talent, cannot be used in speaking of this young actor of such wonderful promise. It is genius in the broadest and largest acceptation of the term.[119]

December 15, Sunday Louisville

December 16, Monday Louisville

Booth appeared as Pescara in *The Apostate*.

December 17, Tuesday Louisville

Booth played Charles de Moor in *The Robbers*:

... to a crowded house, an exquisite performance, realizing to the life the extraordinary character as painted by the greatest of German poets. Mr. Booth appears to have inherited all the genius of his illustrious father, of which he constantly reminds us, more from the manner and the power ... than from ... imitation. In fact, he imitates no one—not even unconsciously. He is guided by his genius alone—a star that is destined to light him to the very summit of the steep "where fame's proud temple shines afar." We are sorry to learn that the engagement of this eminent tragedian is drawing to a close. He has made crowds of admirers....[120]

December 18, Wednesday Louisville

Booth played Shylock in *The Merchant of Venice* and performed the last act of *Macbeth*. The *Democrat* critic was enraptured with Booth's performance, writing that "[t]he audience went with the actor from first to last. He has talent, feeling, and force. No actor has ever so thoroughly carried an audience with him as did Mr. Booth last night."[121]

December 19, Thursday Louisville

Booth appeared in the title role in *The Stranger*, one of his least-performed plays.

December 20, Friday Louisville

Booth appeared as Phidias and Raphael in *The Marble Heart* and as Romeo Jaffier Jenkins in *Too Much for Good Nature*. The *Democrat* anticipated the evening: "The great merits of the artiste ... should draw the largest house of the season. Mr. Booth also appears for the first time in this city, in comedy. A new farce called *Too Much for Good Nature* will be performed."[122]

December 21, Saturday Louisville

Booth played *Richard III*. John Albaugh made his first appearance at Metropolitan Hall in Indianapolis; Booth would follow in a few days.[123]

The *New York Clipper* announced that "John Wilkes Booth, J. S. Clarke, and Miss Bateman are to be the first stars at the Howard Athenaeum, Boston, under the Davenport regime."[124]

December 22, Sunday Louisville

December 23, Monday Louisville

Booth appeared as Phidias and Raphael in *The Marble Heart*, which was a big hit. The *Democrat* advertised:

We are gratified to be able to announce that Mr. Booth has been prevailed on, by the lovers of the drama in the city, to remain for a single night longer, in order that the whole public may witness the representation of *The Marble Heart*, which created so great a sensation on the occasions of Mr. Booth's benefit.[125]

December 24, Tuesday. Indianapolis

The *Indianapolis Daily Journal* noted that Metropolitan Hall in Indianapolis had opened for the season on November 25 and that John Albaugh would be a member of the stock company for the entire season. The article continued:

On tomorrow, Christmas night, we are to be treated to a sight of the famous tragedian, young Booth, who is said to possess all the fire and genius of his father, who was, beyond all question, one of the greatest actors the world ever saw.[126]

December 25, Wednesday Indianapolis

Booth opened his engagement in Indianapolis with *Richard III*. The *Indianapolis Daily Sentinel* noted:

Mr. Booth made his first appearance as *Richard III*. The house was crowded and his performance was wonderful. How so young a man could so perfectly personate the old, crooked-backed tyrant surpassed all our conceptions of theatricals before. We had, years ago, seen the young man's father in the part. He was grand, he was great, he was unapproachable. But the son has all the fire of the old man's genius. He is rash and impetuous, and hurries things through with all the ardor of youth, whereas the elder Booth was, more especially in the soliloquies, deliberate. The young Booth, whom we have among us now, in these respects ought to take his father for an examplar. But in the bustle and stir and vigor and life of the play, he equaled any actor we had previously seen.[127]

December 26, Thursday Indianapolis

Booth played the title role in *Othello*. The *Sentinel* was impressed:

We anticipated a good performance but were not prepared for so great an outburst of genius. We are informed by the bills that Mr. Booth's stay can not be prolonged further than next Monday, therefore we should advise all to see this promising tragedian before that time.[128]

Two days later, the *Sentinel* continued to praise Booth's "matchless performance" in *Othello*.[129]

December 27, Friday Indianapolis

Booth played *Hamlet*. The *Sentinel* called his performance "scholarly, philosophical and finished."[130]

December 28, Saturday Indianapolis

Booth played Charles de Moor in *The Robbers*. The *Journal* was complimentary:

[Booth] has established the fact that his great reputation is not undeserved. His acting may not be entirely acceptable to those who conceive that passion is not always most forcibly expressed by a redundance of passionate exclamations and gestures, yet there is a propriety in every motion, a fitness in every gesture, that shows he does nothing without a purpose, that his acting is not a mere accidental play of hints or gestures.[131]

December 29, Sunday Indianapolis

December 30, Monday Indianapolis

On his benefit night, Booth played *Macbeth* and portrayed Romeo Jaffier Jenkins in *Too Much for Good Nature*.[132] The *Journal* anticipated the performance:

When we say that the house should be overflowing, we but speak simple justice. He deserves it. We never yet had an actor in our midst who so richly deserved it. He is possessed with genius in the highest degree. When we contrast his rendition of the crafty Richard, the played upon Othello, the soul-disturbed Hamlet, we must acknowledge his greatness.[133]

Several days later, the *Journal* continued to discuss the performance:

[Booth's] *Macbeth* gave us many original points—one especially: the reading,—Hang out our banners on the outward wall! The cry is "Still they come!"—met our approval. He is the only actor who ever met our expectations in that passage. We shall be glad to see him again in our midst.... Mr. Albaugh's support of Booth is equal to that rendered by any actor in the country.[134]

December 31, Tuesday Indianapolis

Booth ended his engagement in Indianapolis with *Richard III*. The *Journal* noted:

On the occasion of his first appearance ... he [Booth] appeared as *Richard III*, when hundreds were turned from the doors.... By special request of many of those persons, he will re-appear in this character this evening, and we think very wisely, for we know of many who were disappointed on the first occasion.[135]

1862 *through July 15*

January 1, Wednesday Indianapolis

January 2, Thursday

The Marshall Theatre in Richmond burned to the ground.

January 5, Sunday. St. Louis

January 6, Monday St. Louis

According to the *St. Louis Missouri Democrat*, Booth "had a most rapturous reception" upon opening his engagement in St. Louis with *Richard III*. The newspaper continued:

He is an actor of the highest order, with all the fire and enthusiasm of his father or brother Edwin, being taller and better formed; also a fine expressive face. As a declaimer, he is unexceptionable, careful and correct, never evincing a disposition to rant.[136]

January 7, Tuesday St. Louis

Booth played *Hamlet*.

January 8, Wednesday St. Louis

Booth played *Macbeth*.

January 9, Thursday St. Louis

Booth portrayed *Othello*.

The *Democrat* noted that "Mr. Booth has made a highly favorable impression each night, increasing in the number and the fashion of the audience.... Mr. Booth is in every sense a great actor, well read, and of commanding appearance...."[137]

January 10, Friday St. Louis

Booth, in his benefit, played Pescara in *The Apostate*. The *Democrat* commented that Booth "had a fine house ... and the performance went off admirably. His acting of the arduous character of Pescara was admirable, reminding us much of his late father, who made that part entirely his own."[138]

Booth sent a letter in an envelope bearing the imprint of "Planter's House Stickney & Scollay St. Louis, Mo." to his friend Joe Simonds in Boston:

Dear Joe, Both your letters Recd ... although I hate writing myself, I can read your letters, if you send three or four a-day. My bus[iness] here so far has been fair As you may see by the papers I play here all next week and then *may* go to Chicago, but not sure of it.[139]

January 11, Saturday St. Louis

Booth played *Richard III*.

The memory of Booth's engagement and the battle scene in *Richard III* persisted for many years:

The audience rose to its feet night after night in an agony of suspense, and first Richmond and then Richard would be driven at sword's point over the footlights into the ranks of the audience themselves, who would cheer first the hero and then the villain with wild abandon.[140]

January 12, Sunday St. Louis

January 13, Monday St. Louis

Booth played Charles de Moor in *The Robbers*.

January 14, Tuesday St. Louis

Booth played Julian St. Pierre in *The Wife*.

January 15, Wednesday St. Louis

Booth played Phidias and Raphael in *The Marble Heart*. The *Democrat* reported that "Mr. Booth is nightly attracting full and fashionable houses."[141]

January 16, Thursday St. Louis

Booth played *Richard III*. The *Democrat* puffed:

RICHARD III, in compliance with numerous requests, is repeated to-night, this being positively the last time it can be played. Mr. Booth's acting of the crooked backed tyrant is a great performance. The fight between Richard and Richmond in the last scene is most terrific; indeed we have never seen it equaled on the stage.[142]

January 17, Friday St. Louis

Booth appeared as Claude Melnotte in *The Lady of Lyons* and as Romeo Jaffier Jenkins in *Too Much for Good Nature*.

January 18, Saturday St. Louis

Booth closed his engagement by playing Phidias and Raphael in *The Marble Heart*, followed by a portrayal of Romeo Jaffier Jenkins in *Too Much for Good Nature*.

January 19, Sunday Chicago

January 20, Monday Chicago

Booth opened his engagement at McVicker's Theatre in Chicago with *Richard III*. The *Chicago Tribune* carried a long review of the performance:

The curiosity of the play-going public to know whether the mantle of the illustrious father had fallen upon the shoulders of the son, perhaps influenced in some degree the size and social complexion of the house ... but it is fair to say that those who went to the theatre expecting to see the hackneyed tragedy of Richard, and anticipating a good nap while the play dragged its whole length along, were agreeably disappointed. Nothing more unlike the old-time representation of the hunchback monarch could have been produced. Its old admirers hardly recognized it. J. Wilkes Booth is a very youthful actor, and as a consequence has hardly reached the point at which full appreciation of his powers as a tragedian can be arrived at, but to judge from a single hearing [in *Richard III*], we would at once pro-

nounce him a genius. He undoubtedly has all the elements to hereafter ensure him an eminent position in his profession. Possessing in a remarkable degree the mobility of features, the energy, the fire, the action of his father, a handsome form, a voice though rather sharp yet fully under control, and true inspiration and just appreciation of the play, he must become a popular and, worthy artist. He has also excellent study, yet his action and elocution do not smell of the lamp, but seem to be in every way natural and involuntary. The particular portions of Richard in which Mr. Booth excels are the wooing of Lady Anne, the scene in which he sees the vision of his murdered relations, and the contest with Richmond. In the latter he surpasses in energy any actor we have seen since his father. So fully does he become impressed and identified with the character that those with whom he fights the mimic fight fear him. In the combat with Mr. Pryor [Edwin C. Prior] ... he broke the heavy stage sword used by Richmond and for a moment one half of the audience supposed he would kill the actor himself. It is this very absorption of part and forgetfulness of self that rendered the elder Booth the man he was. In this respect the son certainly follows the sire, yet he cannot be said to copy.[143]

January 21, Tuesday Chicago

Booth played Claude Melnotte in *The Lady of Lyons*.[144]

January 22, Wednesday Chicago

Booth appeared as Pescara in *The Apostate*. The *Chicago Evening Journal* reviewed the performance:

It was reserved for Pescara to bring out Mr. Booth's strong points. His thin, sinewy figure, his cat-like movements, his full, dark eye, his strongly marked features, and above all, his wonderful "facial art," were each and all embodied and personified in *Pescara*.... His delighted audience ... called him twice before the curtain, amid thunders of applause.[145]

January 23, Thursday Chicago

Booth and Jennie Hosmer played *Romeo and Juliet*. Mr. Prior portrayed Mercutio. The afterpiece was *Love and Hunger*.

January 24, Friday Chicago

Booth played *Richard III*. According to the *Journal*:

Mr. Booth's benefit ... was such a one as no other artist has been the recipient of in many months, in this city. The house was filled to overflow. We observed a manifest improvement in the general rendering of *Richard III*, though in the closing scene, the conflict with Richmond, it was the same as before, incapable of improvement—and rendered as no other man ever rendered it.[146]

January 25, Saturday Chicago

Booth appeared as Charles de Moor in *The Robbers*.

January 26, Sunday Chicago

January 27, Monday Chicago

Booth appeared in *Hamlet*. The *Journal* commented:

> Those ... who supposed that the fiery and impetuous Booth, whose *Richard III* and Pescara—two of the most dashing and thrilling characters of the tragic stage—have been so much admired, would not succeed as *Hamlet* ... were agreeably surprised.... Even those who have ... connected *Hamlet* with Mr. Murdock ... were forced to admit that Mr. Booth's impersonation of that difficult character ... was not a whit behind that of Mr. Murdock.[147]

January 28, Tuesday Chicago

Booth played *Hamlet*. The *Journal* predicted "that to-night a brilliant audience will witness" the production.[148]

January 29, Wednesday Chicago

Booth played *Othello* with Mr. Prior as Iago, Mr. Myers as Cassio, Jennie Hosmer as Emilia, and Mrs. Myers as Desdemona. The afterpiece was *Twenty Minutes with a Tiger*.

January 30, Thursday Chicago

Booth appeared as Pescara in *The Apostate*. The *Journal* anticipated:

> It must be borne in mind that Manager [James] McVicker,[149] at the request of three newspapers, has consented to reproduce *The Apostate*, tonight. All who saw this admirable old tragedy, last week, were delighted, and the newspapers were unanimous in pronouncing Mr. Booth's Pescara a most finished and masterly piece of acting. Indeed, we regard it as being much superior to any other character [represented by Booth]....[150]

January 31, Friday Chicago

Booth played *Macbeth*.

February 1, Saturday Chicago

Booth concluded his engagement with *Richard III*. The *Journal* commented:

> To-night Mr. J. Wilkes Booth takes his farewell [in *Richard III*] of Chicago theatre-goers, who, for two weeks, have been entertained in an uncommon degree. Mr. Booth has but few equals upon the tragic stage, which is saying much of a young man not twenty-two years of age. He has

made a splendid beginning—his future lies with himself. He may be the head and front of the American stage, or he may add another to the list of victims of a fatal appetite, upon whose breakers so many bright lights of his profession have perished.[151]

February 2, Sunday Chicago

February 6, Thursday

Union forces captured Fort Henry, Tennessee.

February 14, Friday

The Baltimore American anticipated Booth's upcoming engagement:

> Mr. J. Wilkes Booth—The appearance of this, the youngest scion of the lamented Junius Brutus Booth, in this city [Baltimore], has created some curiosity in the minds of our play-going public, who are anxious to see him. We understand he will shortly appear at the Holliday Street Theatre....[152]

February 15, Saturday Baltimore

The *Baltimore Sun* carried this item under the title RICHARD'S HIMSELF AGAIN:

> It is a subject of congratulations ... to know that Baltimore has added another to the number of her illustrious sons, in the knowledge that with [John Sleeper] Clarke leading the column of American comedians, and Edwin Booth startling England ... we have in his younger brother an actor that with the suddenness of a meteor now illumines the dramatic horizon with a blaze of light, attracting and entrancing in other cities thousands by that hereditary genius which made his sire so famous.... He possesses the electric fire that wins hearts, and a bright, quick intellect that extorts praise....[153]

February 16, Sunday Baltimore

Union General Ulysses S. Grant forced the surrender of Fort Donelson in Tennessee.

February 17, Monday Baltimore

Booth opened at the Holliday Street Theatre with Mary Ann Farren in *Richard III*. In his first Baltimore appearance in a title role, he was billed under the heading "I am Myself Alone," part of a line spoken by the future Richard III in *Henry VI* that begins: "I have no brother, I am no brother...."[154]

The Holliday Street Theatre touted the performance in its advertisement in the next day's *Sun*: "A recognition of home genius.... A bright and glorious success, [Booth was] received ... by an ovation of genuine and continuous applause from an audience tremendous in numbers and brilliant in fashion."[155]

The *Sun* described the performance:

The house was well attended ... despite the very forbidding weather, and by a discriminating audience. We can only say that Mr. Booth was most cordially received, and his personation of the gnarled character of Gloster commanded the free and encouraging applause of the house.... Beyond doubt he will achieve distinction as a dramatic artist.[156]

The *Baltimore American and Commercial Advertiser* offered a review:

The high expectations entertained by his friends and the public were more than satisfied in his masterly performance; in fact we can truly say we have seldom seen the character better performed, it being a chaste and even delineation throughout. His last scene and the combat were very effective, and could not be excelled.[157]

Booth's friend Samuel Knapp Chester was in the Holliday Street Theatre stock company. Edward L. Tilton, another member of the company, played leading roles opposite Booth.[158]

February 18, Tuesday Baltimore

Booth performed *Richard III*. The *Sun* was enthusiastic:

This young artist was favored with another large and discriminating audience ... and the repetition of Richard was received with the warmest demonstrations of cordial esteem. That he is in the career to eminent popularity is quite evident, and that he possesses the elements of true greatness in his profession we cannot doubt. Indeed, with allowance for the exuberance of youth, the energy of an apparently healthy and substantial *physique*, and the consequent *overworking* of some lineaments of character in Richard, the exhibition of great genius, originality and reserved power—that reserve which will chasten and endure with classic grace his maturer performances—is manifest and incontestable. The peculiarity of voice and tone constantly reminds us of his father, and there are frequent graces of expression which carry with them the assurance that the American stage has the acquisition of a good hope in this young man.[159]

Booth wrote to Joe Simonds:

Dear Joe, As usual, I begin with excuses forgive me for not writing sooner, but as you say better late than never. Opened here last night a big house in spite of rain snow & outside show shops. But I do not think my success here will be very great as one's native place is the last place in the world to look for such a thing.[160]

February 19, Wednesday Baltimore

Booth and Annie Graham[161] played *Romeo and Juliet*. During the play Booth struck his nose and delivered some of his lines with his back to the audience to hide the resulting nose bleed.[162] The *Sun* reported:

Mr. Booth's performance of Romeo ... afforded the utmost pleasure to the large audience present to enjoy it, although laboring under a severe cold. He looked and acted the devoted and jealous young lover of Shakespeare's creation with the happiest effect.[163]

The *American and Commercial Advertiser* observed that Booth had given "a fresh and vigorous performance, stamping him at once as an actor of no ordinary genius."[164]

The Holliday Street Theatre's advertisement in the *Sun* called Booth "unexcelled in the originality and delightful freshness of his style." The advertisement continued:

[Booth brings] rare evidence of genius, [and] a passionate earnestness and intense fervor which invests his personations with the charm of reality.... The voice of the people uttered nightly in thunders of heart-cheering applause, has declared his engagement a most brilliant and successful hit![165]

February 20, Thursday Baltimore

Booth played Fabien and Louis in *The Corsican Brothers*. The Holliday Street Theatre's advertisement boasted that its star was "sparkling with the fire of original genius and rendered fervid by the passionate earnestness of youth...."[166]

February 21, Friday Baltimore

Booth appeared as Pescara in *The Apostate* and as Romeo Jaffier Jenkins in *Too Much for Good Nature*. The *Sun* commented:

The passionate interview between Pescara and Florinda, with which the fourth act [of *The Apostate*] closes, was sustained with such power and such influence upon the audience that the house called for a complimentary appearance of Mr. Booth and Mrs. Farren before the curtain, and the demand was reiterated at the close of the piece.[167]

February 22, Saturday Baltimore

Booth closed the week with *Richard III*. The *Sun* reported:

Mr. Booth repeated his personation of Richard III ... to an audience thronging all parts of the house, and the satisfaction enjoyed was manifest in the intense interest and hearty applause bestowed upon the performance. That this young tragedian is destined to achieve great distinction, and, possibly, peculiar eminence in his profession, there cannot be a doubt.[168]

February 23, Sunday Baltimore

February 24, Monday Baltimore

Booth and Mary Ann Farren appeared in *Hamlet*. The *American and Commercial Advertiser* anticipated the performance:

Mr. Booth will appear [in *Hamlet*] ... and from what we have witnessed of his high histrionic abilities, we feel convinced that he will more than realize the sanguine expectations of his numerous friends and admirers. It is a character for which he is peculiarly adapted, as anyone who witnessed his masterly impersonation of Romeo will readily acknowledge. Mr. Booth has every reason to be gratified with his reception in his native city, for seldom have we seen more enthusiastic audiences.[169]

The *American and Commercial Advertiser* reviewed the performance:

We were most agreeably entertained ... in witnessing the admirable representation of this one of the most difficult of Shakespeare's characters, by the above highly gifted young tragedian. We can safely say that it has not been better rendered in this city for years, and Mr. Booth far exceeded the most sanguine expectations of his warmest admirers. From the commencement of the piece to the fall of the curtain he seemed to rivet the attention of the audience, who honored him by a call before the curtain at the end of the third act, and most cordially applauded his efforts.[170]

The *Sun* also offered a review:

The Hamlet of Mr. J. Wilkes Booth ... was a rare treat, and we apprehend a surprise to not a few of those who enjoyed it. It must not savor of disesteem to say that we scarcely expected so excellent a personation of this very subtle and arduous creation of Shakespearean genius, for it certainly could not be fairly demanded of an artist of Mr. Booth's years. It confirms the opinion we have heretofore expressed, therefore, that this young tragedian is to occupy a most distinguished rank on the American stage.[171]

February 25, Tuesday Baltimore

Booth gave a rare performance as *The Stranger*. The *Sun* commented: "The entertainment ... afforded the highest gratification, and the audience seemed to relish it with a zest."[172]

February 26, Wednesday Baltimore

Booth performed *Richard III*.

February 27, Thursday Baltimore

Booth played *Macbeth*. Richard Cary,[173] a friend of Edwin Booth, saw the performance and wrote that Wilkes was much too melodramatic, although in some respects he resembled Edwin

closely. Cary described Booth's face as "wooden." The performance reminded him of "a blood-and-thunder melo-drama full of sheet iron and burnt rosin and ghosts and other horrors."[174]

February 28, Friday Baltimore

Booth played *Hamlet*.

Mary Devlin Booth wrote to Edwin: "I must write a congratulatory letter to John—and in it say what I think of his kindness etc."[175]

March 1, Saturday Baltimore

Booth appeared as Pescara in *The Apostate*.

March 2, Sunday Baltimore

March 3, Monday Baltimore

Booth appeared as Phidias and Raphael in *The Marble Heart*. The *Sun* noted:

The week commences ... with *The Marble Heart*, in which the principal characters are duplicated, the first act appearing in a dream, representing Athens some twenty-five hundred years ago. Mr. Booth as the Sculptor and Miss Annie Graham as Aspasia. In the remaining acts of the play the scene is in modern Paris, and Mr. Booth appears as Raphael Duchatlet, and Miss Graham as Marco, of the marble heart.[176]

Asia and Rosalie Booth witnessed the play.[177]

March 4, Tuesday Baltimore

In a performance of *The Robbers*, Booth played Charles de Moor, a role in which, according to the *Sun*, the actor "has won a very flattering reputation."[178]

March 5, Wednesday Baltimore

Booth appeared as Phidias and Raphael in *The Marble Heart*. The *Sun* reported that the play "was received again ... with great enthusiasm, and its thrilling power was very manifest in several passages of the fourth and fifth acts. Mr. Booth's performance being highly effective."[179]

March 6, Thursday Baltimore

Booth played Romeo in *Romeo and Juliet*. The *Sun* remarked:

Mr. Booth was favored with a very fine audience ... and his performance of Romeo commanded the intelligent applause of the house. The character was effectively developed, and is well suited to the impulsive tone which distinguishes the genius of this young artist.[180]

March 7, Friday Baltimore

Booth appeared as Charles de Moor in *The Robbers*. The afterpiece was *The Merchant of Venice*. The *Sun* reported:

This evening he [Booth] receives a testimonial benefit from his numerous admirers, and the young men of the city, it is understood, will take the occasion to grace the house.... It is a well-deserved compliment to rising talent....[181]

March 8, Saturday Baltimore

Booth closed his engagement in Baltimore with *Richard III*. The *New York Clipper* noted:
Mr. Booth played the character in his usual good style.... In the tent scene on rushing from the couch to the footlights the sword which he wields wildly about broke, the blade ... flew over in the orchestra.... This interruption embarrassed Mr. Booth but he ... proceeded in a masterly manner.[182]

March 9, Sunday Baltimore

The Confederate ironclad *Merrimac* (re-christened the *Virginia)* destroyed Union ships in Hampton Roads, Virginia, but was forced to retire by the USS *Monitor.*

March 10, Monday Baltimore

Maggie Mitchell opened an engagement at the Front Street Theatre. Edwin Forrest[183] and John McCullough opened at the Holliday Street Theatre.[184]

March 11, Tuesday Baltimore

The Front Street Theatre held a complimentary benefit for George Kunkel. Booth, playing the title role, performed the last three acts of *Othello* to honor his former manager.[185]

March 15, Saturday New York

Booth was in New York rehearsing for his March 17 opening. He lodged at the St. Nicholas Hotel at Broadway and Spring Street.[186] The *New York Times* advertisement for Mary Provost's Theatre read: "Engagement and first New York appearance of the young American tragedian, J. Wilkes Booth, whose success in the great characters ... has elicited the wonder and admiration of large and enthusiastic audiences in all the principal cities of the United States will appear Monday."[187]

March 16, Sunday New York

March 17, Monday New York

Booth opened his engagement with *Richard III*. The *New York Herald* reported:
Mr. Booth undertook no small task when he attempted to act a character in which his father was famous, and which his brother Edwin plays so well, but the result justifies the undertaking.... His combat with *Richmond* was a masterpiece.

An audience packed and crammed beyond the usual limits ... applauded him to the echo. [Booth] is almost a facsimile of Edwin ... in the first three acts of the play.... But in the fourth and fifth acts, J. Wilkes Booth is more like his father than his brother.... In the last act he created a veritable sensation. His face blackened and smeared with blood, he seemed *Richard* himself.[188]

March 18, Tuesday New York

Booth again played *Richard III*.

March 19, Wednesday New York

Booth played Charles de Moor in *The Robbers*, described by *Wilkes' Spirit of the Times* as "a play bloody enough to satisfy the appetite of a cannibal."[189] Mary Ann Farren, E. L. Tilton, James Collier, and T. J. Ward played supporting roles. The *New York Evening Express* reported:
There was an overflowing house.... J. Wilkes Booth rendered a very brilliant impersonation of the character. He rendered the softer passages of the play with considerable pathos, and in almost every scene portrayed evidences of genius.... He was rewarded with several floral tributes.[190]

March 20, Thursday New York

Booth played Charles de Moor in *The Robbers*.

March 21, Friday New York

Booth performed *Richard III*. In the last act, according to the *New York Commercial Advertiser*, Booth "fenced so vigorously as to force Richmond into the orchestra over the footlights...."[191] A few days later, the *New York Tribune* described the incident: "In the final scene, Richard dashing at 'shallow Richmond,' went so deep into that peer as to knock him headlong into the orchestra.... Then Richard died, and the curtain went down, and Richmond was found to be hurt."[192]

The *Tribune* offered a review of the performance:
We think Mr. J. W. Booth has great natural gifts for the stage, and an amount of intellectual breadth in one so young that is most remarkable. We apprehend that he is all the better for not having grown into the boards, so to speak; for he is not amenable to the charge of pompous diction and laboriously unnatural sounds. He properly makes Richard III a rough brute, and appears to have mastered especially the rude laconism which Shakespeare puts in the tyrant's mouth; for he never drawls, but goes on quickly and conversationally always as regards time. The diction of the play is almost, every line, as fresh as if written yesterday, and to a player who understands the art of

making talk and action vital, offers supreme advantages as a tragedy.... Mr. J. W. Booth is a head and shoulders above those who ordinarily attempt Richard III, in intellectual breadth and power of concentration. If he would husband his voice a little more in the raving parts, we think the average would be improved.... He was called before the curtain by the generous applause of a full house.[193]

March 22, Saturday New York

Booth again played *Richard III*.

Booth wrote to Joe Simonds:

Dear Joe, Telegraphed you yesterday that Debar wont let me off, so if I come to Boston it must be for the two weeks commencing May 12th.... No news yet of Joe [Booth's brother] have hunted every place I can think of. I cant tell what to do poor Mother will take it so hard....[194]

Joseph Booth was traveling in England and Australia without informing his family of his whereabouts.

March 23, Sunday New York

March 24, Monday New York

Booth performed *Hamlet*. The *Herald* commented:

Mr. Booth's *Hamlet* is not so excellent and consistent a performance as his *Richard III* ... but it is very well read throughout, and has evidently been carefully studied. The melancholic, philosophical scenes were only good; but when the action was hurried and the passion intense, Mr. Booth was more like himself, and marvelously like his father.[195]

March 25, Tuesday New York

Booth appeared in *The Apostate*. *Wilkes' Spirit of the Times* noted that he played:

... that condensed epitome of villainy, Count Pescara.... There is a terrible earnestness in his eye, a waking of every nerve and fiber in his frame, that gives immense effect.... He seems to revel in rascality.... His Mephistophelian sneer ... and pity-murdering laugh, fairly curdle the blood, and haunt one like the specters of a dream.[196]

March 26, Wednesday New York

The *Times* advertised: "Last night but three, of the engagement of the young American tragedian, J. WILKES BOOTH, who will, by particular and general request for this night only, impersonate his great character of *RICHARD III*."[197]

March 27, Thursday New York

Booth played *Richard III*. *Wilkes' Spirit of the Times* commented:

His soliloquies are full of restlessness, gestures

and declamation.... This uneasiness ... gradually increases until, in the last act, it culminates in a whirlwind, in a tornado of rapid execution, hurrying the spectator along with resistless power to a climax unequaled in thrilling effect by any Richard that I have seen, not excepting the father himself.[198]

March 28, Friday New York

Booth, in his benefit, played *Macbeth*. *Wilkes' Spirit of the Times* remarked:

Mr. Booth finely portrays the irresolution of *Macbeth*.... The dagger scene was not great; Mr. B. lacks the delicacy of execution necessary to embody the emotions of supernatural fear. Further on he was better, and went through the murder scene exceedingly well.... In the banquet scene, he was forcible without ranting, a fact greatly in his favor....[199]

March 29, Saturday New York

Booth performed *Richard III*.

March 30, Sunday New York

The *New York Sunday Mercury* noted of Booth:

By his facile, nervous lineaments, soft, and almost womanish voice, and sensitive temperament, he is made to produce great effects, like Kean, by the magnetism of subtle gesture, and the electrical influence of strongly-defined expression of face.[200]

March 31, Monday New York

Booth's engagement was extended and he played *Richard III*.

April 1, Tuesday New York

Booth played *Richard III*.

April 2, Wednesday New York

Booth appeared as Shylock in *The Merchant of Venice*. The *Herald* reported: "He reads carefully and makes an occasional point well, but neither looks, conceives nor acts the character in a style to increase his reputation or satisfy his audience."[201]

April 3, Thursday New York

Booth performed *Richard III*.

April 4, Friday New York

Booth played Charles de Moor in *The Robbers*. *Wilkes' Spirit of the Times* noted: "The play is unfortunate in construction, inasmuch as the climax of acting is the fourth act, the last act being comparatively tame."[202]

April 5, Saturday New York

Booth played *Richard III* for the eleventh time in three weeks.

April 6, Sunday New York

April 7, Monday New York

The *Herald* noted that Booth "leaves town today to fulfill a long list of engagements in the Eastern and Western cities."[203]

Union forces triumphed at Shiloh, or Pittsburg Landing, Tennessee.

April 8, Tuesday New York

Booth presented a silver pocket flask to his friend, minstrel Dan Bryant. It was inscribed "J. Wilkes Booth to Dan Bryant April 8, 1862."[204] Booth also carried a cane presented to him by Dan's brother, Neil Bryant.[205]

Asia Booth Clarke noted in a letter that "John Wilkes is doing excellently in New York."[206]

April 9, Wednesday New York

April 10, Thursday New York

Booth retained a scrap of paper for several years bearing the notation "71 West 45th St., New York, 10 April '62, Thursday."[207]

April 11, Friday New York

April 13, Sunday Philadelphia

Booth, staying in Philadelphia, wrote to Joe Simonds:

No. 923 Chestnut St., Dear Joe, My success in New York continued fair. I will start in a few days for St Louis. Don't you pity me? no news yet from the runaway [Joe Booth]. Expect we shall get a letter in a few weeks, he is doubtless at sea.... Hope to see you in May as lively as ever, for you seem to be the only happy man I have ever met, hope it may last your life-time. God bless you Joe....[208]

April 16, Wednesday

Congress abolished slavery in the District of Columbia.

April 19, Saturday St. Louis

April 20, Sunday St. Louis

April 21, Monday St. Louis

Booth opened his engagement in St. Louis as Charles de Moor in *The Robbers*. Reviewing the performance, the *St. Louis Missouri Democrat* referred to Booth as "the greatest tragedian in the country" and noted that the star had "just concluded a successful engagement in New York City, and was acknowledged by the press and public ... as being equal to his father...."[209]

April 22, Tuesday St. Louis

Booth appeared in *Hamlet*. The *Democrat* remarked:

A full and fashionable house ... witness[ed] his superb performance of *Hamlet*. He is, undoubtedly, the best and most original tragedian now on the American stage; his style is entirely his own, never showing the least symptom of imitation....[210]

April 23, Wednesday St. Louis

Booth played *Macbeth*. The *Democrat* noted: "Mr. J. W. Booth attracted another full and fashionable house, and the performance went off most satisfactorily. This gentleman will prove the most successful star of the season; his performances nightly elicit the most enthusiastic applause."[211]

April 24, Thursday St. Louis

Booth played Pescara in *The Apostate*.

April 25, Friday St. Louis

Booth played *Richard III*. The *Democrat* anticipated the performance:

His rendition of Richard, Duke of Gloster, is pronounced by the press and public unsurpassed by any other living actor; his performance of the part being entirely original, introducing many new and startling effects. The fight with Richmond, in the last scene, has never been equaled by any of his predecessors.[212]

A Federal naval expedition captured New Orleans.

April 26, Saturday St. Louis

Booth appeared in *Richard III*. The *Democrat* explained:

Richard III is, by general desire, repeated to-night for the accommodation of those who were unable to procure seats last night, there being a perfect jam, consequently many were disappointed. Mr. J. W. Booth is now allowed by the press and public to be the only *Richard III* now on the stage. His conception of the part is entirely original, and a decided improvement on all his predecessors.[213]

April 27, Sunday St. Louis

April 28, Monday St. Louis

Booth played Phidias and Raphael in *The Marble Heart*. The *Democrat* anticipated the performance:

This drama has created the greatest excitement wherever it has been produced, the press and public pronouncing it without exception the most intensely interesting and thrilling drama in the language. The characters are strongly cast, and the piece will be well put on the stage, having been long in preparation.[214]

The review in the *Democrat* called this performance "the most decided success of the season" and commented that Booth's acting in the double role "was inimitable. It is by general desire to be repeated ... after which, although so great a success, it must be withdrawn, this being the last night but four of the engagement...."[215]

April 29, Tuesday St. Louis

Booth again played Phidias and Raphael in *The Marble Heart*.

April 30, Wednesday St. Louis

Booth played Shylock in *The Merchant of Venice*.

May 1, Thursday St. Louis

Booth performed *Richard III*. The *Democrat* reported that "To-morrow [Booth] takes his farewell benefit, when he will appear, for the first time in this city, in his renowned character of Romeo.... We understand that a large party of citizens, at whose solicitation this magnificent tragedy is produced, have determined on visiting the theatre on this occasion."[216]

May 2, Friday St. Louis

Booth appeared in *Romeo and Juliet* in his benefit. "The part of Romeo is said to be one of his best representations," remarked the *Democrat*. "We expect to see a crowded house."[217]

May 3, Saturday St. Louis

The *Democrat* announced that "'The Marble Heart,' which proved one of the greatest hits of the season, will, by general desire, be repeated, for positively the last time, to-night, this being the last night of the engagement of Mr. Booth. His acting of the two characters, Phidias and Raphael, in this beautiful drama, is a most artistic performance."[218]

Booth wrote in his copy of *The Marble Heart*, "J. Wilkes Booth St. Louis Theatre, Southern Confederacy May 3 1862."[219]

May 4, Sunday En route to Boston

May 5, Monday En route to Boston

May 6, Tuesday Boston

May 7, Wednesday Boston

May 8, Thursday Boston

May 9, Friday Boston

May 10, Saturday Boston

A man who met Booth on this day was "deeply impressed with his modest bearing and his winning manner.... [Booth] said he felt timid

about appearing before a Boston audience in that character [*Richard*], which had been made famous both by his father and his brother Edwin, and besides he knew that Boston audiences were coldly critical anyway. Still he believed that he could bring out whatever power that was in him...."[220]

May 11, Sunday Boston

May 12, Monday Boston

Booth opened his engagement at the Boston Museum with *Richard III*. The *Boston Daily Evening Transcript* offered a review:

The house was crowded to its utmost capacity by the intelligent, brilliant and sympathetic audience, and he was called twice before the curtain to receive the reward of his exertions in hearty plaudits. His personation was in many respects original, and showed a close study and vivid conception of the individuality of the character. The physical and moral deformity of Richard, and the connection between the two, were closely represented, and the basis of all his wit and intellect in scorn and malignity, was clearly indicated. Richard's jests are more terrible than other men's imprecations, and the essential wickedness which penetrates his whole character, and speech was never lost sight of by Booth for the purpose of making points. Wilkes Booth reminds us of his father in many respects, though he does not imitate him. There are strong indications of genius in his acting, and he is perhaps the most promising young actor on the American stage.[221]

Another observer wrote: "[W]hile the performance was crude in some respects, there were flashes of positive genius that, I was told by those who had seen his father, brought back strikingly memories of that greatest of *Richards*."[222]

After the performance, Booth and William H. Whalley, who played the role of Richmond, had a drink together.[223]

May 13, Tuesday Boston

Booth appeared in *Romeo and Juliet* at the Boston Museum, where his friend Edwin F. Keach was the stage manager.[224] The *Transcript* noted:

From what we have thus far seen of Mr. J. Wilkes Booth, we have no hesitation in declaring him the most promising actor at present upon the American stage. His efforts of Monday and Tuesday evenings were witnessed by extremely fashionable audiences, filling every part of the Museum, and were applauded with a warmth worthy of note. The standard which expectation fixed was a high one, for here it was that the elder Booth was greatly admired, and here it is that the handsome

Edwin Booth has a host of friends, who consider him without a peer, and under those circumstances the success achieved was very flattering.[225]

May 14, Wednesday Boston

Booth played Charles de Moor in *The Robbers*. The *Transcript* described the performance as "a brilliant success," noting that Booth "was thrice called before the curtain by the enthusiastic plaudits of a very large audience.... It is gratifying to record the triumph of one so worthy in every respect of wearing his lamented father's mantle."[226]

May 15, Thursday Boston

Booth played *Richard III*. The *Boston Journal* reported: "Mr. J. Wilkes Booth is creating quite a sensation among theatre-goers. The public verdict is nearly unanimous in favor of the young actor, and the general impression seems to be that he has more traits of the father in him than Edwin, more vivacity and other qualities that greatly interest the spectator."[227]

May 16, Friday Boston

Booth played *Hamlet*. The *Transcript* noted: Mr. J. Wilkes Booth has been rapidly gaining in popular favor during the past week, and it may in truth be said that even his gifted brother Edwin did not win admiration so steadily early in his theatrical career as he has. His shortcoming results from his limited experience on the stage, but he has talents which, if properly cultivated, cannot fail to make him a star performer of the first rank.[228]

May 17, Saturday Boston

Booth appeared in a matinee performance of *Romeo and Juliet*. Mrs. Julia Bennett Barrow, soon to appear with Booth, was playing at the Boston Academy of Music.[229]

May 18, Sunday Boston

May 19, Monday Boston

Booth played Pescara in *The Apostate*. A farce titled *Off to the War* followed.

May 20, Tuesday Boston

Booth appeared in the title role in *The Stranger*.

May 21, Wednesday Boston

Booth appeared as Charles de Moor in *The Robbers* and as Romeo Jaffier Jenkins in *Too Much for Good Nature*. The Boston Museum playbill carried the message: "This Young Artist's histrionic efforts [have] never been equaled by any star at the Museum."[230]

May 22, Thursday Boston

Booth played Claude Melnotte in *The Lady of Lyons*.

May 23, Friday Boston

Booth played *Richard III* with William Whalley as Richmond. The *Transcript* remarked: MR. BOOTH. The engagement of this gifted and promising young actor will close this week. He plays *Richard III* tonight, on occasion of his benefit. He will be greeted by an audience limited only by the capacity of the Museum. Mr. Booth has won many friends during his brief stay in Boston, who will watch with interest his progress in his profession. He has all the elements of success....[231]

May 24, Saturday Boston

Booth closed his engagement with a performance as Claude Melnotte in *The Lady of Lyons*.

May 29, Thursday En Route to Chicago

May 30, Friday En Route to Chicago

May 31, Saturday Chicago

The *Chicago Evening Journal* carried the advertisement: "Monday, the great tragedian, J. WILKES BOOTH."[232]

Mary Ann Booth wrote to Edwin in England: "He [John Wilkes Booth] wrote to me he had arrived there [Chicago] safe but very tired after 51 hours of traveling in cars from Boston."[233]

June 1, Sunday Chicago

The *Chicago Tribune* commented: J. Wilkes Booth commences an engagement at the Theatre on Monday evening appearing as *Richard III*. No other of the present day has advanced so far in public favor as the younger Booth. Since his last engagement in this city he has appeared in New York, Boston and Baltimore, where he has been fairly and justly criticized and come off the acknowledged master of the characters he assumes.[234]

June 2, Monday Chicago

Booth opened his engagement at McVicker's Theatre with *Richard III*. The *Tribune* noted that the theatre was "a crowded house, and to say the audience was delighted is but faint praise. [Booth] was thrice called before the curtain to receive their admiration of his excellent acting."[235] The *Journal* opined that "Booth's Richard is the best and most terrific on the American stage."[236]

June 3, Tuesday Chicago

Booth played Pescara in *The Apostate*. The *Journal* reported:

Another large house awaited Mr. Booth.... Unquestionably his great character is Pescara, the wily, intriguing, vengeful Spaniard. The audience was sensibly pleased throughout, and departed with a keener appreciation of the young tragedian's abilities.[237]

June 4, Wednesday Chicago

Booth played Shylock in *The Merchant of Venice*, drawing another full house. The *Tribune* remarked that "since the death of the elder Kean and Booth, [Shylock] has found few representatives on the American stage. Judging from what we have seen of J. Wilkes Booth's strong facial powers and dramatic tact, we know not why he should not appear to advantage."[238]

June 5, Thursday Chicago

Booth played Claude Melnotte in *The Lady of Lyons*.

June 6, Friday Chicago

Booth chose *Richard III* for his benefit. The afterpiece was *Who Speaks First*.

June 7, Saturday Chicago

The *Tribune* advertised: "Mr. Booth appears for the second time, this evening, as Pescara, in the tragedy of *The Apostate*, the simple announcement of which will fill the theatre."[239]

June 8, Sunday Chicago

June 9, Monday Chicago

Booth played *Hamlet*. The *Tribune* critic commented, "Booth will be as good a *Hamlet* as ever walked the stage."[240] Comments of the *Journal* critic indicate conditions in McVicker's Theatre:

It is great pity that something is not done to remedy a serious defect—a nuisance, in fact.... Something should be put under the carpets, or some means adopted to break the noise of boots upon the stairs in the lobby and down the aisles.[241]

June 10, Tuesday Chicago

Booth played *Hamlet*.

June 11, Wednesday Chicago

Booth appeared in *Romeo and Juliet*.

June 12, Thursday Chicago

Booth played Pescara in *The Apostate*.[242]

The local newspapers reported that many people had stayed up to observe a lunar eclipse.

June 13, Friday Chicago

Booth played Phidias and Raphael in *The Marble Heart*, of which the *Journal* critic had written earlier in the week:

This play, for some reason, has been given up to female stars for the rendition of the character of *Marco*; but most evidently the author intended Raphael for the chief feature of the piece—and Mr. Booth certainly thinks so, and has added it to his repertoire, and the Eastern critics have bestowed high praise upon his performance....[243]

June 14, Saturday Chicago

Booth played *Richard III*.

June 15, Sunday Chicago

June 16, Monday Chicago

Booth played *Macbeth*. The *Tribune* critic anticipated the performance:

... those who remember [Booth's] personation of this character when here last winter, will be sure to be present.... His delineation of *Macbeth* is one of his most powerful efforts, in which his impulsive style of acting shows to great advantage, culminating, as it does, with a combat fully equal to that fought in *Richard III*.[244]

June 17, Tuesday Chicago

Booth played the title role in *Othello*.[245] The *Journal* advertisement claimed that 15,000 people had attended the theatre during Booth's engagement.

June 18, Wednesday Chicago

Booth played Phidias and Raphael in *The Marble Heart*.

June 19, Thursday Chicago

Booth starred in *Richard III*. The afterpiece was *The Obstinate Family*.

President Lincoln signed a measure prohibiting slavery in territories of the United States.

June 20, Friday Chicago

Booth appeared as Charles de Moor in *The Robbers* in his farewell benefit.

A petition appeared in the *Tribune* requesting Booth to perform *The Lady of Lyons*.

June 21, Saturday Chicago

Booth closed his engagement with a portrayal of Claude Melnotte in *The Lady of Lyons*. The *Tribune* reported:

Booth's Farewell. This evening is the last opportunity for those who have not yet witnessed the admirable acting of J. Wilkes Booth, who for three weeks has been the rage in theatrical circles. Those who have seen him should not fail to be present, as by general request of the audiences, he is to appear ... in Bulwer's play of *The Lady of*

Lyons. No actor has ever gained a firmer hold upon a Chicago audience.[246]

June 22, Sunday Chicago

The *Louisville Daily Democrat* remarked: "J. Wilkes Booth, the great tragedian, will appear tomorrow night. Of course, the house will be full." The theatre's advertisement for Monday's performance of *Richard III* boasted that its star was "the greatest tragedian of the day, Mr. J. Wilkes Booth."[247]

June 23, Monday. Chicago?

The *Louisville Daily Journal* noted that "[a]n indisposition will prevent Mr. Wilkes Booth from appearing for a few nights."[248]

June 24, Tuesday Louisville

The *Journal* "expected [Booth] to be well enough to arrive here today."[249]

June 25, Wednesday Louisville

Booth finally opened with *Richard III* at the Louisville Theatre. The *Democrat* noted:
J. Wilkes Booth, the eminent tragedian, was greeted ... with a large and delighted audience. We were pleased to see so many ladies present.... He has greatly improved since we last saw him, and his *Richard III* was indeed a success.[250]

June 26, Thursday Louisville

Booth played *Hamlet*. The *Democrat* reported that "[a] fine audience greeted Mr. Booth."[251]

June 27, Friday Louisville

Booth appeared as Charles de Moor in *The Robbers*. The *Journal* observed:
When commenting upon Wilkes Booth's "moral electricity" in commanding the attention of his audiences, the types made us say "elasticity." He certainly has physical elasticity, but he can only impart that to his hearers by converting them into an applauding army. He has great intensity of style, and that enabled him to make even Charles DeMoor sparkle....[252]

June 28, Saturday Louisville

Booth performed *Richard III*. The *Journal* anticipated that "the 'electricity' of his genius will be seen, and every flash will strike to the hearts of his listeners.... We regard the last two acts of this tragedy, as he performs them, to have never been excelled on the American stage."[253]

The *Democrat* reviewed the performance: There was a fine audience at the theatre last night, notwithstanding the inclemency of the weather. Mr. Booth's personation of Richard was indeed fine—the closing scene was perfection itself. He has kindly consented to appear on Monday evening, which will positively be his last appearance.[254]

June 29, Sunday Louisville

June 30, Monday Louisville

Booth played Shylock in *The Merchant of Venice*. The *Journal* reported:
Mr. Booth closes his engagement this evening, as the arduous labors of the past season require that he should take rest during the summer. On Saturday evening his *Richard* was witnessed by a large and discriminating audience, and the universal verdict was that it was the best sustained personation of the character ever witnessed in our city.[255]

July 1, Tuesday Louisville

July 2, Wednesday

The Battle of the Seven Days near Richmond culminated in the retreat of the Army of the Potomac.

July 11, Friday

An item in the *Vicksburg Daily Whig* for this date stated: "John Booth will leave for Richmond on Friday next, and will take letters for any of the Vicksburg companies in the Richmond army if left at the office of the Provost Marshal." It is unlikely that this man was John Wilkes Booth.[256]

July 15, Tuesday En Route to Chicago

Joseph Booth sailed from Gravesend, England, on or about this date for Australia. His intention in traveling abroad may have been to avoid the Union draft.[257]

6

Success: 1862–1863

John Wilkes Booth lost no time making arrangements for the 1862-1863 theatrical season. In July 1862 he accepted a four-week engagement in Boston for the following January. By August 3 he was booked through March. Booth was in New York early in October to arrange additional engagements. The *New York Tribune* carried a rumor that Edwin and John would appear together "on some special occasion."[1]

Booth opened the season late in October with a two-day engagement in Lexington, Kentucky. A full two-week engagement followed in Louisville, where his appearances attracted large crowds. Louisville playwright George F. Fuller wrote a special introductory scene for Booth to perform in *The Marble Heart; or, The Sculptor's Dream*, a play that soon became a favorite of Booth's audiences. During this engagement Booth reportedly had an argument with the Confederate-sympathizing treasurer of the Louisville Theatre; despite describing himself as a Southerner who liked the people of the South, Booth asserted that the departed states had "no right or occasion to secede, that they had it all their own way in Congress...."[2] If Booth's comment was accurately reported, it marks an odd departure from the pro–Confederate sentiments he generally expressed once the war was underway.

The *Cincinnati Enquirer* announced Booth's November 10 opening at the National Theatre in that city:

J. Wilkes Booth will open in his great character of *Richard III*. Mr. Booth is winning golden opinions wherever he appears, and his name is sure to draw the elite of the city that he favors with his presence. He most happily possesses many of the rare attributes of the elder, without any of his defects.[3]

The *Enquirer* critic thought Booth was "one of the most promising actors of the age" on November 23, but two days later he was less enthusiastic when he concluded that Booth was better qualified to be a leading man in a stock company rather than a touring star.[4] Now that Booth had gained some experience, the critics held him to a higher standard. To make matters worse, attendance at the National Theatre during Booth's engagement was light.

A Cincinnati newspaperman had observed Booth closely and several years later wrote:

He added to his native genius, the advantage of a voice musically full and rich; a face almost classic in outline; features highly intellectual; a piercing black eye, capable of expressing the fiercest and the tenderest passion and emotion, and a commanding figure and impressive stage address. In his transitions from the quiet and reflective passages of a part to fierce and violent outbreaks of passion, his sudden and impetuous manner had in it something of that electrical force and power which made the elder Booth so celebrated, and called up afresh to the memory of men of the last generation the presence, voice and manner of his father. Convivial in his habits, sprightly and genial in his conversation, John Wilkes made many acquaintances and friends among the young men of his own age in the city—an acquaintance that was renewed during two subsequent engagements.

Our recollection of Booth is somewhat indistinct, but, we remember, his features in repose had rather a somber and melancholy cast; yet, under agreeable influences or emotions the expression was very animated and glowing. His hair, jet black and glossy, curled slightly, and set off in fine relief a high intellectual forehead, and a face full of intelligence. Both chin and nose were markedly prominent, and the firm-set lips, and lines about the mouth, indicated firmness of will, decision and resolution. He was scrupulously neat in his dress, and selected his habit with a rare perception of what was becoming to his figure and complexion. He would pass any where, for a neatly, and not overly, dressed man of fashion.[5]

One night in Cincinnati, after a performance of *Money*, a group of young men known as the Peep O'Day Club presented Booth with a pair of splendid swords. "The presentation speech was made by Captain Wilson, U.S.A. and happily responded to by Mr. Booth," the *Cincinnati Enquirer* reported. "Champagne, supper, &c., closed the scene."[6] Lewis Wilson had served as Chief of Police in Cincinnati before the war. He had been severely injured in battle and, in November 1862, was on recruiting duty. Booth's thoughts upon receiving the gift from Wilson are unrecorded.

Booth next appeared at the 1,500-seat Metropolitan Theatre in Indianapolis. He received a negative review from the *Indianapolis Daily Journal*:

His *Othello* was ... a failure.... Mr. Booth, with his thin figure, husky voice, indistinct articulation, exaggerated action, and constant straining to get up to that strength of passion which makes a strong man seem stronger ... was just enough unlike the bold, open and dignified warrior to make one laugh.... There is not enough of him for *Othello*. Riley so far overshadowed Booth that Iago was the hero of the piece.... We don't admire Mr. Booth,

and by what art he became a "star" is more than our astronomy can explain.[7]

Booth went on to McVicker's Theatre in Chicago. After his opening performance in *The Lady of Lyons*, the *Chicago Times* critic placed him in the "first rank among the generation of coming actors." Opinions varied regarding Booth's robust acting style, though, and the critic went on to say that Booth would benefit from a less frenetic approach:

For a young actor, he displays a wonderful adaptation to the profession.... There might have been a shade more of moderation—of gentle toning down, in his action, at times, but as a whole he was very near the true impersonation....[8]

Booth's rendition of *The Merchant of Venice* the next day satisfied the *Times* critic:

It requires an actor of strong delineative power to render it in its true sense. To that class Mr. Booth belongs. His personation was strongly marked, and truthful to the meaning of the author in every part. He showed his power in the first act, when denouncing Antonio's scornful treatment.[9]

Early the next week the same newspaper was much more critical, calling Booth's performance of *The Apostate*:

...a severe dose of Rant. A succession of uproarious dialogues, shouted in thundering tones at the audience, at the ceiling, at the scenery, and at everything else in view, led its plot to its gradual development, and put the audience into nervous tantrums.... Mr. Booth was sufficiently athletic and active to suit the most ardent admirer of the slam-bang style. Occasionally he tempered down to a concentrated and really thrilling exhibition of passion, and in the scene between himself and Florinda, previous to the forced marriage, he was quite effective; throwing aside, as he did, the uproarious method, and rather acting than speaking his passion....[10]

The *Chicago Evening Journal* critic disagreed so thoroughly with this assessment that he attacked the judgment and the past of the *Times* critic:

...he has insulted the very large and intelligent audiences which have witnessed Mr. Booth's admirable acting night after night, by declaring that it is his name alone which draws them, as though a Chicago audience could be so imposed upon more than once. It is an insult to the intelligence and good taste of theatre-goers, and the would-be smart, but really unsophisticated, critic is but rendering himself ridiculous, and a laughing-stock for everybody. It is very evident that this poor critic's recent prison-life has soured his disposition and made his soul as cold as the stone walls that so recently encompassed him.[11]

On December 11 the audience was grateful when two intoxicated patrons were evicted from the theatre during the first scene of *The Stranger*.[12]

Booth closed his Chicago engagement with *Richard III*. The *Journal* noted:

During the entire season McVicker's theatre has been patronized in an unprecedented manner. Money has poured into the box office like rain. And what have those large audiences had in return during the run of five months? Couldock, Coombs, Mitchell, Proctor, Booth. All very good, but not particularly expensive or—well, no matter.[13]

Booth generally attracted large audiences, and he made a considerable amount of money. He sent $800 to his mother in November. He made $900 in his first week in Chicago. He had received, through December, an average of $650 a week for the season.[14]

Booth played a two-week engagement in St. Louis starting late in December. He was supported by Thomas L. Conner, "one of the handsomest and most dashing stock stars of his day." Conner played Richmond to Booth's Richard. Both men were athletes and loved to perform their two-handed broadsword fight. The men appeared to forget themselves during the combat. Often the members of the audience rose and cheered one, then the other, as they fought each other off the stage. In fact, the wild abandon was well-rehearsed, with each actor counting the blows in order

to prevent injury. The stage duels of these men were said to be the best of their generation.[15]

In January Booth returned to Indianapolis for a week. The *Indianapolis Daily Journal* critic praised Booth's portrayal of Hamlet but again criticized his Othello. The *Indianapolis Daily Sentinel*, enamored of Booth, attacked the *Journal* critic's judgment.

Joseph Howard, Jr., a prominent journalist, later expressed a very high opinion of Booth's youthful Hamlet:

I never hesitated to say what I thought of John Wilkes Booth, who had more brains to the square inch in his superbly fashioned head than all the other Booths rolled into one and multiplied by 105. Gifted with unusual personal beauty, supple and graceful in form, dignified and attractive in bearing, essentially dextrous in the use of the sword, with a dare devil in his nature ... he carried with rare brain force a subtle intuition of Shakespearian character which made him an ideal Hamlet, needing only the calming culture of years and the improving toning down of experience to make him absolutely a Shakespearian Hamlet.[16]

Indianapolis was a convenient stop for Booth on his way to Boston for a long, four-week appearance. In mid–January Booth opened in Boston, where Edwin had recently completed a brilliant engagement at the Boston Museum. The *Boston Advertiser* critic wrote:

Mr. J. Wilkes Booth has made improvement in his art; not all that we could wish, nor in many particulars wherein he ought, but still progress is plain. We like as little as ever the occasional slovenliness of his elocution which mars many a passage of the quieter sort....[17]

The theatre was filled for most of Booth's performances. Tickets were sold in advance, an unusual practice for the Boston Museum, to accommodate the demand.[18] Press comments were generally positive. The *Advertiser* critic approved of Booth's energetic acting style:

The great breadth of line and the depth of color with which, when fully aroused, he [Booth] is inclined to portray character, sometimes gives an effect to his tragedy which approaches exaggeration, but they are just what a role of such high Romanticism demands, and their power gives to it a prominence which under less favorable circumstances it could not obtain....[19]

A few days later, the *Advertiser* critic wrote:

The interest manifested when he first came has grown into quite a furor, and the Museum is densely packed every night with contented-looking people ... indeed, the correspondent of the *New York Programme* says that "the carpenter of the establishment has it in contemplation to put a row of hooks and pegs around the lobby and gallery, for the late-comers to hang from."[20]

The *Boston Daily Evening Transcript* was no less enthusiastic:

The engagement of John Wilkes Booth ... might be continued with profit to the management for a month to come at least.... *The Marble Heart* has created a profound sensation, and excited a degree of enthusiasm rarely exhibited by our theatre-goers.[21]

This engagement will long be remembered as having been one of the most successful ever fulfilled by an actor at this place of amusement.[22]

Wilkes' Spirit of the Times (New York) reported that Booth's Boston Museum engagement had been "exceedingly profitable to the management and himself; he has achieved a high artistic reputation."[23] Kate Reignolds[24] appeared with Booth during this engagement and later wrote:

The stage door was always blocked with silly women waiting to catch a glimpse, as he passed, of his superb face and figure. He was ever spoiled and petted, and left to his unrestrained will. He succeeded in gaining position by flashes of genius, and the necessity of ordinary study had not been borne in upon him.[25]

Orlando Tompkins and his family were great friends of the Booths and entertained Edwin and John whenever they visited Boston. Tompkins's mother observed that Edwin "was very quiet and averse to meeting company, while John was full of life and an immediate favorite with all whom he met." Younger brother Eugene Tompkins at the age of twelve would go to Booth's room before he was out of bed to have pillow fights.[26]

John Wilkes Booth visited Edwin's wife, Mary Devlin Booth, on February 16. Mary, living in Dorchester, near Boston, while Edwin performed in New York, had become chilled while waiting for a horse-car. Upon arriving home she felt ill and went to bed. Her condition steadily worsening, she had John take a letter to Edwin in New York.[27] John reached his brother on the 17th and informed him that Mary was ill with a feverish cold.[28] Mary's note asked Edwin not to break his engagement to come to attend her.[29] Edwin had been drinking heavily, and his performances had been affected adversely. A friend wrote to Mary, "Sick or well, you must come [to New York]. Mr. Booth has lost all restraint and hold on himself. Last night there was the grave question of ringing down the curtain before the performance was half over. Lose no time. Come." Mary responded, "I cannot come. I cannot stand. I think sometimes that only a great calamity can save my dear husband. I am going to try and write to him now, and God give me grace to write as a true wife should."[30] On Friday, February 20, Edwin reeled through a performance of *Richard III* in New York.[31] Mary died the next morning at 8:15.[32]

John delayed an engagement at the Arch Street Theatre in Philadelphia to attend Mary's funeral. The theatre's advertisement noted that Booth "has felt the necessity imperative upon him to join his afflicted brother...."[33] Edwin Adams, an acquaintance of Booth since their days in Richmond, was hired to fill his time at the Arch Street Theatre. On Monday, February 23, "Mrs. Booth, Edwin's mother, arrived [in Boston], from Philadelphia ... and later in the day his brother J. Wilkes Booth, and his brother-in-law, Clarke," the *Philadelphia Evening Bulletin* reported.[34] The next day three carriages transported Edwin, John, Asia, their mother, and John Sleeper Clarke from Edwin's Dorchester home to Mount Auburn Cemetery in Cambridge for the funeral service. Abolitionist Julia Ward Howe, who had published her *Battle Hymn of the Republic* the previous year, attended the funeral and wrote that Edwin followed the casket and "beside or behind him walked a young man [John] of remarkable beauty."[35]

Booth finally opened his Philadelphia engagement on March 2. "We welcome Mr. Booth to our stage as a rising man and as the possessor of a name we cannot regard without interest. He has our best wishes for his success," the *Philadelphia Press* remarked.[36] Booth was reunited with old friends John Albaugh and John McCullough during this engagement, and he also appeared on stage with Louisa Lane Drew.[37] She had played *Hamlet* with Junius Brutus Booth many years before. On that occasion Junius had failed to appear for the fifth act; he was finally located on the rafters above the stage when he started crowing like a rooster. He then continued the performance.[38]

During the first week of Booth's engagement, the *Press* critic wrote:

> We have seen enough to justify us in saying that he is a good actor, and may become a great one…. Mr. Booth has far more action, more life, and, we are inclined to think, more natural genius [than Edwin]…. We think he has a wrong conception of the character of the Duke of Gloster. He makes him a slinking, malignant cripple…. It is, perhaps, unfortunate that he [Booth] has become so soon a star; but it shows ambition if not judgment, and he will find the buffs and tumbles of the young tragedian's life a fine field for experience and instruction.[39]

At the beginning of Booth's second week, the *Philadelphia Evening Bulletin* stated:

Critics are dividing as to the great acting ability of Mr. Booth; but all admit him to be the possessor of genius of a high order. The company supports him charmingly….[40]

The *Press* noted:

> Mr. Booth has genius for his profession, but it needs the development of arduous study, if he would reach that eminence which his talented father attained. Possessed of a good figure, an expressive eye, well-marked features, and much nervous power, there is no reason why he should not become a great actor. His voice, inclined to huskiness, which causes an imperfect enunciation, might be much improved and strengthened.[41]

Of Booth's next engagement, in Baltimore, the *American and Commercial Advertiser* was unrestrained:

> The youth, the unmistakable genius, and the personal advantages of the accomplished artist [Booth], coupled with the fact that he is by birth and sympathy identified with the pride and the fame of our city, have invested his efforts with a fervor and speciality of popular regard which no other artist has succeeded in attracting within our recollection.[42]

Booth's mind was on more than acting. He wrote to his friend Joe Simonds inquiring about land in Boston, "Did you or Orlando [Tompkins] send me that catalogue of Back Bay lands to be sold April 9th[?]"[43] He was interested in buying property in the Back Bay, where tidal flats had been filled in. A week later Booth, through the bid submitted for him by Simonds, was successful in buying the land [now 115 Commonwealth Avenue]. One quarter of the purchase price of $8,192.10 was due in fourteen days, with three subsequent semi-annual payments. The recorded owner of the land was not John, but his mother.[44]

In April Booth appeared for the first time in Washington, D.C. "He played not from the stage rule, but from the soul, and his soul is inspired with genius," the *Washington National Intelligencer* commented after his opening performance at Grover's Theatre.[45]

The *Washington Morning Chronicle* noted:

This wonderful young actor [Booth] appeared on Saturday evening to one of the largest, and certainly the most enthusiastic audience of the season. The play of *Richard*, with respect to the principal character has never, to our recollection, been better done.[46]

Several days later the *Chronicle* considered Booth to have gained a "lasting friendship" with the public.[47]

The British actor Charles Wyndham appeared with Booth during this engagement and later described him:

A marvelous man. He was one of the few to whom that ill-used term of genius might be applied with perfect truth. He was a genius and a most unfortunate one. His dramatic powers were of the best. They were untutored, untrained. He lacked the quality of the student that Edwin possessed, but the artist was there.

Seldom has the stage seen a more impressive, or a more handsome, or a more impassioned actor. Picture to yourself Adonis, with high forehead, ascetic face corrected by rather full lips, sweeping black hair, a figure of perfect youthful proportions and the most wonderful black eyes in the world. Such was John Wilkes Booth.

At all times his eyes were his most striking features, but when his emotions were aroused they were like jewels. Flames shot from them. His one physical defect was his height (for certain heroic characters) ... but he made up for the lack by his extraordinary presence and magnetism.

The courtesy and kindliness shown to me by John Wilkes made way for friendship between us, and we frequently were together after the play. He was a most charming fellow, off the stage as well as on, a man of flashing wit and magnetic manner. He was one of the best raconteurs to whom I have ever listened. As he talked he threw himself into his words, brilliant, ready, enthusiastic. He could hold a group spellbound by the hour at the force and fire and beauty of him. He was unusually fluent. And yet throughout the spell he wove upon his listeners there were startling breaks, abrupt contrasts, when his eccentricity and peculiarity cropped to the surface.

He was the idol of women. They would rave of him, his voice, his hair, his eyes. Small wonder, for he was fascinating.[48]

Booth met young David Herold in Washington in the spring of 1863. Herold, despite having studied pharmacy from October 1855 to April 1858 at Georgetown College, was regarded by many as immature and trifling. Booth once told his sister Asia he smuggled quinine to the South; if he engaged in such activity, he may have enlisted Herold in the smuggling operation.[49] Herold said he first encountered Booth when "Booth had a ball taken from his neck by some surgeon in Washington," and that he "met Mr. Booth, off and on, sometimes once a week, or maybe two or three times. We would always stand and have a chat."[50]

On April 13 Booth, accompanied by his former theatre manager Matthew Canning, consulted Dr. John Frederick May about a large lump on his neck. The doctor recommended removal of the fibroid tumor at a later time when an assistant was available. Booth insisted on an immediate operation with Canning being the assistant.[51] When the bloody procedure was complete, Booth asked the doctor to say he removed a bullet if anyone inquired.[52] A few days later Booth wrote to Simonds: "have a hole in my neck you could run your fist in. The doctor had a hunt for my bullet."[53] One may only speculate why Booth would tell Herold and Simonds the operation was for the removal of a bullet rather than a tumor. Lies such as this make it difficult to trust Booth's statements in other matters.

Several days after the operation, Booth's neck wound was reopened during a performance when an actress embraced him. This accident caused a large scar to form and allowed Dr. May to positively identify Booth's body after his death.[54] The *Washington National Republican* referred to the surgery when it noted:

Mr. Booth is a young man of rare abilities, and, considering his experience, really wonderful in his impersonations. His representations, notwithstanding the severe surgical operation of Monday evening last, entitle him to the admiration of the public.[55]

Booth became a manager on April 27 when he leased the Washington Theatre for two weeks. He performed for ten nights, supported by his old friend Samuel Knapp Chester, among others, and sublet the theatre to an opera troupe for two nights. The audiences and Booth's profits were reduced when the Battle of Chancellorsville was fought near Washington. The local newspapers were supportive. The *National Intelligencer* remarked:

> From the encomiums of the press throughout the country bestowed on Mr. Booth we are induced to believe he stands without a rival. Mr. Booth's acting in the fifth act of *Richard* is truly great, while the last scene of the fifth act is terrible. In his battle scenes he is far ahead of any actor now living.[56]

Ford's Athenaeum on Tenth Street had burned on December 30, 1862.[57] While Booth was in Washington, a shortage of bricks briefly halted the reconstruction. Late in April the *National Intelligencer* reported that a "large force of artisans are now engaged in this city and Baltimore in preparing the wood work and ornaments for the interior of the theatre."[58]

Booth returned to Chicago at the end of May. The *Chicago Times* critic was unimpressed:

> Mr. Booth does not abound in power under any circumstances, but he sometimes displays an emotional capacity which wins him a fair share of commendation.... It was hardly necessary ... to go on the rampage and endanger the scenery at the close of the third act [of *The Marble Heart*].[59]

His opinion had not improved several days later:

> He [Booth] has played his usual round of characters during the present visit; some he has played well, some indifferently and some badly. Balancing the whole, he impressed us with a sense of mediocrity.... As a stock actor

he would win a high position, but as a star he is somewhat below the median standard.[60]

The critic objected to Booth's "ranting":

> He fails to appreciate the essential fact that intensity of emotion is not in any sense expressed by fuming rant, and that passion is displayed with the least effect when the actor loses control of himself.... If the audience did not get their money's worth it was not because lungs and muscle failed to do its work.[61]

The *Chicago Tribune* adverted to Booth's shortcomings and attributed them to his inexperience:

> Since his advent in Chicago, some eighteen months ago, no one who has attended his performances, can fail to see an improvement, and we predict ere he has attained his thirtieth year, he will be as great in his delineations as his honored predecessor.[62]

Booth had an idle week and then played two weeks in St. Louis. The day before the engagement opened, authorities in St. Louis apprehended Booth's actor friend Thomas L. Conner for "utterances against the Lincoln administration." Conner was imprisoned for several days until he took the oath of allegiance. Booth was also arrested, according to the later recollection of Lieutenant Colonel Henry L. McConnell, provost marshal of the Department of Missouri, for saying he "wished the whole damned government would go to Hell." He was released upon paying a fine and taking an oath of allegiance. The provost marshal's records document Conner's arrest but do not confirm Booth's arrest. Another J. W. Booth of St. Louis was arrested and took the oath in November 1863 when John Wilkes Booth was elsewhere.[63]

Booth next appeared for four nights in Cleveland, Ohio, at the Academy of Music. The theatre, which opened in 1853, occupied the third and fourth floors of a brick building on the east side of Bank (now West Sixth) Street, near St. Clair Street (now St. Clair Avenue). The theater was 200 feet long, eighty feet wide, and twenty-seven feet high, with an eighty-by-sixty-foot stage. It had good acoustics and seated more than 2,000 people. Among its elegant and grand qualities were gas footlights and a high chandelier that hung from the center of the auditorium.

John Ellsler, manager of the Academy of Music, described Booth at this time: "His figure was of medium height, lithe and symmetrical, well developed and apparently in good condition.... Every feature commanded respect and admiration. His eyes were large, dark, and expressive.... The sparks of genius flashed from those orbs with an effect electrical."[64]

Booth closed the season with a week in Buffalo in July. By the middle of the month he was staying with Edwin and their mother at the home of publisher George P. Putnam[65] in New York City. Adam Badeau, a friend of Edwin and a member of General Ulysses S. Grant's staff, began a convalescence there during Booth's visit. Badeau wrote:

> Wilkes Booth was there and stood in the door when I arrived. He was a strong, stalwart young fellow of twenty-six, and himself helped to lift me out of the carriage, and afterward carried me in his arms to an upper story.[66]

That month, rioters in New York City, protesting the draft, burned twelve buildings, including the United States draft office on Broadway. More than thirty blacks were hanged, shot, or beaten to death. Putnam's house was on 17th Street only half a block from Union Square, a scene of heavy rioting. Badeau described those violent days:

> For a week he [Booth] nursed me tenderly, dressed my wounds, gave me medicines, and, when I was strong enough, again he bore me in his arms daily up and down the stairs. All this while the riot was raging in the street. Several times a day Wilkes went out to learn the situation and when he returned reported it to us all, but he said not one word to indicate he sympathized with the rioters, or with the cause that was their apparent instigation. On the contrary, he spoke with detestation of the burning of houses, shooting Union offi-

cers, and murdering inoffensive Negroes. I had a black servant ... and Edwin Booth took him in, though at the risk of incurring the rage of the rioters. When the murders at the Negro asylum occurred, Wilkes proposed that Randall should be hidden in the cellar. He declared he would protect the boy at the hazard of his life, if the mob came after him.[67]

The riots began to abate. Within several days Federal troops restored order in New York City.

Booth spent a portion of the summer of 1863 in Boston; on an unrecorded date he entered his autograph in an album at the Tremont House.[68] Matthew Canning made several engagements for his young friend for the coming season. Booth subsequently broke the engagements, causing a coolness between the two.[69]

Booth's acting season had been a great success. He had fifteen starring engagements covering twenty-nine weeks. He had performed in the major theatrical cities of Boston (where he had been an outstanding success for four weeks), Chicago (for six weeks), Philadelphia, Baltimore, and Washington. His earnings exceeded $20,000.

1862 *from July 25*

July 25, Friday Philadelphia

Booth wrote to Boston Museum manager Edwin F. Keach and accepted his offer of a four-week engagement to begin January 19, 1863. "Yours recd: -, And as mercy is one of the *many* virtues in my composition, I will display it, for once in my life, by instantly releasing you from The tenter-hooks, upon which I have unwittingly placed you...."[70]

July 26, Saturday Philadelphia

July 27, Sunday Philadelphia

July 28, Monday Philadelphia

July 29, Tuesday Philadelphia

July 30, Wednesday Philadelphia

July 31, Thursday Philadelphia

August 1, Friday Philadelphia

August 2, Saturday Philadelphia

August 3, Sunday Philadelphia

Booth wrote to Valentine Butsch, owner and manager of the Metropolitan Theatre in Indianapolis, noting that he had obtained engagements through March 1863, excepting the weeks of November 24 and January 5. He stated that his terms were to share receipts after the first $80.[71]

August 30, Saturday

The Second Battle of Bull Run (or Manassas) concluded.

September 5, Friday

General Robert E. Lee's Confederate army crossed the Potomac River and invaded Maryland.

September 17, Wednesday

The Battle of Antietam (or Sharpsburg) raged.

September 22, Monday

President Lincoln issued the preliminary Emancipation Proclamation. It declared that slaves in Confederate territory would be freed on January 1, 1863.

September 24, Wednesday

President Lincoln suspended the writ of habeas corpus for those arrested by military authority.

October 6, Monday New York

The *New York Tribune* reported that John Wilkes Booth was in the city and that he and his brothers might "appear together on some special occasion, before the expiration of the present engagement [of Edwin Booth]."[72]

October 7, Tuesday New York

October 8, Wednesday New York

October 9, Thursday New York

October 10, Friday New York

October 11, Saturday New York

October 12, Sunday New York

October 13, Monday New York

The *New York Clipper* noted that "J. Wilkes Booth is in town, but soon leaves for Cincinnati,

etc., to fill engagements. Doubtless we shall have him at some of our city theatres soon."[73]

Edwin Booth was appearing at New York's Winter Garden Theatre.[74]

October 20, Monday

Junius Jr. wrote to Edwin:

Joe [Booth] seems an enigma, but I think I can guess him. I would not say so to Mother but I am afraid he is not sound in mind.... Mind I do not say positive insanity but a crack that way, which father in his highest [?] moments had & which I fear runs more or less thro' the male portion of our family....[75]

October 23, Thursday Lexington

Booth played *Richard III* at the Opera House on the southeast corner of Main and Broadway. The *Lexington Observer and Reporter* noted: "The elite of Lexington theatergoers were thrilled by the first appearance of the greatest tragedian of the age, Mr. John Wilkes Booth."[76]

October 24, Friday Lexington

Booth played Charles de Moor in *The Robbers*.

October 25, Saturday Louisville

October 26, Sunday Louisville

October 27, Monday Louisville

Booth opened at the Louisville Theatre with a portrayal of Claude Melnotte in *The Lady of Lyons; or, Love and Pride*. An observer noted that the "theatre opened ... under the happiest auspices, that is to say, with a suffocating, crowded auditorium...."[77] The lessee of the Louisville Theatre was George F. Fuller.[78]

October 28, Tuesday Louisville

Booth played *Richard III*. The *Louisville Daily Journal* anticipated the performance:

Mr. Wilkes Booth appears tonight in his great personation of *Richard III*, we may say great because it is original and untinctured by stage conventionalities. We regard it as one of the finest pictures of "the crooked-backed tyrant" ever offered.[79]

The *Louisville Daily Democrat* reported afterward that the theatre "was crowded to excess. Mr. Booth fully sustained his character in Richard, with a decided improvement since we last saw him...."[80]

October 29, Wednesday Louisville

Booth appeared as Pescara in *The Apostate*, a part which, according to the *Journal*, "he has made as peculiarly his own as his father did before him.... Mr. Booth is drawing very large audiences, and is well supported by the stock company."[81]

October 30, Thursday Louisville

Booth played *Macbeth*.

October 31, Friday Louisville

Booth appeared as Phidias and Raphael in *The Marble Heart*, which had been a hit in his previous Louisville engagement. Booth performed the play with a special introductory scene "written expressly for him by Mr. Geo. F. Fuller, of this city," the *Democrat* reported.[82] A large audience expressed "delight."[83]

November 1, Saturday Louisville

Booth performed *Richard III* in front of "a full house."[84]

November 2, Sunday Louisville

November 3, Monday Louisville

Booth played Charles de Moor in *The Robbers* for another large audience.

November 4, Tuesday Louisville

Booth played *Macbeth*. The *Democrat* remarked: "The theatre did not have as large an audience as we expected, though there was a very fine audience present."[85]

November 5, Wednesday Louisville

Booth played *Richard III*. "The theatre had a very good audience ... notwithstanding the inclemency of the weather," the *Democrat* reported.[86]

General George B. McClellan was relieved of command of the Army of the Potomac and replaced by General Ambrose Burnside.

November 6, Thursday Louisville

Booth played Shylock in *The Merchant of Venice*.

November 7, Friday Louisville

Booth played the new role of Alfred Evelyn in *Money* in his benefit. "We have seldom, if ever, witnessed so large and appreciative an audience on any former occasion," the *Democrat* noted.[87]

November 8, Saturday Louisville

Booth closed his engagement with *The Corsican Brothers*, in which he played Fabien and Louis.

November 10, Monday Cincinnati

Booth opened his engagement in Cincinnati at the National Theatre with *Richard III*. The *Cincinnati Enquirer* remarked:

The advent of Mr. J. Wilkes Booth ... was a decided success. The gentleman was welcomed by a full house, and enthusiastic applause greeted him during the entire performance. Mr. Booth is [an] actor of rare talent—combining all the virtues of his father and brother.[88]

November 11, Tuesday Cincinnati

Booth played Claude Melnotte in *The Lady of Lyons*. The National Theatre advertisements in the *Cincinnati Daily Commercial* carried Booth's name followed by that of Jennie Parker, "a young lady from the Eastern cities."

November 12, Wednesday Cincinnati

Booth played *Macbeth*. The *Cincinnati Daily Gazette* reported: "J. W. Booth is drawing good houses at the National."[89]

November 13, Thursday Cincinnati

Booth played Fabien and Louis in *The Corsican Brothers*. During a break in the morning rehearsal Booth asked fellow actors Harry A. Weaver and W. H. Hamblin to join him in a drink at an adjoining saloon. After the rehearsal the men continued their conversation, touching on literature and art, poetry and drama, and news of the war. The pleasant discussion continued until they had to go to the theatre for the evening's performance.[90]

November 14, Friday Cincinnati

The advertisement of the National Theatre noted the benefit of Mr. J. Wilkes Booth "on which occasion he will (by particular request) repeat his great character of *Richard III*."[91] The *Enquirer* anticipated the performance: "This is Mr. Booth's masterpiece. No actor now upon the stage can render the character of the humpbacked tyrant with equal effect. In short Booth out-Richards Richard."[92]

November 15, Saturday Cincinnati

Booth played Charles de Moor in *The Robbers*. He wore a pair of gauntlets borrowed from actor M. V. Lingham, who was leading man at Pike's Opera House.[93] The *Enquirer* eagerly awaited the performance:

In the hands of Mr. Booth the character of Charles is so truthfully rendered that all traces of *acting* are lost and we gaze apparently upon a thrilling episode of real life. The dashing cavalier, the reckless profligate, the robber-chief surrounded by the band, and the devoted lover stand before us boldly drawn and true to nature as nature itself. The principal beauty of Mr. Booth's acting is that he does not copy from others, but has acquired an originality of fashion that admits of no imitation. Comparisons may be drawn between him and other actors of celebrity, but there is no parallel.[94]

November 16, Sunday Cincinnati

November 17, Monday Cincinnati

Booth played *Hamlet*. "Mr. J. Wilkes Booth has been re-engaged for another week," the *Gazette* reported."[95]

November 18, Tuesday Cincinnati

Booth played *Othello*.[96] In the opinion of the *Enquirer*:

Booth's *Othello* was a mistake; he would have done Iago better possibly, though the latter is the difficult character in the play. Mr. Booth may be a great actor, but he failed to sustain his reputation as such, in his late engagement. He is the possessor of talents for dramatic personation, of no mean order, however, but should not be starring in it. He would make an admirable leading man, and there is a woeful lack of that commodity here....[97]

November 19, Wednesday Cincinnati

Booth played Pescara in *The Apostate*.[98] The *Enquirer* anticipated the performance:

Perhaps in no other piece does his brilliant genius shine so resplendent as in the *Apostate*. Every passion to which the human mind and heart is heir is in this [play] portrayed by the young actor with terrific strength and wonderful truthfulness. In this particular character Mr. Booth's fine training and judicious acting is more than usually perceptible. Those who witness the impersonation can not fail to pronounce it his masterpiece.[99]

November 20, Thursday Cincinnati

Booth appeared as Charles de Moor in *The Robbers* and, according to the *Enquirer*, "was received by a full house. We have no hesitancy in pronouncing the performance among the best we have ever seen."[100]

November 21, Friday Cincinnati

Booth portrayed Alfred Evelyn in *Money*. According to the *Enquirer*, "Mr. Booth's brilliant acting called forth loud and prolonged bursts of applause."[101]

"After the performance," the *Enquirer* reported, Booth "was waited upon by a party of friends known as the 'Peep O'Day Club,' who presented him with a pair of splendid swords.

The presentation speech was made by Captain [Lewis] Wilson, U.S.A. and happily responded to by Mr. Booth. Champagne, supper, &c., closed the scene."[102]

November 22, Saturday Cincinnati

Booth did not have a role in the matinee performance of *Uncle Tom's Cabin*.

Booth closed his engagement in Cincinnati with a portrayal of Pescara in *The Apostate*. The *Enquirer* commented:

Mr. Booth has endeared himself to the Cincinnati public. Coming among us a stranger, with nothing but the prestige of a great name, he departs bearing with him the goodwill and esteem of everyone who has had the pleasure of witnessing his chaste and matchless impersonations. We have no hesitancy in pronouncing him one of the most promising actors of the age.[103]

Wilkes' Spirit of the Times noted: "Mr. J. Wilkes Booth has copyrighted the new scene in the 'Marble Heart,' and will play it at the East this season."[104]

November 24, Monday Indianapolis

Booth opened with *Macbeth* at the Metropolitan Theatre in Indianapolis, on the northeast corner of Washington and Tennessee [now Capitol] Streets. According to the *Indianapolis Daily Sentinel*, "The theatre could not hold all the people who rushed there to hear and see Mr. Booth.... He was well sustained by Mr. Riley, whose *Macduff* was a fine piece of acting. The fencing in the closing scene was magnificent."[105]

November 25, Tuesday Indianapolis

Booth, supported by Marion Macarthy,[106] played Claude Melnotte in *The Lady of Lyons*.

November 26, Wednesday Indianapolis

Booth appeared in *Hamlet*. According to the *Sentinel*:

Mr. Booth's *Hamlet* was a masterpiece of acting, and held the audience spell-bound from the time the curtain rose in the first act until the green baize fell at its close. Miss Macarthy's Ophelia was much praised, and, indeed, the actors all filled their parts well. A better pleased audience has not left the Metropolitan this season than the one last night.[107]

November 27, Thursday Indianapolis

Booth played the title role in *Othello*. The *Indianapolis Daily Journal* published a negative review:

Mr. Booth has had less reason to complain of his patronage than his audience has of their entertainment. They have treated him better than he has them. His *Othello* ... was, not to put too fine a point upon it, a failure. It may be unjust disparagement of a man's talents that nature has not given him a strong voice, or an imposing appearance, but it certainly indicates by very plain guide-boards in what parts he should seek to exhibit his talents. Unless there is the magic of real genius to blind the eyes to physical unfitness, it is a hazardous step to set the eyes to comparing notes with the imagination. The "disillusion," as the French call it, is apt to make one laugh. Mr. Booth, with his thin figure, husky voice, indistinct articulation, exaggerated action and constant straining to get up a strength of passion which makes a strong man seem stronger, but under which he broke down into paralytic head-shakings, and wild staggerings about the stage, was just enough unlike the bold, open and dignified warrior to make one laugh, if the poet had not put it beyond the power of anybody to make *him* ridiculous.

Mr. Booth may be a good actor in some characters—he certainly played portions of Hamlet admirably—but there is not enough of him for *Othello*. The intense passion of a nature as large as the Moor's would burn on Booth's little boiler in one act. He and Riley should have exchanged parts. The latter has the form, voice and power for the warrior, and Booth's wiry frame is almost one's ideal of the keen, crafty, plausible, inexorable devil Iago. As it was, Riley so far overshadowed Booth that Iago was the hero of the piece and was so hailed by the audience.... We don't admire Mr. Booth, and by what art he became a "star" is more than our astronomy can explain.[108]

November 28, Friday Indianapolis

Booth appeared in *Richard III*. The *Enquirer* was impressed:

The benefit of Mr. Booth called to Metropolitan Hall a large, intellectual and fashionable audience. His *Richard III* was splendid, and he was admirably sustained by Mr. Riley as *Richmond*. It was a rare treat, and highly appreciated. At the conclusion of the play both Mr. Booth and Mr. Riley were called to the front of the curtain to receive the plaudits of those they had so well entertained.[109]

November 29, Saturday Indianapolis

Booth closed his engagement in Indianapolis with a portrayal of Charles de Moor in *The Robbers*.

The *Chicago Evening Journal* carried a "Special Notice" of J. Wilkes Booth's engagement at McVicker's Theatre starting Monday.[110]

November 30, Sunday Chicago

December 1, Monday Chicago

Booth opened his engagement with *The Lady of Lyons*. The *Chicago Times* described the performance:

The house was nearly filled. Mr. Booth is a young man, but he is one of those young men who give promise to become worthy sons of illustrious sires. In common with his brother he may be considered as holding the first rank among the generation of coming actors.... For a young actor, he displays a wonderful adaptation to the profession. He possesses ready and graceful stage action, a full, and at times mellow, and sympathetic voice, and a general ensemble which strikes the audience with pleasure. As Claude Melnotte, he was the young peasant Prince, and here almost to the life. There might have been a shade more of moderation—of gentle toning down, in his action, at times, but as a whole he was very near the true impersonation of his character. As the peasant he was enthusiastic and vivacious—bounding with hope, ambition, or despair. As the Prince, he was graceful and fervent, and, in defiance of his accomplices, eloquent beyond praise. As the unmasked bridegroom, his acting was so earnest, so indicative of the promptings of an honest heart, that many an eye was moistened which had been seized in emotion. He succeeded admirably in attracting the sympathies of his audience, and, through the whole, they were with him in rapt attention.[111]

December 2, Tuesday Chicago

Booth appeared in *Richard III*. The *Times* critic had much to say:

Mr. Booth brought out ... the great tragedy [*RICHARD III*] upon which his father's fame was built. Whether it is politic for so young an actor to aim, at one bound, to gain the place which the veteran occupied only after years of study and experience, we doubt. The character of Gloster is too deep for the fathoming of a youthful mind.... We do not therefore, look with favor upon Mr. Booth's personation of the character. There is always a grace and dignity about his acting, which will attract in any role. There is a mellow cadence in his voice, that rings in modulated strains through the memories of his hearers, long after the tones have ceased. There is pathos and passion in abundance, but there is not that cool, deliberate, sad concentrated villainy which scatters death without a pang, and walks, through blood and desolated affections, steadily to its purpose. The apostate man, cursing at his own destiny and mocking God in a breath, is wanting.

There is a touch of over-acting in the personations—a vigorous reaching for effects which are beyond reach, and a nervous attempt at byplay which can only come from the promptings of a mind wrapt in the subject, and penetrating its every shade of meaning. He was a thousand times more effective as Claude Melnotte, portraying a simple, every day person, than in this subtle essence of things incomprehensible. The part is too heavy for the actor. A load of years, a matured judgment, and the calm, sober bearing which experience will bring, may make Mr. Booth a perfect Richard the III; but he disappoints our expectations now. His audience gathered an unfavorable impression, without perhaps knowing exactly why, and the play is in bad odor thereafter. Indeed there are so few who can do the character any justice that the play is almost always in bad odor. Shakespeare's creation was too deep and subtle for us to hope often to find its counterpart or its counterfeit.[112]

December 3, Wednesday Chicago

Booth played Shylock in *The Merchant of Venice*. According to the *Journal*, the performance "was an admirable piece of acting, and called forth the encomiums of the very large and respectable audience that witnessed it."[113] The *Times* critic noted:

It [*The Merchant of Venice*] requires, therefore, an actor of strong delineative power to render it in its true sense. To that place Mr. Booth belongs. His personation was strongly marked, and truthful to the meaning of the author in every part. He showed his power in the first act.... He rose to a point of superabundant excellence in the scene which follows the loss of his daughter. A raging lion, a bloodthirsty beast, a groaning miser, a fiendish man, intent in the hope of revenge—all by turns, so rapidly the transition confused the sense, and caused the audience to wonder at the conception which created such a being, as well as the imitative power which delineated. In the trial scene he was quite effective. The greed which whetted the man's appetite shown in his eye, lurked on his tongue, and spoke in the nervous play of his fingers.[114]

December 4, Thursday Chicago

Booth played *Othello*. The *Times* appreciated the performance:

Mr. Booth told this tale [*Othello*] in eloquent tones.... The winning pathos of his voice, when he spoke of the fair Desdemona, went home to the hearts of his hearers. But it was when the subtle venom of Iago's ingenuity began to work upon him, that he showed his power. Doubt, hesitancy and reckless passion alternately animated his acting, and made him the absorbing point of interest. And, although Iago is here so prominent a character as to divide the attention, he lost nothing, but carried through with him the palm of su-

periority. In a brief space he was the wreck of all that is noble and good—a raging, jealous man, thirsting for the blood of the being he held dearest—still doubting at intervals, still hesitating; ever and anon accusing his scheming friend, and then invoking the wrath of God on his gentle wife. The death scene was enacted with the same intensity of expression. There was concentrated fire and energy in every word, and, when at last conscience came to accuse him of his great crime, he was a tower of strength and goodness consumed by inward fire.[115]

December 5, Friday Chicago

Booth played *Hamlet*. The *Times* remarked:

In the soliloquies Mr. Booth was very fine. His reading was correct, well-accented, and distinct, and, while more exciting portions of the play failed to command attention at times, he was here listened to in deep silence. If all had been as good, nothing more could have been asked. In the grave-digging scene he was quite effective. "Alas, poor Yorick" came out with a pathos which struck home. The Ghost scene in his mother's closet, gave fine scope, and he improved it well. The intensified horror which sat upon his countenance, and spoke to his tones, thrilled the audience with involuntary tremor.[116]

December 6, Saturday Chicago

Booth played Pescara in *The Apostate* with Betsy Baker.

Booth wrote to Joe Simonds on Tremont House stationery:

Am much obliged to you my dear boy for attending to my bus:[iness] with so much punctuality. Have recd: dresses [costumes]. Am much pleased with them.... My bus:[iness] here has been great near $900. on my first week....[117]

December 7, Sunday Chicago

December 8, Monday Chicago

Booth played Phidias and Raphael in *The Marble Heart*. The *Chicago Tribune* predicted that "[n]o one can witness his beautiful rendition of the aspiring, yet disappointed sculptor, without admiration, and many a tear will flow on beholding the breaking of the marble heart."[118] The *Times* reviewer found that "Mr. Booth, as Raphael, was graceful and self-possessed, and, in the pathetic portions, most effective."[119]

The *Times* critic described the first week of Booth's engagement:

Mr. Booth's engagement at McVicker's Theatre had been a success in a pecuniary point of view. The house has been filled every night. After what we have said from day to day it is hardly necessary to review the performance in detail. He aims to fill the place left vacant by his father. There is a saying that to aim high is to achieve success, and perhaps it is as well for him to place his goal at the pinnacle, and trust to time for its attainment. We award him the position of a rising actor, with a promising future. He has many faults which time will correct, many extravagances which later judgment will modify, and many misconceptions which experience and knowledge of the world will change for the better. Yet, with all for one so young he displays surpassing talent. He can hold an audience enchained in some of his finer delineations, and he has real merit enough to draw them night after night to witness his efforts. That a certain amount of this attention is due to his name, cannot be doubted....[120]

Booth wrote to Boston Museum manager Edwin F. Keach notifying him that he had received costumes by mail and that he would pay for them in person rather than risk the mails. He had sent $800 to his mother two weeks previously. Booth related that he had received an average of $650 a week for the season. He made staging suggestions for his next Boston engagement.[121]

December 9, Tuesday Chicago
Booth played Phidias and Raphael in *The Marble Heart*. The *Times* was complimentary:
Mr. Booth's personation of the principal character is full of interest. From the moment disappointment strikes his hopes to the ground, his voice and manner are full of living pathos, which rings in every tone and is shown in every movement. In the parting scene with Marco, his attitude and gesture were sublime; while the outburst of passion ... was full of manly power.[122]

December 10, Wednesday Chicago
Booth played *Macbeth*. The *Times* commented:
It was in the dagger soliloquy that he was most meritorious. The thrilling earnestness of his voice, the fixed gaze with which his eyes followed the phantom blade, the frantic grasp at air; all went home to his listeners. A natural wildness animated Mr. Booth.... The fencing scene was very fine, and brought down the house; and the curtain fell upon an enthusiastic audience.[123]

December 11, Thursday Chicago
Booth played *The Stranger*. The *Times* critic thought the play was popular because of its "intensity of tone," despite its dramatic weakness, and continued:
The play was well rendered. Mr. Booth as the Stranger, Mr. McVicker as Peter ... bore their

parts well. Mr. Booth was grave, cynical, and moody as the character requires.... The play went smoothly and an agreeable entertainment was the result.[124]

Two intoxicated patrons were evicted from the theatre during the first scene of the play.[125]

December 12, Friday Chicago
Booth played *Richard III*. The *Times* critic found fault:
[Booth's *Richard*] is of ferocious, demonstrative purpose; fierce and ardent in pursuit, and riotous in the joy of accomplishment. Nor is this the only fault. The poetry of the text is too often merged in rant, and then destroyed entirely.[126]

December 13, Saturday Chicago
Booth played Charles de Moor in *The Robbers*.

December 14, Sunday Chicago

December 15, Monday Chicago
Booth played *Money*. The *Times* noted:
[The play] is a sharp parody on popular customs, with a moral for the virtuous.... Mr. Booth, as *Evelyn*, was correct, moderate and pleasing. He was within his bounds, and hence true to himself and his assumed character. In the more sentimental portions of his love experience, he was very attractive, for he can throw a mellow cadence into his voice, which expressed sentiment without words.[127]

December 16, Tuesday Chicago
Booth appeared as Pescara in *The Apostate*, which was followed by *The Two Gregories*. The *Times* critic noted that the "house was the smallest of the past two weeks, whether from an apprehension of the merits of the performance or not, we are unable to say. Whatever kept people at home, they lost but little...."[128]

December 17, Wednesday Chicago
Booth appeared in *Romeo and Juliet*, which was followed by *A Regular Fix*.

December 18, Thursday Chicago
Booth played *Macbeth*. The *Journal* carried a "Special Notice" advertisement for McVicker's Theatre:
The brilliant engagement of this talented young Tragedian must positively end with the present week. In answer to the numerous requests for the repetition of several pieces, the manager respectfully announces that the following plays have been selected for the last three nights—*MACBETH, THE MERCHANT OF VENICE* and *RICHARD III*.[129]

December 19, Friday Chicago

Booth's portrayal of Shylock in *The Merchant of Venice* satisfied the *Times* critic. Booth also played Petruchio in *Katharine and Petruchio*.

December 20, Saturday Chicago

Booth closed his engagement in Chicago with *Richard III*.

December 21, Sunday En Route to St. Louis

December 22, Monday St. Louis

Booth opened at the St. Louis Theatre with *Richard III*. The *St. Louis Missouri Democrat* remarked:

> Mr. J. Wilkes Booth was received ... with a most enthusiastic welcome. The house was well filled, and all present seemed highly delighted with the return to our stage of the legitimate drama. Mr. Booth played *Richard III* as none other can, now on the stage. It is generally conceded by those learned in the matter, that he is now the best *Richard*.[130]

December 23, Tuesday St. Louis

"*Hamlet* was performed ... to a large and fashionable audience, in spite of the rainy weather. Mr. Booth's *Hamlet* was much applauded," the *Democrat* reported.[131]

December 24, Wednesday St. Louis

Booth played Pescara in *The Apostate*. The *Democrat* noted:

> Another crowded house greeted Mr. J. W. Booth.... This gentleman bids fair to play the most successful engagement of the season. His is most decidedly an artist of the highest order, and we are glad to see merit so liberally supported.[132]

December 25, Thursday St. Louis

Booth performed *Macbeth*, a role for which the actor, according to the *Democrat*, "is highly praised by our ablest critics."[133]

December 26, Friday St. Louis

The newspapers did not carry an advertisement for the St. Louis Theatre for this date.

December 27, Saturday St. Louis

Booth played *Richard III*. "This great artist is now playing a highly successful engagement, attracting crowded houses every night of his appearance," the *Democrat* stated.[134]

December 28, Sunday St. Louis

December 29, Monday St. Louis

Booth appeared in *The Marble Heart*, which, according to the *Democrat*:

> proved a great success ... being received by a large and fashionable audience with immense applause. Mr. Booth's acting of the double part of Phidias and Raphael, was really excellent, and drew down the hearty applause of all present. The other parts were admirably given by Mr. Conner, Miss C. Wyette and the rest of the company.[135]

December 30, Tuesday St. Louis

Booth played *Hamlet* before a "full and fashionable house." His performance was "well studied and highly finished," in the estimation of the *Democrat*.[136]

December 31, Wednesday St. Louis

Booth appeared as Phidias and Raphael in *The Marble Heart* by request. The *Democrat* proclaimed Booth's engagement "most brilliant" and opined that the evening's play was "one of the most interesting pieces now on the stage, and was a great success on its first presentation."[137]

1863 *through August 27*

January 1, Thursday St. Louis

Booth played Fabien and Louis in *The Corsican Brothers*.

President Lincoln issued the Emancipation Proclamation.

January 2, Friday St. Louis

Booth played Alfred Evelyn in *Money*.

January 3, Saturday St. Louis

In a benefit that closed his engagement, Booth played Shylock in *The Merchant of Venice* and Petruchio in *Katharine and Petruchio*.

January 4, Sunday En Route to Indianapolis

January 5, Monday Indianapolis

Booth opened his engagement with *Hamlet*. The *Indianapolis Daily Sentinel* reported:

> The Metropolitan was crowded ... with an highly intellectual and appreciative audience to hear Mr. Booth, in the great character of *Hamlet*. Mr. Booth is indeed a great actor, and appears to have a true conception of the character of the melancholy prince.[138]

The *Indianapolis Daily Journal* critic was of the opinion that "[w]hile we think [Booth] is physically unequal to the task of personating such passionate characters as Othello, Macbeth, or Richard, yet he has the ability to play Hamlet with unusually good taste."[139]

January 6, Tuesday Indianapolis

Booth played *Othello*. The *Journal* asserted: "If Booth's *Othello* is a 'truthful performance,' then Shakespeare was an ass."[140] The *Sentinel* replied:

The public were convinced there was an ass around somewhere, but were not sure whether it was Shakespeare, the critic of the *Journal* or Mr. Booth. They decided that the ears did not belong to Mr. Booth, and now the question of ownership lies between the Bard ... and the critic....[141]

The *Indianapolis Gazette* staked out the middle ground:

Mr. Booth played Othello to a good house ... and played it well.... Booth has some defects—who has not? Though in truth we are bound to say his major faults upon the stage are of such a character that to designate them in an unfriendly criticism would be ungenerous, to say the least.

His voice and enunciation are not as clear and effective as Murdoch's or Forrest's, and his physique, perhaps, would not serve as a model for a fighting gladiator. But, in the rendition of the "Moor of Venice" and other master creations of the immortal bard the latter is no sort of obstruction, while his truthful conception of the character, his strict adherence to the form and spirit of the text, and the interpretation of the furtive character of the Turk, make his audience forget the presence of Booth, and think only of a misguided, passionate Moor.

Notwithstanding the fact that asinine qualities [a reference to the *Journal* critic's "ass" comment] have been imputed to the bard, in a certain contingency, we think Mr. Booth's personation a truthful performance, one that will instruct the student of Shakespeare, entertain the gay and thoughtless, and at the same time, cast no discredit upon the legitimate drama—and further that an opportunity of seeing his equal in this and other characters is exceedingly rare in this neck of the woods.[142]

January 7, Wednesday Indianapolis

Booth appeared as Phidias and Raphael in *The Marble Heart*. The *Sentinel* observed:

The Marble Heart was brought out ... and the acting was good. The tableaux of the statues in the final act was magnificent, and marble was never more faithfully represented by flesh and blood. What scenic art gave so faithful a representation of the sculptor's chisel, we know not, but it was true to art. Mr. Booth as Raphael was very happy.... The play has life, vigor, wit and point....[143]

January 8, Thursday Indianapolis

Booth played *The Corsican Brothers* to a full house. The *Sentinel* reported: "Mr. Booth appeared as the twin brothers, and Mr. Riley as Chateau Renaud. The acting of both was excellent, and the tableaux and machinery of the piece was magnificent."[144]

January 9, Friday Indianapolis

Booth appeared as Alfred Evelyn in *Money* and as Petruchio in *Katharine and Petruchio*. He received plaudits for his performance from the *Gazette*:

Money was exceedingly well put upon the stage, and brought round after round of applause from the audience. *Taming of the Shrew* [*Katharine and Petruchio*] was played better than we have ever seen it before, and excited shouts of laughter, in which every one seemed to partake with a gusto that was exhilarating. The acting was unusually happy and appropriate, reflecting credit on the leading man and every member of the company.[145]

January 10, Saturday Indianapolis

Booth closed his engagement with *Richard III*. Marion Macarthy played Lady Ann, and Mr. Riley played Richmond.[146]

January 15, Thursday

Mary Ann Booth wrote to Edwin: "I hope John may do well in Boston. He has been quite successful so far. He plays at the Arch Street in February but shares after $175."[147]

January 17, Saturday Boston

January 18, Sunday Boston

January 19, Monday Boston

Booth opened at the Boston Museum to a crowd of over 2,000 people with *Richard III*. The *Boston Daily Evening Transcript* noted:

The Museum was thronged to its utmost capacity by an audience as fashionable and as critical as any that ever assembled within its walls, and every circumstance of the hour bespoke a complete success as the result of the engagement of John Wilkes Booth. One year has elapsed since Mr. Booth last appeared in Boston, and during that period great progress has been made in the development of his powers. He then gave promise of attaining a foremost position among actors—of worthily wearing the mantle of his lamented father—and his personations engaged the deep interest of our oldest and most intelligent theatre-goers. He now returns with fresh laurels upon his young brow, and our lovers of the drama are again awakened to an exhibition of true enthusiasm.[148]

Another observer recorded:

Mr. Booth has not disappointed the expectation of his friends, and exhibits a professional improvement. The large number who saw him for the first time probably experienced no disappointment of their expectations if we may judge by the applause so lavishly bestowed upon the young actor.... His *Richard*, however, will ever be his favorite character with the generality of playgoers from its vivid earnestness and terrible intensity. In the last scenes the spectator is powerfully impressed by the energy and vigor, seemingly of desperation, he infuses into the part.[149]

January 20, Tuesday Boston

Booth appeared in *The Lady of Lyons*. The playbill noted of Booth: "This Young American Actor, the rapidity of whose professional progress, and brilliance of whose success is almost without parallel in the records of the stage, will make his second appearance this season in the character of Claude Melnotte...."

Laura Keene was appearing at the Howard Athenaeum, a short distance from the Boston Museum.[150]

January 21, Wednesday Boston

Booth appeared as Pescara in *The Apostate* and was cheered wildly. One observer noted that "Mr. Edwin Booth witnessed his brother's performance ... [and] was recognized by the audience on entering, and received a complimentary round of applause, which was repeated as he rose to depart at the termination of the play."[151] Edwin wrote:

> I saw last night—for the first time—my brother act; he played *Pescara*—a bloody villain of the deepest red, you know, an *admiral* of the red, as 'twas, and he presented him—not underdone, but rare enough for the most fastidious "beef-eater"; Jno. Bull himself Esquire never looked more savagely at us poor "mudsills" than did J. Wilkes, himself, Esquire, settle the accounts of last evening. Yet I am happy to state that he is full of the true grit—he has stuff enough in him to make good suits for a dozen such player—folk as we are cursed with; and when time and study round his rough edges he'll bid them all "stand apart" like "a bully boy, with a glass eye"; I am delighted with him & feel the name of Booth to be more of a hydra than snakes and things ever was.[152]

In a letter to a friend, Mary Devlin Booth reported that "we went to see J. Wilkes B—for the first time. We were very much pleased with him—but he has a great deal to learn & unlearn."[153]

January 22, Thursday Boston

Booth played Alfred Evelyn in *Money*. "The character affords fine scope for a display of the

powers of such an actor as the younger Booth," the *Transcript* remarked.[154]

January 23, Friday Boston

Booth played *Richard III*. He had made suggestions to Edwin F. Keach, the manager of the Boston Museum, for staging *Richard*:

> First of all, plenty of supernumeraries (*with one rehearsal.*) And then the Coronation scene, And the scene "Who saw the sun to day," could be made fine pictures, the latter by having the left *flat* painted camp running off in distance.... And on the right flat Archers extending in line of battle. Carrying out that line I draw down right of stage.... Think of it.[155]

"The Museum has been crowded at every performance thus far given by Mr. Booth, but perhaps the greatest success of the week was [Monday's performance of] *Richard III*, which ... aroused the audience present to an exhibition of unusual enthusiasm," the *Transcript* reported.[156]

January 24, Saturday Boston

Booth appeared as Claude Melnotte in *The Lady of Lyons* at the matinee.

January 25, Sunday Boston

January 26, Monday Boston

Booth played *Macbeth*. The *Boston Post* critic wrote: "We like as little as ever the occasional slovenliness of [Booth's] elocution which mars many a passage of the quieter sort that does not sweep away criticism of details by its intensity or by a stroke of genius in acting...."[157]

January 27, Tuesday Boston

Booth played Alfred Evelyn in *Money*.

January 28, Wednesday Boston

Booth played the title role in *Othello*. Kate Reignolds played Desdemona.

January 29, Thursday Boston

Booth played Charles de Moor in *The Robbers*.

Mary Ann Booth wrote to Edwin: "I have had several letters from Wilkes and he tells me he has seen you often...."[158] She asked how Edwin's daughter, Edwina, liked Wilkes and commented that all the little children liked him at once.

January 30, Friday Boston

Booth and Kate Reignolds played *Romeo and Juliet*. Reignolds later wrote:

> In the last scene of *Romeo and Juliet*, one night, I vividly recall how the buttons at his cuff caught

my hair, and in trying to tear them out he trod on my dress and rent it so as to make it utterly useless afterward; and in his last struggle shook me out of my shoes! The curtain fell on Romeo with a sprained thumb [and] Juliet in rags.[159]

January 31, Saturday Boston

Booth appeared as Alfred Evelyn in *Money* in a matinee performance.[160]

February 1, Sunday Boston

February 2, Monday Boston

Booth appeared as Phidias and Raphael in *The Marble Heart*. The *Transcript* anticipated the performance:

It is a play of deep and thrilling interest, its principal situations appealing strongly to the sympathies of an audience, and the character of *Raphael* is one in which young Booth must appear to peculiarly fine advantage. Elsewhere he has achieved great success in it, and there can be no doubt of an equally brilliant triumph here.[161]

After the performance, the *Transcript* reported that "an overflowing audience" had attended and that:

great enthusiasm was excited by John Wilkes Booth's personation of Raphael.... The only complaint to be made ... was the long interval between the acts. The great pecuniary success that the Museum is now enjoying ... should enable the management to increase their corps of stage assistants.[162]

February 3, Tuesday Boston

Booth played Phidias and Raphael in *The Marble Heart*.

John endorsed a check from his brother Edwin.[163]

February 4, Wednesday Boston

Booth played *The Marble Heart* both in the afternoon and in the evening. The *Transcript* commented on Booth's success in Boston:

The engagement of John Wilkes Booth, at the Museum, might be continued with profit to the management for a month to come at least.... The *Marble Heart* has created a profound sensation, and excited a degree of enthusiasm rarely exhibited by our theatre-goers.[164]

February 5, Thursday Boston

Booth played Pescara in *The Apostate*.[165]

February 6, Friday Boston

Booth played *Richard III*.

February 7, Saturday Boston

Booth portrayed Phidias and Raphael in *The Marble Heart*.

February 8, Sunday Boston

February 9, Monday Boston

Booth played *The Corsican Brothers* to begin the fourth and final week of what the *Transcript* called "a truly extraordinary engagement."[166] The newspaper commented after the performance: "The Museum was crowded to excess ... and by an audience whose enthusiasm was extraordinary. Mr. Booth's rendering of the twin brothers Louis and Fabien must add materially to his popularity here."[167]

Edwin Booth opened an engagement at the Winter Garden Theatre in New York. He drank heavily during his engagement and received poor reviews.[168]

February 10, Tuesday Boston

Booth played Fabien and Louis in *The Corsican Brothers*.

February 11, Wednesday Boston

Mary Devlin Booth, Orlando Tompkins, and others saw John in *The Corsican Brothers*.

Mary wrote to Edwin:

He [John] looked badly ... he lacked character. That is one great draw-back to his success, I think—he can't transform himself. The combat was strictly "gladiatorial"—the muscles of his arms ... eclipsing everything else besides. "Look at his arm"—everyone exclaimed—& highly delighted the audience seemed at this exhibition. He was more melo-dramatic than I have ever seen him....[169]

February 12, Thursday Boston

Booth played *Richard III*. According to the *Transcript*, "[t]his engagement will long be remembered as having been one of the most successful ever fulfilled by an actor at this place of amusement."[170]

February 13, Friday Boston

Booth played Shylock in *The Merchant of Venice* and Petruchio in *Katharine and Petruchio*.[171]

February 14, Saturday Boston

Booth closed his engagement in Boston with a portrayal of Fabien and Louis in *The Corsican Brothers*. The *Advertiser* critic wrote:

He [Booth] does not add that elegance to his energy which we could hope, and he cannot stand in the highest position of actors until he shall be willing to perfect his elocution as thoroughly as his sword play. He may be very great, if he will, and we hope he will not relax his efforts because he is a popular favorite.[172]

February 15, Sunday Boston

February 16, Monday Boston

John Wilkes Booth visited Mary Devlin Booth, who was very ill. She gave him a letter to take to Edwin in New York.[173]

February 17, Tuesday New York

Upon arriving in New York, John visited Edwin and told him that Mary had a severe cold.[174] Mary's note to Edwin asked him not to break his engagement to come and attend her.[175]

February 19, Thursday

Friends of Edwin had asked Mary Devlin Booth to come to New York to divert Edwin from drinking. She responded: "I cannot come. I cannot stand. I think sometimes that only a great calamity can save my dear husband. I am going to try and write to him now, and God give me grace to write as a true wife should."[176]

February 20, Friday

Edwin Booth reeled through a performance of *Richard III* in New York.[177]

February 21, Saturday Philadelphia

Mary Devlin Booth died suddenly at 8:15 a.m.

Wilkes' Spirit of the Times reported that John Wilkes Booth's engagement at the Boston Museum had been "exceedingly profitable to the management and himself; he has achieved a high artistic reputation...."[178]

February 22, Sunday Philadelphia

February 23, Monday Boston

Booth was scheduled to begin an engagement in Philadelphia. The *Philadelphia Evening Bulletin* reported that "Mrs. Booth, Edwin's mother, arrived [in Boston], from Philadelphia on Monday forenoon, and later in the day his brother J. Wilkes Booth, and his brother-in-law, Clarke...."[179] The Arch Street Theatre advertisement noted that John "has felt the necessity imperative upon him to join his afflicted brother...."[180]

February 24, Tuesday Boston

Three carriages transported John, Edwin, Asia, their mother, and John Sleeper Clarke from Edwin's Dorchester home to Mount Auburn Cemetery in Cambridge for the funeral service. Julia Ward Howe was one of the few who attended the funeral; she wrote that Edwin followed the casket and "beside or behind him walked a young man [John Wilkes Booth] of remarkable beauty."[181]

February 25, Wednesday Boston?

February 26, Thursday Boston?

February 27, Friday Philadelphia?

In a performance of *Damon and Pythias* at the Chestnut Street Theatre in Philadelphia, Edwin Forrest played Damon and John McCullough played Pythias.[182]

Booth's engagement starting Monday was in opposition to the great Edwin Forrest. The *Philadelphia Daily Dispatch* would call Booth a "rising star" and Forrest a "setting star."[183]

February 28, Saturday Philadelphia

Booth wrote to Joe Simonds in Boston:
I think with you that the water power stock is a good investment and am only sorry that I did not buy long ago When you get this we can not tell what it will be selling for.... I send you by this a draft for Fifteen hundred dollars ($1,500) invest it for me at once dear Joe. I think I will have to make you my banker and give you an interest in my speculations, so that if we are lucky you may be able in a few years to throw aside those musty Ledgers.[184]

March 1, Sunday Philadelphia

Booth was staying at the home of his sister, Asia Booth Clarke, at 1021 Race Street. Concerned about the money he had sent, he again wrote to Joe Simonds:
I sent you a draft yesterday for $1,500. I want you to be as careful of my money as if it were your own (but theres no good in saying that for I know you will, and in fact more so) but what I mean is to "*look before you leap*."[185]

In Washington, D.C., David E. Herold began working for druggist William S. Thompson at Fifteenth and Pennsylvania Avenue. Until his employment ended on July 4, 1864, Herold may have delivered medicines to the White House.[186] Booth would soon meet Herold.

March 2, Monday Philadelphia

Booth opened at the Arch Street Theatre in *Richard III*. Louisa Lane Drew and Booth's old friend John Albaugh were in the cast. The *Bulletin* critic reported:
The performance ... by this young artist proved, beyond a doubt, that he was possessed of true genius—a spark of the electric fire which always finds a responsive thrill in the hearts of an audience. The desperate climax ... must be seen....[187]

March 3, Tuesday Philadelphia

Booth appeared as Phidias and Raphael in *The Marble Heart*. "The audience," according to the *Philadelphia Inquirer*, "was very enthusiastic, the ladies joining in the applause."[188] Booth's sisters Asia and Rosalie attended the performance.

Asia wrote that "John Booth won a beautiful suit of baby clothes at a fair out west and made me a present of them.... John Booth laughs outrageously at me for having babies.... He lies on the floor and rolls over with them like a child."[189]

March 4, Wednesday Philadelphia

Booth played *Richard III*. The *Philadelphia Press* critic wrote: "We have seen enough to justify us in saying that he is a good actor, and may become a great one...."[190]

March 5, Thursday Philadelphia

Booth appeared as Pescara in *The Apostate*. The *Press* critic noted of Booth:

His figure is slender, but compact and well made. He has a small, finely-formed head, with cold, classic features, a bright eye and a face of great expression. He very much resembles his brother Edwin in tone and action. Like Edwin he occasionally minces his words, and uses quaint pronunciation. Indeed, the resemblance is very marked. Without having Edwin's culture and grace, and without that glittering eye that gives so much life to his Iago and Pescara, Mr. Booth has far more action, more life, and, we are inclined to think, more natural genius. He does not play *Richard* as well as Edwin, but he plays some parts of it in a manner that we do not think Edwin can ever equal. His last act, and particularly his dying scene, is a piece of acting that few actors can rival, and it is far above the capacity of Edwin Booth. It is, of course, a different style from that in which we are accustomed to see the elder brother, who is great in quiet scenes, but it was wonderfully done, and shows the possession of a genius that is now rough and rugged, but may become great by constant cultivation.

And having said this much of John Wilkes Booth our commendation must cease. We think he has a wrong conception of the character of the Duke of Gloster. He makes him a slinking, malignant cripple, so deformed as to be almost unpleasant to the eye; one who loved murder for murder's sake alone.... We know it is the custom of actors to make Richard do nothing but murder while he smiles, but Mr. Booth even disdains to smile. His look, from the beginning to the end, is almost demoniac, and it was our constant wonder that he succeeded in making love to Lady Anne, in deceiving the mayor and Buckingham, and making all men his victims, or his tools. The Richard of Mr. Booth is, in these respects, an impossible personage. He dabbles in blood; sprin-

kles it on the stage after the murder of Henry; wipes his sword on his mantle (a very vulgar and disgusting thing for a nobleman to do); and revels in it from the beginning to the end. This all combines to make a very original and effective conception, but so much truth and poetry is sacrificed that we advise Mr. Booth to abandon it. He can be a great Richard, but he must return to his studies and give us Richard as he was.[191]

March 6, Friday Philadelphia

Booth played Shylock in *The Merchant of Venice* and Petruchio in *Katharine and Petruchio* in his benefit. The *Bulletin* commented that "Mr. John Wilkes Booth is rapidly rising in public favor. His benefit ... was quite an ovation, and his Shylock gave immense satisfaction."[192]

Booth bought 25 shares of Boston Water Power Company stock.[193]

March 7, Saturday Philadelphia

Booth played Charles de Moor in *The Robbers*.

March 8, Sunday Philadelphia

The *Philadelphia Sunday Dispatch* critic thought Booth overacted and observed: "He gesticulates too much. He has a motion, a smile or a frown for every sentence. He does not seem satisfied to allow the language of his author to do its work. He wishes to help it along by bodily illustrations...."[194]

March 9, Monday Philadelphia

Booth played *Hamlet* supported by Louisa Lane Drew and Barton Hill.

March 10, Tuesday Philadelphia

John Albaugh and Louisa Lane Drew supported Booth as Alfred Evelyn in *Money*. "Mr. Booth continues to draw excellent houses and is warmly applauded throughout his performances," the *Bulletin* reported.[195]

March 11, Wednesday Philadelphia

Booth played Phidias and Raphael in *The Marble Heart* "by particular request."[196]

March 12, Thursday Philadelphia

Booth, supported by Barton Hill[197] and John Albaugh, played Charles de Moor in *The Robbers*.

Edwin Forrest played *Macbeth* at the New Chestnut Street Theatre. John McCullough played Macduff.[198]

March 13, Friday Philadelphia

Booth chose *Macbeth* for his benefit performance. Edwin Forrest performed the same role at the Chestnut Street Theatre.

March 14, Saturday Philadelphia

Booth closed his engagement in Philadelphia with a portrayal of Pescara in *The Apostate*.

March 15, Sunday Baltimore

March 16, Monday Baltimore

Booth, supported by Alice Gray,[199] opened with *Richard III* at the Holliday Street Theatre. The *Baltimore American and Commercial Advertiser* anticipated the performance:

> [In this] character he has made an abiding impression upon the public mind. The distinguishing features of his performance are its fierce passion and its inherent vigor, qualities which likens it greatly to the elder Booth's impressive performance of the same part. *Richard* is with young Booth, as it was with his father, the touchstone of his genius....[200]

The next day, the *American and Commercial Advertiser* offered a positive review:

> Mr. John Wilkes Booth was welcomed back to his native city ... by an audience which, both in extent and in character, was one of the most brilliant and flattering ever convened here by the attractions of a dramatic performance. *Richard the Third* was rendered by this youthful artist on the occasion with a power and spirit which revived in the minds of those present who had seen the elder Booth's great impersonation of the same character a vivid recollection of his brilliant excellence. There was nothing, however, of the servility of imitation in young Booth's effort. It was, on the contrary, a singularly original performance, and deeply pervaded with the vitality of thought and the creative power of genius. The conception of the character was evidently formed from the elder Booth's point of view. It pictured the usurper in the vivid colors of a brave, cruel and energetic, but still able tyrant, who seized upon the scepter with a grasp as merciless as Ham, and held it with the firmness of Fate. This intellectual portrait of Richard—and it has the sanction of Shakespeare and the popular mind—Mr. Booth realized with great earnestness and with comprehensive power. His energy in the bustling scenes which marked the close of the tyrant's career was irresistible in its fiery force, and established fully the fame of the artist in the minds of his auditors.[201]

The *Baltimore Sun* critic was no less effusive:

> Few artists, young or old, and never one so young, probably have ever enjoyed a more brilliant ovation than that which young Booth received ... at the hands of one of the very largest audiences of

the season. It was perhaps more than he expected, but there was a broad popular confidence in the rising genius, the ascending star, and the people, the elite, the intelligent, assembled *en masse* to witness its bright particular radiance in the freshness of its dawn.[202]

According to the *Baltimore Daily Gazette*:

> Young Booth's conception of the character of *Richard III* is essentially similar to that of his father. Its prominent trait is a ruthless ambition, which regarded no obligation, human or divine, when inimical to its triumph: and its controlling impulse a cruelty as intrepid as it is ferocious. This view of the character—and it is eminently Shakespearean in spirit—was sustained throughout with great clearness and with vital force. The closing scenes of Richard's life, when the usurper, laying aside all dissimulation, devotes to his success all the vast resources of his intellect, his unconquerable energy, and his military skill, were rendered by Mr. Booth with splendid vigor, both of conception and embodiment, and with an effect quite thrilling.[203]

March 17, Tuesday Baltimore

Alice Gray played Juliet with Booth in *Romeo and Juliet*. The *American and Commercial Advertiser* commented:

> Mr. Booth's personation of Romeo, which was witnessed and earnestly applauded by an audience completely filling [the theatre], was a masterly effort, brilliant with the evidence of a pure and vigorous genius, and exhibiting in all its details the care and culture of the thorough artist.[204]

March 18, Wednesday Baltimore

Booth appeared as Phidias and Raphael in *The Marble Heart*. The *American and Commercial Advertiser* was impressed:

> The house was densely crowded, and whether Mr. Booth caught the infection of enthusiasm, or whether the character is specially adapted to his native powers, we will not pause to inquire, but certain it is he acted with surpassing force of passion and skill. It was a splendid effort, his Raphael fraught with the deepest and purest pathos.[205]

March 19, Thursday Baltimore

Booth played Pescara in *The Apostate*. The *Sun* remarked on Booth's popularity:

> A magnificent picture of our brilliant and gifted young townsman [Booth] is exhibited in the window of Canfield & Bro.'s splendid store, southwest corner of Charles and Baltimore Streets. Also another at Harrington & Mills's Picture Store, Baltimore St., north side, between North and Calvert. These pictures are splendid specimens of art, and the subject of them is now drawing immense throngs....[206]

March 20, Friday Baltimore

Booth played Charles de Moor in *The Robbers*, a role in which, according to the *American and Commercial Advertiser*, "his admirers claim he is superior to the eminent James E. Murdoch. It is a character well adapted to display the native power and boldness of young Booth's genius."[207]

The *Gazette* reviewed the performance:

The young favorite acted Charles DeMoor, in Schiller's tragedy of *The Robbers*, with great intensity and a bold originality of conception. The parricide was terrible in its earnestness of passion, and reached, in effect, to the thrilling. We do not hesitate to say that it is the most effective and exciting representation of the character ever presented from the stage of a Baltimore Theatre.[208]

March 21, Saturday Baltimore

Booth closed his engagement with a matinee of *The Marble Heart*, followed by an evening performance of *Richard III*. According to the *American and Commercial Advertiser*:

His performance of *Richard III* was worthy to be remembered in connection with the great Booth's great personation of the same powerful character. Its passion and earnest force were unmistakably evidenced in every speech, and the triumph of the artist culminated at the close of the play, when he wrought the sympathies of his vast auditory up to the highest pitch.[209]

March 22, Sunday Baltimore

March 23, Monday

Maggie Mitchell opened at the Holliday Street Theatre in Baltimore.

April 3, Friday Philadelphia

Booth wrote to Joe Simonds inquiring about land in Boston: "Did you or Orlando [Tompkins, manager of the Boston Theatre] send me that catalogue of Back Bay lands to be sold April 9th[?]."[210] He was interested in buying land in the Back Bay, where tidal flats had been filled in.

April 9, Thursday

At an auction in Boston, Simonds purchased a lot at 115 Commonwealth Avenue, Boston, for Booth. The purchase price was $8,192.10.[211]

April 10, Friday Washington

April 11, Saturday Washington

The Grover's Theatre playbill advertised: "Mr. John Wilkes Booth, First appearance in Washington, A Star of the First Magnitude, Son of Junius Brutus Booth and brother and artistic rival of Edwin Booth." Booth played *Richard III*. British actor Charles Wyndham wrote of the fifth act:

The scene opened with the two contesting parties fighting, forming a long lane diagonally across the stage. On he would come, bursting through this lane, slashing right and left at both friend and foe till aglow with hate and passion he reached the footlights, where Richmond would appear.[212]

The *Washington Morning Chronicle* noted that "J. Wilkes ... appears to have inherited the ability of his father to a greater extent than any of his brothers. His progressive genius has been the admiration of every public save this...."[213]

President Lincoln attended another theatre.

April 12, Sunday Washington

April 13, Monday Washington

Booth played his great double character Phidias and Raphael in the emotional play *The Marble Heart*.

Booth consulted with Dr. John Frederick May[214] and had a fibroid tumor removed from his neck. He asked the doctor to say he removed a bullet if asked.[215]

April 14, Tuesday Washington

Booth performed *Hamlet* with Charles Wyndham as Osric, Effie Germon[216] as Ophelia, and Susan Denin as the Queen.[217]

April 15, Wednesday Washington

Booth appeared as Claude Melnotte in *The Lady of Lyons*.

April 16, Thursday Washington

Grover's Theatre presented the comedy *Money* instead of *Macbeth*. Booth, playing Alfred Evelyn, was hampered by a "severe cold."[218] The *Chronicle* noted:

The manager [of Grover's] had anticipated producing this evening the play of *Macbeth*. It was accordingly advertised ... but the non-arrival of the music, which is a material adjunct of the play in its proper representation, compelled Mr. [Leonard] Grover to submit another programme to-night....[219]

April 17, Friday Washington

Booth appeared as Shylock in *The Merchant of Venice* and as Petruchio in *Katharine and Petruchio*. The *Washington National Republican* stated:

Mr. Booth is a young man of rare abilities, and, considering his experience, really wonderful in his impersonations. His representations, notwithstanding the severe surgical operation of Monday evening last, entitle him to the admiration of the public.[220]

Booth wrote to theatre manager Ben DeBar confirming an engagement in St. Louis to begin June 15.[221]

April 18, Saturday Washington

Booth appeared as Phidias and Raphael in *The Marble Heart*. According to the *Chronicle*:

Mr. Booth has just been in the city long enough to make him well known to us, and to gain for himself a lasting friendship of a critical public to whom he was a stranger but one week ago. The great success of the present engagement has been the thrilling emotional French play of *The Marble Heart*, in which not only Mr. Booth, but also Miss Annette Ince,[222] Miss Susan Denin and the entire company appear.[223]

President Lincoln's ten-year-old son, Tad, was a frequent visitor to Grover's Theatre. Tad and a fourteen-year-old friend attended this performance. The friend later related:

One night [at Grover's Theatre] there was a stirring drama called *The Marble Heart*, in which a dark, handsome man with brilliant black eyes took the leading part. Tad and I looked up his name in the program, for he fascinated us, particularly Tad. "I'd like to meet that man," said Tad. "He makes me thrill." [Between acts the boys were introduced to the actor.] Booth shook hands with us in the pleasantest fashion imaginable. He talked to us while he made up, and when we went away he gave us each a bunch of roses.[224]

April 19, Sunday Washington

Booth wrote to Joe Simonds: "I was idle this week but stay here in hopes to open the other Theatre next Monday for a week or two before going to Chicago.... *[h]ave a hole in my neck you could run your fist in. The doctor had a hunt for my bullet....*"[225] Booth noted in the letter that both he and his sister Rose had sent drafts to Orlando Tompkins for the down-payment on the Back Bay land.

April 20, Monday Washington

April 21, Tuesday Washington

April 22, Wednesday Washington

April 23, Thursday Washington

April 24, Friday Washington

Grau's Opera Company closed its very successful engagement at the Washington Theatre.[226]

April 25, Saturday Washington

Grover's Theatre presented *Our American Cousin* starring Susan Denin and James M. Ward.[227]

April 26, Sunday Washington

April 27, Monday Washington

Booth played *Richard III* at the Washington Theatre, which he was managing for two weeks. The *Washington National Intelligencer* commented:

Our expectations were more than realized ... in witnessing Mr. Booth's rendition of the character of Richard at the Washington Theatre. Although but a youth he has already reached an eminence almost equal to his renowned sire. His genius is wonderful, and displayed itself in the fourth and fifth acts of Richard so strongly as to remind us of the Elder Booth. The effect produced upon the audience was absolutely startling, and bordered nearly upon the terrible. The Theatre was crowded with an appreciative and fashionable audience, who appeared from their frequent bursts of applause, to feel that they were anxious to pay a fitting tribute to that genius which has placed the name of Booth among the foremost on the histrionic stage.[228]

Among the members of the Washington Theatre company during Booth's period as manager were Alice Gray, Effie Germon, and old friend Sam Chester.[229] Booth carried pictures of Gray and Germon in his pocket notebook.

Edwin Adams, who had been in the stock company in Richmond with Booth, opened at Grover's.

April 28, Tuesday Washington

Booth played *The Apostate*. The *National Intelligencer* anticipated the performance:

Mr. Booth appears in his great character of Pescara [in *The Apostate*], a part written expressly for his late lamented father. In this great character Mr. B. is said to stand without a rival. His exhibition of disappointed villainy in the fourth act is said to be entirely beyond description. He has made the part peculiarly his own, and has excited the greatest enthusiasm in every city where he has played it.[230]

April 29, Wednesday Washington

Booth, who, according to the *Chronicle*, "appears to have taken our citizens by storm," appeared as Phidias and Raphael in *The Marble Heart*.[231] The *National Intelligencer* observed of Booth in this play:

In the first act, he says little, but his whole deportment expresses the absorbing enthusiasm of the fierce artist nature, and by that action the audience is almost always magnetized, fascinated, and held; for although his voice is often inarticulate, yet the tones somehow thrill you, although you do not hear the words. We never witnessed a finer piece of acting than Booth's scene with the brilliant lady of his love, Mademoiselle Marco, in which she casts him off forever. She is influenced by worldly considerations; he is influenced only by those burning and bewildering dreams that the ideal nature alone can feel, and which surround the object of its regard with a dazzling halo of merits....[232]

April 30, Thursday Washington

Booth played *Romeo and Juliet.* "On Thursday," the *National Intelligencer* remarked, "we were particularly impressed with the beauty and spirit of Miss Alice Gray's rendition of Juliet."[233]

The *National Intelligencer* commented: The performances of Mr. John Wilkes Booth at the Washington Theatre this week deserve especial notice for our citizens. The engagement is very brief, and he is playing his very best characters. His *Apostate* ... reminded us most vividly of his father's famous impersonation. Although not a great public favorite, this play is nevertheless one demanding prodigious concentration of passion. Booth, the father, used always to thrill the house as Pescara; many single passages in the play were uttered by him with volcanic power. This son seems to us full of his father's genuine inspiration, and he shows it not merely by voice and tone, but in his personal action, his face especially. The play of his features is intensely expressive of the emotion of the words. We have never seen more intense and complicated expressions of agony than his features express in Shylock. J. W. Booth has that which is the grand constituent of all truly great acting, intensity. Intensity is the attribute of genius; learning and study may toil for it, they toil in vain; it is the lightning of the soul, and cannot be taught to the mind. Without it an actor may play level passages, and with a good voice may produce pleasing effects, but he can never strike fire in the hearts of his hearers.[234]

May 1, Friday Washington

On his benefit night, Booth played the title role in *The Stranger* and Petruchio in *Katharine and Petruchio.*

Near Washington, the Battle of Chancellorsville began.

May 2, Saturday Washington

Booth portrayed Charles de Moor in *The Robbers.* The *National Intelligencer* noted:

As a tragedian Mr. Booth deservedly ranks very high. Deep study has mad him conversant with all he has undertaken, and there is much originality in his acting. The talent displayed by Mr. Booth might in one so young be by some deemed precocity were it not that the evidences of study and research are patent in his readings. Time will serve to improve and chasten his style ere he reaches the height of his capacity. His genius is self-evident, and stirred the sensibilities of his audience, as was apparent Saturday night, in his representation of Charles de Moor [in *The Robbers*].... It was absolutely startling and bordered upon the terrible. The strong, passionate, injured, and sometimes penitent robber was portrayed in a manner that will not soon be forgotten by any one in that large assembly.[235]

Lucy Hale, a daughter of Senator John Parker Hale of New Hampshire, witnessed Booth's performance in *The Robbers* during this engagement. She sent him a bouquet of flowers, and they soon became acquainted.[236]

May 3, Sunday Washington

May 4, Monday Washington

"The grand supernatural drama of *The Corsican Brothers* will be produced [at the Washington Theatre] this evening, J. Wilkes Booth appearing as the twin brothers, in which characters it is said he has gained a most enviable renown," wrote the *Chronicle*, which reported the next day that Booth had been greeted by "another large and fashionable audience."[237]

The Battle of Chancellorsville concluded.

May 5, Tuesday Washington

Booth played *Othello*. The Washington Theatre notice in the *National Intelligencer* announced, under the heading "LESSEE AND MANAGER—JOHN WILKES BOOTH," that Grau's Italian Opera Troupe would appear at the theatre on Wednesday and Thursday evenings.

The Union army withdrew from Chancellorsville. As a result of this Union defeat, gloom shrouded Washington and attendance at the theatre fell off.

May 6, Wednesday Washington

Booth relinquished his time to Grau's Italian Opera Troupe for a performance of the opera *Martha*. A severe rainstorm limited the size of the audience and the profits of Manager Booth.[238]

May 7, Thursday Washington

The Opera Troupe had the theatre again and presented the opera *Roberto Il Diavolo*.[239]

May 8, Friday Washington

Booth played *Macbeth*. The *National Intelligencer* was impressed with his engagement:

We regret exceedingly that this favorite and talented young actor is obliged so soon to leave us, but engagements in the West compel him to depart.... He now stands, most unquestionably, among the very first actors in our country.... Mr. Booth has apparently learned early in life the lesson that study and application are necessary in acquiring a high histrionic rank, and to this we are justified in ascribing in a measure the great ability he manifests. He has more than satisfied his friends, has made new admirers and plenty of them, while the size of his audiences has been plainly indicative of the estimation in which he is held here. Mr. Booth's reputation promises to rival his father's, and notwithstanding the resemblances his performance is characterized by marked originality at times, and bears the stamp of merit which genius alone and imitation never could give it. Coming among us a stranger, with nothing but the prestige of a great name, he departs bearing with him, the good will and esteem of every one who has had the pleasure of witnessing his chaste and matchless impersonations. We have no hesitancy in pronouncing him the most promising actor of the age.[240]

May 9, Saturday Washington

Booth closed his engagement with a portrayal of Charles de Moor in *The Robbers*. The *National Intelligencer* anticipated the performance:

Although constantly interfered with by the same causes which have troubled the army of the Potomac, bad weather and rains, yet the young tragedian has played with all his accustomed fire; and his audiences have been always appreciative, and generally large.... This play [*The Robbers*] ... requires more dramatic action than vocal power. And wherever any thing can be exhibited to the eye in illustration of passion Mr. Booth reigns supreme. His soul is filled with terror and enthusiasm, and it exhibits itself in voice and action, but most emphatically in the latter. He *acts* every passion to the eye.[241]

The *National Intelligencer*, summarizing Booth's engagement in Washington, took special note of his work in *The Lady of Lyons*:

In the political and Napoleonic character of Claude Melnotte we think Booth is the handsomest youthful figure on the American stage. Many actors contrive a stage "make-up" like Bonaparte in the famous picture of De la Roche, with the hair drooping over the forehead, but we never saw a more genuine Napoleon profile than Booth's, as he walked the stage in the military costume of the Empire. In conclusion, we have only to say that this young actor plays not from stage rule, but from his soul, and his soul is inspired with genius. Genius is its own schoolmaster, it can be cultivated but not created on earth.[242]

May 10, Sunday Washington

May 11, Monday

James Anderson Wise presented a handwritten copy of the poem *Once I was Pure* to "J. Wilkes Booth, Esq."[243]

May 16, Saturday Chicago

Booth was in Chicago for rehearsals by this date.

May 17, Sunday Chicago

May 18, Monday Chicago

Booth began his engagement at McVicker's Theatre with *The Lady of Lyons*. The *Chicago Tribune* remarked that he "acted Claude Melnotte as few actors on the American stage can do. The applause he received was well bestowed and well merited."[244]

May 19, Tuesday Chicago

Booth played *Richard III*. The *Chicago Times* critic was not impressed:

J. Wilkes Booth appeared at the Theatre ... in his accustomed personation of Gloster, in Richard the Third. He does not display marked difference from his usual style of rendering the character, although one or two palpable improvements have been made since we last heard him. So far as the merits of the performance are concerned, there is really but one valid reason for honoring it with a notice, and that is that he seems to consider it his prime forte. He never neglects an opportunity to put it upon the bills, and wherever his sojourn is made we see in large capitals the title of this favorite play. The most unfavorable criticisms, of which an abundance have emanated from good authority, do not diminish his confidence, but seem rather to stimulate effort than otherwise.

If the appreciation of an audience is a fair index, the effort is a failure in Chicago, for a more unimpassioned gathering seldom sits in the benches of the theatre than the one which occupied them last night. We have said before, and say it again, that the attraction lies in the connection between the name of Booth and the play of Richard the Third. Unfortunately, however, this is not the Booth who created that celebrity. There was one of the name who swept aside all competitors and stood alone in his glory, but he has passed away, and with him the mantle which covered all there was of grandeur and genius in this great conception. His representative, we are sorry to say, lives but in a borrowed light.

There is some tolerable acting in the first and second acts, although it is stilted and stained of the most unnatural hue, when we consider that it represents the actions of a human being. The semblance ceases scarcely, however, when the curtain rises the third time, and from thence onward we have a ranting and roaring stage hero of the first water.... [Booth was] a violent, mouthing stage villain, who could have deceived nobody except by the license of stage forms.... We do not hesitate therefore to say that there is no merit in the performance as a whole, or to add that it is a libel upon the conception of Shakespeare.[245]

May 20, Wednesday Chicago

Booth played Phidias and Raphael in *The Marble Heart*. The *Tribune* critic had a different view from the *Times*:

The name and fame of his father doubtless at first attracted the people toward him, but had he not been a "worthy son of a worthy sire," they would not adhere to him as they do. That there are faults and blemishes in Mr. Booth's acting, no one will deny; but did they not exist with his father, and all great actors at his age? In every part he plays, the auditor will perceive the marks of the student, and this being so, errors of judgment must be eradicated with time and experience. Since his advent in Chicago some eighteen months ago, no one who has attended his performances, can fail to see an improvement, and we predict ere he has attained his thirtieth year, he will be as great in his delineations as his honored predecessor. It is a mere matter of opinion, which is his best character, for certainly he renders all he undertakes far above mediocrity, while at times he sours to the sublimity of his art. No one will ever regret having witnessed him in any of his characters.[246]

The *Times* critic commented:

Mr. Booth's personation is the conventional one, doing ordinary justice perhaps to the character, but furnishing no brilliant points with which to win applause. His audience found no fault certainly, but as certainly received no vivid impressions, for there was no powerful acting to create an impression. Mr. Booth does not abound in power under any circumstances, but he sometimes displays an emotional capacity which wins him a fair share of commendations, and to this peculiarity he was indebted for all the success he acquired.... The inveterate desire for stage display, which is part and parcel of all his acting, was visible as one of the marring features. It was hardly necessary, for instance, to go on the rampage and endanger the scenery at the close of the third act, when a simple act of reckless resolve was to be

perpetrated. The standard text book, it is true, contains the significant hint, in brackets and italics, which instructs him about these times to fall into a fit of "desperation," but standard text books are as stereotyped as standard actors and by no means interpret nature. The same authority also instructs Volage in the same scene to "stand mournfully looking at Madame Duchatlet, pointing to Maria," but Mr. Myers declined to follow the sage advice, and indulged in so sudden and fierce an onslaught upon his unfortunate hat as to bring down the house. The movement was natural and impulsive, and was far the better acting of the two. It is in this adherence to stage forms that Mr. Booth does himself and his same rank injustice. It is that which made a farce of his *Richard the Third*, and which ruins the effect of most of his efforts at high strung acting. He has a native talent which often shows itself, and, when left to the impulse of nature, does credit to its possessor, but when blended with stage rant it is no better than the common trash which we see every day in actors who should have been plowmen.[247]

May 21, Thursday Chicago

Booth repeated *The Marble Heart*. A large party traveled from Beloit, Wisconsin, to witness this performance.[248]

May 22, Friday Chicago

Booth played Alfred Evelyn in *Money*. "He is drawing moderate audiences," reported the *Times*, while the *Tribune* asserted that "Mr. Booth has made, and is making hosts of friends by his beautiful delineations."[249]

May 23, Saturday Chicago

Booth played Charles de Moor in *The Robbers*.

May 24, Sunday Chicago

May 25, Monday Chicago

Booth appeared in *Romeo and Juliet*. The *Times* remarked:

His personation is in many respects an attractive one, and is perhaps the best in his repertoire. He certainly exhibits a better style of acting than in the more violent and demonstrative plays which he seems to prefer. It is in emotional passages that his real strength shows itself, and this play abounds in such.... Mr. Booth can throw a depth and pathos into his voice ... which tells with effect upon an audience. He could not resist the temptation to rant a little before going to fight with Tybalt, and therefore marred an effective scene; and indeed did the same thing more than once. It is a chronic fault, and a most distasteful one. We believe, however, in catering to the capricious fancies of the public, and will in the same connection mention that those who would see a fierce and uncompromising specimen of stage rant should attend the performance of The Apostate [on Tuesday]....[250]

May 26, Tuesday Chicago

Booth played Pescara in *The Apostate*. The *Times* critic continued to find fault with Booth's melodramatic style:

> He fails to appreciate the essential fact that intensity of emotion is not in any sense expressed by fuming rant, and that passion is displayed with the least effect when the actor loses control of himself. It is simply absurd to call that acting which produces an effect contrary to what is intended, and yet the raging scenes of the fourth act bathed the audience in smiles. Its concentrated horrors, accumulating upon one another until better nature seems lost to sight, were simply a burlesque upon tragedy—a heaped up maze of over-acted absurdities, which provoked broad smiles where they should have brought a shudder. To delineate consuming passion by a natural, intense, and concentrated effort which carried with it a thrill of sympathy, is one thing, and to interpret the same sentiment by raging like a wild-beast, splitting the air with hoarse outcry, and fairly fuming into a state of exhaustion, is another. Yet the latter was the letter of Mr. Booth's personation. It was positively agonizing at intervals, always intensity over tragic, and in no sense natural or unaffected. If the audience did not get their money's worth it was not because lungs and muscle failed to do its work.[251]

May 27, Wednesday Chicago

Booth appeared in *The Merchant of Venice*. The *Times* noted that Shylock:

> ...is one of the characters which he [Booth] does justice to by a correct and impressive delineation and the limited exercise of his muscular gifts. It may be listened to from beginning to end without a feeling of distaste, while many portions are calculated to excite the most pleasurable sensations. There is at times a strong emotional capacity in the acting of Mr. Booth; in fact, his strength lies therein, and when that peculiarity is developed, as is largely the case in this character, he acquits himself most creditably.[252]

May 28, Thursday Chicago

Booth played *Richard III*.

May 29, Friday Chicago

Booth played *Hamlet*. The *Times* review was tepid:

> Mr. Booth plays the character in medium style,

without much originality, or a superabundance of striking points. The personation is not particularly calculated to excite enthusiasm in an audience, and may be passed by with the remark that it is of ordinary merit.... There are few actors whose modesty deters them from essaying it [*Hamlet*] and the whole army of spouters have their tilt at it.[253]

May 30, Saturday Chicago

Booth played *Othello*.

May 31, Sunday Chicago

The *Tribune* noted:

> The strangers who are to visit the city during the present week, will be pleased to learn that the young Tragedian, J. Wilkes Booth, is to appear nightly at McVicker's Theatre, in one of his brilliant delineations.... We expect to see the theatre overflowed each evening.[254]

June 1, Monday Chicago

The last week of Booth's Chicago engagement opened with *The Robbers*, in which he played Charles de Moor. The *Times* critic wrote caustically:

> The engagement of Mr. J. Wilkes Booth at the Theatre has not been eminently flattering, in a pecuniary way. He might, perhaps, have done better by putting off the engagement a few months longer, as his appearances here have followed each other in rapid succession during the past twelve months. The highest order of talent will scarcely warrant the familiarity which the public acquires by such frequent engagements, and Mr. Booth does not possess that degree of attraction. He has played his usual round of characters during the present visit; some he has played well, some indifferently and some badly. Balancing the whole, he impressed us with a sense of mediocrity, or something very near it. As a stock actor he would win a high position, but as a star he is somewhat below the medium standard. Time may remedy some of his defects, but as a general thing inherent failings become chronic with experience. The elements of a great actor do not belong to him, and he will consequently never become a great actor. His brother never made, at his age, the displays of bad taste which mark a large portion of his acting, and we firmly believe that an actor who was weak enough to indulge in stereotyped extravagances in early career ever attained celebrity. His *Richard the Third* is a stage conception, full of affected conceits and absurd focus. His *Pescara* is a libel on nature—a complete burlesque on the art of acting. It is positively atrocious in rant. *Shylock* he does fair justice to, as also *Hamlet* and *Romeo*, but in these he is far from a perfect delineation. He possesses a capacity for senti-

mental or emotional parts, and renders them to good advantage, but he is sure to break into a stereotyped outbreak of some kind the moment a shade of violence enters the plot. No greater mistake was ever made than that which leads actors to suppose that passion cannot be interpreted without violence of manner and voice. It is a mistake, however, which is confined to actors of a medium caliber, and is by them alone carried into practice. If they can conquer the habit there is that much gained, and, if they cannot, they must be content with moderate pretensions.[255]

June 2, Tuesday Chicago

Booth performed *Richard III*. The *Times* was dismissive:

Mr. Booth did Richard the Third in his customary style.... Our readers know our opinion of the performance, and we need not enlarge upon it. In an artistic view it is a parody upon nature. In a common sense view it is scarcely worthy of toleration.[256]

June 3, Wednesday Chicago

Booth played Phidias and Raphael in *The Marble Heart*.

June 4, Thursday Chicago

Booth appeared in *Romeo and Juliet*. The *Times* critic wrote:

The audience was not large—not as large as the merits of the play deserved, for it is one of Mr. Booth's best personations. He has a capacity for sentimental parts which should lead him in his search for fame.... As *Romeo* he is impressive and often fervent. There is an emotion, an earnestness, a pathos in the very tones of his voice, which attracts independent of the pervading warmth imparted by the poetic flow of the text. In the balcony scene he is especially conspicuous for sentiment, and is the interview between the new made husband and wife, in the lady's chamber, the same characteristic displays itself. There is a brief but little provocative for rant, and consequently but little ranting is done, and therein lies the virtue of the performance. That there is a virtue to it, compared with some other representations by the same actor, no appreciative mind will deny.[257]

June 5, Friday Chicago

In his benefit performance, Booth played the title role in *The Stranger* and Petruchio in *Katharine and Petruchio*.

June 6, Saturday Chicago

Booth played Shylock in *The Merchant of Venice* and appeared as Petruchio in *Katharine and Petruchio* to close his engagement. *Wilkes'*

Spirit of the Times reported: "J. Wilkes Booth, brother of Edmund [*sic*], was quite successful in Chicago, although he was artistically handled, without gloves, by the local critics."[258] The newspapers announced the opening of Frank Chanfrau at McVicker's Theatre on Monday in *Our American Cousin at Home*.

June 13, Saturday St. Louis

Booth was in St. Louis by this date for rehearsals.

June 14, Sunday St. Louis

Ben DeBar's leading man, Thomas L. Conner, was arrested for making "disloyal expressions." Booth may have been arrested as well, but the provost marshal's records confirm Conner's arrest and do not mention Booth.[259]

June 15, Monday St. Louis

Booth opened at Ben DeBar's St. Louis Theatre in *Richard III* with J. E. Carden as Richmond.

June 16, Tuesday St. Louis

Booth performed *Hamlet*, in which DeBar played the Gravedigger and J. E. Carden played the Ghost. According to the *St. Louis Missouri Democrat*, "J. Wilkes Booth attracted another full and fashionable house ... his artistic rendition of *Hamlet* was warmly applauded and the play throughout was well enacted."[260]

June 17, Wednesday St. Louis

Booth played Pescara in *The Apostate*. The *Democrat* reported that Booth "is nightly greeted by full and fashionable houses; his performance eliciting the most enthusiastic applause. He is well supported by Mr. J. E. Carden, an actor of much merit, Miss Wyette and the rest of the company."[261]

June 18, Thursday St. Louis

Booth appeared as *The Stranger*. The *Democrat* anticipated "an admirable performance."[262]

June 19, Friday St. Louis

Booth appeared as Fabien and Louis in *The Corsican Brothers*.

June 20, Saturday St. Louis

Booth appeared as Fabien and Louis in *The Corsican Brothers*. The *Democrat* stated that "judging from the hearty applause bestowed on the piece last night, we expect to see a full house."[263]

June 21, Sunday St. Louis

June 22, Monday St. Louis

Booth appeared in *The Marble Heart*. The performance "proved a great success," according to the *Democrat*, which remarked that "Mr. Booth in the characters of Phidias and Raphael was most excellent."[264]

R. J. Morgan, a local businessman who fancied himself an actor, asked Booth to relinquish Saturday night. Booth responded, "I will agree to give up Saturday Night 27th on condition you pay me fifty dollars $50 to be paid on or before Friday morning 26th."[265]

June 23, Tuesday St. Louis

Booth played Charles de Moor in *The Robbers*.

June 24, Wednesday St. Louis

Booth appeared as Shylock in *The Merchant of Venice* and as Petruchio in *Katharine and Petruchio*.

June 25, Thursday St. Louis

Booth played *Richard III*. "At the St. Louis Theatre, J. W. Booth, has been playing to a very good average of audiences," the *New York Clipper* reported after the engagement ended.[266]

June 26, Friday St. Louis

Booth played Alfred Evelyn in the comedy *Money*, with Ben DeBar as Graves. Booth's engagement closed on Friday in order to allow R. J. Morgan to appear as the leading player in the Saturday performance.[267]

June 27, Saturday St. Louis?

June 28, Sunday En route to Cleveland

June 29, Monday Cleveland

The *Cleveland Morning Leader* advertisement for the Academy of Music stated: "The Manager announces with no ordinary pride that he has succeeded in inducing the greatest living Tragedian, J. WILKES BOOTH, to appear for FOUR NIGHTS ONLY, commencing on Tuesday evening, June 30th."[268]

June 30, Tuesday Cleveland

Booth opened at the Academy of Music in *Richard III*. John Ellsler, manager of the theatre and an old family friend, wrote:

His fiery, untamed method, if I may so call it, was most noticeable in his *Richard III*. Indeed, to my mind, he was the only Richard, after his father. His fifth act was terribly real, while his fight with Richmond was a task that many a good swords-

man dreaded.... In many instances he wore poor *Richmond* out....[269]

James C. McCollom played Richmond. The *Cleveland Herald* critic noted that the whole audience rose to its feet with excitement during the combat scene in *Richard III*.[270]

July 1, Wednesday Cleveland

Booth appeared as *Hamlet*. The *Herald* observed: "The play was finely performed, and Booth's rendition of the 'Melancholy Dane' drew repeated and enthusiastic applause from a large audience. Mr. Booth has justified the expectations of those who were led to expect something more than ordinarily good...."[271]

James C. McCollom played the Ghost.

The Battle of Gettysburg began.

July 2, Thursday Cleveland

Booth, supported by John Ellsler, played Alfred Evelyn in *Money*.

Union forces repulsed the Confederates at Little Round Top at Gettysburg.

July 3, Friday Cleveland

Booth closed his engagement with a portrayal of Charles de Moor in *The Robbers*. Rachel Noah played a supporting role.

The Army of the Potomac turned back Pickett's Charge at Gettysburg.

July 4, Saturday En route to Buffalo

The Confederate garrison at Vicksburg surrendered to Union forces.

July 5, Sunday Buffalo

July 6, Monday Buffalo

Booth opened at the Metropolitan Theatre with *Richard III*.[272]

July 7, Tuesday Buffalo

Booth played Claude Melnotte in *The Lady of Lyons*. Many businesses in Buffalo decorated their stores in honor of the recent Union victories at Gettysburg and Vicksburg.

July 8, Wednesday Buffalo

Booth played Pescara in *The Apostate*.

July 9, Thursday Buffalo

Booth played *Hamlet*.

July 10, Friday Buffalo

Booth played the double bill of *Money* and *Katharine and Petruchio*. In *Money*, Booth appeared as Alfred Evelyn "and played the part very cleverly," according to the *Buffalo Daily Courier*.[273]

July 11, Saturday Buffalo

Booth played *Macbeth*.

July 12, Sunday New York

Adam Badeau, while on General Grant's staff, had been wounded in the foot and about this date began a convalescence at Edwin Booth's home. He wrote that "Wilkes Booth was there and stood in the door when I arrived. He was a strong, stalwart young fellow of twenty-six, and himself helped to lift me out of the carriage, and afterward carried me in his arms to an upper story."[274]

July 13, Monday New York

Rioters in New York City, protesting the draft, burned twelve buildings, including the United States draft office on Broadway.

July 14, Tuesday New York

The draft riots continued. More than thirty blacks were hanged, shot, or beaten to death.

July 15, Wednesday New York

July 16, Thursday New York

The riots began to abate.

July 17, Friday New York

Federal troops held order in New York City.

July 18, Saturday New York

August 27, Thursday

Ford's Theatre in Washington, D.C., opened to the public.

7

Career End: 1863–1864

John Wilkes Booth began the 1863-1864 season with a two-week engagement at the Howard Athenaeum in Boston alongside veteran actress Julia Bennett Barrow. The audiences were large, and, according to a local newspaper, "their applause has been frequent and merited."[1] Booth, Barrow, and several supporting actors then embarked on a three-week tour of several New England cities, including Worcester and Springfield in Massachusetts, Providence, Rhode Island, and Hartford, Connecticut.[2] The combination played two or three nights in each city. The Worcester Theatre's profits were so high during Booth's visit that an attempt was made to book him for the week of November 2, but a previously arranged engagement in Washington, D.C., prevented his acceptance.[3] The troupe played for two nights in Brooklyn, New York, and concluded its travels with three performances in New Haven, Connecticut, at the end of October. The *Brooklyn Standard* critic wrote of Booth:

> He strongly resembles [Edwin] in features, physique and quality of voice, but he is inferior in several important particulars. His performance lacks the grace, finish and repose of Edwin, his enunciation is indistinct, and he betrays at times a tendency to rant. There are, however, flashes of real power. I was particularly and favorably impressed with the scene of the killing of Henry and with the whole of the fourth act. The difficult wooing scene did not please me as well. The 'terrific broadsword combat,' as it was sensationally described on the bills, was intensely gratifying

to the gallery, Mr. Booth fencing well and introducing some new and effective business.[4]

Fanny Brown,[5] a young actress in the combination, caught Booth's eye. Booth and Fanny reportedly secured adjoining rooms on this tour, in a show of discretion.[6] In November the *New York Clipper* printed a mysterious statement: "Rumor says that J. Wilkes Booth will shortly lead to the hymeneal altar the beautiful and fascinating Fanny Brown. Where's Dolly?"[7] Dolly remains unidentified. Fanny's was one of five photographs found in Booth's pocket diary at the time of his death.

Booth opened with *Richard III* at John T. Ford's new theatre in Washington on November 2. The *Washington Morning Chronicle* critic was not favorably impressed:

> When Mr. Booth comes upon the stage, he looks like a rascal ... he rubs his hands in a coarse, fiendish manner, as though there was as much brutality in his nature as in one of his own murderers.... He insists upon being mentioned in the same sentence as Forrest, Macready, Davenport, Wallack and Edwin Booth. This is an attempt to obtain fame under false pretenses.[8]

The *Washington National Intelligencer* critic thought differently, noting with approval that:

> It has been said of Mr. Booth's rendition of Richard that he is perhaps the best representative of that elegant school of tragedians of which his late honored father was so distinguished a member. Certainly no higher compliment could be paid to the genius of one so young in years.[9]

On November 9 President Lincoln, his secretary John Hay, and a party of several others saw Booth perform *The Marble Heart; or, The Sculptor's Dream*.[10] Ten days later President Lincoln delivered an address at the dedication of the cemetery at Gettysburg.

Booth's engagement at Ford's Theatre was one of the most profitable by any actor outside of New York.[11] John T. Ford, commenting years later on Booth's appearance at his theatre, wrote:

> Doubtless he would have made the greatest actor of his time had he lived. Besides being the handsomest man I ever saw, he was an athlete.... He added a fine physical organization to his marvelous mental powers. His Macbeth and Richard were different from any other I ever witnessed. In the scene in *Macbeth* where he enters the den of the witches, Booth would not content himself with the usual steps to reach the stage, but had a ledge of rocks some 10 to 12 feet high erected in their stead, down which he sprang upon the stage. His Richard was full of marvelous possibilities, and his fighting scene was simply terrific.... He was very fine in *The Apostate*, and his Raphael in *The Marble Heart* was simply matchless. He was an ideal Raphael.... I have paid him $700 a week, and he could easily earn $20,000 a year.[12]

Booth began an engagement at the Academy of Music in Cleveland late in November. The *Cleveland Plain Dealer* critic wrote of Booth:

> Time and study cannot fail to secure for him an exalted place among the most gifted who have ever trod the boards. Let him but wisely use the gifts within his grasp, cultivate nature and develop them and a brilliant future must crown him with an enduring halo of fame.[13]

According to the *New York Clipper*, Booth drew good houses:

> The city of Cleveland has had no reason to complain of amusement, much of it is of the most acceptable class. For the ten days prior to Monday 7th the Academy of Music was nightly crowded to witness Mr. J. Wilkes Booth in his varied and attractive repertoire the result being the thorough establishment

of the young actor as a favorite there and a very gratifying increase of manager Ellsler's treasury.[14]

The *Clipper* correspondent was not a fan of Booth, but he recognized that the public had a different view:

> Though not myself regarding Mr. B. as ever a passable candidate for admission to the circle of stars, the people here formed a different impression, if the attendance may be taken as a criterion. Throughout his engagement he was admirably sustained by Mrs. Ellsler and Mr. McCollom.[15]

Booth narrowly escaped serious injury on November 28 while performing the final act of *Richard III*. In the midst of the terrific sword combat, a blow by Richmond, played by James C. McCollom, broke Booth's sword. Booth caught the blade with his bare hands and continued the fight. The next blow knocked the blade from Booth's hand, and the flying weapon severely cut him through his eyebrow.[16] Clara Morris,[17] a young actress in the stock company, recalled the accident:

> There are not many men who can receive a gash over the eye in a scene at night without at least a momentary outburst of temper, but when the combat between Richard and Richmond was being rehearsed, Mr. Booth had again and again urged Mr. McCollom (that six-foot tall and handsome leading man, who entrusted me with the care of his watch during such encounters) to "come on hard! Come on hot! Hot, old fellow! Harder—faster!" He'd take the chance of a blow, if only they could make a hot fight of it.
>   And Mr. McCollom, who was a cold man, at night became nervous in his effort to act like a fiery one. He forgot he had struck the full number of head blows, and when Booth was pantingly expecting a thrust, McCollom, wielding his sword with both hands, brought it down with awful force fair across Booth's forehead. [Actually he knocked the blade out of Booth's hand.] A cry of horror rose, for in one moment his face was masked in blood, one eyebrow being cut cleanly through. There came, simultaneously, one deep groan from Richard, and the exclamation: "Oh, good God! Good God!" from Richmond, who

stood shaking like a leaf and staring at his work. Then Booth, flinging the blood from his eyes with his left hand, said, as genially as man could speak, "That's all right, old man! never mind me—only come on hard, for God's sake, and save the fight!"

Which he resumed at once, and though he was perceptibly weakened, it required the sharp order of Mr. Ellsler to "ring the first curtain bell," to force him to bring the fight to a close, a single blow shorter than usual. Then there was a running to and fro, with ice and vinegar paper and raw steak and raw oysters. When the doctor had placed a few stitches where they were most required, he laughingly declared there was provision enough in the room to start a restaurant. Mr. McCollom came to try to apologize, to explain, but Booth would have none of it; he held out his hand, crying: "Why, old fellow, you look as if *you* had lost the blood. Don't worry. Now if my eye had gone, that *would* have been bad!" And so, with light words, he tried to set the unfortunate man at ease, and though he must have suffered much mortification as well as pain from the eye, that in spite of all endeavors would blacken, he never made a sigh.[18]

Morris described Booth:

He was so young, so bright, so gay, so kind. I could not have known him well. Of course, too, there are two or three different people in every man's skin, yet when we remember that stars are not generally in the habit of showing their brightest, their best side to the company at rehearsal, we cannot help feeling both respect and liking for the one who does....

He was, like his great elder brother, rather lacking in height, but his head and throat, and the manner of its rising from his shoulders, were truly beautiful. His coloring was unusual, the ivory pallor of his skin, the inky blackness of his densely thick hair, the heavy lids of his glowing eyes, were all Oriental and they gave a touch of mystery to his face when it fell into gravity; but there was generally a flash of white teeth behind his silky mustache, and a laugh in his eyes....

Now it is scarcely an exaggeration to say the sex was in love with John Booth, the name Wilkes being apparently unknown to his family and close friends. At depot restaurants those fiercely unwilling maiden-

slammers of plates and shooters of coffee cups made to him swift and gentle offerings of hot steaks, hot biscuits, hot coffee, crowding round him like doves about a grain basket leaving other travelers to wait upon themselves or go without refreshment. At the hotels, maids had been known to enter his room and tear asunder the already made-up bed, that the "turn-over" might be broader by a thread or two, and both pillows slant at the perfectly correct angle. At the theatre, good heaven! As the sun-flowers turn upon their stalks to follow the beloved sun, so old or young, our faces smiling, turned to him.[19]

Booth's rendition of *The Marble Heart* was an audience favorite. At a rehearsal of the play, three women from the stock company posed, dressed in white with skin and hair powdered white as well, as Grecian statues. Booth, directing the rehearsal, noticed that one of the women had unattractive legs. He told her he was going to "advance" her to the central position where the "statue" wore her draperies to the floor. With this deft compliment, he saved her from embarrassment by not referring directly to his reason for the move. Booth's friend and fellow actor Edwin A. Emerson described him as "the gentlest man I ever knew. He was not feminine, yet gentle as a woman. In rehearsal he was always considerate of the other actors, and if he had a suggestion to make, made it with the utmost courtesy, prefacing it with; 'Now Mr.—, don't you think that perhaps this might be a better way to interpret that?'"[20]

John Ellsler, who had been a friend of Junius Brutus Booth, Sr., managed the theatre in Cleveland. He wrote of John Wilkes Booth:

He was a manly man; a term not easily defined, for there are those, blessed by nature, who have lacked the qualities of manhood. Wilkes Booth was not one of these; he was firm as a rock, honest, sincere, and unassuming in his private associations. If he had not a good word, he never used a bad one, to friend or foe; yet he never brooked an insult or pocketed an affront.

Young, impetuous, fearless, true, he was

also kind, loving and sympathetic; he could wile away hours playing with children, like a big boy (he often did so with mine) and the next moment, he was a man among men. His word was his bond, and men that knew him never doubted it.[21]

Ellsler and Booth became business partners. Oil had been discovered in Pennsylvania, and fortunes were being made. Booth wanted his share. He was tired of constant touring. Perhaps an oil fortune would enable him to retire from acting. Ellsler wrote:

His engagement with us was at the time of the mania for oil territory in Pennsylvania. Through a mutual friend, we were persuaded to invest in a profitable piece of oil land, the understanding being that at the conclusion of the dramatic season, John and myself would repair to our property, purchase the necessary machinery, and develop our investment.[22]

The mutual friend was Thomas Y. Mears. Mears, Ellsler, and Booth, along with Cleveland capitalist George Paunell, formed the Dramatic Oil Company.[23] Mears, Ellsler, and Booth traveled to Franklin, Pennsylvania, in mid–December 1863. The partners leased the oil rights to a farm downstream from Franklin on the east bank of the Allegheny River.[24] Booth soon left Franklin to fulfill an engagement in Leavenworth, Kansas.

The Leavenworth engagement was yet another unusual one in this year of atypical engagements for Booth. Leavenworth was remote and not on the theatrical circuit. Booth took a train from Ohio through Chicago to Hannibal, Missouri, and finally to St. Joseph. He made the short journey from St. Joseph to Leavenworth by steamboat. Abraham Lincoln had visited Leavenworth in December 1859 and had addressed audiences from the stage of Stockton Hall, later renamed Union Hall.[25] Booth performed at the same venue, though he failed to appear on the first night of his engagement. He may have been delayed by weather, or by illness. He arrived a day late[26] and stayed at the Planters' House, where Abraham Lincoln had stayed in 1859.[27]

A Leavenworth theatre employee, writing years after Booth's visit, gave an unflattering portrait of Booth that is inconsistent with all other accounts of Booth's actions and disposition:

I found him behind the scenes to be devoid of gentlemanly manners of any kind, and remarks he made that made many blush and turn away were said regardless of whom there were around him, or who heard them, male or female, and he had a course, reckless manner of throwing himself or anything else around, that those behind the scenes were kept continuously dodging out of his way, in every way acting as a "bully" over small fry.[28]

Booth may have had an "off" night, or perhaps the employee, writing long after the incident and after the assassination of Lincoln, had a distorted memory of Booth.

The theatre critic of the *Leavenworth Daily Conservative* thought well of Booth, writing that he "has not only genius, but careful culture and trained power of intellect. There is no actor now on the stage who displays so much of dramatic force and insight as Mr. J. W. Booth, except, perhaps, his brother Edwin."[29]

Booth, in a letter to Moses Kimball,[30] manager and founder of the Boston Museum, described a visit he made to friends at Fort Leavenworth, north of the city. For reasons he did not explain, he returned to the boat landing at Leavenworth by running the four-mile distance without stopping. At the landing, he learned that the servant who had accompanied him on his western trip, a young black man named Leav, had lost his pocket flask; Booth promptly rented a horse and returned to the Fort. He wrote jocularly that he saw a wagon "just crushing my best friend [the flask]. But I kissed him in his last moments by pressing the snow to my lips *over* which he had spilled his noble blood."[31]

Ice in the river prevented the steamboat from docking. Booth helped cut the ice to allow the boat to reach the shore. The boat then took him across the Missouri River to

Weston, Missouri. The next day he traveled to St. Joseph by train. The weather was bitterly cold, and Booth was chilled. He wrote that he went to bed "a dead man."[32]

Severe cold and heavy snow stalled train traffic and prevented Booth from leaving St. Joseph for his January 4 opening in St. Louis. His Leavenworth earnings must have been meager, for he was low on funds. He gave a reading at a local hall to make some easy money. Anxious to get to St. Louis, Booth hired a four-horse sleigh to take him over thirty-foot snow drifts thirty miles east to Cameron, Missouri, where he spent the night.[33] He took the train to St. Louis the next day. Mrs. McKee Rankin, an actress, sometime after the incident heard Booth tell a story of driving through huge snow drifts in intense cold, of upsetting the sleigh in the darkness and struggling to right it with his servant, and of fighting off wolves.[34] Booth, not averse to making up details to dramatize a story, later told Edwin Adams that he put a gun to the head of a train conductor in order to make him take the train through drifts.[35]

Booth opened his St. Louis engagement on Tuesday, January 12, having lost seven nights of performance—and pay. One of theatre manager Ben DeBar's stock actors wrote:

> He [Booth] told me of his hardships in coming down from Omaha [he meant St. Joseph] to fill his date in St. Louis, and that he had made the greater part of the journey in sleds.... He looked worn out, dejected and as melancholy as the dull, gray sky above us.[36]

Booth had contracted with George Wood, who owned theatres in Louisville, Nashville, and Cincinnati, to appear in those cities for a guarantee of $300 a week.[37] When he opened in Louisville in mid–January, he found that his old friend John Albaugh was in the stock company. The crowds at the theatre were large, and patrons had to be turned away.[38]

Booth opened at Wood's Theatre in Nashville on February 1, 1864. Ada Gray supported him, as she had done in Louisville.[39]

One observer reported being disturbed by noise in an adjoining hotel room and learning the disturbance was caused by "John Wilkes Booth and his leading Woman, who was also his mistress, and they were rehearsing some of their scenes. It sounded like a drunken brawl."[40]

The *Nashville Daily Union* commented:

> Mr. Booth came amongst us a stranger, his reputation as a rising star having preceded him, creating a general desire amongst our playgoers to get a 'taste of his quality.' His first night was a splendid ovation; the Theatre being densely packed, every foot of standing room occupied, and numbers sent away unable to get in. Nobly did he fulfill expectations and establish himself as a favorite. In no part has he failed. His genius appears equal to anything the tragic muse has produced; and the time is not distant when he will attain the highest niche of professional fame. His engagement here will not soon be forgotten by any who have attended the Theatre and the records of that establishment will transmit it to those who follow after him as the best played here during this most wonderful and most eventful of dramatic seasons.[41]

Booth was ill when he started an engagement in Cincinnati in mid–February. He substituted *Othello* for *Richard III*, perhaps to avoid the strenuous combat scene. He struggled through his first two nights of performances and was unable to perform on the third night. He was to suffer from respiratory illness for the next two months. By the end of the week, he seemed to be back in form. The *New York Clipper* reported that "J. Wilkes Booth did a good business last week at Wood's Theatre in Cincinnati."[42]

On February 28, while Booth was traveling to New Orleans for his next engagement, a Federal cavalry unit commanded by Colonel Judson Kilpatrick launched a raid on Richmond. Leading one of Kilpatrick's columns was Colonel Ulric Dahlgren, who was killed near the Confederate capital. Papers found on his body explicitly indicated that the purposes of the raid were to burn Richmond and to assassinate Jefferson Davis and his cabinet. Union General George G. Meade, replying to an inquiry from Confederate General Robert E. Lee, denied that the Union government had approved such plans. However, Dahlgren and others, both Federal and Confederate, believed that assassination of government leaders was a legitimate act of war.

Booth stopped in Memphis, Tennessee, for a day or two on his journey to New Orleans. According to one source, Booth joined the Knights of the Golden Circle, a Copperhead organization, in Memphis.[43] He met and consoled Richard M. Johnson, who, feeling grief for a lost friend, had been drinking when he made Booth's acquaintance. Booth spoke of his interest in the oil business.[44] When Booth left for New Orleans, his new friend remained in Memphis. Johnson came from a prominent St. Louis family, his brother being a leader in the drive against the extension of slavery. Johnson had served as a clerk at General Ulysses S. Grant's headquarters.

Illness delayed Booth's opening in New Orleans by a week, from March 7 to March 14. After he started his engagement at the St. Charles (also known as the Old Drury) Theatre, the *New Orleans Times* noted:

> It is a matter of regret that he is at present laboring under a severe hoarseness, in consequence of which his efforts have been much less satisfactory to himself than to his friends, but we trust his speedy recovery may enable him to consent to the merit of his endeavors. He has certainly created a furor here, which will continue through his engagement.[45]

Furor or not, the audiences were small.[46] Some of the local newspaper critics liked what they saw. The *New Orleans True Delta* remarked:

> Critics have carped at his personalities and found fault with his readings.... He has departed from the traditional renderings of certain personages, and so must any man do who is an actor.... We do not pretend that Mr. Booth is the greatest actor on the stage, but

we have yet to find any ... who gives promise of such excellence.[47]

The *Times* added:

> Seldom have we seen a man whose age and talent so well evinces that dramatic talent is intuitive, and not to be cultivated with years.... Mr. Booth seeks not to play a part, but to be intrinsically of it—not to render it in wonted stage form, but to inhere it, and thus, as an emotional creature to submit his rendition to the public.[48]

The *New York Clipper* succinctly summarized the conflicting views of John Wilkes Booth as an actor:

> The critics, as usual, are at variance respecting his merits. While some praise his performances, others remark that they have seen better performances by actors who were not stars, that he has much to learn and to unlearn ere he can take high rank in his profession, that he is no more successful in comedy than in tragedy etc. People, however, seem to think differently and continue to witness and applaud his performances. Though Mr. Booth is by no means a finished actor, yet there is the stuff in him of which great ones are made and if he will but apply himself assiduously to his profession he will in due course of time become a great actor.[49]

Booth often visited the newspaper editors in the cities in which he performed. The *New York Evening Post* later reported:

> On his arrival [in New Orleans], we are told, [Booth] called upon the editor of one of the leading journals, and in the course of conversation he warmly expressed his sympathy with Secession. Indeed, he was well known as a Secessionist, but he was not one of the "noisy kind." He had the same quiet, subdued, gentlemanly manner in his intercourse with others that marks his whole family.[50]

Booth, according to one source, stayed at the home of George W. Miller on Felicity Street, between Baronne and Dryades Streets. Despite his throat problems, he was quite active in playing billiards and tenpins and riding horseback. He made many friends and seemed always to be the center of attention.[51]

One acquaintance reported that Booth drank, but not so much that it affected his performances. Even when he had been drinking, he remained "an affable, considerate, courteous companion."[52] One night, while walking with friends, Booth was accepted a challenge to sing the banned pro–Confederate song "Bonnie Blue Flag," and, upon doing so, was stopped by Union soldiers. It was said that the act was one of "daredeviltry" rather than a political statement.[53] He was careful to suppress his political sentiments in the company of those with differing opinions. Ensign C. W. Baird met Booth in the bar of the Franklin House, which was frequented by Union Army and Navy officers. Baird recalled that "Booth seemed to be a congenial fellow, with a sense of humor, and I thought very temperate in his habits...."[54]

In the spring of 1864 John wrote to his brother Junius, who was about to leave San Francisco for New York. "Heard from Mother yesterday," the letter read. "God Bless her, she complained at your silence. She and the rest are well. How is dear little Mary [Junius's daughter] Have you ever told her she has an Uncle John?"[55]

During the second week in April, Booth made the long trip from New Orleans to Boston to fulfill a five-week engagement. This engagement was not only his longest, but was also his most successful and his last. The Boston Museum had a reputation for high-quality productions. The *Boston Daily Evening Transcript* explained:

> Words to commend the manner in which affairs are conducted at the Boston Museum are needless. We must point to the pieces which have been brought out during the past week as furnishing fresh illustrations of the truth of the popular saying "They always do things well at the Museum."[56]

The critics offered the young actor advice. According to the *Transcript*:

> A little more distinctness of utterance by Mr. Booth would add much interest to these otherwise pleasant occasions, and those who sit

in the back parts of the auditorium would not be obliged to carry copies of the plays in order to interpret what should be distinctly enunciated.[57]

The *Transcript* critic wrote a week later:

> [Booth], not content with the success which attended him at the outset of his career, has devoted himself assiduously to advancement in his profession. A marked improvement in his acting, since he made his first appearance here—only two years ago—is apparent, much of which is evidently the result of earnest thought and study.
>
> He [Booth] has never acted better than during the past three weeks, and we are most gratified at his success. Although he has faults, and has not yet attained the height which his powers give promise of, yet few actors represent the characters which he assumes more to the satisfaction of the public.[58]

The *Transcript* also sounded a cautionary note:

> Even if this young tragedian [Booth] possesses natural gifts of a high order, as many aver, a continual over-straining and over-taxing of physical power must sooner or later crush those natural endowments and unfit him for the position in which assiduous and intelligent study might have placed him. A grievous and glaring fault of Mr. Booth's acting is, that he attempts to reach things beyond his grasp, and strives to win the applause of those in his immediate presence, rather than to give a correct, truthful, and lasting delineation of the creations of the great dramatic writers—one that will impress the mind from its intrinsic merit. These faults must be overcome before Mr. Booth can hope to occupy a very high position of an artist in the estimation of the truly critical and intelligent patrons of the drama.[59]

Toward the end of the engagement, the *Transcript* remarked:

> Mr. Booth has played a successful engagement, and we hope he will some time return to us, 'toned down' and more finished in manner and declamation, with some of the crudities which invariably follow young actors completely effaced, and with the natu-

ral powers which he evidently possesses rightly developed....[60]

Walter Benn, a member of the Museum's stock company, and Booth were friends from their days in the Arch Street Theatre's stock company in Philadelphia. Benn later wrote:

We were rehearsing "Damon and Pythias" at the Boston Museum. We had reached the famous Senate scene, in act second, and had arrived at the action, where "Damon" rushed on "Dionysius" to stab him. The "Proeles" was entirely too slow to intercept him. After trying the "business" over two or three times, Booth turned and rebuked him, saying, "If you fail to catch me in time tonight there will be a dead "Dionysius." We all smiled then, but, when the performance came we appreciated his remark. At night he was terribly in earnest, he seemed imbued with a patriotic fervor, the tears burst from his eyes and rushing at "Dionysius," he exhibited the frenzy of a madman.... I [Walter Benn] played "Lucillus," and in Act 4, Scene II, where "Damon" learns the horse is slain, he had arranged to grasp me by the throat, keeping his arm taut, I on my knee, both hands on his arm, he was thus to bear my weight and drag me off the stage, giving the appearance that I was striving to tear his hands from my throat. He said at rehearsal, "I won't hurt you Benny."

He had always called me by that name. He was superb in the scene. I did my best to second his efforts, entering heart and soul into the situation. The applause was deafening, and the audience gave us a great curtain call. When I came off the stage, I discovered he had well clawed my neck with his finger nails, and I was bleeding profusely.

"John," I said, "I thought you told me you would not hurt me, look at this," at the same time baring my neck.

"Oh, Benny," he replied, "I did not intend that. Come up to my dressing room and I'll rub something on it." Entering the room he said, "Here is an outer and inner application." So pouring out some Bourbon he rubbed some on my neck, and out of "auld lang syne" we drained a friendly bowl together.[61]

Booth attracted women. Wealthy and poor, well-bred and otherwise, married and unmarried women packed the theatres enraptured by his "striking beauty."[62] They arranged to meet him at performances and at social gatherings. They wrote injudicious letters. He read a few and burned most. Before entrusting a theatre functionary with the letters to be burned, he would tear off the names of the silly women and rip them up himself. With some frequency he thought he was in love; the thought didn't last long.[63]

An observer commented:

Wilkes Booth was extremely popular with everybody. Simple and democratic, he joked with everyone he came in contact with, even the girls in the laundry where he left his collars and cuffs. They always saw to it that Mr. Booth's package was ready when he came for it, and vied with each other as to who should have the honor of delivering it. He joked with the cabmen at the stand corner of the Tremont House. He loved a jest and in his quiet, quizzical way made friends everywhere.[64]

Booth became infatuated with sixteen-year-old Isabel Sumner during the course of his Boston engagement. Isabel was the daughter of a well-to-do grocer. The manner of their meeting is unknown; perhaps Isabel's family was acquainted with one of Booth's Boston friends, or she may have sought an introduction to the actor at the theatre. Six letters that Booth wrote to the young lady during the summer of 1864 reveal the strength of his feelings for her. Isabel's letters to Booth do not survive. Booth presented Isabel with a pearl and diamond ring inscribed "JWB TO IS."[65]

Booth's engagement at the Boston Museum overlapped with appearances by Maggie Mitchell at the Boston Theatre. She had often appeared in Richmond when Booth was in the stock company there. In the subsequent years, they sometimes found themselves in the same city playing opposite each other. Booth's friend James Collier married and then was divorced from Mary Mitchell, Maggie's half-sister. Later Booth's friend John Albaugh married Mary Mitchell. The members of the little group were fast friends. Maggie Mitchell described Booth as "a delightful companion through his great attainments and intellectual superiority. He was a splendid horseman and rode with ease and grace. Being fond of the exercise myself, I was often out with him on horseback."[66]

Harrison W. Huguley, a twenty-year-old member of Surgeon General Joseph K. Barnes's staff, reported an encounter with Booth in Boston. Through a friend, Huguley had arranged an introduction to actress Maggie Mitchell on a Sunday evening at an actors' boarding house on Bullfinch Place. Mitchell introduced the young man to John Wilkes Booth, who, in the course of the evening "gave utterance to his views about the government in terms so intemperate that young Huguley felt that as a government employee he ought not to listen to such treasonable sentiments." Huguley excused himself and, upon returning to Washington, reported the incident to Surgeon General Barnes. Barnes had him repeat the story to Secretary of War Stanton. If this incident actually occurred, it did not prompt Stanton to take further action.[67]

Booth suffered from recurring colds during the theatrical season. His exposure to the frigid weather on the trip from St. Joseph apparently did not cause his illness; the newspapers first reported that he had a cold about five weeks later, in Cincinnati. He cancelled a performance on February 16. By February 22 he thought he had recovered, but he then missed a week of performances starting March 7 in New Orleans and again was unable to appear on March 26 and 27. He rested in New Orleans for a week after his engagement there ended. After arriving in Boston, he had almost two weeks off before beginning his engagement on April 25. Newspapers did not mention the cold after April 26. Booth's five weeks in Boston without missing a performance demonstrated that he had fully recovered his health.

Rail travel in this era was uncomfortable and unsanitary. The rail cars were inadequately heated, if they were heated at all.

Other factors made travel even more difficult. According to the *Alexandria Gazette*, one problem was:

> ...the offensive and disgusting practice of many passengers upon the Rail Road Cars, in spitting great streams of tobacco juice on the heated stoves, thereby rendering the confined atmosphere not only offensive, but sickening to those who have no taste for the "vile weed." But this is not all. Every corner and space under the seats is also filled by the filthy saliva, so that, if by accident you drop your handkerchief, gloves or cloak, they are rendered unfit for decent hands ever after.[68]

The 1863-1864 season was an arduous one for Booth. He had scheduled twenty-seven weeks of engagements, but performed only twenty-five and a half weeks. He gave 148 individual performances. He did not act in Chicago, Baltimore, or Philadelphia, as he had the previous season; apparently, Booth had not earned well in those cities. He continued to be a hit in Boston, where he started the season with a two-week engagement and ended the season with an unprecedented, for him, five-week engagement. John Ford later commented: "When we were playing in Boston [Booth] doubtless made the greatest success of any actor of his day. People waited in crowds after the performance to catch a glimpse of him as he left the theatre."[69]

1863 *from September 17*

September 17, Thursday New York
Booth, staying at Edwin's house in New York, wrote to theatre owner and manager John Ford regarding an engagement in Washington:
> Your telegraph just recd: Now that I understand it. *All right Book me for Nov 2d: for two weeks. I will be there* and I will keep the two following weeks open a time longer. there may be a chance for Baltimore then, or you may want me to keep on in Washington. But consider the two weeks from Nov 2d: settled.[70]

September 20, Sunday New York
The Battle of Chickamauga, near the bor-

der of Georgia and Tennessee, concluded with a Union defeat.

September 21, Monday New York

September 22, Tuesday New York

Booth wrote to Ben DeBar: "Yours of 20th Rec'd. All right. Book me for the two weeks to begin Jan. 4th 64. Share after $140 per night, and benefit each week."[71]

September 23, Wednesday New York

September 24, Thursday New York

September 25, Friday Boston

Booth returned to Boston.[72]

September 26, Saturday Boston

September 27, Sunday Boston

September 28, Monday Boston

Booth opened at the Howard Athenaeum, managed by Henry Willard, in *The Lady of Lyons; or, Love and Pride*, in which he played the role of Claude Melnotte. The *Boston Daily Evening Transcript* noted before the performance that "Mr. Booth has made many friends in Boston during two previous engagements, and Mrs. [Julia Bennett] Barrow is too well known and appreciated to require praise from anyone."[73] Afterward, the newspaper reported that "J. Wilkes Booth and Mrs. Barrow were warmly welcomed ... and 'Claude' and 'Pauline' were never represented more miserable in their misery or happier in their happiness."[74]

September 29, Tuesday Boston

Booth played *Richard III* with Harry Langdon as Richmond. In the opinion of the *Transcript* critic:

The performance was, on the whole, an improvement on his former representations. In many of the principal points he manifested greater intensity than was his wont, while his voice was not allowed that full rant which once characterized his reading. His gestures were more finished, and did not give the impression, as formerly, that he had studied for effect.[75]

September 30, Wednesday Boston

Booth played *Hamlet*. The *Transcript* was complimentary:

[Booth] gave further evidence, by a masterly delineation of this difficult character, of the possession of uncommon histrionic powers. The vacation of the young tragedian has evidently improved [him], and he has returned to the stage showing a decided advance in his art. Mrs. Barrow was excellent as Ophelia.[76]

October 1, Thursday Boston

Booth played Pescara in *The Apostate*.

October 2, Friday Boston

Booth played *Richard III* in his benefit performance. The *Transcript* anticipated the play:

Mr. Booth certainly portrays this difficult character [*Richard*] with a power exhibited by few artists. With great facial expression he unites a well trained and pleasing voice, while his reading is very correct and faithful to the text....[77]

October 3, Saturday Boston

Booth played Charles de Moor in *The Robbers*.

October 4, Sunday Boston

October 5, Monday Boston

Booth played *Othello*. The *Transcript* remarked:

J. Wilkes Booth enters upon the second and last week of his engagement at the Howard Athenaeum this evening. His representations during the past week have been received with great applause. We doubt not that the coming performances of the young tragedian will be as satisfactory to the public, and hope they will be as profitable to Mr. Booth and Manager Willard as those which have taken place.[78]

The *Boston Advertiser* commented that Booth's "popularity does not wane, and he evidently exerts his great energies as steadily as ever to maintain it, throwing into his scenes that strong, fiery power for which he is so eminent...."[79]

October 6, Tuesday Boston

Booth played Phidias and Raphael in *The Marble Heart; or, The Sculptor's Dream*.

October 7, Wednesday Boston

Booth played *Macbeth*. The *Transcript* stated that Booth's "performance in this sublime tragedy is represented to be one of his very best."[80]

October 8, Thursday Boston

Booth played Pescara in *The Apostate*. The *Transcript* observed: "J. Wilkes Booth and Mrs. Barrow are meeting with great success at the Howard. Their assumptions have mainly consisted of those in which both have won an enviable reputation, and the excellent manner in which the plays have been put upon the stage by Manager Willard has greatly added to the interest of their engagement."[81]

October 9, Friday Boston

Booth played Shylock in *The Merchant of Venice* and Petruchio in *Katharine and Petruchio*. "The engagement of the young tragedian has been gratifying to the public, and must have proved quite profitable to himself," the *Transcript* remarked.[82] The *Advertiser* critic wondered whether Booth was trying to improve.[83]

October 10, Saturday Boston

Booth closed his engagement with a matinee performance of *The Marble Heart*. In the evening he played *Richard III* supported by Harry Langdon, his former roommate in Richmond, as Richmond. Harry Hawk played the part of the Lord Mayor.[84]

October 11, Sunday En route to Worcester

The *Worcester Daily Spy* advertised Booth's *Richard III*, to be performed on Monday, as "a prototype of his father's, and is certainly by far the best now on the stage."[85]

October 12, Monday Worcester

Booth played *Richard III* at the Worcester Theatre at 10-14 Front Street. The *Worcester Daily Transcript* reported:

[The play] was a triumphant success. While there is a dash and impulsiveness in the style of Mr. Booth, it is a shallow criticism which would cover his characteristics by those epithets. He sustained the part well, and to do that he was obliged to depict a schemer and shrewd fore-calculator.[86]

October 13, Tuesday Worcester

Booth walked from his Main Street hotel to the theatre, where he performed *The Lady of Lyons*. The *Spy* anticipated:

The capacity of the Theatre will be tested this evening. The role of Claude is peculiarly well suited to the dashing, impulsive style of Mr. Booth; indeed, he has made very many sensations in it.... We hear with regret that tonight positively terminates the visit of the distinguished artist to our city.[87]

October 14, Wednesday Springfield

Booth opened in Springfield with *Richard III*. The *Springfield Daily Republican* review stated:

[The] Music Hall contained ... a large and interested audience. Mr. Booth is young and impulsive, but has unmistakable talent. His readings were at times almost faultless, exhibiting a subtle appreciation of the author's meaning ... at other times his conception was intangible.... In the ex-

pression of intense passion he is very good if not great....[88]

October 15, Thursday Springfield

Booth appeared as Claude Melnotte in *The Lady of Lyons*. According to the *Republican*, "[a]nother good house greeted Mr. Booth and company last night.... Mr. Booth appeared to great advantage in the more passionate and pathetic scenes and the audience was not chary of their applause."[89] The same newspaper also remarked that Booth "does not 'tear a passion to tatters,' but it must be a stout passion to pass whole through the handling he gives some of them."[90]

October 16, Friday Providence

Booth opened at the Academy of Music in Providence with *Richard III*. The *Providence Daily Journal* reported:

The storm did not prevent the attendance of a very large audience at the representation of *Richard III* by John Wilkes Booth, Mrs. Barrow and an efficient company. Mr. Booth's correct reading, and appreciative action were warmly applauded. Mrs. Barrow as Queen Elizabeth was good, as she always is; and the pretty Miss [Fanny] Brown, as Lady Anne, drew largely upon the interest of the audience.[91]

October 17, Saturday Providence

Booth appeared in *The Lady of Lyons*, which, according to the *Journal*, "was very well received by a large audience. Mr. Booth as Claude Melnotte, perhaps, was hardly as effective as in some of his Shakespearean characters...."[92] The *Providence Daily Post* noted: "The description of the palace 'lifting to eternal summer its marble walls,' ... was rendered so admirably that Booth need fear no rivals in artificial love-making."[93]

October 18, Sunday Providence

Booth wrote to Cleveland theatre manager John Ellsler, heading the letter "New York, Oct. 18." He mis-stated either the place or the date.

Have not heard from you of late. November 23d and 30th is the only time I have for Cleveland. I asked for Feb. 1st and 8th in Columbus. I can still give you that time I guess, but let me hear from you at once, as I must answer Nashville.[94]

October 19, Monday Providence

Booth closed his engagement with *Hamlet*. The *Post* raved:

The most astonishing evidence of his true artistic talent was again displayed in his consummate performance.... The soliloquy was a masterpiece of declamation. It was put with a point and empha-

sis so just, a feeling so deep, a passion so re-
pressed, and yet so full, that it seemed to lay bare
a heart torn with distrusts....[95]

October 20, Tuesday Hartford

Booth opened in Hartford with *Richard III*
in front of a large audience at Allyn Hall. The
Hartford Evening Press reported:

Mr. Booth as Richard was in many scenes excellent, and in some reminding one of the senior
Booth who in his time was considered by many
the best *Richard* on the stage. The performance
of the character was not faultless, but on the
whole gave good satisfaction, and Mr. Booth was
frequently applauded.[96]

October 21, Wednesday Hartford

Booth appeared as Claude Melnotte in *The
Lady of Lyons*. The *Hartford Courant* was complimentary:

Of the score of actors who have attempted to represent the character ... we doubt if any have surpassed Mr. Booth in the nice discrimination he
gives to it. There is so much art in love-making
that the skill of an actor must be remarkable to
portray faithfully all the warmth, passion and
"dignity" which is mandatory to give enchant-
ment to the mimicry.[97]

October 22, Thursday Hartford

Booth performed *Hamlet*. The advertisement in the *Courant* proclaimed, "BY SPECIAL
DESIRE MR. J. WILKES BOOTH will appear
as HAMLET, And MRS. JULIA BENNETT
BARROW as OPHELIA, in the celebrated Tragedy of *HAMLET!*" The *Springfield Daily Republican*, anticipating Booth's Friday performance in that city, commented: "There is scarcely
another instance ... where an actor has arisen to
the position now held by Mr. Booth, at so young
an age and in so short a time."[98]

October 23, Friday Springfield

Booth played *Hamlet* at the Music Hall in
Springfield. The review in the *Republican* stated:

Wilkes Booth's Richard is good but his *Hamlet* is
better. He astonished his most enthusiastic admirers with the intensity and power of his representation, and established himself as an actor of
extraordinary merit. Isolated passages were too
hurried and obscure, but his performance as a
whole was masterly.[99]

Merriment reigned when the King of Denmark could not light a gas torch during the
play.[100]

October 24, Saturday Brooklyn

Despite bad weather, the Booth and Barrow

combination drew a large crowd for *Richard III*
at the Academy of Music. The *Brooklyn Standard*
reported:

J. Wilkes Booth made his first appearance in
Brooklyn ... in *Richard III*.... The upper gallery
was well-filled, the deities of the gallery turning
out in force, and making an unusual demonstra-
tion in the scramble for tickets. Such a scene of
pushing, crowding and jamming mingled with expressions more vigorous than polite, is not often
witnessed in the classic precincts of the Academy
and reminded me of the crush and turmoil of a
Bowery theatre when some ear-splitter is announced in *The Corsican Brothers*.... After an orchestra of musicians had made a desperate and
commendable effort to stimulate the chilled and
chilling audience to something like enthusiasm,
the curtain rose on *Richard III*. I should rather
say it rose on the last part of *Henry IV*, Mr. Booth
selecting for his acting version the improvement
(?) on Shakespeare by Cibber & Co. The tragedy
was mounted shabbily to an extreme. Banners,
dresses, scenery, furniture, everything would have
discredited a third-class theatre. The military effects were ludicrous and left the audience in
doubt whether the proportions of the rebellion,
or the power of the established government of
Great Britain, were the more contemptible. *Richmond's* army numbered four men, rank and file,
and Gloster's five, showing clearly that the War of
the Roses could not be carried on much longer
without resort to a draft, or increased activity in
volunteering. Seriously, if Shakespeare's plays cannot be produced at the Academy with a decent
regard to appointment, let us not have them at
all. I do not blame Mr. Booth's management. It is
hardly to be expected that he shall carry a complete theatre over the country with him.[101]

October 25, Sunday Brooklyn

October 26, Monday Brooklyn

Booth played Phidias and Raphael in *The
Marble Heart*. The *Standard* critic wrote:

It is hard to sympathize with a man like Raphael
[Booth] who, foolishly fascinated by a heartless
woman, breaks the heart of an excellent mother
and forsakes so charming a little girl as Marie
(Miss Fanny Brown).... Mr. Booth made what he
could of an unworthy subject....[102]

Booth was hoarse from a severe cold.[103]

October 27, Tuesday New Haven

Booth and his small company rushed to
New Haven, where they played *The Marble Heart*
at the Music Hall at 96 Crown Street. They had
planned to play *Richard III* but were not prepared. The *New Haven Daily Register* thought
Booth "sustained his reputation as a talented

actor," but "Miss Brown frequently dispelled the illusion of the stage by her uncontrollable merriment, which not even her very pretty person could justify."[104]

October 28, Wednesday New Haven

Booth played *Richard III*. The *New Haven Palladium* observed:

> The audience that assembled ... though a fair number, was not as large as the merits of J. Wilkes Booth and Company should call out.... His delineations of the "heavy villain," were received with much applause.... The broadsword combat between Richard and Richmond, and the death of King Richard were admirably rendered.[105]

Stage directions went awry in the last act.[106]

October 29, Thursday New Haven

Booth, supported by Julia Bennett Barrow and Fanny Brown, played *Hamlet*. The *Palladium* was impressed:

> We had before regarded Mr. Booth as a very fine actor, but his impersonation of Hamlet exceeds expectations. He was a genuine Shakespearean Hamlet. The New Haven public has not appreciated the merits of this company as they should.... The manager intends to bring the troupe, or part of it, here again soon.[107]

October 30, Friday

President and Mrs. Lincoln saw *Fanchon, the Cricket* at Ford's Theatre in Washington.[108]

November 1, Sunday Washington

The *Washington Sunday Chronicle* was critical of Booth on the eve of his engagement in that city:

> We do not regard Mr. Booth as an eminent tragedian; we can scarcely call him a tragedian. Unless he has improved very much since we last saw him, he is little more than a second-rate actor, who, as the possessor of a great name, and with a fine presence, sweet voice, and much natural and uncultivated ability, has seen proper to come upon the stage as a representative of tragedy. It is possible that Mr. Booth will in time become a great actor....[109]

November 2, Monday Washington

Booth opened his engagement at the new Ford's Theatre on Tenth Street with *Richard III*. The *Washington Morning Chronicle* was not impressed, stating that Booth "certainly deserves the merit of giving us the very worst Richard now upon the stage. In plainer words his Richard is as bad as it is possible for an actor to make him."[110]

Another observer noted that "[e]very seat, regular or improvised obtainable in the building was occupied, and hundreds were content to [stand]...."[111]

November 3, Tuesday Washington

Booth played Pescara in *The Apostate*. Samuel Knapp Chester was a member of the Ford's Theatre stock company. The *Washington National Intelligencer* noted:

> Mr. Ford's new company is probably the best which has ever appeared before a Washington audience, and in numerical strength and artistic merit are scarcely equaled by any company which has ever performed in America. Seats for ... Mr. Booth's engagement can be secured without extra charge....[112]

November 4, Wednesday Washington

Booth played Charles de Moor in *The Robbers*. The *Chronicle* anticipated the performance:

> Some of the situations of this play are among the best specimens of dramatic effect ever presented before an audience. They are not only powerfully interesting, but leave their traces indelibly fixed upon the memory.... Such is the lesson taught at the end of the second act, where not one among that robber band can be found to turn traitor to their chief.[113]

November 5, Thursday Washington

Booth performed *The Lady of Lyons*. The *National Intelligencer* advertised: "Mr. J. Wilkes Booth appears as Claude Melnotte, a part in which, it is said, he stands without a peer. Tonight's entertainment will doubtless fill Ford's to overflowing."[114]

The *Washington Evening Star* remarked: "There is no doubt but that Mr. Booth has satisfactorily proven himself to our citizens an actor of rare merit, and it is therefore a natural consequence that he should attract large audiences."[115]

November 6, Friday Washington

Booth played Shylock in *The Merchant of Venice* and Petruchio in *Katharine and Petruchio*.

November 7, Saturday Washington

Booth played *Richard III*. The *Evening Star* noted: "FORD'S THEATRE.—The rush to this establishment has continued unabated through the week, and though much of the interest centers in the young tragedian, J. W. Booth, yet there are performers in the combination company worthy to shine as independent stars; such as the beautiful and graceful Miss Annie Waite...."[116]

November 8, Sunday Washington

November 9, Monday Washington

Booth played Phidias and Raphael in *The Marble Heart* before Abraham Lincoln. John Hay, one of President Lincoln's secretaries, recorded in his diary: "Spent the evening at the theatre with the President, Mrs. Lincoln, Mrs. Hunter, Cameron and Nicolay. J. Wilkes Booth was doing *Marble Heart*. Rather tame than otherwise."[117]

Charles Wheatleigh played Volage, the part he had originated with Laura Keene's company five years earlier.

November 10, Tuesday Washington

Booth played *Hamlet*. The *Evening Star* anticipated the performance:

Mr. Booth will essay *Hamlet*, and those who will be disposed to question the resources of his genius and his experience for so arduous a performance will be agreeably disappointed should they witness it. Young Booth has evidently brought to its study the enthusiasm of a true Shakespearean student....[118]

November 11, Wednesday Washington

Booth played *Romeo and Juliet*. The *National Intelligencer* pronounced his Romeo "the most satisfactory of all renderings of that fine character."[119] A fellow actor recalled:

Playing Romeo, he so gave himself up to emotion ... that when he threw himself down ... he wounded himself on the point of the dagger he wore suspended from his girdle. It was on the very spot where he was to fall again....[120]

November 12, Thursday Washington

Booth played Alfred Evelyn in *Money*. The *National Intelligencer* noted:

The engagement of Mr. Booth and the combination which gives him their firm co-exertion has been one of the most brilliant and lucrative ever enacted in any city south of New York. During several days of cold and disagreeable weather there has been no diminution in the attendance at Ford's.... Ford's Theatre has proved itself during the twelve weeks it has been in operation.[121]

November 13, Friday Washington

Booth played *Richard III*. The *National Intelligencer* reported that many people had requested Booth to repeat this role.

November 14, Saturday Washington

Booth closed his engagement with *The Robbers*, in which he played Charles de Moor. The *National Intelligencer* stated:

The Robbers will be given entire, for the first time on the modern stage.... The full talent of the very large and efficient dramatic company will be engaged in the production of the play, and all those parts and lines which political bias have cut away will be produced and no doubt have a telling effect.[122]

November 16, Monday Baltimore

Booth signed a receipt:

Baltimore November 16th—1863 Received of John B. Ray the Sum of $125 Les Comis of 6.25 / $118.75 For Rent of For me in Harford County Md. Due June 1st 1863 By George A. Heisler J. Wilkes Booth. For M. A. Booth.[123]

November 19, Thursday

President Lincoln delivered the Gettysburg Address.

November 22, Sunday Cleveland

November 23, Monday Cleveland

Booth stayed at the American House.[124]

The Battle of Chattanooga began in Tennessee.

November 24, Tuesday Cleveland

November 25, Wednesday Cleveland

The *Cleveland Morning Leader* advertisement proclaimed Thursday as the "FIRST NIGHT of J. WILKES BOOTH, whose engagements in the East have proven One Continuous Triumph!"[125]

The Federal army was victorious at Chattanooga.

November 26, Thursday Cleveland

Booth appeared as Claude Melnotte in *The Lady of Lyons* at the Academy of Music. The *Cleveland Plain Dealer* reviewed the performance:

Mr. Booth's rendition was a beautiful and brilliant performance and drew from the thronged Academy repeated and rapturous applause, culminating in a call for his re-appearance at the close of the play, when he was received with another storm of approval. We were struck, when clothed in the full uniform of a General of the Grand Army, by his remarkable resemblance to Napoleon.[126]

November 27, Friday Cleveland

Booth played *Hamlet*. The *Plain Dealer* was enthusiastic:

Mr. Booth's personation of *Hamlet* was so replete with charms that it is difficult to single out any particular point, where all were so telling, and give it especial praise.... The [closet scene] was given superbly.... The thundering applause which greeted this, as all the other scenes, however, is better testimony and more gratifying of how completely he succeeded in carrying the popular heart.[127]

November 28, Saturday Cleveland

Booth performed *Richard III*. James Mc-Collom, playing Richmond, accidentally struck Booth in the forehead, severing his eyebrow. According to actress Clara Morris: "Then Booth, flinging the blood from his eyes with his left hand, said, as genially as man could speak: 'That's all right, old man! Never mind me—only come on hard, for God's sake, and save the fight!'"[128]

The *Leader* critic opined that the scene was "greatly heightened by the accident."[129]

The *Cleveland Herald* remarked that "Mr. Booth is undoubtedly the best Richard on the stage."[130]

November 29, Sunday Cleveland

November 30, Monday Cleveland

Booth appeared as Phidias and Raphael in *The Marble Heart*. The *Herald* noted:

The powerful and startling drama of *The Marble Heart* was produced, with Mr. Booth as Raphael Duchatlet, the sculptor. The drama is of thrilling interest throughout, and was admirably put upon the stage. Mr. Booth's Raphael was a fine piece of acting, and was received with repeated bursts of applause. The other characters were all well played.[131]

December 1, Tuesday Cleveland

Booth again played *The Marble Heart*. The *Plain Dealer* remarked:

Mr. Booth played *The Marble Heart* for the second time ... and made of the part a very superb performance. [On Wednesday] he appears for the first time in Shakespeare's great character of Iago. This was one of his father's greatest parts, and we doubt not it will be handled with skill and ability by the son, upon whose shoulders the mantle of the great Booth has descended.[132]

December 2, Wednesday Cleveland

Booth played Iago in *Othello*. The *Plain Dealer* noted:

What little we saw of the closing part of *Othello* gave us the warmest admiration for Mr. Booth's portraiture of Iago, which we regretted exceedingly not having witnessed entire. A friend tells us it was a very superior performance, and we think Mr. Booth may congratulate himself upon another triumph in adding this difficult role to his repertoire.[133]

As Booth rushed from the theatre, he accidentally knocked down a small child. He picked up the "dirty, tousled, small heap," told him not to cry, and "took out his handkerchief, and first carefully wiping the dirty little nose and mouth, stooped and kissed him heartily, put some change in each freckled paw, and continued his run to the telegraph office."[134]

December 3, Thursday Cleveland

Booth played *Richard III*.

December 4, Friday Cleveland

Booth played the title role in *The Stranger* and appeared as Petruchio in *Katharine and Petruchio*. According to the *Plain Dealer*:

...he played with consummate ability, and indeed his whole engagement has tended to make a great impression on the lovers of the drama, among whom he has secured many admirers, and from whom he will always receive a hearty welcome. Mr. Booth has genius and talent of a high order, and nature has not been niggard in endowing him with ... a voice capable of much....[135]

December 5, Saturday Cleveland

Booth appeared in *The Robbers*. The *Plain Dealer* was laudatory:

Mr. Booth's ... Charles DeMoor [in *The Robbers*] is, in our judgment, his greatest performance. To a full house he played this part ... and we but utter the simple truth when we say he completely swept the chords of feeling of his crowded and intensely thrilled auditory and carried captive both reason and imagination. Mr. Booth was greeted with a storm of applause at the fall of the curtain....[136]

December 6, Sunday Cleveland

December 7, Monday Cleveland

December 8, Tuesday Cleveland

December 9, Wednesday Cleveland

December 10, Thursday Cleveland

The *Leader* noted that Booth and James Ward, a comedian, were staying at the American House.

December 11, Friday Cleveland

December 14, Monday Franklin?

Booth first visited the oil region in Pennsylvania's Venango County in mid–December, 1863, with John Ellsler, owner and manager of the Cleveland Academy of Music, and Thomas Y. Mears, a strong abolitionist.

President Lincoln attended a performance of *Henry IV*, starring James Hackett, at Ford's Theatre.[137]

December 15, Tuesday　Franklin?

President Lincoln again saw James Hackett perform *Henry IV* at Ford's Theatre.[138]

December 16, Wednesday　Franklin?

December 17, Thursday　Franklin?

President Lincoln attended a performance by James Hackett at Ford's Theatre for the third time this week.[139]

December 18, Friday　En route to Leavenworth

December 19, Saturday　En route

Booth was delayed by heavy snow.

December 20, Sunday　En route

The *Leavenworth Daily Conservative* noted: "WILKES BOOTH.... This distinguished tragedian, an honored member of the famous family of actors, will make his first appearance here tomorrow night."[140]

December 21, Monday　Leavenworth

Booth arrived in Leavenworth in the evening, too late to perform. The *Conservative* carried this item:

When Mr. Booth first appeared in New York, the *Tribune* contained a very elaborate criticism of his style of acting, and represented him as in many respects the most talented of the trio [of brothers]. Since that time, Wilkes Booth has played engagements in all our large cities, and with the most triumphant success.[141]

December 22, Tuesday　Leavenworth

Booth played *Richard III* at the Union Theatre. The *Leavenworth Daily Times* was impressed:

J. Wilkes Booth, as a tragedian, is all he has been represented. His *Richard III* of Tuesday night, was a fine conception. We never witnessed a more thrilling representation of deceit, hate, revenge and ambition combined and intensified than in his *Richard*.[142]

The *Conservative* agreed:

A crowded house greeted Wilkes Booth.... The most ambitious actor would have been gratified with such a reception. The Richard of Mr. Booth is a rare piece of acting, and the splendid touches of the tragedian could hardly have been shown to greater advantage than they were on this occasion.[143]

December 23, Wednesday　Leavenworth

Booth played *Hamlet*, with G. D. Chaplin as Laertes and Mrs. C. F. Walters as Ophelia. The *Times* remarked that Booth's Hamlet was "equally good" as his Richard III, but that "Hamlet had

a cold."[144] The *Conservative* noted that the "face of Mr. Booth is singularly expressive; his eye is bright and keen as that of his matchless brother, Edwin; his elocution is faultless, and his manner is that of a man born for, and at home on the stage."[145]

December 24, Thursday　Leavenworth

Booth performed *The Lady of Lyons*. The Union Theatre advertised: "Immense success of the Talented Young Tragedian, J. WILKES BOOTH, who will appear in his favorite role of Claude Melnotte."[146]

December 25, Friday　Leavenworth

The Union Theatre stock company performed *Uncle Tom's Cabin* in the afternoon. At 7:30 p.m. Booth played Charles de Moor in *The Robbers*.

December 26, Saturday　Leavenworth

In a well-attended benefit, Booth played Alfred Evelyn in *Money* and Petruchio in *Katharine and Petruchio*.

December 27, Sunday　Leavenworth

The *Conservative* carried this item:

Of the merits of Mr. Booth's acting we need scarcely speak. It is unfortunate for our theatre loving public that the weather has been so bad during this talented actor's engagement. Many have been compelled thereby to forego a treat such as seldom falls to the lot of the devotees of Thespis.

Mr. Booth has not only genius, but careful culture and trained power of intellect. There is no actor now on the stage who displays so much of dramatic force and insight as Mr. J. Wilkes Booth, except, perhaps, for his brother Edwin. There is no imitation on the part of the junior, either to his renowned father or his now famous brother. He has a grace and charm all his own, though resembling them in the genius, skill and painstaking care, with which his characters are presented on the stage.[147]

December 28, Monday　Leavenworth

Booth appeared as Phidias and Raphael in *The Marble Heart*. The *Conservative* noted: "The Union was well filled last night to witness the 'Marble Heart.' It was finely rendered. Mr. Booth won fresh laurels and gained warm encomiums by his rendering of the young sculptor."[148]

December 29, Tuesday　Leavenworth

Booth again played *The Marble Heart*. The *Conservative* opined:

[*The Marble Heart*] is a good novel but a bad play. No one with less genius than Mr. Booth could make it endurable, but he played the leading part so well as to be twice called before the curtain by rapturous applause. Our citizens do not half appreciate the jewel they have in Wilkes Booth. We utter commonplaces when we say that he has great genius allied to marvelous familiarity with the stage. Mr. Booth is by far the most intellectual man who has ever appeared on the Western stage.[149]

December 30, Wednesday Leavenworth

Booth, for the first time, played the title role in *Richelieu; or, The Conspiracy*. The character was one which, according to the *Conservative*, "his brother Edwin has rendered almost preeminently his own. We anticipate a rare intellectual treat."[150]

December 31, Thursday Leavenworth

Booth's engagement closed with *Othello*, in which Booth played Iago. The *Conservative* offered some final thoughts about Booth's time in Leavenworth:

We have enjoyed the performances of this brilliant and intellectual young artist as we have done that of no other actor who has ever visited our city, with the exception, perhaps, of Mr. Couldock. Mr. Booth closed his engagement ... by a fine rendering of Iago. A man of intellect, of high culture and attainments, he has well profited by the advantages, which combined with his striking personal appearance, always bespeak for him a welcome. Mr. Booth has dramatic intensity, insight, and a clear conception of characters he seeks to embody. These qualities were strikingly apparent in his rendering of Richelieu on Wednesday evening. We believe it was the first time he has appeared in this difficult character, one which modern masters of the histrionic art have rendered a favorite.... Yet, the younger actor's rendering was striking and original—not by any means a servile imitation, but giving a new idea of the character. His rendering was unequal, but displayed genius. We predict that J. Wilkes Booth's Richelieu will be yet esteemed among the finest impersonations of the American stage.[151]

1864 *through June 5*

January 1, Friday Weston

Booth visited friends at Fort Leavenworth. He ran four miles to the steamboat landing in freezing weather. He had entrusted his flask to a servant accompanying him on this trip. The "boy," as Booth referred to him, had promptly lost it. Booth found the flask crushed by a wagon and salvaged some of its contents by sucking the snow on which it had spilled. Booth helped cut ice to allow the steamboat to reach shore. The boat carried Booth across the Missouri River to Weston, Missouri, where he probably stayed overnight.[152]

January 2, Saturday St. Joseph

Booth made the thirty-mile trip from Weston to St. Joseph on the Platte County Railroad.[153]

When Booth arrived at the Pacific House he went to bed "a dead man." Exposure to the extreme weather resulted in a frost-bitten ear. In bed at 10 p.m. he wrote a letter to Moses Kimball, manager and founder of the Boston Museum.[154] Severely cold weather persisted.

January 3, Sunday St. Joseph

The cold and heavy snows prevented trains from arriving for a week. Eight trains were blocked in the snow on the sixty-mile stretch from St. Joseph to Breckenridge, Missouri. The snows halted all rail traffic in Missouri and parts of Illinois. Many travelers were stalled in St. Joseph.[155]

January 4, Monday St. Joseph

Sixty-eight people, including the mayor, petitioned Booth to give a public reading. In response, Booth wrote:

I have gained some little reputation as an actor, but a dramatic reading I have never attempted. I know there is a wide distinction, as in the latter case it is impossible to identify one's self with any single character. But as I live to please my friends, I will do all in my power to please the kind ones I have met in St. Joseph. I will, therefore, designate Tuesday evening at Corby's Hall.[156]

January 5, Tuesday St. Joseph

Booth, at Corby's Hall, presented a selection of readings consisting of *The Shandon Bells*, the trial scene from *The Merchant of Venice*, selections from *Hamlet*, *Once I Was Pure* [*The Beautiful Snow*], and *The Charge of the Light Brigade*. The *St. Joseph Morning Herald* remarked: "It is seldom that so rare an entertainment is offered in this community, and we are confident our people will show their appreciation ... by turning out...." The notice about Booth's performance appeared immediately below a declaration of the newspaper's political sentiments: "For President—1864, Abraham Lincoln."[157]

The *Herald* reported: "Our people are in a terrible fix. The snow has effectually shut us out from 'all the world and the rest of mankind,' and there is no prospect of relief."[158]

January 6, Wednesday St. Joseph

The *Herald* critic was particularly pleased with the presentation of *Once I Was Pure [The Beautiful Snow]* and *The Charge of the Light Brigade*. The theatre was so cold that the audience made distracting noise with constant movement to keep warm. Booth's proceeds from the box office amounted to $150.[159]

January 7, Thursday St. Joseph

Rail traffic out of St. Joseph was still stalled. The line from St. Louis to Macon in eastern Missouri reopened.

The temperature in St. Joseph at 9 a.m. was twenty-one degrees below zero.[160]

January 8, Friday En route to St. Louis

A man who arrived in St. Joseph related that he had taken the train west from Macon to Breckenridge, where the snow blocked the tracks. On the way from Breckenridge he had passed trains buried in as much as thirty feet of snow. He estimated it would be ten more days before the trains could get through. Anxious to get to St. Louis, Booth rented a four-horse sleigh for $100 to take him sixty miles to Breckenridge.[161]

January 9, Saturday En route to St. Louis

Booth described the hardships of his trip in a letter to John Ellsler several weeks afterwards:

I have had a rough time John scince I saw you. It was hard enough to get to Leavenworth but in coming back was a hundred times worse.... Four days and nights in the largest snow drifts I ever saw Its a long story which I want to tell you.... I never knew what hardship was till then.[162]

Louis J. Weichmann, a man whom Booth would meet in a year, began work as a clerk in the Washington, D.C., office of the Commissary General of Prisoners.[163]

January 10, Sunday En route to St. Louis

January 11, Monday En route to St. Louis

Booth boarded the Hannibal and St. Joseph train at either Cameron or Breckenridge. He changed to the Northern Missouri Line at Macon for the final run to St. Louis. Booth later told fellow actor Edwin Adams that he had put a gun to the head of a train conductor to force him to drive through snow drifts.[164]

January 12, Tuesday St. Louis

Booth played *Richard III* with J. E. Carden as Richmond. The St. Louis Theatre advertisement in the *St. Louis Missouri Republican* read:

Mr. J. Wilkes Booth has arrived and will positively appear this evening as *Richard III*. In consequence of the stoppage of the Railroad by the snow Mr. Booth has lost seven nights of his engagement, consequently he can only appear FIVE NIGHTS. Other engagements prevent the possibility of his remaining over Saturday next.[165]

January 13, Wednesday St. Louis

Booth played *Hamlet*. According to the *St. Louis Missouri Democrat*, he "attracted another full house" and "the performance ... went off admirably in every respect."[166]

January 14, Thursday St. Louis

Booth played Charles de Moor in *The Robbers*.[167]

January 15, Friday St. Louis

On his benefit night, Booth played Alfred Evelyn in *Money*, with Ben DeBar as Graves, and also appeared as Petruchio in *Katharine and Petruchio*.

January 16, Saturday St. Louis

Booth closed his engagement in St. Louis with *Richard III*. A fellow actor wrote:

At the close of the first act of this performance ... he [Booth] whipped out his sword, and ... made such a violent thrust at my side that I apprehended danger.... Thinking that he had stabbed me he was so frightened that ... he stood trembling and repeatedly asked me if I was hurt.[168]

January 17, Sunday En route to Louisville

January 18, Monday Louisville

Booth opened his engagement at Wood's Theatre with *Richard III*.

January 19, Tuesday Louisville

Booth played the title role in *Othello*. The *Louisville Daily Journal* anticipated heavy attendance: "The great tragedian, J. Wilkes Booth, is at Wood's Theatre, and the mere mention of this fact ought to be sufficient to crowd the house nightly.... He stands at the head of the list of American tragedians...."[169]

Afterward, the *Journal* reported that the "rush at Wood's Theatre ... to see the young tragedian [as *Othello*] was unprecedented. A large number of persons were compelled to go away, as the house was crowded...."[170]

January 20, Wednesday Louisville

Booth played *The Robbers*. The *Louisville Daily Democrat* reported:

Notwithstanding the bad weather and a general conspiracy of the elements this popular temple of amusement [Wood's Theatre] was crowded ... to witness J. Wilkes Booth in his masterly impersonations of Charles de Moor, in Schiller's play of "The Robbers." Mr. Booth has improved wonderfully since his last appearance here, and is now one of the most classical and correct artistes on the boards.[171]

The *Democrat* was happy with Booth's engagement:

The weather has been but a trifling impediment to the houses [at Wood's Theatre] since the return of the favorite tragedian, J. Wilkes Booth. He opened on Monday evening to an immense audience. Last night he performed *Othello* to an audience numerically as great, which proves at once conclusively that the sensation his previous engagements have always created is not on the wane.[172]

January 21, Thursday Louisville

Booth played Pescara in *The Apostate*. The *Journal* encouraged attendance at the theatre:

We are pleased to see that our citizens appreciate the great talent of Mr. J. Wilkes Booth, the great tragedian, whose name has become illustrious with the American people. We hope that all of our theatre goers will avail themselves of this opportunity to witness one of the greatest actors of the age. His praise is on every tongue, and he richly merits it.[173]

January 22, Friday Louisville

On his benefit night, Booth appeared in the comedy *Money*. The *Democrat* noted that the role of Alfred Evelyn "is considered one of [Booth's] happiest efforts."[174] The newspaper remarked afterward that the performance "drew together a large and brilliant assemblage, the lower portion of the auditorium being densely packed long before the rise of the curtain."[175]

January 23, Saturday Louisville

Booth played Pescara in *The Apostate*. The *Democrat* opined: "No play produced in this city in the last ten years has been so effectively rendered."[176]

In a letter to John Ellsler, Booth related that he had written to their mutual acquaintance, Tom Mears, asking him to draw up an agreement regarding an oil venture. Though Booth claimed to be hard up for cash, he offered to pay Ellsler's share. He described his difficult journey from St. Joseph to St. Louis.[177]

January 24, Sunday Louisville

January 25, Monday Louisville

Booth played the title role in *Richelieu*. According to one account, Booth had too much wine at dinner and fell asleep while seated on stage. He was finally roused by a shout from the prompter but fell asleep again, causing the curtain to be rung down before a confused audience. Ultimately, Booth finished the performance.[178]

The Union Theatre in Leavenworth, Kansas, burned.[179]

January 26, Tuesday Louisville

Booth played *Richard III*. The *Democrat* reported:

The same old story—house crowded, as usual, to witness Mr. Wilkes Booth as *Richard III*, who riveted the attention of the audience from the commencement to the close of the tragedy. The hold this young artiste has upon the affections of all admirers of the legitimate drama is truly astonishing, and no wonder, either, considering his wonderful histrionic powers.[180]

January 27, Wednesday Louisville

Booth appeared as Fabien and Louis in *The Corsican Brothers*. The *Journal* reported:

The crowd ... was unprecedented. A large number of persons were unable to gain admission [to see *The Corsican brothers*].... Mr. Booth has completely carried our people by storm, and the immense audiences which have filled the house every night during his engagement evince the popularity of this great young tragedian. We are gratified to know that our theatre goers appreciate his eminent talent....[181]

January 28, Thursday Louisville

Booth appeared as Fabien and Louis in *The Corsican Brothers*.

January 29, Friday Louisville

In a benefit for John Albaugh, Booth played the role of Damon for the first time in *Damon and Pythias*. Damon speaks these lines in the second scene of act two:

I am no traitor! But in mine allegiance, To my lost country, I proclaim thee one! [spoken to the tyrant Dionysius, whom Damon tried to kill]

Death's the best gift to one that never yet,
Wished to survive his country. Here are men, Fit
for the life a tyrant can bestow! Let such as these
live on!

January 30, Saturday Louisville

Booth played *Macbeth* in his benefit, which
closed his engagement in Louisville.

Booth wrote to Edwin F. Keach, manager
of the Boston Museum, asking for a written contract stating the time and terms of his next engagement.[182]

January 31, Sunday En route to Nashville

The *Nashville Dispatch* theatre critic noted:
"The engagement of this talented gentleman will
commence to-morrow night, with *Richard III*,
Mr. Booth representing the part of Richard."[183]

February 1, Monday Nashville

Booth opened with *Richard III* at the Nashville Theatre on Cherry Street, near Cedar Street.
The *Dispatch* reported:

The house was packed in every part to see Mr.
Booth's *Richard III*, which appeared to give general satisfaction.... We feel compelled to say, however, that although he possesses many good qualities, his portraiture of Richard was not grand....[184]

The *Nashville Daily Union* was more enthusiastic: "Nothing of late years, equal to it
[Booth's Richard], has been seen here."[185]

February 2, Tuesday Nashville

Booth displayed his boundless energy in the
role of Pescara in *The Apostate*. The *Union* noted:
"With Mr. Booth as the despotic Spaniard there
was much more than satisfaction experienced—
the most unbounded pleasure was felt by all who
appreciate a fine tragedy and splendid acting."[186]
The *Dispatch* critic unfavorably compared Booth's
bombastic style with a more "natural" style, re-
marking:

It may be that we are so firmly wedded to that
quiet school ... as to suppose nothing good can
come from any other school, but if so, we cannot
help it, and therefore cannot commend Mr.
Booth as a finished artiste; he is too violent....[187]

February 3, Wednesday Nashville

Booth played the title role in *Richelieu*.

February 4, Thursday Nashville

Booth played *Hamlet*.

February 5, Friday Nashville

On his benefit night, Booth played Alfred
Evelyn in *Money*. According to the *Dispatch*,

"[t]he house is nightly filled and generally
crowded, with an intelligent audience, who seem
to be delighted with the performance of the
tragedies of the great Bard, as well as the standard
dramas of modern authors."[188] The *Dispatch* reported the next day that Booth's benefit "was a
bumper, alike gratifying and profitable to the
young actor."[189]

February 6, Saturday Nashville

Booth played Charles de Moor in *The Robbers*. The *Union* commented that "it is difficult
for a lady who happens to be late, to get a seat;
and frequently they are compelled to leave because they cannot get one. Shame on the men
who retain their seats and permit this."[190]

February 7, Sunday Nashville

February 8, Monday Nashville

Booth appeared in *Othello* and played the
role of Iago "most ably," according to the *Dispatch*.[191]

Andrew Johnson, Military Governor of
Tennessee, left Nashville for Washington, D.C.[192]

President and Mrs. Lincoln attended a performance starring Laura Keene at the Washington Theatre.[193]

February 9, Tuesday Nashville

Booth played *Richard III* and "continues to
crowd the house," the *Dispatch* reported.[194]

Moses Kimball had written to Booth informing him of the death of Edwin F. Keach.
Booth wrote back: "Poor Keach. I heard of his
death by telegraph and sincerely mourn him, as
will *all* his friends and brother professionals. I
can easily enter into all your regrets."[195]

Booth wrote to Richard Montgomery Field,
Keach's soon-to-be successor at the Boston Museum, arranging the details of his upcoming engagement.[196]

February 10, Wednesday Nashville

Booth played Fabien and Louis in *The Corsican Brothers*. The *Dispatch* observed that
"[e]very night the house is crowded to a perfect
jam, to witness the excellent representations of
sterling tragedies and dramas by Mr. J. W. Booth
and the excellent dramatic company...."[197]

February 11, Thursday Nashville

Booth played Damon in *Damon and Pythias*. "Night after night the crowds pour into the
ancient temple and fill its every nook and corner," noted the *Dispatch*.[198]

The *Dispatch* printed Harriet Beecher Stowe's interview of President Lincoln in which he stated, "Whichever way it [the war] ends, I have the impression that I shan't last long after it is over."[199]

February 12, Friday Nashville

Booth played Shylock in *The Merchant of Venice* and Petruchio in *Katharine and Petruchio*. Of his Petruchio one observer wrote:

> He made it very realistic and frolicked and fumed around the stage. Both he and the actors seemed to enjoy it as much as the spectators. During the banquet scene, he sent the dishes of viands flying over the stage. One of the property hams bounced and hit one of the orchestra in the face and started his nose to bleed, and a loaf of bread landed in a woman's lap. I thought then, and still think, he was under the influence of liquor, for he had such a reckless devil-may-care manner with him.... He was a very handsome dark man, but my impression of him was that he was of a wild undisciplined nature and inclined to dissipation, that he liked to pose and was theatrical.[200]

February 13, Saturday Nashville

Booth closed his engagement with a portrayal of Fabien and Louis in *The Corsican Brothers*.

Booth was presented with a sword at a banquet held by Union officers.[201]

February 14, Sunday En route to Cincinnati

February 15, Monday Cincinnati

Booth opened his engagement at Wood's Theatre by playing Iago in *Othello*, rather than the scheduled *Richard III*, because of "partial illness." The *Cincinnati Daily Commercial* anticipated Booth's engagement:

> The young and rising American tragedian J. Wilkes Booth makes his initial appearance tonight.... With his almost classic name the young actor needs no elaborate introduction.... Genius is not hereditary ... but there was a suspension of the law, if we may call it by so rigid a term, in the Booth family....[202]

February 16, Tuesday Cincinnati

Booth played Pescara in *The Apostate*. One newspaper reported that Booth "labored [Monday and Tuesday nights] under the disadvantage of performing when he should have been in the care of a physician."[203] The *Commercial* reported: "Mr. Booth was himself again last night [Tuesday], though *The Apostate* was never a favorite

with us we were tempted by his striking and powerful Pescara to adopt it as such."[204]

February 17, Wednesday Cincinnati

Booth had to cancel a performance of *The Robbers*. The *Commercial* reported that "Mr. Booth was so ill ... that his physician positively prohibited him from leaving his room [at the Burnett House].... Mr. Booth has really been too ill to appear since his arrival...."[205]

H. C. Young, an acquaintance of Booth of several years, attended Booth in his illness.[206]

February 18, Thursday Cincinnati

Booth appeared as *Richelieu*. The *Commercial* remarked: "The young tragedian gave great satisfaction as the subtle cardinal, and was enthusiastically applauded, though it was evident that he had not fully recovered from his late illness."[207]

February 19, Friday Cincinnati

Booth played Alfred Evelyn in *Money*. The *Commercial* inferred "from the spirited and impassioned acting of Mr. Booth ... in Bulwer's *Money* that he is quite recovered and feels able to cope with his more arduous roles."[208]

President Lincoln saw Edwin Booth perform *Richard III* at Grover's Theatre in Washington.[209]

February 20, Saturday Cincinnati

Booth performed *Richard III*. The *Commercial* reported: "A crowded house—regular Saturday night audience—greeted J. Wilkes Booth ... as he appeared in the character of 'hump-backed Richard,' which he personates remarkably well—both in dress and manner."[210]

Booth's friend Richard Montgomery Field, dramatic critic of the *Boston Post*, became manager of the Boston Museum.

February 21, Sunday Cincinnati

February 22, Monday Cincinnati

Booth played *Hamlet* to a packed house. The *Commercial* described the evening:

> Thousands of our citizens took advantage of the delightful weather last evening to conclude their observance of the 22nd as a holiday, by visiting the different places of amusement.... At Wood's every seat was occupied and standing places were in demand, with many who had visited the place to witness J. Wilkes Booth in his masterly rendition of *Hamlet*.[211]

Booth wrote to Richard Montgomery Field:

Depend on me for April 25th: I start from here (God willing) on Saturday for New Orleans, where I play a five weeks engagement. have two weeks to get from there to Boston.... I have been very sick here, but am all right again. Thank God....[212]

Booth signed a deed.[213]

February 23, Tuesday Cincinnati

Booth played Fabien and Louis in *The Corsican Brothers*.

February 24, Wednesday Cincinnati

Booth played Claude Melnotte in *The Lady of Lyons*.

February 25, Thursday Cincinnati

Booth played *Macbeth*. The *Commercial* commented on Booth's performances in Cincinnati:

Mr. Booth's engagement ... has been progressing for the last fortnight to the satisfaction of fine houses. To say that Mr. Booth has faults is not profound nor original, yet it is true; and, perhaps, we can pay him no more encouraging compliment than to express the conviction that none of them will seriously retard his growth in art.[214]

In Washington, President Lincoln saw another performance by Edwin Booth.

February 26, Friday Cincinnati

Booth played Shylock in *The Merchant of Venice* and Petruchio in *Katharine and Petruchio*. Booth's engagement closed in order to free the theatre for a benefit for Mrs. George H. Gilbert[215] on Saturday evening.[216]

President Lincoln, for the second consecutive night, attended a performance by Edwin Booth in Washington.[217]

February 27, Saturday En route to New Orleans

Booth took passage on a steamboat down the Ohio and Mississippi Rivers to New Orleans, where his engagement was to begin on March 7.

February 28, Sunday En route to New Orleans

February 29, Monday En route to New Orleans

Booth boarded the passenger packet *C. E. Hillman* at Cairo, Illinois. The steamer docked at Columbus and Hickman in Kentucky and New Madrid, Missouri, on its trip to Memphis.[218]

March 1, Tuesday En route to New Orleans

March 2, Wednesday Memphis

The *C. E. Hillman* arrived in Memphis on this day or the next.

Confederate soldiers killed Union Colonel Ulric Dahlgren during a raid near Richmond.

March 3, Thursday Memphis

The *Memphis Bulletin* listed the arrival of the *C. E. Hillman*, though it is unclear whether it arrived on the 2nd or 3rd.

March 4, Friday Memphis

President and Mrs. Lincoln, with Secretary of State William Seward and family, attended Edwin Booth's performance of *Richelieu* at Grover's Theatre.[219]

March 5, Saturday En route to New Orleans

Booth embarked for New Orleans at noon on the packet *J. C. Swon*.[220] Somewhere on the trip south he switched boats and eventually arrived in New Orleans on the *Olive Branch*.

March 7, Monday New Orleans

Illness prevented Booth from opening his engagement as scheduled.

President Lincoln attended a performance by Edwin Booth and Jennie Gourlay at Grover's Theatre in Washington.[221]

March 8, Tuesday New Orleans

March 9, Wednesday New Orleans

March 10, Thursday New Orleans

President Lincoln saw Edwin Booth perform *Richard III* at Grover's Theatre.[222]

March 11, Friday New Orleans

Edwin Booth was performing in Washington. Secretary of State William Seward hosted a dinner party for the actor at his home.[223]

March 12, Saturday New Orleans

Richard M. Johnson, whom Booth had met on the way to Memphis, wrote to Booth from St. Louis and enclosed a picture of himself.[224]

March 13, Sunday New Orleans

March 14, Monday New Orleans

Booth opened with *Richard III* at the St. Charles (also known as the Old Drury) Theatre, where his father had given his final performance. The *New Orleans True Delta* critic was impressed with Booth's "delineation of the 'Bloody-minded Gloster'" and considered John the equal of his brother, noting that his "scenes with Lady Anne, with the Queen mother ... were all masterpieces of satanic dissimulation.... In the tent scene he was absolutely horrifying."[225]

The *New Orleans Daily Picayune* critic observed:

> The announcement that Mr. J. Wilkes Booth would make his first appearance ... and as Gloster, in Richard III, completely filled the house. Great expectations of Mr. Booth's ability as a tragedian had been formed partly from the representations of the press of other cities, but mainly because he is the son of one who, as Gloster, had no equal, and the brother of one who, as a tragedian, already occupies proud position. We think that these expectations have not been fully satisfied. When Mr. Booth first appeared on the stage, he was warmly greeted. He has great personal advantages in a handsome face and fine person. We have neither time nor space for an extended notice of his performance, which, as a whole, disappointed us. His elocution appeared to us to be deficient in clearness, and very labored, and, to our thinking, he displayed great redundancy of action. Throughout the play Mr. Booth was successful in the exhibition of that subtlety which was so prominent in Gloster, as Shakespeare represents him. In the Tent scene, on waking from his horrible dream, his acting was remarkably fine. We cannot imagine a more terrible picture of phrenzied guilt. The combat scene at the close was so protracted, so improbable, that a fine tragic scene was transformed into a ludicrous spectacle.[226]

March 15, Tuesday New Orleans

Booth portrayed *Hamlet* as mad throughout the play, an interpretation at odds with that of the *True Delta* critic, who wrote:

> The large audience seemed pleased with Booth's idea of the Prince of Elsinore. This is perhaps as much as can be said of the efforts of any actor to portray that incomprehensible character. Booth's reading was very pure and chaste ... there was more in the performance to admire than to censure.[227]

The *Picayune* reported:

> The announcement that Mr. J. Wilkes Booth would appear as *Hamlet* ... attracted a large audience. On the whole we were favorably impressed with Mr. Booth's performance. His conception of the character we regard as good, and also his development of it. Some of the soliloquies were finely delivered, others were but so-so. In some scenes he was very impressive, in others, in which we expected he would be as others had been, he was not. He gave some new readings which were not improvements, and in endeavoring to develop new beauties in the text slurred over and sacrificed others dear to all play-goers and Shakespearean students.[228]

March 16, Wednesday New Orleans

Booth appeared as Pescara in *The Apostate*. The *True Delta* was impressed:

> In *The Apostate* Booth realized to the full all of our anticipations. The subtle hate and malignity of Pescara were depicted with a fidelity and an intensity that stamp Mr. Booth as a son worthy of the sire, who excelled in that very line of characters. The scene in which Pescara relates his dream to Florinda was a piece of acting which evinced great power and excellent judgment.[229]

The *Picayune* reported:

> We cannot truly state that Mr. Booth was much more successful in this character than he was in Gloster or Hamlet. In depicting Pescara's malignity and his subtle and fierce hate of Hemaya, Mr. Booth would have been successful if his manner had been less extravagant. Throughout his performance he exhibited an unpleasing mannerism and his action was an exaggerated imitation of his father in the same character. In occasional scenes he was impressive, as in that in which he relates his dream to Florinda, but, as a whole, his Pescara, we think, did not come up to public expectation....[230]

March 17, Thursday New Orleans

Booth played *Richelieu*. The *Picayune* stated:

> There was a large audience.... It would be unfair to compare Mr. Booth's rendition of this character with that of ... Edwin Booth's presentation and conception of this favorite part. Mr. J. Wilkes Booth is as yet an actor of more promise than actual performance, and time, care and study may yet develop in this really promising young actor those evidences of stage talent that made his father so famous, and that have already made his brother Edwin so great a favorite.[231]

March 18, Friday New Orleans

Booth played Alfred Evelyn in *Money*. The *New Orleans Times* noted that the quality of Booth's performances was less than satisfactory because of "severe hoarseness." [232]

The *Picayune* critic believed Booth's acting needed improvement:

> There was a fair house.... Mr. Booth might be disappointed that there was not a larger audience. He could not be more so than, so far as we could observe, the audience was with his performance. He is no more successful in comedy than in tragedy. Experience may improve him and doubtless will, but he has not only much to learn, but much to unlearn.[233]

March 19, Saturday New Orleans

Booth played Charles de Moor in *The Rob-*

bers. The *Picayune* critic was still on watch, writing that "what we saw of the performance ... did not recommend it. Mr. Booth's Charles DeMoor we have seen far excelled by actors who were not stars."[234]

March 20, Sunday New Orleans

Sunday evening performances were traditional in New Orleans. Booth played *Richard III.* According to the *Picayune,* he "is still suffering from hoarseness and his playing suffers in proportion."[235]

March 21, Monday New Orleans

Booth played the title role in *Othello.* Present in the audience were "Gov. [Richard] Yates of Illinois and Gov. [Michael] Hahn of Louisiana who seemed to be greatly pleased with his performance," the *New York Clipper* reported.[236] Yates was closely acquainted with President Lincoln.

March 22, Tuesday New Orleans

Booth played Claude Melnotte in *The Lady of Lyons.* The *Picayune* remained critical:

There was a fair house.... We do not think that the audience saw much to admire either in Mr. Booth's Claude or in the manner in which the other characters were sustained. Mr. Booth's conception of the character of Claude, and his performance, are truly original, but it does not therefore follow that they are good. His Claude is unlike all other Claudes that we have seen, from Anderson down. True, he is a handsome Claude, but he is not a persuasive lover, winning and graceful in manner, and his delivery of the beautiful passages so abounding in his part, was anything but pleasing.[237]

March 23, Wednesday New Orleans

Booth appeared in *Macbeth.* The *Times* remarked:

Booth's Thane was an impressive rendition ... especially in scenes shared by *Lady Macbeth* ... and in the final combat with Macduff. It is so much to be regretted that the obvious talent of Mr. Booth should be so embarrassed with the hoarseness wherewith he has been afflicted for the last ten days. We trust to hear his clear articulation again before his engagement terminates.[238]

The *Picayune* critic, no doubt to Booth's relief, "found greater attraction elsewhere" and thus did not attend.[239]

March 24, Thursday New Orleans

Booth and Mrs. Walters played *Romeo and Juliet.*

March 25, Friday New Orleans

Booth played Shylock in *The Merchant of Venice* and Petruchio in *Katharine and Petruchio.* The *Picayune* critic considered Shylock to be Booth's best role.

March 26, Saturday New Orleans

Booth's cold prevented him from performing. The St. Charles Theatre's advertisement in the *Picayune* announced:

The Management of the St. Charles Theatre regret to inform the public that, in consequence of the severe and continued cold under which Mr. Booth has been laboring for several days, he is compelled to take a short respite from his engagement.[240]

Booth wrote to Richard Montgomery Field of the Boston Museum: "Yours recd: only four days ago Have been sick or would have answered it before...."[241]

March 27, Sunday New Orleans

Booth had to cancel a performance of *Damon and Pythias.*

March 28, Monday New Orleans

The *New York Clipper* noted on April 16 that Booth "has entirely recovered from his indisposition and reappeared on the 28th as Damon in *Damon and Pythias.*"[242]

Booth wrote to Richard M. Johnson: "Yours of 12th: recd:. I am glad to find that you have not forgotten me, and hope I may ever live in your generous remembrance. I enclose in this a picture of myself, *better* (I think) than the one I gave you...."[243]

March 29, Tuesday New Orleans

Booth appeared as Phidias and Raphael in *The Marble Heart* and, according to the *New York Clipper,* "created a very favorable impression."[244]

Actor Lawrence Barrett[245] was appearing at another New Orleans theatre, The Varieties, and was attracting large audiences.[246]

March 30, Wednesday New Orleans

Booth appeared as Fabien and Louis in *The Corsican Brothers.*

March 31, Thursday New Orleans

Booth again played *The Marble Heart.*

April 1, Friday New Orleans

Booth played Claude Melnotte in *The Lady of Lyons* and Petruchio in *Katharine and Petruchio.*

April 2, Saturday New Orleans

Booth played Fabien and Louis in *The Corsican Brothers*. The *Picayune* was conciliatory:

Actors are not over prone to praise each other, but we have heard a good actor say that J. Wilkes Booth had quite as decided theatrical talent as any member of his talented family. It is a matter of regret that a physical disability, we trust temporary, prevented his engagement from being so gratifying to himself or to his friends as was desirable, and we look for his return here next season under more favorable auspices.[247]

April 3, Sunday New Orleans

Booth closed his engagement with *Richard III*. The *Picayune* critic wrote that "Mr. J. Wilkes Booth's engagement ... would have been much more of a success, had he not during his entire stay labored under the disadvantage of a hoarseness that prevented the audience from knowing how really well Booth can do when he is really well himself."[248]

April 4, Monday New Orleans

Booth wrote to an admirer:

I recd: yours yesterday, but was kept (by business) from answering till now. I have come to the conclusion that a noncompliance with your request would be a crime, especially if my *not refusing* will afford you the pleasure you mention. I therefore enclose, (with my best wishes for your future) A picture of my humble self. I start next Saturday for Boston.[249]

April 5, Tuesday New Orleans

April 6, Wednesday New Orleans

April 7, Thursday New Orleans

April 8, Friday New Orleans

President Lincoln saw Edwin Forrest play *King Lear* at Ford's Theatre. Between acts he asked John McCullough, who played Edgar, to come to the presidential box.[250]

April 9, Saturday En route to Boston

Booth left New Orleans for Boston. He probably traveled up the Mississippi River to Cairo, Illinois, or to St. Louis, where rail transportation to the east was available.

April 10, Sunday En route to Boston

April 11, Monday En route to Boston

April 12, Tuesday En route to Boston

April 13, Wednesday Boston

April 14, Thursday Boston

April 15, Friday Boston

General Grant suspended the exchange of Federal and Confederate prisoners of war in order to deny the South additional fighting men, as well as to impose the burden of feeding Union prisoners on the food-poor enemy.[251]

April 16, Saturday Boston

April 17, Sunday Boston

April 18, Monday Boston

April 19, Tuesday Boston

April 20, Wednesday Boston

April 21, Thursday Boston

April 22, Friday Boston

April 23, Saturday Boston

Junius Brutus Booth, Jr., left San Francisco for New York to help Edwin manage the Winter Garden Theatre.[252] On the 300th anniversary of Shakespeare's birth, the cornerstone of a statue of the Bard was laid in Central Park in New York.[253]

April 24, Sunday Boston

April 25, Monday Boston

Booth played *Richard III*. The *Boston Daily Evening Transcript* reported:

Mr. J. Wilkes Booth had a reception ... quite equal to one given to a successful General fresh from a battlefield. The audiences at the Museum are not usually so noisily demonstrative ... and they filled all the parts of the house to repletion. Mr. Booth performed *Richard III* to the satisfaction of his friends, although he was laboring under the effects of a palpable hoarseness.[254]

April 26, Tuesday Boston

Booth appeared in *Money*. According to the *Transcript*:

Mr. Booth played the part of Evelyn at the museum ... with a tact, grace and appreciation of the character such as few but himself can exhibit upon the stage, the only drawback being the cold which restrains his voice. The company, too, put their best feet foremost, and the large audience was kept in excellent humor throughout the evening.[255]

April 27, Wednesday Boston

Booth played Pescara in *The Apostate*. Mary Provost, once Booth's employer, was playing at the Howard Athenaeum.

The *Boston Post* critic commented on Booth's performance as Pescara: "This performance of the young tragedian, reminding one so much of the wild intensity of his lamented father, has always been an unusually popular one here." Although the weather had been stormy since Monday, Booth's performances were well attended.[256]

April 28, Thursday Boston

Booth played Claude Melnotte in *The Lady of Lyons*. The *Post* reported:

Crowded houses have thus far attended the performances of J. Wilkes Booth and this notwithstanding the prevalence of a severe storm from the very commencement of his engagement. Seats are in demand for a week ahead and there is every indication that his present visit to Boston will be crowned with greater success than any heretofore made.[257]

April 29, Friday Boston

Booth performed *Richard III*.

April 30, Saturday Boston

Booth gave a matinee performance as Alfred Evelyn in *Money*.

May 1, Sunday Boston

The *Post* commented: "The great success attending the performances of Mr. J. Wilkes Booth, notwithstanding the extremely disagreeable weather of the past week is a strong indication of the popularity which this young actor enjoys in Boston."[258]

May 2, Monday Boston

Booth played the title role in *Othello*.

May 3, Tuesday Boston

Booth played *Romeo and Juliet* with Kate Reignolds as Juliet.[259]

May 4, Wednesday Boston

Booth appeared as Damon in *Damon and Pythias*. The *Transcript* opined:

He was throughout great and the enthusiastic applause which was bestowed upon him was a genuine expression of the satisfaction of the audience. The scene in the Senate Chamber, when the sturdy patriot is moved by wrath and sorrow, where he appears upon the scaffold in time to save his friend, we have never seen made more impressive.[260]

May 5, Thursday Boston

Booth played Pescara in *The Apostate*.

On behalf of his mother, Booth signed a rent receipt for Tudor Hall to George Heisler.[261]

May 6, Friday Boston

Booth appeared in *Hamlet* on his benefit night.

General Grant's troops fought those of General Lee at the Battle of the Wilderness in Virginia.

May 7, Saturday Boston

Booth appeared in *Romeo and Juliet*. An observer remembered:

Every box was filled with ladies in full evening dress, feathers and flowers in their hair, wearing beautiful jewels and carrying magnificent fans, many of them jeweled and costing hundreds of dollars. The Boston Theatre, with its brilliantly magnificent chandelier lighted, was a gorgeous sight. Between the acts the audience visited and paraded....[262]

"J. Wilkes Booth's engagement at the Boston Museum has thus far proved a brilliant one," the *New York Clipper* reported.[263]

May 8, Sunday Boston

May 9, Monday Boston

Booth played *Richelieu* to a full house at the Boston Museum.[264] The *Transcript* remarked:

In the first act of Richelieu, Mr. Booth betrayed evident nervousness.... But soon ... those who were present enjoyed a performance of much originality and marked by special beauties.... The more impassioned scenes were given with that power for which Mr. Booth is noted.[265]

May 10, Tuesday Boston

Booth played Iago in *Othello* with Kate Reignolds as Desdemona. Reignolds wrote:

How he threw me about! Once even knocked me down, picking me up again with a regret as quick as his dramatic impulse had been vehement. In *Othello*, when, with fiery remorse, he rushed to the bed of Desdemona after the murder, I used to hold my breath, lest the bang of his cimeter [*sic*] should force me back to life with a shriek.[266]

May 11, Wednesday Boston

Booth played Charles de Moor in *The Robbers*.

May 12, Thursday Boston

Booth played *Richard III*. Kate Reignolds, who played Queen Anne, wrote:

He was as undisciplined on the stage as off. When he fought, it was no stage fight. If his antagonist did not strain his nerve and skill, he would either be forced over the stage into the orchestra ... or cut and hurt.... He told me that he generally slept smothered in steak or oysters to cure his own bruises after *Richard The Third*....[267]

May 13, Friday Boston

Booth played Shylock in *The Merchant of Venice* and Petruchio in *Katharine and Petruchio.*

May 14, Saturday Boston

Booth appeared as Claude Melnotte in *The Lady of Lyons* in a matinee.

May 15, Sunday Boston

May 16, Monday Boston

Booth appeared as Phidias and Raphael in *The Marble Heart.* The *Transcript*'s review stated:

Booth played well, and what is more, he enunciated his words far more distinctly than he has been in the habit of doing in many plays since his present engagement. We do not speak of his hoarseness, which was a temporary misfortune....[268]

The *Transcript* also observed that Booth "attempts to reach things beyond his grasp, and strives to win the applause of those in his immediate presence, rather than to give a correct, truthful, and lasting delineation of the creations of the great dramatic writers." Meanwhile, a different column in the same issue of the *Transcript* asserted that Booth "has never acted better than during the past three weeks.... Although he has faults, and has not yet attained the height which his powers give promise of, yet few actors represent the characters which he assumes more to the satisfaction of the public."[269]

May 17, Tuesday Boston

Booth again played *The Marble Heart.*

Junius Brutus Booth, Jr., arrived in New York from California.[270]

May 18, Wednesday Boston

Booth appeared as Damon in *Damon and Pythias.*

Maggie Mitchell was appearing at the Boston Theatre, and Mary Provost was at the Howard Athenaeum.

May 19, Thursday Boston

Booth gave a rare performance as Julian St. Pierre in *The Wife.*

May 20, Friday Boston

Booth, in his benefit, performed *Macbeth.* The *Transcript* advised that "those who wish to see this play brought out as it should be with appointments, etc., complete, should visit the Museum."[271]

May 21, Saturday Boston

Booth played Phidias and Raphael in *The Marble Heart.*

The *New York Clipper* noted that "J. Wilkes Booth continues to be the star at the Boston Museum this week. At the close of his Boston engagement he will probably appear at one of our Broadway theatres."[272]

May 22, Sunday Boston

May 23, Monday Boston

Booth started the week with *The Corsican Brothers,* in which he played Fabien and Louis. The *New York Clipper* reported:

John Wilkes Booth still holds forth at the Boston Museum. He remains this week and next week, then benefits follow after which the dramatic season closes. Mr. J. B. Booth will appear at the Boston Museum next week in the tragedy of *Ugolino,* written by the late J. B. Booth, on the occasion of J. Wilkes Booth's farewell benefit.[273]

May 24, Tuesday Boston

Booth played *The Corsican Brothers.* The *Transcript* anticipated the performance:

The superb manner in which this piece was brought out at the Museum last year, with the same actor in the principal parts, is well remembered by the patrons of the Museum. Mr. Booth will soon appear in the tragedy of *Ugolino.* This piece, written by the elder Booth, has not been performed for many years and will be fresh to the present generation....[274]

May 25, Wednesday Boston

Booth's matinee performance as Phidias and Raphael in *The Marble Heart* was followed in the evening by a portrayal of Fabien and Louis in *The Corsican Brothers.*

May 26, Thursday Boston

Booth appeared as Phidias and Raphael in *The Marble Heart,* which, according to the *Transcript,* "has proved a great success, owing in some measure of course to the tasteful manner in which it is placed upon the stage."[275]

John's brother Junius noted in his diary: "John playing at the Museum. Good bus[iness]."[276]

May 27, Friday Boston

Booth played the title role in *Ugolino.* The *Transcript* announced:

Mr. Booth appears in a new character tonight and doubtless considerable interest will be manifested to witness his performance. We have not the slightest idea what the character is, further than it is call *Ugolino* and that it is said to possess many passages of rare romantic beauty.[277]

The *New York Clipper* had mentioned that

Junius Brutus Booth, Jr., would appear in the performance of *Ugolino*, but he did not.

Booth also appeared as Petruchio in *Katharine and Petruchio*.

May 28, Saturday Boston

Booth appeared as Fabien and Louis in *The Corsican Brothers*, the last performance of his career as a touring star.

May 29, Sunday Boston

May 30, Monday Boston

Booth transferred twenty-five shares of Boston Water Power Company stock to J. W. Fiske[278] and wrote a receipt for his Boston engagement.[279]

May 31, Tuesday Boston?

Booth wrote: "This is to certify that the undersigned has purchased the dressing gown from Mrs. Wilson for seventy-five dollars and which is paid this date."[280]

June 1, Wednesday

Booth signed a receipt.[281]

Junius noted in his diary that he rode out to Mount Auburn Cemetery to see Mary Devlin Booth's grave.[282]

The Battle of Cold Harbor, Virginia, began.

June 2, Thursday

Junius left Boston at 5 p.m. and arrived in New York at 8 a.m. the next day.[283]

June 3, Friday

The Battle of Cold Harbor ended.

June 5, Sunday

Junius noted that it rained all day in New York.[284]

8

Preparations: 1864

John Wilkes Booth closed his acting season at the end of May to search for oil in Pennsylvania. On June 9, 1864, Booth and Joe Simonds left New York for western Pennsylvania.[1] They arrived in Meadville the next day and stayed overnight at the McHenry House. The neophyte oilmen embarked on a stagecoach the next day for Franklin, twenty miles to the south. Upon arriving, Booth wrote to John Ellsler, asking him to come to the oil region and informing him that Thomas Y. Mears was going to Cleveland, Ohio, to buy supplies. Mears had been working with the oilmen for $90 a month. Booth claimed to be short of funds and asked Ellsler to contribute more money.[2]

On June 14 Booth started a two-day walking tour of the oil region. He inspected land along Pithole Creek, seventeen miles up the Allegheny River from Franklin. Several Boston men had formed the Boston Oil Well Company and had purchased promising oil land near the creek for $15,000. Booth invested $1,000 in the venture.[3] During the summer, Simonds became the manager of both the Boston Oil Well Company and the Dramatic Oil Company, which was owned by Booth, Ellsler, and Mears.[4] When Booth returned to Franklin he wrote to Ellsler:

I want to see you here bad. This may be a big thing for us or it may be *nothing*. The last sure if we do not give it our attention. Throw things overboard and come as soon as possible. I must see you. I have seen all the oil regions. I got back the other day from a two

days *walk* of 48 miles. And I know more about these things than anyone can tell me.[5]

Ellsler soon arrived in Franklin and later wrote:

As arranged, Wilkes preceded me to the base of operations, and when I reached him, I found him hard at work, dressed in a slouched hat, flannel shirt, overalls, and boots. He was a sight to behold.... "Shades of Shakespeare!" I exclaimed. "Look down in horror! and behold your Prince of Denmark, digging for the oleaginous, on the banks of the Allegheny!!"[6]

Booth, Ellsler, and Mears had leased three and one-half acres of land on the Fuller farm, one mile south of Franklin on the east bank of the Allegheny River. When Booth was introduced to Henry Sires, who had been hired to drill the well, Sires apologized for his greasy hands. Booth replied, "Never mind, that's what we are after."[7] The Dramatic Oil Company's well, christened "The Wilhelmina" in honor of Mears's wife, was drilled to a depth of 1,900 feet. Work soon began on a second well.[8]

In Franklin, Booth and Simonds secured a room for a few nights, with two other men, at the United States Hotel, and then took up residence at Sarah Webber's rooming house on the corner of Buffalo and Thirteenth Streets. They continued to take their meals at the hotel two blocks away. While walking from the rooming house to the hotel, Booth often stopped at the Watson harness shop to play with the owner's baby, who could be seen sitting in the shop's window.[9] Booth had a way with children. Alfred W. Smiley, a local man who had become acquainted with Booth, remembered:

> When riding horseback through the streets he would frequently stop to gently greet some child.... In walking along the sidewalks, this fondness for children was even more noticeable; his stops were more frequent and his greetings and caresses of the heartiest nature. Stories of the magnetism and fascination in the man's face are strictly true no matter how strongly drawn.[10]

Booth did not spend all his time at his well. Joe Simonds, Robert Brigham, and Booth took long walks in the hills and talked of poetry, the theatre, and literature, but never about politics.[11] Apparently Booth talked politics with others. The local ferryman related:

> Booth was well posted on political facts and figures and very few people could get the better of him in discussing the topic that was in everybody's mind at that time.... Booth had the shrewdest and keenest intellect of any man [I] ever met. [He] had a most striking personality, so much so, that if one saw him once they would know him again wherever or whenever they saw him.[12]

Booth's political feelings came out one day on the Allegheny River ferry when fellow passenger Titus Ridgway made a derogatory remark about Southerners. Booth retaliated with a derisive comment about President Lincoln, which Ridgway called "A damned lie!" Booth drew a pistol from his pocket and was prevented from firing at his antagonist by other passengers.[13] In another incident, Booth was in a barber shop when a black man entered and rejoiced about a Union victory. Booth asked the intruder, "Is that the way you talk among gentlemen, and with your hat on too?" When the man responded with spirit, Booth became agitated and had to be restrained by Tom Mears.[14]

Alexander P. Riddle, who later became lieutenant governor of Kansas, observed that Booth was an avid reader, particularly about current topics.[15] Alfred Smiley described the actor as "very stylish in his dress, rather good looking, cold in manner toward strangers, but when acquainted, quite social and very polite."[16] Booth and Smiley became fast friends. The two often played billiards.[17] One night they attended a dance at the Marshall House near the Allegheny River, and a fight broke out between steamboat and lumber men. When the two friends pushed closer to view the action, they were pulled into the fray and soon were ejected from the hotel, with orders not to return.[18]

Booth was known by some observers for his ability to consume large quantities of alcohol without showing its effect. He usually drank brandy and rum.[19] Others observed that his drinking was moderate during his stay in Franklin.[20]

Booth often rented a chestnut mare and saddle from liveryman Ralph Brigham.[21] Smiley reported:

> Booth spent a great bit of time riding horseback. He was a most graceful rider; suit composed of soft hat, tight fitting coat and high top cavalry boots.... Booth always carried a cane of some kind, usually a gold-headed cane with a figure of a horse accompanied him on his walks or rides, but when no stick of human design was convenient, he would cut a switch from the first bush or tree he passed.[22]

Booth's visit to the oil region of Pennsylvania lasted eighteen days. On June 29, on his way out of the area, he again registered at the McHenry House in Meadville.[23] Later that summer the hotel housekeeper noticed words scratched on the windowpane of room 22: "Abe Lincoln Died Aug 13th/64 By poison." Whether Booth had anything to do with the scratched message is a matter of speculation. He had stayed in another room.[24] He went on to Cleveland, where thousands of people jammed the city to welcome the Seventh and Eighth Ohio Regiments.[25] The Academy of Music manager John Ellsler invited members of the Seventh Regiment to attend the theatre as his guests.[26]

By July 6 Booth was back in New York.[27] Edwin, Junius Jr., and John had planned a mid–July performance of *Julius Caesar* to raise funds for a statue of Shakespeare to be placed in Central Park, but the plans fell through.[28] Edwin wrote to a friend:

> *Julius Caesar* did not take place on account of J. Wilkes' absence—hunting up oil wells in Pennsylvania, and is now postponed until the 9th of August when I hope it will be cool enough to proceed with it. Wilkes was to have played Antony and JB [Junius Brutus Booth, Jr.] to play the role of Cassius.[29]

In the month after he returned to New York, Booth became involved in a plot to capture President Lincoln and take him to Richmond, where he would be exchanged for Confederate prisoners held by the Union. He may have been recruited by representatives of the Confederate government, but that seems unlikely. He may have devised the plot on his own and then sought Confederate approval and support. The inception of the plot seems to have been sudden; otherwise, it is doubtful that Booth would have devoted time and money to oil ventures in June. He soon would take steps to divest himself of those now-distracting interests.

On July 26 Booth registered at the Parker House in Boston. The hotel register shows that H. V. Clinton of Hamilton, Ontario, was also staying at the hotel. A month later, on August 24, Clinton's name appeared on the register of Montreal's St. Lawrence Hall, the Confederate headquarters in that city.[30] While Clinton's presence during Booth's stay in Boston may suggest that Booth was meeting with Confederate agents, no definite conclusion may be drawn.[31] No evidence has been found that Clinton was a Confederate agent or that he and Booth met. It is likely that the purpose of Booth's visit to Boston was to see Isabel Sumner and to spend a few days with his sister Asia and her children in New London, Connecticut, where they were vacationing.

Several plots to capture President Lincoln were afloat in 1864. Confederate General Bradley T. Johnson, a Marylander, proposed to capture the president at his summer residence outside Washington and take him to Virginia. His scheme may have been prompted by the belief that the Kilpatrick-Dahlgren raid on Richmond in February and the raiders' plan to assassinate Confederate leaders had been approved by the United States government, perhaps by President Lincoln himself.

Another plot began to take shape at the end of August, when Confederate Captain Thomas Nelson Conrad, of Virginia, received orders to report to Richmond. Conrad had proposed a plan to capture President Lincoln and convey him to Richmond. Confederate Secretary of War James Seddon was reluctant to endorse the proposal. Conrad later wrote that "[o]n my representations, however, [Seddon] finally gave his consent to the measure as perfectly justifiable in war times, but with the stipulation that no violence should be used in any event."[32] Conrad's preparations in Richmond lasted about two weeks.[33] On September 15 Seddon ordered: "Lt. Col. Mosby and Lieut. Cawood [officer in charge of the Confederate Signal Corps on the Potomac River] are hereby directed to aid and facilitate the movements of Capt. Conrad."[34]

Conrad and three other men left for Washington late in September to prepare to capture President Lincoln.[35] The men followed one of the clandestine routes on which people and mail were moved to and from Richmond and Washington. On the way, Conrad stopped at a tavern in Surrattsville (now Clinton), Maryland, ten miles south of Washington, where he met tavern owner Mary E. Surratt and her son John, a Confederate courier.[36] The Surratt Tavern was a stop, or "safe house," on the Confederate line of communications to the North.[37] The Surratts would become involved in Booth's attempt to capture Lincoln. Booth's plan closely matched that of Conrad.

Booth needed a team to execute the capture. On August 8 or 9 he introduced his friends Samuel Arnold and Michael O'Laughlen at Barnum's Hotel in Baltimore. Arnold had not seen Booth since 1852, when they had been schoolmates. O'Laughlen had lived across the street from Booth in Baltimore when the two were youngsters. Both men had served in the Confederate army, and both agreed to join Booth in a plot to capture the president before the election and use him as a hostage to effect an exchange of prisoners.[38] According to Booth, President Lincoln, accompanied only by a carriage driver, could be abducted on one of his frequent visits to a hospital across the Anacostia River.[39]

Arnold remembered the date of his first meeting with Booth as about September 1. Booth, according to Arnold, returned to New York the next day "to wind up his affairs." While in New York, Booth contracted erysipelas, a subcutaneous infection that afflicted his arm and disabled him for three weeks.[40] Upon recovering, according to Arnold, Booth went to the oil fields, from where he sent Arnold a letter. A notation in Junius Booth's diary fixes the dates of John's illness; on August 28 Junius wrote: "John Booth ill 3 weeks with Erysepalas [sic] in the Right Elbow—Had Dr. Smith."[41] The onset of the illness, three weeks prior to Junius's diary entry, would have been about August 7. On that date John, Edwin, and John Sleeper Clarke traveled from New York to Philadelphia.[42] Booth, contrary to Arnold's recollection, made the short trip to Baltimore to recruit Arnold and O'Laughlen on August 8 or 9. Then he returned to New York, where he became ill.[43]

The infection was serious. The *Medical and Surgical History of the War of the Rebellion* reported a fatality rate of fifteen percent directly attributable to erysipelas among those soldiers suffering from the infection.[44] Asia described John's illness:

[John] was once stopping at Edwin's New York house, and, suffering from a diseased arm, he fainted from the acute pain, and Junius carried him and laid him upon his bed. As he lay there in his shirt-sleeves so pale and death-like, we all felt how wondrously beautiful he was.... Soon he was to lie dead among his foes.... As we saw it [his face] then, pallid and death-like on his bed, we were to ponder it all our lives.[45]

On August 26, Booth wrote:

Dearest Friend Isabel [Sumner], I recd: your sweet flowers yesterday And you know how delighted I must have been in knowing that you sometimes thought of me. God bless you. When your message came this morning I was still in bed waiting for the doctor to come. He came at last; but did not cut my arm. he has put it off til tomorrow.... I have not been out of the house since I saw you....[46]

He wrote another letter to Isabel on the day the doctor "cut" his arm. He wanted to see her in a day or two. For reasons unexplained, this was the last letter of their correspondence.[47]

Junius recalled that "[a]bout this time the latter part of the month of August he [John] had a severe family quarrel on politics."[48] Junius tried to convince John that the North was doing its duty in the prosecution of the war. He later told authorities, "I always feared he might join the South, though he promised me often that he would not, for his mother's and his family's sake."[49] Edwin Booth wrote of his brother John, "I asked him once why he did not join the Confederate army; to which he replied: 'I promised mother I would keep out of the quarrel, if possible, and I am sorry that I said so.'"[50]

By the end of the first week in September Booth's arm had healed. He visited Pennsylvania's oil country again, this time to wrap up his interests. Since the Dramatic Oil Company's drilling rights to the Fuller farm would expire if oil was not discovered, it became necessary for the company to purchase the land outright. Explosives were sunk in the hole and set off, with the hope that oil would flow freely to the surface. Instead, the slight production from the well ceased entirely.[51] Finally, Joe Simonds, at Booth's request, closed out the Booth interests in the Allegheny River property. Two thirds of Booth's share was to be deeded to his brother Junius and one third to Simonds as payment for his assistance. Booth's interest in the Boston Oil Well Company's venture near Pithole Creek was to be deeded to his sister Rosalie. He told Simonds he was divesting himself of the oil interests to concentrate on acting. Booth had invested a total of $6,000 in two oil ventures and not only failed to make a profit, but did not recover his investment. Each of the investments later became moderately profitable. Simonds stayed on in Pennsylvania and soon advertised in the local newspaper "Jo. H. Simonds & Co.—Agents for the Purchase and Sale of Petroleum Lands...."[52]

Early in October Thomas Nelson Conrad, ready to implement his abduction scheme, traveled the proposed route on which the captured President Lincoln was to be taken to Richmond and left instructions that boats should be waiting to ferry the president across the Potomac.[53] Conrad had planned to capture Lincoln when he drove to his summer residence at the Soldiers' Home. Conrad later wrote: "Imagine my astounding surprise and total collapse when we beheld the carriage of Mr. Lincoln moving out of the grounds of the White House, preceded and followed by a squad of cavalry."[54]

When Booth returned to New York from Franklin, he told Junius he was going to Canada to play an engagement.[55] In mid–October Booth traveled to Montreal. One purpose of the trip was to ship his theatrical wardrobe to a southern port. He intended to take up acting again after the execution of his plot. Booth sought out Patrick Charles Martin, who was preparing, for the first time, to run the blockade from Montreal to the Confederacy via Nassau, in the Bahamas. Martin fulfilled another of Booth's needs: the former Baltimore liquor dealer came from southern Maryland and knew the people there. After capturing the president, Booth would need

to transport him to Richmond. The most direct path was through southern Maryland, and the covert Confederate route already in place was perfect. Several doctors, as well as others, were involved in this network; doctors carrying contraband mail could move easily without arousing undue suspicion by Federal patrols. Martin gave Booth a letter of introduction to Dr. William Queen, who was familiar with the route in his neighborhood. He may also have provided a similar letter of introduction to Dr. Samuel A. Mudd.[56] Of course the letters couldn't say, "Help Mr. Booth get President Lincoln to Richmond"; they instead asked for help with real estate investments.[57]

Booth also wanted to either inform or update certain Confederate commissioners in Montreal of his plans. The Confederate government had sent former U.S. Senator Clement Clay and former Secretary of the Interior Jacob Thompson to Canada earlier in 1864. The commissioners supported raids on the Great Lakes and on St. Albans, Vermont, and funded an attempt to burn New York City and poison its water supply. George N. Sanders was Booth's primary Confederate contact in Canada.[58] Sanders had served as United States consul to London, England, in 1853 and had become involved in a plot to assassinate Louis Napoleon, emperor of France. After his return to the United States in 1855, he advocated "death to tyrants."[59] Certainly Booth found a sympathetic ear in Sanders.

Booth's meetings with Sanders were delayed by the aftermath of the October 19 Confederate raid on St. Albans, Vermont. The St. Albans raiders escaped to Canada, where they were arrested. Clement Clay provided funds to Sanders for the legal defense of the raiders.[60] A week after Booth's arrival in Montreal, Sanders returned to that city after visiting the raiders. He registered at St. Lawrence Hall, where Booth was staying. Neither Booth nor Sanders left a record of their discussions. The *Montreal Telegraph* later reported that Booth "was not cordially received by Southern men here, it being reported that he was a Federal spy, and in this light he was generally, although perhaps untruly, regarded."[61]

Intriguing questions concerning Booth's Montreal trip remain unanswered. How had Booth become aware of Patrick C. Martin, who was so helpful in shipping his wardrobe and also in introducing him to the people in southern Maryland? Was this Booth's first contact with the Confederates? Did Booth ask for funds for his project? What was the reaction to his proposal?[62]

Several people claimed to have encountered Booth in Montreal. Confederate Colonel Robert M. Martin said he became acquainted with Booth in the fall of 1864 in Toronto.[63] There is no evidence that Booth was ever in Toronto; Martin may have met Booth in Montreal and incorrectly recalled the meeting place. Martin led a plot sponsored by the Confederate commissioners in Canada to burn New York City on November 25, 1864.[64] A Canadian who met Booth in Montreal wrote: "I was introduced to J. Wilkes Booth at the St. Lawrence Hall ... and indulged in a friendly contest at billiards with him, in the saloon of that establishment, which was continued to a late hour in the evening." Booth, who had been drinking freely, reportedly said, "Abe's contract is near up, and whether re-elected or not, he will get his goose cooked."[65]

Another Montreal acquaintance later wrote of Booth:

A Canadian winter was a novelty to Booth and one afternoon, wearing his yellow foxskin cap with a sheltering peak, he took a sleigh-drive to Lachine, eight miles from Montreal. As far as I know that was his only excursion. A breeze at twenty below zero was more than he bargained for or cared to repeat. In his winter array he was photographed one morning by George Martin....[66]

On his last day in Montreal, Booth, accompanied by Patrick C. Martin, with whom he had been staying for several days, deposited $455 in an account at the Montreal branch of the Ontario Bank. He also exchanged $300 in gold for a bill of exchange and asked the bank teller: "I am going to run the blockade; and, in case I should be captured, can my capturers make use of the exchange?" The teller responded, "No."[67] The sums of money exchanged were not large by Booth's standards. He had earned as much as $20,000 a year, and he was known to be careful with his money. It is likely that Booth was using his own money rather than funds obtained from Confederate sources.

Booth had let it be known that he could not follow his acting profession in the North because of a "bronchial infection" and that he intended to act in the South, where, presumably, the warmer climate would allow the infection to be cured.[68] Booth left his wardrobe with blockade runner Martin to be shipped south via Nassau. Unfortunately for Booth, Martin, his ship *Marie Victoria*, and Booth's wardrobe were lost in a storm.[69]

When Booth returned to New York, he completed the transfer of his oil property to his brother Junius through Charles Nettleton, an out-of-state commissioner of the Commonwealth of Pennsylvania.[70] He sent the deeds to Joe Simonds in Franklin and asked Simonds to write to him at Barnum's Hotel in Baltimore.[71]

Thomas Nelson Conrad's plan to abduct President Lincoln had been developed quickly and was shelved by mid–November.[72] Booth's plot was slow in developing. The initial goal had been to capture the president before the November elections, but that was impossible now. Booth needed to become familiar with the clandestine route to Richmond through southern Maryland, and he needed to make contact with at least some members of the loose network of people who made the route work. He required men who knew the roads, who could transport the kidnappers and their captive across the Potomac River, and who could slow the expected pursuit by Union troops.

Early in November Booth registered at the National Hotel in Washington.[73] It is likely that Booth wrote to Dr. William Queen to ask if he could visit. Having received permission, he took a stage to Bryantown, Maryland, on Friday, November 11. One of the stage stops was at the Surratt Tavern, about ten miles from Washington. The stage continued another fifteen miles to Bryantown. On the way, Booth decided he did not want to be in possession of a weapon if searched by Federal patrols and asked the stage driver to take his pistol and leave it in Washington, probably at the National Hotel.[74] Booth spent the night at the Bryantown Tavern. The next morning Dr. Queen's son Joseph came to town and drove the actor to his father's home, where Booth presented the letter of introduction from Patrick C. Martin. Booth discussed real estate, roads, and people with his host.[75]

On Sunday Booth accompanied Dr. Queen and his son-in-law, John C. Thompson, to St. Mary's Catholic Church near Bryantown. Thompson reportedly introduced Booth to Dr. Samuel A. Mudd in front of the church.[76] The introduction may have occurred on this date, or it may have taken place on Booth's next visit a month later; perhaps the men met on both dates.[77] It is likely that special arrangements had been made for Booth's introduction to Mudd; Dr. Mudd usually attended church at a parish much nearer to his home. Dr. Mudd was young and vigorous and would be more helpful to Booth than the elderly Dr. Queen.

Booth returned to Dr. Queen's home after the Mass.[78] The next day, Booth returned to Washington on a stage driven by another driver and checked into the National Hotel.[79] Not finding his pistol there, he wrote to J. Dominic Burch, a young man he had met in Bryantown:

Hope I shall see you again ere long. Our *friend* of the stage last friday never left what I gave to his charge. You know *what* I had to take from my carpet-bag. It[']s not worth more than $15, but I will give him $20 rather

than lose it. As it saved my life two or three times. He has left the city. If you would be kind enough to get it from him and send it to me I will reimburse you for any outlay. And will never forget you. If you should ever recover it, either send, or give to *our friend* co. Fayette st., where if you wish you can write me. Remember me to all the friends I met while in your country.[80]

On November 16, Booth opened a checking account with Jay Cooke & Co. with an initial deposit of $1,500.[81] He could have done this business before his trip to southern Maryland, but he held off until he was assured of help there. It was certainly possible, given Booth's previous earnings, for him to have $1,500 of his own to deposit; it is also possible he had obtained funds in Canada. After opening the account, Booth left Washington for a two-week visit to Philadelphia and New York.

About this time, a man called at Asia's home in Philadelphia and asked for Dr. Booth. When Asia asked John about it, he responded, "All right, I am he, if to be a doctor means a dealer in quinine."[82] He claimed he was smuggling the drug to the South. His hands, he said, were calloused from nights of rowing. His movements during this period are well known, and he was not near any Confederate lines. On what body of water did the rowing occur? What was the destination? Did Booth tell his sister the truth about smuggling quinine, or was he fabricating a story? After all, he had lied about forcing a conductor to drive a train through snowdrifts, and he had asked Dr. May to lie about the removal of his neck tumor. Booth's statements were not to be trusted. One of his friends referred to Booth's "stories told to him by way of bravado and with no foundation in fact."[83] His hands were actually calloused from frequent exercise in gymnasiums using wooden clubs.[84]

Booth seems to have had several reasons for taking the drastic steps of shelving his acting career and embarking on the dangerous plot to capture the president. He felt patriotism for the South. He felt guilty for living well while his southern "brothers" fought, starved, and died. Perhaps he thought there would be financial gain; at least that is what he told his friend Samuel Knapp Chester. Booth's thoughts are revealed in two letters he wrote at the end of November, one to his mother and another addressed "To whom it may concern." He placed the letters in a sealed envelope and left it with his sister Asia for safekeeping. The envelope also, ironically, contained several United States bonds.[85]

The letter to his mother reveals that Booth felt guilt at not participating in the Southern cause, that he had avoided participation for the sake of his mother, and that, by joining the cause of the South, he understood his life would be in danger. The letter does not explicitly state what he intended to do.[86]

Booth also wrote a letter of explanation for his planned abduction of President Lincoln. The previous July, John Hay had delivered a message from the president to Confederate commissioners in Canada. The message was addressed "To Whom It May Concern" and specified conditions for opening peace discussions. Booth used this phrase to address his own letter, in which he lamented that his beloved Union, once the world's great protector of liberty, justice, and individual rights, had become an engine of oppression and death under Lincoln. The South, he asserted, was not fighting to maintain slavery—though the institution was a "blessing" to both master and slave—but rather to throw off the yoke of a tyranny even crueler than that faced by the Revolutionary generation. Willing to give up his career, his family, and even his life for a Confederacy on the verge of destruction, Booth was prepared to do what he regarded as his "duty": deliver to the South the "man to whom she owes so much misery."[87]

The long-planned benefit for the Shakespeare statue fund in New York was scheduled for November 25. The play starring three sons of the great Junius Brutus Booth would be a big attraction. John Barron described the Booth brothers:

> They all differed, and in some things they were as wide apart as the points of the compass, but in other things they clung together. All four personified generosity. Junius was somewhat phlegmatic, slow of speech and most deliberate in action; Edwin was graceful and decisive; John was quick in action and had eyes that were piercing and most expressive, with a perfect physical beauty and stately bearing; and Joe was the embodiment of ease, comfort and good fellowship. Of dramatic fire, Joe had not one spark. Nature seems to have favored Edwin and John with all the charms that go to make perfect the exquisite art these two sons of an erratic genius adorned. Junius was a fairly good, reliable actor—great in nothing, but perfect in all he did to the limit of his abilities.[88]

The Booth brothers gathered in Philadelphia in the Clarkes' new home to prepare their roles. Then they traveled to New York for the performance at the Winter Garden. John shaved his mustache for the occasion. The theatre was crowded with 2,000 people, some paying as much as $5 for a ticket. When the three brothers came on stage—Junius as Cassius, Edwin as Brutus, and John as Marc Antony—they were greeted by a tremendous round of applause. The play was well underway when it was halted by a warning of a fire next door, one of several fires set by Confederate agents in an attempt to burn the city. Edwin came before the footlights and calmed the crowd. When the danger was over, the play resumed.

At the end of the play, the brothers bowed to the box occupied by Mary Ann Booth and her daughters. Junius escorted the Booth mother to Edwin's residence, while Edwin's business partner, William Stuart, hosted a reception elsewhere. Stuart, apparently inadvertently, forgot to invite Junius and John.[89]

The *New York Herald* reviewed the benefit:

The audience was a great success, and the play was a great success also. The audience was fairly carried by storm from the first entrance of the three brothers side by side in their respective parts.... If there was less of real personality given to Marc Antony [the part played by John Wilkes Booth], the fault was rather in the part than in the actor.[90]

John and Edwin clashed during this visit. "When I told him [Wilkes] that I had voted for Lincoln's re-election," Edwin recalled, "he expressed deep regret, and declared his belief that Lincoln would be made King of America, and this, I believe, drove him beyond the limits of reason."[91] John needed to explain to his family why he was no longer touring as an actor. He told Junius he was forming an oil company in Washington and could make more money in oil than in acting.[92] While John's acting career had ended, Edwin's had reached a peak. On November 26 Edwin began an unprecedented run of 100 performances of *Hamlet*.

Edwin's friend Adam Badeau saw John early in the winter:

As Edwin was very loyal, indeed, even ardent in his sentiment, he and I talked constantly of my desire to rejoin my chief [Major General Ulysses S. Grant], and of the prospect of the war. Again Wilkes Booth restrained in my presence any expressions of sympathy with the South. Edwin indeed told me afterward that he had long and violent political discussions with [John]....[93]

Booth did not neglect the kidnapping plot while he was in New York. He tried to recruit his friend Sam Chester, who was in the stock company at the Winter Garden Theatre. First he asked Chester to go into an "oil" speculation, and then he proposed land speculation in Maryland and Virginia. Chester said he had no money to invest, and the matter temporarily dropped. After Booth returned to Washington, he sent Chester several letters asking him to participate in the land investments.[94] Booth asked John T. Ford to hire Chester for his theatre in Washington

and offered to reimburse him for Chester's salary.[95]

On the morning of December 17 Booth left Washington for southern Maryland and again spent the night at the home of Dr. Queen.[96] He left Queen's house early and apparently did not attend church, as he had on his previous visit.[97] He had arranged to meet Dr. Mudd at the Bryantown Tavern, where Mudd introduced Booth to Thomas H. Harbin. Harbin had served as postmaster in Bryantown and was the principal Confederate signal officer in the lower counties of Maryland. Booth and Harbin met in the privacy of an upstairs room, and Booth asked Harbin to assist in the capture and transportation of Lincoln. Harbin later reported that Booth's proposal was made in a highly dramatic manner, interspersed with looks into the hallways and out the windows to assure that no one was listening. Booth said there was both glory and money in the project. Harbin thought Booth was a "crazy fellow," but he agreed to help move the captured president along the route to Richmond.[98] Either Mudd or Harbin suggested another potentially helpful operative—John H. Surratt. Booth rode home with Mudd. They arrived just after Mrs. Mudd and visitors had finished supper. Mudd introduced Booth to the guests, and, after their supper, Booth joined the Mudds and their visitors in general conversation until 9:30 p.m., when all retired.[99]

The next day, after breakfast, Dr. Mudd and Booth went to the neighboring farm, where Booth bought a one-eyed horse. Booth asked that the horse be delivered to him at Montgomery's Stable in Bryantown the next day.[100] At the local blacksmith shop, accompanied by Dr. Mudd, Booth had the horse shod and bought a saddle and bridle. Several people in the shop found Booth to be quite charming. Mudd and Booth rode away together.[101] Booth certainly needed help navigating the roads; he became lost on the trip back to Washington.[102]

Earlier in December Booth had rented

a substantial brick stable measuring about twenty by thirty feet and located on the south side of the alley behind Ford's Theatre. Edman (Ned) Spangler, a scene-shifter at Ford's and an acquaintance of Booth since 1854, modified the stable to hold two horses and a carriage.[103] When Booth arrived in Washington with the one-eyed horse, however, he boarded the animal at Howard's Stable. He had also acquired a light bay horse that he kept at Howard's.[104]

Booth needed more men to execute the capture of the president. John Surratt, whose name Booth received from Mudd or Harbin, was a Confederate courier who knew at least part of the route from Richmond to Washington and knew the people along the way. Surratt had been appointed postmaster for Surrattsville in September 1862 and was removed a month later for "disloyalty" to the Union.[105] John's mother, Mary Surratt, and her family, including John, had recently moved from their country tavern to a house on H Street in Washington, where she took in lodgers. Howard's Stable, where Booth kept his horses for a time, was about a block away from the Surratt house.

On December 23 Dr. Mudd met Booth in front of the National Hotel. Mudd agreed to introduce Booth to Surratt, and the two started to walk the several blocks to Mary Surratt's boarding house. On the way, they encountered John Surratt and his friend Louis J. Weichmann, a resident of the boarding house. The four men then adjourned to Booth's room at the National Hotel, after which they went to the Pennsylvania House for drinks and discussion. Mudd later claimed he was reluctant to make the introduction and that he took Surratt aside and warned him he suspected Booth of being a spy for the North.[106] At this meeting, or shortly after, Booth described his plot to Surratt, and Surratt agreed to sign on.

Matthew Canning, who had employed Booth in his company at the Montgomery Theatre in Alabama and had later scheduled engagements for Booth elsewhere, was in Washington in December and saw Booth there frequently. On several occasions, Booth missed arranged meetings with Canning, giving the excuse that he was teaching a young friend to shoot at a pistol range. He often practiced with friends at a shooting gallery at Eleventh Street and Pennsylvania Avenue. Canning thought Booth seemed flighty in his ideas, as he spoke of making a fortune by buying land in Virginia and "occasionally he would talk secession sentiments." Booth started to tell Canning about the plot but apparently decided it would be best not to involve him. Canning thought it strange that Booth asked him to talk to the Ford's Theatre management about hiring Sam Chester, and to say that Chester was dissatisfied in New York. Nevertheless, Canning spoke to John Ford, who agreed to employ Chester if he left New York.[107]

Canning related an interesting incident involving Booth and President Lincoln at Grover's Theatre. Canning managed Felicita Vestvali, an opera star who was performing at Grover's in December. On the last night of her engagement, according to Canning, the Lincolns attended the performance, and Booth was present at the theatre. "When the President and lady were passing out, he [Booth] moved after them, eyeing them very intently, while they waited on the steps some moments for a carriage." Canning said he "noticed Booth watching the President with the greatest intensity."[108] He may have been mistaken about the date of the incident, for there is no record of the Lincolns attending the theatre on December 23, the last night Vestvali performed at Grover's.[109]

John returned to New York to spend Christmas with his mother at Edwin's home.[110] On the evening of Christmas Day, Booth called on Sam Chester. Booth described the abduction plot, saying that a team of fifty to 100 men had already been recruited and that Chester was the final addition. Chester's role would be the simple task of keeping the back door of the theatre open: Booth's plan had changed from taking the president from a lightly guarded carriage on a lonely road to abducting him from a crowded theatre. Chester, astonished, flatly refused and kept refusing when Booth continued to badger him. Booth threatened to kill him if he revealed their discussion. Chester was accustomed to inflated stories from Booth and thought this was one of them.[111]

1864 *from June 6*

June 6, Monday New York

Junius Brutus Booth, Jr., recorded in his diary that John had "cut his nose against a clothes line."[112]

June 7, Tuesday New York

Booth wrote to Isabel Sumner and asked her not to show the letter to anyone:

> How, shall I write you; as *lover, friend* or *brother.* I think *so much* of you that (at your bidding) I would even try to school my heart to beat as the latter.... I believe you have *MORE* than *kind feelings* for *me*, but, *I* have been deceived a thousand times.[113]

The National Union Convention assembled at the Front Street Theatre in Baltimore.

June 8, Wednesday New York

The Baltimore convention unanimously renominated Abraham Lincoln for president.

June 9, Thursday En route to Pennsylvania

According to Junius's diary, "John [Wilkes Booth] & Joe Simonds left for Oil City."[114]

June 10, Friday Meadville

Booth and Simonds registered at the McHenry House in Meadville, about twenty miles north of Franklin.

June 11, Saturday Franklin

Booth and Simonds took a stagecoach from Meadville to Franklin, where they secured a room.[115]

Booth talked with Thomas Y. Mears, who was arranging the drilling operation on their Fuller farm land.

Booth wrote to John Ellsler asking him to come to the oil region. Operating expenses were mounting, and Booth wanted Ellsler to share the new expenditures.[116]

June 12, Sunday Franklin

June 13, Monday Franklin

June 14, Tuesday Oil Region

Booth started a two-day walking tour of the oil region.[117]

June 15, Wednesday Oil Region

Booth continued his walking tour.[118]

June 16, Thursday Franklin

Booth completed his tour of the oil region.

June 17, Friday Franklin

Booth again wrote to John Ellsler asking him to come on.[119]

Booth wrote to Isabel Sumner asking several times why she had not written; he explained that no letters from her had been forwarded to him.[120]

June 18, Saturday Franklin

June 19, Sunday Franklin

President Lincoln and John Hay attended a performance at Ford's Theatre.[121]

June 20, Monday Franklin

June 21, Tuesday Franklin

June 22, Wednesday Franklin

June 23, Thursday Franklin

June 24, Friday Franklin

June 25, Saturday Franklin

June 26, Sunday Franklin

June 27, Monday Franklin

The *New York Times* Amusement section noted:

> Central Park Shakespeare Statue—A benefit in aid of this fund is to take place in the course of a few evenings, at the Winter Garden, when the tragedy of "Julius Caesar" is to be presented with the extraordinary attraction of the appearance of the three sons of the late Mr. J. B. BOOTH in the three leading roles, viz; Mr. EDWIN BOOTH as Brutus, Mr. J. WILKES BOOTH as Marc Antony, and Mr. J. B. BOOTH as Cassius, supported by a full corps of volunteer aids. This novel and interesting trio of attractions will, of course, have the effect of filling the house to its utmost capacity, even if the thermometer indicates fever heat.[122]

June 28, Tuesday Franklin

June 29, Wednesday Meadville

Booth registered at the McHenry House.[123]

June 30, Thursday Cleveland

The *Cleveland Morning Leader* noted that "J. Wilkes Booth, the well-known tragedian, was in town [Thursday] and stopping at the Weddell. William Reynolds, Esq., of Meadville, was also at the Weddell...."[124]

The Weddell House, where Booth stayed, was at the northwest corner of Superior and Bank (now West Sixth) Streets.[125]

July 1, Friday Cleveland

Academy of Music manager John Ellsler invited members of the Seventh Regiment to attend the theatre as his guests.[126]

July 2, Saturday

A woodcut portrait of Junius Brutus Booth, Sr., accompanied by biographical notes, appeared on the front page of the *New York Clipper*.

July 6, Wednesday New York

Junius recorded in his diary, "...in NY, Ed & John [Wilkes Booth] home."[127]

July 14, Thursday New York

Booth wrote a letter to Isabel Sumner:
I have just returned from the Mountains of Penn-. God bless you, I was sure you had forgotten me.... I had no idea how much I *cared* for you till the last week or so.... *I LOVE YOU*, and I feel that in the fountain of my heart a *seal is set* to keep its waters, *pure* and *bright* for *thee* alone. God bless you. You see (to follow *your* wishes, NOT MY-OWN) I call myself your FRIEND only....[128]

July 15, Friday New York

July 16, Saturday New York

July 17, Sunday New York

In a letter misdated June 17, rather than July 17, Edwin wrote:
My brother W- is here for the summer, and we intend taking advantage of our thus being brought together, with nothing to do, and will, in the course of a week or two, give a performance of "Julius Caesar" in which I will take the part of *Brutus* instead of *Cassius*—for the benefit of the statue we wish to erect in Central Park.[129]

July 18, Monday New York

July 19, Tuesday New York

July 20, Wednesday

John Hay, representing President Lincoln, delivered a message from the president to Confederate commissioners in Canada. The message, addressed "To Whom It May Concern," specified conditions for opening peace discussions. John Wilkes Booth would later use this phrase in a letter explaining his reasons for participating in a plot to capture the president.

July 23, Saturday

Edwin Booth wrote to a friend that a performance of *Julius Caesar* to benefit the Shakespeare Statue Fund had been postponed because of John Wilkes Booth's trip to the oil region.[130]

July 24, Sunday

Booth wrote to Isabel Sumner:
Have I, in any way, offended you? if so. it has been unwittingly. And God knows how full of repentance, and how anxious I would be to make every atonement. I have been so uneasy, of late, thinking (by your silence) I may have said something in one of my letters to offend....[131]

July 26, Tuesday Boston

Booth registered at the Parker House.[132]

July 27, Wednesday Boston

July 28, Thursday Boston?

July 29, Friday Boston?

The *New York Clipper* noted that "Laura Keene is organizing a company to travel next season."[133]

July 30, Saturday New London

Junius noted in his diary that "John Wilkes came on from Boston...."[134]

A party consisting of John Sleeper Clarke, his wife Asia, their children, Junius and his daughter Marion, and Edwin Booth were vacationing at a friend's home located three miles from New London and one mile from the Pequot House.[135] The friend was probably William Stuart, a business partner of Edwin Booth.

July 31, Sunday New London

August 1, Monday New London

August 2, Tuesday New York

Junius noted that "John [Wilkes Booth] and Edwin left for NY—heavy fog."[136]

August 3, Wednesday New York

The *Official Records of the War of the Rebellion* contain a letter dated August 3 from Major General Lew Wallace to Booth's former teacher, the Rev. Libertus Van Bokkelen, stating that if secessionists in his congregation in Catonsville, Maryland, removed him from the pastorate of St. Timothy's, services would not be allowed unless a successor of undoubted loyalty replaced him.[137]

August 4, Thursday New York

August 5, Friday New York

August 6, Saturday New York

August 7, Sunday Philadelphia

Junius noted in his diary, "Ed & John home ... Clarke [,] Edwin & John [Wilkes Booth] left for Pha [Philadelphia] at 3 pm—very hot...."[138]

August 8, Monday Baltimore?

On or about this date, Booth introduced Samuel Arnold to Michael O'Laughlen at Barnum's Hotel in Baltimore and recruited them in a plot to kidnap President Lincoln.

August 9, Tuesday Baltimore?

August 10, Wednesday New York

Booth became ill with a dangerous infection, erysipelas, of the arm.[139]

August 11, Thursday New York

August 12, Friday New York

On this day, as on many days, Walt Whitman saw President Lincoln riding to the White House from the Soldiers' Home with a cavalry escort.[140]

August 13, Saturday New York

August 14, Sunday New York

August 15, Monday New York

August 16, Tuesday New York

August 17, Wednesday New York

August 18, Thursday New York

Edwin Booth, John Sleeper Clarke, and William Stuart leased the Winter Garden Theatre in New York and opened on this date with an engagement starring Clarke.[141]

August 19, Friday New York

August 20, Saturday New York

Booth's friend Matthew Canning was in New York. The *New York Clipper* reported that "Mr. M. W. Canning, formerly agent for Mary Mitchell, goes out next season with Vestvali."[142]

August 21, Sunday New York

August 22, Monday New York

August 23, Tuesday New York

August 24, Wednesday New York

August 25, Thursday New York

Asia Booth Clarke wrote from Philadelphia that she "had a delightful stay at the seaside and a pleasant time with Mother in New York. Wilkes is quite sick."[143]

August 26, Friday New York

Booth wrote to Isabel Sumner to thank her for flowers she had sent.[144]

August 27, Saturday New York

Confederate Captain Thomas Nelson Conrad received orders to report to Richmond for temporary duty. He had previously proposed a plan to capture President Lincoln and convey him to Richmond. His preparations in Richmond lasted about two weeks.[145]

August 28, Sunday New York

Junius wrote in his diary: "John Booth ill 3 weeks with Erysepalas [*sic*] in the Right Elbow— Had Dr. Smith."[146]

Booth wrote to Isabel Sumner: "I am so sorry I have just recd: your note and not two hours ago had a gash cut in my arm about two inches long I am sure I will be in bed all day tomorrow.... I will try and meet you...."[147]

August 29, Monday New York

August 30, Tuesday New York

August 31, Wednesday New York

September 1, Thursday New York

September 2, Friday New York

Atlanta, which had been under siege for a month, fell to Union forces under General William Tecumseh Sherman. This major victory reduced opposition to Lincoln's re-election which, heretofore, had been in doubt.

September 7, Wednesday Franklin

Booth must have been in Franklin by this date, as Samuel Arnold received a letter from Booth from the oil region on or about September 9.

September 8, Thursday Franklin

September 9, Friday Franklin

September 10, Saturday Franklin

On the 9th, 10th, or 12th, Samuel Arnold received a letter from John Wilkes Booth bearing a postmark from the oil region of Pennsylvania. The letter, written in code, contained $20.[148]

September 11, Sunday Franklin

September 12, Monday Franklin

September 13, Tuesday Franklin

September 14, Wednesday Franklin

September 15, Thursday Franklin

Confederate Secretary of War James Seddon ordered: "Lt. Col. Mosby and Lieut. Cawood [officer in charge of the Secret Line on the Potomac] are hereby directed to aid and facilitate the movements of Capt. [Thomas Nelson] Conrad."[149]

September 16, Friday Franklin

September 17, Saturday Franklin

September 18, Sunday Franklin

Junius recorded in his diary: "John Booth at the Oil Wells, Pa...."[150]

September 19, Monday Franklin

September 20, Tuesday Franklin

September 21, Wednesday Franklin

September 22, Thursday Franklin

September 23, Friday Franklin

September 24, Saturday Franklin

September 25, Sunday Franklin

Thomas Nelson Conrad and his men arrived in Washington by this date. They began preparations to capture President Lincoln.[151]

September 26, Monday Franklin

September 27, Tuesday Franklin

Joe Simonds, at Booth's request, started the process of closing out the Booth interests in the Allegheny River property.[152]

September 28, Wednesday En route

Booth left Franklin for New York.[153]

The first advertisement for "Jo. H. Simonds & Co.—Agents for the Purchase and Sale of Petroleum Lands...." appeared in the *Venango Spectator*.[154]

September 29

Tom Mears deeded his one-third interest in the Fuller farm to Joe Simonds in trust for John Wilkes Booth.[155]

October 3, Monday

Junius Brutus Booth, Jr., opened at the Holliday Street Theatre in Baltimore. The *New York Clipper* reported: "He bids fair to become as great a favorite with the Baltimore people as his two brothers, Edwin and John Wilkes."[156]

October 4, Tuesday

On or about this date, Thomas Nelson Conrad traveled the proposed route on which the captured President Lincoln was expected to be taken to Richmond. He left instructions that boats should be waiting on Saturday night.[157]

October 15, Saturday

Junius Brutus Booth, Jr.'s engagement in Baltimore ended.

October 16, Sunday Newburgh

Booth, on his way to Montreal, arrived in Newburgh, New York, late in the evening and visited several taverns.[158]

October 17, Monday En route

Booth crossed the Hudson River about noon and continued his trip to Montreal.[159]

Booth made his final payment on the Back Bay land in Boston, and a deed was issued in the name of his mother, Mary Ann Booth.[160]

Junius began a two-week engagement at Ford's Theatre in Washington.

October 18, Tuesday Montreal

Booth registered at St. Lawrence Hall at 9:30 p.m.[161]

October 19, Wednesday Montreal

Activities related to a Confederate raid on St. Albans, Vermont, occupied the several Confederate commissioners located in Montreal.

October 20, Thursday Montreal

The St. Albans raiders escaped to Canada and were arrested in the early morning hours.

October 21, Friday Montreal

Joe Simonds, acting for Booth, conveyed one third of Booth's share of the Fuller farm to Moses J. Coleman. Coleman then turned this interest over to Simonds.[162] Simonds, who now had clear title to the land, then wrote a document to transfer the Fuller farm to Junius Brutus Booth, Jr., for the sum of $1,000. He sent the document to John in New York.

October 22, Saturday Montreal

Clement Clay sent funds to George N. Sanders in Montreal for the legal defense of the St. Albans raiders.[163]

October 23, Sunday Montreal

October 24, Monday Montreal

October 25, Tuesday Montreal

George N. Sanders returned to Montreal from a visit to assist the incarcerated St. Albans raiders and lodged in room 169 at St. Lawrence Hall. Booth was seen in the company of Sanders on several unspecified occasions in Montreal.[164]

October 26, Wednesday Montreal

October 27, Thursday En route to Boston

Booth deposited $455 in a bank account at the Montreal branch of the Ontario Bank. He also exchanged $300 in gold for a bill of exchange.[165] Booth left his wardrobe trunks with Patrick Charles Martin, who was to ship them south on a blockade runner. Booth left St. Lawrence Hall and took the train to Boston.

October 28, Friday Boston

Booth wrote to Dr. G. T. Collins, manager of Wood's Theatre in Cincinnati: "I have been in Montreal for the last three or four weeks and as no one (not even myself) knew when I would return home, my letters were not forwarded."[166]

Actor McKee Rankin reported an encounter with Booth:

I was going down Tremont Street on my way to a rehearsal with two ladies of the company, Mrs. Octavia Allen and Miss Louise Anderson. As we neared the Tremont Hotel, Mrs. Allen exclaimed, "Hello, there's John Wilkes Booth!" He was standing in the porch of the hotel talking to Bill Pitcher, one of his close friends, and at that time a sort of steward in the hotel. I had a few words with him in passing, and made an engagement for that afternoon at the Parker House where he was staying. I met him at the appointed time and we had quite a chat about mutual friends, the theater, and things in general. He said he had just come from Montreal from which place he had shipped his wardrobe to Havana [actually Nassau] upon a little blockade runner. He was considerably excited over the state of affairs at the time, the difference between the North and the South. He was dissatisfied with the conditions about him, and said he expected to cross the line somewhere and get into the South to play.... He told me of his plans and prospects, and while he was in a most unsettled frame of mind, he spoke freely and at length upon the continuance of his work in the theatre, in the South, which he considered for him a most congenial field.[167]

October 29, Saturday New York

Booth transferred his oil property to his brother Junius before Charles Nettleton, out-of-state commissioner of the Commonwealth of Pennsylvania.[168] Booth sent the deeds to Joe Simonds in Franklin and asked Simonds to write to him at Barnum's Hotel in Baltimore.[169]

October 30, Sunday New York

Booth often visited his friend Samuel Knapp Chester on Sunday nights, the only night of the week Chester had free. On or about this day Chester asked Booth why he was not acting. Booth explained that he had shipped his wardrobe to the South.[170]

October 31, Monday Philadelphia?

November 1, Tuesday Philadelphia?

Louis J. Weichmann, former schoolmate of John Surratt, took up residence at Mary Surratt's boarding house in Washington. Weichmann would observe the developing plot to capture the president and, later, give testimony against the conspirators.[171]

November 2, Wednesday Philadelphia?

The trial of the St. Albans raiders began in Montreal.[172]

November 3, Thursday Baltimore?

Joe Simonds, in Franklin, addressed a letter to Booth at Barnum's Hotel in Baltimore. Booth had asked Simonds to have the oil property deeds recorded. Simonds said the recording of the deeds would take at least six weeks.[173]

November 4, Friday Baltimore?

November 5, Saturday Baltimore?

November 6, Sunday Baltimore

In Washington, Junius sent a telegram to John Wilkes at Barnum's Hotel in Baltimore: "Will be in Baltimore at six PM tomorrow. Wait for me or come on."[174]

November 7, Monday Baltimore

John Wilkes Booth met Junius at 6 p.m.[175]

November 8, Tuesday Baltimore

President Lincoln was re-elected by a large majority.

November 9, Wednesday Washington

Junius Brutus Booth, Jr., saw John Wilkes in Baltimore.[176]

Booth registered at the National Hotel in Washington in the evening.[177]

November 10, Thursday Washington

On or about this date, Thomas Nelson Conrad abandoned his plot to capture the president.[178] Conrad and his party stayed on in Washington.

November 11, Friday Bryantown

Booth took an early-morning stage to Bryantown. After stopping briefly at the Surratt tavern, the stage continued to Bryantown. Booth asked the stage driver to leave his pistol at his hotel in Washington. Booth stayed overnight at the local tavern.

November 12, Saturday Near Bryantown

Dr. William Queen's son Joseph drove Booth to his father's home, where Booth presented a letter of introduction from Patrick C. Martin.[179] Booth discussed the abduction plot with Dr. Queen. Booth spent the night at the home of Dr. Queen.

November 13, Sunday Near Bryantown

Booth accompanied Dr. Queen and his son-in-law, John C. Thompson, to St. Mary's Catholic Church in Bryantown. Thompson may have introduced Booth to Dr. Samuel A. Mudd. Booth returned to Dr. Queen's home after the Mass.[180]

November 14, Monday Washington

Booth checked into the National Hotel early in the evening.[181]

Booth wrote to J. Dominic Burch in Bryantown asking him to track down the pistol Booth had entrusted to the stage driver.[182]

November 15, Tuesday Washington

President Lincoln saw Edward Loomis Davenport play *Hamlet* at Grover's Theatre.[183]

General Sherman's army started its march to the sea, destroying everything in its path.

November 16, Wednesday Baltimore

Booth opened a checking account with Jay Cooke & Co. with an initial deposit of $1,500.[184]

Booth checked out of the National Hotel and went to Baltimore, where he met his brother Junius.[185] Several trains made the two-hour trip to Baltimore each day.

November 17, Thursday Philadelphia

November 18, Friday Philadelphia

Asia and her family moved from Callowhill Street in Philadelphia to 229 North Eighteenth Street in the same city.[186]

On or about this date, Patrick C. Martin's ship, the *Marie Victoria*, left Montreal carrying Booth's wardrobe.[187]

November 19, Saturday

Confederate Bureau of War records note receipt of a letter from "Doctor J. W. Booth."[188]

November 20, Sunday Philadelphia

November 21, Monday Philadelphia

Junius noted in his diary that John and Edwin were in Philadelphia.[189]

November 22, Tuesday Philadelphia

[Date approximate] Booth left a sealed envelope with his sister Asia for safekeeping. Among the contents of the package were a letter to his mother, a "To whom it may concern" letter, and several United States bonds.[190]

November 23, Wednesday New York

Edwin and John left for New York to attend the 100th night of John Sleeper Clarke's engagement at the Winter Garden Theatre.[191]

November 24, Thursday New York

It is likely that Booth attended rehearsals for the upcoming presentation of *Julius Caesar* with Edwin and Junius.

Sam Chester was in the stock company at the Winter Garden Theatre and talked often with Booth during this period. Booth mentioned an unspecified "speculation" to Chester and asked him to join in. Chester declined.[192]

John Sleeper Clarke closed his engagement at the Winter Garden Theatre.

November 25, Friday New York

Edwin, John, and Junius performed *Julius Caesar* for the benefit of the Shakespeare statue fund. The *New York Herald* claimed that each brother was a better tragedian than any actor in England. Sam Chester related that John Wilkes Booth, portraying Marc Antony, "completely electrified the audience, by his wonderful histrionic genius, especially in his supreme oratorical effects, in the forum scene, over the body of the dead Caesar."[193]

One intriguing, unconfirmed, and likely inaccurate report has future conspirator Lewis Thornton Powell attending this performance. He had been brought to New York, according to this source, to assist in the plot to burn the city, but had refused to participate, not wanting to injure or kill innocent civilians.[194]

November 26, Saturday New York

The *New York Herald* considered Friday's performance a "great success."[195]

In the evening Booth attended a performance of *The Corsican Brothers* at Niblo's Garden.

November 27, Sunday New York

The three Booth brothers donned their costumes from *Julius Caesar* and were photographed by Jeremiah Gurney at a gallery on Broadway just below Fourth Street. Junius asked artist Rufus Wright to paint the actors in costume.[196]

At the Metropolitan Hotel Booth talked to his actor friend Charles Pope and complimented him on his performance in *The Corsican Brothers*. Booth suggested that Pope come to Washington after his engagement, promising him a good time and a chance to make a fortune.[197]

November 28, Monday Philadelphia

John and Junius left New York for Philadelphia.[198]

John told Junius he was forming an oil company in Washington and could make more money in oil than in acting.[199]

November 29, Tuesday Philadelphia

Junius noted in his diary, "John's neck bad with boils...."[200]

Asia Booth Clarke wrote:

A Quaker doctor ... lanced a great carbuncle on [Booth's] neck. The things required were set on the table, and in removing a lampshade the hose of the gas caught in the flame and was burning quickly when Wilkes crushed it in his hands and bound it up hurriedly with a bit of dress braid.[201]

November 30, Wednesday Philadelphia

Booth was still suffering from the boils on his neck.[202] Asia, examining John's burned hands, found them to be rugged and hard. He told her he had been rowing.[203] His hands were probably rough because he frequently exercised with wooden clubs in gymnasiums.[204]

December 1, Thursday Washington

Asia wrote that "Wilkes is in Washington."[205]

December 2, Friday Washington

Booth wrote to Joe Simonds and told him to write to him at Ford's Theatre in Washington.[206]

On or about this date, the *Marie Victoria* sank in a storm. Captain Patrick C. Martin and Booth's wardrobe were lost with the ship.[207]

December 3, Saturday Washington

December 4, Sunday Washington

December 5, Monday Washington

The second session of the 38th United States Congress assembled.

President and Mrs. Lincoln and Secretary of State William H. Seward occupied a private box at Grover's Theatre.[208] This was probably the occasion about which Matthew Canning, Booth's former manager, later reported that "when the President and lady were passing out [of Grover's Theatre], he [Booth] moved after them, eyeing them very intently, while they waited on the steps some moments for a carriage."[209]

December 6, Tuesday Washington

December 7, Wednesday Washington

Joe Simonds addressed a letter to Booth at Ford's Theatre.[210]

December 8, Thursday New York?

December 9, Friday New York?

December 10, Saturday New York?

Ward Hill Lamon wrote to his friend President Lincoln and warned him against going to the theatre unattended. He closed by stating: "And you know, or ought to know, that your life is sought after, and will be taken unless you and your friends are cautious...."[211]

General Sherman's army reached and laid siege to Savannah, Georgia.

December 11, Sunday New York?

The actress Felicita Vestvali opened at Grover's Theatre. Matthew Canning was in Washington for part, if not all, of the two-week engagement.[212]

December 12, Monday Washington

Booth traveled to Washington and registered at the National Hotel.[213]

December 13, Tuesday Washington

The judge of the St. Albans raid trial in Montreal dismissed the charges against the raiders on a technicality and discharged them.[214] A reception at St. Lawrence Hall honored the raiders.[215]

December 14, Wednesday Washington

December 15, Thursday Washington

Confederate agent John Yates Beall attempted to derail a passenger train near Buffalo, New York, and was captured the next day.

December 16, Friday Washington

Booth wrote a $100 check to Matthew W. Canning.[216]

Union General George H. Thomas defeated Confederate General John Bell Hood at Nashville, Tennessee. For practical purposes, the war in the west was over. Prospects for the Confederacy were bleak.

December 17, Saturday Near Bryantown

Booth left early in the morning for southern Maryland and spent the night at the home of Dr. Queen.[217]

December 18, Sunday Near Bryantown

Booth left Dr. Queen's house early.[218] He had arranged to meet Dr. Mudd at the Bryantown Tavern. Mudd introduced Booth to Confederate Secret Service agent Thomas Harbin. Booth asked Harbin to assist in the capture and transportation of Lincoln. Harbin agreed and became an active member of the plot.[219] Booth went home with Dr. Mudd and spent the night there.

December 19, Monday Near Bryantown

Dr. Mudd and Booth walked to the adjoining farm, where Booth bought a one-eyed horse.[220] Booth probably spent the night at Dr. Mudd's house.

President Lincoln attended a play at Ford's Theatre.

December 20, Tuesday Bryantown?

Dr. Mudd and Booth rode to Bryantown. The horse was delivered to Booth in Bryantown.[221] Booth had the horse shod at a local blacksmith shop and bought a saddle and bridle.[222]

Booth did not return to Washington until December 22. It is possible he spent more than one night with Dr. Queen, with Dr. Mudd, or at the Bryantown Tavern.

December 21, Wednesday Bryantown?

Booth explored the roads in the area.
Savannah fell to General Sherman's army.

December 22, Thursday Washington

Booth rode the one-eyed horse to Washington and boarded it at Howard's Stable, which was located behind Mary Surratt's boarding house. Booth also kept a light bay horse there.[223]

Booth returned to the National Hotel early in the evening.[224]

December 23, Friday Washington

Dr. Mudd came to Washington. He met Booth in front of the National Hotel either by arrangement or by accident. Booth asked Mudd to introduce him to John Surratt. They met Surratt and Louis J. Weichmann on the street. Mudd made the introduction. Booth asked Surratt to join the plot.[225]

According to Matthew Canning's recollection, this was the night Booth stared intently at President Lincoln as he exited Grover's Theatre.[226]

December 24, Saturday New York

After withdrawing $50 from his bank account, Booth left Washington on the 11:15 a.m. train.[227] The train was scheduled to arrive in New York at 10:27 p.m.

December 25, Sunday New York

Booth was at Edwin's home for Christmas.[228]

Booth again attempted to recruit Sam Chester. Chester and Booth went to The House of Lords theatrical hotel and bar on Houston Street. While walking, Booth told Chester he was involved in a speculation to capture the heads of the "Government," including the president, and take them to Richmond. When Chester refused, Booth threatened him.[229]

James McVicker wrote to Booth asking him to appear in Chicago for three weeks starting May 29, 1865. Booth had previously scheduled and then canceled a January 1865 engagement at McVicker's Theatre.[230]

December 26, Monday New York?

December 27, Tuesday New York?

[Date approximate] Booth wired Matthew Canning in Louisville, telling him to "push" the matter. The telegraph operator misread the word "push" as "hush." Booth had asked Canning to intervene with John Ford to employ Sam Chester at Ford's Theatre in Washington, and Booth now wanted him to push the matter.[231]

December 28, Wednesday New York

Booth wrote to Joe Simonds and related that he had been sick, that he had been living "fast," and that he needed money.

December 29, Thursday Philadelphia?

Matthew Canning saw Booth in Philadelphia. Booth seemed flighty in his ideas; he spoke of making a fortune by buying land in Virginia and "occasionally he would talk secession sentiments."[232]

December 30, Friday Baltimore

Booth, acting for his mother, signed a receipt for an overdue rent payment on the family farm in Harford County.[233]

John Surratt was hired by the Adams Express Company in Washington.[234]

December 31, Saturday Washington

Booth arrived at the National Hotel.[235]

Junius, in Boston, wrote in his diary: "J. Booth in Washington speculating—all well."[236]

Joe Simonds wrote to Booth and enclosed a check for $500, "which to you I know is not much but it may be of some assistance, until you get to acting again…. I wish while you have been doing nothing you had come out here and staid [sic] with us [Simonds and his mother]."[237]

9

Action: 1865

At the beginning of 1865, John Wilkes Booth could look back at the development of his kidnapping plot over the last five months. He had divested himself of his oil interests as well as his property in Boston. He had tried to prepare for his future by shipping his wardrobe south; unfortunately, the wardrobe was lost in transit. Booth had begun to staff his team by recruiting Samuel Arnold and Michael O'Laughlen. He had made contact with Confederate authorities in Montreal, and, through Dr. Samuel A. Mudd and Thomas Harbin, was familiar with the Confederate clandestine route to Richmond. He had procured weapons and horses. Now, with John H. Surratt on board as of early in January, Booth moved to Washington with the intention of executing his scheme.

An advance view of the development of the plot over the next three and a half months may make it easier to understand the intricacies of that period. From January 1 to April 14, Booth spent sixty-six days in Washington and thirty-eight days elsewhere. In January he added to his team a man who was experienced in ferrying people across the Potomac River. In February Booth brought in another recruit, a man of mystery. Booth's funds were running low, and he spent much of February in New York trying to borrow money. In March, with his men becoming restless, Booth led an *opéra bouffe* attempt to abduct President Lincoln. Most of the team disbanded after this failure, but soon the plot was transmogrified into something more sinister.

As the new year dawned, Booth's plan was to take his band and the captured president through southern Maryland, where they would cross the Potomac on their way to Richmond. Crossing the Potomac was no small matter; a boat and an experienced blockade-runner were essential. Surratt was familiar with the route to Richmond and the people who worked along it. Deputized by Booth, Surratt abandoned his new job at the Adams Express Company in mid–January and went to Port Tobacco, Maryland, where, with Confederate agent Thomas Harbin, he recruited George Andrew Atzerodt for "an extreme plan of blockade running."[1] By day, the German-born Atzerodt, who struck many as cowardly, kept a carriage-painting shop in Port Tobacco; at night, he occasionally rowed paying passengers across the Potomac River, a dangerous activity requiring a strong measure of courage. The thirty-one-year-old Atzerodt was small, unkempt, and a heavy drinker; he was also fun to be around and often told quaint stories.[2]

On the same day he approached Atzerodt, Surratt paid $125 to blockade-runner Richard M. Smoot for immediate possession of a large boat.[3] The boat was turned over to Atzerodt and hidden on King's Creek, which emptied into Nanjemoy Creek and the Potomac. The next day Atzerodt bragged that a party of ten or twelve persons would cross the following night, January 18, and that relays of horses had been stationed between Washington and Port Tobacco.[4] If the party referred to was to include a kidnapped President Lincoln, it was a plot other than that of Booth. Booth did not have enough people to effect a kidnapping at this stage.

Sometime in January, Booth and David Herold renewed their acquaintance, which had begun a year and a half previously. Herold, viewed by most people as "trifling" and unreliable, had certain qualities, particularly a gregarious nature, that were highly valuable to Booth's plans. He spent months each year hunting in southern Maryland and, as a result, knew the land and most of the people in the region. Among his acquaintances and friends were John Surratt, whom he had known since 1856, and George Atzerodt, whom he had known for five years.[5] Shortly after the boat was purchased, Booth, Surratt, and Herold rode to Port Tobacco and, together with Atzerodt, inspected the boat. Booth, using his derringer, shot a vicious dog that barked and nipped at his heels.[6]

Booth had not given up on recruiting his friend Samuel Knapp Chester. On January 9 he sent $50 to Chester in New York and told him to be in Washington by Saturday night.[7] Seeing that Chester was recalcitrant, Booth approached his friend John Mathews, who was a stock player at Ford's Theatre.[8] Mathews, called "Crazy John" by his peers, was rather odd, but, like Herold, fell under the spell of Booth's charisma. Nevertheless, Mathews was too timid to agree to help Booth in the kidnapping scheme.

Around January 11, Booth traveled from Washington to Baltimore, where he had been storing a trunk full of weapons he had previously bought in New York. The contents included two seven-shot Spencer carbines, three pistols, ammunition, three knives, belts with holsters, a set of handcuffs, and a set of leg irons. After purchasing these items, Booth had transported them as far as Baltimore, where he had stashed them upon becoming concerned that the weight of the trunk would arouse suspicion. Now Booth was ready to retrieve the weapons. He visited Sam Arnold and Michael O'Laughlen in Baltimore and gave them the trunk. He also bought a horse and buggy that Arnold selected. The next day Booth returned to Washington, while Arnold removed some of the items to lighten the trunk and shipped it to Booth. Arnold and O'Laughlen then drove the horse and buggy to Washington and met Booth at Ford's Theatre. The horse and buggy were housed in the stable Booth had rented behind the theatre. Booth showed Arnold and O'Laughlen the entrances to the theatre.[9]

Arnold soon began to have doubts about the kidnapping plot. President Lincoln did not visit the residence at the Soldiers' Home in the winter, and therefore it was unlikely he could be abducted on a lonely road. When Booth outlined a plan to capture the president during a performance at Ford's Theatre, Arnold objected on the basis that such a plan was impossible to execute successfully. Booth was undeterred.[10]

The two Baltimoreans took up residence at a boarding house in Washington, but they had little to do in the city. O'Laughlen's brother had a produce and feed business there, which required some of Michael's attention. Booth frequently, sometimes several times a day, called at the boarding house, usually inquiring for O'Laughlen. In turn, O'Laughlen often called on Booth at his hotel. Arnold and Booth were not as eager to see each other. The men spent most of their time at Rullman's Hotel bar drinking and talking with friends from Baltimore. The two men went home to Baltimore on Saturdays and returned on Monday, Tuesday, or even Wednesday of the next week.[11] Booth, demonstrating a rare bit of discipline, did not immediately inform them of the others who had been recruited for the growing conspiracy. On January 27, when Arnold and O'Laughlen called on Booth at his hotel room, Booth introduced them to John Surratt. To them, Booth seemed to be preoccupied with Surratt.[12] Booth and Surratt often practiced marksmanship at a shooting gallery at Pennsylvania Avenue and Eleventh Street.

Louis Weichmann had been a classmate of John Surratt at St. Charles College in Ellicott Mills, Maryland, and now roomed at the boarding house operated by Surratt's mother, Mary E. Surratt. Weichmann had studied for the Catholic priesthood with Surratt, dropped out, and then taught at a boys' school in Washington for two years. He was tall and hefty, intelligent, and sometimes uncomfortably inquisitive about others' affairs. Mary Surratt treated him as if he were a family member. Weichmann had met David Herold when he had visited John Surratt in 1863, at about the time Herold had met Booth. Weichmann began work as a clerk in the Washington office of the Commissary General of Prisoners in January 1864 and had access to information about the number of Confederate prisoners held and where they were imprisoned.[13] He was not a member of the plot, but he observed much of what was going on.

At the end of January, Surratt asked George Atzerodt to come to Washington, where he introduced him to Louis Weichmann in Mary Surratt's parlor. Weichmann and Atzerodt became friends and were seen together frequently. Atzerodt once told Weichmann that he knew people considered him a fool, but in fact he did know "how to behave himself in the company of decent people." Atzerodt visited the Surratt boarding house quite often, while Herold visited the house only once.[14] Arnold and O'Laughlen knew nothing of Mary Surratt or her boarding house.

Yet another member of the plot, Lewis Thornton Powell, was recruited late in January. A native of Alabama, Powell had served the Confederacy in a Florida regiment and had seen action in several major battles. He had been held at a Federal battlefield hospital after he was wounded and captured at Gettysburg. There he met Margaret Branson, a nurse from Baltimore who had Confederate sympathies. Powell recovered sufficiently to help nurse other prisoners and eventually was sent to a hospital in Baltimore, where he continued his friendship with Maggie Branson. Within days he escaped from the hospital. He stopped briefly at the Branson boarding house, where Maggie introduced him to her younger sister, Mary. He then crossed the lines into Virginia, joined Confederate General John Singleton Mosby's cavalry command, and served with distinction. On Christmas Eve, 1864, Powell bravely prevented his Mosby comrades from killing Union prisoners in his charge.[15]

Early in January, the twenty-year-old Powell left Mosby's command and returned to Baltimore. Perhaps he was ordered to go there, or perhaps he was tired of war. He visited the Branson boarding house to call on Margaret and Mary Branson and soon became a boarder there. Somehow—perhaps the Bransons introduced him—he met Confederate sympathizer David Preston Parr, a china dealer. People who sympathized with the Confederacy would drop by his china shop to say hello. Parr could be depended upon to pass messages. Parr knew people, and he had traveled at least part of the secret route through southern Maryland to Richmond.[16]

David Parr and John Surratt had been acquainted for about two years. Surratt would occasionally visit the china shop to chat and perhaps to leave and pick up clandestine mail. The circumstances of how Surratt became aware of Powell are unknown. Parr probably served as a middle-man who made the introductions. Powell, a tall, muscular, well-experienced warrior, was a perfect addition to Booth's team. On January 21 Surratt and Louis Weichmann took the train to Baltimore and registered at a hotel. The next day Surratt, carrying $300 from Booth, went to Parr's shop and was introduced to Powell. It is likely that Surratt started to recruit Powell for the abduction plot.[17] Booth was in Baltimore a week later and may have met with Powell at a gambling house on Monument Square. According to one account, Booth described the kidnapping scheme to Powell in detail. Booth saw Powell the day after their first meeting, and he became a member of the conspiracy.[18]

Booth did not devote all his attention to the abduction plot. On January 20 he appeared at Grover's Theatre in *Romeo and Juliet* in a benefit for Avonia Jones, a friend from his Richmond days. He rode the horse stabled behind Ford's Theatre almost every afternoon and evening, usually returning by 8 or 9 p.m. After Arnold and O'Laughlen brought the buggy from Baltimore, it became his chief mode of transportation. The ever-helpful Edman (Ned) Spangler, a scene shifter at Ford's, harnessed and unharnessed the horse for these excursions. He was never paid for his efforts.[19] Booth often exercised at Brady's gymnasium. John T. Ford later recalled: "He had pluck. He was always training, riding, shooting, at the gymnasium, etc."[20]

Meanwhile, Booth developed yet another romantic interest. He had met Lucy Hale on one of his acting engagements in Washington. Lucy and her sister Elizabeth were daughters of former U.S. Senator and Free Soil Party presidential nominee John Parker Hale, of New Hampshire. Conveniently, the Hale family lived at the National Hotel, where Booth was staying. Lucy was quite popular, and among her friends she counted John Hay, secretary to President Lincoln, young officer Oliver Wendell Holmes, and Robert Todd Lincoln, eldest son of the president. By mid–February Booth and Lucy were engaged. She overcame her objection to his being an actor, and he overcame his objection to her being an abolitionist.[21] Lucy planned to go to Spain with her father, who had been appointed minister to that country. She told Booth she would return within a year, with or without her father, to marry him.[22]

At the same time Booth was proposing marriage, he was involved with a young prostitute, Ellen Starr, a resident at her sister's establishment on Ohio Avenue in Washington, in an area called "Hooker's Division." Booth had known the "rather pretty, light haired

woman" for about three years.[23] Her ardor is shown in a note she wrote to Booth: "My Darling Boy, Please call this evening or as soon as you receive this note and I'll not detain you five minutes—for god's sake come[.] Yours Truly E. S. If you will not come send a note the [reason why]. Washington Feb 7th 1865."[24]

Booth's friend John McCullough was in Washington for most of January supporting the actor Edwin Forrest at Ford's Theatre. McCullough struck up a relationship with Elizabeth Hale. McCullough recalled: "We [Booth and McCullough] used to meet them [possibly the Hale sisters] in Baltimore. They were of high connections and their names required to be protected. We called them in our telegraph dispatches 'Jack' and 'Bob.' Sometimes Booth would telegraph me: 'Jack and Bob are here: come over.' Again I would telegraph him: 'Jack wants you to bring Bob over.'"[25]

Booth did not reveal the abduction plot to McCullough. Whenever McCullough encountered Booth and "those ill-dressed, lowering fellows," Booth would hustle him away saying, "John, you don't want to know those country operators in oil."[26] Booth did, however, take his unknowing friend on a ride to scout the escape route.

Booth's winning ways were such that he couldn't help making new friends and acquaintances. Some were Union officers such as Charles M. Collins, captain's clerk on the U.S.S. *Montauk*, and William W. Crowninshield, acting master in the United States Navy. Another of Booth's associates was the spiritualist Charles J. Colchester. Colchester had conducted séances for the bereaved Mary Lincoln to contact her deceased son, Willie. Colchester called on Booth frequently at the National Hotel, and the two visited local theatres.[27]

Booth often dropped by Ford's Theatre and asked acquaintances to join him in a drink at either of the establishments adjoining the theatre. On entering, he usually invited the patrons of the barrooms to have a drink at his expense.[28] Booth enjoyed sitting up until the early morning hours chatting, smoking, and sipping whiskey with National Hotel night clerk Walter Burton. David Herold occasionally joined them.[29] A fellow hotel guest described Booth as "a very attractive man, winning and soft voiced, and more or less a favorite among those who lived in or frequented the [National] Hotel, with ... graceful and easy manners, he soon fascinated me...."[30] Another observer recalled, "He dressed himself faultlessly, as a rule wore kid gloves, and when his overcoat was not on, it lay over his arm, and his whole pose along the street was as if sitting for a picture."[31]

Some nights Booth dropped into the *Washington Chronicle* offices to call on Colonel Daniel Carpenter Forney, then one of the publishers of that newspaper, usually arriving between 9 p.m. and midnight. The men would visit the local theatres, staying but a short while unless the play was exceptionally gripping. According to Forney, Booth "was an exceedingly interesting man—full of intelligence, and as a conversationalist had few equals. He was a thorough master of all the graces and courtesies of high-bred life...."[32] On previous visits to Washington, Booth had become acquainted with journalist John F. Coyle of the *Washington National Intelligencer*, who had written glowing accounts of Booth's performances. Coyle, who had known Booth's father well, often met the young actor at a club on the corner of Louisiana Avenue and Sixth Street.[33]

By the end of January, Booth was a frequent visitor at Mary Surratt's boarding house on H Street.[34] One evening he visited from 10 p.m. to 1 a.m. Louis Weichmann thought that Mary Surratt and her daughter Annie were "rivals for Booth." Mary referred to Booth as "my Pet."[35] John Surratt wrote to a cousin:

I have just taken a peep in the parlor. Would you like to know what I saw there? Well, Ma was sitting on the sofa, nodding first to one

chair, then to another, next the piano. Anna [his sister] sitting in corner, dreaming, I expect, of J. W. Booth. Well, who is J. W. Booth? She can answer the question.... But hark! The door-bell rings, and Mr. J. W. Booth is announced. And listen to the scamperings.... Such brushing and fixing.[36]

Booth's family and friends were becoming concerned by his inactivity in his profession. John Surratt, at Booth's request, asked Weichmann to write an article for a newspaper "to the effect that John Wilkes Booth, the accomplished actor, in consequence of having erysipelas in his leg, had retired from the stage and was engaged in the oil business."[37] When Booth learned that his mother was sending Junius to Washington to persuade him to come home, he turned one of his horses over to Sam Arnold to avoid having to explain why he kept three horses. When Booth saw his brother Junius, he told him he had given up his intention to act in the South and that he was in Washington speculating in the oil business.[38] Booth also told Junius he was an officer in the Confederate army so that Junius would not insist on taking him home.[39]

Booth spent twenty-five days away from Washington from late in January through February 22. One of his reasons for leaving was to avoid John Sleeper Clarke, who was performing at Ford's Theatre for three weeks. Additionally, according to Arnold:

Booth, through riotous living and dissipation, was compelled to visit the city of New York for the purpose of replenishing his squandered means. His absence continued for most of the first three weeks of February, caused by the great difficulty experienced in borrowing money.[40]

The boat, horses, buggy, and his living expenses were draining his resources. On the other hand, Booth did not seem to be spending much money in support of his team. Sam Arnold claimed he received only $20 during the time he knew Booth. Surratt borrowed money from George Atzerodt. Ned Spangler was never paid for his daily care of Booth's horse. Joe Simonds had sent Booth $500 at the beginning of the year, and Booth borrowed $500 from his childhood friend William O'Laughlen, Michael's brother.[41]

In New York, Booth ran into Adam Badeau, who recalled, "Two months before the end of the war he [John Wilkes] wished me well when I set out to join [General Ulysses S.] Grant. I thought him very captivating, though not so thoroughly distinguished as his greater brother [Edwin]."[42] Edwin and John engaged in long and bitter political discussions during this visit. Booth frequented a shooting gallery at 600 Broadway, where he used a photograph of President Lincoln as a target.[43]

After renewing his efforts to recruit Sam Chester and again being rebuffed, Booth apologized. He told Chester he had also tried to recruit actor John Mathews, who had likewise refused. He called Mathews a coward. Booth revealed that he was short of funds and had spent more than $4,000 of his own money on the project.[44] Despite being low on cash and having borrowed $1,000 from friends, Booth justified to himself spending $150 at Tiffany and Company for a "braiding hair ring," presumably for Lucy Hale.[45]

In February, while visiting his sister Asia in Philadelphia, Booth asked for the packet of documents he had left with her in November. He signed the "To whom it may concern" letter and returned the packet to Asia for safekeeping. Booth did not remove the several United States bonds he had previously placed in the envelope.[46] If he was in need of money, why didn't he cash in the bonds? If he was so dedicated to the cause of the South, why did he support the Union by holding bonds? Asia related that "Wilkes came frequently to me at Philadelphia.... I saw and heard much that distressed and surprised me.... He often slept in his clothes on the couch downstairs, having on his long riding boots. Strange men called at late hours."[47]

Between November 1864 and April 1865, Booth visited Asia about six times. It is difficult to imagine where or why he would have been riding in the environs of Philadelphia with strange men in the middle of the night. Perhaps time had dimmed Asia's memory that on several occasions Booth took the night train from Philadelphia, which arrived in Baltimore at 3:30 a.m.[48]

With some frequency, Confederate couriers traveled the clandestine route from Richmond to Washington and then went on to Montreal. Sarah Antoinette Slater, a young widow, made her first trip as a courier to Montreal starting late in January. Confederate agent Augustus Spencer Howell was assigned to accompany and guide her along the secret line to Washington; this was the same route which Booth intended to use to take the abducted president to Richmond.[49] Howell, or another agent, accompanied Slater as far as New York. Slater was less than five feet tall and incapable of handling much luggage. Therefore, she probably had another escort to Montreal, where she delivered papers to Confederate representatives verifying that the St. Albans raiders were Confederate soldiers.

In February John Surratt traveled to New York in order to accompany Sarah Slater on her return trip. Surratt took the opportunity to visit John Wilkes Booth at Edwin's home in New York. While Surratt was away, Augustus Howell stayed at Mary Surratt's boarding house several days waiting for Slater. The ever-inquisitive Louis Weichmann found Howell interesting. Howell found Weichmann interesting as well when he learned that Weichmann worked at the Commissary of Prisoners Office. Howell taught Weichmann a cipher code, and Weichmann revealed information about prisoners to Howell.[50] George Atzerodt had been recruited to ferry Slater across the Potomac. In order to be informed of what was happening, Atzerodt spent a night at Mary Surratt's. Soon Howell, Weichmann, and Atzerodt were drinking whiskey. Weichmann was commissioned to go out and replace an empty bottle. When Mary found the empty bottles, she blamed Atzerodt.[51]

On February 22 Sarah Slater and John Surratt drove up to Mary Surratt's house in Booth's buggy and conversed with Augustus Howell.[52] Howell took Surratt's place in the buggy, and he and Slater left for Richmond. The next day Atzerodt, riding one of Booth's horses, rode to Port Tobacco to take Slater across the river. Slater, through her association with Surratt, Booth, and Atzerodt, learned about the abduction plot.[53]

Shortly thereafter, probably on the evening of February 23, Lewis Powell knocked on Mary Surratt's door. When Weichmann opened the door, Powell introduced himself as Mr. Wood, a clerk in Preston Parr's china shop. He inquired after John Surratt and, upon finding that he was not home, asked for Mary. Powell believed that Mary knew in general about the plot. Powell stayed one night and was gone when Weichmann awoke the next morning.[54] The purpose of Powell's visit is unknown. If he met with Booth and John Surratt, it was on the day after his arrival.[55] Possibly he was bringing a last-minute message for Howell and Slater sent by or through Preston Parr.

On the evening of March 3 Weichmann encountered Booth and Surratt in Mary Surratt's parlor. The three men went to the Capitol to observe the session of the House of Representatives from the gallery.[56] President Lincoln was also at the Capitol, signing bills passed by Congress. The next day Booth attended President Lincoln's second inauguration with a pass he obtained from Lucy Hale. One observer thought Booth was the man who created an incident at the inauguration by breaking through the crowd and approaching the passing president before being restrained by a policeman.[57] The man was released after the president passed. Booth stood above and behind President Lincoln during the inauguration ceremony. He thought of shooting the president then, but reconsidered. Booth walked back to the National

Hotel with Walter Burton, the hotel's night clerk. Burton, a Lincoln supporter, never heard Booth speak a word against Lincoln.[58]

Booth's conspiracy started to unravel in March. On March 6 Lewis Powell, at his Baltimore boarding house, beat a black woman he thought had insulted him. He was arrested that night and interrogated in the office of the provost marshal. Powell was suspected of being a Confederate spy, but, without proof, he was allowed to take the oath of allegiance. After being held for six days he was released and ordered "to go north of Philadelphia and remain during the war." Powell ignored the order.[59]

John Surratt was again diverted from the kidnapping plot. Sarah Slater returned to Washington in mid–March bearing a new batch of dispatches from the Richmond government for agents in Montreal. She stayed at Mary Surratt's boarding house, displacing Weichmann for a night. The next day Slater left by train for Montreal. John Surratt accompanied her to New York and quickly returned to Washington.[60]

Booth planned a meeting of the conspirators. On March 13, a Monday, he sent a wire to O'Laughlen in Baltimore asking him to come to Washington "at once." Powell was needed as well. Preston Parr apparently kept Surratt informed of Powell's situation. On March 14 Surratt sent a wire to Parr: "Immediately telegraph if my friend is disengaged and can see me this evening in Washington." Parr wired back, "She will be over on the six p.m. train. Parr."[61] This time Powell, forgetting he had previously given his name as Wood, introduced himself at Mary Surratt's house as Mr. Payne, a Baptist preacher.[62] On the same day, Booth asked his actor friend John Mathews to deliver a trunk to a mutual friend in Baltimore on Fayette Street. Back in November Booth had asked that his pistol be delivered to a friend on Fayette Street. The identity of the friend is not known with certainty, but Sam Arnold's father lived on Fayette Street. The trunk contained delicacies intended for the use of the kidnaped president. The abduction seemed imminent.[63]

On March 15 Booth reserved the presidential box at Ford's Theatre for Powell and Surratt, who attended the play with two of Mary Surratt's female boarders.[64] The conspirators needed to know the layout of the theatre if they were to abduct the president there. Booth dropped by the box during the course of the play. After the performance the men returned the female boarders to the Surratt house and then walked to Gautier's Restaurant, where Booth had reserved a private room. After Atzerodt arrived, the group played cards while David Herold went out to get Arnold and O'Laughlen.

This meeting was the first time the conspirators were all in the same place. When Booth made the introductions, Powell was "Mosby" and Atzerodt was "Port Tobacco." Over a table laden with oysters, liquors, and cigars, Booth described the planned abduction of President Lincoln from Ford's Theatre. Booth and "Mosby" would subdue the president. Herold and O'Laughlen would turn off the gas and darken the theatre. Sam Arnold would jump from the box to the stage to help while Booth and "Mosby" lowered their hog-tied victim by rope. John Surratt and "Port Tobacco" would wait on the other side of the Navy Yard Bridge to guide the fleeing pack to the Potomac. With a flair, Booth concluded by saying everything was ready.[65]

A long discussion followed Booth's peroration. John Surratt told the others that "the Government had received information that there was a plot of some kind" and recommended they "throw up the whole project." Arnold immediately recognized the plan as utterly impractical, but he held his tongue for a time until he boldly announced that he objected to the whole scheme. He was willing to take chances, he said, but this plan would surely mean the sacrifice of his life. Besides, he continued, prisoners were now being exchanged, so the purpose of the abduction had been removed. Booth had been imbibing

throughout the meeting, and he flew into a rage. Arnold gave as good as he got, which pushed Booth to threaten to shoot Arnold. The room was quiet when Arnold replied that two could "play at that game." He told the group that he would give the plot one week and then would leave. The meeting ended at 5 a.m.[66]

The next day Booth sought out Arnold and apologized. When he said Arnold must have been drunk, Arnold reacted by saying it was Booth who had overindulged in drink, and he reiterated that he would leave the plot in a week. A day later Booth visited his actor friend John Mathews, who was living at the Petersen house across the street from Ford's Theatre. While lying on the bed there he learned that President Lincoln would attend a performance later in the day at Campbell General Hospital, several miles north of the White House.[67]

Booth quickly made arrangements for the conspirators to meet at a restaurant on Seventh Street. Arnold and O'Laughlen arrived first. Atzerodt, Powell, Surratt, and Booth arrived in turn. They leapt into action by having a few drinks. Booth rode out to the hospital to ascertain the location of the president and found that he was not there. Booth rode back to the restaurant and informed the men, who then disbanded under the impression that Lincoln had changed his plans because the plot had been discovered.[68] Herold had been sent ahead in Booth's buggy with the carbines and other weapons; he expected to meet the others and the abducted president on the road. Herold spent the night at a tavern wondering what had happened. The next day Surratt and Atzerodt found him, and the three men continued on to the Surratt Tavern in Surrattsville. Against the wishes of tenant and tavern-keeper John Lloyd, they hid the carbines and other items in the tavern.[69]

On March 18, the day after the failed abduction, Booth attended a morning rehearsal at Ford's. After the rehearsal Booth and John McCullough relaxed by taking a horseback ride.[70] McCullough recalled:

> I never was a horseback rider, but Booth had a wandering mind and love of physical excitement, and against my will he got me on a horse one day. Instead of taking me to the pleasant places around Washington he rode into by-roads up along the Eastern branch.... [I said] "I am all raw now with riding this old horse. For God's sake take me back to the hotel."[71]

That night Surratt, Weichmann, Atzerodt, and Herold attended Booth's last stage appearance.[72] Booth played Pescara in *The Apostate* for the benefit of McCullough. After the performance McCullough came before the curtain and was applauded. The audience cheered and stamped the floor to encourage Booth to take his bows as well, but, not wanting to upstage McCullough, he refused to come out.[73]

After the failed attempt at kidnapping, Surratt considered the plot to be abandoned.[74] Arnold and O'Laughlen left Washington and the conspiracy. Herold accepted a clerkship to begin April 1 at Base Hospital, Union Army of the James. Booth, unlike the others, wouldn't let go. The following Tuesday Booth took the evening train which, with several changes, would get him to New York at 6 a.m. the next day.[75]

It is likely that Booth, perhaps with his mother, attended his brother Edwin's record one-hundredth consecutive performance of *Hamlet* at the Winter Garden Theatre. Booth had more than one reason for visiting New York; Junius Brutus Booth, Jr., noted in his diary that "John came on to see Miss Hale."[76] Powell had also traveled to New York, where he stayed at the Revere House.[77] When Booth decided to return to Washington, he made arrangements for Powell's return as well. Booth, and perhaps Powell, seems to have associated with like-minded people while in New York, for he later told Atzerodt he learned there of a plot to kill the president by blowing up the White House.[78]

On March 25, when Booth passed through Baltimore on his way to Washington, he sent a note to Sam Arnold asking him to give the abduction plot one more try before abandoning it forever. Arnold then wrote a letter to Booth which later would incriminate him: "You know full that the G—t suspicions something.... Go and see how it will be taken at R—d." This statement seems to confirm John Surratt's claim that the Confederate government in Richmond had not been directly informed of Booth's kidnapping plot.[79]

The day after Booth's return to Washington, Mary Surratt sent Louis Weichmann to ask him to drop by her house. Booth brought Atzerodt along when he called. Mary explained that Augustus Howell was supposed to have escorted Sarah Slater to Richmond, but he had been arrested as a spy at the Surratt Tavern. John Surratt had volunteered to take Howell's place, and Thomas A. Jones, chief of the Confederate signal service north of the Potomac, had crossed the river with Surratt and Slater. To explain her son's absence, Mary told Weichmann that John had gone to Richmond to get a clerkship.[80]

Just before Booth's return to Washington, President Lincoln left the city to visit the front. The date of the president's return was uncertain—in the end, he did not come back until April 9—but Booth thought it would be imminent. He was still planning something. The *Washington Evening Star* announced that the president would attend Ford's Theatre on Wednesday, March 29. Booth wired O'Laughlen: "Get word to Sam. Come on, with or without him, Wednesday morning. We sell that day sure. Don't fail"[81] Lincoln remained at the front and did not show up on Wednesday.

Two days later, Arnold and O'Laughlen traveled from Baltimore to Washington, where they ran into Atzerodt at the train station. They met Booth in his hotel room in the afternoon. Booth said the plot was abandoned forever and that he would return to acting. O'Laughlen asked for, but failed to receive, the $500 which Booth had borrowed from his brother. Back in Baltimore, Arnold soon accepted a job at Fort Monroe, in Virginia, wanting to get far away from Booth and possible trouble.

Not much was happening in Washington. President Lincoln was at the front, and John Surratt was in Richmond. On April 1 Booth took the afternoon train for New York. There he chatted with John McCullough about a summer engagement in Montreal.[82] The next day Richmond was evacuated and occupied by Union forces. With the fall of Richmond, the abduction plot was effectively ended; if Lincoln were captured, there was no place to take him.

On April 4 Booth and a female companion took an overnight steamboat from New York to Newport, Rhode Island. The next morning at the Aquidneck House Booth signed the register "J. W. Booth & Lady, Boston." The couple had breakfast and then left the hotel, ostensibly to walk, from 9 a.m. until 2 p.m. On their return they ordered lunch, but soon changed their minds and took the three o'clock train to Boston, arriving at 6:15 p.m.[83]

In Boston Booth saw Edwin at a rehearsal of *Hamlet*. While at the theatre he told one of the actresses he was tired of travel and that if he acted again, he would confine himself to Boston, New York, and Philadelphia. The following day Booth attracted attention with a fine display of marksmanship at a shooting gallery near the Parker House. He sought out an old family friend, Orlando Tompkins, and bought him a ring inscribed "J.W.B. to O.T."[84]

Booth returned to New York on April 7. When Sam Chester ran into him on Broadway, Booth was drinking heavily. Booth loudly insulted Edwin Adams's agent and tried to pick a fight with a man he perceived to be listening to his conversation. Chester was shocked when his inebriated friend boasted about having had a good chance to kill President Lincoln at the inauguration.[85]

John Surratt and Sarah Slater had left Richmond the day before the city was evacuated. Confederate Secretary of State Judah Benjamin had given Surratt $200 in gold for expenses and asked him to carry dispatches to Canada. A Confederate State Department official who met with Surratt thought he was "unusually mutton-headed."[86] Surratt and Slater arrived in Washington late in the afternoon of April 3. She stayed at the Metropolitan Hotel. Surratt changed clothes at his mother's house, had dinner, and, to avoid possible arrest at home, left to spend the night at a hotel, presumably the one where Slater was staying. The two went to New York the next day. Surratt inquired at Edwin's house in New York and was told that John Wilkes had left for Boston. Surratt then left for Montreal, where he delivered dispatches to Confederate General Edwin G. Lee. Surratt stayed there, fearing arrest in Washington.[87]

Powell kept a low profile in Washington while Booth was away, but he did go out occasionally. He met Mary J. Gardiner, a performer in the "leg show" at Canterbury Hall, and kept a card she gave him with her room number.[88]

Booth was back in Washington on Saturday, April 8. While waiting for a train in Philadelphia, Booth wrote to Chester that he would soon be leaving for Oil City, Pennsylvania.

President Lincoln returned to Washington in the evening on Sunday, April 9. News of General Robert E. Lee's surrender at Appomattox had been received, and the streets were filled with celebrating people. Most people considered the war to be over with the surrender of Lee's army. President Lincoln's first stop in Washington was a visit to Secretary of State William Seward, who had been severely injured in a carriage accident several days previously.

Why did Booth return to Washington on April 8? Yes, Lucy Hale was there and he wanted to spend time with her. The horses and buggy were no longer needed, and he supervised Atzerodt and Spangler in their sale. Why was Powell continuing his stay at the Herndon House? His only draw to Washington had been Booth. Booth struck up a friendship with a widow who lived near the home of Secretary of State William Seward. Booth told Atzerodt that the widow's influence could be used to gain entrance to the Seward house.[89] Powell made several visits of his own to the Seward house. Arnold and O'Laughlen were no longer necessary. Surratt had moved on. Herold was available if needed. But Booth and Powell were waiting to strike.

On Monday, April 10, the city was in a mood of celebration. Booth visited Ford's Theatre and asked Spangler to sell his horse and buggy.[90] Later Booth and a companion identified as Powell ran into his longtime friend, actor H. B. Phillips, and several of Phillips's friends at the corner of Fourteenth Street and Pennsylvania Avenue. When Phillips asked Booth to join them in a drink, Booth said he "would do anything to drive away the blues."[91] They drank at Jesse Birch's saloon.

In the evening Booth visited Mary Surratt. While at the boarding house he saw Louis Weichmann, who joked about the Confederacy having "gone up." Booth pulled out a war map and excitedly showed how the remaining Confederate forces could hide in the mountains and fight a guerrilla war. In response to Weichmann asking why he was not acting, Booth replied that he only wanted to appear in *Venice Preserved*, a play in which there was a conspiracy to kill the leaders of Venice. Booth continued to ponder killing the president.[92]

In the evening Booth practiced at the shooting gallery on Pennsylvania Avenue. Another man, C. H. Pierson, and Booth shot together. Both were excellent shots, and soon Booth became excited and wanted to bet. Pierson won two of their three contests.[93]

On Tuesday Mary Surratt, having business at her country place, sent Weichmann to ask Booth for the use of his buggy. Weichmann called on Booth at his hotel a little after 8 a.m. Booth explained that Spangler had the buggy and was trying to sell it. He gave Weichmann $10 to rent one. On the way to Surrattsville, Mary and Weichmann ran into John Lloyd, her tenant. Lloyd later testified that Mary told him the carbines would be called for soon. When Mary had talked to Booth on the previous day, he apparently asked her to give Lloyd the message about the guns.[94]

A speech by President Lincoln had been announced for Tuesday evening. Booth, Herold, and Powell were in the audience, which cheered wildly before the speech and listened attentively when the president spoke. When Lincoln proposed limited suffrage for black men, Booth said, "That is the last speech he will ever make." He turned to Powell and ordered him to shoot the president. Powell refused.[95]

On Wednesday Spangler sold Booth's horse and buggy. Atzerodt had recently sold the light bay horse, leaving Booth with only the one-eyed horse.[96] In the evening Booth stopped at the Ford's Theatre box office and chatted with Harry Clay Ford. Booth said, "We are all slaves now. If a man were to go out and insult a nigger now he would be knocked down by the nigger and nothing would be done to the nigger." Ticket seller Tom Raybold, egging Booth on, responded, "He should not insult a nigger then." Booth said he could do as much farm work as any white man, but could not keep up with black men, especially those who worked in the southern fields. Booth thought it improper that southern prisoners were being guarded by blacks. Ford responded that if General Lee wanted them to fight for the Confederacy, they were good enough to do guard duty. After thirty minutes Booth had enough and left.[97]

The city had been celebrating all week. To top it off, a "grand illumination" was planned for Thursday, April 13. Many workers had the day off. The streets were crowded with parades and marching bands. In the evening nearly all the windows in the city would be adorned with gas lights and candles. Some of Washington's residents were not celebrating; on Thursday morning, Lewis Powell walked past Secretary of State Seward's house and chatted with George Robinson, Seward's nurse.[98] Michael O'Laughlen and a few friends came over from Baltimore late in the afternoon. O'Laughlen called for Booth at the National Hotel, but he was out.[99]

When Booth stopped at Ford's Theatre to pick up his mail, he told actor E. A. Emerson that when Lincoln had visited the White House of the Confederacy, he had "squirted tobacco juice all over the place. Somebody ought to kill the old scoundrel."[100] Harry Ford observed Booth, alone, on the gallery steps. Booth next stopped at Taltavull's saloon next to the theatre.[101]

In mid-afternoon Booth visited Grover's Theatre. Manager C. D. Hess and his stage director were reading a play. Hess said, "Hello John, how is trade?" Booth responded, "Pretty fair." Booth, who usually waited to be asked to come into the office, walked right in. He asked whether Hess was going to illuminate the theatre that night. Hess responded in the affirmative but added that Friday, the anniversary of the fall of Fort Sumter, would be Grover's big night. Booth asked if the president had been invited. Hess said he was going to invite the president to attend Friday night's performance.[102]

Later on Thursday Booth, Herold, Atzerodt, and Powell met in Powell's room at the Herndon House. Atzerodt was assigned to register at the Kirkwood House in order to scout Vice President Johnson, who lived there. Herold was directed to ride into southern Maryland and pass the word that the next night several men would be heading for the Potomac on an urgent basis. Certainly Booth and Powell knew their assignments for the following night—murder the president, Gen-

eral Grant, and Secretary Seward. Perhaps Atzerodt and Herold were kept in the dark, perhaps not. The men would meet again the next night for last-minute coordination.[103]

On the morning of April 14, 1865, as desk clerk Walter Burton was going off duty at the National Hotel, he ran into David Herold in the hall. Herold explained that he was looking for Booth, so Burton took him to Booth's room, opened the door, and found that the room was empty and the bed was still made.[104] Burton's account appeared forty-four years after the event; perhaps he was mistaken. It is likely Booth walked about the city on Thursday night to see the Grand Illumination. He may have spent time with Lucy Hale. There may have been an overnight visit to Ellen Starr. The prospect of the planned murder may have kept him awake. It is possible that Booth returned to his hotel room and slept on top of the bed covers. In the morning Michael O'Laughlen, in Washington for the Grand Illumination, also looked for Booth at the National Hotel; it is unknown whether he found him.[105] Booth did connect with Herold sometime in the morning, for he sent Herold to tell Atzerodt to go to Surrattsville and "see after" items, certainly the carbines, he had left there.[106]

Booth wrote a letter to his mother with the date heading, "April 14, 2:00 a.m." The letter may have been written at that time; there is a chance, however, that he wrote it at about 4 p.m. in the National Hotel lobby, when he asked the clerk, "Is it 1864 or 1865?"[107]

Atzerodt executed the assignment he had been given the day before. He checked into the Kirkwood House before 8 a.m. without baggage and paid a day in advance. He did not go to his room.[108] Now he, and his visitors, had a legitimate reason for being in the hotel. Lewis Powell again walked past Seward's house and chatted with Seward's nurse.[109]

Booth had breakfast at his hotel. Accounts vary. He dined with Lucy Hale.[110] Or he ate alone in the hotel's dining room. He stopped at the hotel barbershop. He passed through the lobby alone, noticing that the time was past eleven o'clock.[111] Booth walked up Sixth Street, turned left on H Street, and walked up the steps to Mary Surratt's front door. In the course of his conversation with Mary, she revealed that she would be traveling to Surrattsville in the afternoon. Now there was no need for Atzerodt to make the trip; later Booth told Atzerodt that Mary had gone to Surrattsville "to get out the guns."[112]

Leaving the Surratt house, Booth walked several blocks to Ford's Theatre, perhaps stopping to see Powell at the Herndon House. He arrived just before noon. There, on the steps, he encountered Harry Ford and a few others. Harry Ford, remembering that Booth had criticized General Lee in conversation the previous day, said, "Here is a man who don't like Gen. Lee." Booth, provoked, repeated his criticisms. Ford then asked Booth if he would loan him money for a business venture. Booth was non-committal.[113] Before he left Ford's, Booth learned that the president would attend Ford's that night, not Grover's, to see *Our American Cousin*, starring Laura Keene. Originally General Grant was going to attend the play with the Lincolns, but the plans changed and Grant headed for New Jersey.[114]

James Ford, carrying flags he had borrowed from the Treasury Department to decorate the president's box at the theatre, ran into Booth at E and Tenth Streets. After leaving Ford, Booth took a few steps and encountered his friend John F. Coyle, an editor of the *National Intelligencer*.[115]

Booth then walked to Pumphrey's Stable on C Street, just across from his hotel. The horse he usually rented was not available, but he was able to reserve an active bay mare, which he said he would pick up later. James W. Pumphrey, the stableman, observed that Booth was calm. He declined Booth's offer to go for a drink.[116]

At noon Herold went to the Kirkwood House to see Atzerodt. They left together.

Herold rented a horse at Nailor's Stable, and Atzerodt rented one at Keleher's on Eighth Street. The men, on their horses, were seen near the Navy Yard in the afternoon. Herold's family lived near the Navy Yard. It was also the area where the men had arranged to meet after the events planned for that night. Late in the afternoon the men both stabled their horses at Nailor's.[117]

Booth retrieved his field glasses from either the stable or his hotel and walked to Mary Surratt's house, arriving at about 2:30. As Weichmann was leaving to rent a buggy for the trip to Surrattsville, he observed Booth chatting with Mary. Booth gave her a package containing his binoculars; he asked her to leave it at her country place and explain that it would be called for that night. He also asked her to have the guns taken from their hiding place. Upon arriving in Surrattsville, Mary gave the package to tavern-keeper John Lloyd and told him to have the "shooting irons" ready that night.[118]

Booth may have walked from Mary Surratt's house to his hotel. He needed to get his riding boots and spurs preparatory to picking up his horse. He asked desk clerk Henry Merrick for a sheet of paper and an envelope and asked admittance to the hotel office so he could write in privacy. Strangely, he asked whether the year was 1864 or 1865. Merrick noticed that Booth seemed agitated, unlike his usual self. On his way out of the hotel he urged the clerks to see the play at Ford's that night, commenting, "There is going to be some splendid acting tonight."[119]

Booth returned to Pumphrey's Stable to pick up the horse he had reserved. The small, light bay mare was very lively and had a nervous temperament. She would not allow herself to be tied; someone must hold her reins. The horse was equipped with an English saddle, a snaffle bit, and a single rein. Before he mounted the horse, Booth took a single spur from his pocket and placed it on his right boot. He rode east and then west on C Street and turned north on Sixth Street. He had told Pumphrey he was going to "the theatre to write a letter and would leave the horse in a stable in the alley behind the theatre." Pumphrey assumed Booth meant Grover's Theatre, but Booth meant Ford's.[120]

Later in the afternoon, Booth, on horseback, ran into John Mathews on Pennsylvania Avenue between Thirteenth and Fourteenth Streets near the Willard Hotel. Booth had written a letter explaining his actions and addressed it to John F. Coyle of the *National Intelligencer*. He asked Mathews to hold the letter until the next day and then give it to Coyle for publication.[121] Just as Booth handed the sealed letter to Mathews, General and Mrs. Grant rode by on their way to the train station. Booth galloped after their carriage, peering into it as he passed and again after he turned around and rode by a second time. Mrs. Grant thought she recognized him as one of four men who had stared at her a few hours before at lunch at Willard's.[122]

A little after five o'clock Booth stopped at the Kirkwood House. As he was walking up the steps, he saw John A. Deveney, an acquaintance from Canada. Booth tapped him in the shoulder and asked, "How d'ye do Jack, when did you get back from Canada?" Booth explained that he was not acting, but was in the oil business. Then Booth entered the hotel and left a note for Vice President Johnson with the clerk: "Don't wish to disturb you. Are you at home?"[123] If Johnson had been there, Booth would have explained that he wanted to open a theatre and asked him for a pass to Richmond, even though a pass was no longer necessary.[124] His real intent was to determine whether Johnson was in the hotel and in which room. Deveney saw Booth leave the hotel and ride down Pennsylvania Avenue headed in the direction of the Capitol.[125]

Booth rode up Tenth Street to Ford's Theatre, where he encountered several Ford's employees and James Ferguson, who ran a restaurant on the north side of the theatre. Booth said to Ferguson, "See what a nice horse I have got? Now watch, she can run just like a cat." He spurred the animal, which then accelerated up Tenth Street.[126] He rode into Baptist Alley behind Ford's and put the horse in his stable. He removed the saddle and replaced the distinctive yellow trimmed saddle blanket with his shawl. After locking the stable door, he walked out to Tenth Street to treat some of the men from the theatre to a drink.

Booth walked from Ford's to his hotel. On the bureau there was a half-pound of Killikinick tobacco, a clothes brush, a broken comb, and a pair of embroidered slippers. In the bureau there was a shirt, two pairs of "drawers," several pairs of socks, a bottle of hair oil, and a pair of black cashmere pants marked "J. Wilkes Booth" on the fob pocket. There was a trunk on the floor with the label "theatre," a valise, and a pair of boots.[127]

Booth was wearing a dark sack coat, double-breasted vest, pants of a dark mixed color, a dark slouch hat, and riding boots. He was nearly five feet, ten inches tall when wearing the boots. The well-worn boots were twenty-three inches high with a diameter of twenty inches at the thigh. The heel to toe measurement was eleven inches. Booth was known to be bowlegged, but, strangely, the heel and sole of his right boot were worn on the inside, about a quarter of an inch, indicating that his ankles turned in when he walked, as if he were slightly knock-kneed.[128]

Herold apparently came to Booth's room, where Booth gave him a knife, a loaded pistol, and a coat to take to Atzerodt at the Kirkwood House. The knife and pistol were to be used by Atzerodt to kill Vice President Johnson. The coat belonged to Booth, and in the pockets were Booth's Ontario bank book, a map of Virginia, a pair of new gauntlets, several handkerchiefs, three boxes of cartridges, a toothbrush, a spur, a pair of socks, and two collars.[129] The contents of the coat indicate that Booth had packed it with a few items for use in his escape. Herold, or perhaps Atzerodt, was supposed to bring the coat to Booth when they met later.

Herold found Atzerodt in his room at the Kirkwood House and left the weapons and coat.[130] Herold was supposed to bring Atzerodt to a restaurant to meet Booth, but when Booth did not appear they went to the National Hotel; he was not there either. Herold went in search of Booth, telling Atzerodt to wait at the hotel. Atzerodt immediately headed to a bar for a drink. He returned to the Kirkwood House and asked a man where he could find the vice president. The man pointed out Johnson in the dining room.[131] Atzerodt was back in his room when Herold came in and told him Booth and "Wood," Powell's alias, wanted to see him at the Herndon House.

Booth walked to the Herndon House and waited with Powell for Atzerodt and Herold to arrive.[132] When the four men were in the room, Booth went over the plan, which was to be executed at about 10:15. Booth would kill the president and General Grant at Ford's Theatre.[133] Powell was to kill Secretary of State Seward in his home. Atzerodt peremptorily refused when Booth ordered him to kill Vice President Johnson. Booth threatened Atzerodt with death, but to no avail. Finally the assignment to kill Johnson was given jointly to Herold and Atzerodt. The four men planned to meet at the Navy Yard Bridge, where Atzerodt would guide them to the Potomac.[134]

Booth walked several blocks to Mary Surratt's house. According to Louis Weichmann's later recollection, Booth was waiting in the Surratt parlor when Weichmann and Mary returned from the country. Mary had told John Lloyd to have the "shooting irons" ready because they would be called for that night. She had also given Lloyd Booth's package containing the binoculars.[135]

Booth walked to his stable and led his horse to the back door of the theatre. He opened the door and, in a loud voice, called for Ned Spangler three times. Booth handed him the reins and asked him to hold the horse for ten or fifteen minutes. The request was not unusual; Spangler had held Booth's horse on twenty or more previous occasions.[136] As Spangler started to explain that he was needed on the stage, Booth walked past him into the theatre. Spangler had duties and did not have time to hold the horse, so he sent for Peanut John, another Ford's Theatre subaltern, and held the horse until he came.[137] Booth's handoff of the horse was amazingly nonchalant given that his life would depend on the horse being ready in a few minutes.

When Booth entered the theatre, he could not cross to the other side of the stage without being seen by the audience, so he used an underground passageway. He climbed the stairs on the other side and exited the theatre to an alleyway that led to Tenth Street. There he saw several people at the front of Ford's Theatre as well as the president's carriage.

He entered the first door of the theatre. The ticket office was on the right. On the left was a door into the main or parquet level, which Booth entered. He observed the play for several minutes; he then left the theatre and entered the Star Saloon just to the south. In a hurried manner he addressed the bartender, "Give me some whiskey." After he was served, Booth asked for water in a more urgent tone.[138] Booth left the saloon and walked back to Ford's. He encountered an acquaintance, Captain William Williams, who asked him to join him in a drink. Booth declined.[139] He entered the theatre and parquet again briefly. On returning, he asked ticket-taker John Buckingham the time. Buckingham pointed out a clock in the lobby. Booth looked at the clock and then climbed the stairs to the first balcony, called the dress circle, where the entrance to the president's box was located.[140]

Booth approached the door, paused for a moment, and surveyed the entrance of the presidential box. A man seated nearby observed Booth and thought he had a glare in his eye and that he was intoxicated.[141] Booth took his hat off and held it in his left hand. He took something, perhaps a visiting card, from his coat pocket and showed it to the man seated at the outer door of the box. In a moment he entered the passageway to the box and shut the door. Placing his hat on his head, he retrieved a bar he had hidden behind the door earlier and wedged the door shut.

The passageway was about four feet wide and eight feet long, with a closed door to Box 7 on the left side and an open door to Box 8 at the end. The two boxes had been combined for the presidential party by removing a partition. The far box, occupied by Major Henry Rathbone and his fiancée, Clara Harris, was about nine feet deep and a little more than six feet wide at the stage. The near box was smaller, about five feet deep, with the same exposure to the stage. Rathbone's back was to the open door, and he did not see Booth enter.[142]

Booth acted quickly. After barring the door, he walked to the far end of the passageway, passing the closed Box 7 door and probably ignoring the peep hole someone had drilled in it. With his single shot derringer pistol in his right hand, he walked through the open door to Box 8, turned left, and immediately shot President Lincoln in the back of the head at close range.

Major Rathbone heard the shot, saw black smoke, and heard Booth say, "Freedom." Others heard him say, "Sic Semper Tyrannis!" Booth dropped the pistol and pulled out his Rio Grande camp knife as Rathbone rushed at him and grabbed him by the throat. Booth broke free and attempted to stab Rathbone in the chest. Rathbone parried the blow upward with his left arm. The ten-inch blade entered at the elbow and pierced nearly to the shoulder. Booth needed strength to extricate the blade. Booth lost his hat in the scuffle.[143]

Booth then rushed to the front of the box, placed his left hand and then his right on the rail, and leapt over, leading with his right leg.[144] Rathbone grabbed at Booth's clothes as he went over the rail, throwing Booth off balance. Rathbone heard a tearing

sound and thought he had torn Booth's clothes. The sound was caused by Booth's spur ripping a flag that adorned the box. Rathbone shouted, "Stop that man!" When Booth landed on the stage, he fell to his right knee with the knife still in his right hand. He sprang to his feet and may have repeated, "Sic Semper Tyrannis!" Booth, knife theatrically raised, ran "with lightning speed" across the stage with his upper body slightly turned left toward the audience. About two-thirds of the way across the stage he said, "The South shall be free!" or "The South is avenged!" and then, "I have done it!"[145]

If Booth injured his leg in jumping to the stage, it did not affect his ability to run. After crossing the stage Booth turned sharply right. In order to make a running right turn—"cut right," in athletic terms—the left leg must be firmly planted and bear the entire weight of the runner, dissipate some of the forward momentum, and direct it to the right. He made the turn with ease.

Saying "Do let me pass!" he shoved hapless orchestra leader William Withers out of his way, his knife cutting through the man's vest and shirt. As Booth rushed toward the back door, stage carpenter Jacob Ritterspaugh, who had heard someone call, "Stop that man," prepared to do so, but he backed off when he saw the knife in Booth's hand. Booth opened the back door and rushed into the alley, pulling the door shut. The time from the shot to Booth's exit was very short, perhaps eight seconds according to one witness, fifteen seconds according to another.[146]

Peanut John, having heard the shot, was approaching the rear door and was about four feet away when it burst open. Booth rushed out shouting, "Give me my horse!" Booth put his left boot into the stirrup but was hindered in mounting because Peanut was still holding the horse's bridle. Booth pushed him away with the butt of the dagger and kicked him. A theatre patron who later claimed he was in hot pursuit opened the door and tried, but failed, to grab the reins of Booth's horse.[147]

1865 *through April 14*

January 1, Sunday Washington

Booth left his one-eyed horse at Cleaver's Stable. It had previously been kept at Howard's Stable.[148]

Booth may have visited at Mary E. Surratt's boarding house.[149]

On or about this date, twenty-year-old Lewis Thornton Powell left Confederate partisan ranger John Singleton Mosby's cavalry command. The muscular, six-foot-tall soldier would soon become involved in the plot to kidnap President Lincoln.

January 2, Monday Washington

John H. Surratt accepted Booth's offer to join the plot on or about this date.[150]

Booth wrote to Samuel Knapp Chester: "You must come to Washington, I cannot do without you."[151]

Booth's friend John McCullough appeared at Ford's Theatre with Edwin Forrest from January 2 through February 3.

January 3, Tuesday Washington

John Surratt, recognizing the danger he was in, deeded his interest in the family properties to his mother.[152]

January 4, Wednesday Washington

Booth wrote a letter to Joe Simonds.[153]

January 5, Thursday Washington

Booth deposited $250 in his account with Jay Cooke & Company in Washington. It is likely this money was part of the $500 that Joe Simonds had sent on the last day of December.[154]

January 6, Friday Washington

[Date approximate] Booth renewed his acquaintance with fellow National Hotel residents Lucy and Elizabeth Hale, daughters of former Senator John P. Hale, of New Hampshire.

January 7, Saturday Washington

Booth withdrew $150 from his account with Jay Cooke & Company.[155]

On or about this date, Eddy Martin, a New York cotton broker, engaged blockade-runner George Andrew Atzerodt to ferry him across the Potomac River.[156] Atzerodt would soon be recruited for the abduction plot.

President and Mrs. Lincoln with their son Tad saw Avonia Jones perform at Grover's Theatre.[157]

January 8, Sunday Washington

January 9, Monday Washington

Booth withdrew $750 from his account with Jay Cooke & Company.[158] Some of the money would be used to pay for a boat to ferry Lincoln across the Potomac River.

On or about this date, Booth sent $50 to Sam Chester and told him to be in Washington by Saturday night.[159]

January 10, Tuesday Baltimore

Booth left for Baltimore at 7:30 p.m.[160]

January 11, Wednesday Baltimore

[Probable date] Booth met with Samuel Arnold and Michael O'Laughlen and left them with a trunk containing two Spencer carbines and other weapons he had purchased previously in New York. He also bought a horse, a buggy, and a harness selected by Arnold.[161]

In Montreal, the St. Albans raiders' hearing was recessed so that papers certifying that the raiders were acting under Confederate orders could be sent from Richmond.

Thomas Nelson Conrad wrote to Confederate Secretary of War James Seddon asking for funds to continue unspecified activities in Washington. Seddon responded that only Confederate President Jefferson Davis could approve such funds.[162]

January 12, Thursday Washington

Booth returned to Washington from Baltimore.

[Probable date] After Sam Arnold and Michael O'Laughlen shipped Booth's trunk to Washington, they drove the horse and buggy to that city and met Booth at Ford's Theatre. Booth showed them the entrances to the theatre.[163] Booth kept the horse and buggy in the stable behind Ford's Theatre. On or about this date, Booth lodged his light bay horse at Cleaver's Stable.[164]

January 13, Friday Washington

John Surratt asked the Adams Express Company for a leave of absence so he could take his mother to Surrattsville. His request was denied.[165]

On several occasions George Atzerodt attempted to make arrangements for Eddy Martin to cross the Potomac.[166]

Lewis Powell entered Union lines and was paroled in Alexandria, Virginia.[167]

January 14, Saturday Washington

Booth withdrew $75 from his account with Jay Cooke & Company.[168]

Mary Surratt appeared at the Adams Express Company office and asked for a leave for her son. Her request was refused. John Surratt left the office, never to return, and went to Port Tobacco, Maryland, where, with Confederate agent Thomas Harbin, he recruited George Atzerodt to ferry the president across the Potomac River.[169]

January 15, Sunday Washington

January 16, Monday Washington

John Surratt paid $125 in trust to blockade-runner Richard M. Smoot for immediate possession of a large boat, which was then turned over to George Atzerodt and hidden on King's Creek, a tributary of Nanjemoy Creek on the Potomac. Surratt told Smoot he wanted two more boats.[170]

Eddy Martin, still waiting to cross the river, was introduced to John Surratt at Brawner's Hotel in Port Tobacco.[171]

Junius Brutus Booth, Jr., played *Richard III* for the first time in Philadelphia. That city's *North American and United States Gazette* identified him as "a son of the great tragedian whose name he bears, and a brother of the popular actors, Edwin Booth and J. Wilkes Booth."[172]

January 17, Tuesday Washington

On this day or the next, Booth and two other men had breakfast in the "big saloon" at Gautier's Restaurant.[173]

Booth wrote Junius explaining that he was staying in Washington, rather than New York, to avoid Edwin.[174]

George Atzerodt told Eddy Martin that a party of ten or twelve persons would cross the Potomac on Wednesday night and that relays of horses had been stationed between Washington and Port Tobacco.[175]

[Date approximate] Sam Arnold and Michael O'Laughlen moved to Mitchell's Hotel near Grover's Theatre in Washington.[176]

January 18, Wednesday Washington

Booth withdrew $600 from his account with Jay Cooke & Company, reducing his balance to $25.[177]

President Lincoln had intended to attend Edwin Forrest's performance of *Jack Cade* at Ford's Theatre but did not.[178]

January 19, Thursday Washington

Booth probably attended a morning rehearsal at Grover's Theatre to prepare for his Friday appearance as Romeo in Avonia Jones's benefit.

Booth wrote a letter to Joe Simonds.[179]

Lewis Powell, who had been living in a Baltimore hotel, moved to the Branson boarding house in Baltimore.[180]

January 20, Friday Washington

Booth played *Romeo and Juliet* with Avonia Jones in her farewell benefit at Grover's Theatre. The *Washington National Intelligencer* critic wrote:

> ...we have never seen a Romeo bearing any near comparison with the acting of Booth.... His death-scene was the most remarkable and fearfully natural that we have seen for years upon the stage.... His elocution was faultless. His step was "light as vanity." His readings were perfect....[181]

Two days later, the *Intelligencer* continued to discuss the performance, noting that Booth "suffered from huskiness of voice—but, then, what perfect acting! His likeness to his remarkable father is very striking.... He is full of genius, and almost as perfect an artist as his brother Edwin."[182]

January 21, Saturday Washington

John Surratt and Louis Weichmann took the train to Baltimore and registered at the Maltby House.[183]

January 22, Sunday Washington

John Surratt, without Louis Weichmann, met Lewis Powell at Preston Parr's china shop. Surratt was carrying $300, received from Booth. Surratt evaluated Powell's potential use and may have initiated a discussion of the abduction plot. Powell had no means of support, and it is possible Surratt provided him with some of Booth's money.[184]

January 23, Monday Washington

[Date approximate] John Surratt asked Louis Weichmann to write an article for a newspaper "to the effect that John Wilkes Booth, the accomplished actor, in consequence of having erysipelas in his leg, had retired from the stage and was engaged in the oil business."[185]

In "the latter part of January" John Surratt introduced George Atzerodt to Louis Weichmann in Mary Surratt's parlor. Thereafter, Weichmann and Atzerodt became friends and were seen together frequently.[186]

January 24, Tuesday Washington

Booth met with Sam Arnold and Michael O'Laughlen several times a week.[187]

[Date approximate] Booth and David Herold rode to Port Tobacco and, together with Atzerodt, inspected the boat. Booth, using his derringer, shot a vicious dog which barked and nipped at his heels.[188]

General Grant resumed prisoner exchanges with the South.[189]

January 25, Wednesday Washington

Booth met John Surratt at Cleaver's Stable in the evening. Surratt told William Cleaver he was going to a dance, but he later said he was going to help someone cross the river. Surratt also boasted that he and Booth were going to "kill Abe Lincoln." Booth and Surratt rode away in heavy rain.[190]

Jefferson Davis had approved Thomas Nelson Conrad's request for funds, and the monies were made available on this date.[191]

January 26, Thursday Washington

January 27, Friday Washington

[Date approximate] Arnold and O'Laughlen called on Booth at his hotel. Booth introduced them to John Surratt.

[Date approximate] Booth told Arnold that his mother was sending Junius to Washington to persuade him to come home. Booth turned one of his three horses over to Arnold to avoid having to explain to Junius why he kept several horses.[192]

Booth saw Junius and told him he had given up his intention to act in the South.[193]

January 28, Saturday Baltimore?

Booth left Washington on the 7:30 p.m. train to Baltimore.[194]

Booth revealed to Arnold that he had told Junius he was an officer in the Confederate army so that Junius would not insist on taking him home.[195]

January 29, Sunday Baltimore?

[Date approximate] Booth met Lewis Powell for the first time. Booth, according to one report, frequented a gambling house on Monument Square in Baltimore, where he met Powell late in January or early in February.[196] Booth described the abduction plot to Powell in detail.

January 30, Monday Baltimore?

Booth saw Powell the day after their first meeting, and he became a member of the abduction plot.[197]

January 31, Tuesday New York?

February 1, Wednesday New York?

John Surratt, for reasons unexplained, checked into the National Hotel in Washington.[198]

February 2, Thursday New York?

President Lincoln left Washington for a peace conference at Hampton Roads in Virginia.[199]

February 3, Friday New York?

[Date approximate] Confederate courier Sarah Antoinette Slater, escorted by Confederate agent Augustus S. Howell, crossed the Potomac. Slater was on her way to Montreal with papers from Richmond verifying that the St. Albans raiders were Confederate soldiers.[200] Booth and other members of his band would soon become acquainted with Slater.

The engagement of Edwin Forrest and John McCullough at Ford's Theatre concluded.

February 4, Saturday New York?

President Lincoln returned to Washington from Hampton Roads at 9:30 a.m.[201]

February 5, Sunday New York

Booth told Sam Chester he had tried to recruit actor John Mathews and had been rebuffed.[202]

Booth repeated his request, and Chester refused again. Chester returned the $50 Booth had sent. Booth said he wouldn't accept it if he were not short of funds. Booth apologized and released him.

February 6, Monday New York

John Surratt wrote to his cousin Bell Seaman: "I have just taken a peep into the parlor [of his mother's boarding house].... The doorbell rings and Mr. J. W. Booth is announced. Just listen to the scamperings. Such brushing and fixing."[203] Surratt was describing what it was like when Booth was there, but Booth was not actually present when the letter was written. Surratt also wrote that he was leaving for Europe in a week.[204]

John Sleeper Clarke opened a three-week engagement at Ford's Theatre in Washington.

February 7, Tuesday New York

[Date approximate] Prostitute Ellen Starr wrote to Booth pleading that he see her this evening.[205] Perhaps she didn't know Booth was in New York, or possibly she mis-dated her message.

February 8, Wednesday New York

The one-eyed horse and the light bay horse were moved from Cleaver's Stable to Howard's Stable, near Mary Surratt's boarding house.[206]

President and Mrs. Lincoln and family attended the Washington Theatre to see Laura Keene in *Sea of Ice*.[207]

February 9, Thursday Philadelphia

Booth wrote to his friend Orlando Tompkins asking for one dozen *cartes de visite* of himself in which he was "*seated, with cane & Black cravat*." He claimed that his oil stock had risen in value from $1,000 to $15,000 per share.[208]

February 10, Friday Philadelphia

Booth saw Junius in Philadelphia.[209]

Arnold and O'Laughlen took rooms at 420 D Street in Washington. O'Laughlen, apparently with Arnold's help, sometimes attended to his brother's produce and feed business.[210]

President Lincoln and Generals Ulysses S. Grant and Ambrose E. Burnside attended a play at Ford's Theatre starring John Sleeper Clarke.[211]

February 11, Saturday New York

Booth took the train from Philadelphia to New York.[212] A woodcut portrait of Edwin Booth appeared on the front page of the *New York Clipper*.

February 12, Sunday New York

[Date approximate] Adam Badeau saw Booth, presumably at Edwin Booth's house.[213]

Edwin and John Wilkes had long and bitter political discussions during this period.[214]

February 13, Monday New York

Booth was awake until 3:30 a.m. on Tuesday morning writing a valentine for "Miss Hale." He slept on a sofa in order to be up early to mail the letter.[215]

Junius was informed, probably by Joe Simonds, that John was not making money in oil, as had been represented.[216]

February 14, Tuesday New York

Booth frequented a shooting gallery at 600 Broadway, where he used a photograph of President Lincoln as a target.[217]

February 15, Wednesday Philadelphia

Booth probably left New York for Philadelphia.[218]

Sarah Slater arrived in Montreal and delivered papers for the St. Albans raiders.[219]

February 16, Thursday Philadelphia

Booth wrote to Joe Simonds, who replied, "Your strange note of the 16th rec'd. I hardly know what to make of you this winter—so different from your usual self. Have you lost ambition or what is the matter."[220]

February 17, Friday Philadelphia

[Date approximate] During one of Booth's visits to his sister Asia, he asked for the packet of documents he had left previously. He signed his November letter addressed "To whom it may concern" and had Asia return it to her safe.

February 18, Saturday New York

Richard M. Johnson, whom Booth had met a year before, wrote to the actor from St. Louis, enclosing a picture of himself, and asking Booth for another photograph. Johnson had given his own photo of Booth to a young lady in St. Louis who died shortly afterwards.[221]

February 19, Sunday New York

Booth's friend Orlando Tompkins in Boston wrote to Booth saying he had obtained the photographs Booth had requested and was mailing them to Ford's Theatre in Washington.[222]

February 20, Monday En route to Baltimore

John Surratt traveled to New York to escort Sarah Slater to Washington. Surratt visited Booth in New York and was introduced to Edwin Booth at his home at 28 E. Nineteenth St.[223]

Booth bought a "braiding hair ring" for $150 at Tiffany & Co. in New York and left for Baltimore on the night train.[224]

Confederate agent Augustus Howell, awaiting Slater's return from Montreal, stayed at Mary Surratt's boarding house. Howell taught Louis Weichmann a Confederate cipher code. Weichmann gave Howell information about Confederate prisoners.[225]

February 21, Tuesday Baltimore

Booth arrived in Baltimore at 3:30 a.m.[226]

At Barnum's Hotel, Booth sent a telegram to John P. H. Wentworth, a cousin of the Hale sisters, in Washington: "Will you keep promise to-day or tomorrow. Let me know. I cannot stay."[227]

Atzerodt stayed one night at Mary Surratt's boarding house. Howell, Atzerodt, and Weichmann finished a bottle of whiskey, and Weichmann went out to get another bottle.[228] Later, Mary placed the blame on Atzerodt after she found the liquor bottles.[229]

John Sleeper Clarke played *Our American Cousin* at Ford's Theatre in Washington.

February 22, Wednesday Washington

Booth took the 6 p.m. train from Baltimore to Washington.[230]

Booth, John P. H. Wentworth, and John McCullough checked into the National Hotel.[231]

In the afternoon Sarah Slater and John Surratt, who had escorted her from New York, drove up to Mary Surratt's boarding house in a buggy and conversed with Augustus Howell.[232] Howell and Slater left for Richmond in the buggy.

John Surratt left instructions at Howard's Stable to allow Atzerodt to use "his" horse whenever he desired. Atzerodt would need the horse to get to Port Tobacco to ferry Sarah Slater across the Potomac.[233]

February 23, Thursday Washington

Atzerodt rode one of Booth's horses to Port Tobacco so he could take Slater across the river.[234]

[Date approximate] Powell, giving his name as Mr. Wood, visited the Surratt boarding house for the first time. He asked Weichmann, who answered the door, for John Surratt and, upon finding that he was not home, asked for Mary Surratt. Powell stayed one night.[235]

February 24, Friday Washington

[Date approximate] Powell returned to Baltimore.

Confederate agent John Yates Beall was hanged at Governor's Island, New York.[236]

February 25, Saturday Washington

John Sleeper Clarke closed his three-week run at Ford's Theatre.

February 26, Sunday Washington

February 27, Monday Washington

Booth sent a telegram to Michael O'Laughlen in Baltimore: "As you could not stay here to see me I will be in Baltimore tomorrow. See me there Booth. Sure."[237]

Confederate courier James H. Fowle was introduced to John Surratt in Surrattsville on or about this date.[238]

Atzerodt rowed Augustus Howell, Sarah Slater, and James Fowle across the Potomac to the Tannant Farm in Virginia. Shortly thereafter, Atzerodt, driving the buggy used by Howell and Slater and trailing the horse he had ridden, returned to Washington.[239]

February 28, Tuesday Baltimore

Booth took the 8:15 a.m. train to Baltimore.[240]

Booth had telegraphed to arrange a meeting with Arnold and O'Laughlen and apparently did so. It is possible he met with Powell as well.

John Surratt and Sarah Slater arrived in Richmond.

March 1, Wednesday Washington

Booth returned to Washington and registered at the National Hotel.

March 2, Thursday Washington

Booth asked the hotel clerk to call him at 8 a.m.

March 3, Friday Washington

In the evening Weichmann saw Booth and Surratt in Mary Surratt's parlor and proposed that they go to the Capitol. The three men observed the session of the House of Representatives from the gallery.[241]

President Lincoln was also at the Capitol, signing bills passed by Congress.[242]

March 4, Saturday Washington

Booth requested the hotel to awaken him at 8 a.m.

Booth nearly attacked John McCullough when he unexpectedly entered his hotel room a few hours before the inauguration.[243]

Booth attended Lincoln's second inauguration with a pass he obtained from Lucy Hale. He stood above and behind the president. He left the Capitol with Walter Burton, night clerk at the National Hotel.[244]

Booth had a drink with O'Laughlen at the Lichau House at about 10:30 p.m.[245]

In the evening President Lincoln shook hands with 6,000 people at a public reception at the White House.

March 5, Sunday Washington

Booth wrote a bit of poetry to Lucy Hale, who he entertained in his room. She added these lines from John Greenleaf Whittier's poem, *Maude Muller*: "For all sad words from tongue or pen, The saddest are these—it might have been. March 5, 1865 In John's room."[246]

March 6, Monday Washington

In Baltimore Lewis Powell beat a black woman he thought had insulted him.[247]

President Lincoln attended an inaugural ball at the Patent Office in the evening.[248]

Booth may have escorted Lucy Hale to the inaugural ball.

March 7, Tuesday Washington

President and Mrs. Lincoln attended Grover's Theatre.

March 8, Wednesday Washington

Booth visited Arnold and O'Laughlen often, generally riding in his buggy.[249]

March 9, Thursday Washington

March 10, Friday Washington

In Baltimore Lewis Powell was arrested and interrogated in the office of the provost marshal.[250]

President Lincoln appointed former Senator John P. Hale to the post of Minister to Spain.

March 11, Saturday Washington

[Date approximate] Sarah Slater, bearing dispatches from the Richmond government for agents in Montreal, arrived in Washington about this date.[251] She stayed at Mary Surratt's boarding house, displacing Weichmann for a night.

John McCullough registered at the National Hotel.[252]

March 12, Sunday Washington

Powell was suspected of being a spy, but, without proof, he was allowed to take the oath of allegiance and was ordered "to go north of Philadelphia and remain during the war."[253]

Sarah Slater and John Surratt left by train for New York. Slater went on to Montreal, and Surratt returned to Washington.[254]

March 13, Monday Washington

Booth telegraphed O'Laughlen in Baltimore: "You had better come at once." O'Laughlen came to Washington.[255]

John McCullough and Edwin Forrest started a one week engagement at Ford's Theatre.

March 14, Tuesday Washington

Booth asked John Mathews to deliver a

trunk containing delicacies to a friend in Baltimore. The items in the trunk were intended for the use of the abducted president. The trunk was to be shipped to southern Maryland.[256]

John Surratt sent a telegram to Preston Parr in Baltimore asking him to have Powell come to Washington. Powell arrived in Washington on the 6 p.m. train.[257] He introduced himself at Mary Surratt's boarding house as Mr. Payne, a Baptist preacher.[258]

March 15, Wednesday Washington

Booth reserved the presidential box at Ford's Theatre for Powell and Surratt, who attended the evening performance with two of Mary Surratt's female boarders.[259]

After the play Booth gathered Herold, Surratt, Atzerodt, Powell, Arnold, and O'Laughlen together at Gautier's Restaurant and proposed to capture the president in a theatre. Arnold and Booth argued, and the meeting broke up at 5 a.m.[260]

President and Mrs. Lincoln attended a performance at Grover's Theatre accompanied by Clara Harris, daughter of Senator Ira Harris, of New York.[261]

March 16, Thursday Washington

After leaving Gautier's, Powell and Surratt returned to Mary Surratt's house at 7 a.m. They were still there when Weichmann returned from work at 4:30 p.m.[262]

Arnold met Booth at 2 p.m. and said he would quit the conspiracy in a week.[263]

Booth closed out his bank account by withdrawing $25.[264]

March 17, Friday Washington

Booth visited John Mathews at the Petersen boarding house across from Ford's Theatre and learned that President Lincoln would attend a play at Campbell General Hospital later in the day.[265]

Booth, Surratt, Powell, Arnold, Atzerodt, and O'Laughlen rode out Seventh Street to intercept and capture President Lincoln. Lincoln did not appear, and the group disbanded.[266]

David Herold, driving Booth's buggy, took the weapons-filled trunk to the town of T.B. in southern Maryland.[267]

Sarah Slater signed in at St. Lawrence Hall in Montreal using her mother's maiden name, A. Reynaud.[268]

President Lincoln gave a short speech at 4 p.m. at the National Hotel. Booth, by one account, was present.[269]

March 18, Saturday Washington

John Surratt and George Atzerodt met David Herold, took the weapons to the Surratt Tavern, and asked innkeeper John Lloyd to hide them.[270]

Booth attended a morning rehearsal at Ford's Theatre. After the rehearsal Booth and McCullough rode horses along the by-roads near the Anacostia River.[271]

Booth played Pescara in *The Apostate* in the evening for the benefit of John McCullough. Surratt, Weichmann, Atzerodt, and Herold attended this, Booth's last stage appearance.[272]

After the play, Booth had a drink with Atzerodt, Herold, and Weichmann.[273]

Atzerodt checked into the Pennsylvania House Hotel, where he would stay until April 12.[274]

Powell traveled to New York.[275]

Arnold and O'Laughlen notified their landlord that they were moving out.[276]

March 19, Sunday Washington

Roderick D. Watson, a neighbor of Thomas Jones, wrote to John Surratt asking him to come to New York "on important business." He probably wanted Surratt to escort Sarah Slater to Washington.[277]

March 20, Monday Washington

Through a mix-up, Booth was scheduled to appear at a theatre in Louisville.[278]

John Surratt told Weichmann he had received a letter from "Wood" [Powell] from New York.[279]

Arnold and O'Laughlen checked out of their D Street boarding house and returned to Baltimore.[280] For them, the plot was over.

March 21, Tuesday En route to New York

Booth took the 7:30 p.m. train, which would get him to New York the next morning.[281]

President and Mrs. Lincoln attended a performance of an opera at Grover's Theatre.[282]

March 22, Wednesday New York

Booth was standing on the steps of the Metropolitan Hotel on Broadway when he spotted John Barron, his friend and fellow member of the Richmond stock company several years before.

Barron thought Booth looked either troubled or ill. Later, Barron thought Booth was about to confide in him about the plot, but when Barron opened his civilian overcoat Booth saw his Union uniform and cut the conversation short.[283]

[Date approximate] Booth told Sam Chester the "affair" had fallen through because certain parties had backed out. He said the horses were being sold and he would recoup some of the $4,000 he had spent.[284]

Edwin Booth completed a record 100 performances of *Hamlet* at the Winter Garden Theatre in New York. It is likely that John witnessed this performance, in which his friend Sam Chester had a role.

Junius Brutus Booth, Jr., noted in his diary: "John came on to see Miss Hale."[285]

March 23, Thursday New York

At the St. Nicholas Hotel, Booth telegraphed Weichmann: "Tell John to telegraph number and street at once."[286] John Surratt had arranged a room in Washington for Powell. Upon receiving this information, Booth informed Powell of the address of the Herndon House in Washington.

Sarah Slater arrived in New York on her way to Richmond.[287]

Dr. Mudd was in Washington but did not see any of the conspirators.[288]

President Lincoln left Washington to confer with General Grant at City Point, Virginia.[289] He would not return until April 9.

March 24, Friday En route to Baltimore

Augustus Howell, who was to take Sarah Slater to Richmond, was arrested as a spy at the Surratt Tavern in Surrattsville.[290]

March 25, Saturday Washington

Booth arrived at Barnum's Hotel in Baltimore shortly after 3:30 a.m., having taken the train from Philadelphia.[291] He may have been escorting Slater.

Booth left Sam Arnold a card asking him to come to Barnum's Hotel. When Arnold arrived Booth had departed, but he had left a note asking Arnold to give the abduction plot one more try and then abandon it forever.[292]

Booth took the 7 a.m. train for Washington.[293]

Booth registered at the National Hotel in Washington.

It is possible Booth had escorted Sarah Slater from New York or Baltimore to Washington. In the morning John Surratt and Slater drove up to Mary Surratt's boarding house in a two-horse carriage. Mary got into the carriage and traveled with the two as far as Surrattsville; she then returned to Washington by stage. In Surrattsville they learned that Augustus Howell had been arrested. John Surratt volunteered to escort Slater to Richmond. Later, Mary told Weichmann that John had gone to Richmond to get a clerkship.[294]

Confederate Captain Robert Cobb Kennedy, who had attempted to burn New York, was hanged in that city.[295]

March 26, Sunday Washington

Newspaperman George Alfred Townsend encountered Booth at the Metropolitan Hotel on Pennsylvania Avenue. Soon several others joined them, and they adjourned to a private club room.[296]

Weichmann, sent by Mary Surratt to ask Booth to drop by, found him with John McCullough.[297]

David Barry, a friend of John Surratt, returned the carriage and horses to Howard's Stable and stopped by Mary Surratt's house to tell her John had gone to Richmond. Mary introduced Barry to Booth and Atzerodt, who were at her house.[298] Mary Surratt told Booth of Howell's arrest and that her son had escorted Sarah Slater to Richmond.

John Surratt sent a note from Port Tobacco asking his stable keeper to allow Booth to use "his" horses.[299]

John McCullough left Washington for New York on the evening train.[300]

March 27, Monday Washington

The *Washington Evening Star* advertised that the president would be at Ford's Theatre on Wednesday.[301] The reservation was canceled later.

Booth wired O'Laughlen: "Get word to Sam. Come on, with or without him, Wednesday morning. We sell that day sure. Don't fail."[302]

Powell came to Washington and registered at the Herndon House under the name of Kincheloe.[303]

Atzerodt left the Pennsylvania House Hotel and returned the next day.[304]

Arnold wrote to Booth: "You know full

that the G—t suspicions something.... Go and see how it will be taken at R—d."[305]

March 28, Tuesday Washington

Booth received a letter from his mother written on March 26 in which she affirmed: "I have never yet doubted your love and devotion to me—in fact I always gave you praise for being the fondest of all my boys, but since you leave me in grief I must doubt it.... Heaven guard you, is my constant prayer."[306]

Atzerodt, who had been in Port Tobacco, returned to Washington.[307]

March 29, Wednesday Washington

On or about this date, Booth visited Ellen Starr at the brothel on Ohio Avenue.[308]

Booth paid the stable bill for the one-eyed horse and the light bay horse at Howard's Stable.[309]

John Surratt and Sarah Slater arrived in Richmond in the evening.[310]

March 30, Thursday Washington

On or about this date, Booth attended a performance at Ford's Theatre with Elizabeth and Lucy Hale.[311]

March 31, Friday Washington

Arnold and O'Laughlen traveled from Baltimore to Washington, where they ran into Atzerodt at the train station. The two met Booth in his hotel room at 2 p.m. Booth said the plot was abandoned forever and that he would return to acting. O'Laughlen asked Booth for $500, which Booth had borrowed from his brother.[312]

Atzerodt and Herold took the one-eyed horse and the light bay horse away from Howard's Stable.[313]

At 6:30 p.m. Booth and Atzerodt boarded the one-eyed horse and the light bay horse at Nailor's Stable. Booth told Atzerodt to sell the one-eyed horse.[314]

Atzerodt bragged to hotel clerk John Greenawalt that some day he would leave and return "with as much gold as will keep me all my lifetime." The plot was not over as far as he was concerned.[315]

April 1, Saturday Baltimore?

Booth left Washington for Baltimore on the afternoon train.[316]

Confederate Secretary of State Judah Benjamin asked John Surratt to carry dispatches to Canada.[317] Later, Surratt told Weichmann he had seen both Benjamin and President Jefferson Davis.[318]

John Surratt and Sarah Slater left Richmond for Washington in the morning.[319]

Benjamin Franklin Stringfellow, a Confederate agent who had been working in Washington, started his return trip to Richmond, leaving in the afternoon. He spent the night twelve miles from Washington, probably at the Surratt Tavern. Mary Surratt travelled in a buggy to Surrattsville, and it is likely she transported Stringfellow. Mary's brother, John Zadoc Jenkins, then returned to Washington with her.[320]

Sam Arnold left Baltimore for Fort Monroe, Virginia, where he obtained a job as a clerk.[321]

April 2, Sunday New York

John McCullough chatted with Booth at the Metropolitan Hotel about a proposed summer engagement in Montreal.[322]

Booth responded to Junius's suggestion that he could make more money in the oil region by saying that he would not live in the oil region for all the wealth in the area. He stated that he was in love with a lady in Washington, and that the relationship was worth more to him than all the money he could make.[323]

Before church, Mary Surratt sent Weichmann to ask Booth to visit her. If he could not be found, she asked him to bring Atzerodt. Mary did not know Booth had left the city. Weichmann found Atzerodt, and they rode horses from the Pennsylvania House to the Surratt boarding house on H Street. Atzerodt and Mary Surratt had a private conversation.[324]

In the afternoon Mary Surratt again sent Weichmann for Atzerodt. She wanted to borrow one of the horses for the use of her brother. Atzerodt went to the Herndon House to ask Powell for approval to use one of Booth's horses, and he refused.[325]

Richmond was evacuated and fell to Union forces.

April 3, Monday New York

At 4 p.m. John Surratt and Sarah Slater arrived in Washington on the Leonardtown, Maryland, stage. Slater took a room at the Metropolitan Hotel.[326]

John Surratt advised Atzerodt to go home to Port Tobacco and go to work.[327]

At 8:30 p.m. John Surratt came to the Surratt boarding house. At about 9:30 Surratt and Weichmann went out for oysters. Surratt told Weichmann he was leaving for Montreal. He did not return with Weichmann because a detective had called at the house earlier. Weichmann told Mary Surratt her son had left for Montreal.[328]

April 4, Tuesday En route to Newport

John Surratt and Sarah Slater left Washington for New York.[329]

Booth and a female companion boarded the steamer *Empire State* at 4 p.m. The ship traveled along Long Island Sound and reached Newport, Rhode Island, the next morning.[330]

President Lincoln toured Richmond.[331]

April 5, Wednesday Boston

John Surratt inquired at Edwin's house in New York and was told that John Wilkes had left for Boston. Surratt then left for Montreal.[332]

The steamboat carrying Booth and his companion arrived in Newport, Rhode Island, at about 8 a.m. He registered as "J. W. Booth & Lady, Boston" at the Aquidneck House. After a long walk the couple left for Boston on the three o'clock train.[333]

Booth saw Edwin play *Hamlet* and talked to actress Rachel Noah backstage.[334]

[Date approximate] Mary Surratt, returning from an evening service at church, called on Powell at his hotel.[335]

April 6, Thursday Boston

Booth attracted attention with a fine display of marksmanship at a shooting gallery near the Parker House.[336]

Booth visited Edwin at the theatre.[337]

Booth encountered his friend Orlando Tompkins on Washington Street and took him to a jewelry store, where he bought a ring inscribed "J.W.B. to O.T. April 6, 1865" for Tompkins. As he handed it to Tompkins he said, "Here, Doctor, I never gave you anything before and I may never see you again."[338]

John Surratt delivered dispatches to Confederate General Edwin G. Lee in Montreal and stayed in Montreal, fearing arrest in Washington.[339]

April 7, Friday New York

Booth traveled from Boston to New York.

Booth was drinking heavily and was loudly drunk when Sam Chester saw him. He bragged that he'd had a splendid chance to kill the president at the inauguration.[340]

April 8, Saturday Washington

While waiting for train connections in Philadelphia, Booth wrote to Sam Chester, relating that he would soon be leaving for Oil City.[341]

Booth went on to Washington and registered at the National Hotel.[342]

[Date approximate] Lucy Hale agreed to return from Spain within a year, with or without her father, to marry Booth.[343]

April 9, Sunday Washington

General Robert E. Lee surrendered his Confederate army to General Ulysses S. Grant at Appomattox Court House, Virginia.

President Lincoln returned to Washington in the evening.[344]

April 10, Monday Washington

Booth called at the Surratt boarding house in the afternoon and asked Mary Surratt about John. He also chatted with Weichmann.[345]

H. B. Phillips, an actor at Ford's Theatre, saw Booth on Pennsylvania Avenue. In response to Phillips' request to join him for a drink, Booth replied that he would do "anything to drive away the blues."[346]

Booth practiced shooting at a gallery at Ninth and Pennsylvania Avenue.[347]

Booth told Ned Spangler he would be leaving Washington and asked him to attempt to sell his horse, harness, and buggy at an auction.[348]

April 11, Tuesday Washington

Mary Surratt, needing to go to Surrattsville on business, sent Weichmann to ask Booth for the loan of his buggy. Booth explained that his buggy was being sold and gave Weichmann money to rent a buggy.[349]

Booth again practiced shooting at a gallery.[350]

Mary Surratt and Weichmann passed her tenant John Lloyd on the road. Mary said the carbines which Surratt had Lloyd hide on March 18 would be called for soon.

At 6 p.m. Spangler informed Booth that he had attempted to sell the horse and buggy at a horse auction, but the reserve price of $260 had not been met. Booth asked Spangler to keep trying to sell them.[351]

At the White House, Booth, Herold, and Powell heard President Lincoln propose limited suffrage for black men. Booth said, "That is the last speech he will ever make."[352]

April 12, Wednesday Washington

Blockade-runner Richard M. Smoot called at Mary Surratt's house to get the balance of payment for his boat. Mary informed him that the boat might be needed this night.[353]

In the morning Atzerodt checked out of the Pennsylvania House, saying he would be gone for a few days.[354]

Atzerodt took the one-eyed horse away from Nailor's Stable. He had recently sold the light bay. Spangler sold the horse and buggy, which had been kept together in the stable behind Ford's Theatre, for $260.[355]

[Date approximate] Between four and five o'clock Atzerodt visited the Kirkwood House and asked for Vice President Andrew Johnson's room number. A patron showed him the room and pointed out the Vice President in the dining room.[356]

In the evening Booth visited the ticket office at Ford's Theatre for half an hour and talked derogatorily about blacks.[357]

John Surratt, sent by Confederate General Edwin Lee, arrived in Elmira, New York, to ascertain the layout of the prison holding captured Confederate soldiers. He may have been accompanied by Sarah Slater.[358]

April 13, Thursday Washington

Booth went to Ford's Theatre in the morning.[359]

Booth asked the manager of Grover's Theatre if he intended to invite the president to the theatre that night.[360]

General Grant and Captain Robert Lincoln, a member of Grant's staff, arrived in Washington.

Powell was seen at Secretary of State Seward's house.[361]

Michael O'Laughlen and friends came to Washington to see the Grand Illumination. O'Laughlen looked for Booth at the National Hotel between four and five o'clock.[362]

Booth, Herold, Atzerodt, and Powell met in the latter's room at the Herndon House. Booth asked Atzerodt to register at the Kirkwood House the next morning in order to establish a reason for being there.[363]

April 14, Friday Surrattsville and
Bryantown

Booth wrote to his mother at 2 a.m.[364]

Booth had breakfast at his hotel.

Powell again strolled past Seward's house.[365]

Herold asked Atzerodt to rent a horse so he could go to the Surratt Tavern, operated by John Lloyd, and "see after" some items there.[366]

Atzerodt registered at the Kirkwood House at 8 a.m.[367]

O'Laughlen looked for Booth, but seems not to have found him.[368]

Booth walked to Mary Surratt's boarding house and learned that she was going to drive to Surrattsville on business, making it unnecessary for Atzerodt to go. Booth said he would return with his binoculars before she left so that she could drop them off at the Surratt Tavern. He also asked her to tell tavern-keeper John Lloyd to take the carbines from their hiding place; they would be picked up that night.[369]

At about noon Booth came down Tenth Street to Ford's Theatre and stopped there to read a letter. Theatre manager Harry Ford told him that President Lincoln and General Grant would attend the performance of *Our American Cousin* that night.

At 12:30 p.m. Booth reserved a horse at Pumphrey's Stable.[370]

At 2:30 p.m. Booth returned to the Surratt boarding house with his binoculars.[371]

At about 4:30 p.m. Booth picked up his rented horse at Pumphrey's Stable.[372]

Booth saw John Mathews on Pennsylvania Avenue near Willard's Hotel and gave him a letter to be delivered the next day. Booth galloped after General Grant's passing carriage.[373]

Booth left a note for Vice President Andrew Johnson at the Kirkwood House.[374]

At about sundown Mary Surratt and Weichmann gave Booth's message to John Lloyd at the Surratt Tavern.[375]

Booth stabled his rented horse behind Ford's Theatre.

Booth walked to his hotel.

At 8 p.m. at the Herndon House, Booth said he would kill the president and General Grant. He assigned Powell to kill Secretary of State Seward and Herold and Atzerodt to kill Vice President Johnson. Atzerodt refused to cooperate.

At 9 p.m., according to Weichmann, Booth visited Mary Surratt, perhaps to confirm that she had seen Lloyd and delivered his binoculars.[376]

At 9:30 p.m. blockade-runner Richard M. Smoot again called on Mary Surratt. In "feverish excitement" she said the boat would be needed this night. She warned him to leave the city.[377]

At about 9:30 p.m. Booth led his horse to the rear door of Ford's Theatre.

Booth walked through a passage to the front of Ford's Theatre and passed through the box office into the theatre. He had a drink at the Star Saloon.

Booth entered the theatre again, surveyed the house, climbed the stairs to the Dress Circle, entered the president's box, and shot President Lincoln from behind.

Booth jumped to the stage, ran to the back door, mounted his horse, and rode away.

Booth was seen riding furiously on the south side of the Capitol.[378]

Booth and Herold met on the road to Surrattsville.

10

Useless: 1865–1869

John Wilkes Booth spurred his horse to a gallop, passed his stable, slowed to turn left into Baptist Alley, and again slowed to turn right on F Street. He rode past the Capitol Building to Pennsylvania Avenue; a right turn on Eleventh Street then led him to the Navy Yard Bridge, which would take him south. As Booth, riding rapidly, approached the bridge, a sentry brought him to a halt. At twenty to twenty-five minutes before eleven o'clock, Sergeant Silas T. Cobb stepped forward to interview Booth. Cobb noticed that the horse had been ridden hard and was restive. In contrast to the horse, the rider—a muscular man with a black mustache and clear, white skin—seemed calm. Possibly Cobb, a very keen observer, was mistaken when he recalled that the rider was wearing a dark, felt hat. Booth's hat had been left at the theatre.

In response to Cobb's questions, Booth calmly gave his name as "Booth" and said he was going to his home near Beantown (now Waldorf, Maryland). Cobb explained that the bridge was closed after nine o'clock. Booth replied that he had waited for the moon to rise to light his way. The moon, four days past full, had risen at 10:01 p.m. When Cobb allowed him to pass, Booth said, "Hell! I guess there'll be no trouble about that." Booth then rode his horse at a walk across the bridge.

About ten minutes after Booth left, David Herold rode up. Cobb described Herold as heavier than Booth. Herold did not ask any questions to determine whether Booth

had already crossed the river. Cobb soon allowed him to cross.[1]

Earlier in the evening, after the Herndon House meeting broke up, Booth had parted from Herold and George Atzerodt on Ninth Street in front of the hotel. The plan started to crumble immediately. Atzerodt refused to give Herold the key to his room at the Kirkwood House. Herold's gun was in the room, and so was Booth's coat, packed with items for the escape. Herold rushed back to Booth, who told him to bring Atzerodt to him. Herold found Atzerodt, still uncooperative, at the Oyster Bay bar.[2] He probably tried to reason with the stubborn German and may have had a drink or two with him. Herold soon left the bar and retrieved his rented horse. Atzerodt held his post at the Oyster Bay until nearly ten o'clock. Previously, he had asked the stableman at Nailor's Stable to leave the saddle on his rented horse and said he would pick it up at 10 p.m. When Atzerodt returned to the stable, he appeared to be drunk and was very excited. After having a drink with the stableman, he mounted his horse, rode a block and a half to the Kirkwood House, tied the horse, and entered.[3] If he intended to carry out his assignment to kill Vice President Johnson, he soon changed his mind.

Atzerodt rode out C Street and passed between the Old Capitol Prison and the new Capitol Building. Possibly he was trying to intercept one or more of the others on their way to the Navy Yard Bridge. He returned on

Pennsylvania Avenue, where he encountered cavalry and heard that President Lincoln had been assassinated. He rode up Eighth Street and dropped his horse off at the stable. He then walked to the Herndon House, probably hoping to find Lewis Powell or the others; having no luck, he took a horse car to the Navy Yard. Finally, he settled into a room at the Pennsylvania House, alternatively known as the Kimmel House.[4]

Herold's movements after leaving Atzerodt at the Oyster Bay at about nine o'clock are not known with certainty. A reporter later quoted Herold as saying he "consented to see that Powell undertook his work" and then was to guide Booth and Powell through Maryland.[5] This description of events was different from his initial assignment to aid Atzerodt and suggests that Herold again saw Booth or Powell, or both, after leaving the Oyster Bay. Perhaps Herold explained that Atzerodt simply would not cooperate, and Booth assigned him to go with Powell and guide him to the Navy Yard Bridge. The reporter must have garbled Herold's words at least partially, for certainly Herold's role, whatever it may have been, was not to assure that Powell would do his work. Powell did not have much confidence in Herold; he had called him a "little blab" and had told Booth he was never satisfied with him.[6]

Powell, accompanied perhaps by Herold, rode the one-eyed horse to Secretary of State William Seward's house on the square opposite the White House. If Herold was there, he waited in the shadows while Powell coordinated his entry into the Seward house to about the same time Booth was going to assassinate the president. Powell attempted to enter the building by claiming he had medicine which he needed to deliver personally to Seward, who was in bed recovering from a carriage accident. When that approach failed, he forced his way in. With some difficulty, Powell found the room in which Seward was convalescing and attempted to kill the Secretary of State with a knife. He left a scene of carnage, having severely assaulted Seward and three others. Powell fled through the maze of Washington streets and soon became lost.[7]

Herold, perhaps hearing the commotion in the Seward house, rode his horse south on Fifteenth Street and east on Pennsylvania Avenue. This was the most direct route to the Navy Yard Bridge and would possibly allow him to connect with Atzerodt. Herold was soon spotted and chased by Nailor's stableman, John Fletcher, who had rented him the now-overdue horse. Herold turned his horse, galloped up Fourteenth Street, and turned right on F Street. Any thoughts of meeting Atzerodt or picking up Booth's coat were gone. He may have noticed a commotion to his right at Ford's Theatre as he crossed Tenth Street. Fletcher, wanting to retrieve his horse, saddled another and rode toward the Navy Yard Bridge, where he assumed Herold was heading. Fletcher ended his pursuit at the bridge.[8]

Booth, meanwhile, rode into Uniontown (now Anacostia), turned left, and started to ascend Good Hope Hill. Polk Gardiner, heading to Washington with a friend, observed Booth approaching and riding "very fast." Booth stopped and asked whether Gardiner had passed another horseman. Gardiner responded in the negative. Booth now knew Herold was not ahead of him. Then Booth asked directions and rode on. When Gardiner reached the bottom of the hill, he saw Herold approaching at a gallop. He heard Herold ask some teamsters at the side of the road whether a horseman had passed. Yes, they said.[9]

First Booth, then Herold, passed the forts at the top of Good Hope Hill. Then Booth may have slowed his pace a bit to preserve his horse and to allow Herold to catch up. At Soper's Hill, about eight miles from Washington, Herold caught up with Booth. The men told each other what they had done as they rode on. Booth's leg was broken. It may have been injured when he jumped to the stage; if so, the break did not hinder his running out of the theatre, mounting his horse, or riding at a fast pace. It is more likely that Booth's horse fell on the dark road, resulting in the injury. Booth and Herold traded horses so Booth could ride the gentler horse.[10]

The men soon approached a broken-down wagon at the side of the road, where George Thompson and Henry Butler were waiting for help to arrive. Wanting to mislead any pursuers, Booth or Herold asked the two men to say they had taken the Marlboro Road.[11]

The fugitives arrived at the Surratt Tavern, twelve miles from Ford's Theatre, just after midnight. John Lloyd, the tavern's lessee, was drunk. Herold jumped off his horse and knocked on the door. When Lloyd opened it, Herold urgently requested, "For God's sake, make haste and get those things!" The "things" were the field glasses and two carbines that Mary Surratt had asked him to have ready. While Lloyd retrieved them, Herold went to the bar for a bottle of whiskey and brought it to Booth, who remained mounted on the large horse. Lloyd soon brought the items out and gave them to Herold, who took the binoculars, ammunition, and one of the carbines. Herold then took the bottle of whiskey inside and returned.[12]

Booth explained to Lloyd that he could not carry the other carbine because his horse had fallen and his leg was broken. He told Lloyd he wanted to find a surgeon to set the leg. Lloyd thought Booth was drunk and appeared to be in great pain.[13]

As the men were about to ride away, Booth bragged to Lloyd, "I am pretty certain that we have assassinated the President and Secretary Seward." The men's stop had lasted only five minutes. They rode away at a full gallop, hoping to cross the Potomac River as quickly as possible and find the protection of friends. Booth was in such pain, however, that he could not continue without medical attention. When Booth said he must go to Dr. Mudd's house for treatment, Herold tried to dissuade him because it would delay their crossing. Booth insisted.[14]

Four hours and fifteen miles after leaving the Surratt Tavern, the fugitives arrived at the home of Dr. Samuel A. Mudd. Herold knocked on the door while Booth remained on his horse. Receiving no response, Herold repeated his knock. Finally Dr. Mudd opened the door. Mudd did not know Herold, but he did know Booth and must have recognized him immediately. The men explained that Booth's leg was injured. Mudd and Herold helped Booth off his horse. While Herold held the horses, Mudd helped Booth into the house to a sofa in the parlor. Mrs. Mudd thought Booth, who had red and swollen eyes, looked as if he had been "drinking very hard."[15] After Mudd obtained a lamp, Booth was carried upstairs to the front room. The doctor cut the boot from Booth's left leg and found that the small outer bone, the fibula, had a clean break two inches above the instep. Booth complained of severe pain in his back. Dr. Mudd and Herold left Booth to rest.[16]

After setting the leg, the doctor went back to bed until seven o'clock, when he and Herold had breakfast. In Washington, President Lincoln died at 7:22 a.m. After breakfast Herold asked for a razor for Booth. When Mudd went upstairs a short time later, Booth had shaved off his mustache.[17] Dr. Mudd thought Booth was "much debilitated" and very pale. The doctor then went about the farm giving directions for the day's work. He returned just before noon to check on Booth. Then he went to the barn and helped one of his workers make a pair of crutches. He also found a low-cut shoe for Booth.[18]

At the midday meal Herold asked Mudd where he could get a carriage; the two men rode out to attempt to borrow one. While Herold was gone, Mrs. Mudd visited Booth for about five minutes. Concerned because he had not eaten anything all day, she brought him wine, cake, and oranges. When he asked for brandy, she offered him whiskey. He declined. He told her that when his horse fell he had broken his leg and injured his back by striking a stone. The left front leg of the bay mare was lame, which was consistent with a fall.[19] Herold soon returned, having been gone only half an hour.[20]

Dr. Mudd rode into Bryantown, where he found Federal cavalry searching for Booth. When Mudd observed that the troops were preventing people from leaving the town, he evaded them.[21] Mudd later said that when he returned home, the fugitives were about to leave. It seems most likely Mudd told them to leave because he was afraid of the consequences of Booth being found at his house.[22] Booth pulled out a thick roll of greenbacks and paid Dr. Mudd $25 for setting his leg.[23]

Herold helped Booth down the stairs and then went out the front door, where his horse was tied. Booth could have had his horse brought to him but, instead, hobbled on his crutches to the stable over a hundred yards from the house.[24]

While Booth had freely told Lloyd he had assassinated the president, it is not clear that Booth also told Dr. Mudd. It was in Booth's nature to tell what he had done. Dr. Mudd had aided the plot considerably by introducing Booth to Thomas Harbin and John Surratt. Mudd may have been aware of the plan to capture the president; Atzerodt later said that Booth had sent "liquors & provisions for the trip with the President" to Mudd.[25] But Mudd probably knew nothing in advance of the assassination.[26]

In the following days both Mudd and Lloyd would tell investigators that Booth said his leg had been broken when his horse slipped and fell. If Booth had told them he broke his leg when he jumped to the stage after shooting the president, it is unlikely they would have reported that to investigators; doing so would have been admission that they knowingly helped the assassin escape. Several days after the assassination, for the benefit of posterity, Booth wrote in his diary that he had broken his leg while jumping. In whatever manner his leg had been broken, the pain oc-casioned by riding and the pain in the lower back had slowed his progress considerably.[27]

Dr. Mudd's house was near the northern end of Zekiah Swamp, a morass that extends fifteen miles to the Potomac River. Perhaps in an attempt to mislead authorities, Dr. Mudd later stated that Booth and Herold headed west across the swamp to Piney Church, about five miles away.[28] Booth and Herold soon changed direction and crossed the north/south road to the east of Dr. Mudd's farm. Before long the men were lost. They had traveled about two miles and were near the home of Henry Mudd, Dr. Mudd's father. At dusk Electus Thomas, who worked for Henry Mudd, saw David Herold approaching on foot. Herold asked, "Uncle, where am I at?" Which way was east, west, north, south? Somewhat oriented, Herold walked back to where he had left Booth.[29]

The men slowly worked their way south, swinging east of Bryantown to avoid the cavalry there. They soon were lost in the dark. At about nine o'clock they encountered Oswell Swan, a black tobacco farmer. Swan provided them with milk, whiskey, and bread. The fugitives asked Swan to guide them to the home of William Burtle, about a mile away. While on the way they determined that Burtle wasn't needed; Swan could take them across the swamp to their next objective, the home of Samuel Cox, a leader of the Confederate underground in southern Maryland. Cox's place was about twelve miles south and on the west side of the swamp, only three miles from the Potomac River.[30]

The fugitives arrived at the Cox plantation, known as "Rich Hill," at about 1 a.m. Herold rode up to the house, leaving Booth and Swan some distance away. Responding to Herold's knock, Cox opened a window and asked who was there. Herold explained that he and another man wanted to come in. Cox asked their identity, and Herold prevaricated. Herold revealed that his friend had an injured foot. Cox had heard of the assassination the previous day and quickly surmised the identity of the men. When he came out of his house with a candle, Booth rode up. After he verified that he was speaking to Cox, Booth told him what he had done. He showed his tattooed hand to identify himself. Cox invited the men into the house.[31]

Swan, who had been paid $12 for his services, waited outside, perhaps hoping to earn more. Sometime between 3 and 4 a.m. on Sunday, the men came out. When Herold absent-mindedly headed for his horse, Booth, annoyed, called, "Don't you know I can't get on." Herold directed Swan to put his hands under Booth's crotch and lift him onto his horse. One of the fugitives, perhaps hoping to give Cox cover, said, "I thought Cox was a man of Southern feeling," as if Cox had rejected them.[32]

Cox swung into action. He had his overseer, Franklin Robey, provide the men with food and guide them to a thick growth of pines about a mile away.[33] Cox also sent for his foster brother, Thomas A. Jones. Cox told Jones that the assassin had been at his house and needed assistance in crossing the river. Jones agreed to help. Jones was a vital part of the loose network which had moved mail and people between Richmond and Washington during the war. As chief Confederate signal agent in Maryland, he often transported people across the Potomac. Further, Jones was a brother-in-law of Thomas Harbin.[34]

It was late morning now as Jones left Cox and headed for the hiding place. As Jones approached, he found Booth's bay mare saddled and un-tethered. When Jones gave the signal whistle, Herold emerged from the pines holding a cocked carbine. Herold took Jones to Booth, who was lying on the ground, wrapped in a blanket, his head supported on his hand, his leg bandaged and propped up. Booth identified himself by the tattooed initials on his hand. Jones observed that Booth was quite pale and in great pain. Jones explained that Union troops were in the neighborhood, so they would have to wait for a propitious time to cross the river. Booth, with

his pistols and knife close at hand, made it clear that he would not allow himself to be taken alive.[35] Jones found Booth interested in getting food, crossing the river, and finding out what was being said about the assassination. Jones later wrote that Booth "seemed very desirous to know what the world thought of his deed, and asked me to bring him some newspapers," which Jones then did.[36]

A huge manhunt was underway. Secretary of War Edwin M. Stanton coordinated the efforts of Washington Provost Marshal James R. O'Beirne, Washington Police Superintendent Almarin C. Richards, and Major General Christopher C. Auger, who commanded the defenses of the capital. Hundreds of troops were in the immediate area where Booth and Herold were hiding. The fugitives often heard troops ride by. The presence of the horses threatened to give them away, and soon they were removed; accounts vary as to their fate.

Booth recorded his thoughts in his notebook:

April 14, Friday, the Ides.—Until today nothing was ever thought of sacrificing to our country's wrongs. For six months we had worked to capture, but our cause being almost lost, something decisive and great must be done. But its failure was owing to others, who did not strike for their country with a heart. I struck boldly, and not as the papers say. I walked with a firm step through a thousand of his friends, was stopped, but pushed on. A colonel was at his side. I shouted Sic semper before I fired. In jumping broke my leg. I passed all his pickets, rode sixty miles that night with the bone of my leg tearing the flesh at every jump. I can never repent it though we hated to kill. Our country owed all her troubles to him and God simply made me the instrument of his punishment. This country is not what it was. This forced Union is not what I have loved. I care not what becomes of me. I have no desire to outlive my country....

Booth's propensity to exaggerate, even fabricate, and glorify his actions is evident in his diary entries. Booth did not shout "Sic

Semper Tyrannis" before he fired. He rode about thirty miles that night, not sixty. Certainly he did not take note of Rathbone's rank as they struggled, but he referred to him in his diary as a colonel even though he knew Rathbone was a major from newspaper accounts. And, quite possibly, Booth did not break his leg in jumping to the stage.

Cox sent his overseer to visit the men several times.[37] Jones visited them briefly each day at mid-morning, bringing bread, butter, ham, fish, whiskey, coffee, and newspapers. Booth continued to read the newspapers with great interest. Each day Jones observed Booth's leg become more swollen, inflamed, and painful. The cold, cloudy, and damp weather chilled the bones; the ground was cold, and Booth wore a light suit. Jones found Booth to be a sympathetic figure. Once, when Booth pressed Jones to take them across the Potomac, a troop of cavalry passed close by. When the sound died away, Jones said, "You see my friend, we must wait." Booth replied, "Yes, I leave it all with you."

As evening approached on Thursday, April 20, Jones learned that the cavalry troops who had been camped nearby would be searching elsewhere. He reached the fugitives just after dark and told them they must cross the river that night. Jones and Herold lifted Booth, who groaned at each movement, onto Jones's horse. The night was damp, and dew drenched the men as they slipped past wet trees and shrubs. Jones led Booth and Herold about two and three-quarter miles to his house, "Huckleberry," and had them wait outside while he went in to get food. Jones related their conversation:

JONES: Wait here, while I go in and get you some supper, which you eat here while I get something for myself.

BOOTH: Oh, can't I go in and get some of your hot coffee?

JONES: Oh, my friend, it would not be safe. This is your last chance to get away. I have Negroes at the house; and if they see you, you are lost and so am I.[38]

Jones led Booth on his horse down a ravine about three quarters of a mile to the river, where a boat was hidden. Jones found the boat and positioned it in the water. The men carried Booth to the boat and settled him in the stern. With the aid of a candle and Booth's compass, Jones pointed out the way to Machodoc Creek on the other side. There a Mrs. Quesenberry might help if Jones's name were mentioned.[39]

As the men prepared to shove off, according to Jones, Booth offered to pay for the boat. Jones took $18, the amount he had paid for the boat. With some emotion, Booth said to Jones, "God bless you, my dear friend for all you have done for me. Good bye, old fellow."[40] However, Herold's description of the scene a few days later was less benign. Herold reported that "the damn scalawag" had gouged them $150 for the small skiff.[41]

The boat was equipped with only one paddle and a broken oar.[42] Booth, in the stern, steered with the oar. Keeping a straight line in the flat-bottomed, twelve-foot-long boat would be difficult. Their objective, the mouth of Machodoc Creek in Virginia, was southwest and down the river about eight miles away. Somehow they traveled about seven miles northwest and up the river to the mouth of Nanjemoy Creek on the Maryland side. They may have been lost in the fog at the mercy of tide and currents, or they may have drifted north to avoid a lightship and/or gunboat they encountered.

Rowing north up Nanjemoy Creek, they soon encountered King's Creek on the east shore, where the boat Surratt had bought in January had been hidden. Peregrine Davis's Indiantown Farm was just south of King's Creek. One of Atzerodt's assignments had been to lead the men to Indiantown, and that is exactly where they found themselves, despite Atzerodt's absence.[43] The men found a secluded spot and beached the boat. Herold helped Booth ashore. Herold, who knew the location well having hunted there, approached the house and asked Colonel John

J. Hughes for help. Hughes provided food and directed the fugitives to an unoccupied small frame house on the waterfront.[44]

Booth had sore arms. He had not been walking much, so the soreness was not caused by his crutches. Possibly he and Herold had taken turns at the oars.[45] Needing rest, the men did not attempt to cross to Virginia on Friday night.

Booth knew from the newspapers that he was not receiving the popular acclaim he had anticipated. His state of mind is evident from his diary entry written at Nanjemoy Creek:

Friday 21st—After being hunted like a dog through swamps, woods, and last night being chased by gun-boats till I was forced to return wet cold and starving, with every mans hand against me, I am here in despair. And why; For doing what Brutus was honored for, what made Tell a Hero. And yet I for striking down a greater tyrant than they ever knew am looked upon as a common cutthroat. My action was purer than either of theirs. One, hoped to be great himself. The other had not only his country's but his own wrongs to avenge. I hoped for no gain. I knew no private wrong. I struck for my country and that alone. A country groaned beneath this tyranny and prayed for this end. Yet now behold the cold hand they extend to me. God *cannot* pardon me if I have done wrong. Yet I cannot see any wrong except in serving a degenerate people. The little, the very little I left behind to clear my name, the Govrnt will not allow to be printed. So ends all. For my country I have given up all that makes life sweet and Holy, brought misery upon my family, and am sure there is no pardon in Heaven for me since man condemns me so.

I have only *heard* of what has been done (except what I did myself) and it fills me with horror. God try and forgive me and bless my mother. To night I will once more try the river with the intent to cross, though I have a greater desire to return to Washington and in a measure clear my name which I feel I can do.

I do not repent the blow I struck. I may before my God, but not to man. I think I have done well, though I am abandoned, with the curse of Cain upon me. When if the world knew my heart, *that one* blow would have made me great, though I did desire no greatness.

To night I try to escape these blood hounds once more. Who who can read his fate. God's will be done. I have too great a soul to die like a criminal. Oh may he, may he spare me that and let me die bravely. I bless the entire world. Have never hated or wronged anyone. This last was not a wrong, unless God deems it so. And its with Him, to damn or bless me. As for this brave boy with me, who often prays (yes before and since) with a true and sincere heart, was it crime in him, if so why can he pray the same I do not wish to shed a drop of blood, but "I must fight the course." Tis all thats left me.[46]

The Saturday edition of the *New York Tribune* noted: "LUCY HALE'S GRIEF— The unhappy lady—the daughter of a New England Senator—to whom Booth was affianced, is plunged in profoundest grief; but with womanly fidelity is slow to believe him guilty of this appalling crime, and asks, with touching pathos, for evidence of his innocence."[47]

Crossing from Nanjemoy Creek to Virginia was no easy matter; Thomas Nelson Conrad had been arrested attempting to cross earlier that week.[48] On Saturday at dusk Booth and Herold pushed off and rowed three miles to the Potomac, where they passed the Upper Cedar Point Lightship.[49] Herold later reported that "at sundown, we crossed the mouth of Nanjemoy Creek, passed within 300 yards of a gunboat, and landed at Mathias Point."[50] The distance from Nanjemoy to Mathias Point is four miles. If Herold knew of and attempted to find the Confederate spy camp located near the point, he failed. The men rowed south along the Virginia shoreline and pulled into Gambo Creek when they sighted a gunboat.

Herold, leaving Booth under a tree beside the creek, found a local farmer called "Old Sic," who directed him to the home of Elizabeth Quesenberry about a mile away. Quesenberry's house had been a stop on the clandestine Confederate mail route, and she was familiar with the Confederate operatives. Herold knocked on the door at 10 a.m. and chatted with Quesenberry's daughter, Lucy. They were soon joined by Joseph N. Baden, a paroled Confederate soldier who was staying with the Quesenberrys for a few days. Quickly Baden recognized that he was acquainted with Herold, a fact that seemed to embarrass the young man. Herold explained that he had a brother with a broken leg and asked for a conveyance or a horse. Quesenberry claimed later that she refused to help and that Herold as a result seemed surprised. She did agree, however, to send food out to the men at Gambo Creek.[51]

Quesenberry quickly located Thomas Harbin, who had crossed the river several days previously, perhaps attempting to find and aid the fugitives. Harbin and Baden, carrying food prepared by Mrs. Quesenberry, soon found Booth and Herold. Booth must have been surprised and pleased to see his acquaintance and one-time co-conspirator. Harbin knew it was dangerous to help the fugitives; he quickly departed after directing them to the nearby farm of William L. Bryant.[52]

Herold walked to the Bryant farm, arriving an hour before sundown. Herold paid Bryant $10 to take him and his "brother" on horseback eight miles to the summer home of Dr. Richard Stuart. Bryant saddled two horses. The men found Booth and headed for Dr. Stuart's house. Along the way another man joined the group. His identity is unclear; he may have been local resident Cadwallader W. Crismond, or possibly John Lewis Crismond, a Confederate private on detached duty. On the way Herold did all the talking; Booth said little. Herold told Bryant that Dr. Stuart had been recommended to them.[53]

At 8 p.m. Dr. Stuart answered a knock at his door and outside in the dark observed Herold carrying a carbine and Booth wrapped in a large shawl. When Herold asked for accommodations for the night, Stuart refused, but he agreed to feed them. The men walked into the house, ate, and departed after only fifteen minutes. They persisted in asking Stuart to let them stay. Stuart recalled, "I was suspicious of the urgency of the lame man. He desired to tell something I did not care to hear." When Booth told him, "We are Marylanders and want to go to [Confederate partisan ranger John Singleton] Mosby," Stuart told him Mosby had surrendered. When Booth said Dr. Mudd had set his leg and had recommended that they seek Stuart's help, Stuart claimed he did not know Mudd.[54]

When Bryant and Crismond started to ride away, Stuart ran several hundred yards after them and said the men could not stay with him. He told Bryant to take them away. Bryant guided them a quarter mile to the cabin of William Lucas, a black man. When Lucas answered their knock, the men forced their way into the cabin and told him they were going to stay overnight. When Lucas objected, Booth pulled out his knife and said, "Old man, how do you like that?" Lucas replied, "I do not like that at all." The fugitives slept in the cabin while Lucas and his sick wife spent the night on the front step, afraid to sleep for fear their horses would be stolen.[55]

When there was light in the morning Booth wrote a long note—more than a hundred words—to Dr. Stuart. While the note, which offered $5 for the food Stuart provided, was meant as an insult, it also gave the man cover. Booth ended the note, "I not only thank you but on account of the reluctant manner in which it was bestowed, I feel bound to pay for it. Yours respectfully, Stranger." The man who was being hunted by an angry nation then re-wrote the note to increase the insult by offering only $2.50.[56]

Before Booth and Herold left at seven o'clock on Monday morning, April 24, Booth handed $25 to Lucas's wife. Lucas's son Charley drove Booth and Herold in his wagon ten miles to the Rappahannock River. Booth seemed very fatigued and tried to sleep in the bed of the wagon. The wagon arrived at the ferry wharf in Port Conway between 10 and 11 a.m. Herold approached local resident William Rollins and asked for a drink of water. During the war Rollins had assisted the Confederate Signal Corps line of communication.[57] Herold took the dipper to his "brother," who remained in Lucas's wagon. At parting, Booth gave Charley Lucas the note for Dr. Stuart.

On returning the dipper, Herold asked Rollins to take them to Orange Court House. Orange, Virginia, had been in Mosby's area of operation, and perhaps the fugitives would find friends there. Rollins refused but offered to take them to Bowling Green for $10. Booth offered to pay more than the going rate to be rowed across the Rappahannock River, but Rollins refused; the tide was coming in, and he needed to place his fishing nets. Rollins then went fishing.[58]

As the fugitives waited for the tide to rise, three mounted Confederate soldiers who had served in Mosby's command rode up: Lieutenant Mortimer B. Ruggles, Private Absalom R. Bainbridge, and Private Willie Jett. Ruggles's father was Daniel Ruggles, a Confederate general then serving as Commissary General of Prisoners. The young lieutenant had been Thomas Nelson Conrad's second-in-command. The meeting of the soldiers and Booth may have been accidental, or perhaps the three had been sent to find and assist the fugitives.[59]

Herold approached the soldiers and asked what command they belonged to and where they were going. Soon, Booth, using his crutches, walked over to the group of men. Herold proposed they have a drink, which they refused. Herold asked Jett to step aside and then, with trembling voice, revealed that he and Booth were the "assassinators" of the president. Pointing at Booth, Herold said, "Yonder is J. Wilkes Booth, the man who killed the President." The soldiers agreed to help, and Rollins was informed that his services would not be needed.[60]

At about one o'clock, when the ferry finally arrived, Booth mounted Ruggles's horse and sat on it as the scow crossed the Rappahannock to Port Royal. Ruggles had borrowed the horse from his superior, Thomas Nelson Conrad.[61] Ruggles carried Booth's crutches.

On the Port Royal side of the river, Jett rode a few blocks to the home of the William Peyton family and asked the Peyton sisters if they would help a wounded Confederate soldier. They agreed but soon changed their minds after Booth entered the house and sat on a lounge. Booth, un-shaven and un-bathed, wore a black slouch hat, clothes that were raveled by contact with thorny undergrowth, and a long gray shawl.[62] The men rode on and stopped at several farms asking for shelter for Booth; at each they were rejected.[63]

Booth rode alone on Ruggles's horse, while the four other men rode double on the other two horses.[64] Herold began to speak of the assassination. Booth stopped him by saying, "That's nothing to brag about." Booth also said he did not intend to be taken alive. Booth told Ruggles that if he had known the South would not fight on, "he would never have struck the blow he did."[65] Finally, they came to Richard Garrett's farm, about three miles from the river.

At about 3 p.m. Bainbridge and Herold parted from the others at the outer gate to Garrett's farm. Herold's feet were sore, and he was badly in need of a new pair of shoes, which he hoped to get in Bowling Green.[66] As they parted, Herold said to Booth, "I'll be with you soon, John. Keep in good spirits." Booth replied, "Have no fear about me, Herold. I am among friends now." He turned his horse and rode to the farmhouse with Jett and Ruggles.[67]

Jett did the talking at the house. He introduced Booth to farm owner Richard Henry Garrett as John W. Boyd, a Confederate soldier wounded at Petersburg. Garrett agreed to take "Boyd" in until Wednesday morning, when Jett and the others would return. Booth got down, and the men rode away saying, "We will see you in a day or so."[68] John Garrett and Booth took seats on the porch and chatted.

The Garrett family consisted of Mr. and Mrs. Garrett, nine children, and Mrs. Garrett's sister, Lucinda Holloway. Booth soon captivated the younger ones, those not engaged in the work of the farm. They gathered around him on the grass as he demonstrated his pocket compass to them.

After supper, about eight o'clock, Booth sat on the front steps and smoked a pipe. Soon Jack Garrett, one of Richard's sons, proposed they go to bed. Booth ascended the stairs to the second floor of the house. As he disrobed, he removed a belt in which he carried two pistols and his knife and hung it at the head of the bed. As Garrett helped in removing Booth's boot he noticed the swelling of his "wounded" leg. Booth explained that it was not painful unless touched. Booth went to bed. Garrett and his younger brother William slept in another bed.

When Booth awoke on Tuesday morning, the family had already eaten breakfast. Refreshed from a long night's sleep, he walked with the aid of his crutches to the barn and about the farm. When Mrs. Garrett asked if he would like her to dress his wound, he turned her down, saying that it caused him no pain. Soon he was asleep again, this time on a bench on the front porch. After another walk he sat on the grass under an apple tree and told stories to the younger children.[69]

At the noon meal Jack Garrett revealed that he had heard the president had been assassinated and that a large reward had been offered for his capture. One of the boys said he would turn the assassin in for the reward given the chance. Booth responded, "Would you do such a thing?" When one of the daughters speculated that the assassin had been paid, Booth returned his own speculation that he had done it for "notoriety's sake."[70] Mr. Garrett asked "Boyd" if he had ever seen John Wilkes Booth. Yes, Booth replied, he

had seen the man in Richmond when he was quite young, around the time of the John Brown raid.[71]

After the noon meal Booth asked Jack Garrett to take down a map from the wall and lay it on the table. He said he wanted to go to Orange Court House and join others who were headed for Mexico. Soon Booth was sitting on a bench on the porch writing in his memorandum book: "I have too great a soul to die like a criminal. O may He spare me that, and let me die bravely! I do not wish to shed a drop of blood, but 'I must fight the course.' 'Tis all that's left me."

On the previous day, after leaving Booth with the Garretts, Ruggles and Jett rode away to join Herold and Bainbridge at a tavern run by Martha Carter and her four accommodating daughters. The men then rode several miles to Bowling Green. Herold and Bainbridge spent the night at a neighboring farm. By noon they were back in Bowling Green at the Star Hotel, where Jett was staying. Herold, Bainbridge, and Ruggles rode back to the Garrett farm, where they left Herold at the gate at about 3:30 p.m. When Booth heard the approaching horses, he demanded of Jack Garrett, "You go and get my pistols!" Booth strapped on the pistol belt and walked down the lane to meet Herold. After engaging in private conversation for about half an hour, they walked back to the house, where Booth introduced Herold as his cousin. Jack, having become suspicious of the men, told them that only his father, who was not present, could give permission to Herold to stay overnight.[72]

A half hour after they had left, Bainbridge and Ruggles returned to the Garrett farm, riding fast. Booth and Herold walked to meet them and were told Union cavalry was on the way. The two soldiers rode off. Herold helped Booth to the woods beyond the barn to hide and soon returned. Two hours later, after the Federal force had passed, Herold returned to the woods and brought Booth back to the house.[73]

Jack Garrett, sure now that something was amiss, told the guests they were no longer welcome to stay in the house. With no horses, Booth and Herold could not leave. Jack tried to hire a neighbor to take the men away, but the neighbor was out. Finally he agreed to take the men to Orange Court House the next morning. When Garrett told the men they could not stay in the house, Herold proposed that they sleep under the porch with the dogs. Garrett responded that the dogs would bite them. Garrett then agreed to let the men stay in the tobacco barn. After supper they went to the barn to sleep. As a precaution to prevent the men from taking the horses, William Garrett locked the men in the barn with their consent.[74] The Garrett brothers spent the night in a nearby corn crib to keep watch. The barn was a substantial building measuring forty-eight by fifty feet, with a plank floor throughout. It was packed with farm equipment and animal feed.[75]

The troops, a unit of twenty-six men led by Lieutenant Edward P. Doherty of the 16th New York Cavalry, were looking for Booth. Accompanying Doherty and his men were two civilian detectives, ex-army officers Lieutenant Colonel Everton Conger and Lieutenant Luther Byron Baker. Baker had shown pictures of Booth and Herold at the ferry landing, where the locals had recognized them. Baker learned that Willie Jett had accompanied the men and that Jett was courting a girl in Bowling Green. The troopers set out to find Jett, thinking Booth might be with him. At Bowling Green they found Jett, who agreed to lead them to Booth. At about 2 a.m. on Wednesday, April 26, the troopers descended on the Garrett farm and surrounded the house and barn. Baker woke Richard Garrett and was interrogating him when Jack Garrett came forward and led the troops to the barn.

Baker forced Jack Garrett to go into the barn, where he told the men they were surrounded and that surrender was their only option. Garrett pleaded with Booth to surrender to avoid having the barn burned. When Booth accused him of betrayal and reached behind him for a revolver, Garrett made a swift exit. Baker and Conger decided to fire the barn. A half hour was consumed as the men dismounted two at a time and led their horses away from the barn and secured them.

A part of the long conversation which ensued is reconstructed from the reports of the several participants[76]:

BAKER: You men had better come out of there. You are surrounded by fifty armed men. We know who you are. If you don't come out in five minutes, we will set the barn on fire.

BOOTH: Captain, This is a hard case. I don't know who you are. It may be that I am to be taken by my friends. Who do you take me for?

BAKER: Never mind who we are. We know who you are. You had better come out and deliver yourselves up.

Silence.

BOOTH: Give me time for reflection. I am alone, there is no one in here with me.

BAKER: We know that two men were in there and two must come out.

BAKER: We did not come to have a fight. We came to make you prisoners and we will, dead or alive.

BOOTH: This is a hard case, it may be that I am to be taken by my friends. Be fair and give me a show, I could have killed you a dozen times tonight, but I took you to be a brave man, and I believe you to be an honorable man. I am a cripple. I have but one leg. Draw your men back a hundred yards and I will fight you all. Give me a fair fight.

Col. Conger directed Will Garrett to pile brush at the side of the barn.

BOOTH TO WILL GARRETT: Young man, you had better stop that. If you put any more brush I will shoot you.

Silence.

BOOTH TO HEROLD: You damn coward! Will you leave me now? Surrender if you want, but I will fight and die like a man.

BOOTH: There is a man in here very anxious to surrender.

BAKER: Come to the door, deliver your arms to Mr. Garrett who will receive them and you can come out.

BOOTH: He has no arms; they are mine.

BAKER: I know what arms he carried in there and he has to bring the same out.

BOOTH: Upon my word of honor, he has no arms.

HEROLD: I know nothing of this man.

Doherty grabbed Herold's wrists as he left the barn.

BAKER: We will fire the barn in two minutes if you do not come out.

BOOTH: Give me a chance for my life, and I will come out and fight you.

Silence.

BAKER: Your time is up.

BOOTH: Well, my brave boys, you can prepare a stretcher for me. One more stain upon the old banner.

Conger set fire to a rear corner of the barn, and the flames spread rapidly. Booth dropped his crutch and, holding the carbine, approached the fire as if to put it out. Seeing that it was out of control, he limped toward the door, his carbine in one hand and a pistol in the other. Sergeant Boston Corbett took aim with his pistol through the wide openings between the boards of the barn and fired from a distance of about twelve feet. The bullet pierced Booth's neck, cutting through the vertebrae and severing the spinal cord. Booth fell on his back. Baker, Conger, and Doherty, still holding Herold, rushed into the barn. Baker had to twist the pistol to free it from Booth's grip. Doherty and Herold tried to find a rope to secure Booth, but it quickly became evident that restraint was not needed.

After Baker, Conger, and a soldier dragged Booth to a grassy patch outside the barn, he began to show signs of life. Water was splashed on his face and mouth. Conger saw that Booth was moving his lips and, with his ear close to Booth's mouth, heard him say, "Tell my mother I die for my country." Conger repeated it and Booth indicated yes. Booth then said, "Tell my mother I did what I thought was for the best." Conger noted the time of Booth's shooting as 3:15 a.m.

Soon the heat from the fire caused the men to move Booth to the front porch of the house. A mattress was obtained to support Booth's head. Booth's face was distorted, his chin being drawn down and to the side. His skin had a blue tinge, and he seemed to be in the greatest agony. Dr. Charles Urquhart had been summoned from Port Royal, and, upon examining the wound, said Booth would die in a short time. Baker bathed Booth's head and dipped a rag in water and moistened Booth's lips. Eventually he turned this duty over to Mrs. Garrett's sister, Lucinda Holloway. Herold, tied to a tree several yards from Booth, observed the scene.

BOOTH: Kill me. Kill me. Kill me.

BAKER: No Booth, we do not wish to kill you. We hope you may live.

BOOTH (seeing Willie Jett): Did Jett betray me?

CONGER: Jett has been taken prisoner.

BAKER: Oh, never mind about Jett.

BOOTH: My hands.

Baker raised his hands.

BOOTH: Useless, useless.

Booth asked to be turned on his back and began to choke. He was turned back. Booth was conscious for about forty minutes after being shot and then remained unconscious until he died at about 7:15 a.m.[77]

Conger went through Booth's clothing and took possession of the diary, a bill of exchange, $45 in greenbacks, a compass, keys, matches, wood shavings, a pipe, tobacco, a Catholic medal, a pin with a crystal inscribed "Dan Bryant to J. W. Booth," and a pocket knife. In a pocket of the diary Conger found five *cartes de visite* bearing the images of Lucy Hale and four actresses.

Mrs. Garrett washed the face of the corpse and knotted a handkerchief over the face to protect it. Then the body was sewn into a saddle blanket. Lieutenant Luther Byron Baker and Garrett neighbor Ned Freeman loaded the corpse into a one-horse wagon. They arrived at Port Royal at 9 a.m., crossed the Rappahannock River, and started for Belle Plain, expecting that the troops would catch up with them. The troops, less familiar with the area than Freeman, branched off on another road. The men and the wagon finally reached the Potomac at an old landing three miles above Belle Plain where the steamship *John S. Ide* was anchored and waiting to convey the party to Washington. Baker and Freeman carried the body to the edge of the river and hid it in bushes. Baker made his way to the military dock, obtained a rowboat and oarsmen, and retrieved the body.[78]

On the day the news of Booth's death was reported in the New York newspapers, Mary Ann Booth was handed a newspaper as she boarded a train from New York to Philadelphia to help her daughter Asia. On the train she read the details of her son's death and the message, "Tell mother I died for my country."[79]

The *John S. Ide* arrived at the Washington Navy Yard, and Booth's body and Herold were transferred to the monitor U.S.S. *Montauk* at 1:45 a.m. on April 27. The body, still wrapped in a blanket, was placed on a carpenter's bench. Sometime in the morning an unidentified lady accompanied by two Naval officers was allowed to visit the ship. It is difficult to imagine who other than Lucy Hale would have the desire and connections necessary to get on the ship.[80]

At 11 a.m. Surgeon General Joseph K. Barnes, Judge Advocate General Joseph Holt, Major Thomas T. Eckert, Colonel Lafayette C. Baker (head of the National Detective Police), his cousin Luther Byron Baker, Everton J. Conger, Charles Dawson (chief clerk of the National Hotel), photographer Alexander Gardner, Dr. John Frederick May, a steward

carrying surgical instruments, and several others came on board. Barnes started the autopsy by removing the splint from Booth's left leg. He placed the wrappings on the center of the body, and when someone attempted to take a pin, Barnes warned that nothing was to be taken. Next, Barnes examined the neck wound. First the body was placed in a sitting position for observation of the path of the bullet; then a narrow board was placed under the shoulders, allowing the head to hang backwards. The throat and upper part of the chest were explored, and the section of vertebrae through which Corbett's bullet had passed was removed. Booth's shirt and jacket were pulled aside as necessary; the clothing was not removed. After the autopsy, the body was wrapped in a gray blanket.[81]

Surgeon General Barnes' report to Secretary of War Stanton stated:

> The left leg and foot were encased in an appliance of splints and bandages, upon the removal of which, a fracture of the fibula (small bone of leg) 3 inches above the ankle joint, accompanied by considerable ecchymosis [skin discoloration caused by blood escaping into the tissues] was discovered.
>
> The cause of death was a gun shot wound in the neck—the ball entering just behind the sterno-cleido muscle—2½ inches above the clavicle—passing through the bony bridge of fourth and fifth cervical vertebrae—severing the spinal cord and passing out through the body of the sterno-cleido of right side, 3 inches above the clavicle.
>
> Paralysis of the entire body was immediate, and all the horrors of consciousness of suffering and death must have been present to the assassin during the two hours he lingered.[82]

An inquest was held. William W. Crowninshield and Charles M. Collins, who both had known Booth for only six weeks, identified the body, as did Charles Dawson of the National Hotel. Dr. John Frederick May identified the body by the scar left when he had removed a tumor from Booth's neck in April 1863.

At 2:15 p.m. Lafayette Baker, Luther

Byron Baker, and several soldiers quickly and without notice lowered Booth's body to a small boat and rowed away. The move was so sudden that the box prepared for the body was not used. The men rowed down the Eastern Branch of the Potomac River (now the Anacostia River) about two miles to the Washington Arsenal on the north bank at the junction with the Potomac River (now the site of Fort Lesley J. McNair). The arsenal had been developed in 1803. Eventually a fifty-foot by 300-foot federal penitentiary was built on the grounds. During the Civil War the penitentiary was converted to arsenal use. The men manning the boat unloaded Booth's body at the arsenal wharf and unceremoniously dropped it on the floor of an open summer house. The body, wrapped in a blanket, remained in the summer house under guard until midnight, when it was loaded into a horse cart and taken to a large room, forty by fifty feet, in the old penitentiary building. The body was placed in a pine ammunition box and buried in the floor of the storeroom.[83]

While Booth had been attempting his escape, the others in the plot had been apprehended. Lewis Powell, without Herold to guide him, had soon become lost in Washington. He lost his horse, then hid in a tree. Desperate after several days, he decided to seek help from Mary Surratt. He waited until late on Monday, April 17, to knock on her door. In a strange coincidence, authorities had come to the house to arrest Mary Surratt minutes before. Hearing a knock, an officer opened the door and soon arrested the hapless Powell. Earlier the same day Samuel Arnold was arrested at Old Port Comfort, Virginia, where he had taken a job. Michael O'Laughlen gave himself up in Baltimore when he learned he was a suspect. Edman (Ned) Spangler came under suspicion and was arrested the same night. He was taken to the Old Capitol Prison.

George Atzerodt had been assigned to kill Vice President Johnson. He drank instead. He made his way to the home of his cousin in Montgomery County, Maryland, where he was arrested on Thursday, April 20.

Dr. Mudd was interviewed by investigators several times. Finally, ten days after the assassination, he was taken into custody.

President Andrew Johnson ordered those allegedly involved in the conspiracy to assassinate President Lincoln to be tried by a military tribunal rather than the civil court of the District of Columbia. A military commission consisting of nine Federal army officers convened on May 8, 1865, in a large room at the eastern end of the old penitiary building at the Washington Arsenal. Booth had been secretly buried 300 feet away at the western end of the building. On May 10 the military commission brought charges against the alleged conspirators: Samuel Arnold, George A. Atzerodt, David E. Herold, Samuel A. Mudd, Michael O'Laughlen, Lewis Paine [Powell], Edman Spangler, and Mary E. Surratt. The prosecution closed its case on May 23 after calling 131 witnesses. The defense closed on June 29 after examining 128 witnesses. The next day the military commission sentenced Atzerodt, Herold, Powell, and Mary Surratt to be hanged. Ned Spangler received a sentence of six years imprisonment at hard labor. The commission sentenced Arnold, Mudd, and O'Laughlen to imprisonment at hard labor for life.

On July 5 President Johnson ordered:

The foregoing sentences in the cases of David E. Herold, G. A. Atzerodt, Lewis Paine [Powell] and Mary E. Surratt are hereby approved, and it is ordered that the sentences ... be carried into execution by the proper military authority under the direction of the Secretary of War on the 7th day of July, 1865, between the hours of 10 o'clock a.m. and 2 o'clock p.m. of that day.

On Friday, July 7, under a brutally hot sun, Atzerodt, Herold, Powell, and Mary Surratt were hanged on the grounds of the Washington Arsenal.

Late in July Sam Arnold, Dr. Mudd, Michael O'Laughlen, and Ned Spangler arrived at Fort Jefferson off the Florida Keys to serve their sentences. O'Laughlen died there on September 23, 1867, during an outbreak of yellow fever.

On the night of the assassination John Surratt was in Elmira, New York, scouting the prison for captured Confederates. When he learned of the assassination, he headed for Canada, where he hid for several months. He crossed the Atlantic to England and then traveled on to the Papal States, where he enlisted in the Papal Zouaves. He was arrested after he was recognized and reported by an old acquaintance. He escaped and made his way to Egypt, where he was arrested and deported to the United States. In the summer of 1867 he stood trial in the Criminal Court for the District of Columbia. Even though the jury failed to agree on a verdict, Surratt was not immediately released from custody. He was let out on bail in June 1868, and eventually the charges were dropped.[84]

Sarah Slater kept a low profile when the news of the Lincoln assassination reached Montreal. Within a month she resumed a quiet, civilian life at her 84th Street residence in New York City.[85]

John Wilkes Booth's family wanted his body to be buried in a new family plot in Green Mount Cemetery in Baltimore. Shortly after the assassination Edwin Booth asked New York political boss Thurlow Weed to inquire about the release of the body to the family. Secretary of War Stanton responded that when the public interest in the assassination abated, something would be arranged.[86] In the next several years Edwin's requests for the body were rejected or ignored.

The inauguration of Ulysses S. Grant as president was quickly approaching when Edwin Booth again attempted to recover his brother's body. This time he was successful. On February 15, 1869, the bodies of Booth and the four executed conspirators were exhumed.[87] Booth's body was taken to the Har-

vey and Marr undertaking establishment in Washington and then sent to Baltimore.

On February 18, the remains of John Wilkes Booth were placed without ceremony in the vault of undertaker John Weaver at Green Mount Cemetery.[88] In the next several months the bodies in the Booth family plot, as well as the monuments in Baltimore Cemetery, were moved to a new plot in Green Mount Cemetery. On Saturday afternoon, June 26, John Wilkes Booth's casket was carried from the Weaver vault to the Booth plot by members of the acting profession. The Rev. Fleming James read the Episcopal service in the presence of Mary Ann, Rosalie, Junius Jr., and Edwin, who "were much stricken with the sorrow of the occasion." A box containing the remains of three siblings who had died in youth was placed atop John's coffin. The casket and box were interred at the foot of the monument of Junius Brutus Booth, Sr.[89]

For years after the assassination, those with kind memories of John Wilkes Booth kept quiet. With the passage of time, more and more of these friends and acquaintances shared their memories. There was no thought of forgiveness for his horrible act. Perhaps they simply wished to let it be known that there was more to Booth than that act. On November 14, 1891, the *Washington Evening Star* carried an article from which the following is extracted:

> It's an odd circumstance that nearly every old-time actor, actress and manager believes firmly that John Wilkes Booth was the greatest star of his day. His crime has not shaken their belief in his genius. There is still no faltering in their worship of his brilliant and meteoric stage achievements, which, after the lapse of a quarter century, have gained rather than lost luster. It is the delight of the "has-beens" among our players to tell of Wilkes Booth's eccentricities, of his triumphs before the footlights and his conquests behind the scenes....[90]

1865 *from April 15*

April 15, Saturday Bel Alton

Booth and David Herold arrived at the Surratt Tavern at about midnight and picked up a carbine, ammunition, and the binoculars Mary Surratt had delivered earlier.

The fugitives rode to the home of Dr. Samuel A. Mudd, arriving at 4 a.m. Mudd splinted Booth's leg.

The two men left Dr. Mudd's house late in the afternoon. Their route took them to the east side of Zekiah Swamp, which extends south from the Mudd farm. The fugitives got lost in the dark. At about 9 p.m. they met Oswell Swan, a black tobacco farmer, and induced him to guide them to William Burtle's home. Soon they changed their minds and had Swan lead them to the home of Samuel Cox, a Confederate sympathizer. Cox lived on the west side of the swamp about twelve miles to the south.

April 16, Sunday Bel Alton

Booth, Herold, and Swan arrived at "Rich Hill," the home of Samuel Cox, at about 1 a.m. Cox had Booth and Herold come into the house.

The men came out of Cox's house between 3 and 4 a.m. Swan, still waiting, was paid $12. Herold warned Swan not to say anything or he wouldn't live long.

Samuel Cox had his overseer, Franklin Robey, guide the men to a pine thicket and sent for Thomas A. Jones, chief of the Confederate signal service north of the Potomac.

Jones found the men late in the morning. Booth asked Cox to bring newspapers.[91]

April 17, Monday Bel Alton

Jones brought food at mid-morning.

Samuel Cox or his overseer also carried substantial provisions to the fugitives.[92]

The horses were disposed of so they wouldn't attract attention from passing troops.

Samuel Arnold was arrested at Fort Monroe in Virginia.

Michael O'Laughlen, upon learning he was a suspect, turned himself in to the Baltimore police.

Ned Spangler was arrested and incarcerated in the Old Capitol Prison.

At 9 p.m. Michael O'Laughlen was imprisoned on the U.S.S. *Saugus* at the Navy Yard in Washington.

Authorities had come to Mary Surratt's boarding house in Washington late in the evening. Lewis Powell, who had attempted to murder Secretary of State William Seward at the same time Booth attacked Lincoln, appeared at the boarding house as Mary Surratt was being arrested. He was taken into custody.

April 18, Tuesday Bel Alton

Thomas Jones visited Booth and Herold at mid-morning. Jones's conversations with Booth centered on food, crossing the river, and on what was being said about the assassination.[93]

Later in the day, in Port Tobacco, Jones was offered a $100,000 reward by a Federal captain for information regarding Booth. Jones kept silent.[94]

John Surratt and Sarah Slater returned to Montreal from Elmira, New York, and checked into St. Lawrence Hall as "Harrison" and "A. Reynaud."[95]

At 5 a.m. Lewis Powell was imprisoned on the U.S.S. *Saugus*. Later, in daylight, Alexander Gardner photographed Powell.[96]

April 19, Wednesday Bel Alton

At 2 a.m. Sam Arnold was imprisoned on the U.S.S. *Saugus*.

Jones visited Booth and Herold at mid-morning.

Booth recorded his thoughts in his diary.

April 20, Thursday En route

In the evening Jones led Booth and Herold to the Potomac River. They descended a steep embankment to the mouth of a small creek, where a boat was hidden. With Booth in the stern and Herold at the oars, they headed down river for the mouth of Machodoc Creek, where Mrs. Elizabeth Quesenberry might help them. Tide, fog, and a desire to avoid gunboats carried them off course. They found themselves at the mouth of Nanjemoy Creek in Maryland. They rowed up a small creek at Indiantown Farm and pulled the boat ashore.

George Atzerodt was taken into custody at the home of his cousin in Montgomery County, Maryland.

At 11:30 p.m. George Atzerodt was imprisoned on the U.S.S. *Saugus*.

April 21, Friday Near Indiantown

Herold recognized their location as the farm "Indiantown" owned by Peregrine Davis.

Davis's son-in-law, John J. Hughes, fed the fugitives.[97]

Booth, describing himself as "wet, cold and starving" wrote in his diary: "For my country I have given up all that makes life sweet and Holy...." Booth and Herold failed to cross the Potomac on Friday night.

April 22, Saturday En route

Booth and Herold pushed off for Virginia at sundown and rowed all night. The night was chilly.[98]

April 23, Sunday Lucas's cabin

Booth and Herold landed on the Virginia side of the river at Gambo Creek. Herold walked to the home of Elizabeth Quesenberry, a stop on the Confederate mail route. She sent for Thomas Harbin, who took Booth and Herold to the farm of Will Bryant. Booth, Herold, and Bryant rode on horseback eight miles to the home of Dr. Richard Stuart, who provided food but denied lodging.[99]

The fugitives slept in William Lucas's cabin, forcing the black man and his wife to sleep outside.[100]

At 3 p.m. George Atzerodt was moved from the U.S.S. *Saugus* to the U.S.S. *Montauk*.

At 11:30 p.m. Ned Spangler was imprisoned on the U.S.S. *Montauk*.

April 24, Monday Garrett farm

William Lucas's son Charley drove Booth and Herold in his wagon ten miles to Port Conway on the Rappahannock River.[101]

Booth and Herold revealed their deed to three Confederate soldiers—Mortimer B. Ruggles, Absalom R. Bainbridge, and Willie Jett.

Willie Jett took the fugitives to the William Peyton house, where the Peyton sisters first agreed to take them in and then reconsidered.

Upon reaching the Garrett farm, the men split up. Herold and Bainbridge rode on, while Jett and Ruggles accompanied Booth to the farmhouse to ask whether Booth could stay. Richard Garrett agreed to take in the stranger for a night or two. Jett and Ruggles then rode toward Bowling Green.[102]

April 25, Tuesday Garrett farm

Refreshed by a good night's rest, Booth walked about the farm after breakfast. He played with the Garrett children.

Leaving Jett in Bowling Green, Bainbridge and Ruggles took Herold to Garrett's farm at 3:30 p.m. before riding onward. Booth was sitting on the porch when Jack Garrett said, "There goes some of your party now." They were heading in the direction of Port Royal. Booth excitedly asked Garrett to get his pistols. Soon Herold, who had been dropped off, was seen walking toward the house. Booth buckled on his pistols and hobbled about fifty yards to meet Herold. The pain from his leg was not so severe as to prevent him from walking.

Bainbridge and Ruggles returned in a short time to report that Union cavalry was headed their way. Booth hid in the woods until the troops had passed. The Federal cavalry rode to Bowling Green, where they found Jett, who agreed to lead them to Booth.[103]

Booth and Herold slept in the Garrett tobacco barn.

Alexander Gardner conducted a second photography session on the U.S.S. *Saugus* at the Washington Navy Yard.

April 26, Wednesday

At about 2:30 a.m. men of the 16th New York Cavalry surrounded the tobacco barn and ordered Booth and Herold to surrender. Herold soon gave up. The barn was set afire and, as Booth was hobbling to the door, Sergeant Boston Corbett shot him through the neck. Booth was placed on a mattress with his head and shoulders inside the house and his body and legs on the porch.

John Wilkes Booth died at about 7:15 a.m.

Luther Byron Baker and a black wagon driver transported Booth's corpse thirty miles to Belle Plain and loaded it aboard a steamer bound for Washington.[104]

April 27, Thursday

David Herold and Booth's body were transferred to the monitor U.S.S. *Montauk* at the Washington Navy Yard at 1:45 a.m.

Several acquaintances of Booth, as well as Dr. John Frederick May, who had removed a tumor from Booth's neck two years before, positively identified the body at a court of inquiry.[105] An autopsy concluded at 2 p.m.

Booth's body was lowered to a boat, rowed to the Arsenal wharf, unloaded, and unceremoniously deposited on the floor of an open summer house.[106]

Alexander Gardner photographed David Herold on the U.S.S. *Montauk*.

April 28, Friday

Booth's body, wrapped in blankets, remained in the summer house under guard until midnight, when it was loaded into a horse cart and taken to a large room, forty by fifty feet, in the penitentiary building. The body was buried in a pine box in the floor on the southwest corner of the storeroom.[107]

Edwin Booth was picked up by a detective in New York and brought to Washington.[108] There he was questioned by Lafayette Baker, head of the National Detective Police, and Judge Advocate General Joseph Holt before being released.

April 29, Saturday

Shortly after midnight the prisoners held on the U.S.S. *Saugus* and U.S.S. *Montauk* were transferred to the steamer *Keyport* and taken to the Arsenal Penitentiary.

May 4, Thursday

The body of Abraham Lincoln was placed in a temporary vault in Oak Ridge Cemetery in Springfield, Illinois.

May 10, Wednesday

A military commission brought charges against the alleged conspirators: Samuel Arnold, George A. Atzerodt, David E. Herold, Samuel A. Mudd, Michael O'Laughlen, Lewis Paine [Powell], Edman Spangler, and Mary E. Surratt.

May 11, Thursday

Joseph Booth had left San Francisco on April 13. He arrived in New York on this date and was immediately arrested. Secretary of War Stanton ordered a thorough examination to determine whether he was involved in the conspiracy.[109]

May 12, Friday

Joe Booth was examined by Major General John A. Dix. He revealed that he had been in Australia until June 1864, when he went to San Francisco and worked as a letter carrier. He said he had received a letter from John Wilkes about five months previously.[110]

May 20, Saturday

The *Philadelphia Inquirer* reported:
W. Stewart [sic], of the Winter Garden Theatre, New York, is here [in Washington] to try and

procure the body of Booth for his family. It is needless to say that it will not be granted, as he is buried deep, and none can ever resurrect him or find his grave.[111]

May 22, Monday

Asia Booth Clarke wrote to her friend Jean Anderson:
I can give you no idea of the desolation which has fallen upon us. The sorrow of [John Wilkes's] death is very bitter but the disgrace is far heavier.... I was shocked and grieved to see the names of Michael O'Laughlin [sic] and S. Arnold. I am still more surprised to learn that all engaged in the plot are Roman Catholics. Wilkes was of the faith professedly, and I was glad that he had fixed his faith on one religion, for he was always of a pious mind.... I told you, I believe, that Wilkes was engaged to Miss Hale. They were devoted lovers and she has written heart-broken letters to Edwin about it.[112]

May 23, Tuesday

The prosecution in the trial of the conspirators closed its case after calling 131 witnesses.

June 3, Saturday

Oil was struck on the Pithole Creek property once owned in part by John Wilkes Booth. The well was very productive.[113]

June 5, Monday

The *New York Times* carried an affidavit of John Sleeper Clarke summarizing his contacts with John Wilkes Booth over the last year. In addition to the letters Booth had left with Asia, he also left $4,000 in bonds—$3,000 in "five-twenty bonds" and $1,000 in "Philadelphia City 6's."[114]

June 7, Wednesday

The *Quebec Gazette* reported under "THE EFFECTS BELONGING TO JOHN WILKES BOOTH" that his trunks labeled "J. Wilkes Booth" had been recovered from the wreck of the schooner *Marie Victoria* and brought to Quebec and:
On examination of the contents the trunks were found to contain a magnificent theatrical wardrobe, consisting of crowns, rings, capes, doublets, swords, &c., &c., also play-books, parts written out, tickets, memoranda, letters, &c. We understand that all the written documents were, after a close examination, handed over to the American Consulate for safe-keeping, to be transmitted by him to Washington.[115]

June 29, Thursday

The defense in the trial of the conspirators closed its case after examining 128 witnesses.

June 30, Friday

The military commission sentenced Atze-rodt, Herold, Powell, and Mary Surratt to be hanged. Arnold, Mudd, and O'Laughlen were sentenced to imprisonment at hard labor for life and Ned Spangler to six years imprisonment at hard labor.

July 5, Wednesday

President Johnson approved the findings of the military commission and ordered the executions to be carried out on July 7.

July 6, Thursday

Major General John F. Hartranft, Governor of the Military Prison, accompanied by the members of the military commission, went to the cell of each prisoner and read the verdict.

July 7, Friday

The day of the execution dawned light and clear. The *Washington National Intelligencer* reported that "[a]t seventeen minutes after one o'clock, the work of adjusting the nooses over the heads of the condemned was commenced."[116]

Atzerodt, Herold, Powell, and Mary Surratt were hanged at 1:21 p.m. on the grounds of the Arsenal Penitentiary. The bodies were buried near the scaffold.

July 18, Tuesday

The *Quebec Morning Chronicle* of July 19 carried this item:

The theatrical wardrobe of the late John Wilkes Booth, recovered about a month ago from the wreck of the schooner *Marie Victoria,* at Bic, last autumn, was disposed of by decree of the vice-admiralty court by public auction [on the 18th]. Among the wardrobe, which unfortunately has been injured by salt water, there was a splendid collection of theatrical clothes....[117]

July 25, Tuesday

Sam Arnold, Dr. Mudd, Michael O'Laughlen, and Ned Spangler arrived at Fort Jefferson off the Florida Keys.

September 16, Saturday

John Surratt, who had been in hiding since he learned of the assassination, boarded a ship in Quebec bound for England.

September 27, Wednesday

John Surratt arrived in Liverpool, England.

November 6, Monday

Edwin Booth wrote to Secretary of War Stanton:

At the earnest solicitation of my Mother I write to ask if you think the time is yet arrived for her to have the remains of her unhappy son.... If I am premature in this I hope you will understand the motive which actuates me—arising purely from a sense of duty to assuage—if possible, the anguish of an aged mother.[118]

Stanton did not reply.

December 9, Saturday

John Surratt, in Rome, enlisted in the Papal Zouaves.

1866

November 7, Wednesday

John Surratt, serving in the Papal army at Veroli, Italy, was arrested by request of the American minister at Rome.

November 8, Thursday

John Surratt escaped from his captors by jumping over a wall to a ledge thirty-five feet below.

November 23, Friday

John Surratt was arrested at Alexandria, Egypt, by order of the American Consul there.

1867

February 18, Monday

John Surratt, under arrest, arrived in Washington on board the U.S.S. *Swatara,* which tied up next to the monitor U.S.S. *Montauk.*

March 21, Thursday

McKee Rankin claimed he encountered fellow actor Barton Hill, a member of Edwin Booth's company, at New York's Metropolitan House Cafe. Hill convinced Rankin to sell him John Wilkes Booth's wardrobe trunk.[119]

March 22, Friday

Rankin claimed he relinquished the trunk. He learned that night that Hill bought the trunk for Edwin Booth.[120]

March 23, Saturday

New York's Winter Garden Theatre burned. Edwin Booth's costumes, along with those of his father and his brother John, were stored at the theatre and were destroyed.[121]

June 10, Monday

The case of *United States of America v. John Harrison Surratt* opened in the Criminal Court of the District of Columbia.

August 10, Saturday

The jury in the trial of John Surratt, voting eight to four for acquittal, announced that it was deadlocked. A mistrial was declared, and the jury was dismissed. Surratt remained in custody.[122]

August 15, Thursday

The *New York World* later reported:
On the 15th of August, 1867, public opinion extorted out of ... Edwin M. Stanton, the place, time and circumstances of the burial of the man who killed Abraham Lincoln, and the secret of the grave of John Wilkes Booth became known, not only for the first time to the country, but for the first time to his relatives who are few, and to his friends who are many. Since then the secluded room in the first of the warehouses in the military buildings on the old arsenal ground has been visited by many hundreds of people, actuated by all the mingled motives which run between and connect curiosity and affection.[123]

September 11, Wednesday

Edwin Booth, at Barnum's Hotel in Baltimore, wrote to Ulysses S. Grant, asking for the release of John Wilkes Booth's body.
I now appeal to you—on behalf of my heartbroken mother—that she may receive the remains of her son. You, sir, can understand what a consolation it would be in an aged parent to have the privilege of visiting the grave of her child, and I feel assured that you will, even in the midst of your most pressing duties, feel a touch of sympathy for her—one of the greatest sufferers living.[124]
Once again Edwin's request was ignored.[125]

September 23, Monday

Michael O'Laughlen died of yellow fever at Fort Jefferson.

October 1, Tuesday

In September 1867, the Secretary of War had ordered demolition of the portion of the old penitentiary in which Booth was buried. A long search was required to find the key to the storeroom. The bodies of Booth, the executed conspirators, and Captain Henry Wirz, the executed commandant of Andersonville prison, were exhumed. They were re-interred in a fifty-by-thirty-foot room at the northeast corner of Warehouse 1 on the east side of the Arsenal parade grounds. The common grave in the middle of the room under the flagstone floor held Atzerodt, Herold, Powell, Mary Surratt, Wirz, and Booth.[126]

1868

June 22, Monday

John Surratt was released from custody after posting bail of $25,000.[127]

November 5, Thursday

The case against John Surratt was finally dismissed.[128]

1869

February 8, Monday

President Johnson pardoned Dr. Mudd.

February 10, Wednesday

Edwin Booth, in New York, wrote to President Johnson, asking that the remains of his brother be released to the family. He promised secrecy. John Weaver, sexton of Christ Church in Baltimore and an undertaker by profession, carried the letter to Washington.[129]

February 12, Friday

Baltimore undertaker John Weaver and Washington undertaker Richard H. Harvey carried Edwin Booth's letter to the president at the White House. Johnson directed the two men to return on Monday to receive an order authorizing removal of the body.[130]

February 15, Monday

At 4 p.m. a wagon driven by undertaking assistant Willis R. Speare carried John Weaver and Richard Harvey to the Washington Arsenal. Five soldiers were put to work removing the dirt in the warehouse floor to access the box holding Booth's corpse. The painted name "Booth" was observed on the top of the box when the soil was scraped away. Four soldiers carried the box to the waiting wagon.[131] At five o'clock the wagon containing Booth's body drove to the rear of the Harvey and Marr undertaking establishment. The rear of the business faced Baptist Alley near the rear of Ford's Theatre. The wagon, reversing the route of Booth's escape, was driven through the alley and parked in the Harvey and Marr stable—the very stable which had been Booth's.[132]

The box was carried into the shop, where

the men used the gray blanket in which the body was wrapped to lift it and place it in a plain transfer coffin for the trip to Baltimore. When the body was transferred, the head became entirely detached from the body. According to some accounts, Booth's dentist, William Merrill, was there and identified his dental work. A witness claimed that Booth's face was "perfect," except for a hole in each cheek. The hair appeared as if he had come from a barber's shop. The lips had receded, showing the teeth. The skin looked like parchment. The boot and shoe were still on the feet and in good condition. Soon the casket was on the train to Baltimore, where it arrived at 9 p.m. The body was taken to Weaver's undertaking establishment on Fayette Street, across from the Holliday Street Theatre.[133]

February 16, Tuesday

At 3 p.m. the body of John Wilkes Booth was transferred to a metal coffin.[134]

February 17, Wednesday

Mary Ann Booth, Rosalie, and Joseph gathered at Weaver's on Fayette Street. Harry Clay Ford and his future wife, Blanche Chapman, were also there. Several actors and employees came over from the theatre. The body was identified to the satisfaction of the family.[135]

The body was moved to the Weaver vault at Green Mount Cemetery at 11:45 p.m.

February 18, Thursday

According to the *Baltimore Sun* of February 19:

> The remains of J. Wilkes Booth were quietly put away in the vault of Mr. J. H. Weaver, the undertaker, at Greenmount [*sic*] Cemetery yesterday morning [February 18], without ceremony. There

was no one present on the occasion but Mr. Weaver and his assistants.[136]

March 2, Tuesday

President Johnson, two days before leaving office, signed pardons for Sam Arnold and Ned Spangler.

March 11, Thursday

Dr. Samuel A. Mudd, now free, boarded a ship for home from Fort Jefferson.

March 13, Saturday

Laura Keene performed *Our American Cousin* at Wall's Opera House in Washington.[137]

March 20, Saturday

Dr. Samuel A. Mudd arrived home.

April 6, Tuesday

Sam Arnold and Ned Spangler, now free men, arrived in Baltimore.

June 13, Sunday

Mary Ann Booth paid $250 for the title to lots 9 and 10 in Green Mount Cemetery. On May 25, 1874, Edwin Booth paid $200 for perpetual care for the plots.[138]

June 26, Saturday

John Wilkes Booth's remains were interred at the foot of the monument of Junius Brutus Booth in Green Mount Cemetery in the afternoon. The Rev. Fleming James read the service in the presence of about fifty people, including Mary Ann Booth, Rosalie, Joseph, Junius Jr., and Edwin, who "were much stricken with the sorrow of the occasion." The remains of three siblings who died in youth were placed atop John Wilkes's coffin in one box.[139]

Chapter Notes

Short titles used in Chapter Notes: **Arnold Confession of 1865**—Samuel Arnold statement, 18 April 1865, in Michael W. Kauffman, ed., *Samuel Bland Arnold: Memoirs of a Lincoln Conspirator* (Bowie, MD: Heritage Books, 1995), 133–137. **Arnold Confession of 1867**—Samuel Arnold statement, 3 December 1867, in Michael W. Kauffman, ed., *Samuel Bland Arnold: Memoirs of a Lincoln Conspirator* (Bowie, MD: Heritage Books, 1995), 22–37. **Atzerodt Statement, 1 May 1865**—"Statement of George A. Atzerodt to Prov. Mar. McPhail, May 1, 1865," *Surratt Courier* 13 (October 1988): 2–3. **LASE**—William C. Edwards and Edward Steers, Jr., eds., *The Lincoln Assassination: The Evidence* (Urbana: University of Illinois Press, 2009). **Poore**—Ben Perley Poore, ed., *The Conspiracy Trial for the Murder of the President* (Boston: J. E. Tilton, 1865 and 1866). **Surratt Trial**—*Trial of John H. Surratt in the Criminal Court of the District of Columbia*, 2 vols. (Washington, D.C.: Government Printing Office, 1867).

Chapter 1. Youth: 1838–1857

1. Richard Booth (1759–1839) was an attorney in London. Eventually he followed his son to the United States.

2. Stephen M. Archer, *Junius Brutus Booth: Theatrical Prometheus* (Carbondale: Southern Illinois University Press, 1992), 67.

3. Stanley Kimmel, *The Mad Booths of Maryland* (New York: Dover, 1969), 39.

4. Archer, *Junius Brutus Booth*, 5.

5. Constance Head, "The Booth Sisters of Bel Air," *Lincoln Herald* 84 (1981): 761.

6. John Sleeper Clarke (1833–1899) changed his name from John Clarke Sleeper for stage reasons. He and Edwin Booth were the same age, and they engaged in amateur theatricals in Baltimore in their youth. After the Lincoln assassination he and his wife moved to England.

7. Kimmel, *Mad Booths*, 324.

8. Alonzo J. May, "May's Dramatic Encyclopedia, 1750–1904," microfilm, Manuscript Division, Library of Congress, Washington, D.C. (original in Baltimore Theater Papers, Maryland Historical Society, Baltimore).

9. Typed note, Stanley Kimmel Papers, Macdonald-Kelce Library, University of Tampa, Tampa, Florida.

10. "George L. Stout's Recollections," Stanley Kimmel Papers.

11. David Rankin Barbee, "Lincoln and Booth," typescript, 211, David Rankin Barbee Papers, Georgetown University Library, Washington, D.C.

12. Asia Booth Clarke, *The Unlocked Book: A Memoir of John Wilkes Booth by his Sister Asia Booth Clarke*, ed. Eleanor Farjeon (New York: G.P. Putnam's Sons, 1938), 43–44.

13. James J. Williamson, *Prison Life in the Old Capitol* (West Orange, NJ, 1911), 79.

14. Typed note, Stanley Kimmel Papers.

15. Kimmel, *Mad Booths*, 70.

16. "Milton Academy in Retrospect," *Federation P.T.A. News* (March-April 1935).

17. Clarke, *Unlocked Book*, 55.

18. Clarke, *Unlocked Book*, 58.

19. Rules and Regulations for the Government of the Students at St. Timothy's Hall, Catonsville, Baltimore County, Maryland (Baltimore: Joseph Robinson, 1852), 4. Copy in author's files.

20. The Rev. Libertus Van Bokkelen (1815–1889) established St. Timothy's in 1845 at the suggestion of his bishop.

21. Henry Onderdonk (1822–1895) was suspended as president of the Maryland Agricultural College in 1864 for harboring Confederate troops on college grounds.

22. Neal A. Brooks and Eric G. Rockel, *A History of Baltimore County* (Towson, MD: Friends of the Towson Library, 1979), 224.

23. Clarke, *Unlocked Book*, 153–155.

24. "St. Timothy's Hall Circular," 29. September 1853, 1, Maryland Diocesan Archives, Baltimore, Maryland.

25. Barbee, "Lincoln and Booth," 216. Samuel Arnold (1834–1906) was the son of the leading baker in Baltimore. Arnold served briefly in the Confederate army but was discharged for disability. He continued to serve as a civilian clerk.

26. James W. Shettel, "J. Wilkes Booth at School: Recollections of a Retired Army Officer Who Knew Him Then," *New York Dramatic Mirror*, 26 February 1916, 3.

27. Asia Booth Clarke to Jean Anderson, autumn 1854, BCLM Works on Paper Collection, ML 518, Box 37, Maryland Historical Society, Baltimore.

28. Kimmel, *Mad Booths*, 100.

29. Clarke, *Unlocked Book*, 76–77.

30. Clarke, *Unlocked Book*, 63.

31. Clarke, *Unlocked Book*, 105.

32. Asia Booth Clarke, *John Wilkes Booth: A Sister's Memoir*, ed. Terry L. Alford (Jackson: University Press of Mississippi, 1996), 71–72; John Wilkes Booth to William O'Laughlen, 8 August 1854, in John H. Rhodehamel and Louise Taper, eds., *Right or Wrong, God Judge Me: The Writings of John Wilkes Booth* (Urbana: University of Illinois Press, 1997), 38–39.

33. Court Records Department, Historical Society of Harford County, Bel Air, Maryland. Research provided by Dinah Faber.

34. Clarke, *Unlocked Book*, 107; *Baltimore Sun*, 14 August 1855.

35. *Bel Air Southern Aegis*, 18, 25 July, 1, 8, 15 August 1857.

36. *Baltimore Sun*, 6 April 1838.

37. *Baltimore Sun*, 3 May 1838. The performances of *Junius Brutus Booth* in Baltimore indicate the dates he was certainly at home. The theatres referred to in this chapter are in Baltimore (and are identified as such the first time each is mentioned), unless otherwise noted.

38. *Baltimore Sun*, 1 May 1838.

39. *Baltimore Sun*, 3 May 1838.

40. A place name in a date entry indicates where John Wilkes Booth spent the night.

41. Archer, *Junius Brutus Booth*, 5.

42. *Baltimore Sun*, 15 May 1838.

43. *Baltimore Sun*, 12 June 1838.

44. *Baltimore Sun*, 15 July 1839.

45. *Baltimore Sun*, 22 October 1839. The Front Street Theatre was also known as the American Theatre.

46. *Baltimore Sun*, 26 October 1839.

47. Kimmel, *Mad Booths*, 58.

48. Asia Booth Clarke, *Personal Recollections of the Elder Booth* (London: Privately printed, n.d.), 36.

49. *Baltimore Sun*, 23, 24 January 1840.

50. "Interview of Joseph A. Booth," *New York Mail and Express*, 8 June 1893.

51. *Baltimore Sun*, 2 March 1840.

52. Clarke, *Personal Recollections*, 37.

53. Typed note, Stanley Kimmel Papers.

54. Typed note, Stanley Kimmel Papers.

55. Archer, *Junius Brutus Booth*, 268.

56. *Baltimore Sun*, 8 March 1841.

57. *Baltimore Sun*, 1 April 1841.

58. *Baltimore Sun*, 26 July 1841.

59. *Baltimore Sun*, 9 October 1841.

60. *Baltimore Sun*, 12 April 1842.

61. *Baltimore Sun*, 13 June 1842.

62. *Baltimore Sun*, 3 September 1842.

63. *Baltimore Sun*, 16 March 1843.

64. *Baltimore Sun*, 29 September 1843.

65. *Baltimore Sun*, 9 November 1843.

66. Kimmel, *Mad Booths*, 60.

67. *Baltimore Sun*, 29 April 1844.

68. *Baltimore Sun*, 27 March 1845.

69. *Baltimore Sun*, 1 July 1845.

70. May, "May's Dramatic Encyclopedia."

71. Kimmel, *Mad Booths*, 63–64; *New York Press*, 9 August 1891.

72. Typed note, Stanley Kimmel Papers.

73. *Baltimore Sun*, 8 March 1847.

74. *Baltimore Sun*, 5 April 1847.

75. Booth file, Maryland Historical Society, Baltimore.

76. *Baltimore Sun*, 17 May 1847.

77. Archer, *Junius Brutus Booth*, 181.

78. *Baltimore Sun*, 30 June 1847.

79. *Baltimore Sun*, 2 July 1847.

80. *Baltimore Sun*, 20 October 1847.

81. *Baltimore Sun*, 5 November 1847.

82. *Baltimore Sun*, 10 November 1847.

83. *Baltimore Sun*, 29 May 1848.

84. *Baltimore Sun*, 10 July 1848.

85. *Baltimore Sun*, 13 July 1848.

86. Archer, *Junius Brutus Booth*, 185, 274.

87. *Baltimore Sun*, 25 November 1848.

88. *Baltimore Sun*, 18 June 1849.

89. Kimmel, *Mad Booths*, 73.

90. "Circular of Milton Boarding School," 4, Maryland Historical Society, Baltimore.

91. Kimmel, *Mad Booths*, 64.

92. "Circular of Milton Boarding School," 4.

93. Playbill, Valentine Richmond History Center, Richmond, Virginia.

94. Playbill, Valentine Richmond History Center.

95. Kimmel, *Mad Booths*, 74.

96. *Baltimore Sun*, 27 May 1850.

97. "Circular of Milton Boarding School," 4.

98. Kimmel, *Mad Booths*, 75–76.

99. "Circular of Milton Boarding School," 4.

100. *Baltimore Sun*, 31 October 1850.

101. *Baltimore Sun*, 1 November 1850.

102. *Baltimore Sun*, 2 November 1850; May, "May's Dramatic Encyclopedia."

103. "Circular of Milton Boarding School," 4.

104. Archer, *Junius Brutus Booth*, 196; *New York Dramatic News*, 1 August 1891.

105. Records of the Baltimore Cemetery Company, Baltimore, Maryland.

106. Archer, *Junius Brutus Booth*, 197.

107. Archer, *Junius Brutus Booth*, 197.

108. Charles F. Fuller, Jr., "Kunkel and Company at the Marshall Theatre, Richmond, Virginia, 1856–1861" (MA Thesis, Ohio University, 1968), 27.

109. Asia Booth Clarke, *Booth Memorials: Passages, Incidents, and Anecdotes in the Life of Junius Brutus Booth (the elder)* (New York: Carleton, 1866), 82.

110. Playbill, Valentine Richmond History Center.

111. Playbill, Valentine Richmond History Center.

112. "Circular of Milton Boarding School," 4.

113. Kimmel, *Mad Booths*, 79.

114. "Circular of Milton Boarding School," 4.

115. *Baltimore Sun*, 3 October 1851.

116. *Baltimore Sun*, 4 October 1851.

117. Archer, *Junius Brutus Booth*, 198.

118. James J. Gifford also was the architect of Ford's Theatre in Washington, D.C., in 1863. See George J. Olszewski, *Restoration of Ford's Theatre* (Washington, D.C.: United States Department of the Interior, 1963), 7.

119. *Baltimore Sun*, 1 January 1852.

120. *Baltimore Sun*, 2 January 1852.

121. *Baltimore Sun*, 3 January 1852.

122. *Baltimore Sun*, 10 January 1852.

123. *Baltimore Sun*, 12 February 1852.

124. *Baltimore Sun*, 24 February 1852.

125. *Baltimore Sun*, 16 March 1852.

126. *Baltimore Sun*, 17 March 1852.

127. *Baltimore American*, 6 May 1852.

128. *Baltimore Sun*, 31 May 1852.

129. *Baltimore Sun*, 1 June 1852.

130. *Baltimore Sun*, 2 June 1852.

131. *Baltimore Sun*, 3 June 1852.

132. *Baltimore Sun*, 4 June 1852.

133. *Baltimore Sun*, 5 June 1852.

134. Kimmel, *Mad Booths*, 85.

135. Clarke, *Unlocked Book*, 58.

136. Archer, *Junius Brutus Booth*, 218.

137. Kimmel, *Mad Booths*, 89.

138. Archer, *Junius Brutus Booth*, 222.

139. *New York Clipper*, 2 July 1864.

140. *New York Clipper*, 2 July 1864.

141. *New York Clipper*, 2 July 1864.

142. *New York Clipper*, 2 July 1864.

143. *New York Clipper*, 2 July 1864; *Baltimore Sun*, 3 December 1852.

144. *Baltimore Sun*, 11 December 1852.

145. *Baltimore Sun*, 13 December 1852; May, "May's Dramatic Encyclopedia."

146. Clarke, *Personal Recollections*, 35.

147. Records of The Baltimore Cemetery Company, Baltimore, Maryland.

148. Baptismal Record of St. Timothy's Church, Catonsville, Maryland.

149. "St. Timothy's Hall Circular," 2.

150. Asia Booth Clarke to Jean Anderson, 11 October 1853, BCLM Works on Paper Collection.

151. Asia Booth Clarke to Jean Anderson, 20 December 1853, BCLM Works on Paper Collection. T. William O'Laughlen, born in 1838, lived with his family at 57 North Exeter Street in Baltimore across the street from the Booth family. William's younger brother, Michael, was also a boyhood friend of John Wilkes Booth.

152. Asia Booth Clarke to Jean Anderson, 8 January 1854, BCLM Works on Paper Collection.

153. John Wilkes Booth to William O'Laughlen, 25 January 1854, in Rhodehamel and Taper, eds., *Right or Wrong*, 36–37.

154. Rhodehamel and Taper, eds., *Right or Wrong*, 25.

155. John Wilkes Booth to William O'Laughlen, 30 April 1854, in Rhodehamel and Taper, eds., *Right or Wrong*, 37–38.

156. John Wilkes Booth to William O'Laughlen, 30 April 1854, in Rhodehamel and Taper, eds., *Right or Wrong*, 37–38.

157. Clarke, *Unlocked Book*, 58. Billy Bowlegs (ca. 1810–1864), born Holata Micco, was a leader of the Seminoles in Florida.

158. *Baltimore Sun*, 15 June 1854; Dinah Faber research at Baltimore Cemetery.

159. Dinah Faber, who consulted the conflicting cemetery records and *Baltimore Sun* notices, determined the date of the burial.

160. Clarke, *John Wilkes Booth, A Sister's Memoir*, 71–72; Court Records Department, Historical Society of Harford County, Bel Air, Maryland.

161. Kimmel, *Mad Booths*, 109.

162. John Wilkes Booth to William O'Laughlen, 8 August 1854, in Rhodehamel and Taper, eds., *Right or Wrong*, 38–39.

163. Kimmel, *Mad Booths*, 115.

164. John Wilkes Booth to William O'Laughlen, 8 November 1854, in Rhodehamel and Taper, eds., *Right or Wrong*, 40.

165. John Wilkes Booth to William O'Laughlen, 25 January 1855, in Rhodehamel and Taper, eds., *Right or Wrong*, 40–41.

166. Kimmel, *Mad Booths*, 117.

167. Asia Booth Clarke to Jean Anderson, 22 May 1855, BCLM Works on Paper Collection.

168. John Wilkes Booth to William O'Laughlen, 18 June 1855, in Rhodehamel and Taper, eds., *Right or Wrong*, 41–42.

169. Asia Booth Clarke to Jean Anderson, 28 June 1855, BCLM Works on Paper Collection.

170. Asia Booth Clarke to Jean Anderson, 1 August 1855, BCLM Works on Paper Collection.

171. *Baltimore Sun*, 14 August 1855. John Albaugh (1837–1909) was born in Baltimore. His family was not in the theatrical profession, but Albaugh had a strong desire to be an actor. He made his professional debut at the Baltimore Museum on February 1, 1855, several months before John Wilkes Booth made his debut. Albaugh and Booth were fast friends, and their paths often crossed during Booth's short career. Albaugh married Mary Mitchell in 1866, and he worked steadily in many cities as an actor, manager, or theatre owner. He accumulated great wealth. He developed a 250-acre farm just north of Washington, D.C., and had a home in Baltimore as well as a 23-room house in Long Branch, New Jersey.

172. John Wilkes Booth to William O'Laughlen, 14 September 1855, in Rhodehamel and Taper, eds., *Right or Wrong*, 42.

173. John Wilkes Booth to William O'Laughlen, 14 September 1855, in Rhodehamel and Taper, eds., *Right or Wrong*, 42.

174. John Wilkes Booth to William O'Laughlen, 14 September 1855, in Rhodehamel and Taper, eds., *Right or Wrong*, 42.

175. John Wilkes Booth to William O'Laughlen, 12 November 1855, in Rhodehamel and Taper, eds., *Right or Wrong*, 43.

176. Kimmel, *Mad Booths*, 130.

177. Asia Booth Clarke to Jean Anderson, 10 September 1856, BCLM Works on Paper Collection.

178. *Baltimore Sun*, 15 October 1856; Kimmel, *Mad Booths*, 135.

179. *Baltimore Sun*, 25 October 1852; Kimmel, *Mad Booths*, 135.

180. T. Allston Brown, *History of the American Stage from 1733 to 1870* (New York: Dick & Fitzgerald, 1870), 69. Samuel Knapp Chester (1836–1921) was born Samuel Chester Knapp. He married Anne E. Hodges on January 2, 1862, in Baltimore.

181. *Bel Air Southern Aegis*, 18 July 1857.

Chapter 2. Philadelphia: 1857–1858

1. William Wheatley (1816–1876), born in New York City, made his first public appearance on stage at age ten. He was a popular actor and theatre manager.

2. George S. Bryan, *The Great American Myth* (New York: Carrick & Evans, 1940), 84.

3. *Philadelphia Press*, 10 November 1857.

4. *Philadelphia Press*, 4 January 1858.

5. *Philadelphia Press*, 19 December 1857.

6. *Philadelphia Press*, 20 February 1858.

7. John Edward McCullough (1837–1885) was born in Ireland and came to America at the age of sixteen. He became a very popular actor, but his career and life were cut short by the effects of syphilis.

8. Walter Benn, "The Great National Conspiracy," *Wilkes-Barre* [Pennsylvania] *Times,* 19 December 1894.

9. Playbill, 19 February 1858, Mr. Roland Reed's playbills, Arch Street Theatre, Philadelphia, 1857–1858, Founders Library, Howard University, Washington, D.C. Michael W. Kauffman kindly provided the author with a copy of the notes from his examination of the Roland Reed playbills.

10. *Philadelphia Evening Bulletin*, 18 February 1858.

11. George Alfred Townsend, *The Life, Crime, and Capture of John Wilkes Booth* (New York: Dick & Fitzgerald, 1865), 21.

12. *Philadelphia Evening Bulletin*, 25 February 1858.

13. Townsend, *Life, Crime, and Capture of John Wilkes Booth*, 21; Pandolfo Petrucci (c. 1452–1512) ruled the Italian city of Siena during the Renaissance. Townsend thought the incident proved Booth had little talent.

14. George Alfred Townsend, "A Philistine's Diary," unidentified newspaper, 30 July 1882, George Alfred Townsend Papers, Maryland State Archives, Annapolis.

15. Townsend, *Life, Crime, and Capture of John Wilkes Booth*, 25.

16. Townsend, *Life, Crime, and Capture of John Wilkes Booth*, 26.

17. Mary Ann Holmes Booth to Junius Brutus Booth, Jr., 3 February 1858, in John H. Rhodehamel and Louise Taper, eds., *Right or Wrong, God Judge Me: The Writings of John Wilkes Booth* (Urbana: University of Illinois Press, 1997), xi.

18. St. Nicholas Hotel register, New-York Historical Society.

19. *New York Sun*, 28 March 1897. Charles Pope (1832–1899) was born in Germany. He made his American debut in Rochester, New York.

20. *Baltimore Sun*, 27 August 1858; Stanley Kimmel, *The Mad Booths of Maryland* (New York: Dover, 1969), 151–152.

21. James Henry Stoddart, *Recollections of a Player* (New York: The Century Co., 1902), 117.

22. Quoted in Bryan, *Great American Myth*, 84. Perhaps the information that "Wilks" was "from the N. York Theatres" was meant to mislead the public regarding Booth's identity.

23. *Philadelphia Public Ledger & Daily Transcript*, 11 August 1857.

24. *Philadelphia Press*, 14 August 1857.

25. Bryan, *Great American Myth*, 84.

26. Playbill, 15 August 1857, Mr. Roland Reed's playbills; *Philadelphia Press*, 15 August 1857. Unless otherwise noted, the dates and plays performed during this season were derived from the Reed collection.

27. *Bel Air Southern Aegis*, 15 August 1857.

28. Booth's role, if any, is unknown unless otherwise stated.

29. On the first mention of a play, the full name, including subtitle, is used. Subsequent occurrences do not include the subtitle.

30. *Philadelphia Press*, 26 August 1857.

31. *Philadelphia Press*, 28 August 1857.

32. *Philadelphia Press*, 1 September 1857.

33. *Philadelphia Inquirer*, 21 September 1857.

34. *Philadelphia Press*, 21 September 1857.

35. *Philadelphia Press*, 19 October 1857.

36. *Philadelphia North American and United States Gazette*, 22 October 1857.

37. *Philadelphia North American and United States Gazette*, 28 October 1857.

38. Deirdre Kincaid, "Rough Magic: The Theatrical Life of John Wilkes Booth" (unpublished manuscript, 2009), Chronology, 2.

39. Kincaid, "Rough Magic," Chronology, 2.

40. *Philadelphia Press*, 2 November 1857.

41. *Philadelphia Press*, 10 November 1857.

42. *Philadelphia North American and United States Gazette*, 11 November 1857.

43. *Philadelphia Press*, 16 November 1857.

44. *Philadelphia North American and United States Gazette*, 21 November 1857.

45. *Philadelphia Press*, 24 November 1857.

46. *Philadelphia Press*, 12 December 1857.

47. *Philadelphia Press*, 14 December 1857.

48. *Philadelphia Evening Bulletin*, 16 December 1857.

49. *Philadelphia North American and United States Gazette*, 19 December 1857.

50. *Philadelphia Evening Bulletin*, 22 December 1857.

51. *Philadelphia Evening Bulletin*, 26 December 1857.

52. *Philadelphia Evening Bulletin*, 30 December 1857.

53. *Philadelphia Press*, 4 January 1858.

54. *Philadelphia Evening Bulletin*, 30 January 1858.

55. Kincaid, "Rough Magic," Chronology, 4.

56. Rhodehamel and Taper, eds., *Right or Wrong*, 26.

57. *Philadelphia Evening Bulletin*, 19 February 1858.

58. Mary Ann Farren, born Mary Ann Russell, was the wife of George P. Farren. She began her stage career in 1824.

59. *Philadelphia Press*, 20 February 1858.

60. *Philadelphia Press*, 22 February 1858.

61. Townsend, *Life, Crime, and Capture of John Wilkes Booth*, 21.

62. *Philadelphia Evening Bulletin*, 25 February 1858.

63. Susan Denin (1835–1875) traveled widely as an actress. She died from the effects of a fall while acting in Indianapolis.

64. Mme. Ponisi (1818–1899), born Elizabeth Hanson, had a long career as an American actress.

65. *Philadelphia Evening Bulletin*, 1 March 1858.

66. *Philadelphia Press*, 1 March 1858, quoted in Kincaid, "Rough Magic," Chapter 3, 11.

67. Kincaid, "Rough Magic," Chronology, 5.

68. *Philadelphia Evening Bulletin*, 6 March 1858.

69. Kimmel, *Mad Booths*, 63–65; Louis J. Weichmann, *A True History of the Assassination of Abraham*

Lincoln and of the Conspiracy of 1865, ed. Floyd E. Risvold (New York: Vintage, 1975), 36.

70. *Philadelphia Evening Bulletin*, 29 March 1858.

71. *Philadelphia Press*, 30 March 1858.

72. *Philadelphia Evening Bulletin*, 6 April 1858.

73. Kincaid, "Rough Magic," Chronology, 5.

74. Alonzo J. May, "May's Dramatic Encyclopedia, 1750–1904," microfilm, Manuscript Division, Library of Congress, Washington, D.C. (original in Baltimore Theater Papers, Maryland Historical Society, Baltimore).

75. Sotheby-Parke-Bernet (auction catalog), Sang Sale, part 5, 4 December 1981.

76. *Philadelphia Evening Bulletin*, 26 April 1858.

77. Asia Booth Clarke, *The Elder and the Younger Booth* (Boston: James R. Osgood, 1882), 107.

78. Charlotte Cushman (1816–1876), born in Boston, made her stage debut in 1836 in New Orleans. She went on to become one of the greatest actresses of her era in America as well as in England.

79. *Philadelphia Evening Bulletin*, 24 May 1858.

80. *Philadelphia Press*, 25 May 1858.

81. *Philadelphia Evening Bulletin*, 25 May 1858.

82. Playbill, 26 May 1858, Mr. Roland Reed's playbills.

83. Gordon Samples, *Lust for Fame: The Stage Career of John Wilkes Booth* (Jefferson, NC: McFarland, 1982), 23.

84. *Philadelphia Evening Bulletin*, 31 May 1858. Charles William Couldock (1815–1898), born in London, immigrated to the United States in 1849.

85. *Philadelphia Press*, 31 May 1858.

86. *Philadelphia Evening Bulletin*, 7 June 1858.

87. Mary Ann Holmes Booth to Junius Brutus Booth, Jr., undated fragment, Harvard Theatre Collection, Harvard College Library, Cambridge, Massachusetts. This letter is described in Kincaid, "Rough Magic," chapter 4, 1, and in Rhodehamel and Taper, eds., *Right or Wrong*, xi.

88. *Philadelphia Press*, 14 June 1858; *Philadelphia Evening Bulletin*, 14 June 1858.

89. St. Nicholas Hotel register, New-York Historical Society.

90. St. Nicholas Hotel register, New-York Historical Society.

91. Adam Badeau, "A Night with the Booths," *New York Times*, 7 August 1858. Adam Badeau (1831–1895) was seriously wounded at Port Hudson, Louisiana, in 1863. Upon recovering, he served on the staff of General Ulysses S. Grant as military secretary.

92. T. Allston Brown, *History of the American Stage from 1733 to 1870* (New York: Dick & Fitzgerald, 1870), 388.

93. Kimmel, *Mad Booths*, 151–152.

94. Stoddart, *Recollections of a Player*, 117.

95. Quincy Kilby, undated typescript quoting a letter from Mary Ann Booth to Junius Brutus Booth, Jr., William Seymour Family Papers, Manuscripts Division, Department of Rare Books and Special Collections, Princeton University Library, Princeton, New Jersey.

96. Quincy Kilby, undated typescript quoting a letter from Mary Ann Booth to Junius Brutus Booth, Jr., William Seymour Family Papers.

Chapter 3. Richmond: 1858–1860

1. John H. Rhodehamel and Louise Taper, eds., *Right or Wrong, God Judge Me: The Writings of John Wilkes Booth* (Urbana: University of Illinois Press, 1997), 46, n. 6; Mary Ann Holmes Booth to Junius Brutus Booth, Jr., 3 October 1858, in Louise and Barry Taper Collection, Abraham Lincoln Presidential Library, Springfield, Illinois. George Kunkel (1823–1885), born in Pennsylvania, began his career at the age of nineteen as a black-face performer. While he occasionally managed theatres, he spent the greater part of his career as a minstrel performer and was described as a "giant of burnt cork."

2. Charles F. Fuller, Jr., "Kunkel and Company at the Marshall Theatre, Richmond, Virginia, 1856–1861" (MA Thesis, Ohio University, 1968), 108; John Wilkes Booth to Edwin Booth, 10 September 1858, in Rhodehamel and Taper, eds., *Right or Wrong*, 45–46, and in George S. Bryan, *The Great American Myth* (New York: Carrick & Evans, 1940), 85.

3. David Rankin Barbee, "Lincoln and Booth," typescript, 235, David Rankin Barbee Papers, Georgetown University Library, Washington, D.C.

4. *Richmond Daily Dispatch*, 1 October 1858.

5. Asia Booth Clarke, *The Unlocked Book: A Memoir of John Wilkes Booth by his Sister Asia Booth Clarke*, ed. Eleanor Farjeon (New York: G.P. Putnam's Sons, 1938), 111.

6. Fuller, "Kunkel and Company," 120.

7. Robert M. Sillard, *Barry Sullivan and His Contemporaries: A Histrionic Record* (London: T. Fisher Unwin, 1901), 2:20.

8. Sillard, *Barry Sullivan and His Contemporaries*, 2:4.

9. Sillard, *Barry Sullivan and His Contemporaries*, 2:18.

10. George Crutchfield to Edward V. Valentine, 5 July 1909, quoted in Bryan, *Great American Myth*, 86.

11. John M. Barron, "With John Wilkes Booth in His Days as an Actor," *Baltimore Sun*, 17 March 1907. John M. Barron observed Booth at times during the 1859–1860 season, but his comments are applicable here.

12. Edward M. Alfriend, "Recollections of John Wilkes Booth," *The Era* 8 (October 1901): 604. For more on Alfriend, see John T. Kneebone, et al., eds., *Dictionary of Virginia Biography* (Richmond: Library of Virginia, 1998), 1:64–65.

13. Charles M. Wallace, Sr., "Richmond in By Gone Days," *Richmond Times-Dispatch*, 24 June 1906.

14. John Wilkes Booth to Edwin Booth, 10 September 1858, in Rhodehamel and Taper, eds., *Right or Wrong*, 45–46.

15. "Dr. James Beale Dead," *Richmond Times*, 2 July 1890. James Beale (1803–1890) at first studied law but switched to medicine. He was a social leader in Richmond for decades.

16. J.N. Upshur, *Medical Reminiscences of Richmond During the Past Forty Years* (Richmond: privately printed, 1906), 12.

17. Interview of Mary Bella Beale Brainerd in *Philadelphia Daily News*, 31 December 1887, in Barbee Papers.

18. Interview of Mary Bella Beale Brainerd.

19. *Philadelphia Daily News*, 26 December 1887.

20. Barron, "With John Wilkes Booth in His Days as an Actor."

21. Second Annual Directory for the City of Richmond, 1860.

22. *Richmond Examiner*, 1 October 1858, quoted in Fuller, "Kunkel and Company," 108.

23. Mary Ann Holmes Booth to Junius Brutus Booth, Jr., 3 October 1858, Taper Collection. A different portion of this letter is quoted in Rhodehamel and Taper, eds., *Right or Wrong*, 46, n. 6; Francis Wilson, *John Wilkes Booth: Fact and Fiction of Lincoln's Assassination* (Boston: Hougton Mifflin, 1929), 18.

24. Rhodehamel and Taper, eds., *Right or Wrong*, xi.

25. Stanley Kimmel, *The Mad Booths of Maryland* (New York: Dover, 1969), 153.

26. *Richmond Daily Dispatch*, 29 September 1858.

27. *Richmond Daily Dispatch*, 7 October 1858.

28. *Richmond Daily Dispatch*, 15 October 1858.

29. *Richmond Whig*, 24 December 1858.

30. Fuller, "Kunkel and Company," 216.

31. Clarke, *Unlocked Book*, 110–111.

32. *Richmond Dispatch*, 2 February 1902.

33. Edwin Adams (1834–1877) became one of America's best light comedians. In 1869 he joined Edwin Booth's acting company.

34. "The Harpers Ferry Invasion," *New York Herald*, 23 November 1859.

35. John O. Taylor, "John Brown Hanging: Recollections of a Member of the Richmond Grays," *Richmond Times-Dispatch*, 1 May 1904, quoted in Angela Smythe, "Bound for Glory: John Wilkes Booth and the Richmond Grays," www.antebellumrichmond.com/bound-for-glory.html (accessed 31 July 2013), 39. Angela Smythe's remarkable research provides the best view of the Richmond Grays and John Wilkes Booth in Charlestown. In addition to "Bound for Glory," see "Has He Been Hiding in Plain Sight? John Wilkes Booth and the Richmond Grays," www.antebellumrichmond.com/hiding.html (accessed 31 July 2013), and "Out of Hiding: John Wilkes Booth and the Richmond Grays," www.antebellumrichmond.com/out-of-hiding.html (accessed 31 July 2013).

36. Wirt Armistead Cate, "A History of Richmond, 1607–1861," unpublished manuscript, Valentine Richmond History Center, Richmond, Virginia, quoted in Smythe, "Bound for Glory," 32.

37. George W. Libby, "John Brown and John Wilkes Booth," *Confederate Veteran* 38 (April 1930): 138–139.

38. "John Taylor manuscript," typescript, file 36–10–22-T, Virginia Historical Society, Richmond, Virginia, quoted in Smythe, "Bound for Glory," 40.

39. Taylor, "John Brown Hanging."

40. Militia pay audit records for the period of 19 November–6 December 1859, John Brown's Raid unit records, 1859–1911, Virginia, Department of Confederate Military Records, accession 27684, State Government Records Collection, Library of Virginia, Richmond.

41. Libby, "John Brown and John Wilkes Booth," 138–139.

42. Alfriend, "Recollections of John Wilkes Booth."

43. John S. Alfriend, *History of Zion Episcopal Church, Saint Andrew's Parish, Charles Town, West Virginia* (1973).

44. Libby, "John Brown and John Wilkes Booth," 138–139.

45. Smythe, "Out of Hiding," 32.

46. *Richmond Daily Dispatch*, 5 December 1859.

47. Smythe, "Out of Hiding," 32.

48. Smythe, "Out of Hiding," 44.

49. *Richmond Daily Dispatch*, 1 December 1859.

50. "An Old Time Hanging," *Philadelphia Inquirer*, 7 May 1896.

51. Philip Whitlock, "The Life of Philip Whitlock, Written by Himself," 1, Beth Ahabah Museum and Archives Trust, Richmond, Virginia.

52. James O. Hall, "John Wilkes Booth and John Brown," *Surratt Society News* 10 (November 1985).

53. Alfriend, "Recollections of John Wilkes Booth."

54. Mary Devlin (1840–1863) made her stage debut at the age of twelve. She met Edwin Booth in 1856. They were engaged in July 1858, with the understanding that she would give up the stage.

55. Mary Devlin to Edwin Booth, 28 November 1859, in Mary Devlin Booth, *The Letters and Notebooks of Mary Devlin Booth*, ed. L. Terry Oggel (New York: Greenwood Press, 1987), 22.

56. James W. Collier (1834–1898) was a novice actor along with Booth in Richmond. He married and later divorced actress Mary Mitchell, half-sister of Maggie Mitchell.

57. *Daily Richmond Enquirer*, 31 May 1860.

58. *Richmond Daily Dispatch*, 31 May 1860.

59. *Daily Richmond Enquirer*, 4 June 1860.

60. Mary Devlin to Edwin Booth, 1 March 1860, in Booth, *Letters and Notebooks of Mary Devlin Booth*, 45. Joseph Jefferson (1829–1905) was born in Philadelphia to an acting family. He became a first-rate actor.

61. *Richmond Daily Dispatch*, 6 September 1858; Fuller, "Kunkel and Company," 106–107. The establishment will be referred to as the Marshall Theatre in this book.

62. *Richmond Daily Dispatch*, 7 September 1858. Unless otherwise noted, the sources of performances and characters played in Richmond are the *Richmond Daily Dispatch*, the *Daily Richmond Enquirer*, or the *Richmond Examiner*.

63. John Wilkes Booth to Edwin Booth, 10 September 1858, in Rhodehamel and Taper, eds., *Right or Wrong*, 45–46.

64. John Wilkes Booth to Edwin Booth, 10 September 1858, in Rhodehamel and Taper, eds., *Right or Wrong*, 45–46. Maggie Mitchell (1832–1918) began her stage career as a child. She became a national star in 1861 when her role in *Fanchon, The Cricket*, became a hit.

65. *Daily Richmond Enquirer*, 13 September 1858.

66. *Daily Richmond Enquirer*, 22 September 1858.

67. *Richmond Daily Dispatch*, 29 September 1858.

68. *Daily Richmond Enquirer*, 1 October 1858.

69. *Daily Richmond Enquirer*, 1 October 1858; Fuller, "Kunkel and Company," 114–115.

70. *Richmond Daily Dispatch*, 4 October 1858.

71. *Richmond Daily Dispatch*, 2 October 1858.

72. Rhodehamel and Taper, eds., *Right or Wrong*, 46, n. 6; Mary Ann Holmes Booth to Junius Brutus Booth, Jr., 3 October 1858, Louise and Barry Taper Collection.

73. Alfriend, "Recollections of John Wilkes Booth." I have found no supporting evidence that Booth played Horatio on this occasion.

74. *Richmond Daily Dispatch*, 7 October 1858.

75. Fuller, "Kunkel and Company," 211.

76. *Richmond Whig*, 15 October 1858, quoted in Fuller, "Kunkel and Company," 116.

77. *Richmond Daily Dispatch*, 15 October 1858.

78. *Daily Richmond Enquirer*, 16 October 1858.

79. Clarke, *Unlocked Book*, 18.

80. *Richmond Daily Dispatch*, 25 October 1858.

81. Edward V. Valentine Diary, Valentine Richmond History Center, Richmond.

82. *Lynchburg Daily Virginian*, 1 November 1858. Unless otherwise noted, the performances during this engagement are derived from the *Daily Virginian*.

83. *Lynchburg Daily Virginian*, 2 November 1858.

84. *Lynchburg Daily Virginian*, 5 November 1858.

85. *Lynchburg Daily Virginian*, 5 November 1858.

86. *Lynchburg Daily Virginian*, 6 November 1858.

87. *Lynchburg Daily Virginian*, 8 November 1858.

88. *Lynchburg Daily Virginian*, 10 November 1858.

89. *Lynchburg Daily Virginian*, 12 November 1858.

90. *Lynchburg Daily Virginian*, 13 November 1858.

91. Avonia Stanhope Jones (1839–1867) made her acting debut in Philadelphia in 1856. She died of pneumonia while in England in 1867.

92. Fuller, "Kunkel and Company," 210; *Richmond Whig*, 19 November 1858.

93. James William Wallack, Jr. (1818–1873), born in England, moved to the United States in 1852 and was a leading actor in comedy and melodrama as well as a theatre manager.

94. Gordon Samples, *Lust for Fame: The Stage Career of John Wilkes Booth* (Jefferson, NC: McFarland, 1982), 36.

95. Julia Dean was born in 1830 in Pleasant Valley, New York. Her acting career began in 1845. She married, and then divorced, Arthur P. Hayne. She married again and died in childbirth.

96. *Daily Richmond Enquirer*, 20 December 1858.

97. *Richmond Whig*, 24 December 1858. It is possible that Kate Fisher, a popular actress and ballet dancer born in 1840, was the girl Booth saved.

98. John Andrew Jackson Neafie (1815–1892) made his acting debut in New York in 1838. He toured for a time as the principal supporting player to Edwin Forrest.

99. *Richmond Daily Dispatch*, 24 January 1859.

100. *Richmond Whig*, 28 January 1859, quoted in Fuller, "Kunkel and Company," 126.

101. *Richmond Whig*, 1 February 1859

102. *Richmond Whig*, 4 February 1859.

103. *Petersburg Daily Express*, 14 February 1859. Unless otherwise noted, the plays and reviews of the Petersburg engagement are found in the *Petersburg Daily Express*.

104. *Petersburg Daily Express*, 16 February 1859.

105. *Petersburg Daily Express*, 17 February 1859.

106. *Petersburg Daily Intelligencer*, 17 February 1859.

107. *Petersburg Daily Express*, 19 February 1859.

108. *Petersburg Daily Intelligencer*, 21 February 1859.

109. Letter dated 22 February in *Richmond Daily Dispatch*, 25 February 1859.

110. Barbee, "Lincoln and Booth," 240.

111. *Richmond Daily Dispatch*, 1 March 1859.

112. *Richmond Daily Dispatch*, 5 March 1859.

113. *Richmond Whig*, 11 March 1859, quoted in Fuller, "Kunkel and Company," 119.

114. William Jermyn Florence and Malvina Pray Florence (1830–1906). She was also known as Mrs. Joseph Litrell.

115. *Daily Richmond Enquirer*, 18 April 1859.

116. *Daily Richmond Enquirer*, 26 April 1859.

117. *Richmond Daily Dispatch*, 27 April 1859.

118. Kimmel, *Mad Booths*, 142.

119. Asia Booth Clarke, *John Wilkes Booth: A Sister's Memoir,* ed. Terry L. Alford (Jackson: University Press of Mississippi, 1996), 79.

120. *Petersburg Daily Intelligencer*, 27 April 1859.

121. *Richmond Whig*, 2 May 1859.

122. Fuller, "Kunkel and Company," 216.

123. *Lynchburg Daily Virginian*, 18 May 1859. Unless otherwise noted, the *Lynchburg Daily Virginian* is the source for information about this Lynchburg engagement.

124. *Lynchburg Daily Virginian*, 18 May 1859.

125. *Lynchburg Daily Virginian*, 19 May 1859.

126. *Lynchburg Daily Virginian*, 20 May 1859.

127. *Lynchburg Daily Virginian*, 23 May 1859.

128. *Lynchburg Daily Virginian*, 25 May 1859.

129. *Lynchburg Daily Virginian*, 26 May 1859.

130. *Lynchburg Daily Virginian*, 27 May 1859.

131. *Lynchburg Daily Virginian*, 30 May 1859.

132. *Lynchburg Daily Virginian*, 1 June 1859.

133. *Lynchburg Daily Virginian*, 30 May 1859.

134. This version of the play was likely the same as *Our Eastern Shore Cousin in Richmond*.

135. *Richmond Daily Dispatch*, 5 September 1859.

136. *Richmond Daily Whig*, 12 September 1859.

137. *Lynchburg Daily Virginian*, 17 October 1859. Unless otherwise noted, the *Lynchburg Daily Virginian* is the source for information about this Lynchburg engagement.

138. *Lynchburg Daily Virginian*, 20 October 1859.

139. *Daily Richmond Enquirer*, 7 November 1859.

140. Barron, "With John Wilkes Booth in His Days as an Actor."

141. Barron, "With John Wilkes Booth in His Days as an Actor."

142. Barron, "With John Wilkes Booth in His Days as an Actor."

143. William Evan Burton (1804–1860) studied for the ministry in London, where he was born. His acting career began in England. He came to the United States in 1834 and opened Burton's Theatre in New York.

144. Hall, "John Wilkes Booth and John Brown"; *Richmond Daily Dispatch*, 21 November 1859.

145. *Richmond Daily Dispatch*, 23 November 1859.

146. "Charlestown Intelligence, November 21," *Richmond Whig*, 25 November 1859.

147. *Richmond Daily Dispatch*, 21 November 1859.

148. Smythe, "Hiding in Plain Sight," 12.

149. Alfriend, *History of Zion Episcopal Church.*

150. Mary Devlin to Edwin Booth, 28 November 1859, in Booth, *Letters and Notebooks of Mary Devlin Booth*, 22.

151. *Daily Richmond Enquirer*, 28 November 1859.

152. Asia Booth Clarke to Jean Anderson, undated, BCLM Works on Paper Collection, ML 518, Box 37, Maryland Historical Society, Baltimore, Maryland.

153. "The Hanging of John Brown," *Philadelphia Inquirer*, 2 May 1897, quoted in Smythe, "Out of Hiding," 31.

154. Smythe, "Out of Hiding," 31.

155. Whitlock, "Life of Philip Whitlock," 1.

156. Hall, "John Wilkes Booth and John Brown."

157. *Richmond Daily Dispatch*, 5 December 1859.

158. *Richmond Daily Dispatch*, 5 December 1859.

159. George Marsh organized the Marsh Juvenile Troupe, also known as the Marsh Troupe, in June 1855. The Troupe, consisting of about ten girls mostly under the age of ten, performed plays and skits.

160. *Richmond Whig*, 26 December 1859.

161. Mary Devlin to Edwin Booth, 28 December 1859, in Booth, *Letters and Notebooks of Mary Devlin Booth*, 27.

162. Caroline Richings (1827–1882) was born in England as Mary Caroline Reynoldson. She became a concert pianist while still a girl. She was adopted by actor Peter Richings (1797–1871). Peter Richings was born in England and immigrated to the United States in 1821.

163. Rhodehamel and Taper, eds., *Right or Wrong*, 47.

164. Mary Devlin to Edwin Booth, 1 March 1860, in Booth, *Letters and Notebooks of Mary Devlin Booth*, 45.

165. Rosalie A. Booth to Edwin Booth, 12 March 1860, Billy Rose Theatre Division, New York Public Library.

166. Asia Booth Clarke to Jean Anderson, 7 March 1860, BCLM Works on Paper Collection.

167. Rosalie A. Booth to Edwin Booth, 12 March 1860, Billy Rose Theatre Division, New York Public Library.

168. The author has not found evidence placing John Wilkes Booth in either Petersburg or in Richmond.

169. *Richmond Daily Dispatch*, 2 April 1860.

170. Harpers Ferry Fund Accounts and Receipts, 1860–1861, Auditor of Public Accounts, entry 145, box 448, Library of Virginia.

171. Asia Booth Clarke to Jean Anderson, 29 April 1860, BCLM Works on Paper Collection.

172. *Petersburg Press*, 30 April 1860. No newspapers or other records describing this Norfolk engagement seem to exist.

173. Frank Chanfrau (1824–1884) began his career playing bit parts and doing impressions of star actors. He managed theatres in New York and traveled as a star.

174. *Richmond Daily Dispatch*, 30 April 1860.

175. *Richmond Whig*, 8 May 1860.

176. John Wilkes Booth to Robert Whittle, 8 May 1860, John Hay Library, Brown University.

177. *Richmond Daily Dispatch*, 25 May 1860.

178. *Richmond Daily Dispatch*, 31 May 1860.

179. *Daily Richmond Enquirer*, 31 May 1860.

180. *Daily Richmond Enquirer*, 4 June 1860.

Chapter 4. Novice: 1860–1861

1. George Alfred Townsend, "How John Wilkes Booth Was Started in the Theatrical Profession," *Cincinnati Enquirer*, 19 January 1886, 1.

2. *Columbus Daily Times*, 30 September 1860, quoted in Helen B. Keller, "The History of the Theater in Columbus, Georgia from 1828 to 1865" (MA Thesis, University of Georgia, 1957), 142.

3. *Montgomery Daily Mail*, 16 October 1860.

4. *New York Clipper*, 27 October 1860.

5. Townsend, "How John Wilkes Booth Was Started in the Theatrical Profession"; *Columbus Weekly Enquirer*, 16 October 1860.

6. *Columbus Daily Sun*, 13 October 1860, quoted in Keller, "History of the Theater in Columbus, Georgia," 147.

7. *Columbus Daily Sun*, 13 October 1860, quoted in Keller, "History of the Theater in Columbus, Georgia," 147.

8. Alonzo J. May, "May's Dramatic Encyclopedia, 1750–1904," microfilm, Manuscript Division, Library of Congress, Washington, D.C. (original in Baltimore Theater Papers, Maryland Historical Society, Baltimore).

9. *Columbus Daily Times*, 17 October 1860, quoted in Keller, "History of the Theater in Columbus, Georgia," 148.

10. Keller, "History of the Theater in Columbus, Georgia," 149.

11. *Columbus Daily Sun*, 20, 22 October 1860, quoted in Keller, "History of the Theater in Columbus, Georgia," 150.

12. Keller, "History of the Theater in Columbus, Georgia," 151.

13. *Montgomery Daily Mail*, 26 October 1860.

14. *Montgomery Daily Mail*, 31 October 1860.

15. Kate Bateman (1843–1917) came from an acting family. She made her debut in New York at the age of six.

16. *Washington Sunday Herald*, 25 January 1874.

17. *Montgomery Daily Mail*, 1 December 1860.

18. *Montgomery Daily Mail*, 25 October 1860.

19. *Montgomery Daily Mail*, 26 (quotation), 27 October 1860.

20. *Montgomery Daily Mail*, 27 October 1860.

21. *Montgomery Daily Mail*, 6 November 1860.

22. John A. Ellsler, *The Stage Memories of John A. Ellsler*, ed. Effie Ellsler Weston (Cleveland: The Rowfant Club, 1950), 129. John Ellsler (1821–1903) became an actor at an early age. He managed theatres in Cleveland for more than 30 years.

23. Louise C. Wooster, *The Autobiography of a Magdalen* (Birmingham, AL: Birmingham Publishing Co., 1911), 50–53.

24. *Montgomery Daily Mail*, 27 September 1860.

25. *New York Herald*, 10 December 1860.

26. Asia Booth Clarke to Jean Anderson, 16 December 1860, BCLM Works on Paper Collection, ML 518, Box 37, Maryland Historical Society, Baltimore.

27. Text printed in John H. Rhodehamel and Louise Taper, eds., *Right or Wrong, God Judge Me: The Writings of John Wilkes Booth* (Urbana: University of Illinois Press, 1997), 55–64. Rhodehamel and Taper present an excellent analysis of the speech. See also Jeannine Clarke Dodels, "Water on Stone: A Study of John Wilkes Booth's Political Draft Preserved at the Players Club NYC," unpublished manuscript, the first scholarly treatment of Booth's speech draft.

28. Otis Skinner, *The Last Tragedian: Booth Tells His Own Story* (New York: Dodd, Mead, 1939), 136.

29. *New York Clipper*, 9 February 1861.

30. *New York Clipper*, 23 February 1861; *Baltimore Sun*, 14 February 1861; *New York Herald*, 13 February 1861.

31. Henry P. Phelps, *Players of a Century: A Record of the Albany Stage* (Albany: Joseph McDonough, 1880), 319.

32. *Albany Atlas and Argus*, 18 February 1861.

33. Henry Dickinson Stone, *Personal Recollections of the Drama, or Theatrical Reminiscences* (Albany: Charles van Benthuysen & Sons, 1873), 70.

34. *Albany Atlas and Argus*, 18 February 1861.

35. Phelps, *Players of a Century*, 326.

36. *Albany Evening Journal*, undated quote in the *Albany Times Union*, 10 February 1963.

37. *New York Clipper*, 9 March 1861.

38. *Albany Atlas and Argus*, 2 March 1861.

39. Phelps, *Players of a Century*, 325.

40. *Albany Atlas and Argus*, 22 February 1861.

41. Phelps, *Players of a Century*, 326.

42. *Portland Daily Advertiser*, 16 March 1861. William B. English was the manager of the Portland Theatre. He married the widowed mother of Lucille and Helen Western, who had been born in New Orleans in 1843 and 1844.

43. *Portland Sunday Telegram*, 13 April 1902.

44. T. Allston Brown, *History of the American Stage from 1733 to 1870* (New York: Dick & Fitzgerald, 1870), 121.

45. *Philadelphia Press*, 1 March 1858, quoted in Deirdre Kincaid, "Rough Magic: The Theatrical Life of John Wilkes Booth" (unpublished manuscript, 2009), Chapter 3, 11.

46. *Portland Daily Advertiser*, 29 April 1861.

47. *New York Clipper*, 25 May 1861.

48. Townsend, "How John Wilkes Booth Was Started in the Theatrical Profession."

49. May, "May's Dramatic Encyclopedia."

50. May, "May's Dramatic Encyclopedia."

51. E.B. Long, *The Civil War Day By Day: An Almanac, 1861–1865* (Garden City, NY: Doubleday, 1971), 74.

52. May, "May's Dramatic Encyclopedia"; *Baltimore Sun*, 16 May 1861.

53. Charles Wyndham (1837–1919) was born in Liverpool. He was educated as a doctor but preferred an acting career. He served briefly in the American Civil War, acted in the United States, and returned to England, where he became a theatre manager. He was knighted in 1902.

54. *New York Herald*, 27 June 1909, quoted in Francis Wilson, *John Wilkes Booth, Fact and Fiction of Lincoln's Assassination* (Boston: Hougton Mifflin, 1929), 157.

55. Asia Booth Clarke to Jean Anderson, 27 June 1861 [mis-dated 1862], BCLM Works on Paper Collection.

56. Adam Badeau, "Dramatic Reminiscences," *St. Paul and Minneapolis Pioneer Press*, 20 February 1887.

57. "*The Military Occupation of Bel Air*," *Bel Air Southern Aegis*, 20 July 1861, 2. Herman Stump, Jr. (1837–1917) was a lawyer in Bel Air. In August 1861 he fled to Canada to escape arrest by federal authorities. He went on to become a state senator and, under President Grover Cleveland, Superintendent of Immigration.

58. "Harford Historical Society," *Bel Air Southern Aegis*, 22 January 1886.

59. *New York Clipper*, 30 June 1860.

60. Richard Lockridge, *Darling of Misfortune: Edwin Booth, 1833–1893* (New York: The Century Co., 1932), 85.

61. Eleanor Ruggles, *Prince of Players: Edwin Booth* (New York: W.W. Norton, 1953), 108.

62. *New York Clipper*, 14 July 1860, column dated 9 July 1860.

63. *Montgomery Advertiser*, 12 September 1860.

64. *Columbus Daily Times*, 30 September 1860, quoted in Keller, "History of the Theater in Columbus, Georgia," 142. Unless otherwise noted, the sources of characters and plays are the *Columbus Daily Times* or *Columbus Daily Sun*.

65. *New York Clipper*, 21 October 1860.

66. *Columbus Daily Sun*, 4 October 1860, described in Keller, "History of the Theater in Columbus, Georgia," 143.

67. Michael W. Kauffman, "Information Circular No. 1: Booth on Stage," typescript summary of the plays in which Booth appeared, 1981. Copy in author's files.

68. *Columbus Daily Sun*, 3 October 1860, quoted in Keller, "History of the Theater in Columbus, Georgia," 142.

69. *Columbus Daily Times*, 5 October 1860, quoted in Keller, "History of the Theater in Columbus, Georgia," 144.

70. *Columbus Daily Sun*, 10 October 1860, quoted in Keller, "History of the Theater in Columbus, Georgia," 145.

71. Keller, "History of the Theater in Columbus, Georgia," 145.

72. *Columbus Daily Sun*, 11 October 1860, quoted in Keller, "History of the Theater in Columbus, Georgia," 146.

73. *New York Clipper*, 27 October 1860.

74. May, "May's Dramatic Encyclopedia."

75. *Columbus Daily Sun*, 13 October 1860, quoted in Keller, "History of the Theater in Columbus, Georgia," 147.

76. *Columbus Daily Sun*, 13 October 1860, quoted in Keller, "History of the Theater in Columbus, Georgia," 147.

77. *Montgomery Evening Mail*, 16 October 1860.

78. *Columbus Daily Times*, 17 October 1860, quoted in Keller, "History of the Theater in Columbus, Georgia," 148.

79. *Montgomery Evening Mail*, 18 October 1860.

80. Keller, "History of the Theater in Columbus, Georgia," 149.

81. *Columbus Daily Sun*, 20 October 1860, quoted in Keller, "History of the Theater in Columbus, Georgia," 150.

82. *Columbus Daily Sun*, 22 October 1860, quoted in Keller, "History of the Theater in Columbus, Georgia," 150.

83. Keller, "History of the Theater in Columbus, Georgia," 151.

84. *New York Clipper*, 3 November 1860.

85. *Columbus Daily Sun*, 23 October 1860, quoted in Keller, "History of the Theater in Columbus, Georgia," 151; *Montgomery Daily Mail*, 22, 23 October 1860.

86. *Montgomery Daily Mail*, 25 October 1860.

87. *Montgomery Daily Mail*, 26 October 1860.

88. *Montgomery Daily Mail*, 25 October 1860.

89. *Montgomery Daily Mail*, 26 October 1860.

90. *Montgomery Daily Mail*, 27 October 1860.

91. *Montgomery Daily Mail*, 26, 27, 29 October 1860.

92. *Montgomery Daily Mail*, 30 October 1860.

93. *Montgomery Daily Mail*, 31 October 1860.

94. *Montgomery Daily Mail*, 1 November 1860.
95. *Montgomery Daily Mail*, 1 November 1860.
96. *Montgomery Daily Mail*, 2 November 1860.
97. *Montgomery Daily Mail*, 2 November 1860.
98. *Montgomery Daily Mail*, 3 November 1860.
99. *Montgomery Post*, 5 November 1860.
100. *Montgomery Daily Mail*, 6 November 1860.
101. *Montgomery Daily Mail*, 6 November 1860.
102. Long, *Civil War Day By Day*, 4.
103. *Montgomery Daily Mail*, 15 November 1860.
104. *Montgomery Daily Mail*, 17 November 1860.
105. *New York Clipper*, 17 November 1860.
106. *New York Clipper*, 24 November 1860.
107. *Montgomery Daily Mail*, 29 November 1860.
108. *Montgomery Daily Mail*, 30 November 1860.
109. W.H.F. Gurley in William C. Edwards and Edward Steers, Jr., eds., *The Lincoln Assassination: The Evidence* (Urbana: University of Illinois Press, 2009), 623. This book is hereafter cited as LASE. Investigation materials gathered for the Lincoln assassination conspiracy trial are housed at the National Archives and Records Administration in Record Group 153, Records of the Office of the Judge Advocate General (Army). The National Archives published this material on 16 rolls of microfilm known as Microcopy M599, which some authors have cited as "LAS" for Lincoln Assassination files. Each page has a reel and frame number. The book edited by Edwards and Steers, a transcription of these documents, has revolutionized access to the trial evidence.
110. *Montgomery Daily Mail*, 1 December 1860.
111. *Montgomery Daily Mail*, 2 December 1860.
112. *New York Clipper*, 15 December 1860.
113. *New York Herald*, 10 December 1860.
114. *Wilkes' Spirit of the Times* (New York), 22 December 1860.
115. Asia Booth Clarke to Jean Anderson, 16 December 1860, BCLM Works on Paper Collection.
116. *New York Clipper*, 5 January 1861.
117. Rhodehamel and Taper, eds., *Right or Wrong*, 55–64.
118. Skinner, *Last Tragedian*, 136.
119. Asia Booth Clarke, *The Elder and the Younger Booth* (Boston: James R. Osgood, 1882), 153.
120. *Rochester Union and Advertiser*, 22 January 1861. The sources for reviews and plays for this engagement are the *Rochester Union and Advertiser* and the *Rochester Evening Express*.
121. *Rochester Union and Advertiser*, 22 January 1861.
122. *Rochester Evening Express*, 23 January 1861.
123. *Rochester Evening Express*, 24 January 1861.
124. *Rochester Union and Advertiser*, 25 January 1861.
125. *Wilkes' Spirit of the Times* (New York), 26 January 1861.
126. *Rochester Union and Advertiser*, 30 January 1861.
127. *New York Clipper*, 9 February 1861.
128. *Albany Atlas and Argus*, 9 February 1861.
129. Phelps, *Players of a Century*, 326.
130. *New York Clipper*, 23 February 1861; *Baltimore Sun*, 14 February 1861; Phelps, *Players of a Century*, 325; Stanley Kimmel, *The Mad Booths of Maryland* (New York: Dover, 1969), 158–159.
131. *Albany Evening Journal*, 13 February 1861.
132. *Albany Evening Journal*, 14 February 1861.
133. *Albany Atlas and Argus*, 14 February 1861.

134. Paul M. Angle, *Lincoln 1854–1861: Being the Day by Day Activities of Abraham Lincoln from January 1, 1854 to March 4, 1861* (Springfield, IL: The Abraham Lincoln Association, 1933), 373.
135. Phelps, *Players of a Century*, 326.
136. *Albany Times and Courier*, undated clipping, filed in the William Seymour Family Papers, Manuscripts Division, Department of Rare Books and Special Collections, Princeton University Library, Princeton, New Jersey. Part of this review was quoted in the *Portland Daily Advertiser*, 19 March 1861.
137. *New York Clipper*, 9 March 1861.
138. *Albany Atlas and Argus*, 2 March 1861.
139. *Albany Atlas and Argus*, 2 March 1861.
140. *Albany Express*, 5 March 1861.
141. *Albany Express*, 6 March 1861.
142. *Albany Express*, 7 March 1861. Performances for this engagement are as advertised in the *Express* unless otherwise noted.
143. Kincaid, "Rough Magic," Chronology, 13.
144. *New York Clipper*, 9 March 1861.
145. *Albany Atlas and Argus*, 11 March 1861.
146. *Albany Times and Courier*, 11 March 1861.
147. *Albany Times and Courier*, 15 March 1861.
148. *Albany Times and Courier*, 16 March 1861.
149. Herb Adams of Portland responded with intelligence, industry, and wit to my many inquiries regarding Booth in Portland.
150. *Portland Eastern Argus*, 19 March 1861.
151. *Portland Daily Advertiser*, 20 March 1861. Performances for this engagement are found in the *Daily Advertiser* unless otherwise noted.
152. *Portland Daily Advertiser*, 22 March 1861.
153. *Portland Eastern Argus*, 23 March 1861.
154. *Portland Daily Advertiser*, 25 March 1861.
155. *Baltimore Sun*, 25 March 1861.
156. "Post Scrapbook," vol. 2, n.d., 102–104, Maine Historical Society, Portland, quoted in Gordon Samples, *Lust for Fame: The Stage Career of John Wilkes Booth* (Jefferson, NC: McFarland, 1982), 61.
157. *Portland Eastern Argus*, 5 April 1861.
158. *Portland Daily Advertiser*, 8 April 1861.
159. *Portland Daily Advertiser*, 11 April 1861.
160. *Portland Daily Advertiser*, 10 April 1861.
161. *New York Clipper*, 11 May 1861.
162. James Moreland, "A History of the Theatre in Portland, 1794–1932" (unpublished manuscript, 1938), 244 (available at the Portland Public Library).
163. *Albany Atlas and Argus*, 22 April 1861. Performances for this engagement are found in the *Atlas and Argus* unless otherwise noted.
164. *Madison* [Indiana] *Courier*, 11 May 1861.
165. *New York Clipper*, 4 May 1861.
166. *Baltimore Sun*, 16 May 1861; May, "May's Dramatic Encyclopedia."
167. George Alfred Townsend, "GATH's Etchings," *St. Louis Post-Dispatch*, 8 May 1880. Townsend wrote that on May 18 Booth began a six-week stay ending on June [*sic*] 11. Actually, the stay was meant to be for eight weeks ending July 11; it was then extended two weeks to July 25.
168. Asia Booth Clarke to Jean Anderson, 27 June 1861 [mis-dated 1862], BCLM Works on Paper Collection.

169. "The Military Occupation of Bel Air," *Bel Air Southern Aegis*, 20 July 1861. The article reports that the invasion occurred at 4:30 a.m. on the night of Saturday, 13 July 1861. More precisely, the invasion occurred at 4:30 on Sunday morning.

170. "Harford Historical Society," *Bel Air Southern Aegis*, 22 January 1886; Townsend, "GATH's Etchings."

Chapter 5. Rising Star: 1861–1862

1. Joseph H. Simonds (1839–1888) and John Wilkes Booth seem to have become acquainted in the summer of 1861. Booth, to his credit, recognized that Simonds had business sense and came to rely on him more and more in the next several years. Simonds was "a well-built man.... He was an immaculate dresser, had sandy hair, a mustache, and was a little austere in appearance. He had a deep interest in the stage as well as an intense desire to advance to a position more affluent than that of a bank teller." Description of Simonds in Ernest C. Miller, *John Wilkes Booth—Oilman* (New York: The Exposition Press, 1947), 26.

2. *Buffalo Daily Courier*, 1 November 1861.

3. *Chicago Tribune*, 30 April 1865.

4. T. Allston Brown, *History of the American Stage from 1733 to 1870* (New York: Dick & Fitzgerald, 1870), 286.

5. Alonzo J. May, "May's Dramatic Encyclopedia, 1750–1904," microfilm, Manuscript Division, Library of Congress, Washington, D.C. (original in Baltimore Theater Papers, Maryland Historical Society, Baltimore).

6. "No. 2 Bullfinch Place," *Chicago Daily Inter Ocean*, 27 August 1893.

7. John Wilkes Booth to Joseph H. Simonds, 23 November 1861, in John H. Rhodehamel and Louise Taper, eds., *Right or Wrong, God Judge Me: The Writings of John Wilkes Booth* (Urbana: University of Illinois Press, 1997), 74–75.

8. *Cincinnati Daily Commercial*, 23 November 1861.

9. *Cincinnati Daily Commercial*, 17 April 1865.

10. *Louisville Daily Democrat*, 8, 15 December 1861.

11. *Indianapolis Daily Journal*, 28 December 1861.

12. *Indianapolis Daily Sentinel*, 30 December 1861.

13. *Indianapolis Daily Journal*, 4 January 1862.

14. Albert G. Porter, "Recollections of John Wilkes Booth," Albert G. Porter Papers, Indiana State Library, Indianapolis.

15. Benedict DeBar (1812–1877), born in London, came to the United States in 1834. He was an actor, stage manager, and theatre owner.

16. Grant M. Herbstruth, "Benedict DeBar and the Grand Opera House in St. Louis, Missouri, from 1855 to 1879" (Ph.D. diss., University of Iowa, 1954), 27.

17. Herbstruth, "Benedict DeBar and the Grand Opera House," 94.

18. James H. Baker in William C. Edwards and Edward Steers, Jr., eds., *The Lincoln Assassination: The Evidence* (Urbana: University of Illinois Press, 2009), 100. This book is hereafter cited as LASE.

19. *New York Clipper*, 18 January 1862.

20. *New York Clipper*, 30 January 1862 (correspondence dated 15 January).

21. *St. Louis Missouri Democrat*, 15 January 1862.

22. Richard J.S. Gutman and Kellie O. Gutman, *John Wilkes Booth Himself* (Dover, MA: Hired Hand Press, 1979), 46.

23. Gutman and Gutman, *John Wilkes Booth Himself*, 46–51.

24. *Chicago Tribune*, 19 January 1862.

25. *Chicago Evening Journal*, 21 January 1862.

26. *Chicago Evening Journal*, 23 January 1862.

27. Unidentified clipping from Harvard Theatre Collection, quoted in Deirdre Kincaid, "Rough Magic: The Theatrical Life of John Wilkes Booth" (unpublished manuscript, 2009), Chapter 5, 28.

28. *Chicago Evening Journal*, 1 February 1862.

29. *Baltimore Sun*, 17 February 1862.

30. *Baltimore Sun*, 21 February 1862.

31. *Baltimore Sun*, 24 February 1862.

32. Mary Provost (1835–1914) was an American actress and theatre manager.

33. *New York Times*, 19 March 1862.

34. *Wilkes' Spirit of the Times*, 5 April 1862.

35. Brown, *History of the American Stage*, 510.

36. *New York Clipper*, 29 March 1862.

37. *Wilkes' Spirit of the Times*, 7 March 1863.

38. John Joseph Jennings, *Theatrical and Circus Life; or, Secrets of the Stage, Green-room and Sawdust Arena* (St. Louis: Sun, 1882), 487–488.

39. Obituary of Edward L. Tilton, *New York Times*, 20 March 1887. Edward Lafayette Tilton (1824–1886) was born in Massachusetts and spent most of his life in New York City. He was steadily employed as an actor and occasionally as a stage manager. One of his pallbearers was J.W. Collier, another associate of John Wilkes Booth.

40. "No. 2 Bullfinch Place," *Chicago Daily Inter Ocean*, 27 August 1893; Brown, *History of the American Stage*, 37.

41. *New York Tribune*, 21 March 1862.

42. *New York Times and Messenger*, 23 March 1862.

43. *Wilkes' Spirit of the Times*, 5 April 1862.

44. *Wilkes' Spirit of the Times*, 29 March 1862.

45. *New York Herald*, 25 March 1862.

46. Gordon Samples, *Lust for Fame: The Stage Career of John Wilkes Booth* (Jefferson, NC: McFarland, 1982), 80.

47. *New York Herald*, 7 April 1862.

48. *Wilkes' Spirit of the Times*, 31 March 1862.

49. *St. Louis Missouri Democrat*, 23 April 1862. Stuart Robson (1836–1903) was born Henry Robson Stuart in Annapolis, Maryland. In 1850 the Robson family moved to Baltimore, where Stuart, along with Edwin Booth, John Sleeper Clarke, and John Wilkes Booth, participated in amateur theatricals. He became an "eccentric comedian" with a voice described as the "Robson Squeek."

50. *St. Louis Missouri Democrat*, 24 April 1862.

51. James H. Baker in LASE, 100.

52. *Boston Daily Evening Transcript*, 9 May 1862.

53. *Boston Post*, 13 May 1862.

54. *Boston Post*, 19 May 1862.

55. *Boston Advertiser*, 19 May 1862.

56. *Saturday Evening Express*, 15 April 1865, quoted in Kincaid, "Rough Magic," Chapter 6, 19.

57. *Chicago Evening Journal*, 3 June 1862.

58. *Chicago Evening Journal*, 10 June 1862.

59. *Chicago Evening Journal*, 11 June 1862.

60. *Chicago Tribune*, 15 June 1862.

61. *Chicago Tribune*, 20 June 1862.

62. *Louisville Daily Journal*, 23 June 1862.

63. John Wilkes Booth to Joseph H. Simonds, 9 October 1861, in Rhodehamel and Taper, eds., *Right or Wrong*, 72.

64. Stanley Kimmel, *The Mad Booths of Maryland* (New York: Dover, 1969), 163.

65. John Wilkes Booth to Joseph H. Simonds, 9 October 1861, in Rhodehamel and Taper, eds., *Right or Wrong*, 72.

66. *New York Clipper*, 19 October 1861.

67. *Providence Daily Post*, 22 October 1861.

68. *Providence Daily Post*, 21 October 1861.

69. *Providence Daily Post*, 23 October 1861.

70. *Providence Daily Post*, 24 October 1861.

71. *Providence Journal*, 24 October 1861.

72. *Providence Daily Post*, 25 October 1861.

73. *Buffalo Post*, 29 October 1861.

74. *Buffalo Daily Courier*, 30 October 1861.

75. *Buffalo Morning Express*, 29 October 1861.

76. *Buffalo Daily Courier*, 29 October 1861.

77. "No. 2 Bullfinch Place," *Chicago Daily Inter Ocean*, 27 August 1893.

78. *Buffalo Daily Courier*, 2 November 1861.

79. *Buffalo Daily Courier*, 1 November 1861.

80. *Buffalo Daily Courier*, 4 November 1861.

81. *Buffalo Morning Express*, 5 November 1861.

82. *Buffalo Morning Express*, 5 November 1861.

83. *Buffalo Morning Express*, 6 November 1861.

84. *Buffalo Morning Express*, 7 November 1861.

85. John Wilkes Booth to Joseph H. Simonds, 23 November 1861, in Rhodehamel and Taper, eds., *Right or Wrong*, 74–75.

86. *Buffalo Daily Courier*, 8 November 1861.

87. *Buffalo Morning Express*, 9 November 1861.

88. *Detroit Free Press*, 12 November 1861. Unless otherwise noted, the sources of reviews and plays for this engagement are issues of the *Detroit Free Press*.

89. *Detroit Free Press*, 13 November 1861.

90. *Detroit Free Press*, 15 November 1861.

91. *Detroit Free Press*, 17 November 1861.

92. *Detroit Free Press*, 16 November 1861.

93. Account statement from Russell House in LASE, 170.

94. John Wilkes Booth to Fanny, 20 November 1861, in Rhodehamel and Taper, eds., *Right or Wrong*, 74.

95. John Wilkes Booth to Joseph H. Simonds, 23 November 1861, in Rhodehamel and Taper, eds., *Right or Wrong*, 74–75.

96. *Cincinnati Daily Commercial*, 26 November 1861. Unless otherwise noted, the sources of reviews and plays for this engagement are issues of the *Cincinnati Daily Commercial*.

97. *Cincinnati Daily Gazette*, 26 November 1861.

98. Murat Halstead (1829–1908), born in Ohio, was a journalist, editor, and author.

99. *Cincinnati Daily Commercial*, 27 November 1861.

100. *Cincinnati Daily Commercial*, 28 November 1861.

101. *Cincinnati Daily Commercial*, 29 November 1861.

102. *Cincinnati Daily Commercial*, 28 November 1861.

103. *Cincinnati Daily Commercial*, 30 November 1861.

104. "No. 2 Bullfinch Place," *Chicago Daily Inter Ocean*, 27 August 1893.

105. *Cincinnati Daily Gazette*, 30 November 1861.

106. *Cincinnati Daily Commercial*, 3 December 1861.

107. *Cincinnati Daily Press*, 3 December 1861.

108. *Cincinnati Daily Commercial*, 5 December 1861.

109. *Cincinnati Daily Commercial*, 6 December 1861.

110. *Cincinnati Daily Commercial*, 7 December 1861.

111. *Cincinnati Daily Commercial*, 17 April 1865.

112. *Cincinnati Daily Gazette*, 7 December 1861.

113. *Louisville Daily Democrat*, 8 December 1861.

114. *Louisville Daily Democrat*, 10 December 1861. Unless otherwise noted, the sources of reviews and plays for this engagement are issues of the *Louisville Daily Democrat*.

115. *Louisville Daily Journal*, 10 December 1861.

116. *Louisville Daily Democrat*, 12 December 1861.

117. *Louisville Daily Democrat*, 13 December 1861.

118. *Louisville Daily Democrat*, 14 December 1861.

119. *Louisville Daily Democrat*, 15 December 1861.

120. *Louisville Daily Democrat*, 18 December 1861.

121. *Louisville Daily Democrat*, 19 December 1861.

122. *Louisville Daily Democrat*, 20 December 1861.

123. *Indianapolis Daily Sentinel*, 21 December 1861.

124. *New York Clipper*, 21 December 1861.

125. *Louisville Daily Democrat*, 22 December 1861.

126. *Indianapolis Daily Journal*, 24 December 1861.

127. *Indianapolis Daily Sentinel*, 28 December 1861.

128. *Indianapolis Daily Sentinel*, 27 December 1861.

129. *Indianapolis Daily Sentinel*, 28 December 1861.

130. *Indianapolis Daily Sentinel*, 28 December 1861.

131. *Indianapolis Daily Journal*, 28 December 1861.

132. Kincaid, "Rough Magic," Chronology, 16.

133. *Indianapolis Daily Journal*, 30 December 1861.

134. *Indianapolis Daily Journal*, 4 January 1862.

135. *Indianapolis Daily Journal*, 31 December 1861.

136. *St. Louis Missouri Democrat*, 7 January 1862. Unless otherwise noted, the sources of reviews and plays for this engagement are issues of the *St. Louis Missouri Democrat*.

137. *St. Louis Missouri Democrat*, 9 January 1862.

138. *St. Louis Missouri Democrat*, 11 January 1862.

139. John Wilkes Booth to Joseph H. Simonds, 10 January 1862, in Rhodehamel and Taper, eds., *Right or Wrong*, 76.

140. *Boston Herald*, 5 June 1890.

141. *St. Louis Missouri Democrat*, 15 January 1862.

142. *St. Louis Missouri Democrat*, 16 January 1862.

143. *Chicago Tribune*, 21 January 1862.

144. *Chicago Evening Journal*, 23 January 1862. Unless otherwise noted, the sources of reviews and plays for this engagement are issues of the *Chicago Evening Journal*.

145. *Chicago Evening Journal*, 23 January 1862.

146. *Chicago Evening Journal*, 25 January 1862.

147. *Chicago Evening Journal*, 28 January 1862.

148. *Chicago Evening Journal*, 28 January 1862.

149. James H. McVicker (1822–1896) was born in New York. He began acting at the age of eighteen. He became famous as a theatre owner and manager. His daughter Mary was the second wife of Edwin Booth.

150. *Chicago Evening Journal*, 30 January 1862.

151. *Chicago Evening Journal*, 1 February 1862.

152. *Baltimore American*, 14 February 1862.

153. *Baltimore Sun*, 15 February 1862.

154. *Baltimore Sun*, 17 February 1862.

155. *Baltimore Sun*, 18 February 1862.

156. *Baltimore Sun*, 18 February 1862.

157. *Baltimore American and Commercial Advertiser*, 18 February 1862.

158. David Rankin Barbee, "Lincoln and Booth," typescript, 271, David Rankin Barbee Papers, Georgetown University Library, Washington, D.C.

159. *Baltimore Sun*, 19 February 1862.

160. John Wilkes Booth to Joseph H. Simonds, 18 February 1862, in Rhodehamel and Taper, eds., *Right or Wrong*, 77.

161. Annie Graham and her sister Lillie were born in Philadelphia and made their acting debut there in 1855.

162. *Wilkes' Spirit of the Times*, 8 March 1862.

163. *Baltimore Sun*, 20 February 1862.

164. *Baltimore American and Commercial Advertiser*, 20 February 1862.

165. *Baltimore Sun*, 19 February 1862.

166. *Baltimore Sun*, 20 February 1862.

167. *Baltimore Sun*, 22 February 1862.

168. *Baltimore Sun*, 24 February 1862.

169. *Baltimore American and Commercial Advertiser*, 24 February 1862.

170. *Baltimore American and Commercial Advertiser*, 25 February 1862.

171. *Baltimore Sun*, 25 February 1862.

172. *Baltimore Sun*, 26 February 1862

173. Richard F. Cary and his wife, Emma, were friends of Edwin Booth. Richard, serving as a captain, was killed in the Battle of Antietam in September 1862.

174. Eleanor Ruggles, *Prince of Players: Edwin Booth* (New York: W.W. Norton, 1953), 123. Cary's account of Booth's performance was found in his effects after his death.

175. Mary Devlin Booth to Edwin Booth, 28 February 1862, in Mary Devlin Booth, *The Letters and Notebooks of Mary Devlin Booth*, ed. L. Terry Oggel (New York: Greenwood Press, 1987), 69.

176. *Baltimore Sun*, 3 March 1862.

177. Kincaid, "Rough Magic," Chapter 7, 7.

178. *Baltimore Sun*, 4 March 1862.

179. *Baltimore Sun*, 6 March 1862.

180. *Baltimore Sun*, 7 March 1862.

181. *Baltimore Sun*, 7 March 1862.

182. *New York Clipper*, 22 March 1862.

183. Edwin Forrest (1806–1872), born in Philadelphia, made his debut there at the age of fourteen. He became a top-rank actor.

184. *Baltimore Sun*, 10 March 1862.

185. *Baltimore Sun*, 11 March 1862.

186. *New York Times*, 17 March 1862.

187. *New York Times*, 15 March 1862.

188. *New York Herald*, 18 March 1862.

189. *Wilkes' Spirit of the Times*, 29 March 1862.

190. *New York Evening Express*, 20 March 1862.

191. *New York Commercial Advertiser*, 24 March 1862.

192. *New York Tribune*, 25 March 1862.

193. *New York Tribune*, 21 March 1862.

194. John Wilkes Booth to Joseph H. Simonds, 22 March 1862, in Rhodehamel and Taper, eds., *Right or Wrong*, 78.

195. *New York Herald*, 25 March 1862.

196. *Wilkes' Spirit of the Times*, 31 March 1862.

197. *New York Times*, 26 March 1862.

198. *Wilkes' Spirit of the Times*, 29 March 1862.

199. *Wilkes' Spirit of the Times*, 29 March 1862.

200. *New York Sunday Mercury*, 30 March 1862.

201. *New York Herald*, 3 April 1862.

202. *Wilkes' Spirit of the Times*, 5 April 1862.

203. *New York Herald*, 7 April 1862.

204. *Toledo Blade*, 2 January 1899.

205. George S. Bryan, *The Great American Myth* (New York: Carrick & Evans, 1940), 372. Three O'Brien brothers changed their last name to Bryant. Dan Bryant (1833–1875), with his brothers Neil (1830–1902) and Jerry (1828–1861), formed Bryant's Minstrels in 1857 and became very popular in New York in the 1860s. Dan Emmet, a member of the group, wrote the song "Dixie," which was first performed by Bryant's Minstrels in 1859.

206. Asia Booth Clarke to Jean Anderson, 8 April 1862, BCLM Works on Paper Collection, ML 518, Box 37, Maryland Historical Society, Baltimore.

207. Fragment in LASE, 564.

208. John Wilkes Booth to Joseph H. Simonds, 13 April 1862, in Rhodehamel and Taper, eds., *Right or Wrong*, 79.

209. *St. Louis Missouri Democrat*, 22 April 1862.

210. *St. Louis Missouri Democrat*, 23 April 1862.

211. *St. Louis Missouri Democrat*, 24 April 1862.

212. *St. Louis Missouri Democrat*, 25 April 1862.

213. *St. Louis Missouri Democrat*, 26 April 1862.

214. *St. Louis Missouri Democrat*, 28 April 1862.

215. *St. Louis Missouri Democrat*, 29 April 1862.

216. *St. Louis Missouri Democrat*, 1 May 1862.

217. *St. Louis Missouri Democrat*, 2 May 1862.

218. *St. Louis Missouri Democrat*, 3 May 1862.

219. W.H.F. Gurley in LASE, 622.

220. J.E. Buckingham, *Reminiscences and Souvenirs of the Assassination of Abraham Lincoln* (Washington, D.C.: Rufus H. Darby, 1894), 49.

221. *Boston Daily Evening Transcript*, 13 May 1862. Unless otherwise noted, the sources of reviews and plays for this engagement are issues of the *Boston Daily Evening Transcript*.

222. Buckingham, *Reminiscences and Souvenirs*, 49.

223. Kincaid, "Rough Magic," Chapter 6, 12. William H. Whalley, born in Ireland in 1837, came to America and made his debut in Philadelphia in 1853.

224. Edwin Frank Keach (1824–1864) was the stage manager of the Boston Museum.

225. *Boston Daily Evening Transcript*, 14 May 1862.

226. *Boston Daily Evening Transcript*, 15 May 1862.

227. *Boston Journal*, 15 May 1862.

228. *Boston Daily Evening Transcript*, 16 May 1862.

229. Mrs. Julia Bennett Barrow was born in England in 1824, the daughter of an English actor. She was, at this time, one of the most popular actresses in Boston.

230. Copy of Boston Museum playbill for 21 May 1862 in author's files.

231. *Boston Daily Evening Transcript*, 23 May 1862.

232. *Chicago Evening Journal*, 31 May 1862.

233. Mary Ann Booth to Edwin Booth, 10 June 1862, Edwin Booth Collection, Hampden-Booth Theatre Library, The Players, New York.

234. *Chicago Tribune*, 1 June 1862.

235. *Chicago Tribune*, 3 June 1862.

236. *Chicago Evening Journal*, 2 June 1862.

237. *Chicago Evening Journal*, 4 June 1862.

238. *Chicago Tribune*, 4 June 1862 (quotation); *Chicago Evening Journal*, 5 June 1862.

239. *Chicago Tribune*, 7 June 1862.

240. *Chicago Tribune*, 10 June 1862.

241. *Chicago Evening Journal*, 9 June 1862.

242. Kincaid, "Rough Magic," Chronology, 18.

243. *Chicago Evening Journal*, 10 June 1862.

244. *Chicago Tribune*, 15 June 1862.

245. Kincaid, "Rough Magic," Chronology, 18.

246. *Chicago Tribune*, 21 June 1862.

247. *Louisville Daily Democrat*, 22 June 1862. Unless otherwise noted, the sources of reviews and plays for this engagement are from issues of the *Louisville Daily Democrat*.

248. *Louisville Daily Journal*, 23 June 1862.

249. *Louisville Daily Journal*, 24 June 1862.

250. *Louisville Daily Democrat*, 26 June 1862.

251. *Louisville Daily Democrat*, 27 June 1862.

252. *Louisville Daily Journal*, 28 June 1862.

253. *Louisville Daily Journal*, 28 June 1862.

254. *Louisville Daily Democrat*, 29 June 1862.

255. *Louisville Daily Journal*, 30 June 1862.

256. *Vicksburg Daily Whig*, 11 July 1862.

257. John C. Brennan, "John Wilkes Booth's Enigmatic Brother Joseph," *Maryland Historical Magazine* 78 (Spring 1983): 23.

Chapter 6. Success: 1862–1832

1. *New York Tribune*, 6 October 1862.

2. *Cincinnati Daily Commercial*, 17 April 1865.

3. *Cincinnati Enquirer*, 9 November 1862.

4. *Cincinnati Enquirer*, 23, 25 November 1862.

5. *Cincinnati Daily Commercial*, 17 April 1865.

6. *Cincinnati Enquirer*, 23 November 1862.

7. *Indianapolis Daily Journal*, 29 November 1862.

8. *Chicago Times*, 2 December 1862.

9. *Chicago Times*, 4 December 1862.

10. *Chicago Times*, 8 December 1862.

11. *Chicago Evening Journal*, 8 December 1862.

12. *Chicago Tribune*, 13 December 1862.

13. *Chicago Evening Journal*, 18 December 1862.

14. John Wilkes Booth to Edwin F. Keach, 8 December 1862, in John H. Rhodehamel and Louise Taper, eds., *Right or Wrong, God Judge Me: The Writings of John Wilkes Booth* (Urbana: University of Illinois Press, 1997), 83.

15. "Stage Duels as a Drawing Card," *New York Herald*, 5 January 1890.

16. Joseph Howard, Jr., "Some Hamlet Studies," *Chicago Herald*, 30 November 1890. Joseph Howard, Jr., was a widely known journalist and biographer of Henry Ward Beecher.

17. *Boston Advertiser*, 26 January 1863.

18. *Boston Daily Evening Transcript*, 22 January 1863.

19. *Boston Advertiser*, 26 January 1863.

20. *Boston Advertiser*, 1 February 1863.

21. *Boston Daily Evening Transcript*, 5 February 1863.

22. *Boston Daily Evening Transcript*, 12 February 1863.

23. *Wilkes' Spirit of the Times*, 21 February 1863.

24. Kate Reignolds (1836–1911) was born in England, the daughter of the Duke of Wellington's aide-de-camp. She acted in both the United States and England.

25. Catherine (Kate) Mary Reignolds Winslow, *Yesterday with Actors* (Boston: Cupples and Hurd, 1887), 142.

26. Quincy Kilby, typescript note, William Seymour Family Papers, Manuscripts Division, Department of Rare Books and Special Collections, Princeton University Library, Princeton, New Jersey.

27. Mrs. Thomas Bailey Aldrich, *Crowding Memories* (Boston: Houghton Mifflin, 1920), 35.

28. Eleanor Ruggles, *Prince of Players: Edwin Booth* (New York: W.W. Norton, 1953), 137.

29. Aldrich, *Crowding Memories*, 35.

30. Aldrich, *Crowding Memories*, 35.

31. Ruggles, *Prince of Players*, 139.

32. *New York Evening Post*, 21 February 1863.

33. *Philadelphia Evening Bulletin*, 23 February 1863.

34. *Philadelphia Evening Bulletin*, 27 February 1863.

35. Ruggles, *Prince of Players*, 141.

36. *Philadelphia Press*, 5 March 1863.

37. Louisa Lane Drew (1818–1897) was born Louisa Lane in England. She made her acting debut in 1827 in Philadelphia in a production of *Richard III* with Junius Brutus Booth, Sr., starring as Richard. She married John Drew in 1850.

38. Stanley Kimmel, *The Mad Booths of Maryland* (New York: Dover, 1969), 57.

39. *Philadelphia Press*, 5 March 1863.

40. *Philadelphia Evening Bulletin*, 9 March 1863.

41. *Philadelphia Press*, 9 March 1863.

42. *Baltimore American and Commercial Advertiser*, 20 March 1863.

43. John Wilkes Booth to Joseph H. Simonds, 3 April 1863, in Rhodehamel and Taper, eds., *Right or Wrong*, 86. Orlando Tompkins (ca. 1819–1884) made a fortune by selling "hot soda water." He managed the Boston Theatre from 1862 to 1875.

44. Richard Gutman and Kellie Gutman, "Boston: A Home for John Wilkes Booth?" *Surratt Society News* 10 (September 1985): 1.

45. *Washington National Intelligencer*, 12 April 1863.

46. *Washington Morning Chronicle*, 13 April 1863.

47. *Washington Morning Chronicle*, 18 April 1863.

48. Charles Wyndham, "John Wilkes Booth: An Interview with the Press with Sir Charles Wyndham," *New York Herald*, 27 June 1909.

49. Michael W. Kauffman, "David Edgar Herold, the Forgotten Conspirator," *Surratt Society News* 6 (November 1981).

50. David Herold statement in William C. Edwards and Edward Steers, Jr., eds., *The Lincoln Assassination: The Evidence* (Urbana: University of Illinois Press, 2009), 666–667. This book is hereafter cited as LASE.

51. George Alfred Townsend, "How John Wilkes Booth was Started in the Theatrical Profession," *Cincinnati Enquirer*, 19 January 1886, 1.

52. John Frederick May, "Mark of the Scalpel," *Records of the Columbia Historical Society* 13 (1910): 53.

53. John Wilkes Booth to Joseph H. Simonds, 19

April 1863, in Rhodehamel and Taper, eds., *Right or Wrong*, 88.

54. May, "Mark of the Scalpel," 55.

55. *Washington National Republican*, 17 April 1863.

56. *Washington National Intelligencer*, 27 April 1863.

57. George J. Olszewski, *Restoration of Ford's Theatre* (Washington, D.C.: United States Department of the Interior, 1963), 11.

58. *Washington National Intelligencer*, 27 April 1863.

59. *Chicago Times*, 21 May 1863.

60. *Chicago Times*, 1 June 1863.

61. *Chicago Times*, 27 May 1863.

62. *Chicago Tribune*, 21 May 1863.

63. Lt. Col. Henry L. McConnell in LASE, 852; Kimmel, *Mad Booths*, 175. Missouri's Union Provost Marshal Papers, 1861–1866, www.sos.mo.gov/archives/provost/default.asp.

64. John A. Ellsler, *The Stage Memories of John A. Ellsler*, ed. Effie Ellsler Weston (Cleveland: The Rowfant Club, 1950), 123.

65. George Palmer Putnam (1814–1872) founded the publishing companies which eventually became G.P. Putnam's Sons. He was a patron of the arts and a founder the Metropolitan Museum of Art.

66. Adam Badeau, "Dramatic Reminiscences," *St. Paul and Minneapolis Pioneer Press*, 20 February 1887.

67. Badeau, "Dramatic Reminiscences."

68. Joseph Rubinfine Autographs, West Palm Beach, Florida, catalog 96, item 19, 1988.

69. John H. Jack in LASE, 738.

70. John Wilkes Booth to Edwin F. Keach, 25 July 1862, in Rhodehamel and Taper, eds., *Right or Wrong*, 80.

71. John Wilkes Booth to T. Valentine Butsch, 3 August 1862, in Rhodehamel and Taper, eds., *Right or Wrong*, 81.

72. *New York Tribune*, 6 October 1862.

73. *New York Clipper*, 18 October 1862, column dated 13 October.

74. *New York Clipper*, 18 October 1862.

75. Junius Brutus Booth, Jr., to Edwin Booth, 20 October 1862, Edwin Booth Collection, Hampden-Booth Theatre Library, The Players, New York.

76. *Lexington Observer and Reporter*, 25 October 1862.

77. Quoted in Gordon Samples, *Lust for Fame: The Stage Career of John Wilkes Booth* (Jefferson, NC: McFarland, 1982), 93.

78. *Wilkes' Spirit of the Times*, 22 November 1862.

79. *Louisville Daily Journal*, 28 October 1862.

80. *Louisville Daily Democrat*, 29 October 1862. Unless otherwise noted, plays and reviews for this engagement are found in issues of the *Louisville Daily Democrat*.

81. *Louisville Daily Journal*, 29 October 1862.

82. *Louisville Daily Democrat*, 31 October 1862.

83. *Louisville Daily Democrat*, 1 November 1862.

84. *Louisville Daily Democrat*, 2 November 1862.

85. *Louisville Daily Democrat*, 5 November 1862.

86. *Louisville Daily Democrat*, 6 November 1862.

87. *Louisville Daily Democrat*, 8 November 1862.

88. *Cincinnati Enquirer*, 11 November 1862. Unless otherwise noted, plays and reviews for this engagement are found in issues of the *Cincinnati Enquirer*.

89. *Cincinnati Daily Gazette*, 12 November 1862.

90. "No. 2 Bullfinch Place," *Chicago Daily Inter Ocean*, 27 August 1893.

91. *Cincinnati Daily Commercial*, 14 November 1862.

92. *Cincinnati Enquirer*, 14 November 1862.

93. "No. 2 Bullfinch Place," *Chicago Daily Inter Ocean*, 27 August 1893.

94. *Cincinnati Enquirer*, 15 November 1862.

95. *Cincinnati Daily Gazette*, 17 November 1862.

96. *Cincinnati Daily Gazette*, 18 November 1862.

97. *Cincinnati Enquirer*, 25 November 1862.

98. *Cincinnati Daily Gazette*, 19 November 1862.

99. *Cincinnati Enquirer*, 19 November 1862.

100. *Cincinnati Enquirer*, 21 November 1862.

101. *Cincinnati Enquirer*, 22 November 1862.

102. *Cincinnati Enquirer*, 23 November 1862.

103. *Cincinnati Enquirer*, 23 November 1862.

104. *Wilkes' Spirit of the Times*, 22 November 1862.

105. *Indianapolis Daily Sentinel*, 25 November 1862. Unless otherwise noted, plays and reviews for this engagement are found in issues of the *Indianapolis Daily Sentinel*.

106. Marion Macarthy (1838–1865) was a minor British actress of the period. She became ill in October 1863, was confined to an asylum in Indianapolis, and died on April 1, 1865.

107. *Indianapolis Daily Sentinel*, 27 November 1862.

108. *Indianapolis Daily Journal*, 29 November 1862.

109. *Indianapolis Enquirer*, 29 November 1862.

110. *Chicago Evening Journal*, 29 November 1862.

111. *Chicago Times*, 2 December 1862. Unless otherwise noted, plays and reviews for this engagement are found in issues of the *Chicago Times*.

112. *Chicago Times*, 3 December 1862.

113. *Chicago Evening Journal*, 4 December 1862.

114. *Chicago Times*, 4 December 1862.

115. *Chicago Times*, 5 December 1862.

116. *Chicago Times*, 6 December 1862.

117. John Wilkes Booth to Joseph H. Simonds, 6 December 1862, in Rhodehamel and Taper, eds., *Right or Wrong*, 82.

118. *Chicago Tribune*, 7 December 1862.

119. *Chicago Times*, 9 December 1862.

120. *Chicago Times*, 8 December 1862.

121. John Wilkes Booth to Edwin F. Keach, 8 December 1862, in Rhodehamel and Taper, eds., *Right or Wrong*, 83.

122. *Chicago Times*, 10 December 1862.

123. *Chicago Times*, 11 December 1862.

124. *Chicago Times*, 12 December 1862.

125. *Chicago Tribune*, 13 December 1862.

126. *Chicago Times*, 13 December 1862.

127. *Chicago Times*, 16 December 1862.

128. *Chicago Times*, 17 December 1862.

129. *Chicago Evening Journal*, 18 December 1862.

130. *St. Louis Missouri Democrat*, 23 December 1862. Unless otherwise noted, plays and reviews for this engagement are found in issues of the *St. Louis Missouri Democrat*.

131. *St. Louis Missouri Democrat*, 24 December 1862.

132. *St. Louis Missouri Democrat*, 25 December 1862.

133. *St. Louis Missouri Democrat*, 25 December 1862.

134. *St. Louis Missouri Democrat*, 27 December 1862.

135. *St. Louis Missouri Democrat*, 30 December 1862.

136. *St. Louis Missouri Democrat*, 31 December 1862.

137. *St. Louis Missouri Democrat*, 31 December 1862.

138. *Indianapolis Daily Sentinel*, 6 January 1863.

139. *Indianapolis Daily Journal*, 5 January 1863.

140. *Indianapolis Daily Journal*, 6 January 1863.

141. *Indianapolis Daily Sentinel*, 7 January 1863.

142. *Indianapolis Gazette*, 7 January 1863.

143. *Indianapolis Daily Sentinel*, 8 January 1863.

144. *Indianapolis Daily Sentinel*, 9 January 1863.

145. *Indianapolis Gazette*, 10 January 1863.

146. *Indianapolis Daily Sentinel*, 10 January 1863.

147. Mary Ann Holmes Booth to Edwin Booth, 15 January 1863, Edwin Booth Collection, Hampden-Booth Theatre Library, The Players, New York.

148. *Boston Daily Evening Transcript*, 20 January 1863.

149. "The Stage-Drama Green Room," unidentified clipping, January 1863.

150. *Boston Daily Evening Transcript*, 20 January 1863.

151. "The Stage-Drama Green Room," unidentified clipping, January 1863.

152. Ruggles, *Prince of Players*, 135.

153. Mary Devlin Booth to Emma C. Cushman, 22 January 1863, in Mary Devlin Booth, *The Letters and Notebooks of Mary Devlin Booth*, ed. L. Terry Oggel (New York: Greenwood Press, 1987), 101.

154. *Boston Daily Evening Transcript*, 22 January 1863.

155. John Wilkes Booth to Edwin F. Keach, 8 December 1862, in Rhodehamel and Taper, eds., *Right or Wrong*, 83.

156. *Boston Daily Evening Transcript*, 23 January 1863.

157. *Boston Post*, 26 January 1862.

158. Mary Ann Holmes Booth to Edwin Booth, 29 January 1863, Edwin Booth Collection, Hampden-Booth Theatre Library, The Players, New York.

159. Winslow, *Yesterday with Actors*, 142.

160. *Boston Daily Evening Transcript*, 31 January 1863.

161. *Boston Daily Evening Transcript*, 2 February 1863.

162. *Boston Daily Evening Transcript*, 3 February 1863.

163. Rhodehamel and Taper, eds., *Right or Wrong*, 27.

164. *Boston Daily Evening Transcript*, 5 February 1863.

165. *Boston Daily Evening Transcript*, 5 February 1863.

166. *Boston Daily Evening Transcript*, 9 February 1863.

167. *Boston Daily Evening Transcript*, 10 February 1863.

168. Kimmel, *Mad Booths*, 170.

169. Mary Devlin Booth to Edwin Booth, 12 February 1863, in Booth, *Letters and Notebooks of Mary Devlin Booth*, 105–106.

170. *Boston Daily Evening Transcript*, 12 February 1863.

171. *Boston Daily Evening Transcript*, 13 February 1863.

172. *Boston Advertiser*, 16 February 1863.

173. Aldrich, *Crowding Memories*, 34.

174. Ruggles, *Prince of Players*, 137.

175. Aldrich, *Crowding Memories*, 35.

176. Aldrich, *Crowding Memories*, 35.

177. Ruggles, *Prince of Players*, 139.

178. *Wilkes' Spirit of the Times*, 21 February 1863.

179. *Philadelphia Evening Bulletin*, 27 February 1863.

180. *Philadelphia Evening Bulletin*, 23 February 1863.

181. Ruggles, *Prince of Players*, 141.

182. *Philadelphia Evening Bulletin*, 27 February 1863.

183. *Philadelphia Daily Dispatch*, 15 March 1863.

184. John Wilkes Booth to Joseph H. Simonds, 28 February 1863, in Rhodehamel and Taper, eds., *Right or Wrong*, 84.

185. John Wilkes Booth to Joseph H. Simonds, 1 March 1863, in Rhodehamel and Taper, eds., *Right or Wrong*, 85.

186. William S. Thompson in *Trial of John H. Surratt in the Criminal Court of the District of Columbia*, 2 vols. (Washington, D.C.: Government Printing Office, 1867), 1:517. This source is hereafter cited as Surratt Trial.

187. *Philadelphia Evening Bulletin*, 3 March 1863.

188. *Philadelphia Inquirer,* 4 March 1863.

189. Asia Booth Clarke to Jean Anderson, 3 March 1863, BCLM Works on Paper Collection, ML 518, Box 37, Maryland Historical Society, Baltimore.

190. *Philadelphia Press*, 5 March 1863.

191. *Philadelphia Press*, 5 March 1863.

192. *Philadelphia Evening Bulletin*, 7 March 1863.

193. Rhodehamel and Taper, eds., *Right or Wrong*, 85, n. 2.

194. *Philadelphia Sunday Dispatch*, 8 March 1863.

195. *Philadelphia Evening Bulletin*, 10 March 1863.

196. *Philadelphia Evening Bulletin*, 11 March 1863.

197. Charles Barton Hill (1827-after 1884) was a British-born actor. He managed the California Theatre in San Francisco.

198. *Philadelphia Evening Bulletin*, 12 March 1863.

199. Alice Gray or Grey (1833-after 1874), born in Boston, made her acting debut in 1849.

200. *Baltimore American and Commercial Advertiser*, 16 March 1863.

201. *Baltimore American and Commercial Advertiser*, 17 March 1863.

202. *Baltimore Sun*, 17 March 1863.

203. *Baltimore Daily Gazette,* quoted in *Baltimore Sun*, 21 March 1863.

204. *Baltimore American and Commercial Advertiser*, 18 March 1863.

205. *Baltimore American and Commercial Advertiser*, 19 March 1863.

206. *Baltimore Sun*, 19 March 1863.

207. *Baltimore American and Commercial Advertiser*, 20 March 1863.

208. *Baltimore Daily Gazette*, 21 March 1863.

209. *Baltimore American and Commercial Advertiser*, 23 March 1863.

210. John Wilkes Booth to Joseph H. Simonds, 3 April 1863, in Rhodehamel and Taper, eds., *Right or Wrong*, 86.

211. Rhodehamel and Taper, eds., *Right or Wrong*, 87, n. 2.

212. Wyndham, "John Wilkes Booth," *New York Herald*, 27 June 1909.

213. *Washington Morning Chronicle*, 11 April 1863.

214. John Frederick May (1812–1891) was a leading surgeon in the District of Columbia.

215. May, "Mark of the Scalpel," 55.

216. Euphemia (Effie) Germon (1845–1914) made her acting debut in Baltimore in the 1857–1858 season. One of five *cartes de visite* that Booth carried at the time of his death was that of Effie Germon.

217. *Washington Morning Chronicle*, 14 April 1863.

218. *Washington Morning Chronicle*, 17 April 1863.

219. *Washington Morning Chronicle*, 16 April 1863.

220. *Washington National Republican*, 17 April 1863.

221. John Wilkes Booth to Benedict DeBar, 17 April 1863, in Rhodehamel and Taper, eds., *Right or Wrong*, 87.

222. Annette Ince (died in 1892) began her career as a dancer. She made her acting debut in 1853 in Philadelphia.

223. *Washington Morning Chronicle*, 18 April 1863.

224. "Lincoln's Son Met Booth before Shooting," *Springfield* [Ohio] *News Sun*, 1 February 1999, A5. The *News Sun* quotes the 7 July 1905 *New York Sun* obituary of Gustav Albert Schurmann. Schurmann's account and memorabilia in the possession of his descendants lend credence to his description of the incident.

225. John Wilkes Booth to Joseph H. Simonds, 19 April 1863, in Rhodehamel and Taper, eds., *Right or Wrong*, 88.

226. *Washington Morning Chronicle*, 24 April 1863.

227. *Washington Morning Chronicle*, 25 April 1863.

228. *Washington National Intelligencer*, 28 April 1863.

229. *Washington Morning Chronicle*, 27 April 1863.

230. *Washington National Intelligencer*, 28 April 1863.

231. *Washington Morning Chronicle*, 29 April 1863.

232. *Washington National Intelligencer*, 9 May 1863.

233. *Washington National Intelligencer*, 4 May 1863.

234. *Washington National Intelligencer*, 30 April 1863.

235. *Washington National Intelligencer*, 4 May 1863.

236. "The House That Booth Built," Ella Mahoney Papers, Historical Society of Harford County, Bel Air, Maryland.

237. *Washington Morning Chronicle*, 4, 5 May 1863.

238. *Washington Evening Star*, 7 May 1863.

239. *Washington Morning Chronicle*, 7 May 1863.

240. *Washington National Intelligencer*, 8 May 1863.

241. *Washington National Intelligencer*, 9 May 1863.

242. *Washington National Intelligencer*, 9 May 1863.

243. James Anderson Wise to John Wilkes Booth, 11 May 1863, Edwin Booth Collection, Hampden-Booth Theatre Library, The Players, New York. The poem is attributed to John Whitaker Watson.

244. *Chicago Tribune*, 19 May 1863.

245. *Chicago Times*, 20 May 1863.

246. *Chicago Tribune*, 21 May 1863.

247. *Chicago Times*, 21 May 1863.

248. *Chicago Tribune*, 19 May 1863.

249. *Chicago Times*, 22 May 1863; *Chicago Tribune*, 22 May 1863.

250. *Chicago Times*, 26 May 1863.

251. *Chicago Times*, 27 May 1863.

252. *Chicago Times*, 28 May 1863.

253. *Chicago Times*, 30 May 1863.

254. *Chicago Tribune*, 31 May 1863.

255. *Chicago Times*, 1 June 1863.

256. *Chicago Times*, 3 June 1863.

257. *Chicago Times*, 5 June 1863.

258. *Wilkes' Spirit of the Times*, 13 June 1863.

259. Lt. Col. Henry L. McConnell in LASE, 852; Kimmel, *Mad Booths*, 175. Missouri's Union Provost Marshal Papers, 1861–1866, http://www.sos.mo.gov/archives/provost/default.asp.

260. *St. Louis Missouri Democrat*, 17 June 1863. Unless otherwise noted, reviews and plays are found in issues of the *St. Louis Missouri Democrat*.

261. *St. Louis Missouri Democrat*, 18 June 1863.

262. *St. Louis Missouri Democrat*, 18 June 1863.

263. *St. Louis Missouri Democrat*, 20 June 1863.

264. *St. Louis Missouri Democrat*, 23 June 1863.

265. John Wilkes Booth to R.J. Morgan, 22 June 1863, in Rhodehamel and Taper, eds., *Right or Wrong*, 89.

266. *New York Clipper*, 4 July 1863.

267. Grant M. Herbstruth, "Benedict DeBar and the Grand Opera House in St. Louis, Missouri, from 1855 to 1879" (Ph.D. diss., University of Iowa, 1954), 594.

268. *Cleveland Morning Leader*, 29 June 1863.

269. Ellsler, *Stage Memories*, 124.

270. *Cleveland Herald*, 2 July 1863.

271. *Cleveland Herald*, 2 July 1863.

272. *Buffalo Express*, 6 July 1863. Unless otherwise noted, reviews and plays are found in issues of the *Buffalo Express*.

273. *Buffalo Daily Courier*, 11 July 1863.

274. Badeau, "Dramatic Reminiscences."

Chapter 7. Career End: 1863–1864

1. *Boston Daily Evening Transcript*, 2 October 1863.

2. *New York Clipper*, 10 October 1863.

3. *Worcester* [Massachusetts] *Sunday Telegram*, 17 December 1944.

4. *Brooklyn Standard*, 31 October 1863.

5. Fanny Brown (1837- died after 1870) began her stage career at the age of six.

6. Typed note summarizing gossip gathered in Boston theatres, Stanley Kimmel Papers, Macdonald-Kelce Library, University of Tampa, Tampa, Florida.

7. *New York Clipper*, 28 November 1863.

8. *Washington Morning Chronicle*, 3 November 1863.

9. *Washington National Intelligencer*, 12 November 1863.

10. John Hay, *Lincoln and the Civil War in the Diaries and Letters of John Hay*, ed. Tyler Dennett (New York: Dodd, Mead, 1939), 118.

11. *Washington National Intelligencer*, 12 November 1863.

12. *Washington Evening Star*, 7 December 1881.

13. *Cleveland Plain Dealer*, 5 December 1863.

14. *New York Clipper*, 19 December 1863.

15. *New York Clipper*, 19 December 1863. James C. McCollom (ca. 1838–1883) was born in Buffalo and acted in that vicinity. He was secretly married to Mrs. D.P. Bowers, with whom he often appeared on stage.

16. *Cleveland Morning Leader*, 30 November 1863.

17. Clara Morris (1849–1825) was an actress and a prolific writer.

18. Clara Morris, *Life on the Stage: My Personal Experiences and Recollections* (London: Morris, Isbister, 1902), 97–98.

19. Morris, *Life on the Stage*, 97–99.

20. "The Night That Lincoln Was Shot," *The Theatre* 17 (June 1913), quoted in Gordon Samples, *Lust for Fame: The Stage Career of John Wilkes Booth* (Jefferson, NC: McFarland, 1982), 90.

21. John A. Ellsler, *The Stage Memories of John A. Ellsler*, ed. Effie Ellsler Weston (Cleveland: The Rowfant Club, 1950), 125, 127.

22. Ellsler, *Stage Memories*, 127.

23. Ernest C. Miller, "John Wilkes Booth in the Pennsylvania Oil Region," *Western Pennsylvania Historical Magazine* 31 (March-June 1948): 61.

24. Joseph H. Simonds in William C. Edwards and Edward Steers, Jr., eds., *The Lincoln Assassination: The Evidence* (Urbana: University of Illinois Press, 2009), 1154–1155. This book is hereafter cited as LASE.

25. Alan W. Farley, "Abraham Lincoln in Kansas Territory, December 1 to 7, 1859," pamphlet, Fort Leavenworth, Kansas, 1959.

26. *Leavenworth Daily Times,* 22 December 1864.

27. *Leavenworth Daily Times*, 25 February 1940.

28. Jerome Manuscript, Kansas Historical Society, Topeka.

29. *Leavenworth Daily Conservative*, 27 December 1863.

30. Moses Kimball (1809–1895) was a prominent and wealthy Boston businessman. He was a rival, and later partner, of showman P.T. Barnum. Kimball founded and managed the Boston Museum.

31. John Wilkes Booth to Moses Kimball, 2 January 1864, in John H. Rhodehamel and Louise Taper, eds., *Right or Wrong, God Judge Me: The Writings of John Wilkes Booth* (Urbana: University of Illinois Press, 1997), 93–94.

32. John Wilkes Booth to Moses Kimball, 2 January 1864, in Rhodehamel and Taper, eds., *Right or Wrong*, 93–94.

33. "Snowbound with John Wilkes Booth at Cameron, Missouri," *St. Louis Republic Magazine*, 4 August 1901.

34. Mrs. McKee Rankin, "The News of Lincoln's Death," *American Magazine* (January 1909): 261. Mrs. McKee Rankin (1847–1911), born Kitty Blanchard, started dancing professionally at age 10 to support her mother and herself after her father died.

35. Edwin Adams in LASE, 5.

36. Charles A. Krone, "Recollections of an Old Actor," *Missouri Historical Society Collections* 4, no. 2, 343.

37. *New York Clipper*, 20 February 1864.

38. *Louisville Daily Journal*, 28 January 1864.

39. Charles E. Holding, "John Wilkes Booth Stars in Nashville," *Tennessee Historical Quarterly* 23 (March 1964): 75.

40. Sarah Jane Full Hill, *Mrs. Hill's Journal: Civil War Reminiscences*, ed. Mark M. Krug (Chicago: Lakeside Press, 1980), 222.

41. *Nashville Daily Union*, 12 February 1864, quoted in Holding, "John Wilkes Booth Stars in Nashville," 79.

42. *New York Clipper*, 5 March 1864.

43. Miller, "John Wilkes Booth in the Pennsylvania Oil Region," 61. Copperheads were Democrats who opposed the war and wished to achieve peace through negotiations with the Confederacy.

44. R.M. Johnson to John Wilkes Booth, 18 February 1865, in LASE, 754–755. Richard Marshall Johnson (1842–1922) served on General Grant's headquarters staff early in the Civil War. President Grant appointed him consul to Hankow, China, in 1869. At the end of Grant's presidency, Johnson returned to St. Louis and practiced law. In 1866 he married Annie M. Blow, whose grandfather, Peter Blow, had brought the slave Dred Scott to Missouri in 1830.

45. *New Orleans Times*, 19 March 1864, quoted in Ernest C. Miller, *John Wilkes Booth—Oilman* (New York: The Exposition Press, 1947), 17.

46. *New Orleans Daily Picayune*, 26 March 1864.

47. *New Orleans True Delta*, quoted in John S. Kendall, *The Golden Age of the New Orleans Theatre* (Baton Rouge: Louisiana State University Press, 1952), 502.

48. *New Orleans Times*, 18 March 1864.

49. *New York Clipper*, 9 April 1864.

50. *New York Evening Post*, 15 April 1865.

51. Kendall, *Golden Age of the New Orleans Theatre*, 497.

52. Kendall, *Golden Age of the New Orleans Theatre*, 499.

53. Kendall, *Golden Age of the New Orleans Theatre*, 498.

54. Clara M. Laughlin, *Traveling Through Life* (Boston: Houghton Mifflin, 1934), 107.

55. John Wilkes Booth to Junius Brutus Booth, Jr., ca. April 1864, in Rhodehamel and Taper, eds., *Right or Wrong*, 105.

56. *Boston Daily Evening Transcript*, 2 May 1864.

57. *Boston Daily Evening Transcript*, 10 May 1864.

58. *Boston Daily Evening Transcript*, 16 May 1864.

59. *Boston Daily Evening Transcript*, 16 May 1864.

60. *Boston Daily Evening Transcript*, 27 May 1864.

61. Walter Benn, "The Great National Conspiracy," *Wilkes-Barre Times*, 19 December 1894.

62. Clara Morris account in *Boston Herald*, 10 January 1890.

63. Clara Morris account in *Boston Herald*, 10 January 1890.

64. A.F. Norcross, "A Child's Memory of the Boston Theatre," *Theatre Magazine* 43 (May 1926): 37, quoted in Deirdre Kincaid, "Rough Magic: The Theatrical Life of John Wilkes Booth" (unpublished manuscript, 2009), Chapter 6, 20.

65. Rhodehamel and Taper, eds., *Right or Wrong*, 107.

66. "Maggie Mitchell's Dream," *Washington Critic-Record*, 30 September 1881.

67. Quincy Kilby, typescript note, William Seymour Family Papers, Manuscripts Division, Department of Rare Books and Special Collections, Princeton University Library, Princeton, New Jersey. Harrison Whitfield Huguley (1844–1913) was a prominent wine importer and held several government offices. The fact that Maggie Mitchell was appearing in Boston at the same time as Booth lends credence to the account of the incident.

68. "Hit them Again," *Alexandria Gazette*, 12 January 1874, quoted in Angela Smythe, "Bound for Glory: John Wilkes Booth and the Richmond Grays," www.antebellumrichmond.com/bound-for-glory.html (accessed 31 July 2013), 83.

69. *Washington Evening Star*, 7 December 1881.

70. John Wilkes Booth to John T. Ford, 17 September

1863, in Rhodehamel and Taper, eds., *Right or Wrong*, 90.

71. John Wilkes Booth to Ben DeBar, 22 September 1863, in LASE, 100.

72. Edwin Booth to Adam Badeau, 26 September 1863, Edwin Booth, Collection, Hampden-Booth Theatre Library.

73. *Boston Daily Evening Transcript*, 28 September 1863.

74. *Boston Daily Evening Transcript*, 29 September 1863. Unless otherwise noted, reviews and plays for this engagement are found in issues of the *Boston Daily Evening Transcript*.

75. *Boston Daily Evening Transcript*, 30 September 1863.

76. *Boston Daily Evening Transcript*, 1 October 1863.

77. *Boston Daily Evening Transcript*, 2 October 1863.

78. *Boston Daily Evening Transcript*, 5 October 1863.

79. *Boston Advertiser*, 5 October 1863.

80. *Boston Daily Evening Transcript*, 7 October 1863.

81. *Boston Daily Evening Transcript*, 8 October 1863.

82. *Boston Daily Evening Transcript*, 9 October 1863.

83. *Boston Advertiser*, 9 October 1863.

84. Playbill, private collection. Harry Hawk (1839–1916) specialized in comedic roles. He died, and is buried, on the Island of Jersey, Channel Islands.

85. *Worcester Daily Spy*, quoted in James Lee, "When Lincoln's Assassin Acted in Worcester," *Worcester Sunday Telegram*, 17 December 1944.

86. *Worcester Daily Transcript*, 13 October 1863.

87. *Worcester Daily Spy*, 13 October 1863.

88. *Springfield Daily Republican*, 15 October 1863.

89. *Springfield Daily Republican*, 16 October 1863.

90. *Springfield Daily Republican*, 15 October 1863. Booth was sometimes criticized for "ranting" or using a robust, over-the-top acting style, especially in scenes with high emotions. The critic here cleverly conveys that Booth was not the worst of the ranters.

91. *Providence Daily Journal*, 17 October 1863.

92. *Providence Daily Journal*, 19 October 1863.

93. *Providence Daily Post*, 19 October 1863.

94. John Wilkes Booth to John A. Ellsler, 18 October 1863, in Rhodehamel and Taper, eds., *Right or Wrong*, 92; Charles E. Kennedy, *Fifty Years of Cleveland, 1875–1925* (Cleveland: Weidenthal, n.d.), 89.

95. *Providence Daily Post*, 20 October 1863.

96. *Hartford Evening Press*, 21 October 1863.

97. *Hartford Courant*, 22 October 1863.

98. *Springfield Daily Republican*, 22 October 1863.

99. *Springfield Daily Republican*, 24 October 1863.

100. *Springfield Daily Republican*, 24 October 1863.

101. *Brooklyn Standard*, 31 October 1863.

102. *Brooklyn Standard*, 31 October 1863.

103. *New York Clipper*, 7 November 1863.

104. *New Haven Daily Register*, 28 October 1863.

105. *New Haven Palladium*, 29 October 1863.

106. *New Haven Daily Register*, 29 October 1863.

107. *New Haven Palladium*, 30 October 1863.

108. George J. Olszewski, *Restoration of Ford's Theatre* (Washington, D.C.: United States Department of the Interior, 1963), 105.

109. *Washington Sunday Chronicle*, 1 November 1863.

110. *Washington Morning Chronicle*, 3 November 1863.

111. A.I. Mudd, "The First Appearance and Last Appearance of John Wilkes Booth at the National Capital," Mudd file, New York Public Library for the Performing Arts.

112. *Washington National Intelligencer*, 3 November 1863.

113. *Washington Morning Chronicle*, 4 November 1863.

114. *Washington National Intelligencer*, 5 November 1863.

115. *Washington Evening Star*, 5 November 1863.

116. *Washington Evening Star*, 7 November 1863.

117. Hay, *Lincoln and the Civil War*, 118.

118. *Washington Evening Star*, 9 November 1863.

119. *Washington National Intelligencer*, quoted in Stanley Kimmel, *The Mad Booths of Maryland* (New York: Dover, 1969), 177.

120. W.J. Ferguson, *I Saw Booth Shoot Lincoln* (1930; reprint, Austin, Texas: Pemberton Press, 1969), 15.

121. *Washington National Intelligencer*, 12 November 1863.

122. *Washington National Intelligencer*, 14 November 1863.

123. Profiles in History Catalog 19 (Spring 1993): 17.

124. *Cleveland Morning Leader*, 23 November 1863.

125. *Cleveland Morning Leader*, 25 November 1863.

126. *Cleveland Plain Dealer*, 27 November 1863.

127. *Cleveland Plain Dealer*, 28 November 1863.

128. Morris, *Life on the Stage*, 98.

129. *Cleveland Morning Leader*, 30 November 1863.

130. *Cleveland Herald*, 30 November 1863.

131. *Cleveland Herald*, 1 December 1863.

132. *Cleveland Plain Dealer*, 2 December 1863.

133. *Cleveland Plain Dealer*, 3 December 1863.

134. Morris, *Life on the Stage*, 102–103. Clara Morris places this incident the day after a performance of *The Marble Heart*.

135. *Cleveland Plain Dealer*, 5 December 1863.

136. *Cleveland Plain Dealer*, 9 December 1863.

137. Olszewski, *Restoration of Ford's Theatre*, 105. Olszewski mistakenly lists the performance as taking place on November, rather than December, 14.

138. Olszewski, *Restoration of Ford's Theatre*, 105.

139. Olszewski, *Restoration of Ford's Theatre*, 105.

140. *Leavenworth Daily Conservative*, 20 December 1863.

141. *Leavenworth Daily Conservative*, 21 December 1863. Unless otherwise noted, reviews and plays for this engagement appear in issues of the *Leavenworth Daily Conservative*.

142. *Leavenworth Daily Times*, 24 December 1863.

143. *Leavenworth Daily Conservative*, 23 December 1863.

144. *Leavenworth Daily Times*, 24 December 1863.

145. *Leavenworth Daily Conservative*, 23 December 1863.

146. *Leavenworth Daily Conservative*, 23 December 1863.

147. *Leavenworth Daily Conservative*, 27 December 1863.

148. *Leavenworth Daily Conservative*, 29 December 1863.

149. *Leavenworth Daily Conservative*, 30 December 1863.

150. *Leavenworth Daily Conservative*, 30 December 1863.

151. *Leavenworth Daily Conservative*, 1 January 1864.

152. John Wilkes Booth to Moses Kimball, 2 January 1864, in Rhodehamel and Taper, eds., *Right or Wrong*, 93–94.

153. The *St. Joseph Morning Herald,* 8 January 1864, comments on the rail line between Weston and St. Joseph.

154. John Wilkes Booth to Moses Kimball, 2 January 1864, in Rhodehamel and Taper, eds., *Right or Wrong*, 93–94.

155. *St. Joseph Morning Herald*, 3 January 1864.

156. *St. Joseph Morning Herald*, 5 January 1864. Correspondence dated 4 January. Unless otherwise noted, reviews and plays for this engagement appear in issues of the *St. Joseph Morning Herald*.

157. *St. Joseph Morning Herald*, 5 January 1864.

158. *St. Joseph Morning Herald*, 5 January 1864.

159. *St. Joseph Morning Herald*, 6 January 1864; John Wilkes Booth to John A. Ellsler, 23 January 1864, in Rhodehamel and Taper, eds., *Right or Wrong*, 96.

160. *St. Joseph Morning Herald*, 8 January 1864.

161. *St. Joseph Morning Herald*, 8, 9 January 1864.

162. John Wilkes Booth to John A. Ellsler, 23 January 1864, in Rhodehamel and Taper, eds., *Right or Wrong*, 96.

163. Louis J. Weichmann in *Trial of John H. Surratt in the Criminal Court of the District of Columbia* (Washington, D.C.: Government Printing Office, 1867), 1:409. This source is hereafter cited as Surratt Trial.

164. Edwin Adams in LASE, 5.

165. *St. Louis Missouri Republican*, 12 January 1864.

166. *St. Louis Missouri Democrat*, 14 January 1864.

167. *St. Louis Missouri Democrat*, 14 January 1864.

168. Krone, "Recollections of an Old Actor," 323.

169. *Louisville Daily Journal*, 19 January 1864.

170. *Louisville Daily Journal*, 20 January 1864.

171. *Louisville Daily Democrat*, 21 January 1864.

172. *Louisville Daily Democrat*, 20 January 1864.

173. *Louisville Daily Journal*, 21 January 1864.

174. *Louisville Daily Democrat*, 22 January 1864.

175. *Louisville Daily Democrat*, 23 January 1864.

176. *Louisville Daily Democrat*, 24 January 1864.

177. John Wilkes Booth to John A. Ellsler, 23 January 1864, in Rhodehamel and Taper, eds., *Right or Wrong*, 96.

178. Rankin, "News of Lincoln's Death," 261.

179. *New York Clipper*, 6 February 1864.

180. *Louisville Daily Democrat*, 27 January 1864.

181. *Louisville Daily Journal*, 28 January 1864.

182. John Wilkes Booth to Edwin F. Keach, 30 January 1864, in Rhodehamel and Taper, eds., *Right or Wrong*, 98.

183. *Nashville Dispatch*, 31 January 1864.

184. *Nashville Dispatch*, 2 February 1864.

185. *Nashville Daily Union*, 2 February 1864.

186. *Nashville Daily Union*, 3 February 1864.

187. *Nashville Dispatch*, 3 February 1864.

188. *Nashville Dispatch*, 5 February 1864.

189. *Nashville Dispatch*, 6 February 1864.

190. *Nashville Daily Union*, 6 February 1864.

191. *Nashville Dispatch*, 9 February 1864.

192. *Nashville Dispatch*, 9 February 1864.

193. "Washington Theatre—Mrs. Laura Keene," *Washington Evening Star,* 9 February 1864.

194. *Nashville Dispatch*, 9 February 1864.

195. John Wilkes Booth to Moses Kimball, 9 February 1864, in Rhodehamel and Taper, eds., *Right or Wrong*, 99.

196. John Wilkes Booth to Richard Montgomery Field, 9 February 1864, in Rhodehamel and Taper, eds., *Right or Wrong*, 100.

197. *Nashville Dispatch*, 10 February 1864.

198. *Nashville Dispatch*, 11 February 1864.

199. *Nashville Dispatch*, 11 February 1864.

200. Hill, *Mrs. Hill's Journal*, 225.

201. James R. Harvey, "Recollections of the Early Theatre," *Colorado Magazine* 17 (1940): 163, quoted in Kincaid, "Rough Magic," Chapter 8, 12.

202. *Cincinnati Daily Commercial*, 15 February 1864.

203. Samples, *Lust for Fame*, 140.

204. *Cincinnati Daily Commercial*, 17 February 1864.

205. *Cincinnati Daily Commercial*, 18 February 1864.

206. H.C. Young in LASE, 1400. Henry Clay Young was born about 1834 and died in Paris on 7 April 1907. He had lived in Paris since 1883 and was one of the best-known men in the American colony there.

207. *Cincinnati Daily Commercial*, 19 February 1864.

208. *Cincinnati Daily Commercial*, 20 February 1864.

209. The Lincoln Log website, www.thelincolnlog.com.

210. *Cincinnati Daily Commercial*, 22 February 1864.

211. *Cincinnati Daily Commercial*, 23 February 1864.

212. John Wilkes Booth to Richard Montgomery Field, 22 February 1864, in Rhodehamel and Taper, eds., *Right or Wrong*, 101.

213. Rhodehamel and Taper, eds., *Right or Wrong*, 28. The editors note that Booth signed a deed on this date. The unidentified deed is in a private collection.

214. *Cincinnati Daily Commercial*, 25 February 1864.

215. Mrs. George H. Gilbert (1821–1904) was born Anne Jane Hartley in England. She began her career as a dancer but later became a popular and respected actress.

216. *Cincinnati Daily Commercial*, 26 February 1864.

217. David Chambers Mearns, *Largely Lincoln* (New York: St. Martin's Press, 1961), 142.

218. *Memphis Bulletin*, 3 March 1864.

219. *Washington National Republican*, 5 March 1864.

220. *Memphis Bulletin*, 5 March 1864.

221. *Washington Morning Chronicle*, 8 March 1864. Jennie Gourlay (1845–1928) was born into a family of actors in Edinburgh, Scotland. As a youth she and her sister Maggie toured the United States with the Marsh Troupe of juvenile actors. She retired from the stage in 1878.

222. *Washington Evening Star*, 11 March 1864.

223. Michael W. Kauffman, *American Brutus: John Wilkes Booth and the Lincoln Conspiracies* (New York: Random House, 2004), 127.

224. John Wilkes Booth to Richard M. Johnson, 28 March 1864, in Rhodehamel and Taper, eds., *Right or Wrong*, 103.

225. *New Orleans True Delta*, 15 March 1864.

226. *New Orleans Daily Picayune*, 16 March 1864.

227. *New Orleans True Delta*, 17 March 1864.

228. *New Orleans Daily Picayune*, 17 March 1864.

229. *New Orleans True Delta*, quoted in Kendall, *The Golden Age of the New Orleans Theatre*, 502.

230. *New Orleans Daily Picayune*, 18 March 1864.

231. *New Orleans Daily Picayune*, 19 March 1864.

232. *New Orleans Times*, quoted in Kimmel, *Mad Booths*, 180.

233. *New Orleans Daily Picayune*, 20 March 1864.

234. *New Orleans Daily Picayune*, 20 March 1864.

235. *New Orleans Daily Picayune*, 21 March 1864.

236. *New York Clipper*, 9 April 1864.

237. *New Orleans Daily Picayune*, 24 March 1864.

238. *New Orleans Times*, 25 March 1864.

239. *New Orleans Daily Picayune*, 25 March 1864.

240. *New Orleans Daily Picayune*, 26 March 1864.

241. John Wilkes Booth to Richard Montgomery Field, 26 March 1864, in Rhodehamel and Taper, eds., *Right or Wrong*, 102.

242. *New York Clipper*, 16 April 1864.

243. John Wilkes Booth to Richard M. Johnson, 28 March 1864, in Rhodehamel and Taper, eds., *Right or Wrong*, 103.

244. *New York Clipper*, 16 April 1864.

245. Lawrence Barrett (1838–1891) was born Lawrence Brannigan in New Jersey. Barrett toured with his friend Edwin Booth in the years after the Civil War.

246. *New Orleans Daily Picayune*, 29 March 1864.

247. *New Orleans Daily Picayune*, 3 April 1864.

248. *New Orleans Daily Picayune*, 3 April 1864.

249. John Wilkes Booth to "My Dear Miss," 4 April 1864, in Rhodehamel and Taper, eds., *Right or Wrong*, 104.

250. Olszewski, *Restoration of Ford's Theatre*, 105; The Lincoln Log, www.thelincolnlog.org; Noah Brooks, *Washington in Lincoln's Time* (1896; reprint, New York: Rinehart, 1958), 71–72.

251. Benjamin P. Thomas and Harold M. Hyman, *Stanton: The Life and Times of Lincoln's Secretary of War* (New York: Alfred A. Knopf, 1962), 131.

252. Kimmel, *Mad Booths*, 183.

253. *New York Clipper*, 30 April 1864.

254. *Boston Daily Evening Transcript*, 26 April 1864.

255. *Boston Daily Evening Transcript*, 27 April 1864.

256. *Boston Post*, 29 April 1864.

257. *Boston Post*, 29 April 1864.

258. *Boston Post*, 1 May 1864.

259. *Boston Daily Evening Transcript*, 3 May 1864.

260. *Boston Daily Evening Transcript*, 18 May 1864.

261. Rhodehamel and Taper, eds., *Right or Wrong*, 29. No other information is provided.

262. Norcross, "A Child's Memory of the Boston Theatre."

263. *New York Clipper*, 7 May 1864.

264. *Boston Daily Evening Transcript*, 10 May 1864.

265. *Boston Daily Evening Transcript*, 16 May 1864.

266. Catherine (Kate) Mary Reignolds Winslow, *Yesterday with Actors* (Boston: Cupples and Hurd, 1887), 141.

267. Winslow, *Yesterday with Actors*, 141.

268. *Boston Daily Evening Transcript*, 17 May 1864.

269. *Boston Daily Evening Transcript*, 16 May 1864.

270. *New York Clipper*, 28 May 1864.

271. *Boston Daily Evening Transcript*, 20 May 1864.

272. *New York Clipper*, 21 May 1864.

273. *New York Clipper*, 28 May 1864, column dated 23 May.

274. *Boston Daily Evening Transcript*, 23 May 1864.

275. *Boston Daily Evening Transcript*, 26 May 1864.

276. Junius Brutus Booth, Jr., "Diary of Junius Brutus Booth, Jr., for 1864," Folger Shakespeare Library, Washington, D.C.

277. *Boston Daily Evening Transcript*, 27 May 1864.

278. Rhodehamel and Taper, eds., *Right or Wrong*, 29. Fiske is possibly Joseph Winn Fiske, whose New York company was one of the preeminent makers of ornamental metalwork in the second half of the nineteenth century.

279. Rhodehamel and Taper, eds., *Right or Wrong*, 29.

280. Rhodehamel and Taper, eds., *Right or Wrong*, 106.

281. Rhodehamel and Taper, eds., *Right or Wrong*, 29. No further information is provided.

282. Booth, "Diary of Junius Brutus Booth, Jr., for 1864."

283. Booth, "Diary of Junius Brutus Booth, Jr., for 1864."

284. Booth, "Diary of Junius Brutus Booth, Jr., for 1864."

Chapter 8. Preparations: 1864

1. Junius Brutus Booth, Jr., "Diary of Junius Brutus Booth, Jr., for 1864," Folger Shakespeare Library, Washington, D.C.

2. John Wilkes Booth to John A. Ellsler, 11 June 1864, in John H. Rhodehamel and Louise Taper, eds., *Right or Wrong, God Judge Me: The Writings of John Wilkes Booth* (Urbana: University of Illinois Press, 1997), 111–112.

3. Ernest C. Miller, *John Wilkes Booth—Oilman* (New York: The Exposition Press, 1947), 32.

4. Joseph H. Simonds in William C. Edwards and Edward Steers, Jr., eds., *The Lincoln Assassination: The Evidence* (Urbana: University of Illinois Press, 2009), 1154–1155. This book is hereafter cited as LASE.

5. John Wilkes Booth to John A. Ellsler, 17 June 1864, in Rhodehamel and Taper, eds., *Right or Wrong*, 113.

6. John A. Ellsler, *The Stage Memories of John A. Ellsler*, ed. Effie Ellsler Weston (Cleveland: The Rowfant Club, 1950), 127–128.

7. Ernest C. Miller, "John Wilkes Booth in the Pennsylvania Oil Region," *Western Pennsylvania Historical Magazine* 31 (March-June 1948): 29.

8. Miller, "John Wilkes Booth in the Pennsylvania Oil Region," 28.

9. Miller, *John Wilkes Booth—Oilman*, 30.

10. Hildegarde Dolson, *The Great Oildorado: The Gaudy and Turbulent Years of the First Oil Rush: Pennsylvania, 1859–1880* (New York: Random House, 1959), 150.

11. Miller, "John Wilkes Booth in the Pennsylvania Oil Region," 39.

12. Miller, "John Wilkes Booth in the Pennsylvania Oil Region," 34.

13. Miller, *John Wilkes Booth—Oilman*, 33.

14. Miller, *John Wilkes Booth—Oilman*, 36.

15. Miller, "John Wilkes Booth in the Pennsylvania Oil Region," 31.

16. Alfred Wilson Smiley, *A Few Scraps, Oily and Otherwise* (Oil City, PA: Derrick, 1907), 79.

17. Smiley, *A Few Scraps*, 82.

18. Miller, *John Wilkes Booth—Oilman*, 31.

19. Miller, *John Wilkes Booth—Oilman*, 40.

20. Miller, "John Wilkes Booth in the Pennsylvania Oil Region," 39.

21. Dolson, *Great Oildorado*, 149.

22. Miller, "John Wilkes Booth in the Pennsylvania Oil Region," 44.

23. J. Heron Foster in LASE, 561.

24. J. Heron Foster in LASE, 562.

25. *Cleveland Morning Leader*, 30 June 1864.

26. *Cleveland Morning Leader*, 2 July 1864.

27. Booth Jr., "Diary of Junius Brutus Booth, Jr., for 1864."

28. Edwina Booth Grossman, *Edwin Booth: Recollections by his Daughter* (New York: The Century Co., 1894), 153.

29. Edwin Booth to Emma F. Cary, 23 July 1864, in private collection of the late Donald P. Dow, Fort Worth, Texas.

30. Cordial Crane in LASE, 402.

31. William A. Tidwell, with James O. Hall and David Winfred Gaddy, *Come Retribution: The Confederate Secret Service and the Assassination of Lincoln* (Jackson: University Press of Mississippi, 1988), 263.

32. Thomas N. Conrad, *A Confederate Spy: A Story of the Civil War* (New York: J. Ogilvie, 1892), 69. For more on Conrad, see John T. Kneebone, et al., eds., *Dictionary of Virginia Biography* (Richmond: Library of Virginia, 2006), 3:408–410.

33. Thomas N. Conrad, *The Rebel Scout: A Thrilling History of Scouting Life in the Southern Army* (Washington, D.C.: National Publishing Co., 1904), 117, 119.

34. Conrad, *Rebel Scout*, 119.

35. Tidwell, Hall, and Gaddy, *Come Retribution*, 20.

36. Tidwell, Hall, and Gaddy, *Come Retribution*, 409.

37. Letters and Telegrams Received, 1861–1865, Records of the Office of the Secretary of War, War Department Collection of Confederate Records, RG 109, M437, reel 121, frame 59, National Archives and Records Administration, Washington, D.C.; James O. Hall, "You Have Mail," *Surratt Courier* 25 (July 2000): 8–9.

38. Samuel Arnold statement, 3 December 1867, in Michael W. Kauffman, ed., *Samuel Bland Arnold: Memoirs of a Lincoln Conspirator* (Bowie, MD: Heritage Books, 1995, 22–37), 22–23. This source is hereafter cited as Arnold Confession of 1867.

39. Kauffman, ed., *Samuel Bland Arnold*, 42.

40. Arnold Confession of 1867, 23.

41. Booth Jr., "Diary of Junius Brutus Booth, Jr., for 1864."

42. Booth Jr., "Diary of Junius Brutus Booth, Jr., for 1864."

43. Edward Steers, *Blood on the Moon: The Assassination of Abraham Lincoln* (Lexington: University Press of Kentucky, 2001), 62, states that previous authors have accepted Arnold's dates. In 1991, however, the first edition of *John Wilkes Booth: Day By Day* presented for the first time the logic which leads to the early August meeting of Booth, Arnold, and O'Laughlen.

44. Joseph H. Barnes, *The Medical and Surgical History of the War of the Rebellion* (Washington, D.C.: Government Printing Office, Second Issue, 1888), 855.

45. Asia Booth Clarke, *The Unlocked Book: A Memoir of John Wilkes Booth by his Sister Asia Booth Clarke*, ed.

Eleanor Farjeon (New York: G.P. Putnam's Sons, 1938), 118.

46. John Wilkes Booth to Isabel Sumner, 26 August 1864, in Rhodehamel and Taper, eds., *Right or Wrong*, 116–117.

47. John Wilkes Booth to Isabel Sumner, 27 or 28 August 1864, in Rhodehamel and Taper, eds., *Right or Wrong*, 117.

48. Junius B. Booth, Jr., in LASE, 181.

49. Junius B. Booth, Jr., in LASE, 181.

50. Edwin Booth to Nahum Capen, 28 July 1881, in Clarke, *Unlocked Book*, 203.

51. Miller, *John Wilkes Booth—Oilman*, 35.

52. Joseph H. Simonds in LASE, 1154–1155; Miller, *John Wilkes Booth—Oilman*, 75.

53. Conrad, *Rebel Scout*, 123.

54. Conrad, *Rebel Scout*, 124.

55. Junius B. Booth, Jr., in LASE, 181.

56. Ben Perley Poore, ed., *The Conspiracy Trial for the Murder of the President* (Boston: J.E. Tilton, 1865 and 1866), hereafter cited as Poore. Eaton G. Horner in Poore, 1:430, testified that Sam Arnold had said that Booth had told him he had letters of introduction to both Dr. Mudd and Dr. Queen. However, in the Arnold Confession of 1867, 33–34, Arnold stated: "He [Booth] told me he had a letter of introduction either to Dr. Queen or Dr. Mudd. I am not sure which.... That was the only time I ever heard Booth mention Dr. Mudd's name." See also James O. Hall, "Dr. Mudd—Again—Part 1," *Surratt Courier* 23 (July 1998): 4–7.

57. George Alfred Townsend, "Thomassen: The Dynamite Fiend Amongst the Assassins of President Lincoln," *New York Graphic*, 22 March 1876.

58. William E. Wheeler in Poore, 1:33.

59. Tidwell, Hall, and Gaddy, *Come Retribution*, 332.

60. Oscar A. Kinchen, *Confederate Operations in Canada and the North* (North Quincy, MA: Christopher, 1970), 137.

61. *Montreal Telegraph* clipping reproduced in Lincoln Obsequies Scrapbook, 63, Manuscript Division, Library of Congress, Washington, D.C. The *Montreal Telegraph* article was also reprinted in the *Sacramento* [California] *Daily Union*, 20 May 1865.

62. Townsend, "Thomassen." Booth told Martin he hoped to see George P. Kane of Baltimore in Montreal. Martin's curiosity was aroused. He wrote to Kane, in Baltimore, asking what he knew about Booth. Kane knew nothing of Booth or his plot.

63. Tidwell, Hall, and Gaddy, *Come Retribution*, 336.

64. Nat Brandt, *The Man Who Tried To Burn New York* (Syracuse: Syracuse University Press, 1986), 71.

65. *New York Clipper*, 20 May 1865.

66. George Iles, "John Wilkes Booth," handwritten memo dated 11 September 1935, Stanley Kimmel Papers, Macdonald-Kelce Library, University of Tampa, Tampa, Florida.

67. Robert Anson Campbell in Poore, 2:87.

68. *Montreal Telegraph* quoted in *Quebec Gazette*, 24 April 1865.

69. Tidwell, Hall, and Gaddy, *Come Retribution*, 331; Townsend, "Thomassen." Townsend asserts that Martin's business partner placed bombs aboard the ships and later collected on a $100,000 insurance policy. Booth's wardrobe was recovered late in the spring of 1865.

70. Dolson, *Great Oildorado*, 161.

71. Joseph H. Simonds to John Wilkes Booth, 3 November 1864, in LASE, 143–144.

72. Conrad, *Rebel Scout*, 130.

73. G.W. Bunker in Poore, 1:30.

74. David Rankin Barbee, "Lincoln and Booth," typescript, 538, David Rankin Barbee Papers, Georgetown University Library, Washington, D.C.

75. John C. Thompson in Poore, 2:269.

76. John C. Thompson in Benn Pitman, comp., *The Assassination of President Lincoln and The Trial of The Conspirators*, facsimile ed. (New York: Funk & Wagnalls, 1954), 178.

77. The testimony of several witnesses to the meeting of Booth and Dr. Mudd, including that of Dr. Mudd, may be interpreted to place the meeting in November or in December. See Edward Steers, Jr., *His Name Is Still Mudd: The Case Against Doctor Samuel Alexander Mudd* (Gettysburg, PA: Thomas, 1997), 39–43, for an interpretation of the former and Michael W. Kauffman, *American Brutus: John Wilkes Booth and the Lincoln Conspiracies* (New York: Random House, 2004), 432, note 7, for the latter.

78. John C. Thompson Pitman, *Assassination*, 178.

79. Thomas Ewing, Jr., in Pitman, *Assassination*, 330.

80. John Wilkes Booth to J. Dominic Burch, 14 November 1864, in Rhodehamel and Taper, eds., *Right or Wrong*, 123; Barbee, "Lincoln and Booth," 538.

81. "Jay Cooke & Co. in acc't with J. Wilkes Booth," cited in Rhodehamel and Taper, eds., *Right or Wrong*, 30.

82. Clarke, *Unlocked Book*, 116.

83. Samuel Knapp Chester in LASE, 341.

84. John T. Ford in LASE, 528.

85. Clarke, *Unlocked Book*, 125–127.

86. John Wilkes Booth to Mary Ann Holmes Booth, November 1864, in Rhodehamel and Taper, eds., *Right or Wrong*, 130–131. See also Richard E. Sloan, ed., *The Lincoln Log* 2 (May–June 1977): 1–2.

87. John Wilkes Booth to "To Whom It May Concern," November 1864, in Rhodehamel and Taper, eds., *Right or Wrong*, 124–127. See also Richard E. Sloan, ed., *The Lincoln Log* 2 (May–June 1977): 3–4.

88. John M. Barron, "With John Wilkes Booth in His Days as an Actor," *Baltimore Sun*, 17 March 1907.

89. Kauffman, *American Brutus*, 150.

90. *New York Herald*, 26 November 1864.

91. Edwin Booth to Nahum Capen, 28 July 1881, in Clarke, *Unlocked Book*, 203.

92. Junius B. Booth, Jr., in LASE, 182.

93. Adam Badeau, "Dramatic Reminiscences," *St. Paul and Minneapolis Pioneer Press*, 20 February 1887.

94. Samuel Knapp Chester in LASE, 340–341.

95. John T. Ford in U.S. Congress, House, *Impeachment Investigation: Testimony Taken Before the Judiciary Committee of the House of Representatives in the Investigation of the Charges Against Andrew Johnson*, 2d session, 39th Congress, and 1st session, 40th Congress (Washington, D.C.: Government Printing Office, 1867), 535.

96. John C. Thompson in Poore, 2:271–272.

97. John C. Thompson in Pitman, *Assassination*, 178.

98. Tidwell, Hall, and Gaddy, *Come Retribution*, 337; George Alfred Townsend interview of Thomas H. Harbin, 1885, in *Cincinnati Enquirer*, 18 April 1892; "Statement of George A. Atzerodt to Prov. Mar. McPhail,

May 1, 1865," *Surratt Courier* 13 (October 1988): 2–3, hereafter cited as Atzerodt Statement, 1 May 1865.

99. Samuel Mudd, *The Life of Dr. Samuel A. Mudd*, ed. Nettie Mudd (New York: Neale, 1906), 29.

100. Samuel A. Mudd in LASE, 940; Thomas L. Gardiner in Poore, 1:361–363.

101. Osborn H. Oldroyd, *The Assassination of Abraham Lincoln: Flight, Pursuit, Capture, and Punishment of the Conspirators* (Washington, D.C.: O.H. Oldroyd, 1901), 259.

102. John F. Hardey in Poore, 3:435.

103. James L. Maddox in LASE, 831–832; Ned Spangler's statement in Mudd, *Life of Dr. Samuel A. Mudd*, 323–324.

104. Brooke Stabler in Poore, 1:177–178, 204; John A. Foster in LASE, 532. Stabler testified incorrectly that the one-eyed horse was brought to the stable in October.

105. James O. Hall, *The Surratt Family & John Wilkes Booth* (Clinton, MD: Surratt Society, 1976), 9.

106. "Rockville Lecture of John H. Surratt," in Clara Elizabeth Laughlin, *The Death of Lincoln: The Story of Booth's Plot, His Deed and the Penalty* (New York: Doubleday, Page, 1909), Appendix VI, 226; William H. Gleason Statement, 19 December 1867, Benjamin F. Butler Papers, Manuscript Division, Library of Congress.

107. John H. Jack in LASE, 738.

108. John H. Jack in LASE, 738.

109. President and Mrs. Lincoln, with Secretary Seward, attended a performance of the opera *Faust* at Grover's Theatre on December 5, 1864. On occasion Lincoln attended theatrical performances alone, and most of these are not documented. But occasions when he attended with Mrs. Lincoln did not escape public notice. The December 5 performance at Grover's seems to be the best candidate for the incident, despite the fact that Vestvali's engagement had not begun. Vestvali's last performance was on the 23rd, according to the *Washington Daily Constitutional Union*, 27 December 1864.

110. Stanley Kimmel, *The Mad Booths of Maryland* (New York: Dover, 1969), 198.

111. Samuel Knapp Chester in LASE, 340–343; Samuel Knapp Chester in Poore, 1:45–47.

112. Booth Jr., "Diary of Junius Brutus Booth, Jr., for 1864."

113. John Wilkes Booth to Isabel Sumner, 7 June 1864, in Rhodehamel and Taper, eds., *Right or Wrong*, 110–111.

114. Booth Jr., "Diary of Junius Brutus Booth, Jr., for 1864."

115. Smiley, *A Few Scraps*, 77.

116. John Wilkes Booth to John A. Ellsler, 11 June 1864, in Rhodehamel and Taper, eds., *Right or Wrong*, 111–112.

117. John Wilkes Booth to John A. Ellsler, 17 June 1864, in Rhodehamel and Taper, eds., *Right or Wrong*, 113.

118. John Wilkes Booth to John A. Ellsler, 17 June 1864, in Rhodehamel and Taper, eds., *Right or Wrong*, 113.

119. John Wilkes Booth to John A. Ellsler, 17 June 1864, in Rhodehamel and Taper, eds., *Right or Wrong*, 113.

120. John Wilkes Booth to Isabel Sumner, 17 June 1864, in Rhodehamel and Taper, eds., *Right or Wrong*, 113–114.

121. Barbee, "Lincoln and Booth," 173.

122. *New York Times*, 27 June 1864. The performance did not take place until November 25.

123. J. Heron Foster in LASE, 561.

124. *Cleveland Morning Leader*, 1 July 1864.

125. *Cleveland Morning Leader*, 1 July 1864.

126. *Cleveland Morning Leader*, 2 July 1864.

127. Booth Jr., "Diary of Junius Brutus Booth, Jr., for 1864."

128. John Wilkes Booth to Isabel Sumner, 14 July 1864, in Rhodehamel and Taper, eds., *Right or Wrong*, 114–115.

129. Grossman, *Edwin Booth: Recollections by his Daughter*, 153–154. The performance did not occur until November 25.

130. Edwin Booth to Emma F. Cary, 23 July 1864, in private collection of the late Donald P. Dow, Fort Worth, Texas.

131. John Wilkes Booth to Isabel Sumner, 24 July 1864, in Rhodehamel and Taper, eds., *Right or Wrong*, 115–116.

132. Cordial Crane in LASE, 402.

133. *New York Clipper*, 30 July 1864.

134. Booth Jr., "Diary of Junius Brutus Booth, Jr., for 1864."

135. Booth Jr., "Diary of Junius Brutus Booth, Jr., for 1864."

136. Booth Jr., "Diary of Junius Brutus Booth, Jr., for 1864."

137. U.S. War Department, *The War of the Rebellion: A Compilation of the Official Records of the Union and Confederate Armies*, ser. 1, vol. 37, part 2, 590.

138. Booth Jr., "Diary of Junius Brutus Booth, Jr., for 1864."

139. Samuel Bland Arnold, *Defence and Prison Experiences of a Lincoln Conspirator: Statements and Autobiographical Notes* (Hattiesburg, MS: The Book Farm, 1943), 19.

140. Earl Schenck Miers, et al., eds., *Lincoln Day By Day: A Chronology, 1809–1865* (Dayton, OH: Morningside, 1991), 3:178.

141. Asia Booth Clarke, *The Elder and the Younger Booth* (Boston: James R. Osgood, 1882), 158.

142. *New York Clipper*, 20 August 1864.

143. Asia Booth Clarke to Jean Anderson, 25 August 1864, BCLM Works on Paper Collection, ML 518, Box 37, Maryland Historical Society, Baltimore, Maryland.

144. John Wilkes Booth to Isabel Sumner, 26 August 1864, in Rhodehamel and Taper, eds., *Right or Wrong*, 116–117.

145. Conrad, *Rebel Scout*, 117, 119.

146. Booth Jr., "Diary of Junius Brutus Booth, Jr., for 1864."

147. John Wilkes Booth to Isabel Sumner, 27 or 28 August 1864, in Rhodehamel and Taper, eds., *Right or Wrong*, 117.

148. Arnold, *Defence and Prison Experiences*, 19. Littleton P.D. Newman testified about the date Arnold received the letter in Poore, 1:423.

149. Conrad, *Rebel Scout*, 119.

150. Booth Jr., "Diary of Junius Brutus Booth, Jr., for 1864."

151. Tidwell, Hall, and Gaddy, *Come Retribution*, 20.

152. Joseph H. Simonds in LASE, 1154–1155.

153. Joseph H. Simonds in Poore, 1:42.

154. Miller, *John Wilkes Booth—Oilman*, 75.

155. Deed to oil properties, 21 October 1864, cited in Kauffman, *American Brutus*, 429.

156. *New York Clipper*, 22 October 1864.

157. Conrad, *Rebel Scout*, 123.

158. *Newburgh* [New York] *Telegraph*, 19 April 1865.

159. *Newburgh* [New York] *Telegraph*, 19 April 1865.

160. Richard Gutman and Kellie Gutman, "Boston: A Home for John Wilkes Booth?" *Surratt Society News* 10 (September 1985): 1.

161. Charles Brombach, "The Canadian Phase of Lincoln's Murder" (1953), 2, typescript in Columbia University Library, New York.

162. Miller, *John Wilkes Booth—Oilman*, 59–60.

163. Kinchen, *Confederate Operations*, 137.

164. William E. Wheeler in Poore, 1:33.

165. Robert Anson Campbell in Poore, 2:87.

166. *Cincinnati Daily Commercial*, 1 May 1865.

167. David Beasley, *McKee Rankin and the Heyday of the American Theater* (Waterloo, Ontario: Wilfrid Laurier University Press, 2002), 45–46.

168. Dolson, *Great Oildorado*, 161.

169. Joseph H. Simonds to John Wilkes Booth, 3 November 1864, in LASE, 143–144.

170. Samuel Knapp Chester in Poore, 1:44.

171. *Trial of the Assassins and Conspirators for the Murder of Abraham Lincoln* (Philadelphia: Barclay & Co., 1865), 22.

172. Clayton Gray, *Conspiracy in Canada* (Montreal: L'Atelier Press, 1959), 61.

173. Joseph H. Simonds to John Wilkes Booth, 3 November 1864, in LASE, 143–144.

174. Junius Brutus Booth, Jr., to John Wilkes Booth, 6 November 1864, in LASE, 147.

175. Junius Brutus Booth, Jr., to John Wilkes Booth, 6 November 1864, in LASE, 147.

176. Booth Jr., "Diary of Junius Brutus Booth, Jr., for 1864."

177. G.W. Bunker in Poore, 1:30.

178. Conrad, *Rebel Scout*, 130.

179. John C. Thompson in Poore, 2:269.

180. John C. Thompson in Pitman, *Assassination*, 178. See Steers Jr., *His Name Is Still Mudd*, 39–43.

181. Thomas Ewing, Jr., in Pitman, *Assassination*, 330.

182. John Wilkes Booth to J. Dominic Burch, 14 November 1864, in Rhodehamel and Taper, eds., *Right or Wrong*, 123.

183. Miers, et al., eds., *Lincoln Day By Day*, 3:296.

184. "Jay Cooke & Co. in acc't with J. Wilkes Booth," cited in Rhodehamel and Taper, eds., *Right or Wrong*, 30. Rhodehamel and Taper state: "The two original checks that remain unaccounted for and for which the payee remains unknown are 20 December 1864 (for $100) and 9 January 1865 (for $750)." Actually, the 20 December transaction is accounted for. John Wilkes Booth wrote a $100 check to Matthew Canning on 16 December 1864. The bank received and processed the check on 20 December. A $600 check for a 18 January 1865 transaction is not extant.

185. Kimmel, *Mad Booths*, 191.

186. Booth Jr., "Diary of Junius Brutus Booth, Jr., for 1864."

187. Tidwell, Hall, and Gaddy, *Come Retribution*, 331.

188. U.S. Congress, House, *Report Relating to the Assassination of President Lincoln*, First Session, 39th Congress, Report No. 104. It seems doubtful that John Wilkes Booth sent this letter.

189. Booth Jr., "Diary of Junius Brutus Booth, Jr., for 1864."

190. John Wilkes Booth to Mary Ann Holmes Booth, November 1864, in Rhodehamel and Taper, eds., *Right or Wrong*, 130–131; John Wilkes Booth to "To Whom It May Concern," November 1864, in Rhodehamel and Taper, eds., *Right or Wrong*, 124–127.

191. Booth Jr., "Diary of Junius Brutus Booth, Jr., for 1864"; Winter Garden Theatre advertisement, *New York Herald*, 23 November 1864.

192. Samuel Knapp Chester in Poore, 1:44–45.

193. Alonzo J. May, "May's Dramatic Encyclopedia, 1750–1904," microfilm, Manuscript Division, Library of Congress (original in Baltimore Theater Papers, Maryland Historical Society, Baltimore). Sam Chester related this information to Alonzo May.

194. David Homer Bates, *Lincoln in the Telegraph Office: Recollections of the United States Military Telegraph Corps During the Civil War* (New York: The Century Co., 1907), 380.

195. *New York Herald*, 26 November 1864.

196. Photograph and Rufus Wright's commentary on display at the National Portrait Gallery, Washington, D.C.; Booth Jr., "Diary of Junius Brutus Booth, Jr., for 1864."

197. Charles Pope in *New York Sun*, 28 March 1897.

198. Booth Jr., "Diary of Junius Brutus Booth, Jr., for 1864."

199. Junius B. Booth, Jr., in LASE, 182.

200. Booth Jr., "Diary of Junius Brutus Booth, Jr., for 1864."

201. Clarke, *Unlocked Book*, 119.

202. Booth Jr., "Diary of Junius Brutus Booth, Jr., for 1864."

203. Clarke, *Unlocked Book*, 119.

204. John T. Ford in LASE, 528.

205. Asia Booth Clarke to Jean Anderson, 1 December 1864, BCLM Works on Paper Collection.

206. Joseph H. Simonds to John Wilkes Booth, 7 December 1864, in LASE, 147.

207. Tidwell, Hall, and Gaddy, *Come Retribution*, 331. The wardrobe was recovered late in the spring of 1865.

208. *Washington National Republican*, 6 December 1864.

209. John H. Jack in LASE, 738. Canning reported that the incident happened on the last night of Felicita Vestvali's engagement at Grover's, but there is no evidence that the Lincolns attended the theatre that night (December 23; see *Washington Daily Constitutional Union*, 27 December 1864). On occasion Lincoln attended theatrical performances alone, and most of these are not documented. But occasions when he attended with Mrs. Lincoln did not escape public notice. The December 5 performance at Grover's seems to be the best candidate for the incident, despite the fact that Vestvali's engagement had not begun.

210. Joseph H. Simonds to John Wilkes Booth, 7 December 1864, in LASE, 147.

211. Ward Hill Lamon, *Recollections of Abraham Lincoln, 1847–1865*, ed. Dorothy Lamon Teillard (Chicago: A.C. McClurg, 1895), 260–270.

212. *Washington Evening Star*, 11 December 1864.

213. G.W. Bunker in Poore, 1:32.

214. Gray, *Conspiracy in Canada*, 73.

215. Gray, *Conspiracy in Canada*, 74.

216. "Jay Cooke & Co. in acc't with J. Wilkes Booth," cited in Rhodehamel and Taper, eds., *Right or Wrong*, 30.

217. John C. Thompson in Poore, 2:272.

218. John C. Thompson in Pitman, *Assassination*, 178, and in Poore, 2:272.

219. George Alfred Townsend interview of Thomas H. Harbin, 1885, in *Cincinnati Enquirer*, 18 April 1892.

220. Samuel A. Mudd in LASE, 940.

221. Thomas L. Gardiner in Pitman, *Assassination*, 71, and in Poore, 1:363.

222. Oldroyd, *Assassination of Abraham Lincoln*, 259.

223. Brooke Stabler in Poore, 1:177–178, 204; John A. Foster in LASE, 532. Stabler testified incorrectly that the one-eyed horse was brought to the stable in October.

224. George W. Bunker in *Trial of John H. Surratt in the Criminal Court of the District of Columbia* (Washington, D.C.: Government Printing Office, 1867), 1:330. This source is hereafter cited as Surratt Trial.

225. "Rockville Lecture of John H. Surratt" in Laughlin, *Death of Lincoln*, 226.

226. John H. Jack in LASE, 738. See also entry for December 5, 1864.

227. "Jay Cooke & Co. in acc't with J. Wilkes Booth," cited in Rhodehamel and Taper, eds., *Right or Wrong*, 30.

228. Kimmel, *Mad Booths*, 198.

229. Samuel Knapp Chester in LASE, 341–347; Samuel Knapp Chester in Poore, 1:45–47.

230. George S. Bryan, *The Great American Myth* (New York: Carrick & Evans, 1940), 103.

231. John H. Jack in LASE, 739.

232. John H. Jack in LASE, 738.

233. Rhodehamel and Taper, eds., *Right or Wrong*, 30.

234. Henry R. McDonough in Surratt Trial, 1:356.

235. G.W. Bunker in Pitman, *Assassination*, 46.

236. Booth Jr., "Diary of Junius Brutus Booth, Jr., for 1864."

237. Joseph H. Simonds to John Wilkes Booth, 31 December 1864, in LASE, 152–154.

Chapter 9. Action: 1865

1. Atzerodt Confession, *Baltimore American*, 18 January 1869. According to Louis J. Weichmann, *A True History of the Assassination of Abraham Lincoln and of the Conspiracy of 1865*, ed. Floyd E. Risvold (New York: Vintage, 1977), 385, Atzerodt wrote this confession on the night before his execution. See also George A. Atzerodt in William C. Edwards and Edward Steers, Jr., eds., *The Lincoln Assassination: The Evidence* (Urbana: University of Illinois Press, 2009), 61. This book is hereafter cited as LASE.

2. Weichmann, *True History*, 76. Several witnesses at the trial of the conspirators testified about Atzerodt's cowardice in an attempt to show he was easily influenced by Booth. See Benn Pitman, comp., *The Assassination of President Lincoln and The Trial of The Conspirators*, facsimile ed. (New York: Funk & Wagnalls, 1954), 153.

3. Atzerodt said $300 was paid. See "Statement of George A. Atzerodt to Prov. Mar. McPhail, May 1, 1865,"

Surratt Courier 13 (October 1988): 2–3, hereafter cited as Atzerodt Statement, 1 May 1865.

4. Eddy Martin in in *Trial of John H. Surratt in the Criminal Court of the District of Columbia* (Washington, D.C.: Government Printing Office, 1867), 1:215. This source is hereafter cited as Surratt Trial.

5. Michael W. Kauffman, "David Edgar Herold, the Forgotten Conspirator," *Surratt Society News* 6 (November 1981): 5; Laurie Verge, "That Trifling Boy," *Surratt Courier* 27 (January 2002): 4–9.

6. George Alfred Townsend, *Katy of Catoctin; or, The Chain-Breakers* (1895; reprint, Cambridge, MD: Tidewater, 1959), 473. Townsend's novel, while fictional, contains factual notes derived from his first-hand research. This incident was related to him by Thomas A. Harbin.

7. Samuel Knapp Chester in Ben Perley Poore, ed., *The Conspiracy Trial for the Murder of the President* (Boston: J.E. Tilton, 1865 and 1866), 1:47. This source is hereafter cited as Poore.

8. John Mathews signed his name with one "t," and his name on his tombstone is spelled with one "t." His statements in interrogations, trial testimony, and newspaper articles are especially labyrinthine. The reader is directed to these articles which make sense of Mathews's involvement with Booth. James O. Hall, "That Letter to the National Intelligencer," *Surratt Courier* 18 (November 1993): 4–8; Terry Alford, "John Matthews: A Vindication of the Historical Consensus," *Surratt Courier* 19 (April 1994): 4–8.

9. Samuel Arnold statement, 3 December 1867, in Michael W. Kauffman, ed., *Samuel Bland Arnold: Memoirs of a Lincoln Conspirator* (Bowie, MD: Heritage Books, 1995, 22–37), 23, hereafter cited as Arnold Confession of 1867; Samuel Arnold statement, 18 April 1865, in Kauffman, ed., *Samuel Bland Arnold* (133–137), 134, hereafter cited as Arnold Confession of 1865. For the horse and buggy being housed behind Ford's Theatre, see Mary Jane Anderson in LASE, 10; John Bohran (Joseph Burroughs) in LASE, 140; James L. Maddox in LASE, 832; and Joe Simms in LASE, 1154.

10. Kauffman, ed., *Samuel Bland Arnold*, 44–45.

11. Mary Ann Van Tyne in LASE, 1294.

12. Arnold Confession of 1867, 24.

13. Louis J. Weichmann in Surratt Trial, 1:409.

14. Weichmann, *True History*, 75–76; Louis J. Weichmann in Surratt Trial, 1:434; Louis J. Weichmann in LASE, 1317, 1325.

15. Betty J. Ownsbey, "Saving Private Lockner: Lewis Powell and his Yankee Prisoner," *Lincoln Assassination Occasional Papers* 1 (November 2011): 25.

16. Powell supposedly told the Reverend Gillette he was a member of the Confederate Secret Service. See Amy Bassett, *Red Cross Reveries: On the Homefront and Overseas* (Harrisburg, PA: Stackpole, 1961), 89.

17. Louis J. Weichmann in Surratt Trial, 1:373; Weichmann, *True History*, 74–75; Edwards Pierrepont summary in Surratt Trial, 2:1269.

18. Argument of W.E. Doster in Pitman, *Assassination*, 314. William E. Doster, a competent attorney who defended both Atzerodt and Powell before the military commission, related a tale told by Powell that Powell had met and become friends with Booth in Richmond at the beginning of the war. Then, the story went, Powell, starv-

ing and homeless, ran into Booth in Baltimore in March 1865. Booth asked him to come into the oil business. Powell likely made this story up to protect Preston Parr. The part about the meeting with Booth at Monument Square seems to contain some truth mixed in with the misinformation. See David Rankin Barbee, "Lincoln and Booth," typescript, 570, David Rankin Barbee Papers, Georgetown University Library, Washington, D.C.; David Homer Bates, *Lincoln in the Telegraph Office* (New York: The Century Co., 1907), 382.

19. Ned Spangler's statement in Samuel Mudd, *The Life of Dr. Samuel A. Mudd*, ed. Nettie Mudd (New York: Neale, 1906), 323–324.

20. *New York Graphic*, 6 November 1873; John T. Ford in LASE, 528.

21. Samuel Knapp Chester in LASE, 346.

22. Asia Booth Clarke to Jean Anderson, 22 May 1865, BCLM Works on Paper Collection, ML 518, Box 37, Maryland Historical Society, Baltimore.

23. William E. Doster, *Lincoln and Episodes of the Civil War* (New York: G.P. Putnam's Sons, 1915), 276; John A. Kennedy in LASE, 767. Booth was no stranger to prostitutes in Washington and elsewhere. According to John Kennedy, Superintendent of New York Metropolitan Police, Booth was known as a frequent visitor at houses of prostitution in New York. At only one "was he regarded as a lover; that of Sally Andrews, No. 67 West 25th Street."

24. Ellen Starr to John Wilkes Booth, 7 February 1865, in LASE, 1192. The note seems to be mis-dated; Booth was in New York on that date. Starr also used the names Nellie Starr, Ella Turner, and Fannie Harrison.

25. George Alfred Townsend, "A Philistine's Diary," unidentified newspaper, 30 July 1882, in George Alfred Townsend Papers, Maryland State Archives, Annapolis.

26. "Echoes from the Capital," *New York Daily Graphic*, 6 November 1873.

27. William C. Edwards, ed., *The Lincoln Assassination—The Trial Transcript: A Transcription of NARA Microfilm M599, Reels 8 thru 16* (2012), 23.

28. Harry Clay Ford in LASE, 517.

29. *Washington Evening Star*, 24 January 1909; "Before Booth Killed Lincoln: Col. Burton's Reminiscences of the Assassination," *Baltimore American*, 26 February 1905.

30. Jesse W. Weik, "A New Story of Lincoln's Assassination: An Unpublished Record of an Eye-Witness," *The Century Magazine* 135 (February 1913): 559–562.

31. Frank A. Burr in *Washington Post*, 5 April 1891.

32. D.C. Forney, "Thirty Years After: Col. D.C. Forney's Recollections of a Stirring Time," *Washington Evening Star*, 27 June 1891.

33. John F. Coyle, "Booth's Letter Again," *Washington Post*, 30 March 1902, 35.

34. John A. Foster in LASE, 544.

35. Joan Lee Chaconas, "George Alfred Townsend's Papers," *Surratt Society News* 5 (October 1980): 4–6.

36. John Surratt to Bell Seaman, 6 February 1865, quoted in L.C. Baker, *History of the United States Secret Service* (Philadelphia: L.C. Baker, 1867), 562. Booth was not in Washington on February 6; I believe Surratt wrote that Booth was there to make the letter more interesting. If Booth had been there, Surratt would not have been writing a letter.

37. Louis J. Weichmann in Surratt Trial, 1:407.

38. Junius B. Booth, Jr., in LASE, 182.

39. Arnold Confession of 1867, 37.

40. Samuel Bland Arnold, *Defence and Prison Experiences of a Lincoln Conspirator: Statements and Autobiographical Notes* (Hattiesburg, MS: The Book Farm, 1943), 43.

41. Joseph H. Simonds to John Wilkes Booth, 24 January 1865, in LASE, 1159–1160.

42. Adam Badeau, "Dramatic Reminiscences," *St. Paul and Minneapolis Pioneer Press*, 20 February 1887.

43. Edwin A. Ely, *Personal Memoirs of Edwin A. Ely*, ed. Ambrose E. Vanderpoel (New York: Charles Francis Press, 1926), 231.

44. Samuel Knapp Chester in Poore, 1:48; Samuel Knapp Chester in LASE, 344.

45. LASE, 161.

46. John Wilkes Booth in LASE, 175.

47. Asia Booth Clarke, *The Unlocked Book: A Memoir of John Wilkes Booth by his Sister Asia Booth Clarke*, ed. Eleanor Farjeon (New York: G.P. Putnam's Sons, 1938), 123.

48. John H. McCumber in LASE, 862.

49. James O. Hall, "The Saga of Sarah Slater, Part 1," *Surratt Society News* 7 (January 1982): 3–6, and James O. Hall, "The Saga of Sarah Slater, Part 2," *Surratt Society News* 7 (February 1982): 2–6; Augustus S. Howell in Poore, 2:358.

50. Louis J. Weichmann in Poore, 1:382–384.

51. Louis J. Weichmann in Surratt Trial, 1:439.

52. Augustus S. Howell in Pitman, *Assassination*, 134. Weichmann, *True History*, 85, states that Sarah Slater stayed overnight at Mary Surratt's house on or about the night of February 22. Her overnight stay was on March 11, not February 22.

53. Atzerodt Statement, 1 May 1865.

54. "The Assassins Executed," *Boston Daily Advertiser*, 8 July 1865; Weichmann, *True History*, 84–85.

55. Louis J. Weichmann in Poore, 1:75–76, 88, 109.

56. Weichmann, *True History*, 88.

57. Benjamin Brown French to Francis O. French, Benjamin B. French Papers, Manuscript Division, Library of Congress, Washington, D.C.; Michael W. Kauffman, "Booth's First Attempt, Revisited," *Surratt Courier* 29 (August 2004): 3–4.

58. "Lincoln Memoirs in Washington," *Washington Evening Star*, 24 January 1909.

59. Henry B. Smith, *Between the Lines: Secret Service Stories Told Fifty Years After* (New York: Booz Brothers, 1911), 256–258.

60. Hall, "Saga of Sarah Slater, Part 1," 3–6, and Hall, "Saga of Sarah Slater, Part 2," 2–6.

61. John Wilkes Booth telegram to Michael O'Laughlen, 13 March 1865, in Rhodehamel and Taper, eds., *Right or Wrong*, 140; John H. Surratt to Preston Parr, 14 March 1865, in LASE, 1382; Preston Parr to John H. Surratt, 14 March 1865, in LASE, 1383.

62. Weichmann, *True History*, 97.

63. Frank A. Burr, "Booth's Bullet," *Washington Evening Star*, 7 December 1881. Atzerodt stated: "Booth sent (as he told me) liquor & provisions for the trip with the President to Richmond, about two weeks before the murder to Dr. Mudd." See Atzerodt Statement, 1 May 1865. Atzerodt was incorrect about the timing; the provisions

were sent about a month before the murder. See March 15 entry.

64. Weichmann, *True History*, 98; Louis J. Weichmann in Surratt Trial, 1:378.

65. Arnold Confession of 1867, 25–26.

66. "Rockville Lecture of John H. Surratt" in Clara Elizabeth Laughlin, *The Death of Lincoln: The Story of Booth's Plot, His Deed and the Penalty* (New York: Doubleday, Page, 1909), Appendix VI, 227; Arnold Confession of 1867, 25–26.

67. Burr, "Booth's Bullet"; Harry Clay Ford in LASE, 522, describes a visit to John Mathews and Charles Warwick in the room they shared, "where the President died."

68. Arnold Confession of 1867, 26–27.

69. Arnold Confession of 1867, 27; John M. Lloyd in LASE, 811–812; "John M. Lloyd—Star Witness," *Surratt Society News* 2 (March 1977): 3.

70. W.J. Ferguson, *I Saw Booth Shoot Lincoln* (1930; reprint, Austin: Pemberton Press, 1969), 20.

71. Townsend, "Philistine's Diary."

72. Weichmann, *True History*, 119.

73. Weik, "A New Story of Lincoln's Assassination."

74. "Rockville Lecture of John H. Surratt" in Laughlin, *Death of Lincoln*, 229.

75. Billy Williams in Pitman, *Assassination*, 223.

76. Junius B. Booth, Jr., "Diary of Junius Brutus Booth, Jr., for 1865," Muger Memorial Library, Boston University. The entry was mis-dated March 25.

77. Mary Branson in LASE, 200. Atzerodt, never especially precise in his several statements, placed Powell in New York in February. Powell made only one trip to New York, and the date of his return to Washington fixes the date he was in New York.

78. Atzerodt Statement, 1 May 1865.

79. "Rockville Lecture of John H. Surratt" in Laughlin, *Death of Lincoln*, 227; Samuel B. Arnold to John Wilkes Booth, 27 March 1865, in Kauffman, *Samuel Bland Arnold*, 9.

80. Louis J. Weichmann in Surratt Trial, 1:383–384; Hall, "Saga of Sarah Slater, Part 1," 3–6, and Hall, "Saga of Sarah Slater, Part 2," 2–6; George Alfred Townsend, "How Wilkes Booth Crossed the Potomac," *The Century Magazine* 27 (April 1884): 826.

81. Edward C. Stewart in Pitman, *Assassination*, 223; John Wilkes Booth telegram to Michael O'Laughlen, 27 March 1865, in Rhodehamel and Taper, eds., *Right or Wrong*, 143.

82. John McCullough to John T. Ford, 21 June 1865, John T. Ford Papers, Manuscript Division, Library of Congress.

83. Alfred Smith in LASE, 1163; "Traveling Directory," *Newport* [Rhode Island] *Mercury*, 1 April 1865, 4. See copy of register in Carl Sandburg, *Abraham Lincoln: The War Years* (New York: Harcourt, Brace, 1939), 4:331.

84. Joseph George, Jr., "F. Lauriston Bullard as a Lincoln Scholar," *Lincoln Herald* 62 (Winter 1960): 173–182; Richard Gutman and Kellie Gutman, "Boston: A Home for John Wilkes Booth?" *Surratt Society News* 10 (September 1985): 1.

85. Samuel Knapp Chester in LASE, 345.

86. George Alfred Townsend interview of L.Q. Washington, 5 January 1867, quoted in Hall, "Saga of Sarah Slater, Part 2," 5.

87. "Rockville Lecture of John H. Surratt" in Laugh-

lin, *Death of Lincoln*, 233; Hall, "Saga of Sarah Slater, Part 1," 3–6, and Hall, "Saga of Sarah Slater, Part 2," 3–6. Atzerodt, in one of his rambling confessions, claimed that Booth had told him he was going to Canada; apparently he did not go. It is possible Atzerodt or his interviewer inadvertently substituted Booth's name for Surratt's.

88. Betty Ownsbey to Arthur F. Loux, email, 8 August 2011.

89. Atzerodt Confession, *Baltimore American*, 18 January 1869.

90. Ned Spangler's statement in Mudd, *Life of Dr. Samuel A. Mudd*, 324.

91. Maxwell Whiteman, ed., *While Lincoln Lay Dying: A Facsimile Reproduction of the First Testimony Taken in Connection with the Assassination of Abraham Lincoln as Recorded by Corporal James Tanner* (Philadelphia: The Union League, 1968), n.p.; H.R. Tracy in LASE, 1279; Barbee, "Lincoln and Booth," 663.

92. Weichmann, *True History*, 131.

93. John H. Jack in LASE, 738; C.H. Pierson in LASE, 1048.

94. Louis J. Weichmann in Poore, 1:74–75, 136–137; John M. Lloyd in Poore, 1:117–118.

95. U.S. Congress, House, *Impeachment Investigation: Testimony Taken before the Judiciary Committee of the House of Representatives in the Investigation of the Charges against Andrew Johnson*, 2d session, 39th Congress, and 1st session, 40th Congress (Washington, D.C.: Government Printing Office, 1867), 674.

96. For the sale of the horse and buggy, see Ned Spangler's statement in Mudd, *Life of Dr. Samuel A. Mudd*, 324; for the sale of the light bay horse, see John Fletcher in LASE, 512, and Atzerodt Confession, 25 April 1865, in LASE, 62.

97. Harry Clay Ford in LASE, 516–517.

98. George Foster Robinson in LASE, 1111.

99. Benjamin T. Early in LASE, 458.

100. Barbee, "Lincoln and Booth," 680.

101. Harry Clay Ford in LASE, 517.

102. George Wren in LASE, 1391; C. Dwight Hess in LASE, 687.

103. Atzerodt Confession, 25 April 1865, in LASE, 62–63. Atzerodt in LASE, 62, puts the meeting at "two or three days before the President was killed," but in LASE, 63, he states that "we agreed to meet the next day at the National." The meeting the next day was on Friday morning, based on Atzerodt's description of the meeting and subsequent events, so the meeting the day before was clearly on Thursday. He then describes a Friday evening meeting at the Herndon House in which he was assigned to kill Vice President Johnson. Herold's and Atzerodt's assignments are inferred from their subsequent actions.

104. *Washington Sunday Star*, 24 January 1909, quoted in Allen C. Clark, *Abraham Lincoln in the National Capital* (Washington, D.C.: W.F. Roberts, 1925), 95.

105. Benjamin T. Early in LASE, 459.

106. Atzerodt Confession, 25 April 1865, in LASE, 64.

107. Henry Merrick in *Baltimore Sun*, 18 April 1865, quoted in Michael W. Kauffman, *American Brutus: John Wilkes Booth and the Lincoln Conspiracies* (New York: Random House, 2004), 223.

108. R.R. Jones in LASE, 757–758. Atzerodt told investigators that he had registered at the Kirkwood House on Thursday (see Atzerodt Confession, 25 April 1865, in LASE, 63).

109. George Foster Robinson in LASE, 1111.

110. *Washington National Intelligencer*, 29 April 1865; Burr, "Booth's Bullet."

111. John T. Ford, "Behind the Curtain of a Conspiracy," *North American Review* 148 (April 1889): 484–493.

112. John T. Ford, "The 14th of April, 1865," *Washington Evening Star*, undated clipping; Atzerodt Statement, 1 May 1865; Burr, "Booth's Bullet."

113. Harry Clay Ford in LASE, 518.

114. Henry Clay Ford in Poore, 2:548–549; Harry Clay Ford in LASE, 518.

115. James R. Ford in Surratt Trial, 1:580; Burr, "Booth's Bullet."

116. James W. Pumphrey in LASE, 1065; James W. Pumphrey in Poore, 1:175.

117. John Fletcher in LASE, 513; John Fletcher in Poore, 1:327; Atzerodt Confession, 25 April 1865, in LASE, 64; John A. Foster in LASE, 539; James Steele in LASE, 1195.

118. John M. Lloyd in Poore, 1:117–118; John M. Lloyd in Surratt Trial, 1:280; John M. Lloyd in LASE, 812; Louis J. Weichmann in Surratt Trial, 1:443–444; Atzerodt Statement, 1 May 1865.

119. Henry Merrick in *Baltimore Sun*, 18 April 1865, quoted in Kauffman, *American Brutus*, 223.

120. James W. Pumphrey stated a few days after the assassination that Booth said "theatre" and he "assumed" Booth meant Grover's. A month later Pumphrey, in Poore, 1:175, quoted Booth as saying, "I am going to Grover's Theatre." The manager of Grover's Theatre, C. Dwight Hess, testified on April 16 that he had last seen Booth on Thursday, April 13. See Hess in LASE, 687. Hess's sister-in-law wrote in 1909 that she and Hess saw Booth at Grover's in the morning of April 14, which would have been before Booth picked up the horse. See M. Helen Palmes Moss, "Lincoln and Wilkes Booth as Seen on the Day of the Assassination," *The Century Magazine* 77 (April 1909): 950.

121. Hall, "That Letter to the National Intelligencer," 4–8. After the shooting Mathews returned to his room and read the letter, which he said was written on both sides of a single sheet. Afraid of the implications of having the letter, he burned it. Years later he claimed to recall the contents; the text, according to Mathews, was nearly identical to Booth's "To Whom It May Concern" letter. Booth did not have time to write a letter that long, and a letter of that length would certainly not fit on a single sheet of paper.

122. Horace Porter, *Campaigning with Grant* (New York: The Century Co., 1897), 498. Strangely, there seem to be no corroborating witnesses to the encounter at lunch at Willard's.

123. John A. Deveney in LASE, 434; John Wilkes Booth to Andrew Johnson, 14 April 1865, in Rhodehamel and Taper, eds., *Right or Wrong*, 146.

124. Atzerodt Confession, 25 April 1865, in LASE, 62–63.

125. John A. Deveney in LASE, 434.

126. James P. Ferguson in LASE, 483; James P. Ferguson in Poore, 1:189–190.

127. "The Great National Calamity," *The Baltimore Sun*, 18 April 1865, 1.

128. William W. Crowninshield noted Booth's height in LASE, 408; "New Interest in Booth Relics Keeps War Department Busy," *Washington Evening Star*, 17 May 1925.

129. Atzerodt Confession, *Baltimore American*, 18 January 1869; John Lee in Poore, 1:63–66.

130. R.R. Jones in LASE, 60.

131. Atzerodt Confession, 25 April 1865, in LASE, 63.

132. Martha Murray, the proprietress of the Herndon House, testified in Poore 1:470 that Powell paid his bill and asked for dinner early at four o'clock. She also said he left at "about 4:00." However, Atzerodt's several confessions make it clear that the conspirators met in Powell's room on both Thursday and Friday at about 8 p.m. Powell demonstrated that he had some measure of character by paying his hotel bill.

133. Atzerodt Confession of 21 June 1865 in *Trial of the Assassins and Conspirators for the Murder of Abraham Lincoln* (Philadelphia: Barclay & Co., 1865), 67.

134. Atzerodt Confession, 25 April 1865, in LASE, 63; Atzerodt Confession, *Baltimore American*, 18 January 1869.

135. Louis J. Weichmann in LASE, 1331; John Lloyd in LASE, 807; Bennett F. Gwynn in Surratt Trial, 2:755.

136. Ned Spangler conversation with Captain Dutton in "Conspirators, Incidents of the Voyage to the Tortugas," in Lincoln Obsequies Scrapbook, 112, Manuscript Division, Library of Congress.

137. John Miles in LASE, 898; Ned Spangler in LASE, 1174–1175; Mary Ann Turner in LASE, 1288; John Bohran (Joseph Burroughs) in LASE, 141; "Who Held Booth's Horse?" *Surratt Courier* 31 (April 2006): 1–5.

138. Peter Taltavull in Poore, 1:179.

139. John E. Buckingham, *Reminiscences and Souvenirs of the Assassination of Abraham Lincoln* (Washington, D.C.: Press of R.H. Darby, 1894), 62.

140. John Buckingham in Poore, 1:188; Ford, "The 14th of April, 1865," *Washington Evening Star*, undated clipping.

141. A.M.S. Crawford in LASE, 405.

142. Henry A. Rathbone in LASE, 1080–1081.

143. Henry A. Rathbone in LASE, 1081; David Herold in LASE, 682; Dave Taylor, "Cloak and Daggers," *Surratt Courier* 37 (March 2012): 8.

144. "The Assassination of Lincoln," *Texas Siftings*, 4 August 1883. The article quotes General Charles Hamlin's observations.

145. John A. Deveney in LASE, 433; Henry A. Rathbone in LASE, 1081; Ferguson, *I Saw Booth Shoot Lincoln*, 36–40; Ronald D. Rietveld, ed., "An Eyewitness Account of Abraham Lincoln's Assassination," *Civil War History* 22 (1976): 64; John B. Stewart in LASE, 1197–1199.

146. William Withers in LASE, 1364–1365; Jacob Ritterspaugh in LASE, 1109; Rietveld, ed., "Eyewitness Account of Abraham Lincoln's Assassination," 64; Harry Hawk letter to his father in Lincoln Obsequies Scrapbook, 62, Manuscript Division, Library of Congress. Hawk, the only actor on the stage at the time of the assassination, heard Booth say "Sic Semper Tyrannis" in the box after the shot was fired and "The South shall be free" as he regained his feet.

147. John Bohran (Joseph Burroughs) in LASE, 141; Joseph B. Stewart in Poore, 2:70–72.

148. William E. Cleaver in Surratt Trial, 1:205; John A. Foster in LASE, 532.

149. Elizabeth Steger Trindal, *Mary Surratt: An American Tragedy* (Gretna, LA: Pelican, 1996), 88.

150. "Rockville Lecture of John H. Surratt" in Laughlin, *Death of Lincoln*, 226. Surratt does not state the precise date.

151. Samuel Knapp Chester in LASE, 343.

152. Hall, *Surratt Family & John Wilkes Booth*, 12.

153. Joseph H. Simonds to John Wilkes Booth, 24 January 1865, in LASE, 154.

154. "Jay Cooke & Co. in acc't with J. Wilkes Booth," cited in Rhodehamel and Taper, eds., *Right or Wrong*, 30.

155. "Jay Cooke & Co. in acc't with J. Wilkes Booth," cited in Rhodehamel and Taper, eds., *Right or Wrong*, 30.

156. Eddy Martin in Surratt Trial, 1:214–215.

157. Earl Schenck Miers, et al., eds., *Lincoln Day By Day: A Chronology, 1809–1865* (Dayton, OH: Morningside, 1991), 3:306.

158. "Jay Cooke & Co. in acc't with J. Wilkes Booth," cited in Rhodehamel and Taper, eds., *Right or Wrong*, 30. The Jay Cooke & Co. bank record indicates $750 was withdrawn from Booth's account on this date. No check has been found for this transaction. It is probable that Booth withdrew the money directly from the bank.

159. Samuel Knapp Chester in Poore, 1:47.

160. G.W. Bunker in Poore, 1:32.

161. Arnold Confession of 1867, 23.

162. U.S. Congress, House, *Report Relating to the Assassination of President Lincoln*, First Session, 39th Congress, Report No. 104 (Washington, D.C.: Government Printing Office, 1866).

163. Arnold Confession of 1865, 134.

164. William E. Cleaver in Surratt Trial, 1:205.

165. Charles C. Dunn in Surratt Trial, 1:437.

166. Eddy Martin in Surratt Trial, 1:214–215.

167. Smith, *Between the Lines*, 258.

168. "Jay Cooke & Co. in acc't with J. Wilkes Booth," cited in Rhodehamel and Taper, eds., *Right or Wrong*, 30.

169. Atzerodt Confession, *Baltimore American*, 18 January 1869; Atzerodt Confession, 25 April 1865, in LASE, 62.

170. Richard Mitchell Smoot, *The Unwritten History of the Assassination of Abraham Lincoln* (Clinton, MA: Press of W.J. Coulter, 1908), 9.

171. Eddy Martin in Surratt Trial, 1:215.

172. *Philadelphia North American and United States Gazette*, 16 January 1865.

173. John Thomas Miles in LASE, 901.

174. John Wilkes Booth to Junius Brutus Booth, Jr., 17 January 1865, in Rhodehamel and Taper, eds., *Right or Wrong*, 131–132.

175. Eddy Martin in Surratt Trial, 1:215.

176. Arnold Confession of 1867, 24.

177. "Jay Cooke & Co. in acc't with J. Wilkes Booth," cited in Rhodehamel and Taper, eds., *Right or Wrong*, 30.

178. Theodore Roscoe, *The Web of Conspiracy: The Complete Story of the Men who Murdered Abraham Lincoln* (Englewood Cliffs, NJ: Prentice-Hall, 1959), 72–74. Roscoe concludes that Booth, Surratt, Atzerodt, Harbin,

and others were prepared to abduct the president and take him to Richmond. It seems unlikely that an abduction would have been attempted with only Booth, Surratt, Arnold, and O'Laughlen available in Washington.

179. Joseph H. Simonds to John Wilkes Booth, 24 January 1865, in LASE, 154.

180. Roscoe, *Web of Conspiracy*, 67; Margaret Branson in Poore, 3:81.

181. *Washington National Intelligencer*, 21 January 1865.

182. *Washington National Intelligencer*, 22 January 1865.

183. Louis J. Weichmann in Surratt Trial, 1:373.

184. Weichmann, *True History*, 75; Louis J. Weichmann in Surratt Trial, 2:1269.

185. Louis J. Weichmann in Surratt Trial, 1:407.

186. Weichmann, *True History*, 75–76; Louis J. Weichmann in Surratt Trial, 1:434.

187. Arnold Confession of 1865, 134.

188. Townsend, *Katy of Catoctin*, 473.

189. E.B. Long, *The Civil War Day By Day: An Almanac, 1861–1865* (Garden City, NY: Doubleday, 1971), 628.

190. William E. Cleaver in Surratt Trial, 1:206. Tidwell, Hall, and Gaddy have John Surratt leaving Cleaver's Stable and then traveling to Richmond and meeting with Confederate Secretary of State Judah Benjamin. I believe they are mistaken. As is often the case, the dates given in the testimony seem to have been recalled incorrectly with the passage of time. Surratt did see Benjamin in Richmond, but it was on April 1, 1865. See William A. Tidwell, with James O. Hall and David Winfred Gaddy, *Come Retribution: The Confederate Secret Service and the Assassination of Lincoln* (Jackson: University Press of Mississippi, 1988), 340–341.

191. Tidwell, Hall, and Gaddy, *Come Retribution*, 324.

192. Arnold Confession of 1867, 24–25; William E. Cleaver in Surratt Trial, 1:213.

193. Junius B. Booth, Jr., in LASE, 179.

194. G.W. Bunker in Poore, 1:32.

195. Arnold Confession of 1867, 37.

196. Argument of W.E. Doster in Pitman, *Assassination*, 314. Doster relates a tale told by Powell that Powell had met and become friends with Booth in Richmond at the beginning of the war. Then, the story went, Powell, starving and homeless, ran into Booth in Baltimore in March 1865, and Booth asked him to come into the oil business. Powell likely made up parts of the story to protect Preston Parr. The meeting with Booth in Baltimore probably took place but was prearranged and not accidental.

197. Argument of W.E. Doster in Pitman, *Assassination*, 314.

198. Tidwell, Hall, and Gaddy, *Come Retribution*, 340.

199. Miers, et al., eds., *Lincoln Day By Day*, 3:311.

200. Hall, "Saga of Sarah Slater, Part 1," 3–6, and Hall, "Saga of Sarah Slater, Part 2," 2–6; Augustus S. Howell in Poore, 2:358.

201. The Lincoln Log, www.thelincolnlog.org.

202. Samuel Knapp Chester in Poore, 1:48.

203. Roscoe, *Web of Conspiracy*, 53.

204. Trindal, *Mary Surratt: An American Tragedy*, 91.

205. Ellen Starr in LASE, 1192.

206. Weichmann, *True History*, 76; Brooke Stabler in Surratt Trial, 1:216.

207. *Washington Evening Star*, 9 February 1864.

208. John Wilkes Booth to Orlando Tompkins, 9 February 1865, in Rhodehamel and Taper, eds., *Right or Wrong*, 134–135. Booth wrote "Washington, DC" on top of the letter as if writing from there, but at the end of the letter he stated, "I return to this city in about a week." He wanted Tompkins to send the cards to him in Washington.

209. Booth Jr., "Diary of Junius Brutus Booth, Jr., for 1865."

210. Mary Van Tine [Tyne] in Poore, 1:139; P.H. Maulsby in Poore, 2:225–226; Arnold Confession of 1865, 134.

211. *Washington Evening Star*, 11 February 1865.

212. John Wilkes Booth to Orlando Tompkins, 9 February 1865, in Rhodehamel and Taper, eds., *Right or Wrong*, 134–135.

213. Badeau, "Dramatic Reminiscences."

214. Adam Badeau quoted in Izola Forrester, *This One Mad Act* (Boston: Hale, Cushman & Flint, 1937), 160.

215. Junius Brutus Booth, Jr., to Asia Booth Clarke, February 1865, in Clarke, *Unlocked Book*, 199.

216. Junius B. Booth, Jr., in LASE, 179.

217. Ely, *Personal Memoirs*, 231.

218. Clarke, *Unlocked Book*, 200.

219. Hall, "Saga of Sarah Slater, Part 1," 3–6, and Hall, "Saga of Sarah Slater, Part 2," 2–6.

220. Hildegarde Dolson, *The Great Oildorado: The Gaudy and Turbulent Years of the First Oil Rush: Pennsylvania, 1859–1880* (New York: Random House, 1959), 162.

221. Richard M. Johnson in LASE, 754–755.

222. Orlando Tompkins in LASE, 1276.

223. Louis J. Weichmann in Surratt Trial, 1:375.

224. Tiffany & Co. receipt found in Booth's trunk in LASE, 161. The receipt is dated February 21, but Booth arrived in Baltimore on the 3:30 a.m. train on that date. I assume the receipt is mis-dated.

225. Louis J. Weichmann in Poore, 1:382–384; Weichmann, *True History*, 86.

226. John McCumber in LASE, 862.

227. John Wilkes Booth telegram to John Parker Hale Wentworth, 21 February 1865, in Rhodehamel and Taper, eds., *Right or Wrong*, 137.

228. Louis J. Weichmann in Surratt Trial, 1:439.

229. Statement of Mary E. Surratt, 17 April 1865, in LASE, 1245.

230. John McCumber in LASE, 862.

231. George W. Bunker in Surratt Trial, 1:330.

232. Augustus S. Howell in Pitman, *Assassination*, 134. Some have speculated that Booth escorted Sarah Slater from New York to Washington. Slater was in Washington in the afternoon, and Booth did not arrive until about 8 p.m. so it seems John Surratt had escorted the lady.

233. Brooke Stabler in Surratt Trial, 1:223. Actually, the horse belonged to Booth.

234. Hall, "Saga of Sarah Slater, Part 1," 3–6, and Hall, "Saga of Sarah Slater, Part 2," 2–6.

235. Weichmann, *True History*, 84–85; Louis J. Weichmann in Pitman, *Assassination*, 114.

236. Some authors have claimed that Booth pleaded with Lincoln to spare Beall's life. No supporting evidence has been found.

237. John Wilkes Booth telegram to Michael O'Laughlen, 27 February 1865, in Rhodehamel and Taper, eds., *Right or Wrong*, 138.

238. James H. Fowle statement in Benjamin F. Butler Papers, Manuscript Division, Library of Congress.

239. Tidwell, Hall, and Gaddy, *Come Retribution*, 340–341; Hall, "Saga of Sarah Slater, Part 1," 3–6, and Hall, "Saga of Sarah Slater, Part 2," 2–6.

240. G.W. Bunker in Poore, 1:32. The date he took the 8:15 train is shown as February 18, but from context it was obviously February 28.

241. Weichmann, *True History*, 88.

242. Miers, et al., eds., *Lincoln Day By Day*, 3:317.

243. Stanley Kimmel, *The Mad Booths of Maryland* (New York: Dover, 1969), 202.

244. "Lincoln Memoirs in Washington," *Washington Evening Star*, 24 January 1909.

245. George L. Grillet in LASE, 620.

246. John Wilkes Booth verse, 5 March 1865, in Rhodehamel and Taper, eds., *Right or Wrong*, 139. The handwriting matches other samples of Lucy Hale's writing.

247. Smith, *Between the Lines*, 257.

248. Miers, et al., eds., *Lincoln Day By Day*, 3:318.

249. Mary Van Tine [Tyne] in Poore, 1:139.

250. Smith, *Between the Lines*, 256.

251. Hall, "Saga of Sarah Slater, Part 1," 3–6, and Hall, "Saga of Sarah Slater, Part 2," 2–6.

252. G.W. Bunker in Poore, 3:61.

253. Smith, *Between the Lines*, 258.

254. Hall, "Saga of Sarah Slater, Part 1," 3–6, and Hall, "Saga of Sarah Slater, Part 2," 2–6.

255. John Wilkes Booth telegram to Michael O'Laughlen, 13 March 1865, in Rhodehamel and Taper, eds., *Right or Wrong*, 140; P.H. Maulsby in Pitman, *Assassination*, 232.

256. Burr, "Booth's Bullet."

257. John H. Surratt to Preston Parr, 14 March 1865, in LASE, 1382; Preston Parr to John H. Surratt, 14 March 1865, in LASE, 1383.

258. Weichmann, *True History*, 97; Louis J. Weichmann in Surratt Trial, 1:378.

259. Weichmann, *True History*, 98.

260. Arnold Confession of 1867, 25–26; John Howard in LASE, 714–715; Thomas Manning in LASE, 836–837.

261. Miers, et al., eds., *Lincoln Day By Day*, 3:320.

262. Louis J. Weichmann in Surratt Trial, 1:378.

263. Arnold Confession of 1867, 26.

264. "Jay Cooke & Co. in acc't with J. Wilkes Booth," cited in Rhodehamel and Taper, eds., *Right or Wrong*, 30. See also note about check on page 31.

265. Burr, "Booth's Bullet."

266. Arnold Confession of 1867, 27.

267. Arnold Confession of 1867, 27.

268. John F. Stanton, "Who Was Kate Thompson?" *Surratt Courier* 34 (February 2009): 5–9.

269. *Boston Globe*, 17 June 1878.

270. "John M. Lloyd—Star Witness," 3.

271. Townsend, "Philistine's Diary."

272. Weichmann, *True History*, 119.

273. Louis J. Weichmann in Pitman, *Assassination*, 115.

274. John Greenawalt in Poore, 1:346.

275. Louis J. Weichmann in Surratt Trial, 1:380.

276. Mary Van Tine [Tyne] in Poore, 1:142.

277. Roderick D. Watson to John H. Surratt, 19 March 1865, in LASE, 1315.

278. *New York Clipper*, 22 April 1865.

279. Louis J. Weichmann in Surratt Trial, 1:380.

280. Mary Van Tine [Tyne] in Pitman, *Assassination*, 222; Arnold Confession of 1867, 27.

281. G.W. Bunker in Poore, 1:32.

282. Miers, et al., eds., *Lincoln Day By Day*, 3:321.

283. "With John Wilkes Booth In His Days As An Actor," *Baltimore Sun*, 17 March 1907.

284. Samuel Knapp Chester in LASE, 344, states that Booth said the affair had ended late in January or early in February. However, in Poore, 1:48, Chester states that Booth was still trying to recruit him early in February. Almost certainly, Booth mentioned this after the failure on March 17.

285. Booth Jr., "Diary of Junius Brutus Booth, Jr., for 1865," entry mis-dated March 25.

286. John Wilkes Booth telegram to Louis J. Weichmann, 23 March 1865, in Rhodehamel and Taper, eds., *Right or Wrong*, 142.

287. Hall, "Saga of Sarah Slater, Part 1," 3–6, and Hall, "Saga of Sarah Slater, Part 2," 2–6.

288. Thomas L. Gardiner in Pitman, *Assassination*, 196.

289. Miers, et al., eds., *Lincoln Day By Day*, 3:322.

290. Louis J. Weichmann in Pitman, *Assassination*, 114; Hall, "Saga of Sarah Slater, Part 1," 3–6, and Hall, "Saga of Sarah Slater, Part 2," 2–6.

291. John H. McCumber in LASE, 861.

292. Arnold Confession of 1867, 28.

293. John H. McCumber in LASE, 861.

294. Louis J. Weichmann in Pitman, *Assassination*, 114.

295. Tidwell, Hall, and Gaddy, *Come Retribution*, 336.

296. Terry Alford, "John Wilkes Booth and George Alfred Townsend: A Marriage Made in Hell," Paper Delivered at the Third Biennial Tudor Hall Conference, Aberdeen, Maryland, 3 May 1992.

297. Louis J. Weichmann in Surratt Trial, 1:412.

298. Honora Fitzpatrick in Surratt Trial, 1:715; Hall, "Saga of Sarah Slater, Part 1," 3–6, and Hall, "Saga of Sarah Slater, Part 2," 2–6.

299. Brooks Stabler in Surratt Trial, 1:217.

300. Henry E. Merrick in Poore, 3:43; John McCullough to John T. Ford, 21 June 1865, John T. Ford Papers, Manuscript Division, Library of Congress.

301. Champ Clark, *The Assassination: Death of the President* (Alexandria, VA: Time-Life Books, 1987), 54.

302. Edward C. Stewart in Pitman, *Assassination*, 223; John Wilkes Booth telegram to Michael O'Laughlen, 27 March 1865, in Rhodehamel and Taper, eds., *Right or Wrong*, 143.

303. Weichmann, *True History*, 121; John A. Foster in LASE, 542.

304. John Greenawalt in Poore, 1:346.

305. Samuel B. Arnold to John Wilkes Booth, 27 March 1865, in Kauffman, *Samuel Bland Arnold*, 9; William H. Terry in Pitman, *Assassination*, 236.

306. Mary Ann Booth to John Wilkes Booth, 28 March 1865, in LASE, 166.

307. Henry M. Bailey in LASE, 97.

308. Ellen Starr in LASE, 1194.

309. Brooke Stabler in Poore, 1:178, 204, and in Surratt Trial, 1:222.

310. J.B. Tinsley in Surratt Trial, 2:791.

311. James R. Ford in Surratt Trial, 1:581.

312. Arnold Confession of 1867, 28–29, 36.

313. Brooke Stabler in Poore, 1:178, 204.

314. John Fletcher in Poore, 1:326–327, in LASE, 512, and in Surratt Trial, 1:230. Fletcher was sure that a man matching Booth's description and Atzerodt brought the horses to Nailor's on April 3, but Booth had left town on April 1. March 31, the date the horses were taken from Howard's Stable, seems the more likely date.

315. John Greenawalt in Poore, 1:342.

316. G.W. Bunker in Poore, 1:32, and Surratt Trial, 1:331.

317. "Rockville Lecture of John H. Surratt" in Laughlin, Death of Lincoln, 230.

318. Louis J. Weichmann in Pitman, Assassination, 114.

319. Hall, "The Saga of Sarah Slater, Part 1," 3–6, and Hall, "The Saga of Sarah Slater, Part 2," 2–6.

320. Louis J. Weichmann in Surratt Trial, 1:438; James O. Hall, "Stringfellow Notes," 21 July 1999 (notes in author's files); Tidwell, Hall, and Gaddy, Come Retribution, 411–412.

321. Arnold Confession of 1867, 29.

322. John McCullough to John T. Ford, 21 June 1865, John T. Ford Papers, Manuscript Division, Library of Congress. Circumstantial and inconclusive evidence suggests that Booth may have taken a train to Montreal on April 2 and returned April 4.

323. Junius Brutus Booth, Jr., in LASE, 179.

324. Louis J. Weichmann in LASE, 1325; Weichmann, True History, 126–127.

325. Weichmann, True History, 126–127.

326. Hall, "Saga of Sarah Slater, Part 1," 3–6, and Hall, "Saga of Sarah Slater, Part 2," 2–6; Louis J. Weichmann in Pitman, Assassination, 114.

327. Weichmann, True History, 130.

328. Honora Fitzpatrick in Surratt Trial, 1:713; Trindal, Mary Surratt: An American Tragedy, 114; Louis J. Weichmann in Poore, 1:80.

329. "Rockville Lecture of John H. Surratt" in Laughlin, Death of Lincoln, 232.

330. "Pour Boston, via Newport," New York Courrier des Etats-Unis, 7 April 1865, 4.

331. Miers, et al., eds., Lincoln Day By Day, 3:325.

332. "Rockville Lecture of John H. Surratt" in Laughlin, Death of Lincoln, 232.

333. See facsimile in Sandburg, Abraham Lincoln: The War Years, 4:331; Alfred Smith in LASE, 1163; "Traveling Directory," Newport [Rhode Island] Mercury, 1 April 1865.

334. George Jr., "F. Lauriston Bullard as a Lincoln Scholar."

335. Louis J. Weichmann in Surratt Trial, 1:385; Weichmann, True History, 122.

336. George Jr., "F. Lauriston Bullard as a Lincoln Scholar."

337. Samuel Knapp Chester in LASE, 345.

338. Gutman and Gutman, "Boston: A Home for John Wilkes Booth?" 1; Quincy Kilby, typescript note, William Seymour Family Papers, Manuscripts Division, Department of Rare Books and Special Collections, Princeton University Library, Princeton, New Jersey.

339. "Rockville Lecture of John H. Surratt" in Laughlin, Death of Lincoln, 233; Alexandra L. Levin, "The Canada Contact: Edwin Gray Lee," Civil War Times 18 (June 1979): 43.

340. Samuel Knapp Chester in LASE, 345, and Poore, 1:49–50.

341. Samuel Knapp Chester in LASE, 346.

342. G.W. Bunker in Poore, 1:32, and Surratt Trial, 1:331.

343. Asia Booth Clarke to Jean Anderson, 22 May 1865, BCLM Works on Paper Collection.

344. Miers, et al., eds., Lincoln Day By Day, 3:327.

345. Weichmann, True History, 130–131.

346. H.R. Tracy in LASE, 1279.

347. Clem H. Pierson in LASE, 479.

348. Ned Spangler's statement in Mudd, Life of Dr. Samuel Mudd, 324.

349. Louis J. Weichmann in Poore, 1:74.

350. John H. Jack in LASE, 739.

351. Ned Spangler's statement in Mudd, Life of Dr. Samuel Mudd, 324.

352. U.S. Congress. House, Impeachment Investigation, 674.

353. Smoot, Unwritten History, 11–13.

354. John Greenawalt in LASE, 615, and in Poore 1:346.

355. John Fletcher in LASE, 512, and Atzerodt Confession, 25 April 1865, in LASE, 62; Ned Spangler's statement in Mudd, Life of Dr. Samuel Mudd, 324.

356. William R. Nevins in Poore, 2:278. Nevins confidently testified that he showed Johnson's room to Atzerodt on April 12. Based on other evidence, April 14, or even April 13, would be a better fit.

357. Harry Clay Ford in LASE, 516.

358. "Rockville Lecture of John H. Surratt" in Laughlin, Death of Lincoln, 233–234; Baker, History of the United States Secret Service, 557. Surratt had a companion dressed as a man who was about five feet tall and didn't speak.

359. Harry Clay Ford in LASE, 517.

360. C.D. Hess in Pitman, Assassination, 99.

361. George Foster Robinson in LASE, 1111.

362. James B. Henderson in Poore, 3:510.

363. Atzerodt Confession, 25 April 1865, in LASE, 62–63.

364. John Wilkes Booth to Mary Ann Holmes Booth, 14 April 1865, in Rhodehamel and Taper, eds., Right or Wrong, 144.

365. George Foster Robinson in LASE, 1111.

366. Atzerodt Confession, 25 April 1865, in LASE, 63–64.

367. R.R. Jones in LASE, 757–758. Atzerodt told investigators that he had registered at the Kirkwood House on Thursday (see Atzerodt Confession, 25 April 1865, in LASE, 63).

368. Edward Murphy in LASE, 955–957; James B. Henderson in Poore, 3:510.

369. John M. Lloyd in Surratt Trial, 1:280.

370. James W. Pumphrey in LASE, 1065.

371. Louis J. Weichmann in Surratt Trial, 1:443, 445.

372. James W. Pumphrey in LASE, 1065.

373. Hall, "That Letter to the National Intelligencer," 4–8; Horace Porter, *Campaigning with Grant* (New York: The Century Co., 1897), 498.

374. John Wilkes Booth to Andrew Johnson, 14 April 1865, in Rhodehamel and Taper, eds., *Right or Wrong*, 146.

375. "John M. Lloyd—Star Witness," 3.

376. Louis J. Weichmann in LASE, 1331; Louis J. Weichmann in Surratt Trial, 1:395.

377. Smoot, *Unwritten History*, 13; "Some Damaging Evidence?" *Surratt Courier* 30 (June 2005): 3–5.

378. John A. Foster in LASE, 533.

Chapter 10. Useless: 1865–1869

1. Silas T. Cobb in William C. Edwards and Edward Steers, Jr., eds., *The Lincoln Assassination: The Evidence* (Urbana: University of Illinois Press, 2009), 363–366. This book is hereafter cited as LASE. There is abundant evidence that Booth lost his hat in the theatre. Yet he was wearing a hat when he reached the Navy Yard Bridge.

2. Atzerodt Confession, *Baltimore American*, 18 January 1869. According to Louis J. Weichmann, *A True History of the Assassination of Abraham Lincoln and of the Conspiracy of 1865*, ed. Floyd E. Risvold (New York: Vintage, 1977), 385, Atzerodt wrote this confession on the night before his execution.

3. John Fletcher in Ben Perley Poore, ed., *The Conspiracy Trial for the Murder of the President* (Boston: J.E. Tilton, 1865 and 1866), 1:328. This source is hereafter cited as Poore.

4. Atzerodt Confession, *Baltimore American*, 18 January 1869; Atzerodt Confession of 21 June 1865 in *Trial of the Assassins and Conspirators for the Murder of Abraham Lincoln* (Philadelphia: Barclay & Co., 1865), 67.

5. "The Assassins Executed," *Boston Daily Advertiser*, 8 July 1865.

6. U.S. Congress, House, *Impeachment Investigation: Testimony Taken Before the Judiciary Committee of the House of Representatives in the Investigation of the Charges Against Andrew Johnson*, 2d session, 39th Congress, and 1st session, 40th Congress (Washington, D.C.: Government Printing Office, 1867), 674.

7. Betty J. Ownsbey, *Alias "Paine": Lewis Thornton Powell, the Mystery Man of the Lincoln Conspiracy* (Jefferson, NC: McFarland, 1993), 70–85.

8. John Fletcher in Poore, 1:328–329.

9. Polk Gardiner in Poore, 1:255–257; Polk Gardiner in LASE, 584–585.

10. David Herold in LASE, 682.

11. William P. Wood in LASE, 1372–1374.

12. John M. Lloyd in LASE, 810, 812–814.

13. Herold also thought Booth had been drinking that night: "I thought Booth must have been drinking. I am quite confident he had been." See David Herold in LASE, 671. Dr. Samuel A. Mudd's wife, Nettie, also thought he was inebriated.

14. The stop at John Lloyd's is described by Lloyd in LASE, 806–817; Lloyd in Poore, 1:118–120, 123–125, 129–132; Lloyd in *Trial of John H. Surratt in the Criminal Court of the District of Columbia* (Washington, D.C.: Government Printing Office, 1867), 1:282–287, 289–302. This source is hereafter cited as Surratt Trial. Herold's attempt to dissuade Booth from going to Dr. Mudd's house is described in Samuel A. Mudd file, Pardon Case Files, 1853–1963, Records of the Office of the Pardon Attorney, RG 204, National Archives and Records Administration, Washington, D.C. Herold related the incident to his lawyer, Frederick Stone, who, in turn, related it to Mudd's lawyer, Thomas Ewing.

15. "Dr. Mudd at Home," *Port Tobacco Times and Charles County Advertiser*, 9 April 1869, 1.

16. The visit to Dr. Mudd is described in Lt. Alexander Lovett in Poore, 1:258–272, and LASE 822–824; Col. Henry Horatio Wells in Poore, 1:281–293 and in LASE 1336–1347; Joshua Lloyd in Poore, 1:273–281; William Williams in Poore, 1:294–301; Samuel A. Mudd in LASE, 938–942, and LASE, 942–950; Thomas Davis in LASE, 418–421; Frank Washington in LASE, 1313–1314.

17. Booth may also have cut off his large forelock of hair. See Seaton Munroe, "Recollections of Lincoln's Assassination," *North American Review* 162 (March 1896): 431; George L. Porter, "How Booth's Body Was Hidden," *Columbian Magazine* 4 (April 1911): 68. Both Munroe and Porter assert that Booth cut off his forelock, but Porter has clearly copied Munroe's article.

18. H.H. Wells in Poore, 1:283.

19. Thomas David in LASE, 419.

20. Samuel Mudd, *The Life of Dr. Samuel A. Mudd*, ed. Nettie Mudd (New York: Neale, 1906), 33.

21. William H. Gleason Statement, 19 December 1867, Benjamin F. Butler Papers, Manuscript Division, Library of Congress, Washington, D.C.

22. Mudd's round trip to Bryantown with the stops he later mentioned would have brought him home about 5 p.m. However, witnesses later revealed that he returned home between 6 and 7 p.m. Mudd may have visited William Burtle, who lived three miles south of Bryantown. Burtle could help the fugitives through Zekiah Swamp along to the next stop on the covert route to Richmond. There may have been a second reason for visiting Burtle; Dr. Mudd was carrying Confederate contraband mail, and Burtle was a contact on the underground mail route. Booth and Herold departed shortly after Mudd's return and headed for Burtle's place. See Edward Steers, Jr., "Dr. Mudd's Sense of Timing: The Trip into Bryantown," *Surratt Courier* 24 (September 1999): 4–8.

23. At his death, on April 26, Booth had "a one hundred dollar note" and $60 in gold. See Herold statement in LASE, 683.

24. Sarah F. Mudd statement dated 6 July 1865, in Samuel A. Mudd file, Pardon Case Files, 1853–1963, Records of the Office of the Pardon Attorney, RG 204, National Archives and Records Administration; original in Ewing Family Papers, Manuscript Division, Library of Congress. Sarah Mudd stated that Booth (she called him "Tyler") was wearing a heavy, false beard when he left the house. This was a weak attempt to support her fiction that she and her husband had not recognized Booth despite the fact that he had been an overnight visitor at their house on a previous occasion.

25. "Statement of George A. Atzerodt to Prov. Mar.

McPhail, May 1, 1865," *Surratt Courier* 13 (October 1988): 2–3, hereafter cited as Atzerodt Statement, 1 May 1865.

26. If Booth did not reveal what he had done, how did he explain his 4 a.m. arrival and his haste to move on? Some researchers conclude from the evidence that Booth did not inform Dr. Mudd of his deed, and that Dr. Mudd first learned of the assassination and of Booth's involvement when he was in Bryantown. I believe almost certainly Booth and Herold told Mudd of Booth's deed. The reader may make up his or her own mind.

27. Rick Smith, "Break a Leg," *Surratt Courier* 28 (June 2003): 4–6; Michael W. Kauffman, *American Brutus: John Wilkes Booth and the Lincoln Conspiracies* (New York: Random House, 2004), 273.

28. William C. Edwards, ed., *The Lincoln Assassination—The Trial Transcript: A Transcription of NARA Microfilm M599, Reels 8 thru 16* (2012), 291.

29. Alexis (Electus) Thomas in LASE, 1266–1268.

30. Oswell Swan in LASE, 1251–1252.

31. The visit to Cox's house is derived from several, sometimes conflicting, sources. See Thomas A. Jones, *J. Wilkes Booth: An Account of His Sojourn in Southern Maryland After the Assassination of Abraham Lincoln, His Passage Across the Potomac, and His Death in Virginia* (Chicago: Laird & Lee, 1893), 71; Oswell Swan in LASE, 1251; Mary Swan in LASE, 1252; David Herold statement in LASE, 665–683.

32. Oswell Swan in LASE, 1251–1252.

33. Jones, *J. Wilkes Booth: An Account*, 73.

34. Kauffman, *American Brutus*, 153; Jones, *J. Wilkes Booth: An Account*, 111–112.

35. Jones, *J. Wilkes Booth: An Account*, 78.

36. Jones, *J. Wilkes Booth: An Account*, 80.

37. George Alfred Townsend, "How Wilkes Booth Crossed the Potomac," *The Century Magazine* 27 (April 1884): 829.

38. Townsend, "How Wilkes Booth Crossed the Potomac," 830.

39. Jones, *J. Wilkes Booth: An Account*, 109–110. Some evidence points to Thursday, some to Friday, for Booth and Herold leaving Dent's Meadow. The evidence is presented in Tidwell, "Booth Crosses the Potomac: An Exercise in Historical Research," *Civil War History* 36 (December 1990). Tidwell concludes the men left on Friday.

40. Jones, *J. Wilkes Booth: An Account*, 110.

41. W.N. Walton, "Booth's Flight and Death," 3 May 1865, newspaper clipping in Lincoln Obsequies Scrapbook, 83, Manuscript Division, Library of Congress. Walton accompanied L.B. Baker's troops when they followed the escape trail to gather evidence. Herold commented on the "scalawags" as he sat on Rollins's steps.

42. Stanley Kimmel, *The Mad Booths of Maryland* (New York: Dover, 1969), 362. According to Kimmel, an unidentified newspaper report described the boat as being in very dilapidated condition with oars that appeared to have been cobbled together from several distinct pieces of wood.

43. Atzerodt Confession, 25 April 1865, in LASE, 64.

44. Michael W. Kauffman, "John Wilkes Booth and the Murder of Abraham Lincoln," *Blue & Gray Magazine* 7 (April 1990): 38.

45. David Herold in LASE, 674.

46. John H. Rhodehamel and Louise Taper, eds., *Right or Wrong, God Judge Me: The Writings of John Wilkes Booth* (Urbana: University of Illinois Press, 1997), 154–155.

47. *New York Tribune*, 22 April 1865, quoted in Gene Smith, *American Gothic: The Story of America's Legendary Theatrical Family, Junius, Edwin, and John Wilkes Booth* (New York: Simon & Schuster, 1992), 181.

48. John F. Stanton, "The Arrest of Thomas Nelson Conrad and Fannie Byrd Dade," *Surratt Courier* 29 (October 2004): 3.

49. John F. Stanton, "Booth and the Lightships: Booth's Route and Timing, Crossing the Potomac," *Lincoln Assassination Occasional Papers* 1 (February 2012).

50. David Herold in LASE, 674.

51. Elizabeth Rousby Quesenberry in LASE, 1074; Walton, "Booth's Flight and Death."

52. Joseph E. "Rick" Smith and William L. Richter, "Elizabeth Rousby Quesenberry and the Escape of Lincoln's Assassin," *Surratt Courier* 33 (September 2008): 4; John F. Stanton, "Another Look at Crismond," *Surratt Courier* 38 (April 2013): 3; William L. Bryant in LASE, 216; John Stewart, *Confederate Spies at Large: The Lives of Lincoln Assassination Conspirators Tom Harbin and Charlie Russell* (Jefferson, NC: McFarland, 2007), 87.

53. Joseph E. "Rick" Smith and William L. Richter, "'Behold! I Tell You a Mystery': Who Was Mr. Chrisman?" *Surratt Courier* 38 (March 2013): 13; William L. Bryant in LASE, 216–217; Kauffman, *American Brutus*, 299.

54. Richard H. Stuart in LASE, 1201–1203. Where did Booth get a shawl? He had replaced the saddle blanket of the horse he had rented in Washington with his shawl. Apparently when Herold had disposed of the horses, Booth had retrieved the shawl.

55. William L. Bryant in LASE, 216; Richard H. Stuart in LASE, 1201–1202; William Lucas in LASE, 824–825.

56. James O. Hall, "Two Pages from Booth's Diary: Dr. Richard H. Stuart Meets John Wilkes Booth," *Surratt Courier* 21 (August 1996): 3–5; Richard H. Stuart in LASE, 1202.

57. Tidwell, Hall, and Gaddy, *Come Retribution*, 464.

58. William Rollins in LASE, 1113–1114.

59. Willie S. Jett in LASE, 746.

60. Willie S. Jett in Poore, 1:312.

61. Tidwell, Hall, and Gaddy, *Come Retribution*, 465.

62. Prentiss Ingraham, "Pursuit and Death of John Wilkes Booth," *The Century Magazine* 39 (January 1890): 444.

63. Walton, "Booth's Flight and Death." Possibly reporter Walton garbled the Peyton name into Pritian.

64. Willie S. Jett in LASE, 748.

65. Ingraham, "Pursuit and Death of John Wilkes Booth," 445.

66. Willie S. Jett in LASE, 748; John C. Brennan, "Hobbledehoy David Edgar Herold," *Surratt Courier* 12 (August 1987): 6–7.

67. Ingraham, "Pursuit and Death of John Wilkes Booth," 445.

68. U.S. Congress. House. Richard H. Garrett War Claim, 22 June 1874. First Session, 43rd Congress, Report No. 743, 5; Ingraham, "Pursuit and Death of John Wilkes Booth," 444–445. Writing years after the event, Bainbridge claimed the Garretts were informed of Booth's identity. Other witnesses do not support that claim.

69. John M. Garrett statement, 20 May 1865, in "Mr. Booth Visits the Garrett Family," *Surratt Courier* 24 (April 1999): 3; William H. Garrett statement, 20 May 1865, in "Mr. Booth Visits the Garrett Family," *Surratt Courier* 24 (April 1999): 5.

70. William H. Garrett, "True Story of the Capture of John Wilkes Booth," *Confederate Veteran* 29 (1921): 129; Lucinda Holloway, "The Capture and Death of John Wilkes Booth by an Eye-witness," in James O. Hall, comp., *On the Way to Garrett's Barn: John Wilkes Booth and David E. Herold in the Northern Neck of Virginia, April 22–26, 1865* (Clinton, MD: The Surratt Society, 2001, 178–183): 180.

71. U.S. Congress, House, Richard H. Garrett War Claim, 22 June 1874. First Session, 43rd Congress, Report No. 743, 6.

72. John M. Garrett statement in "Mr. Booth Visits the Garrett Family"; Michael W. Kauffman, "Booth's Escape Route: Lincoln's Assassin on the Run," *Blue & Gray Magazine* 7 (June 1990): 46. Kauffman concludes that this entry was written at this time and place.

73. Richard H. Garrett letter to Grandison Manning, 5 April 1866, in Hall, comp., *On the Way to Garrett's Barn*, 171–173.

74. Walton, "Booth's Flight and Death," 83.

75. U.S. Congress, House, Richard H. Garrett War Claim, 22 June 1874. First Session, 43rd Congress, Report No. 743, 4.

76. Hall, comp., *On the Way to Garrett's Barn*, contains the reports of the various Garrett family members and the soldiers. See also Stephen G. Miller, "You have doubtless heard of Booth the murderer of President Lincoln," *Surratt Courier* 31 (April 2006): 5–7.

77. Everton J. Conger in Surratt Trial, 1:308; Conger in U.S. Congress, House, *Impeachment Investigation*, 326.

78. Luther Byron Baker's Interrogation Aboard the Montauk in Hall, comp., *On the Way to Garrett's Barn*, 82.

79. Francis Wilson, *John Wilkes Booth: Fact and Fiction of Lincoln's Assassination* (Boston: Houghton Mifflin, 1929), 289.

80. "Guarding Booth's Body," *Washington Evening Star*, 15 April 1890. David Rankin Barbee stated that the lady was "undoubtedly" Lucy Hale in "Lincoln and Booth," typescript, 1016, David Rankin Barbee Papers, Georgetown University Library, Washington, D.C.

81. John Peddicord, "About John Wilkes Booth, Roanoke Gentleman Saw Corpse," *Roanoke Evening News*, 6 June 1903. Dr. John Peddicord, then a Marine sergeant, witnessed the autopsy. See also "Booth's Body—The Post Mortem and What It Disclosed," *New York Clipper*, 20 May 1865; *Boston Herald*, 7 May 1865, quoted in Barbee, "Lincoln and Booth," 996; Charles O. Paullin, "The Navy and the Booth Conspirators," *Journal of the Illinois State Historical Society* 33 (September 1940): 270–278.

82. "The Booth Autopsy," *Surratt Courier* 18 (July 1993): 3.

83. Porter, "How Booth's Body Was Hidden"; Michael W. Kauffman, "Fort Lesley J. McNair and the Lincoln Conspirators," *Lincoln Herald* 80 (Winter 1978): 176–186.

84. F.L. Black, "Lincoln's Murder—Amazing Manhunt," *Dearborn* [Michigan] *Independent*, 10 April 1926.

85. John F. Stanton, "A Mystery no Longer: the Lady in the Veil (con't)," *Surratt Courier* 36 (August 2011): 5.

86. Edwin Booth to Edwin M. Stanton, 6 November 1865, Edwin M. Stanton Papers, Manuscript Division, Library of Congress, quoted in Barbee, "Lincoln and Booth," 1258.

87. Herman Henry Kohlsaat, "[Edwin] Booth's Letter to Grant," *The Saturday Evening Post*, 9 February 1924, 20.

88. *Baltimore Sun*, 19 February 1869.

89. Asia Booth Clarke, *The Unlocked Book: A Memoir of John Wilkes Booth by his Sister Asia Booth Clarke*, ed. Eleanor Farjeon (New York: G.P. Putnam's Sons, 1938), 185–186.

90. "Theatrical Gossip," *Washington Evening Star*, 14 November 1891, 11. The author is grateful to Angela Smythe for finding and sharing this article.

91. Jones, *J. Wilkes Booth: An Account*, 78.

92. James R. O'Beirne, "Diary," in private collection of the late Donald P. Dow, Fort Worth, Texas.

93. Jones, *J. Wilkes Booth: An Account*, 80.

94. Jones, *J. Wilkes Booth: An Account*, 93.

95. Louis J. Weichmann in Benn Pitman, comp., *The Assassination of President Lincoln and The Trial of The Conspirators*, facsimile ed. (New York: Funk & Wagnalls, 1954), 114; John F. Stanton, "Attention Sarah Slater Seekers," *Surratt Courier* 30 (September 2010): 4.

96. John E. Elliott and Barry M. Cauchon, "A Peek Inside the Walls," booklet prepared for the Surratt Society and Surratt House Museum 2012 Conference, March 16–18, 2012. All information regarding imprisonments and photography at the Navy Yard is taken from this booklet.

97. Kauffman, "John Wilkes Booth and the Murder of Abraham Lincoln," 38.

98. Jeremiah Lockwood Diary, Jeremiah T. Lockwood Papers, Manuscript Division, Library of Congress.

99. Smith and Richter, "Elizabeth Rousby Qusenberry," 4; William L. Bryant in LASE, 216; Stewart, *Confederate Spies at Large*, 87.

100. William Lucas in LASE, 824–825.

101. William Lucas in LASE, 825.

102. Ingraham, "Pursuit and Death of John Wilkes Booth," 445.

103. Walton, "Booth's Flight and Death."

104. Luther Byron Baker's Interrogation Aboard the Montauk in Hall, comp., *On the Way to Garrett's Barn*, 82.

105. Barbee, "Lincoln and Booth," 993.

106. Porter, "How Booth's Body Was Hidden," 65.

107. Julian E. Raymond, "History of Fort Lesley J. McNair," typescript (1951), 54; Kauffman, "Fort Lesley J. McNair and the Lincoln Conspirators," 178.

108. James O. Hall, "That Ghastly Errand," *Surratt Courier* 21 (October 1996): 4.

109. Brennan, "John Wilkes Booth's Enigmatic Brother Joseph," *Maryland Historical Magazine* 78 (Spring 1983): 26.

110. Brennan, "John Wilkes Booth's Enigmatic Brother Joseph," 26.

111. "Special Despatches to the Inquirer," *Philadelphia Inquirer*, 20 May 1865.

112. Asia Booth Clarke to Jean Anderson, 22 May 1865, BCLM Works on Paper Collection, ML 518, Box

37, Maryland Historical Society, Baltimore, Maryland. Of the "conspirators," only Mary Surratt, John Surratt, and Dr. Samuel Mudd were Catholic. There is no corroboration that Booth converted to Catholicism.

113. Ernest C. Miller, "John Wilkes Booth and the Land of Oil," *Pennsylvania Heritage* 7 (Summer 1981): 5.

114. *New York Times*, 5 June 1865.

115. *Quebec Gazette*, 7 June 1865.

116. *Washington National Intelligencer*, 8 July 1865.

117. *Quebec Morning Chronicle*, 19 July 1865.

118. Edwin Booth to Edwin M. Stanton, 6 November 1865, quoted in Barbee, "Lincoln and Booth," 1258.

119. David Beasley, *McKee Rankin and the Heyday of the American Theater* (Waterloo, Ontario: Wilfrid Laurier University Press, 2002), 68.

120. Beasley, *McKee Rankin*, 68.

121. Deirdre Kincaid, "Rough Magic: The Theatrical Life of John Wilkes Booth" (unpublished manuscript, 2009), Chapter 8, 35, quoting Francis Wilson. Kincaid makes a convincing argument that McKee Rankin's account is suspect.

122. Surratt Trial, 2:1379.

123. "The Disinterment," *New York World*, 15 February 1869, quoted in Clarke, *Unlocked Book*, 181.

124. Wilson, *John Wilkes Booth*, 286.

125. Kauffman, "Fort Lesley J. McNair and the Lincoln Conspirators," 185.

126. Kauffman, "Fort Lesley J. McNair and the Lincoln Conspirators," 185; *Baltimore Gazette*, 26 October 1867, quoted in Joan Chaconas, "Tearing Down the Old Penitentiary," *Surratt Courier* 26 (July 2001): 7.

127. F.L. Black, "Lincoln's Murder—Amazing Manhunt," *Dearborn* [Michigan] *Independent*, 10 April 1926.

128. *U.S. vs John H. Surratt*, Criminal Court for the District of Columbia, case no. 5920, Records of District Courts of the United States, RG 21, National Archives and Records Administration, Washington, D.C.

129. Kohlsaat, "Booth's Letter to Grant," 20.

130. *Baltimore Sun*, 17 February 1869.

131. *New York World*, 16 February 1869, quoted in Barbee, "Lincoln and Booth," 1263.

132. *Washington Evening Star*, 16 February 1869, quoted in Barbee, "Lincoln and Booth," 1264.

133. "Funeral of the Five Conspirators After the Execution," *Boston Traveler*, n.d., clipping from a bound scrapbook belonging to George Alfred Townsend in the Library of Congress Manuscript Room; Harlowe Hoyt, "She Clipped a Lock from Booth, the Dead Assassin," unidentified newspaper clipping in author's files; "Body of Wilkes Booth Certainly Lies in a Baltimore Cemetery," *Washington Evening Star*, 6 June 1903; *Baltimore Sun*, 17 February 1869.

134. "Reinterment of the Remains of J. Wilkes Booth," *New York Times*, 17 February 1869; "Card from Mr. J.B.H. Weaver Relative to the Remains of J. Wilkes Booth," *New York Times*, 18 February 1869. No crowds gathered nor were admitted to view the remains.

135. Hall, "That Ghastly Errand," 4.

136. *Baltimore Sun*, 19 February 1869.

137. *Washington Evening Star*, 13 March 1869, 2.

138. Records of Green Mount Cemetery, Baltimore, Maryland.

139. Clarke, *Unlocked Book*, 185–186; "Reinterment of the Remains of John Wilkes Booth," *New York Times*, 28 June 1869, 1.

Bibliography

Resources

Abraham Lincoln Presidential Library, Springfield, IL.
Cleveland Public Library, Cleveland, OH.
Connecticut Historical Society, Hartford, CT.
Dallas Public Library, Dallas, TX.
Detroit Public Library, Detroit, MI.
Donald P. Dow Collection, Fort Worth, TX.
Folger Shakespeare Library, Washington, D.C.
Ford's Theatre National Historic Site, Washington, D.C.
Founders Library, Howard University, Washington, D.C.
Georgetown University Library, Washington, D.C.
Hampden-Booth Theatre Library, The Players, New York, NY.
Harvard College Library, Cambridge, MA.
Historical Society of Harford County, Bel Air, MD.
Historical Society of Pennsylvania, Philadelphia, PA.
Huntington Library, San Marino, CA.
Illinois State Historical Library, Springfield, IL.
Indiana Historical Society Library, Indianapolis, IN.
Indiana State Library, Indianapolis, IN.
James O. Hall Research Center, Surratt House Museum, Clinton, MD.
John Hay Library, Brown University, Providence, RI.
Jones Memorial Library, Lynchburg, VA.
Kansas State Historical Society, Topeka, KS.
Lexington Public Library, Lexington, KY.
Library of Congress, Washington, D.C.
Library of Virginia, Richmond, VA.
Louis A. Warren Lincoln Library and Museum, Fort Wayne, IN.
Louisville Free Public Library, Louisville, KY.
Macdonald-Kelce Library, University of Tampa, Tampa, FL.
Maryland Diocesan Archives, Baltimore, MD.
Maryland Historical Society, Baltimore, MD.
Maryland State Archives, Annapolis, MD.
Massachusetts Historical Society, Boston, MA.
Missouri Historical Society, Columbia, MO.
Muger Memorial Library, Boston University.
Mutter Medical Museum, Philadelphia, PA.
National Archives and Records Administration (NARA), Washington, D.C.
New Haven Colony Historical Society, New Haven, CT.
New Haven Free Public Library, New Haven, CT.
New Orleans Public Library, New Orleans, LA.
New-York Historical Society, New York, NY.
New York Public Library, Lincoln Center Branch, Billy Rose Theatrical Library, New York.
Newark Public Library, Newark, NJ.
Petersburg Public Library, Petersburg, VA.
Philadelphia Free Library, Philadelphia, PA.
Portland Public Library, Portland, ME.
Princeton University Library, Princeton, NJ.
Public Library of Cincinnati and Hamilton County, OH.
Public Library of Nashville and Davidson County, TN.
Rhode Island Historical Society, Providence, RI.
Rochester Public Library, Rochester, NY.
St. Louis Public Library, Local History Division, St. Louis, MO.
Shelby County Public Library & Information Center, Memphis, TN.
Troy Public Library, Troy, NY.
Union League of Philadelphia, PA.
University of Tulsa, Tulsa, OK.
Valentine Richmond History Center, Richmond, VA.
Western Reserve Historical Society, Cleveland, OH.
Yale University, New Haven, CT.

Documents and Manuscripts

Booth, Edwin. Collection. Hampden-Booth Theatre Library. New York.
Booth, John Wilkes. Draft of a Speech. Hampden-Booth Theatre Library. New York.
Booth, Junius Brutus, Jr. "Diary of Junius Brutus Booth, Jr. for 1864." Folger Shakespeare Library. Washington, D.C.
Booth, Junius Brutus, Jr. "Diary of Junius Brutus Booth, Jr. for 1865." Muger Memorial Library. Boston University.
Butler, Benjamin F. Papers. Manuscript Division. Library of Congress. Washington, D.C.
"Circular of the Milton Boarding School." Maryland Historical Society. Baltimore.

Clarke, Asia Booth. Letters to Jean Anderson. BCLM Works on Paper Collection. Maryland Historical Society. Baltimore.

Cox, Samuel, Jr. Letter to Mrs. Bradley T. Johnson, July 20, 1891. Photocopy. Cox file. James O. Hall Research Center. Surratt House Museum. Clinton, MD.

Cox, Samuel, Jr. Notes dated August 7, 1893, in the margins of the book titled *J. Wilkes Booth* by Thomas A. Jones. Maryland Historical Society. Baltimore.

Ewing Family Papers. Manuscript Division. Library of Congress. Washington, D.C.

"Examination of John Wilkes Booth's Diary, October 3, 1977." File numbers 95–216208, D-770615073 PN, D-770520035 PN. Federal Bureau of Investigation. Washington, D.C.

Ford, John T. Papers. Manuscript Division. Library of Congress. Washington, D.C.

French, Benjamin B. Papers. Manuscript Division. Library of Congress. Washington, D.C.

Harpers Ferry Fund Accounts and Receipts, 1860–1861. Auditor of Public Accounts. Library of Virginia. Richmond.

Investigation and Trial Papers Relating to Suspects in the Assassination of Abraham Lincoln. RG 153. Microcopy M599. 16 reels. NARA. Washington, D.C.

Kimmel, Stanley. Papers. Macdonald-Kelce Library. University of Tampa. Tampa, FL.

Letters and Telegrams Received, 1861–1865. Records of the Office of the Secretary of War. War Department Collection of Confederate Records. RG 109. Microcopy 437. NARA. Washington, D.C.

Letters Received by the Office of the Adjutant General (Main Series), 1861–1870. Records of the Adjutant General's Office. RG 94. Microcopy M619. NARA. Washington, D.C.

Lincoln Obsequies Scrapbook. Manuscript Division. Library of Congress. Washington, D.C.

May, Alonzo. "May's Dramatic Encyclopedia, 1750–1904." Microfilm. Manuscript Division. Library of Congress. Washington, D.C.

Militia pay audit records for the period of 19 November–6 December 1859. Library of Virginia. Richmond.

Mudd, Samuel A. Pardon File. Pardon Case Files, 18531963. Records of the Office of the Pardon Attorney. RG 204. NARA. Washington, D.C.

O'Beirne, James R. Diary. Donald P. Dow Collection. Fort Worth, TX.

Porter, Albert G. "Recollections of John Wilkes Booth." Indiana State Library. Indianapolis.

Reed, John Roland. Mr. Roland Reed's Playbills. Founders Library. Howard University. Washington, D.C.

"St. Timothy's Hall Circular." September 29, 1853. Maryland Diocesan Archives. Baltimore.

Seymour, William. Family Papers. Princeton University Library. Princeton, NJ.

Stanton, Edwin M. Papers. Manuscript Division. Library of Congress. Washington, D.C.

Taper, Louise, and Barry. Collection. Abraham Lincoln Presidential Library. Springfield, IL.

Townsend, George Alfred. Papers. Maryland State Archives. Annapolis.

U.S. vs. John H. Surratt. Criminal Court for the District of Columbia, case no. 5920. Records of District Courts of the United States. RG 21. NARA. Washington, D.C.

Valentine, Edward V. Collection. Valentine Richmond History Center. Richmond, VA.

Published Primary Sources

Atzerodt, George A. "Confession of George A. Atzerodt." *Baltimore American*, January 18, 1869; rpt. *Surratt Courier* 13 (December 1988): 3–5.

Atzerodt, George A. "Statement of George A. Atzerodt to Prov. Mar. McPhail, May 1, 1865." *Surratt Courier* 13 (October 1988): 2–3.

Bates, Edward. *Bates Diary, 1859–1866.* Ed. Howard K. Beale. *American Historical Association Annual Report* 4. Washington, D.C.: Government Printing Office, 1930.

Booth, Mary Devlin. *The Letters and Notebooks of Mary Devlin Booth.* Ed. L. Terry Oggel. New York: Greenwood Press, 1987.

Browning, Orville Hickman. *The Diary of Orville Hickman Browning, 1850–1864.* 2 vols. Ed. Theodore Calvin Pease and James G. Randall. Springfield: Illinois State Historical Library, 1925 and 1933.

Chaconas, Joan Lee. "Unpublished Atzerodt Confession Revealed Here For The First Time." *Surratt Courier* 13 (October 1988): 1–3.

Edwards, William C., ed. *The Lincoln Assassination— The Trial Transcript. A transcription of NARA Microfilm M599, Reels 8 thru 16*, 2012.

Edwards, William C., and Edward Steers, Jr., eds. *The Lincoln Assassination: The Evidence.* Urbana: University of Illinois Press, 2009.

The Great Impeachment and Trial of Andrew Johnson, President of the United States. Philadelphia: T.B. Peterson & Brothers, 1868; rpt., New York: Dover, 1974.

Kauffman, Michael W., ed. *Samuel Bland Arnold: Memoirs of a Lincoln Conspirator.* Bowie, MD: Heritage Books, 1995.

Lincoln, Abraham. *The Collected Works of Abraham Lincoln.* Ed. Roy P. Basler. New Brunswick, NJ: Rutgers University Press, 1953.

Pitman, Benn, comp. *The Assassination of President Lincoln and the Trial of the Conspirators.* Facsimile Edition. New York: Funk & Wagnalls, 1954.

Poore, Ben Perley. *Perley's Reminiscences of Sixty Years in the National Metropolis.* Philadelphia: Hubbard Brothers, 1886.

_____, ed. *The Conspiracy Trial for the Murder of the President.* 3 vols. Boston: J.E. Tilton, 1865 and 1866.

Rhodehamel, John H., and Louise Taper, eds. *Right*

or Wrong, God Judge Me: The Writings of John Wilkes Booth. Urbana: University of Illinois Press, 1997.

St. Timothy's Hall. *Rules And Regulations for the Government of the Students at St. Timothy's Hall, Catonsville*. Baltimore: Joseph Robinson, 1852.

Trial of John H. Surratt in the Criminal Court of the District of Columbia. 2 vols. Washington, D.C.: Government Printing Office, 1867.

The Trial of the Assassins and Conspirators at Washington City, D.C., May and June, 1865. Philadelphia: T. B. Peterson & Brothers, 1865.

Trial of the Assassins and Conspirators for the Murder of Abraham Lincoln. Philadelphia: Barclay & Co., 1865.

U.S. Congress. House. *Impeachment Investigation: Testimony Taken Before the Judiciary Committee of the House of Representatives in the Investigation of the Charges Against Andrew Johnson*. Second Session, 39th Congress, and First Session, 40th Congress. Washington, D.C.: Government Printing Office, 1867.

_____. *Report Relating to the Assassination of President Lincoln*. First Session, 39th Congress, Report No. 104. Washington, D.C.: Government Printing Office, 1866.

_____. *War Claims Report No. 743, Petition of Richard H. Garrett for compensation for barn and other property burned*. First Session, 43rd Congress. Washington, D.C.: Government Printing Office, 1874.

U.S. War Department. *The War of the Rebellion: A Compilation of the Official Records of the Union and Confederate Armies*. 128 vols. Washington, D.C.: Government Printing Office, 1880–1901.

Whiteman, Maxwell. *While Lincoln Lay Dying: A Facsimile Reproduction of the First Testimony Taken in Connection with the Assassination of Abraham Lincoln as Recorded by Corporal James Tanner*. Philadelphia: The Union League, 1968.

Newspapers

Albany Atlas and Argus
Albany Evening Journal
Albany Express
Albany Times and Courier
Albany Times Union
Alexandria Gazette
Baltimore American and Commercial Advertiser
Baltimore Sun
Bel Air [Maryland] *Southern Aegis*
Boston Daily Advertiser
Boston Daily Evening Transcript
Boston Herald
Boston Post
Boston Sunday Herald
Brooklyn Standard
Buffalo Courier Express
Buffalo Daily Courier
Buffalo Express
Chicago Daily Inter Ocean
Chicago Evening Journal
Chicago Herald
Chicago Times
Chicago Tribune
Cincinnati Daily Commercial
Cincinnati Daily Gazette
Cincinnati Daily Press
Cincinnati Enquirer
Cleveland Herald
Cleveland Morning Leader
Cleveland Plain Dealer
Columbus Daily Sun
Columbus Daily Times
Columbus Weekly Enquirer
Daily Richmond [Virginia] *Enquirer*
Detroit Free Press
Hartford Courant
Hartford Evening Press
Indianapolis Daily Journal
Indianapolis Daily Sentinel
Indianapolis Enquirer
Indianapolis Gazette
Leavenworth Daily Conservative
Leavenworth Daily Times
Lexington Observer and Reporter
Louisville Daily Democrat
Louisville Daily Journal
Lynchburg Daily Virginian
Madison [Indiana] *Courier*
Memphis Bulletin
Montgomery Advertiser
Montgomery Daily Mail
Montgomery Post
Nashville Daily Union
Nashville Dispatch
New Haven Daily Register
New Haven Palladium
New Orleans Daily Picayune
New Orleans Times
New Orleans True Delta
New York Clipper
New York Commercial Advertiser
New York Courier des Etats-Unis
New York Daily Graphic
New York Dramatic News
New York Evening Express
New York Evening Post
New York Herald
New York Mail and Express
New York Press
New York Sun
New York Sunday Mercury
New York Times
New York Tribune
New York World
Newburgh [New York] *Telegraph*
Newport [Rhode Island] *Mercury*
Petersburg Daily Express

Petersburg Daily Intelligencer
Philadelphia Daily Dispatch
Philadelphia Daily News
Philadelphia Evening Bulletin
Philadelphia Inquirer
*Philadelphia North American and United States
   Gazette*
Philadelphia Press
Philadelphia Public Ledger & Daily Transcript
Port Tobacco [Maryland] *Times and Charles County
   Advertiser*
Portland [Maine] *Daily Advertiser*
Portland Eastern Argus
Portland Sunday Telegram
Providence Daily Journal
Providence Daily Post
Quebec Gazette
Richmond Daily Dispatch
Richmond Times
Richmond Times-Dispatch
Richmond Whig
Roanoke Evening News
Rochester Evening Express
Rochester Union and Advertiser
St. Joseph Morning Herald
St. Louis Missouri Democrat
St. Louis Missouri Republican
St. Louis Post-Dispatch
St. Paul and Minneapolis Pioneer Press
Springfield [Massachusetts] *Daily Republican*
Springfield [Ohio] *News Sun*
Toledo Blade
Vicksburg Daily Whig
Washington Critic-Record
Washington Daily Constitutional Union
Washington Evening Star
Washington Morning Chronicle
Washington National Intelligencer
Washington National Republican
Washington Post
Washington Sunday Globe
Washington Times
Washington Tribune
Wilkes-Barre [Pennsylvania] *Times*
Wilkes' Spirit of the Times
Worcester [Massachusetts] *Daily Spy*
Worcester Daily Transcript
Worcester Sunday Telegram

Books

Aldrich, Mrs. Thomas Bailey. *Crowding Memories.*
   Boston: Houghton Mifflin, 1920.
Alfriend, John S. *History of Zion Episcopal Church, St.
   Andrew's Parish, Charles Town, West Virginia.* 1973.
Angle, Paul M. *Lincoln 1854–1861: Being the Day-by-
   Day Activities of Abraham Lincoln from January 1,
   1854 to March 4, 1861.* Springfield, IL: The Abra-
   ham Lincoln Association, 1933.

Archer, Stephen M. *Junius Brutus Booth: Theatrical
   Prometheus.* Carbondale: Southern Illinois Univer-
   sity Press, 1992.
Arnold, Samuel Bland. *Defence and Prison Experiences
   of a Lincoln Conspirator: Statements and Autobio-
   graphical Notes.* Hattiesburg, MS.: The Book Farm,
   1943.
Baker, L.C. *History of the United States Secret Service.*
   Philadelphia: Published by L.C. Baker, 1867.
Barnes, Joseph K. *The Medical and Surgical History of
   the War of the Rebellion.* 6 vols. Washington, D.C.:
   Government Printing Office, 1875–1888.
Bassett, Amy. *Red Cross Reveries: On the Homefront
   and Overseas.* Harrisburg: Stackpole, 1961.
Bates, David Homer. *Lincoln in the Telegraph Office:
   Recollections of the United States Military Telegraph
   Corps during the Civil War.* New York: The Cen-
   tury Co., 1907.
Bauer, Charles J. *The Odd Couple Who Hanged Mary
   Surratt!* Silver Spring, MD: Silver Spring Press,
   1980.
Beasley, David. *McKee Rankin and the Heyday of the
   American Theater.* Waterloo, Ontario: Wilfrid Lau-
   rier University Press, 2002.
Blum, Daniel. *A Pictorial History of the American The-
   atre, 1860–1970.* New York: Crown, 1969.
Brandt, Nat. *The Man Who Tried To Burn New York.*
   Syracuse: Syracuse University Press, 1986.
Brennan, John C. *Pictorial Primer Having to Do with
   the Assassination of Abraham Lincoln and with John
   Wilkes Booth, the Assassin.* Laurel, MD: Minute-
   man, 1979.
Brooks, Neal A., and Eric G. Rockel. *A History of Bal-
   timore County.* Towson, MD: Friends of the Tow-
   son Library, 1979.
Brooks, Noah. *Washington in Lincoln's Time.* New
   York: The Century Co., 1896.
Brown, T. Allston. *History of the American Stage from
   1733 to 1870.* New York: Dick & Fitzgerald, 1870.
_____. *A History of the New York Stage from the First
   Performance in 1732 to 1901.* 3 vols. New York:
   Dodd, Mead, 1903.
Bryan, George S. *The Great American Myth.* New
   York: Carrick & Evans, 1940.
Buckingham, John E. *Reminiscences and Souvenirs of
   the Assassination of Abraham Lincoln.* Washington,
   D.C.: Press of R.H. Darby, 1894.
Carpenter, F.B. *Six Months at the White House with
   Abraham Lincoln: The Story of a Picture.* New York:
   Hurd and Hougton, 1866.
Carter, Samuel, III. *The Riddle of Dr. Mudd: A Biog-
   raphy of One of the Most Enigmatic Figures in Amer-
   ican History.* New York: G.P. Putnam's Sons, 1974.
Chamlee, Roy Z., Jr. *Lincoln's Assassins: A Complete
   Account of Their Capture, Trial, and Punishment.*
   Jefferson, NC: McFarland, 1990.
Clark, Allen C. *Abraham Lincoln in the National Cap-
   ital.* Washington, D.C.: W.F. Roberts, 1925.
Clark, Champ. *The Assassination: Death of the Presi-
   dent.* Alexandria, VA: Time-Life Books, 1987.

Clarke, Asia Booth. *Booth Memorials: Passages, Incidents, and Anecdotes in the life of Junius Brutus Booth (the elder)*. New York: Carleton, 1866.

_____. *The Elder and the Younger Booth*. Boston: James R. Osgood, 1882.

_____. *John Wilkes Booth: A Sister's Memoir*. Ed. Terry Alford. Jackson: University Press of Mississippi, 1996.

_____. *Personal Recollections of the Elder Booth*. London: Privately printed, n.d.

_____. *The Unlocked Book: A Memoir of John Wilkes Booth by His Sister Asia Booth Clarke*. Ed. Eleanor Farjeon. New York: G.P. Putnam's Sons, 1938.

Conrad, Thomas N. *A Confederate Spy: A Story of the Civil War*. New York: J. Ogilvie, 1892.

_____. *The Rebel Scout: A Thrilling History of Scouting Life in the Southern Army*. Washington, D.C.: National Publishing Co., 1904.

DeWitt, David Miller. *The Assassination of Abraham Lincoln and its Expiation*. New York: Macmillan, 1909.

_____. *The Impeachment and Trial of Andrew Johnson, Seventeenth President of the United States*. New York: Macmillan, 1903; rpt. with introduction by Stanley I. Kutler, Madison: State Historical Society of Wisconsin, 1967.

_____. *The Judicial Murder of Mary E. Surratt*. Baltimore: John Murphy, 1895.

Dolson, Hildegarde. *The Great Oildorado: The Gaudy and Turbulent Years of the First Oil Rush, Pennsylvania, 1859–1880*. New York: Random House, 1959.

Doster, William E. *Lincoln and Episodes of the Civil War*. New York: G.P. Putnam's Sons, 1915.

Douglas, Henry Kyd. *I Rode with Stonewall*. Chapel Hill: University of North Carolina Press, 1940.

Eisenschiml, Otto. *In the Shadow of Lincoln's Death*. New York: Wilfred Funk, 1940.

_____. *Why Was Lincoln Murdered?* Boston: Little, Brown, 1937.

Ellsler, John A. *The Stage Memories of John A. Ellsler*. Ed. Effie Ellsler Weston. Cleveland: The Rowfant Club, 1950.

Ely, Edwin A. *Personal Memoirs of Edwin A. Ely*. Ed. Ambrose E. Vanderpoel. New York: Charles Francis Press, 1926.

Ferguson, W.J. *I Saw Booth Shoot Lincoln*. Boston: Houghton Mifflin, 1930; rpt., Austin: Pemberton Press, 1969.

Ford, George D., and J. Kirk Merrick. *These Were Actors: A Story of the Chapmans and the Drakes*. New York: Library Publishers, 1955.

Forrester, Izola. *The One Mad Act: The Unknown Story of John Wilkes Booth and His Family*. Boston: Hale, Cushman & Flint, 1937.

Graham, Franklin. *Histrionic Montreal: Annals of the Montreal Stage*. Montreal: J. Lovell and Son, 1902.

Gray, Clayton. *Conspiracy in Canada*. Montreal: L'Atelier Press, 1959.

Grossman, Edwina Booth. *Edwin Booth: Recollections by His Daughter*. New York: The Century Co., 1894.

Gutman, Richard J.S., and Kellie O. Gutman. *John Wilkes Booth Himself*. Dover, MA: Hired Hand Press, 1979.

Hall, James O., comp. *On the Way to Garrett's Barn*. Clinton, MD: Surratt Society, 2001.

_____. *The Surratt Family & John Wilkes Booth*. Clinton, MD: Surratt Society, 1976.

Hanchett, William. *The Lincoln Murder Conspiracies*. Urbana: University of Illinois Press, 1983.

Hay, John. *Lincoln and the Civil War—In the Diaries and Letters of John Hay*. Ed. Tyler Dennett. New York: Dodd, Mead, 1939.

Headley, John W. *Confederate Operations in Canada and New York*. New York: Neale, 1906.

Hibben, Henry B. *Navy-Yard, Washington: History from Organization, 1799, to Present Date*. Washington, D.C.: Government Printing Office, 1890.

Hill, Sarah Jane Full. *Mrs. Hill's Journal: Civil War Reminiscences*. Ed. Mark M. Krug. Chicago: Lakeside Press, 1980.

Houmes, Blaine V. *Abraham Lincoln Assassination Bibliography: A Compendium of Reference Materials*. Clinton, MD: Surratt Society, 1997.

Howe, Julia Ward. *Reminiscences, 1819–1899*. New York: Houghton Mifflin, 1899.

Jefferson, Joseph. *The Autobiography of Joseph Jefferson*. New York: The Century Co., 1890.

Jennings, John Joseph. *Theatrical and Circus Life; or, Secrets of the Stage, Greenroom and Sawdust Arena*. St. Louis: Sun, 1882.

Jones, Thomas A. *J. Wilkes Booth: An Account of His Sojourn in Southern Maryland after the Assassination of Abraham Lincoln, His Passage Across the Potomac, and His Death in Virginia*. Chicago: Laird & Lee, 1893.

Kauffman, Michael W. *American Brutus: John Wilkes Booth and the Lincoln Conspiracies*. New York: Random House, 2004.

Kendall, John S. *The Golden Age of the New Orleans Theatre*. Baton Rouge: Louisiana State University Press, 1952.

Kennedy, Charles E. *Fifty Years of Cleveland, 1875–1925*. Cleveland: Weidenthal, 1925.

Kennedy, James H., ed. *History of the Ohio Society of New York, 1885–1905*. New York: Grafton Press, 1906.

Kimmel, Stanley. *The Mad Booths of Maryland*. New York: Dover, 1969.

Kinchen, Oscar A. *Confederate Operations in Canada and the North*. North Quincy, MA: Christopher, 1970.

Kneebone, John T., et al, eds. *Dictionary of Virginia Biography*. 3 vols. Richmond: Library of Virginia, 1998–2006.

Kunhardt, Dorothy Meserve, and Philip B. Kunhardt, Jr. *Twenty Days: A Narrative in Text and Pictures of the Assassination of Abraham Lincoln*. New York: Castle Books, 1965.

Lamon, Ward Hill. *Recollections of Abraham Lincoln, 1847–1865.* Ed. Dorothy Lamon Teillard. Chicago: A.C. McClurg, 1895.

Lattimer, John K. *Kennedy and Lincoln: Medical and Ballistic Comparisons of Their Assassinations.* New York: Harcourt Brace Jovanovich, 1980.

Laughlin, Clara M. *The Death of Lincoln: The Story of Booth's Plot, His Deed and the Penalty.* New York: Doubleday, Page, 1909.

_____. *Traveling Through Life.* Boston: Houghton Mifflin, 1934.

Leech, Margaret. *Reveille in Washington, 1860–1865.* New York: Harper and Brothers, 1951.

Lewis, Lloyd. *Myths After Lincoln.* New York City: Harcourt, Brace, 1929.

Life, Trial and Extraordinary Adventures of John H. Surratt, the Conspirator. Philadelphia: Barclay & Co., 1867; rpt. Port Tobacco, MD: James L. Barbour, 1988.

Lockridge, Richard. *Darling of Misfortune: Edwin Booth, 1833–1893.* New York: The Century Co., 1932.

Long, EB. *The Civil War Day By Day: An Almanac, 1861–1865.* Garden City, NY: Doubleday, 1971.

Mahoney, Ella V. *Sketches of Tudor Hall and the Booth Family.* Bel Air, MD: Tudor Hall, May 1925.

Matheny, H. E. *Major General Thomas Maley Harris.* Parsons, WV: McClain, 1963.

McLaurin, John J. *Sketches in Crude-Oil.* Harrisburg, PA: McLaurin, 1896.

Mearns, David Chambers. *Largely Lincoln.* New York: St. Martin's Press, 1961.

Miers, Earl Schenck, ed. *Lincoln Day By Day: A Chronology, 1809–1865.* 3 vols. Dayton, OH: Morningside, 1991.

Miller, Ernest C. *John Wilkes Booth—Oilman.* New York: The Exposition Press, 1947.

Moore, Guy W. *The Case of Mrs. Surratt: Her Controversial Trial and Execution for Conspiracy in the Lincoln Assassination.* Norman: University of Oklahoma Press, 1954.

Morris, Clara. *Life on the Stage: My Personal Experiences and Recollections.* London: Morris, Isbister, 1902.

Mudd, Samuel. *The Life of Dr. Samuel A. Mudd.* Ed. Nettie Mudd. New York: Neale, 1906.

Mullin, Donald, ed. *Victorian Actors and Actresses in Review: A Dictionary of Contemporary Views of Representative British and American Actors and Actresses, 1837–1901.* Westport, CT: Greenwood Press, 1983.

Munson, John W. *Reminiscences of a Mosby Guerrilla.* New York: Moffat, Yard, 1906.

Neely, Mark E., Jr. *The Abraham Lincoln Encyclopedia.* New York: McGraw Hill, 1982.

Oldroyd, Osborn H. *The Assassination of Abraham Lincoln: Flight, Pursuit, Capture, and Punishment of the Conspirators.* Washington, D.C.: Oldroyd, 1901.

Olszewski, George J. *Restoration of Ford's Theatre.* Washington, D.C.: United States Department of the Interior, 1963.

Ownsbey, Betty J. *Alias "Paine": Lewis Thornton Powell, the Mystery Man of the Lincoln Conspiracy.* Jefferson, NC: McFarland, 1993.

Parsons, John E. *Henry Deringer's Pocket Pistol.* New York: William Morrow, 1952.

Phelps, H.P. *Players of a Century: A Record of the Albany Stage.* Albany: Joseph McDonough, 1880.

Porter, Horace. *Campaigning with Grant.* New York: The Century Co, 1897.

Porter, Mary Abbie. *The Surgeon in Charge.* Concord, NH: Rumford Press, 1949.

Pratt, Harry E. *Lincoln 1840–1846: Being the Day-by-Day Activities of Abraham Lincoln from January 1, 1840 to December 31, 1846.* Springfield, IL: Abraham Lincoln Association, 1939.

Reck, W. Emerson. *A. Lincoln: His Last 24 Hours.* Jefferson, NC: McFarland, 1987.

Reignolds, Catherine (Kate) Mary. *Yesterday with Actors.* Boston: Cupples and Hurd, 1887.

Reuter, William L. *The King Can Do No Wrong.* New York: Pageant Press, 1958.

Roscoe, Theodore. *The Web of Conspiracy: The Complete Story of the Men Who Murdered Abraham Lincoln.* Englewood Cliffs, NJ: Prentice-Hall, 1960.

Ruggles, Eleanor. *Prince of Players: Edwin Booth.* New York: W.W. Norton, 1953.

Samples, Gordon. *Lust for Fame: The Stage Career of John Wilkes Booth.* Jefferson, NC: McFarland, 1982.

Sandburg, Carl. *Abraham Lincoln: The War Years.* Vol. 4 of 4 vols. New York: Harcourt, Brace, 1939.

Seward, Frederick W. *Reminiscences of a War-Time Statesman and Diplomat.* New York: G.P. Putnam's Sons, 1916.

Shaw, Dale. *Titans of the American Stage: Edwin Forrest, the Booths, the O'Neills.* Philadelphia: The Westminster Press, 1971.

Sillard, Robert M. *Barry Sullivan and His Contemporaries: A Histrionic Record.* 2 vols. London: T. Fisher Unwin, 1901.

Skinner, Otis. *The Last Tragedian: Booth Tells His Own Story.* New York: Dodd, Mead, 1939.

Smiley, Alfred Wilson. *A Few Scraps, Oily and Otherwise.* Oil City, PA: Derrick, 1907.

Smith, Gene. *American Gothic: The Story of America's Legendary Theatrical Family, Junius, Edwin, and John Wilkes Booth.* New York: Simon & Schuster, 1992.

Smith, H.B. *Between The Lines: Secret Service Stories Told Fifty Years After.* New York: Booz Brothers, 1911.

Smoot, Richard Mitchell. *The Unwritten History of the Assassination of Abraham Lincoln.* Clinton, MA: Press of W. J. Coulter, 1908.

Starr, John W., Jr. *Lincoln's Last Day.* New York: Frederick A. Stokes, 1922.

Steers, Edward, Jr. *Blood on the Moon: The Assassination of Abraham Lincoln.* Lexington: University Press of Kentucky, 2001.

_____. *His Name Is Still Mudd: The Case Against Doctor Samuel Alexander Mudd*. Gettysburg, PA: Thomas, 1997.

Steers, Edward, Jr., and Joan L. Chaconas. *The Escape and Capture of George A. Atzerodt*. Brandywine, MD: Marker Tours, 1989.

Stern, Philip Van Doren. *The Man Who Killed Lincoln: The story of John Wilkes Booth and His Part in the Assassination*. New York: Random House, 1939.

_____. *Secret Missions of the Civil War*. New York: Bonanza Books, 1959.

Stewart, John. *Confederate Spies at Large: The Lives of Lincoln Assassination Conspirators Tom Harbin and Charlie Russell*. Jefferson, NC: McFarland, 2007.

Stoddart, James H. *Recollections of a Player*. New York: The Century Co., 1902.

Stone, Henry D. *Personal Recollections of the Drama, or Theatrical Reminiscences*. Albany: Charles van Benthuysen & Sons, 1873.

Surratt Society. *From War Department Files*. Clinton, MD: Surratt Society, 1980.

_____. *In Pursuit of... Continuing Research in the Field of the Lincoln Assassination*. Clinton, MD: Surratt Society, 1990.

Thomas, Benjamin P., and Harold M. Hyman. *Stanton: The Life and Times of Lincoln's Secretary of War*. New York: Alfred A. Knopf, 1962.

Tidwell, William A., with James O. Hall and David Winfred Gaddy. *Come Retribution: The Confederate Secret Service and the Assassination of Lincoln*. Jackson: University Press of Mississippi, 1988.

Tompkins, Eugene. *The History of the Boston Theatre*. Boston and New York: Houghton Mifflin, 1908.

Townsend, George Alfred. *Katy of Catoctin; or The Chain-Breakers*. New York: D. Appleton, 1895; rpt., Cambridge, MD: Tidewater, 1959.

_____. *The Life, Crime, and Capture of John Wilkes Booth*. New York: Dick & Fitzgerald, 1865.

Trefousse, Hans L. *Impeachment of a President: Andrew Johnson, the Blacks, and Reconstruction*. Knoxville: University of Tennessee Press, 1975.

Trindal, Elizabeth. *Mary Surratt: An American Tragedy*. Gretna, LA: Pelican, 1996.

Turner, Thomas Reed. *Beware the People Weeping: Public Opinion and the Assassination of Abraham Lincoln*. Baton Rouge: Louisiana State University Press, 1982.

U.S. Congress. *Biographical Directory of the American Congress, 1774–1961*. Washington, D.C.: Government Printing Office, 1961.

Upshur, J.N. *Medical Reminiscences of Richmond During the Past Forty Years*. Published by resolution of the Richmond Academy of Medicine and Surgery, 1906.

Weichmann, Louis J. *A True History of the Assassination of Abraham Lincoln and of the Conspiracy of 1865*. Ed. Floyd E. Risvold. New York: Vintage, 1975.

Williamson, James J. *Prison Life in the Old Capitol*. West Orange, NJ, 1911.

Wilson, Francis. *John Wilkes Booth: Fact and Fiction of Lincoln's Assassination*. Boston: Houghton Mifflin, 1929.

Wilson, Rufus Rockwell. *Lincoln among His Friends*. Caldwell, ID: The Caxton Printers, 1942.

Winter, William. *In Memory of John McCullough*. New York: The De Vinne Press, 1889.

Wooster, Louise C. *The Autobiography of a Magdalen*. Birmingham: Birmingham Publishing Co., 1911.

Articles and Websites

Alford, Terry. "John Matthews: A Vindication of the Historical Consensus." *Surratt Courier* 19 (April 1994): 4–8.

Alfriend, Edward M. "Recollections of John Wilkes Booth." *The Era* 8 (October 1901): 603–605.

"The Assassination of Lincoln." *Texas Siftings*, August 4, 1883.

Badeau, Adam. "A Night with the Booths." *New York Sunday Times*, August 7, 1858.

_____. "Dramatic Reminiscences." *St. Paul and Minneapolis Pioneer Press*, February 20, 1887.

_____. "Edwin Booth, On and Off the Stage." *McClure's Magazine* 1 (August 1893): 255–267.

Barber, Deirdre. "Colonel's Journal Slams Thesp! or, Two Reviews of John Wilkes Booth." *Surratt Courier* 12 (February 1987): 1, 5–8.

Barron, John M. "With John Wilkes Booth in His Days as an Actor." *Baltimore Sun*, March 17, 1907.

Benn, Walter. "The Great National Conspiracy." *Wilkes-Barre Times*, December 19, 1894.

Black, F.L. "Lincoln's Murder—Amazing Manhunt." *Dearborn Independent*, April 10, 1926.

Bone, Beverly. "Edwin Stanton in the Wake of the Lincoln Assassination." *Lincoln Herald* 82 (Winter 1980): 508–521.

"The Booth Autopsy." *Surratt Courier* 18 (July 1993): 3.

Booth, Edwin. "Edwin Booth and Lincoln." *The Century Magazine* 77 (April 1909): 919–920.

Brennan, John C. "The Confederate Plan to Abduct President Lincoln." *Surratt Society News* 6 (March 1981): 4–7.

_____. "Confederate Spy—Captain Thomas Nelson Conrad." *Surratt Society News* 2 (June-July 1977): 3–4.

_____. "General Bradley T. Johnson's Plan to Abduct President Lincoln." *Chronicles of St. Mary's* 22 (November 1974): 413–427.

_____. "Hobbledehoy David Edgar Herold." *Surratt Courier* 12 (August 1987): 6–8.

_____. "John Wilkes Booth's Enigmatic Brother Joseph." *Maryland Historical Magazine* 78 (Spring 1983): 22–34.

_____. "The Three Versions of the Testimony in the 1865 Trial." *Surratt Society News* 8 (March 1983): 3–6.

_____. "Why the Attempt to Assassinate Secretary of

State William H. Seward?" *Surratt Courier* 12 (January 1987): 1, 4–8.

Bullard, F. Lauriston. "Boston's Part in Lincoln's Death." *Boston Sunday Herald*, April 11, 1915.

_____. "When—If Ever—Was John Wilkes Booth in Paris?" *Lincoln Herald* 50 (June 1948): 28–34.

Burr, Frank A. "Booth's Bullet." *Washington Evening Star*, December 7, 1881.

Carter, Samuel, III. "J.W. Booth and Lady." *Yankee Magazine* 40 (February 1976): 59.

Chaconas, Joan Lee. "George Alfred Townsend's Papers." *Surratt Society News* 5 (October 1980): 4–6.

_____. "Tearing Down the Old Penitentiary." *Surratt Courier* 26 (July 2001): 7.

Clampitt, John W. "The Trial of Mrs. Surratt." *The North American Review* 131 (September 1880): 221–240.

Crook, William H. "Lincoln's Last Day." *Harper's Monthly Magazine* 115 (September 1907): 519–530.

Culyer, John Y. "The Assassination of Abraham Lincoln." *The Magazine of History* 22 (March 1916): 58–60.

Davis, Curtis Carroll. "In Pursuit of Booth Once More: A New Claimant Heard From." *Maryland Historical Magazine* 79 (Fall 1984): 220–234.

Dodels, Jeannine Clarke. "John Wilkes Booth as Richard III." *Surratt Society News* 10 (December 1985): 5–7.

_____. "John Wilkes Booth's Secession Crisis Speech of 1860." In *John Wilkes Booth, Actor: The Proceedings of a Conference Weekend in Bel Air, Maryland, May 1988*, 48–52. Ed. Arthur Kincaid. North Leigh, Oxfordshire: Published privately, 1989.

Ford, John T. "Behind the Curtain of a Conspiracy." *North American Review* 148 (April 1889): 484–493.

_____. "The 14th of April, 1865." *Washington Evening Star*, undated clipping.

Forney, D.C. "Thirty Years After; About Col. D.C. Forney and His Associations with Lincoln and Booth." *Washington Evening Star*, June 27, 1891.

Frank, Seymour J. "The Conspiracy to Implicate the Confederate Leaders in Lincoln's Assassination." *Mississippi Valley Historical Review* 40 (March 1954): 629–656.

Freiberger, Edward. "Grave of Lincoln's Assassin Disclosed At Last." *Boston Sunday Herald Magazine*, February 26, 1911.

_____. "True Story of John Wilkes Booth's Death and Burial." *Washington Post*, February 1916.

Fuller, Charles F., Jr. "Edwin and John Wilkes Booth, Actors at the Old Marshall Theatre in Richmond." *Virginia Magazine of History and Biography* 79 (October 1971): 477–483.

Garrett, Richard Baynham. "A Chapter of Unwritten History." Ed. Betsy Fleet. *Virginia Magazine of History and Biography* 71 (October 1963): 387–407.

Garrett, William H. "True Story of the Capture of John Wilkes Booth," *Confederate Veteran* 29 (1921): 129–130.

George, Joseph, Jr. "F. Lauriston Bullard as a Lincoln Scholar." *Lincoln Herald* 62 (Winter 1960): 173–182.

_____. "Nature's First Law: Louis J. Weichmann and Mrs. Surratt." *Civil War History* 28 (June 1982): 101–127.

_____. "The Night John Wilkes Booth Played Before Abraham Lincoln." *Lincoln Herald* 59 (Summer 1957): 11–15.

Gleason, D. H. L. "Conspiracy Against Lincoln." *The Magazine of History* 13 (February 1911): 59–65.

Gray, John A. "The Fate of the Lincoln Conspirators." *McClure's Magazine* 37 (October 1911): 626–636.

Gutman, Richard, and Kellie Gutman. "Boston: A Home for John Wilkes Booth?" *Surratt Society News* 10 (September 1985): 1, 6–8.

Hall, James O. "About Those Guns." *Surratt Society News* 4 (June 1979): 4.

_____. "The Dahlgren Papers." *Civil War Times Illustrated* 22 (November 1983): 30.

_____. "Dr. Mudd—Again—Part 1." *Surratt Courier* 23 (July 1998): 4–7.

_____. "The Guerrilla Boyle." *Surratt Society News* 10 (April 1985): 1, 5–6 and (May 1985): 6–8.

_____. "John Wilkes Booth and John Brown." *Surratt Society News* 10 (November 1985): 1, 4.

_____. "John Wilkes Booth Escape Route, Notes by James O. Hall." Clinton, MD: The Surratt Society, 1980.

_____. "Joseph H. Simonds—Booth's Partner." *Surratt Society News* 8 (August 1983): 4.

_____. "The Saga of Sarah Slater." *Surratt Society News* 7 (January 1982): 3–6 and (February 1982): 3–6.

_____. "That Ghastly Errand." *Surratt Courier* 21 (October 1996): 4.

_____. "That Letter to the National Intelligencer." *Surratt Courier* 18 (November 1993): 4–8.

_____. "Two Pages from Booth's Diary: Dr. Richard H. Stuart Meets John Wilkes Booth." *Surratt Courier* 21 (August 1996): 3–5.

_____. "You Have Mail." *Surratt Courier* 25 (July 2000): 8–9.

Hanchett, William. "Booth's Diary." *Journal of the Illinois State Historical Society* 72 (February 1979): 39–56.

_____. "The Eisenschiml Thesis." *Civil War History* 25 (September 1979): 197–217.

_____. "Lincoln's Assassination Revisited." *Lincoln Herald* 99 (Spring 1997): 34–43.

_____. "The War Department and Booth's Abduction Plot." *Lincoln Herald* 82 (Winter 1980): 499–508.

Head, Constance. "The Booth Sisters of Bel Air." *Lincoln Herald* 84 (Winter 1981): 759–764.

_____. "Insights on John Wilkes Booth from His Sister Asia's Correspondence." *Lincoln Herald* 82 (Winter 1980): 540–544.

_____. "J.W.B.: His Initials in India Ink." *Virginia Magazine of History and Biography* 90 (July 1982): 359–366.

_____. "John Wilkes Booth as a Hero Figure." *Journal of American Culture* 5 (Fall 1982): 22–28.

Holding, Charles E. "John Wilkes Booth Stars in Nashville." *Tennessee Historical Quarterly* 23 (March 1964): 73–79.

Holloway, L.K.B. "The Capture and Death of John Wilkes Booth—By an Eyewitness." Museum of the Confederacy, Richmond.

Holt, Joseph. "New Facts about Mrs. Surratt, Correspondence of Judge Holt and Hon. James Speed." *The North American Review* 147 (July 1888): 83–94.

Howard, Joseph, Jr. "Some Hamlet Studies." *Chicago Herald*, November 30, 1890.

Ingraham, Prentiss. "Pursuit and Death of John Wilkes Booth." *The Century Magazine* 39 (January 1890): 443–449.

Isacsson, Alfred. "The Status of Weichmann Studies." *Surratt Courier* 11 (January 1986): 1, 6–11.

_____. "A Study of Louis J. Weichmann." *Lincoln Herald* 80 (Spring 1978): 25–38.

"John M. Lloyd—Star Witness." *Surratt Society News* 2 (March 1977): 3–4.

Kauffman, Michael W. "Booth's Escape Route: Lincoln's Assassin on the Run." *Blue & Gray Magazine* 7 (June 1990): 9–61.

_____. "Booth's First Attempt, Revisited." *Surratt Courier* 29 (August 2004): 3–4.

_____. "David Edgar Herold, the Forgotten Conspirator." *Surratt Society News* 6 (November 1981): 4–5.

_____. "Edman Spangler: A Life Rediscovered." *Surratt Courier* 11 (November 1986): 1, 7–10.

_____. "Fort Lesley J. McNair and the Lincoln Conspirators." *Lincoln Herald* 80 (Winter 1978): 176–188.

_____. "John Wilkes Booth and the Murder of Abraham Lincoln." *Blue & Gray Magazine* 7 (April 1990): 8–62.

Keeler, William F. "Aboard the USS *Florida*: 1863–1865; letters of William F. Keeler." *Naval Letters Series*, Vol. 2, United States Naval Institute, Annapolis, Maryland.

Keesler, Robert. "The Education of John Wilkes Booth." *Lincoln Log* 2 (February-March 1977): 7.

Kincaid, Arthur. "The Book Unlocked Again." *Surratt Courier* 11 (June 1986): 5–7.

Kohlsaat, H.H. "[Edwin] Booth's Letter to Grant." *The Saturday Evening Post* (February 9, 1924): 20–24.

Krone, Charles A. "Recollections of an Old Actor." *Missouri Historical Society Collections* 4, no. 2, 343.

Levin, Alexandra Lee. "The Canada Contact: Edwin Gray Lee." *Civil War Times Illustrated* 19 (June 1979): 4–8, 42–47.

Libby, George W. "John Brown and John Wilkes Booth." *Confederate Veteran* 38 (April 1930): 138–139.

The Lincoln Log, www.thelincolnlog.org.

Loux, Arthur F. "The Accident-Prone John Wilkes Booth." *Lincoln Herald* 85 (Winter 1983): 262–268.

_____. "The Mystery of the Telegraph Interruption." *Lincoln Herald* 81 (Winter 1979): 234–238.

Martin, Percy E. "The Hookstown Connection." *Surratt Society News* 5 (July 1980): 5–6.

_____. "Sam Arnold and Hookstown." *History Trails* 16 (Summer 1982): 13–16.

_____. "Surprising Speed in the Identification of Two Baltimore Conspirators." *Surratt Society News* 3 (October 1978): 3–5.

May, John Frederick. "The Mark of the Scalpel." *Records of the Columbia Historical Society* 13 (1910): 122–130.

Merrifield, Richard. "John Wilkes Booth." *Yankee Magazine* 17 (October 1953).

Miller, Ernest C. "John Wilkes Booth and the Land of Oil." *Pennsylvania Heritage* 7 (Summer 1981): 9–15.

_____. "John Wilkes Booth in the Pennsylvania Oil Region." *Western Pennsylvania Historical Magazine* 31 (March-June 1948): 26–47.

Miller, Stephen G. "You have doubtless heard of Booth the murderer of President Lincoln." *Surratt Courier* 31 (April 2006): 5–8.

"Milton Academy in Retrospect." *Federation P.T.A. News* (March-April 1935).

"Mr. Booth Visits the Garrett Family." *Surratt Courier* 24 (April 1999): 4–7.

Morcom, Richard. "They All Loved Lucy." *American Heritage* 21 (October 1970): 12–15.

Morrison, Michael. "Young Booth in Buffalo." *Buffalo Courier Express*, April 12, 1981.

Moss, M. Helen Palmes. "Lincoln and Wilkes Booth as Seen on the Day of the Assassination." *The Century Magazine* 67 (April 1909): 950–953.

Munroe, Seaton. "Recollections of Lincoln's Assassination." *North American Review* 162 (March 1896): 426–434.

Neely, Mark E., Jr., ed. *Lincoln Lore: Bulletin of the Louis A. Warren Lincoln Library and Museum*. Fort Wayne, IN.

Norcross, A.F. "A Child's Memory of the Boston Theatre." *Theatre Magazine* 43 (May 1926).

Ownsbey, Betty. "Lewis Powell: Mystery Man of the Conspiracy." *Surratt Society News* 5 (June 1980): 5–6.

_____. "Saving Private Lockner: Lewis Powell and His Yankee Prisoner." *Lincoln Assassination Occasional Papers* 1 (November 2011): 25–34.

Pathways. The Journal of the Booth Family, Lincoln's Assassination & Historic Preservation Law, Bel Air, MD.

Paullin, Charles G. "The Navy and the Booth Conspirators." *Journal of the Illinois State Historical Society* 33 (September 1940): 67–79.

Peddicord, John. "About John Wilkes Booth, Roanoke Gentleman Saw Corpse." *Roanoke Evening News*, June 6, 1903.

Porter, George L. "How Booth's Body Was Hidden." *Columbian Magazine* 4 (April 1911): 62–82.

Pryor, Leon O. "Lewis Payne, Pawn of John Wilkes Booth." *Florida Historical Quarterly* 43 (July 1964): 1–20.

Rankin, Mrs. McKee. "The News of Lincoln's Death." *American Magazine* (January 1909).

Rietveld, Ronald D., ed. "An Eyewitness Account of Abraham Lincoln's Assassination." *Civil War History* 22 (March 1976): 60–69.

Riggs, David F. "The Dahlgren Papers Reconsidered." *Lincoln Herald* 84 (Summer 1981): 658–667.

Shettel, James W. "J. Wilkes Booth at School: Recollections of a Retired Army Officer Who Knew Him Then." *The New York Dramatic Mirror*, February 26, 1916, 1, 5.

Skinner, Otis. "The Last of John Wilkes Booth." *American Magazine* (November 1908).

Sloan, Richard E., ed. *The Lincoln Log.* Seaford, NY, November 1975 to January 1981.

Smith, Joseph E. "Rick," and William L. Richter. "'Behold! I Tell You a Mystery': Who Was Mr. Chrisman?" *Surratt Courier* 38 (March 2013): 11–14.

_____. "Elizabeth Rousby Quesenberry and the Escape of Lincoln's Assassin." *Surratt Courier* 33 (September 2008): 4–7.

Smith, Rick. "Break a Leg." *Surratt Courier* 28 (June 2003): 4–6.

Smythe, Angela. "Bound for Glory, John Wilkes Booth and the Richmond Grays." Web, published May 10, 2012, www.antebellumrichmond.com/bound-for-glory.html.

_____. "Has He Been Hiding in Plain Sight? John Wilkes Booth and the Richmond Grays." Web, published May 10, 2010, www.antebellumrichmond.com/hiding.html.

_____. "Out of Hiding—John Wilkes Booth and the Richmond Grays." Web, published May 10, 2011, www.antebellumrichmond.com/out-of-hiding.html.

"Snowbound with John Wilkes Booth at Cameron, Missouri." *St. Louis Republic Magazine*, August 4, 1901.

"Some Damaging Evidence." *Surratt Courier* 30 (June 2005): 3–5.

Stanton, John F. "Another Look at Crismond." *Surratt Courier* 38 (April 2013): 3–5.

_____. "The Arrest of Thomas Nelson Conrad and Fannie Byrd Dade." *Surratt Courier* 29 (October 2004): 3.

_____. "Attention Sarah Slater Seekers." *Surratt Courier* 35 (September 2010): 4.

_____. "Booth and the Lightships: Booth's Route and Timing, Crossing the Potomac." *Lincoln Assassination Occasional Papers* 1 (February 2012): 48–50.

_____. "Mrs. Fannie B. Dade: An Introduction to a Spy." *Surratt Courier* 11 (August 1986): 1, 5–9.

_____. "A Mystery No Longer: The Lady in the Veil (con't)." *Surratt Courier* 36 (August 2011): 5.

_____. "Who Was Kate Thompson?" *Surratt Courier* 34 (February 2009): 5–9.

Steers, Edward, Jr. "Dr. Mudd's Sense of Timing: The Trip into Bryantown." *Surratt Courier*, 24 (September 1999): 4–6.

Storey, Moorefield. "Dickens, Stanton, Sumner, and Storey." *Atlantic Monthly* 145 (April 1930): 463–465.

Surratt, John H. "Lecture on the Lincoln Conspiracy." *Lincoln Herald* 51 (December 1949): 20–33.

Tarbell, Ida M. "Booth's Plot to Kidnap Lincoln." Ed. Ernest C. Miller. *Pennsylvania History* 21 (July 1954): 201–213.

Taylor, Dave. "Cloak and Daggers." *Surratt Courier* 37 (March 2012): 3–9.

Taylor, John O. "John Brown Hanging: Recollections of a Member of the Richmond Grays." *Richmond Times-Dispatch*, May 1, 1904.

Tidwell, William A. "Booth Crosses the Potomac: An Exercise in Historical Research." *Civil War History* 36 (December 1990): 325–333.

Townsend, George Alfred. "GATH's Etchings," *St. Louis Post-Dispatch*, 8 May 1880.

_____. "How John Wilkes Booth was Started in the Theatrical Profession." *Cincinnati Enquirer*, January 19, 1886.

_____. "How Wilkes Booth Crossed The Potomac." *The Century Magazine* 27 (April 1884): 822–832.

_____. "A Philistine's Diary." Unidentified newspaper, 30 July 1882, in George Alfred Townsend Papers, Maryland State Archives, Annapolis.

_____. "Thomassen: The Dynamite Fiend Amongst the Assassins of President Lincoln." *New York Graphic*, 22 March 1876.

Tucker, Glenn. "John Wilkes Booth at the John Brown Hanging." *Lincoln Herald* 78 (Spring 1976): 3–11.

Verge, Laurie. "That Trifling Boy." *Surratt Courier* 27 (January 2002): 4–9.

Wallace, Charles M., Sr. "Richmond in By Gone Days." *Richmond Times-Dispatch*, June 24, 1906.

Weik, Jesse. "A New Story of Lincoln's Assassination: An Unpublished Record of an Eye-Witness." *The Century Magazine* 135 (February 1913): 559–562.

Whitlock, Philip. "The Life of Philip Whitlock, Written by Himself." Beth Ahabah Museum and Archives Trust, Richmond, VA.

Wyndham, Charles. "John Wilkes Booth: An Interview with the Press with Sir Charles Wyndham." *New York Herald*, June 27, 1909.

Unpublished Papers, Theses and Dissertations

Alford, Terry. "John Wilkes Booth and George Alfred Townsend: A Marriage Made in Hell." Paper delivered at the Third Biennial Tudor Hall Conference, Aberdeen, MD, May 3, 1992.

_____. "The Silken Net: Plots to Abduct Abraham Lincoln During The Civil War." Paper presented to the Lincoln Group of the District of Columbia, Washington, April 21, 1987.

Arnold, Claude Ahmed. "The Development of the Stage in Nashville, Tennessee 1807–1870." Typescript, Public Library of Nashville and Davidson County, 1933.

Barbee, David Rankin. "Lincoln and Booth." Typescript, David Rankin Barbee Papers, Georgetown University Library, Washington, D.C.

Brombach, Charles. "The Canadian Phase of Lincoln's Murder." Typescript, Columbia University Library, New York.

Dodels, Jeannine Clarke. "Water on Stone: A Study of John Wilkes Booth's Political Draft Preserved at the Players Club NYC." Unpublished manuscript, copy in possession of author.

Elliott, John E., and Barry M. Cauchon. "A Peek Inside The Walls." Paper prepared for the Surratt Society and Surratt House Museum 2012 Conference, March 16–18, 2012.

Farley, Alan W. "Abraham Lincoln in Kansas Territory." Pamphlet, Fort Leavenworth, KS, 1959.

Fuller, Charles F., Jr. "Kunkel and Company at the Marshall Theatre, Richmond, Virginia, 1856–1861." M.A. thesis, Ohio University, 1968.

Herbstruth, Grant M. "Benedict DeBar and the Grand Opera House in St. Louis, Missouri, from 1855 to 1879." Ph.D. diss., University of Iowa, 1954.

Kamphausen, Debra. Letter to Frank Hebblethwaite, August 8, 1988. Copy in author's files.

Kauffman, Michael W. "Booth, Republicanism and the Lincoln Assassination." Special Scholars thesis, University of Virginia, 1980.

_____. "Information Circular No. 1: Booth on Stage." Typecript summary of the plays in which Booth appeared, 1981. Copy in author's files.

Keller, Helen B. "The History of the Theater in Columbus, Georgia from 1828 to 1865." M.A. thesis, University of Georgia, 1957.

Kincaid, Deirdre. *Rough Magic: The Theatrical Life of John Wilkes Booth*. Manuscript, North Leigh, Whitney, United Kingdom, 2009.

Langley, William Osler. "The History of Theatre in Columbus, Georgia, from 1828 to 1878." M.S. thesis, Alabama Polytechnic Institute, n.d.

Mahoney, Ella. "The House That Booth Built." Ella Mahoney Papers, Historical Society of Harford County, Maryland.

Moreland, James. "A History of the Theatre in Portland, 1794–1932." Typescript, Portland Public Library, 1938.

Mudd, A. I. "The First Appearance and Last Appearance of John Wilkes Booth at the National Capital." Mudd file, New York Public Library at Lincoln Center.

Mundy, Rick. "Theatrical Pariah: John Wilkes Booth and the Literature of the Theatre." Ph.D. diss., University of Kansas, 1999.

Porter, George Loring. "The Tragedy of the Nation." Lecture text, Library of Congress, 1896.

Raymond, Julian E. "History of Fort Lesley J. McNair." Typescript, Fort McNair Library, Washington, D.C., ca. 1960.

Shull, Mary E. "The Misunderstood Mitchells." Talk presented to the Surratt Society, Clinton, MD, November 13, 1989.

Sollers, John Ford. "The Theatrical Career of John T. Ford." Ph.D. diss., Stanford University, 1962.

Trueson, Gerald. Letter to Arthur F. Loux, March 12, 1986. Copy in author's files.

Webster, William H. "The Lincoln Assassination and its Investigation." Talk presented to the Abraham Lincoln Association, Springfield, IL, February 12, 1979.

Withers, Nan Wyatt. "The Acting Style and Career of John Wilkes Booth." Ph.D. diss., University of Wisconsin-Madison, 1979.

Index